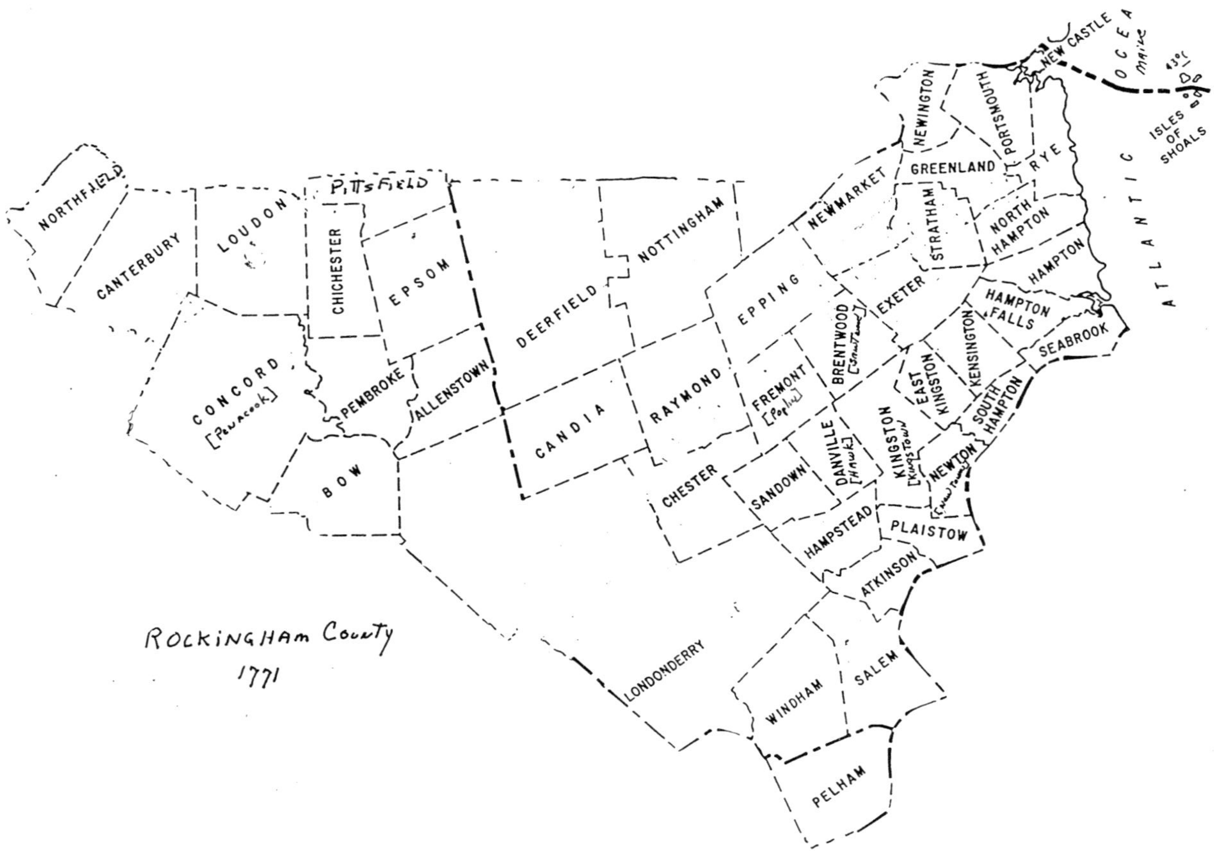
ROCKINGHAM COUNTY
1771
ATLANTIC
ISLES OF SHOALS
NEW CASTLE
NEWINGTON
PORTSMOUTH
RYE
GREENLAND
NEWMARKET
STRATHAM
NORTH HAMPTON
HAMPTON
EXETER
HAMPTON FALLS
SEABROOK
KENSINGTON
EAST KINGSTON
SOUTH HAMPTON
KINGSTON [Kingstown]
NEWTON [Newtown]
PLAISTOW
ATKINSON
HAMPSTEAD
DANVILLE [Hawk]
BRENTWOOD
FREMONT [Poplin]
SANDOWN
CHESTER
EPPING
RAYMOND
NOTTINGHAM
DEERFIELD
CANDIA
LONDONDERRY
WINDHAM
SALEM
PELHAM
ALLENSTOWN
EPSOM
PITTSFIELD
CHICHESTER
PEMBROKE
BOW
CONCORD [Penacook]
LOUDON
CANTERBURY
NORTHFIELD

Abstracts of the Probate Records of Rockingham County, NH 1771-1799

Volume 2

Helen F. Evans

Heritage Books, Inc.

Another book by the author:
Strafford County, NH, Probate Records, 1771-1799
CD-ROM also available: Abstracts of the Probate Records of Rockingham County, NH, 1771-1799

Published 2000 by

HERITAGE BOOKS, INC.
1540E Pointer Ridge Place
Bowie, Maryland 20716

1-800-398-7709
www.heritagebooks.com

ISBN 0-7884-1477-1

MaCARTNEY. See also McCartney

1628. MaCARTNEY, JOHN (1776) #4263
EST. Londonderry yoeman decd. testate. WILL: Drawn 9/5/1772. Legatees: Sons-George and John; Daus.-Joan, Mary and Margaret McCartney. Execs.-Friends Peeter Patterson and Moses Barnet. His sig. Witnesses: Robert Barnett, Samuel Wason and James Barnett. He instructs his execs. to dispose of all his est. for the benefit of his children. His sig. CERT. WILL (D23:375): 9/25/1776 Presented by Execs. and witnesses Wason and James Barnett. INVY.: Appr. 1/26/1776. "Invy. was taken on advice without a warrant." Comm.: James Wallace and James Alexander, chosen by Capt. Barnet and Peeter Paterson. Value L435.19.6 3/4. Oaths 9/23/1776 Comm. to Matthew Thornton, JP. Oaths 9/25/1776 Execs. to judge. ACCOUNT: 11/28/1781. Of Execs. Allowed 11/28/1781.

1629. MACE, JOHN (1799) #6604
EST. Gosport mariner decd. testate. WILL: Drawn 7/1/1799. Legatees: Wife-Sarah; Mother-Elizabeth Kiswell; Bro.-Joseph Mace; Sister-Molly Kiswell. Execs.-wife Sarah and Reuben Shapley of Portsmouth. His sig. Witnesses: Dr. William Cutter, Benjamin C. Shapley and Reuben S. Randall. CERT. WILL (D33:133): 8/29/1799. Presented by Sarah Mace, an Exec., and witnesses Shapley and Randall. ADMIN.: 8/29/1799. Exec. Sarah Mace, Gosport widow. Bond $3,000.00. Sureties: Benjamin C. Shapley and Reuben S. Randall, Portsmouth mariners. Witnesses: Sally Adams and W. Parker.

MacGREGOR. See also McGregore, McGregor

1630. MacGREGOR, REV. DAVID (1777) #4367
EST. Londonderry clerk decd. testate. WILL.: Drawn 4/13/1777. Legatees: Wife-unnamed; Sons-David, James and Robert; Five daus.-unnamed. Exec.-James oldest son. His sig. Witnesses: John McKeen, Robert Morison and Robert Boid. CERT. WILL: (D24:52). 6/25/1777. Presented by Exec. and witnesses McKeen and Morison.

1631. MACKAY, BENJAMIN (1779) #4554
Est. Portsmouth saddler decd. ADMIN.: 7/22/1779. Admx.: Elizabeth Mackay, Portsmouth widow. Bond: L2000.0.0. Sureties: Thomas Bickford, yoeman and Samuel Bowles, merchant, both of Portsmouth. Witnesses: Saml. Drowne and Ann Leigh. INVY. WARR.:7/22/1779.Comm.: Samuel Bowles, merchant; Samuel Drowne, goldsmith and Nehemiah Rowell, saddler, all of Portsmouth. INVY.: Appr. 9/27/1779. Value L243.18.2 1/2. Oaths 9/27/1779 Bowles and

Drowne to H. Wentworth, JP. Oath 9/27/1779 Admx. to judge. ACCOUNT: 3/8/1789. Of Admx. Includes main. of sons Joseph and Hampden and dau. Ann until she died. PETITION: 4/9/1789. Of Admx. For Comm. of Insolvency. Gives list claims of L320.9.4. Witnesses: Danl. Humphries and Saml. (Waterhouse?-poor copy). CLAIMS WARR.: 4/15/1789. Comm.: Supply Clap, Thomas Martin and Isaac Rindge, esquires; John Evans and Samuel Bowles, traders, all of Portsmouth. CLAIMS: 2/26/1790. Total L275.3.7. Oaths 2/26/1790 Clap, Martin and Bowles to Nathl. Adams, JP. LICENSE (D30:15): 2/16/1791. To Admx. To sell real est. to amount of L106.0.0.

MacMURPHY. See also McMurphy

1632. MacMURPHY, JAMES (1792) #5795
EST. Londonderry yoeman decd. testate. WILL: Drawn 5/16/1792. Legatees: Wife-Mary; Sons-Alexander and Benjamin; Daus.-Jean McMurphy, Jenet McMurphy, Peggy McMurphy, Mary McMurphy, Elisabeth McMurphy and Elis McMurphy. Execs-wife Mary and son Alexander. His sig. Witnesses: John Bell, William Willson and Jean McMurphy. CERT. WILL (D30:279): 8/15/1792. Presented by Execs. and witnesses Bell and Willson. ADMIN.: 8/15/1792. Execs.: Mary McMurphy, widow and Alexander McMurphy, yoeman, both of Londonderry. Bond L1000.0.0. Sureties: John Bell, Londonderry esq. and William Willson of Chester. Witnesses: James Nesmith Jr. and W. Parker. INVY.: Comm.: John Bell, James Aiken and Abraham Duncan. Value not tallied. Esti. L359.0.0+. Oaths 10/4/1792 Aiken, Duncan and Execs. to John Bell, JP.

1633. MAGOON, ABIGAIL (1794) #6006
GDP. Exeter spinster adjudged n.c.m. PETITION: 6/4/1794. Of Simeon Gordon, Exeter yoeman. States his aunt, Abigail Magoon, is n.c.m. Requests appointment of a Gdn. Order: 6/4/1794. To Exeter Selectmen. To conduct an inquisition into the state of mind of Abigail Magoon. Report: 6/5/1794. Of: Elipht. Giddinge, Gideon Lamson, Geo. Odiorne and Jeremiah Leavitt, Exeter Selectmen. They find Abigail to be n.c.m. and in need of a Gdn. GDP.: 7/8/1794. Of Abigail, an adult adjudged n.c.m. Gdn. Benjamin Magoon, Kingston yoeman. Bond L1000.0.0. Sureties: Benjamin Gordon and Simeon Gordon, Exeter yoemen. Witnesses: Nathl. Fogg and W. Parker. Note: This is a clerk's error, the other papers show that it was Benjamin Gordon who was the Gdn. and Benjamin Magoon, Kingston yoeman, therefore, a Surety. INVY.: Appr. 10/14/1797. Comm.: Joseph Loveren, Samuel Hobart and Nathl. Gordon. Value not tallied. Esti. L35.0.0+. Oaths 10/15/1794 Hobart, Nathl. Gordon and Gdn. Benja.

Gordon to judge. ACCOUNT: 1/30/1797. Of Gdn. Allowed 1/30/1797. PETITION: 3/28/1797. Of Ephm. Robinson, Gideon Lamson and Benj. C. Gilman, Exeter Selectmen and Overseers of the Poor. They are dissatisfied with the Account allowed, being suspicious that there are many over charges. Request an appeal from allowance. Granted 3/28/1797. BOND: 3/28/1797. Of Ephraim Robinson, esq.; Gideon Lamson, trader and Benja. Clark Gilman, clockmaker, Exeter Selectmen. Bond $100.00. To appeal Decree allowing Gdp. Account. Witnesses: Mary S. Parker and W. Parker. ADDL. ACCOUNT: Of Gdn. Allowed 12/28/1797.

1634. MAN. See also Mann

MAN, JAMES & JOHN (1782) #4764
GDP. Of the children of Joseph Man, Canterbury yoeman decd. GDP.: 9/25/1782. Of James, a minor over 14 and of John, a minor under 14. Gdn. Benjamin Blanchard Jr. of Canterbury. Bond L1000.0.0. Surety Samuel Hobart of Exeter. Witness Abiel Foster. Note: The file jacket says "other papers missing."

1635. MAN, JAMES (1789) #5463
EST. Epsom yoeman decd. ADMIN.: 6/17/1789. Admx. Sarah Man, Epsom widow. Bond L1000.0.0. Sureties: Jonathan Perkins, Pittsfield yoeman and Joseph Saterly, Hampton Falls cordwainer. Witnesses: Nathl. Parker and W. Parker. INVY.: 7/6/1789. Comm.: Hilyard Shaw and James Marden. Value L63.11.0. Oaths 8/26/1789 Comm. to Jonathan Leavitt, JP. Oath 9/16/1789 Admx. to judge. PETITION: 9/16/1789. Of Jonathan Perkins atty to Admx. For Comm. Insolvency. Gives list claims of L90.8.2. DOWER WARR.: 9/16/1789. Comm.: Jonathan Leavitt, esq.; Hilyard Shaw, yoeman; Dyer Hook and Dudley Sanborn, gentlemen, all of Chichester and Michael McClary, Epsom esq. Of Widow Sarah Man. CLAIMS WARR.: 9/16/1789. Comm.: Michael McClary, Epsom esq.; Dyer Hook and Dudley Sanborn, Chichester gentlemen. CLAIMS EXTENSION: 3/17/1790. Comm. granted 3 months longer. CLAIMS: Total L87.5.11. Oaths 5/19/1790 Comm. to judge. DOWER: Oaths 4/21/1790 Leavitt, Hook and Sanborn to Michael McClary, JP. Allowed 5/19/1790. ACCOUNTL Of Admx. Allowed 5/19/1790. Account includes main. one child. LICENSE: 5/19/1790. To Admx. To sell 2/3 of the real est. and reversion of Dower. ADDL. ACCOUNT: Of Jonathan Perkins atty. to Admx. Allowed 10/27/1790.

1636. MAN, JOSEPH (1783) #4900
EST. Canterbury yoeman decd. ADMIN.: 5/28/1783. Admr. Benjamin Blanchard Jr., Canterbury yoeman. Bond L1000.0.0. Sureties: Samuel Hobart, esq. and Benjamin Dearben, yoeman, both of Exeter. Witnesses: Nathl. Parker, Saml. Robinson and Samuel Shannon. INVY. WARR.: 5/28/1783. Comm.: Archelaus Moore, esq.; Samuel Gerrish and David Foster, husbandmen, all of Canterbury. Invy.: 6/2/1783. Value L92.9.9. Oaths 6/2/1783 Comm. to Archelaus Moore, JP. Oath 8/26/1783 Admr. to W. Parker, Reg. Includes cert. of Comm. that they had attended to the business of the Warr. The following Dower Warr. and Dower recorded as #4920 James Meloney (1783) belong here. DOWER WARR.: 5/28/1783. Comm.: Archelaus Moore, esq.; Samuel Gerrish, David Foster and Jonathan Blanchard, all of Canterbury and Chandler Lovejoy of Concord. Of Elizabeth Meloney wife of James, her Dower in est. Joseph Man late of Canterbury. Cert.: Of Comm. They have attended to business of Warr. DOWER: 6/2/1783. Oaths Gerrish, Foster, Lovejoy and Blanchard to Archelaus Moore, JP. Allowed.

1637. MAN, PETER (1794) #5969
EST. Portsmouth barber decd. testate. WILL: Drawn 1/23/1793. Legatees: Sons-William, Joseph, John, Thomas and Peter (oldest); Daus.-Elizabeth, Mehitabel, Patience and Sarah Loud wife of Edward Brown Loud. Exec.-son John. His sig. Witnesses: George Gains, Danl. Humphreys and Joseph Akerman Jr. CERT. WILL (D31:192): 2/19/1794. Presented by Exec. and witnesses Humphreys, esq. and Akerman. ADMIN.: 2/19/1794. Exec. John Man, Portsmouth barber. Bond L1000.0.0. Sureties: Jeremiah Libbey, esq. and Robt. Odiorne Treadwell, merchant, both of Portsmouth. Witness Saml. Morrison. INVY.: Appr. 1/25/1794. Comm.: Jeremiah Libbey, Thomas Chadbourn and James Hill. Value L353.8.6. Oaths 1/27/1794 Exec. and Comm. to Geo. Gains, JP. PETITION: 7/20/1795. Of Exec. For License to sell all the land. Person interested in the real est., with Exec., is a minor. Selling part would be injurious. Consent 7/24/1795 of Jeremiah Libbey, Gdn. of minor. LICENSE: 7/25/1795. To Exec. To sell all the land. BOND: 7/25/1795. Of Exec. Bond $900.00. To Account for sale of land by License. Sureties: John Nelson, goldsmith and Joseph Man, boatbuilder. Witnesses: E. Hall and Nathanael Melcher. ACCOUNT: 2/17/1796. Of Exec. Allowed 2/17/1796. Jeremiah Libbey as Gdn. of Thos. Man, an heir, has no objections to Account.

MANN. See also Man

1638. MANN, THOMAS (1795) #6124
GDP. Of the son of Peter Mann, Portsmouth barber decd. GDP.: 7/21/1795. Of Thomas, a minor over 14. Gdn. Jeremiah Libbey, Portsmouth esq. Bond $1,000.00. Sureties: John Man, barber and John Nelson, goldsmith, both of Portsmouth. Witnesses: Nathaniel Dean and James Rundlett.

1639. MANN, WILLIAM (1784) #5037
EST. Pembroke yoeman decd. ADMIN.: 9/15/1784. Admx. Mary Man, Pembroke widow. Bond L500.0.0. Sureties: Samuel McConnel, esq. and Joseph Man, yoeman, both of Pembroke. Witness: W. Parker. INVY.: Appr. 12/23/1784. Comm.: Samuel McConnel, James Cunningham and John Knox. Value L357.12.7.Oaths 12/23/1784 Admx. and Comm. to Richard Bartlett, JP. PETITION: Dated by clerk 9/1785. Signed by Joseph Man. For License. Gives list debts paid and some still due in amount of L93.12.6.1. LICENSE (D25:523): 9/29/1785. To Admx. To sell the real est. ACCOUNT: 9/19/1787. Of Admx. Allowed 9/19/1787.

1640. MANNING, THOMAS (1777) #4371
EST. Portsmouth innholder decd. ADMIN.: 7/2/1777. Admr. Thomas Manning Portsmouth mariner. Bond L500.0.0. Sureties: Richard Salter, mariner and Joseph Ayers, cordwainer, both of Portsmouth. Witnesses: Jeremiah Parker and Wm. Parker. INVY.: Appr. 7/3/1777. Comm.: Jno. Parker, esq.; Richard Salter and Jos. Ayers. Value L319.6.0. Oaths 7/11/1777 Comm. and on 7/16/1777 Admr. to Saml. Penhallow, JP. CLAIMS: 4/2/1779. Comm.: Jacob Treadwell and Thomas Martin. Total L95.18.0 1/2. Oaths 4/17/1779 Comm. to George Gains, JP. DOWER: 5/11/1779. Comm.: Samuel Hale, esq.; Richd. Salter, Jeremiah Libbey "and others." Of Sarah Arney late wife of Thomas Manning. Oaths 5/11/1779 Comm. to Saml. Penhallow, JP. Allowed. LICENSE: 9/29/1779. To Admr. To sell sufficient real est. to pay debts. ACCOUNT: 11/1779. Of Admr. Allowed 11/24/1779. Account includes main. 2 children.

1641. MARBLE, CALEB (1795) #6137
EST. Salem yoeman decd. ADMIN.: 8/20/1795. Admr. Samuel Marble, Salem yoeman. Bond $3,000.00. Sureties: Thomas Dow, gent. and Robert Ellingwood, cordwainer, both of Salem. Witnesses: Joseph Blanchard and Wm. Parker. INVY.: Appr. 12/1/1795. Comm.: Thomas Dow, William Clement and Robert Ellingwood Jr. Value $269.85. Oaths 12/1/1795 Clement and Ellingwood to Jos. Wardwell, JP. Oath 12/16/1795 Admr. to judge. ACCOUNT: 8/1796. Of Admr. Allowed 8/17/1796.

1642. MARBLE, SAMUEL JR. & WALTER WEEKS (1794) #6043
PET. DIV. PETITION: 11/8/1794. Of Samuel Marble Jr., Stratham mariner. For div. of land in Stratham which he holds as tanant in common, in equal shares, with Walter Weeks, Stratham yoeman. Order: For hearing, petitioner to serve Weeks with copy of Petition and Order. See also #3914 Walter Weeks (1772) who may be the other divisee.

1643. MARCH, CLEMENT (1777) #4366
EST. Greenland esq. decd. testate. WILL: Drawn 5/21/1777. Legatees: Sons-George, Joseph of Deerfield, Clement and Stephen; Daus.-Eleanor Weeks, Mary Clark, Hannah Storer, Abigail Weeks, Anne Bracket, Martha March, Elizabeth March and Sarah March. Execs.-sons Clement and Stephen and he appoints his friends John Pickering and Joseph Peirce overseers and advisors to the Execs. His sig. Witnesses: Joshua Haines, John Savage and John Pickering. CERT. WILL (D24:50): 6/25/1777. Presented by Execs. and witnesses Haines and Savage. ADMIN.: 6/25/1777. Execs. Clement March and Stephen March, Greenland gentlemen. Bond L2000.0.0. Sureties: Richard Downing, Newington esq. and Thomas Martin, Portsmouth merchant. Witnesses: James Betton and James Macgregore Jr.

1644. MARCH: CLEMENT & NATHANIEL BARREL (1796) #6225
GDP. Of the sons of Nathaniel March of Portsmouth decd. GDP.: 6/15/1796. Of: Clement, a minor over 14 and of Nathaniel Barrel March, a minor under 14. Gdn. John March, Portsmouth saddler. Bond $1,000.00. Sureties: Jotham Rindge, yoeman and William Sowersby, chaisemaker, both of Portsmouth. Witnesses: Jeremiah Libbey and W. Parker.

1645. MARCH, JAMES (1786) #5200
Est. Portsmouth joiner decd. ADMIN.: 5/26/1786. Admx. Margery March, Portsmouth widow. Bond L1000.0.0. Sureties: John Banfill, yoeman and Thomas Chadbourn, esq., both of Portsmouth. Witnesses: W. Parker and John Calife.

1646. MARCH, STEPHEN (1772) #3921
EST. Portsmouth blacksmith decd testate. PETITION: 3/25/1772. Of Nathl. Brackett of Greenland in right of his wife, an heir. States that Stephen was n.c.m. when he wrote his ill and requests a hearing and that the will not be proved. Judge's notation: 3/7772. Bracket, in his right and on behalf of the other heirs, reserves the right to dispute this Will at common law. On back he further notes "Nothing done on it. I suppose agreed." WILL: Drawn 1/27/1762. Legatees: Wife-Elizabeth. Exex. Wife Elizabeth. His sig. Witnesses: Simon Pope, Peter Pearse and Mary Pearse.

Judge notes Will was offered for probate on 3/25/1772. A hearing ordered for 4/6/1772 at which time it was proved by the oaths of witnesses Peter and Mary Pearse. INVY. WARR.: 4/6/1772. Comm.: Nathanael Folsom of Exeter, Saml. Hale of Portsmouth and Richard Jenness of Rye, esquires. INVY: Appr. 2/3/1773. Value L1192.9.7. Oaths (D22:56): 2/3/1773 Comm. and Exex. to judge.

1647. MARDEN, ISRAEL (1798) #6454
EST. Portsmouth husbm. decd. testate. WILL: Drawn 4/3/1798. Legatees: Wife-unnamed; Sons-John, Francis, Thomas and Israel; Dau.-Sabra Morill; Heirs of dau. Sarah Morill decd.; Heirs of dau. Prudence Cate decd. Exec.- son Francis. His sig. Witnesses: Francis Jenness, Samuel Walker and William Norton. CERT. WILL (D32:475): 4/30/1798. Presented by Exec. and all witnesses. ADMIN.: 4/30/1798. Exec. Francis Marden, Portsmouth gent. Bond $3,000.00. Sureties: Samuel Walker of Portsmouth and Francis Jenness of Rye, yoemen. Witnesses: W. Parker and Saml. Parker. INVY.: Comm.: Peter Garland, Francis Jenness and Levi Jenness. Value $2,518.25. Oaths 6/4/1798 Garland and Levi Jenness to Joseph Parsons, JP. Oath 6/20/1798 Exec. to judge. Note: The card Index gives Israel's res. as Rye, but Will and all papers say Portsmouth.

1648. MARDEN, JAMES (1777) #4387
EST. Rye yoeman decd. testate. PETITION: 9/8/1777. Of Judith Marden, widow of James. She accepts the provision made for her in Will and Executorship. Requests Will be proved and allowed. Witnesses: W. Parker and Nathl. Parker. WILL: Drawn 9/8/1770. Legatees: Wife-Judath; Sons-Nathan, James and William; Daus.-Mary Foss, Hannah Clark, Judath Marden and Oli Marden; Grandchildren-John Marden and his sister Sarah and Bithiah Johnson. Execs.-wife Judath and son William. His sig. Witnesses: Stephen Marden, Samuel Murry and Christopher Gold. CERT WILL: 9/24/1777. Presented by Execs. and Samuel Murry only surviving witness, Marden and Gould now decd. ADMIN.: 9/24/1777. Exec. William Marden, Rye yoeman. Bond L500.0.0. Sureties: Samuel Murry, yoeman and Nathaniel Rand, gent., both of Rye. Witnesses: James Taggart and W. Parker. Note: There is no explanation as to why Widow Judath was not included in Admin.

1649. MARDEN, JAMES (1791) #5698
EST. Chichester gent. decd. ADMIN.: 10/15/1791. Admx. Sarah Marden, Chichester widow. Bond L1000.0.0. Sureties: Nathan Marden Jr. and Daniel Shaw, yoeman, both of Epsom. Witnesses: Michl. McClary and Dudley Sanborn. INVY.: Appr. 10/19/1791. Comm.: Michl. McClary, Dudley Sanborn and Abraham True. Value L182.16.6. Oaths 10/19/1791

Sanborn, True and Admx. to Michl. McClary, JP. PETITION: 1/18/1792. Of Admx. For Comm. Insolvency. Gives list claims of L82.0.0. plus her Dower. Witness Michl. McClary. DOWER: 5/5/1792. Comm.: Amos Morrill, Michl. McClary, Dudley Sanborn, Jonathan Leavitt and Moses Seavey. Of Widow Sarah Marden. Oaths 5/5/1792 Morrill, Sanborn, Leavitt and Seavey to Michl. McClary, JP. Allowed. ADDL. INVY.: Appr. 8/30/1792. Value L22.16.0. Oaths 8/30/1792 Sanborn and True to Michl. McClary. Plus appr. 9/19/1792 another piece of land valued at L20.0.0. Signed by McClary and Sanborn. PETITION: 9/19/1792. Of Admx. For license. States claims are L1099.9.4. Granted. LICENSE (D30:300): 9/19/1792. To Admx. To sell real est. to L1000.0.0. CLAIMS: 9/19/1792. Comm.: Michl. McClary, Dudley Sanborn and Amos Morrill. Total L1099.9.4. Oaths 9/19/1792 Comm. to W. Parker, JP. ACCOUNT: 5/16/1793. Of Admx. Allowed 5/16/1793. Account includes main. 3 children. PROP. &SETTLM.: Claims L1099.9.4. Amount to be proportioned L81.8.9 1/2. Allowed 6/3/1793 with order to Admx. to pay.

1650. MARDEN, STEPHEN (1781) #4755
EST. Chester joiner decd. ADMIN.: 12/11/1781. Admx. Elizabeth Marden, Chester widow. Bond L500.0.0. Sureties: William Lock, gent. and Nathan Knowles, cordwainer, both of Chester. Witnesses: Abigail Marden and John Dudley. INVY. WARR.: 12/11/1781. Comm.: Jonathan Swain, gent. and Matthias Hains, yoeman, both of Raymond and Nathan Knowles, Chester yoeman. INVY. Appr. 1/22/1781. Value L191.3.6. Oaths 2/23/1782Swain, Knowles and Admx. to John Dudley, JP. ACCOUNT: 2/7/1790. Of Admx. Allowed 5/19/1790. Account includes main. 3 children. LICENSE (D29:387): 5/19/1790. To Admx. To sell real est. to amount of L27.0.0. STATEMENT: Of: David Bagley, Archelaus Moore, John Stevens and Josiah Marden, heirs of est. They have agreed to give the income of est. to the widow.

1651. MARSH: BETTY, POLLY & SARAH (1787) #5305
GDP. Of the daus. of John Marsh, Pelham yoeman decd. GDP.: 11/21/1787. Of: Sarah, a minor over 14 and of Betty and Polly, minors under 14. Gdn. John Ferguson, Pelham gent. Bond L1000.0.0. Sureties: Josiah Gage and Robt. Young, Pelham esquires. Witnesses: Jeremiah Gage and Henry Gage.

1652. MARSH: ISABELLA, SAMUEL & SARAH (1793) #5884
GDP. Of the children of Samuel Marsh, Londonderry gent. decd. GDP.: 4/16/1793. Of Samuel, a minor over 14. Gdn. Andrew Mack, Londonderry yoeman. Bond L1000.0.0. Sureties: Edward Ela and Daniel Reynolds, esq., both of Londonderry. GDP.: 4/17/1793. Of: Sarah and

Isabella, minors over 14. Gdn. William Anderson, Londonderry yoeman. Bond L1000.0.0. Sureties: Jonathan Adams, gent. and Daniel Reynolds, esq., both of Londonderry. Witnesses: Robt. Barnet and N. Parker.

1653. MARSH, JOHN (1776) #4233
EST. Pelham husbm. decd. testate. WILL: Drawn 3/12/1776. Legatees: Wife-Martha; Sons-Ezra (oldest), John (2d), James (3d) and Jacob (4th); Daus.-Martha Marsh, Ruth Marsh, Elizabeth, Hannah and Salla. Execs.: wife Martha and son James. His sig. Witnesses: Job Hardy, Benj. Coburn and James Richardson. Note: The Will is so faded and the writing so very tiny it is difficult to read, but has been checked against the Docket copy. CERT. WILL: 5/29/1776. Presented by Execs. and witnesses Hardy and Colburn. INVY. WARR.: 5/28/1776. Comm.: Job Hardy, Joshua Atwood and Benjamin Coburn, all of Pelham. Includes oaths 6/8/1776 of Comm. to Jno. Varnum, JP. INVY.: Appr. 6/8/1776. Value L421.4.5. Oaths. 6/8/1776 Execs. to Jno. Varnum, JP

1654. MARSH, JOHN (1778) #4495 & (1779) #4521
EST. Pelham yoeman decd. ADMIN. (#4495): 10/29/1778. Admx. Sarah Marsh, Pelham widow. Bond L500.0.0. Sureties: Josiah Gage and James Gibson, Pelham esquires. Witnesses: Joshua Attwood and Jesse Wilson. INVY. (#4521): Appr. 12/28/1778. Comm.: Josiah Gage, esq.; Joshua Attwood, yoeman and Jesse Wilson, gent. Value L1081.5.8. Oaths 3/1/1779 Comm. to Timothy Ladd, JP. Oath 3/18/1779 Admx. to Josiah Gage, JP. The following Account and Citation found in #4765 John Marsh (1782) belong here. CITATION: 4/17/1793. To Timothy Davis and Sarah his wife, Admx., of Pelham. To appear and exhibit Account. ACCOUNT: Of Timothy Davis and Sarah his wife, Admx. est. John Marsh, Pelham yoeman. Allowed 4/19/1786. Account includes main. Sarah, Betty and Molley. LICENSE (D28:505): 4/19/1786. To Timothy Davis and Sarah his wife, Admx. To sell the real est. Oath 4/13/1682 Sarah Davis to Josiah Gage, JP.

1655. MARSH, JOHN (1782) #4765
EST. Portsmouth merchant decd. ADMIN.: 5/15/1782. Admx. Sarah Marsh, Portsmouth widow. Bond L1000.0.0. Sureties: Thomas Sheafe and James Sheafe, Portsmouth merchants. Witnesses: John Pickering and Abigail Pickering. INVY. WARR.: 5/15/1782. Comm.: Samuel Hale, Joshua Brackett and William Hart, Portsmouth esquires. INVY.: Appr. 8/8/1782. Value L625.6.11 1/2. Oaths: 8/8/1782 Comm. to H. Wentworth, JP. Oath: 8/12/1782 Admx. to Saml. Penhallow, JP. Note: This file includes a Citation and Account which be belong with #4495 (1778) & #4521 (1779 John Marshal of Pelham and are recorded there.

1656. MARSH, MARTHA (1787) #5300
EST. Pelham widow decd. intestate. ADMIN.: 11/7/1787. Admr. Ezra Rolfe Marsh, Pelham gent. Bond L1000.0.0. Sureties: Josiah Gage and Robert Young, Pelham esquires. Witnesses: Amos Gage and Mehitabel Gage. INVY.: Appr. 11/16/1787. Comm.: Jacob Butler Jr., Joshua Atwood and John Ferguson. Value L240.13.5. Oaths 11/16/1787 Comm. to Josiah Gage, JP. Oath 11/21/1787 Admr. to judge. ACCOUNT: 4/15/1789. Of Admr. Allowed 3/18/1789. ADDL. ACCOUNT: 4/15/1789. Of Admr. Allowed 4/15/1789.

1657. MARSH, SAMUEL (1780) #4653
EST. Londonderry yoeman decd. testate. WILL: Drawn 6/20/1780. Legatees: Wife-Maryann; His 3 children, only Samuel named; Cousin-Daniel Marsh. Execs.-wife Maryann and John Nesmith. His sig. Witnesses: Robt. Barnett, James Willson and Moses Barnett. CERT. WILL (D25:371).: 9/27/1780. Presented by Execs. and witnesses Robert Barnett and Willson. INVY.: Comm.: Moses Barnett, John McKeen and James Willson. Value not tallied. Esti. L15821.0.0+. Oaths 12/19/1780 Comm. and Execs. to John Bell, JP. ACCOUNT: 11/1789. Of Execs. Allowed 11/18/1789 the heirs being minors not notified. PETITION: 11/18/1789. Of Execs. For License. LICENSE: 11/18/1789. To Execs. To sell real est. out of the homestead to amount of L36.0.0. ACT OF NH GENERAL COURT: 2/4/1791. Allowing John Nesmith, surviving Exec., to sell all the real est. which, in his Will, Samuel ordered to be sold to pay his debts. The demands against est. are a considerable sum and selling part would be injurious to heirs and legatees, who are minors. Signed by John Samuel Sherburne, Speaker P. Tem.; Josiah Bartlett, Pres. and Joseph Pearson, Secy. BOND: 4/8/1791. Of John Nesmith, an Exec. Bond L1000.0.0. To account for sale of real est. Sureties: William Anderson, yoeman and John Nesmith III, gent., both of Londonderry. Witnesses: James Aiken, Arthur Nesmith, James Morrison and Hugh Anderson. ADDL. ACCOUNT: 12/17/1794. Of Exec. Nesmith. Allowed 12/17/1794 the Gdns. of heirs present and not objecting.

1658. MARSHALL, GEORGE (1782) #4839
EST. Portsmouth sailmaker decd. intestate. ADMIN.: 10/24/1782. Admx. Eleanor Marshall, Portsmouth widow. Bond L1000.0.0. Sureties: George Wentworth, Portsmouth merchant and Samuel Shackford, Newington gent. Witnesses: James Grouard and John Marshall. INVY. WARR.: 10/30/1782. Comm.: John Furnald, Samuel Drowne and Nathaniel Marshall, all of Portsmouth. INVY.: 12/4/1782. Value L185.0.0. Oaths 12/6/1782 Comm. and Eleanor Shackford wife of Samuel Shackford, Newington gent., Admx. and late wife of George Marshall, to Saml.

Pemhallow, JP. PETITION: 12/9/1782. Of Samuel Shackford. For License. Gives list claims of L209.0.0. Granted. CLAIMS COMM.: 12/9/1782. Comm.: Thomas Martin and John Parker, Portsmouth esquires. LICENSE (D27:133): 12/25/1782. To Admrs. To sell sufficient real est. to pay debts. DOWER: 6/24/1783. Comm.: Wm. Knight, Pierce Long, Jno. Parker, Geo. Wentworth and Geo. Gains. Of Eleanor Shackford in est. George Marshall. Oaths 6/24/1783. Of Samuel Shackford that he had shown Comm. all the real est. and Comm. to Saml. Penhallow, JP. Allowed 6/25/1783. CLAIMS: 12/15/1783. Total L233.11.4. Oaths 12/15/1783 Comm. to Saml. Penhallow, JP. ACCOUNT: 12/27/1783. Of Admrs. Account includes main. Eleanor and Deborah.

1659. MARSHALL, JAMES (1792) #5738
GDP.: Of the son of Simeon Marshall, Exeter shipwright decd. GDP.: 2/3/1792. Of James. Gdn. Seth Fogg, Exeter yoeman. Bond L300.0.0. Sureties: James Folsom 3d, Exeter joiner and Simon Sanborn, Hampton yeoman. Witnesses: Thos. Chase and W. Parker.

1660. MARSHALL, JOHN (1771) #3858
EST. Of Portsmouth boatbuilder decd. intestate. ADMIN.: 7/26/1771. Admr. David Griffith, Portsmouth shopkeeper. Bond L500.0.0. Sureties: John Griffeth, shopkeeper and George King, mariner, both of Portsmouth. INVY.: Comm.: Jona. Ayers and Joseph Cotton. Value L42.7.3. Allowed 10/30/1771. CLAIMS WARR.: 10/30/1771. Comm.: Saml. Hale and Saml. Griffith, both of Portsmouth. CLAIMS: 1/28/1773. Total L6.1.5. Allowed 3/3/1773.

1661. MARSHALL, DEACON JOHN (1784) #4979
EST. Portsmouth boatbuilder decd. intestate. ADMIN.: 3/16/1784. Admr. John Marshall, Portsmouth boatbuilder. Bond L3000.0.0. Sureties: Pearse Long and Woodbury Langdon, Portsmouth esquires. Witness Nathl. Parker. INVY. WARR.: 3/17/1784. Comm.: Captains William Knight, George Wentworth and Ephraim Hall, all of Portsmouth. INVY.: Appr. 3/25/1784. Value L782.9.3. Oaths 4/12/1784 Comm. to Saml. Penhallow, JP. Oath 8/18/1784 Admr. to W. Parker, Reg. DIV.: 10/12/1784. Comm.: Jacob Sheafe, Jno. Parker, Pearse Long, Tho. Martin and Jos. Wentworth. To div. the real est. between the heirs. Divisees: John Marshall, Lucy Snell, Martha Janvrin, Elizabeth Hills and Abigail Marshall. Oaths 10/12/1784 Comm. to George Gains, JP. Allowed 10/20/1784. Includes Map. ACCOUNT: 7/16/1794. Of Admr. (of est. his father). Allowed 7/20/1794. Consent: Elisha Hill, Lucy Snell, Martha Janvrin and Saml. Haven Jr. have examined the Account and are satisfied with it.

1662. MARSHALL, SAMUEL (1749) A#1458
Portsmouth potter decd. DIV. WARR. (D35:221): 2/15/1804. Comm.: Isaac Rindge, Edward Sargent, George Gains, Saml. Hutchins and Nathaniel Marshall, all of Portsmouth. The judge informs Comm. that George Wentworth, esq., Exec. of Will of Eleanor Shackford, Portsmouth widow, has represented to him that Samuel Marshall, Portsmouth potter decd. intestate, left a dwelling house and land and a son and 4 daus., viz. Mary Jackson, who left an only child, Thomas Jackson; Eleanor Shackford; Deborah Shackford and Elizabeth Waters. Samuel Marshall, the son, died c1768 unmarried and d.s.p. so his share went to his mother Eleanor decd. and now belongs to her heirs. 1/6 belongs to Thomas Jackson as heir of Thomas decd. and 1/6 to each of the surviving daus. of Samuel the elder, holding as tenants in common. Div., setting off to the heirs of Eleanor decd. 2/6; to Eleanor Shackford wife of Samuel Shackford 1/6; to Elizabeth Waters 1/6; to Deborah Shackford wife of Josiah Shackford 1/6 and to Thomas Jackson 1/6. Orig. Archives file includes Admin., Invy. and Div.

1663. MARSHALL, SIMEON (1780) #4679
EST. Exeter shipwright decd. ADMIN.: 12/27/1780. Admrs. Seth Fogg, yoeman and Elizabeth his wife, of Exeter. Bond: L10000.0.0. Sureties: Josiah Robinson and James Leavitt. gent., both of Exeter. Witness Nathl. Parker. INVY. WARR.: 3/27/1780. Comm.: Josiah Sanborn, Joseph Cram and Josiah Rawlings, Exeter yoemen. INVY.: Appr. 1/6/1781. Value L1784.2.0. Oaths 1/30/1781 Sanborn, Rawlings and Admrs. to judge. PETITION: Dated by clerk 10/1781. Of Seth Fogg, an Admr. For Comm. Insolvency as there are 2 children to support and claims which the creditors refuse to present. ACCOUNT: 4/24/1782. Of Admrs. Allowed 2/24/1784. Account includes main. 2 children.

1664. MARSHALL, CAPT. WILLIAM (1771) #3855
EST. Portsmouth mariner decd. intestate. ADMIN.: 6/26/1771. Admx. Margaret Marshall, Portsmouth widow. Bond L500.0.0. Sureties: John Marshall, boatbuilder and George Marshall Jr., sailmaker, both of Portsmouth. INVY.: Appr. 8/29/1771. Comm.: Jno. Marsh and Robt. Robertson. Value L71.4.6. Oaths 8/29/1771 Admx. and Comm. to judge. Allowed 8/29/1771. ACCOUNT: Of Admx. Allowed 2/26/1772. CLAIMS: 2/30/1772. Comm.: J. Brackett and Jno. Marsh. Total L3.3.4 1/2. Allowed 2/26/1772. Account includes main 2 children.

1665. MARSTES, DR. JOHN (1799) #6608
EST. Newmarket physician decd. ADMIN.9/9/1799. Admr. Dudley Watson, trader. Bond L1000.0.0. Sureties: John Shute, innholder and Josiah Adams, esq., both of Newmarket. Witnesses: John Shute Jr. and Mary Branscombe. INVY.: Appr. 10/9/1799. Comm.: Josiah Adams, Danl. Hill and John Shute. Value $83.62. Oaths 10/9/1799 Comm. to Natl. Rogers, JP. Oath 10/16/1799 Admr. to judge. PETITION: 10/15/1799. Of Admr. for Comm. Insolvency. Gives list claims of $270.00. Granted with Comm. of Josiah Adams and Danl. Hill, esquires and John Shute. Note: The file also contains a fragment with figures which appears to est. expenses.

1666. MARSTON: ASAHEL & MARY (1789) #5436
GDP. Of the children of John Marston, Hampton yoeman decd. GDP.: 4/15/1789. Of: Ashahel and Mary, minors over 14. Gdn. Abigail Marston, Hampton widow. Bond L500.0.0. Sureties: Jacob Marston of Hampton and Isaac Brown of Hampton Falls, yoemen. Witness W. Parker.

1667. MARSTON, CALEB (1770) A#3754 & (1791) #4448 1/2
EST. Newmarket yoeman decd. intestate. LICENSE (D21:23): 5/30/1771. To Admr. To sell sufficient real est. to pay debts. ADDL. ACCOUNT (#4448 1/2): 4/18/1791. Of Admr. Allowed 3/22/1791. ADDL. PROP. & SETTLM. (D30:42): Claims L296.3.6. Amount to be proportioned L49.5.6. Allowed 4/20/1791 with order to Admr. to pay. Note: The Addl. Prop. & Settlm. Was made because the Admr. posted the Addl. Account after the orig. Prop. was made. Orig. Archives file includes Will, Invy., Account 1771, Prop. & Settlm. 1771 and Dower.

1668. MARSTON, CALEB (1778) #4448
EST. North Hampton gent. decd. testate. WILL: Drawn 5/9/1774. Legatees: Wife-Tabitha; Sons-Paul Smith Marston, John and Simeon; Daus.-Anna Sanborn wife of Thomas Sanborn; Abigail Marston and Lydia Marston. Execs.-sons John and Simeon. His sig. Witnesses: John Moulton, Jonathan Moulton 3d and Josh. Moulton. CERT. WILL: (D24:269).4/29/1778.Presented by Execs. and witnesses John Moulton and Josiah Moulton. ADMIN.: 4/29/1778. ACCEPTANCE: 4/28/1778. Of Tabitha Marston, widow of Caleb. She accepts what Caleb left her in his Will instead of her Dower and fully consents to the proof and acceptance of Will. Her mark. Witnesses: David Marston and Isaac Marston. ADMIN.: 4/29/1778. Execs.: John Marston and Simeon Marston, North Hampton yeomen. Bond L500.0.0. Sureties: John Moulton, esq. and Josiah Moulton 3d, gent., both of Hampton. Witnesses: Nathl. Parker and W. Parker.

1669. MARSTON: CALEB & ELIZABETH (1779) No#
GDP. Of the children of David Marson, North Hampton gent. decd. GDP.(D25:203): 6/30/1779. Of: Caleb and Elizabeth, minors over 14. Gdn. John Lamprey, North Hampton gent. Sureties: Isaac Marston, yoeman and Moses Leavitt, esq., both of North Hampton.

1670. MARSTON, CALEB (1791) #4448 ½
See Caleb Marston A#3754 (1770)

1671. MARSTON, DAVID (1779) #4524
EST. North Hampton gent. decd. intestate. RENUN.: 3/12/1779. Of Abigail Marston, widow of David. Of Admin. Requests appointment of her oldest son, Isaac. Witnesses: Joseph Towle Jr. and Moses Elkins. ADMIN.: 3/12/1779/. Admr. Isaac Marston, North Hampton yoeman. Bond L1000.0.0. Sureties: Levi Dearborn of North Hampton and Josiah Moulton of Hampton, esquires. Witnesses: Nathl. Parker and W. Parker. INVY. WARR.: 3/12/1779. Comm.: Henry Bachelder of Hampton; Joseph Towle Jr. and Moses Elkins, Hampton yoemen. INVY.: Appr. 3/29/1779. Value L2456.0.0. Oaths 3/29/1779 Comm. to Joseph Dow Jr., JP. Oath 3/31/1779 Admr. to W. Parker, Reg. ACCOUNT: 6/31/1779. Of Admr. Allowed 6/30/1779.

1672. MARSTON, DOROTHY (1796) #6257
GDP. North Hampton spinster adjudged n.c.m. PETITION: 9/21/1796. Of Morris Hobbs, neighbor. Requests court appoint a Gdn. ORDER: To North Hampton Selectmen. To hold an inquisition concerning Dorothy's condition. CERT.: 9/27/1796. Of: Thomas Leavitt and Samuel Dearborn, North Hampton selectmen. They certify that Dorothy is n.c.m. and request appointment of a Gdn. They recommend Morris Hobbs. GDP.: 9/27/1796 Gdn. Morris Hobbs, North Hampton yoeman. Bond $2,000.00. Sureties: Thomas Leavitt, esq. and Thomas Loveren, gent., both of North Hampton. INVY.: Appr. 9/27/1796. Comm.: Thomas Leavitt, Increase Batchelder and Thomas Loverin. Value $120.00. Oaths 9/27/1796 Comm. to W. Parker. ACCOUNT: 2/6/1797. Of Gdn. ADDL. ACCOUNT: 9/1797. Of Gdn. Allowed 9/25/1797.

1673. MARSTON, ELISHA (1766) A#3308
EST. Brentwood yoeman decd. intestate. LICENSE (D22:310): 10/27/1773. To Admx. Anna Marston. To sell sufficient real est. to pay debts. Orig. Arvices file includes Admin., Invy., Dower Warr., Dower, Claims Warr., Claims, Petition to Account and Account.

1674. MARSTON, JAMES (1777) #4348
EST. Chichester yoeman decd. ADMIN.: 4/30/1777. Admx. Phebe Marston, Chichester widow. Bond L200.0.0. Sureties: Thomas Hunniford and Nathaniel Pease, Newmarket yoemen. Witnesses: Nathl. Parker and W. Parker. INVY.: Appr. 7/29/1777. Comm.: Jeremiah Sanborn, Edmund Rand Leavitt and Jonathan Stanyan. Value L51.8.6 less L40.16.6 sold. Oath 7/29/1778 Admx. to judge. Judge notes Comm. sworn before appr. and oaths are on back of Warr. CLAIMS: 8/13/1781.Comm.:Edmund Rand and Smith Morrill. Total L116.9.5. Oaths 6/21/1783 Comm. to John Cram, JP. ACCOUNT: 8/1773. Of Admx. Allowed 8/26/1783. Account includes main. 2 children. PROP. & SETTLM.: Claims L117.8.7. Amount to be proportioned L7.11.6. Allowed 11/19/1783 with order to Admx. to pay.

1675. MARSTON, JAMES (1786) #5172
EST. Hampton husbandman decd. testate. WILL: Drawn 10/16/1784. Legatees: Wife-Abigail; Sons-Samuel, Jacob and Ashel; Daus.-Comfort Peas wife of Samuel Peas, Sarah Marston and Mary Marston. Execs.-sons Samuel and Jacob and Nathaniel Shannon. His sig. Witnesses: Joseph Dow, Jona. Garland and Joseph Philbrick Jr. CERT. WILL (D28:434): 2/15/1786. Presented by Execs. and witnesses Garland and Philbrick.

1676. MARSTON, JOHN (1795) #6117
EST. Nottingham yoeman decd. ADMIN.: 6/22/1795. Admr. John Marston, Nottingham joiner. Bond $3,000.00. Sureties: John Kelsa and William Kelsa, Nottingham yoemen. Witnesses: Mary S. Parker and W. Parker. INVY.: Appr. 7/10/1795. Comm.: Bradbury Cilley, John Gile and Thomas Odel. Value $390.00. Oaths 9/12/1795 Comm. to Benjamin Butler, JP. Oath 9/14/1795 Admr. to W. Parker. PETITION: 4/16/1796. Of Admr. For Comm. Insolvency. Gives claims already in as $300.00 and others not ascertained. Granted. CLAIMS WARR.: 4/16/1796. Comm.: Thomas Bartlett, esq. and John Kelsa, yoeman, both of Nottingham. CLAIMS: Total $224.59. Oaths 1/16/1797 Comm. to Jos. Cilley, JP. PETITION: 2/19/1797. Of Admr. For License and for an allowance to widow out of personal est. License granted. LICENSE (D32:250): 2/9/1797. To Admr. To sell real est. to amount of $260. DOWER: Comm.: Josiah Bartlett, Gideon Randel, John Kelsa, Thomas Odal and Joseph Nealey. Of Widow Mary Marston. Oaths 2/16/1797 Bartlett, Randel and Kelsa to Thos. Bartlett, JP. Allowed. ACCOUNT: 3/1797. Of Admr. Allowed 3/7/1797.

1677. MARSTON, JONATHAN (1799) #6574
EST. Hampton husbm. decd. testate. WILL: Drawn 11/19/1794. Legatees: Wife-Hannah; Sons-Jonathan and Abraham; Dau.-Mary Dearborn; Children of his dau. Abigail Nudd decd.: Josiah, Thomas and James. Execs.-sons Jonathan and Abraham. His sig. Witnesses: Caleb Toppan, Philip Towle and Oliver Whipple. CERT. WILL (D33:94): 6/5/1799. Presented by Execs. and witnesses Toppan and Whipple, esq. ADMIN.: 6/5/1799. Execs.: Jonathan Marston and Abraham Marston, Hampton husbandmen. Bond $3,000.00. Sureties: Caleb Toppan, yoeman and Oliver Whipple, esq., both of Hampton. Witnesses: Saml. Parker and W. Parker.

1678. MARSTON, WINTHROP (1795) #6142
EST. Brentwood yoeman decd. testate. WILL: Drawn 1/1/1793. Legatees: Wife-Martha; Sons-Samuel, Jonathan, James, Winthrop and Jeremiah; Daus.-Hannah Gordon, Hephzebah Young, Ruhamah Burleigh, Molly Sanborn and Betty Robinson. Execs.-sons Samuel and Jonathan. His sig. Witnesses: Nathan Tuck, Edward Tucke and Saml. Shepard. CERT. WILL (D32:51): 10/1/1795. Presented by Execs. and on oath of Nathan Tuck and affirm. Edward Tucke. ADMIN.: 10/1/1795. Execs.: Samuel Marston and Jonathan Marston, Brentwood yoemen. Bond $3,000.00. Sureties: Edward Tucke and Nathan Tuck, Brentwood yoemen. Witnesses: Mary S. Parker and Wm. Parker. INVY.: Appr. 10/19/1795. Comm.: Ezekl. Godfrey and Jabez Smith, esquires and Porter Kimball. Value $1,444.26. Oaths 12/7/1795 Godfrey, Smith and Samuel Marson, and Exec., affirm. of Jonathan Marston, and Exec. to John Scribner, JP.

1679. MARTIN, JAMES (1781) #4737
EST. Pembroke gent. decd. ADMIN.: 9/13/1781. Admx. Elizabeth Martin, Pembroke widow. Bond L40000.0.0. Sureties: James Cochran and William Cochran, Pembroke gentlemen. Witnesses: John McDaniel and Robert Martin. INVY. WARR.: 12/28/1781. Comm.: William Cochran, gent. and John McDaniel, both of Pembroke. INVY.: Value L180.8.0. Oaths 1/28/1782. Comm.: to Timo. Walker, Jr. JP. Oath 1/30/1782 Admx. to Wm. Parker, Reg.

1680. MASON, BENJAMIN (1792) #5784
EST. Hampton taylor decd. testate. WILL: Drawn 9/15/1787. Legatees: Sons-Benjamin, Edmund and Josiah; Daus.-Martha Moulton wife of Small Moulton; Sarah Mason wife of Benjamin Mason, Mary Mason and Abigail Mason. Exec.- son Edmund. His sig. Witnesses: Abraham P. Towle, Issac Marston and Moses Elkins. CERT. WILL D30:248): 6/18/1792. Presented by Exec. and witnesses Towle and Marston. ADMIN.: 6/20/1792. Exec. Edmund Mason, Hampton yoeman. Bond L500.0.0. Sureties: Abraham

Towle of Hampton and Isaac Marston of North Hampton, yoemen. Witnesses: Nat Parker and W. Parker. INVY.: Comm.: Abraham P. Towle, Isaac Marston and Joseph Towle Jr. Value L93.1.0. Oaths 3/12/1793 Abraham P. Towle, Marston and Exec. to Christo. Toppan, JP.

1681. MASON, EDWARD (1785) #5069
EST. Stratham husbm. decd. testate. WILL: Drawn 12/4/1784. Legatees: Wife-Molly; Sons-Edward, Ward and Noah; Dau.-Molly Marvel. Exec. son-Edward. His sig. Witnesses: Samuel Pottle, Jonathan Chase, Levi Pottle and Saml. Shepard. CERT. WILL:1/19/1785. Presented by Exec. and oath of witness Samuel Pottle and affirm. Rev. Shepard. INVY.: Appr. 4/20/1785. Comm.: Paine Wingate, gent. and Jonathan Chase and Samuel Pottle, yoemen. Value L584.5.0. Oaths 4/20/1785 Comm. and Exec. to judge. DOWER WARR.: 3/21/1787. Comm.: Samuel Lane, esq.; Paine Wingate, Jona. Robinson and Joseph Norris, gentlemen, all of Stratham and Saml. Pottle of Exeter. Of Widow Molly Mason. Dower: 7/18/1787. Oaths 7/18/1787 Lane, Wingate and Robinson to judge. Allowed.

1682. MASON, JOHN (1777) #4299
GDP. Of the son of John Mason, Deerfield yoeman decd. GDP.: 1/22/1777. Of John. Gdn. John McClary, Londonderry (& Epsom) esq. Bond L200.0.0. Sureties: Michael McClary, gent. and Henry Parkinson, both of Londonderry. Witnesses: Noah Sinkler and Enoch Cates.

1683. MASON, JOHN TUFTON (1791) #5673
EST. Bridgon, Huntington Co., Great Britain esq. PETITION: 6/14/1791. Of Sarah Cath. Moffatt, dau. of John Tufton Mason. States that her father's Will was approved by the court in Great Britain and his widow, Mrs. Mary Tufton Mason, appointed sole Exex. While the Exex. may have executed the Will in Great Britain, she has done nothing about the est. in this country and has not invested some other person to do so. As in the Will Mary was devised part of both the real and personal est. in America, she requests the appointment of her son-in-law Nathaniel Appleton Haven as Admr. WILL: An attested copy filed with Mixed Records 1771-1772 p.37. Drawn 6/24/1780. Legatees: Present wife Mary. He confirms a prenuptial agreement made 12/13/1763. Dau.-Sarah Catherine wife of Samual Moffatt of Demorara, esq. and her children living at her death; Grandchildren-Anne, Elizabeth, Susanna and Charlotte Livius; Nephews-Thos. Sackville Tufton and John Tufton Mason; Nieces-Elizabeth Tufton and Susanna Tufton. Exec.-wife Mary; His sig. Witnesses: A. Winterbottom, merchant of Taylors Hall, London and Samuel Bicknell Jr. of Bishop Gate St., McHeylen, clk. to Mr. Winterbottom. Proved 9/5/1787 on oaths of Wid. Mary Mason, Exex.; Henry Stevens; Gorb Gortling and James Townley, actuaries. 8/13/1788 entered agreeable to the abstract: per

W. Parker, Reg. Follows Admin. of Mary Tufton Mason as Exex. and cert. as a true copy of will. PETITION: 7/11/1791. Of Nathl. Appleton Haven, Portsmouth physician. For Admin. as he has an interest in est. in right of his wife. ADMIN.: 8/15/1791. Admr. Nathaniel Appleton Mason, Portsmouth physician. Bond L1000.0.0. Sureties: Joseph Haven and John Haven, Portsmouth merchants. Witnesses: Clement Storer and Oliver Briard. LETTER ADMIN.: 8/15/1791. To Admr. Nathl. Appleton Haven. To admin. all of the est. in N.H. according to his will. ACT OF N.H. GENERAL COURT: Passed House 12/14/1791 and Senate 12/19/1791. Allows Mary Tufton Mason of Brigdon, Huntington Co., Great Britain to appeal the Decree allowing admin. to Dr. Nathl. Appleton Haven. CAVEAT: 1/25/1792. Of Thomas Martin of Portsmouth atty. to Exex. Mary Tufton Mason of Brigdon, Great Britain. Requests appeal from Decree appointing Haven Admr. as Martin believes the office belongs to him. Granted 1/25/1792. BOND: 1/25/1792. Of Thomas Martin, Portsmouth esq. Bond L1000.0.0. To appeal Decree of Admin. Surety Joseph Peirce, New Durham Gore, Strafford Co., esq. Witnesses: Charlotte Martin and Thomas Hart. ACCOUNT: 11/21/1792. Of Tho. Martin atty. to Exec. Allowed 11/21/1792.

1684. MASON, JOSEPH (1784) #4980
EST. Epping yoeman decd. testate. WILL: Drawn 5/23/1777. Legatees: Wife-Esther; Dau.-Sarah Mason; Cousins-Children of Benjamin Mason decd.: Mary Mason, Joseph Mason and Benjamin Mason; Sarah Shaw. Exec.-Benjamin Barker of Stratham. His mark. Witnesses: Jonathan Wiggin, Josiah Thirston and Benjamin Barker Jr. CERT. WILL (D27:408): 3/17/1794. Presented by Exec. and all witnesses: INVY. WARR.: 3/17/1784. Comm.: Jona. Wiggin and Pain Wingate, gentlemen and Jonah Thurstin, yoeman, all of Stratham. INVY.: Appr. 4/21/1784. Value L157.8.0. Oaths 4/21/1784 Wingate, Wiggin and Exec. to judge. ACCOUNT: 7/16/1788. Of Exec. Allowed 7/16/1788.

1685. MASON, NOAH (1797) #6397
EST. Stratham yoeman decd. ADMIN.: 12/12/1797. Admx. Comfort Mason, Stratham widow. Bond $3,000.00. Sureties: Jonathan Wiggin, gent. and John Marble, mariner, both of Stratham. Witnesses: Joseph Hoit and W. Parker. INVY. WARR.: 12/12/1797. Comm.: Jonathan Wiggin, gent.; Phinehas Merrill and Thomas Veasey, yoeman, all of Stratham. Invy.: Value $846.12. Oaths 3/10/1798 Wiggin, Merrill and Admx. to W. Parker. ADMIN. D.B.N.: 6/27/1799. Admr. d.b.n. Francis Mason, Exeter miller. Bond $2,000.00. Sureties: James Folsom, painter and Daniel Thurston, joiner, both of Exeter. Witnesses: Samuel Parker and W. Parker. LETTER ADMIN. D.B.N.: 6/27/1799. To Francis Mason, Admr., the former Admx. having married before finishing admin.

1686. MASSEY, DANIEL (1787) #5263
EST. Salem yoeman decd. ADMIN.: 3/21/1787. Admr. Jonathan Massey of Salem. Bond L500.0.0. Sureties: William Rogers of Salem and Robert Young, Pelham esq. Witnesses: Isaac Hills and Nathl. Parker. INVY.: Appr. 6/14/1787. Comm.: William Rogers, Richard Kimball and Silas Wheeler. Value L273.12.6. Oaths 6/14/1787 Comm. to Moody Morse, JP. Oath 6/20/1787 Admr. to judge.

1687. MATTHES: AGIGAIL, FRANCIS & TAMISON (1772) #3955
GDP. Of Abigail and Francis, minors under 14 and of Tamison, a minor over 14. Of Lee(?-sic). GDP.: 7/30/1772. Gdn. Gideon Matthes, Lee, Strafford Co. yoeman. Bond L500.0.0. Sureties: Joseph Sias of Lee, Strafford Co. and John Dudley of Raymond, esquires. Witnesses: Henry Moore and Samuel Parker. See also Pet. Div. (1784?) #5046 of Francis Matthew, Isaac Meder and Tamson his wife, Eldad Langley and Nathaniel Jones.

1688. MATTHES, FRANCIS; ISAAC MEDER & TAMSEN HIS WIFE (1784) #5046
PET. for Div. PETITION: Of: Francis Matthes of Lee and Isaac Meder and Tamsen his wife of Durham, all Strafford Co. For div. of about 100acresof land in Nottingham they hold in common with Eldad Langley of Nottingham and Nathaniel Jones, son of Ebenezer Jones, Lee, Strafford Co. yoeman decd., a minor, on which Langley now lives. Order: 10/20/1784. For hearing, Petitioners to send copies of Petition and Order to all concerned, including the Gdn. of Jones.

McALESTER. See also McAllaster

1689. McALESTER, JOHN (1780) #4634
EST. Londonderry yoeman decd. testate. WILL: Drawn 4/24/1780. Legatees: Wife-Rebacca; Sons-Benjamin (youngest) and Isaac; Dau.-Sarah; Child his wife is now pregnant with. Execs.-wife Rabecca and Thomas Wallace Jr. His mark. Witnesses: Peter Patterson, Thomas Patterson and James Betton. CERT. WILL (D25:350): 6/28/178. Presented by Execs. and witnesses Betton, esq. and Thomas Patterson. INVY.: Appr. 7/12/1780. Comm.: James Betton, Andrew Mack and Thomas Patterson. Value L40300.0.0. Oaths 8/23/1780 Mack, Patterson and Exex. to James Betton, JP. PETITION: 12/23/1785. Of Rebecca McAllester, Exex. For setting off of her Dower. Requests Comm. of John Clark, John Dwinel, Andrew Mack and Robert Thompson, Londonderry yoeman and James Betton, Windham esq. She also notes that the personal est. is not sufficient to pay debts and requests License. LICENSE (D25:529):.1/18/1786.To Exex. To sell the real est.

McALLASTER. See also McAlester

1690. McALLASTER, ARCHIBALD (1778) #4469
EST. Londonderry yoeman decd. testate. WILL: Drawn 7/23/1778. Legatees: Wife-Jane; Son-David; Daus.-Margaret Clark McAllester and Lydia McAllester. Execs.-Thomas Patterson and Andrew Mack, both of Londonderry. His mark. Witnesses: Josiah Jones, Petter Paterson and John McAllester. CERT. WILL (D24:318): 8/26/1778. Presented by Execs. and witnesses Paterson and Jones. INVY. WARR.: 8/26/1778. Comm.: Petter Paterson, Josiah Jones and Henry Campbell, Londonderry yeomen. INVY.: Value L974.9.0. Oaths 2/6/1779 Comm. to John Bell, JP. DOWER WARR.: 9/30/1778. Comm.: Petter Paterson, John Clark, Robert Thompson, Abel Plummer and Henry Campbell all of Londonderry. Of Widow Jane McAllaster. DOWER: 1/6/1779. Oaths 2/6/1779 Clark, Paterson and Campbell to John Bell, JP. Allowed 3/31/1779. ACCOUNT: 11/27/1782. Of Execs. Allowed 11/27/1782.
1691. McALLASTER, DAVID (1791) #5648
GDP. Of the son of Archibald McAllaster of Londonderry decd. GDP.: 4/20/1791. Of David, a minor over 14. Gdn. Edward Ela, Londonderry yoeman. Bond L1000.0.0. Sureties: Capt. Saml. Allison and Deacon Samuel Fisher, both of Londonderry. Witnesses: George Russell and Nathl. Parker.

1692. McBRIDE, JAMES (1783) #4944
EST. Exeter laborer decd. intestate. ADMIN.: 10/29/1783. Admr. James Thurston, Exeter blacksmith. Bond L200.0.0. Sureties: Daniel Jones, blacksmith and James Burleigh, joiner, both of Exeter. Witnesses: Nathl. Parker and W. Parker.

1693. McBRIDGE, BARNABAS (1783) No#
EST. Of Exeter decd. ADMIN. (D27:328): 10/29/1783. Admr. James Thurston. Sureties: Daniel Jones and James Burleigh, all of Exeter.

McCARTNEY. See also MaCartney

1694. McCARTNEY, JANE (1778) #4451
GDP. Of the dau. of John McCartney, Londonderry yoeman decd. GDP.: 5/22/1778. Of Jane, a minor over 14. Gdn. John Davidson, Windham yoeman. Bond L500.0.0. Sureties: James Davidson, yoeman and James Betton, esq., both of Windham. Witnesses: James Cochran and Samuel Betton.

1695. McCARTNEY: JOHN & MARY (1781) #4741
GDP. Of the children of John McCartney, Londonderry yoeman decd. GDP.: 9/26/1787. Of John and Mary, minors over 14. Gdn. James Anderson of Londonderry. Bond L1000.0.0. Sureties: Moody Morse of Salem and Willm. Rogers of Londonderry. Witnesses: Moses Harnett and Peter Patterson.

1696. McCARTNEY, MARGARET (1786) #5189
GDP. Of the dau. of John McCartney, Londonderry yoeman decd. GDP.: 4/21/1786. Of Margaret, a minor. Gdn. Mary Alexander, Londonderry widow. Bond L1000.0.0. Sureties: Hugh Alexander, Londonderry yoeman and James Betton, Windham esq. Witnesses: William Alexander and Agness Alexander.

1697. McCAY: DAVID & ROBERT (1779) No#
GDP. Of the sons of Charles McCay, Londonderry yoeman decd. GDP. (D25:201): 6/18/1779. Of: David and Robert, minors over 14. Gdn. Adam Taylor. Sureties: William Taylor and David Taylor, all Londonderry yoemen. The following Citation found in #5801BenjaminBrown (1792) belongs here. CITATION: 10/31/1792. To Capt. Adam Taylor, Londonderry gent., Gdn. of Robert McKay, of whom he was appointed Gdn 1779. To appear and exhibit his Account Gdp. for settlm. Cert.: 10/30/1792. Of John Morrison, Dept. Sheriff. He notified Taylor by reading the Citation to him. Note: The clerk erroneously marked this as Invy. est. of Benja. Brown.

1698. McCLARY, MAJOR ANDREW (1775) #4184
EST. Epsom innholder and esq. decd. intestate. ADMIN.: 11/11/1775. Admx. Elizabeth McClary, Epsom widow. Bond L1000.0.0. Sureties: John McClary, Epsom esq. and Eliphalet Giddinge, Exeter innholder. Witnesses: Ephraim Lock, Henry McCrellis, Israel Morey and Wm. Parker. INVY. WARR.: 11/11/1775. Comm.: Jeremiah Eastman and Daniel Page, both of Deerfield. Invy.: Appr. 10/1776 (sic.).Value L1122.4.6. Oaths 10/1/1776 Comm. to John McClary, JP. Oath 10/30/1776 Admx. to Wm. Parker, JP. & Reg. ACCOUNT: 11/27/1782. Of Admx. Allowed 12/4/1782. Account includes main. of William, Elizabeth and Nancy. Oath 5/19/1790 Admr. to judge, but also says she gave oath to judge 12/4/1782. LICENSE (D27:132): 12/1782. To Admx. To sell sufficient real est. to pay debts. DOWER: 3/26/1788. Comm.: Jeremiah Eastman, Joseph March, Daniel Page, Thomas Babb and Saml. Osgood. Of Widow Elizabeth McClary. Oaths 3/26/1788 Comm. to John McClary JP. Allowed 6/17/1788.ADDL.ACCOUNT: 5/1790. Of Admx. Allowed 5/19/1790. PETITION: Of Admx. For Comm. of Insolvency.

1699. McCLARY, ANDREW (1781) #4730
GDP. Of the son of Andrew McClary, Epsom esq. decd. GDP.: 6/28/1781. Of Andrew, a minor over 14. Gdn. Elizabeth McClary, widow. Bond L20000.0.0. Sureties: John McClary, esq. and Thomas Babb, husbm. Note: This file also includes the Will of John Mcclary, Epson esq. #6857 (1801) which is not included in this book.

1700. McCLURE: ANDREW, BETSEY, DAVID & POLLY (1797) #6304.
GDP. Of the children of Jonathan McClure, Deerfield yoeman decd. GDP.: 2/8/1797. Of: Andrew, David and Betsey, minors over 14 and of Polly, a minor under 14. Gdn. Moses Barnard, Deerfield esq. Bond $2,000.00. Sureties: Peter Sanborn, gent. and Jonathan McClure, yoeman, both of Deerfield. Witnesses: Sam. Colcord and W. Parker.
1701. McCLURE, JAMES (1791) #5667
EST. Exeter mariner decd. testate. WILL: Drawn 1/26/1789 ("going to sea.") Legatees: Wife-Elizabeth; All his children living at wife's death. Exex.-wife Elizabeth. His sig. Witnesses: Wm. Parker Jr., James Rundlett and Oliver Peabody. CERT. WILL (D30:79): 6/9/1791. Presented by Exex. and witnesses Parker and Rundlett. ADMIN.: 6/9/1791. Exex. Elizabeth McClure, Exeter widow. Bond L1000.0.0. Sureties: Nathl. Gilman, esq. and Gideon Lamson, shopkeeper, both of Exeter. Witnesses: Henry S. (Randel?) and Peggy Warren.

1702. McCLURE, JONATHAN (1787) #5297
EST. Deerfield yoeman decd. intestate. ADMIN.: 10/31/1787. Admx. Mary Mcclur, Deerfield widow. Bond L500.0.0. Sureties: Samuel McClure and Chase Prescott, Deefield yoemen. Witnesses: John Parker and W. Parker. INVY.: Appr. 1/10/1788. Comm.: Jeremiah Eastman, Moses Barnard and Patton Simpson. Value L290.2.3. Oaths 1/10/1788 Comm. to Richard Jenness, JP. Oath 1/10/1788 Admx. to Jeremiah Eastman, JP. APPR. WARR.: 9/18/1793. Comm.: William Smith, gent.; Benjamin Fellows and Dudley Leavitt, yoemen, all of Deerfield. To view 2/3 of real est. to see if it can be div. among all his children. Div. or appr. Appr.: 10/1/1793. Value with reversion of Dower L217.10.0. Oaths 10/1/1793 Comm. to George Evens, JP. DECREE SETTLM. (D32:246): 2/8/1797. Jonathan McClur, oldest son, appearing and consenting, real est. is settled on him, Jonathan to pay each of his co-heirs $103.57, Sally Evans and David McClure in one year, Andrew McClure and Betsey McClure in 3 years and Polly McClure in 5 years, with interest. Jonathan is entitled to 2 shares. BOND: 2/8/1797. Of Jonathan McClur, Deerfield yoeman. Bond $1,450.00. To pay co-heirs per Decree Settlm. Sureties: Peter Sanborn, Deerfield gent. and Peter Sanborn, Kingston yoeman. Witnesses: W. Parker and Thos. Page.

McCOLLOM. See also McCollum

1703. McCOLLOM, ALEXANDER (1781) #4728
EST. Londonderry yoeman decd. testate. WILL: Drawn 1/21/1781. Legatees: Sons-Thomas and Robert; Heirs of his son Alexander decd.; Sons-in-law-Isaac Brewster and Jane his wife, Abraham Morison and Elizabeth his wife, John Gordon and Jannet his wife; Grandau.-Jennet McColom dau. of his son Robert. Exec.- son Robert. His mark. Witnesses: Josiah McNeill, Samuel Alls and Archibald McMurphy. CERT. WILL (D26:143): 7/25/1781. Presented by Exec. and witnesses Alls and McMurphy. INVY. WARR.: 7/25/1781. Comm.: Samuel Alls, Archibald McMurphy and William Adams, Londonderry gentlemen. INVY.: Appr. 9/5/1781. Value L28.16.11 + 40 dollars old emission. Oaths 9/5/1781 Comm. and Exec. to John Bell, JP.

McCOLLUM. See also McCollum

1704. McCOLLUM, ROBERT (1799) #6626
EST. Londonderry gent. decd. ADMIN.: 12/18/1799. Admx. Martha McCollum, Londonderry widow. Sureties: Archibald McMurphy, esq. and David Brewster, yoeman, both ofLondonderry.Bond$3,000. Witnesses: Alesd. McColom and Wm. Parker. INVY.: Comm.: John Pinkerton and Willm. Adams, esquires and James Pinkerton, merchant. Value $2,158.64. Oaths 4/14/1800 Comm. and Admx. to John Bell, JP. DOWER WARR.: 5/21/1804. Comm.: John Bell, John Pinkerton and William Adams, esquires; James Pinkerton and John Pinkerton Jr., gentlemen, all of Londonderry. Of Widow Martha MacCollum. DOWER: 5/28/1804. Oaths 7/5/1804 Adams, James Pinkerton and James Pinkerton Jr. to John Bell, JP. Allowed.

McCRELLIS. See also McCrillis

1705. McCRELLIS, WILLIAM (1775) #4186
EST. Nottingham yoeman decd. ADMIN.: 12/6/1775. Admx. Lydia McCrellis, Epping widow. Bond L500.0.0. Sureties: William Morrill, Epping yeoman and Joseph Sias, Lee, Strafford Co. esq. Witnesses: James Kelse and James Sanborn. INVY. WARR.: 12/6/1775. Comm.: Joseph Sias, Lee, Strafford Co. esq. and James Sambon, Epping yoeman. INVY.: 2/26/1776. Appr.2/26/1776. Value L118.15.4. Oaths 5/29/1776 Comm. and Admx. to judge. PETITION: 5/30/1786.OfJohn McCrillis, Nottingham gent. For div. of Dower held in common by heirs, one of whom is a minor. Agreed to by Jonathan Hutchins, Nathaniel Demerit and William Morrill, Gdn. of the minor. They recommend a Comm. of: Joseph Sias, Miles

Randell and James Bracket, Lee, esquires and John Thompson, Durham yoeman, all of Strafford Co. and John Gile, Nottingham gent. DIV. WARR.: 6/24/1786. Comm. as requested. To div. Dower, giving 2/5 to oldest son and one share to each of the other heirs. DIV.: 6/26/1786. Divisees: John McCrillis (oldest son); Daus.-Jane Huckins and Mary Demerit; Granddau.-Jane McCrillis. Oaths 7/3/1786 Brackett and Gile to Joseph Sias, JP. Oath 12/20/1786 Sias, esq. to judge. ACCOUNT: 7/20/1791. Of John Sias and wife Lydia, Admx. Allowed 7/20/1791. Account includes main. of Jane.

McCRILLIS. See also McCrellis

1706. McCRILLIS, JANE (1782) #4788
GDP. Of the dau. of William McCrillis, Nottingham yoeman decd. GDP.: 3/27/1782. Of Jane, a minor under 14. Gdn. William Morrill, Epping yoeman. Bond L500.0.0. Sureties: Robert Page, Deerfield yoeman and Joseph Sias, Lee, Strafford co. esq. Witness Nathl. Parker. GDP.: 4/25/1788. Of Jenny, a minor over 14. Gdn. William Plumer, Epping yoeman. Bond L500.0.0. Sureties: Samuel Plumer, husbm. and Samuel Plumer Jr., yoeman, both of Epping. Witnesses: Rebecca Plumer and Daniel Plumer.

1707. McCRILLIS, JANE (1786) #5204
EST. Nottingham widow decd. intestate. ADMIN.: 5/29/1786. Admr. John McCrillis, Nottingham gent. Bond L2000.0.0. Sureties: Israel Randel, gent. and Samuel Dame, yoeman, both of Nottingham. Witnesses: Saml. Hobart and Nathl. Parker. INVY.: Comm.: Israel Randel and John Gile. Value L46.13.5. Oaths 12/16/1786. Comm. to James Brackett, JP. Oath 12/20/1786 Admx. to judge.

1708. McCURDY, NANNY (1785) #5106
EST. Londonderry widow decd. intestate. ADMIN.: 6/8/1785. Admr. Samuel McFarland, Londonderry yoeman. Bond L1000.0.0. Sureties: Archibald McMurphy of Londonderry and Henry Moore of Chester, esquires. Witnesses: John Shaw and W. Parker. LETTER ADMIN.: 6/8/1785. To Samuel McFarland, Londonderry yoeman, Admr. Witness W. Parker, Reg.

1709. McCURDY, ROBERT (1778) #4470
EST. Londonderry yeoman decd. testate. WILL: Drawn 6/8/1778. Legatees: Wife-Nanny; Sons-John and Robert; Daus.-Mary Cochran wife of Peter Cochran, Jennet McCurdy, Ann McCurdy, Elisabeth McCurdy and Nanny McCurdy; Mary Stinson and Jane Stinson, daus. of his dau.

Margaret Stinson who married Nathan Stinson: Grandson-James McCurdy son of his son John. He also specifically mentions "all my unmarried children. Execs.-Matthew Thornton esq. and wife Nanny. His sig. Witnesses: Robert McFarland, Jonathan Kelsey and Bemste Plummer. CERT. WILL: (D24:327) Presented by Admrs. and witnesses McFarland and Kelsey. INVY.: Comm.: John Gilmore, Robert Archibald and Samuel Dodge, yoemen. Value L4043.9.0. Oaths 11/1778 Comm. to John Bell, JP. Oath 11/25/1778 Matthew Thornton, an Exec., to Wm. Parker, Reg.
McDaniel. See also McDonald

1710. McDANIEL, JOHN (1796) #6214
EST. Pembroke yoeman decd. testate. WILL: Drawn 6/26/1793. Legatees: Wife-Mary; Sons-Nehemiah and John; Daus.-Hannah McDaniel, Mary McDaniel, Jeney McDaniel, Betty McDaniel and Maryann McDaniel. Exec.-William Cochran. His sig. Witnesses: Samuel Martin, Natt Martin and Daniel Cochran. CERT. WILL (D32:138): 5/18/1796. Presented by Exec. and witnesses Samuel Martin and Nathaniel Martin. ADMIN.: 5/18/1796. Exec. William Cochran, Pembroke gent. Bond $3,000.00. Sureties: Samuel Martin and Nathaniel Martin, Pembroke yoemen. Witnesses: Allen Gilman and W. Parker. INVY. (D32:189): Comm.: Saml. Daniels, Caleb Lovejoy and Robert Martin. Value L492.19.2. Oaths 8/23/1796 Comm. to Daniel Knox, esq. Oath 9/21/1796 Exec. to judge.

1711. McDANIEL, NEHEMIAH (1799) #6567
EST. Pembroke yoeman decd. testate. CAVEAT: 5/15/1799. Of Samuel Gault of Canterbury. Requests Will not be proved as it was obtained unfairly, Nehemiah being of unsound mind and incompetent at time of signing and for some time previous. Order: For hearing on Caveat. WILL: Drawn 4/9/1798. Legatees: Wife-Margaret; Daus.-Moley Cochran, Nally Knox, Margret Cochran, Jenny Martin and Martha Gault; Heirs of Robert McDaniel his oldest son; Heirs of John McDaniel his youngest son. Exec.-Daniel Knox, esq. His mark. Witnesses: Eben. Moses, Nehem. Cochran and William Cochran. CERT. WILL (D33:81): 5/15/1799. Presented by Exec. and witnesses Nehemiah Cochran and William Cochran, the objections of Samuel Gault not with standing. ADMIN.: 5/15/1799. Exec. Daniel Knox, Pembroke esq. Bond $2,000.00. Sureties: Deacon William Cochran and Joseph Emery Jr., both of Pembroke. Witnesses: John Knox Jr. and Nath. Parker.

1712. McDANIEL, ROBERT (1771) #3897
EST. Barrington yoeman decd. testate. WILL: Drawn 11/28/1771. Legatees: Sons-Nehemiah, John, William and James; Daus.-Eleonor and Margaret McDaniels. Exec.-son John. His mark. Witnesses: William

McDaniel Jr., Patrick Tobyne and Jeremiah McDaniel. Noted by clerk as proved 12/30/1771. ADMIN.: 12/30/1771. Exec. John McDaniel of Barrington. Bond L500.0.0. Sureties: Patrick Tobyne and William McDaniel Jr., both of Barrington. Witnesses: John Goffe and Samuel Penhallow.

McDONALD. See also McDaniel

1713. McDONALD, ROBERT (1787) #5273
EST. Pembroke yoeman decd. ADMIN.: 6/20/1787. Admx. Lydia McDaniel, Pembroke widow. Bond L500.0.0. Sureties: William Cochran and John McDonald, Pembroke yoemen. Witnesses: Nehemiah McDaniel and Eben. Moses. INVY.: Comm.: William Cochran, John Cochran and Solomon Whitehouse. Value L475.17.0. Oaths 3/28/1788 Comm. to Saml. Daniell, JP.

1714. McFARLAND, ELIZABETH (1798) #6420
EST. Chester spinster decd. ADMIN.: 2/15/1798. Admr. Daniel McFarland, Antrim, Hillsborough Co. gent. Bond $3,000.00. Sureties: Henry Moore, Chester esq. and James Thurston, Exeter gent. Witness W. Parker. INVY.: Appr. 2/20/1798. Comm.: Henry Moore, Robert Forsith and Jabez Hoit. Value $45.00. Oaths 2/20/1798 Moore and Forsith to Jabez Hoit, JP. "Admr. not sworn."

McGREGOR. See also McGregore, Macgregore

1715. McGREGOR, JAMES (1776) #4244
EST. Londonderry gent. decd. testate. WILL: Draw 6/7/1776. Legatees: Daus. of friends James Adams and Robt. Moor; Children of his bro. Rev. David MacGregor; Children of his sister Jane; Only surviving child of his sister Margaret; Surviving children of his bro. Alexander. Exec.-bro. Rev. David MacGregor. His mark. Witnesses: John Moor, Moses Lankester and Mary Whiten. CERT. WILL: 6/21/1776. Presented by Exec. and all witnesses. INVY. WARR.: 6/21/1776. Comm.: John Moor, gent; John McKeen and John Hunter, yoemen, all of Londonderry. INVY: Value L2075.3.11 3/4. Oaths 11/26/1776 McKeen, Moor and Exec. to Moses Barnett, JP. LIST OF NOTES OF HAND DUE EST.: Total L378.18.8. PETITION: 10/18/1776. Of James Macgregore of Londonderry. Requests div. One of the divisees is a minor. Order: For hearing, the other divisees to be notified. DIV.: Comm.: Moses Barnett, Thomas Christy, James Ramsey and John Clark. To div. the real est. in 16 equal shares among the heirs. Divisees: The children of Rev. David Macgregor: sons-Lt. David; Robert, Goffstown, Hillsborough Co esq. and James Jr.; Daus.-Mary

Means wife of Robert Means, Amherst, Hillsborough Co. merchant; Margaret Rogers wife of Col. James Rogers of Kent, Cumberland Co., NY; Maryann Hopkins wife of James Hopkins of Londonderry; Jane Macgregore and Elizabeth Macgregore. The children of Dr. Alexander Clark decd.: Sons-Alexr., Archibald and Mathew; Dau.-Mary Clark. The children of Alexander Macgregore: Son-James. Daus.-Susannah Burnside wife of Thomas Burnside, Stonington, Grafton Co. esq. and Margaret Comstock; Agness Warner wife of Tobias Warner of Portsmouth dau. of Margaret Catswell. Oaths 12/9/1776 Comm. to John Bell, JP. CAVEAT: 3/12/1777. Of Tobias Warner, Portsmouth yeoman in right of his wife who is a legatee of her uncle James McGregore. Requests that he be notified of the time of the examination of the Exec.'s Account and that acceptance of the Account be withheld until he has been heard on it.

1716. McHARD, JAMES (1781) #4683
EST, Haverhill, Essex Co., MA esq. decd. testate. WILL: Drawn 10/1/1769. Legatees: Wife-Margaret; Son-James; Daus.-Sarah Duncan and Abigail White; Grand-sons-Thomas McHard White, Richard White, and James White children of his dau. Abigail White; Also children of his dau. Abigail White-not named; Son-in-law-John White; Nephews-Joseph Johnson, John McHard, Joseph McHard and William Dixon of Newburyport, Essex Co., MA.; Malatto girl Jane bequeathed to wife. Exec.- son James. His sig. Witnesses: Nathl. Saltonstall, John Wingate and Nathl. Peaslee Sargeant. Proved: 7/16/1772. Presented by Exec. and witnesses Wingate and Sargeant, esquires. Cert.: Of Daniel Noyes, Reg. Probate, Essex Co., MA as a true copy.

1717. McILVAINE, DANIEL JR. (1785) #5137
EST. Windham taylor decd. testate. WILL: Drawn 7/3/1785. Legatees: Parents-Daniel and Mary McIlvaine; Bros.(?)-Robert, Jno., William, Ebenezer and James McIlvaine and Sister Mary; Nephew-Daniel McIlvaine son of Ebenezer and Mary McIlvaine; Cousin-Elizabeth Davison; The child now a minor. Exec.-bro. Robert. His sig. Witnesses: John Davison, John Simpson and Jesse Davison. CERT. WILL (D28:288): 9/21/1785. Presented by Exec. and witnesses Simpson and Jesse Davison. INVY. (D29:364): Comm.: Gain Armour, Benja. Thom and John Simpson. Value L277.16.3. Oaths 4/20/1790 Comm. and Exec. to James Betton, esq.

1718. McINTIRE, WILLIAM (1786) #5208
EST. Portsmouth mariner decd. ADMIN.: 8/3/1786. Admx.: Ruth McIntire, Portsmouth widow. Bond L1000.0.0.Sureties:James Haslet, leather dresser and Danl. Peirce, both of Portsmouth. Witnesses: George

Gains and Patty Haslett. INVY.: Appr. 8/15/1786. Comm.: Danl. Peirce and Joseph Low. Value L1.16.6. Oaths 8/15/1786 Admx. and Comm. to George Gains, JP.

1719. McKACHAN, JOHN (1793) #5905
EST. Tabago merchant decd. ADMIN.: 6/29/1793. Admr. Jacob Sheafe, Portsmouth merchant. Bond L1000.0.0. Sureties: Thomas Sheafe, merchant and James Sheafe, esq., both of Portsmouth. Witnesses: Gilbert Horney and Matt. S. Marsh.

1720. McKAY, ROBERT (1779) No#
GDP. Of Londonderry? The following item found in #5801 Benjamin Brown (1792) and mistakenly noted by clerk as "Invy. est. Benja. Brown of Epping. CITATION: 12/31/1792. To Capt. Adam Taylor, Londonderry gent, Gdn. of Robert McKay, of whom he was appointed Gdn. 1779. To appear and exhibit his Account of Gdp. for settlm.

McKEAN. See also McKeen

1721. McKEAN, MARY (1798) #6519
EST. Of Londonderry decd. ADMIN. (D33:7): 12/19/1798. Admr. Joseph McKean, Beverly, Essex Co., MA clerk. Sureties: Daniel McKean and Samuel McKean, Londonderry yeomen. INVY. (D33:66): Appr. 12/20/1798. Comm.: Geo. Reid, John Nesmith and Aaron Choat. Value $367.00. Oaths 4/17/1799 Comm. and Admr. to judge.

McKEEN. See also McKean

1722. McKEEN, DEA. JOHN (1793) #5949
EST. Of Londonderry decd. ADMIN.: 12/18/1793. Adnmx. Mary McKeen, Londonderry widow. Bond L2000.0.0. Sureties: John McKeen, Londonderry gent. and Joseph McKeen, Beverly, Essex Co., MA clerk. Witnesses: Daniel McKeen and Samuel McKeen. INVY.: Appr. 12/20/1793. Comm.: John Cochran and James Orr. Value L350.18.7 3/4. Oaths 4/17/1794 Comm. and on 12/17/1794 Admx. to judge.

1723. McMASTERS, JAMES (1781) #4694
EST. Portsmouth merchant, an absentee. INVY.: 4/26/1779. Comm. Nathl. Cooper. Copy of an Invy. of the goods and articles delivered to Caleb Hodgdon and John B. Hanson, a Comm., being part of the est. of James McMasters & Co. which Cooper had in care. Items are listed without any appr. and include 77 notes due. RECEIPT: 2/14/1780. Of Nichl. Gilman, treasurer. He received from Caleb Hodgdon, esq. L145.4.0. for Capt.

Dalling's note of which James McMasters was possessed, for which sum Gilman is accountable to the State. TRUSTEESHIP: 3/28/1781. Of the est. of James McMasters, late Portsmouth merchant, confiscated to the State of N.H. Trustee Wentworth Cheswill, Newmarket yoeman. Bond L50000.0.0. Sureties: John Tash of New Durham and David Folsom of Tamworth, Strafford Co. esquires. Witnesses: Andrew Freese and Nathl. Parker. ACCOUNT: 3/7/1782. Of Joseph Badger, Caleb Hodgdon and John B. Hanson, a Comm. appointed by the Court to take care of and dispose of ests. of the absentees in Strafford Co., N.H. An Account of the income and expenses of sales of sundry goods which were the property of James McMasters & Co. Allowed 3/7/1782, presented by Hodgdon and Burnham. Account also includes an item, "an Invy. of the Account of the Sales of goods which belonged to John Wentworth, esq. (Gov.) at L64.6.4." RECEIPT:3/8/1782. Of Nichl. Gilman, treasurer. He received of John B. Hanson and Maj. Hodgon, agents or trustees of McMasters' est., Bounty Notes amounting to L15.17.5 for which sum he is accountable to the state. ACCOUNT: 4/1/1784. Of Wentworth Cheswill, Trustee. An account of some of the Notes listed in the Invy. He notes that Note #67 listed in the name of Stephen Parsons should be Joseph Parsons. Allowed 4/21/1781. See also #4695 for est. John McMasters who was in partnership with James. Note: This file also includes a torn and incomplete bond of Peter Hopkinson which is recorded under his name.

1724. McMASTERS, JOHN (1781) #4695
EST. Portsmouth merchant, an absentee. TRUSTEESHIP: 2/28/1781. Of the est. of John McMasters, late Portsmouth merchant, an absentee from the state, whose est. is by law declared forfeit to the use of the state. Trustee Wentworth Cheswill, Newmarket yoeman. Bond L100000.0.0. Sureties: Josiah Adams, esq. and Hubartus Neal, gent., both of Newmarket. Witnesses: Mark Wiggin and Simon Wiggin. ORDER: 9/5/1781. To Joseph Badger, Caleb Hodgdon and John Burnham Hanson, esquires, a Comm. appointed to take possession of the estates in Strafford Co. of certain persons named in the Act entitled "An Act to Confiscate the Estates of Sundy Persons," enacted 11/28/1778. In accordance with a Resolve of the NH General Court dated 8/29/1781, they are required to deliver to Wentworth Cheswill, who has been appointed Trustee of the confiscated estates of John McMasters and James McMasters, late of Portsmouth, absentees from the state, all the books, papers and other effects of the confiscated estates. Cert.: 9/26/1781. Of Trustee. He called on John Burnham Hanson, showed him the Order, and demanded the books, papers and other effect of John McMasters and James McMasters which he supposed to be in Hanson's possession, but Hanson has neglected to do so. ADDL. ACCOUNT: 7/30/1791. Of Trustee. Of ests. of James

McMasters and John McMasters. Allowed 8/15/1791. See also #4694 est. of James McMasters who was in partnership with John.

1725. McMASTERS, WILLIAM (1782) #4797
GDP. Of Chester yoeman n.c.m. RECOMMENDATION: 4/22/1782. Of: Jabez Hoit, Stephen Morse and Joseph Blanchard, Chester Selectmen. They state that William has become n.c.m., has no wife, child, bro. or sister to care for him and needs a Gdn. They recommend as Gdns. Thomas McMaster, a nephew who lives near William, and Daniel Hunter of Londonderry, a near kinsman. GDP.: 4/24/1782. Of William, an adult adjudged n.c.m. Gdns.: Thomas McMasters of Chester and Daniel Hunter of Londonderry. Bond L1000.0.0. Sureties: William Gilmore and John Moore of Londonderry. Witnesses: Josiah Brown and W. Parker. The following 2 items are in #4833 William McMasters (1782), William's est., but belong here. INVY. WARR.: 4/24/1782. Comm.: David Weatherspoon, David Dickey and William Gilchrist, all of Chester. To take an Invy. of est. of William, an adult n.c.m. INVY. Appr. 7/29/1782. Value not tallied. Esti. L350.0.0.+. Oaths 7/29/1782 Comm. and on 7/31/1782 Gdns. to Saml. Emerson, JP. See #4833 William McMasters (1782) for William's est.

1726. McMASTERS, WILLIAM (1782) #4833
EST. Chester adult adjudged n.c.m. decd. ADMIN.: 8/28/1782. Admrs.: Thomas McMasters of Chester and Daniel Hunton of Londonderry, yoemen. Bond L1000.0.0. Sureties: Isaac Blasdel of Chester and Robert Boyd, New Boston, Hillsborough Co. yoemen. Witnesses: Paul Jewett and Nathl. Parker. INVY. WARR.: 8/28/1782. Comm.: David Wetherspoon, gent.; David Dickey, yoeman and William Gilchrist, all of Chester. INVY.: Appr. 11/19/1782. Value not tallied. Esti. L400.0.0+. Oaths 11/19/1782 Comm. and Admrs. to Saml. Emerson, JP. Note: This file also contains an Invy. Warr. and Invy. which belong with William's Gdp. #4832 (1782) and are recorded there.

McMURPHY. See also MacMurphy

1727. McNEIL, DANIEL (1782) #4784
EST. Of Londonderry. PETITION: 3/14/1782. Of Thomas Willson, George Russell, William Parker, William McNeill and Alexdr. McNeill. Request appointment of James Macgregore Jr. as Admr. of est. of their bro. Daniel McNeal decd. The est. has been left in a critical situation and Macgregore is the greatest creditor. There is no other person except themselves and one bro. of McNeal who lives in Walpole, Cheshire Co. who can pretend to the admin. Consent: 3/25/1782. Of Alexander McNeill

of Walpole, Cheshire Co. ADMIN. (D26:318): 3/27/1782. Admr. James Macgregore, Londonderry merchant. Sureties: Jeremiah Fogg, Kensington esq. and James Thurston, Exeter innholder. Note: The following letter found in #4960 William McNeil (1783) belongs here. LETTER: 4/16/1783. From Admr. To judge. Macgregore is unable to attend court and all he has is his account against the est. He has paid each of the heirs as much as he can consent to pay until they give bond for future demands, in which case he will set a time to account. He notes that except for one, the heirs are persons of no fixed property. PETITION: 8/17/1791. Of: George Russell and Thomas Willson, heirs of decd. Request permission to sue Bond of Admin. since Admr. neglects to settle est., though cited to do so, thus keeping heirs from benefit of est. BOND.: 4/16/1794. Of John Prentice, Londonderry esq. Bond L60.0.0. To sue Bond of Admin. Witnesses: Ed. Livermore and Mo. Neal.

1728. McNEIL, WILLIAM (1783) #4960
EST. Chester yoeman decd. ADMIN.: 12/18/1783. Admx. Jennet McNeal, Chester widow. Bond L500.0.0. Sureties: Samuel Pilsbury, gent. and Isaac Thom, physician, both of Londonderry. Witnesses: Paul Jewett, Nathl., Parker and W. Parker. INVY. WARR.: 12/18/1783. Comm.: Samuel Pilsbury, gent. and James Macgregore, merchant, both of Londonderry and James Miller, Chester yoeman. INVY.: Appr. 3/8/1784. Value L219.9.11. Oaths 3/8/1784 Comm. to John Webster, JP. Oath 3/17/1784 Admx. to W. Parker, Reg. LICENSE (D27:405): 3/17/1787. To Admx. To sell sufficient real est. to pay debts. CITATION: 8/15/1787. To Admx. In response to a complaint, she is cited to appear and present her Account. Cert.: Of Stephen Merrill. He read the Citation to Jannet McNeal on 9/4 before a witness. ACCOUNT: 9/1787. Of Admx. Allowed 9/19/1787.

1729. McSHANNON, ELEANOR (1798) #6492
EST. Canterbury single woman decd. PETITION: Of Samuel Moor of Canterbury. States his sister, Eleanor McShannon, Canterbury single woman, has died leaving an est. but no bros. or parents. As husb. of her only sister, requests Admin. Granted. ADMIN. (D32:525): 9/19/1798. Admr. Samuel Moor of Canterbury. Sureties: Obadiah Mooney and Samuel Stevens, both of Canterbury. INVY.: Comm.: Marston Morrill, Obadiah Mooney and David McCrilles. Value $388.83. Oaths 1/23/1799 Mooney and McCrilles to Jereh. Clough, JP. Oath 1/25/1799 Admr. to judge. Note: The #4480 file is recorded as Shannon.

1730. McSHANNON, JOHN (1777) #4359 & AS SHANNON (1778) #4480
EST. Of Salem, Essex Co., MA. RENUN. (4359): 5/27/1777. Of Anna McShannon, Canterbury widow. Of Admin. of est. of her son John of Salem, Essex Co. MA. Requests appointment of her dau. Elennor McShannon, Canterbury single woman. Witnesses: Obadiah Mooney and Stephen Webster. ADMIN. (#4359): 5/28/1777. Admx. Elennor McShannon, Canterbury spinster and single woman. Bond L500.0.0. Sureties: John Molony, Canterbury mariner and John Casey of Epsom. Witness Samuel Huston. INVY. (#4480): Comm.: John Moloney, Archelaus Moore and Jeremiah Clough Jr. Value not tallied. Esti. L335.0.0+. Oaths 11/12/1777 Moloney and Moore to Jeremiah Clough, JP. Oath 9/30/1778 Admx. to judge.

1731. MELONEY, JAMES (1783) #4920
See #4900 Joseph Man (1783)
1732. MELOON, ENOCH (1794) #6007
EST. Portsmouth joiner decd. testate. WILL: Drawn 2/25/1794. Legatees: Wife-Mary; Son-Joseph; Daus.-Polly (changed to Mary), Libbey, Peggy (changed to Margaret) and Olive. Will notes changes made before signing. Exec.-wife Mary. His sig. Witnesses: Richard Jackson, Isaac Rindge and Jno. March. CERT. WILL (D31:304): 6/18/1794. Presented by Exex. and all witnesses. ADMIN.: 6/18/1794. Exex. Mary Meloon, Portsmouth widow. Bound L1000.0.0. Sureties: John Pitman, cooper and John March, saddler, both of Portsmouth. Witnesses: Joseph Clark and Alice Nason. INVY.: Appr. 3/31/1794. Comm.: Richard Jackson, Jno. March and John Pitman. Value L226.3.7. Oaths 3/31/1794 Comm. and on 6/17/1794 Exex. to Nathl. Adams, JP. Note: All papers in this file are photocopies except Will, which is in very fragile condition. They appear to have been water damaged.

1733. MELOON, JOSEPH (1774) #4118
EST. Greenland yoeman decd. intestate. RENUN.: 7/10/1774. Of Hannah Meloon, widow. Of Admin. Requests appointment of Major Wm. Weeks, esq. and Nathan Johnson, gent. Witnesses: John Folsom and Clemt. Weeks. ADMIN.: 8/11/1774/ Admrs.: William Weeks, esq. and Nathan Johnson, gent., both of Greenland. Bond L1000.0.0. Sureties: John Penhallow and Joseph Peirce, Portsmouth merchants. Witnesses: Saml. Hale Jr. and Benja. Mackay. INVY.: Appr. 11/8/1774. Comm.: Walter Bryent and Greenleaf Clark. Value L309.12.6. Oaths 11/9/1774 Comm. and Execs. to judge. PETITION: 1/1775. Of Widow Hannah Meloon. That her Dower be set off. Allowed 1/27/1775 with Comm. of Walter Bryent, esq.; Greenleaf Clark, John Huzzene, Ichabod Weeks and Thomas

Johnson. DOWER: 2/14/1775. Oaths 2/14/1775 Bryent, Clark and Johnson to judge. Includes Map. PETITION: 2/21/1775. Of Admrs. for License. Allowed 2/21/1775. LICENSE (D23:560): 2/21/1775. To Admrs. To sell sufficient real est. to pay debts. PETITION: 2/16/1804. Of John B. Hill on behalf of the heirs. States that both Admrs. are dead and during their lifetimes submitted no accounting. Requests Execs. of the ests. of Admrs. be cited to settle Account. ORDER: 2/16/1804. Citation be issued to Execs. of ests. of the Admrs. to appear 3d Wed. March. Order: 3/23/1804. Hearing postponed. Petitioner to furnish the Petitioner (sic.) with a copy of the proper amount they shall then lay before the judge ten days before the hearing. ACCOUNT: Of: Clement Weeks Exec. of est. of William Weeks, esq. and Nathan Johnson Exec. est. Nathan Johnson. DECREE: 6/29/1804. The Account was presented by Clement Weeks, Exec. of one Admr., examined and allowed on 6/20/1804. John B. Hill in right of his wife, an heir, objected to sundry items. Further consideration was deferred to this date, at which hearing the parties with their legal counsel were heard. Decree: The Admrs., by License, sold all the homeplace at private sale to Joshua Weeks, a son of William, who soon after conveyed the same to William. From evidence, it would have sold for more at public auction. The Execs. are to charge the Account with the further sum of L32.05.0 as addl. proceeds of the homeplace sold. Also, the Execs. are to strike out various sums listed, including the amount paid to the Widow, which was more than 1/3 of the personal est., and a sum said to be still due on the mortgage. An adjustment is to be made on the mortgage accounting. The final total due to heirs is $862.01.Note: Decree includes ref. to death of widow. Petition: 8/11/1804. Of Clement Weeks of Greenland and Nathan Johnson, Execs. of Meloon's Admrs. Request appeal from Decree on Account. BOND: 8/11/1804. Of Clement Weeks and Nathan Johnson. Bond $100.00. To appeal Decree on Account. Surety John Weeks, Greenland esq. Witnesses: Stephen M. Weeks and Mary Johnson.

1734. MENDUM, FRANCES (1771) #3883
EST. Portsmouth widow decd. DIV.: 10/24/1771. Divisees: Eleanor Shackford wife of William Shackford esq. 1/3; The children and legal reps. of Elizabeth Janvrin decd. late wife of George Janvrin 1/3; The legal reps. of Mary Wentworth late wife of Ebenezer Wentworth, both decd. 1/3. Oaths 10/24/1771 Comm. to judge. Allowed. NOTE: For Div. Warr. see Est. Nathaniel Mendum (1771) #3869.

1735. MENDUM, NATHANIEL (1771) #3869
EST. Portsmouth esq. decd. testate. WILL: Drawn 12/27/1770. Legatees: Dau.-Eleanor Shackford wife of William Shackford, esq.; Grandsons-Mendum Janvrin, John Janvrin and Ebenezer Janvrin children of his decd.

dau. Mary Janvrin; Granddau.-Rebecca Wentworth wife of Capt. George Wentworth; Great Grandson-George Long; Nathan Wentworth son of Capt. George Wentworth by his present wife; Great Granddau.-Mary Wentworth dau. Of George Wentworth and Rebecca his wife. Execs.- William Knight, esq.; Capt. George Wentworth and William Shackford, esq. His sig. Witnesses: John Wendell, Peter Coues and Zachariah Allen. Proved 9/5/1771 on oaths of Wendell and Coues. Note: In Will Nathaniel says "dau. Mary Janvrin." However all papers show that it was his dau. Elizabeth who married George Janvrin and his dau. Mary married Ebenezer Wentworth. INVY.WARR.: 9/6/1771. Comm.: John Marshall, boatbuilder and Joshua Brackett, physician, both of Portsmouth. INVY: Appr. 9/20/1771.Value not tallied. Esti. L3362.0.0+. Oaths 10/2/1771 Comm. and Execs. to judge. Plus a note that Dr. Brackett was paid in full for Invy. CERT.: 9/10/1771. Of William Shackford. He agrees to give security as provided in Will. Witnesses: John Marshall and Martha Marshall. DIV. WARR.: 10/12/1771. Comm.: Jonathan Warner, Daniel Rogers, Samuel Hale and John Parker, esquires and William Whipple, merchant. To div. the real est. which was Frances Mendrum's decd., of which she and her hus. Nathaniel were seized in her right at her death. Divisees: Eleanor Shackford wife of William Shackford, esq.; Children and legal heirs of Elizabeth Janvrin decd. late wife of George Janvrin; Legal reps. of Mary Wentworth late wife of Ebenezer Wentworth, both decd. Includes judge's notation that John Janvrin, a co-heir, is absent and his father George Janvrin is his agent and atty. and is also Gdn. of a minor heir. Note: See #3883 Frances Mendum (1771) for Div. DIV. WARR.: 10/25/1771. Comm.: Samuel Hale and John Parker, esquires; John Penhallow, Thomas Martyn and William Whipple, merchants, all of Portsmouth. To div. the real est. of Nathaniel. Div.: 11/4/1771. Divisees: William Shackford and Eleanor his wife in her right; Heirs of Elizabeth Janvrin decd.-Ebenezer Janvrin, Mendum Janvrin, John Janvrin and George Long only son of Mary decd. dau. Of Elizabeth Janvrin; N. Wentworth; George Wentworth and Rebecca his wife dau. of Mary Wentworth decd. Includes Map. ACCOUNT: 2/25/1774. Of George Wentworth and William Knight, surviving Execs. Allowed.

MERILL. See also Merriel, Merril, Merrill

1736. MERILL, JOHN (1792) #5834
EST. Salem yoeman decd. testate. Will: Drawn 3/18/1792. Legatees: Wife-Deborah; Sons-Daniel, John, Phinehas, Enoch, Josiah and Jonathan; Daus.-Ruth wife of John Clark, Easter wife of Asa Pattengale and Martha wife of Daniel Heath; Heirs of son Peter decd. Execs.-wife Deborah and son Jonathan. His sig. Witnesses: Timothy Ladd, Phinehas Gordon and

Caleb Morse. CERT. WILL (D30:343): 12/19/1792. Presented by Execs. and witnesses Gordon and Morse. ADMIN.: 12/19/1792. Execs.: Deborah Merril, widow and Jonathan Merril, yoeman, both of Salem. Bond L1000.0.0. Sureties: Phinehas Gordon, yoeman and Caleb Morse, gent., both of Salem. Witnesses: John Morrison and W. Parker. INVY.: Comm.: Timothy Ladd, Phinehas Gordon and Caleb Morse. Value L209.18.0. Oaths 1/4/1793 Gordon, Morse and Execs. to Timothy Ladd, JP.

MERRIEL. See also Merill, Merril, Merrill

1737. MERRIEL, ENOCH (1787) #5250
EST. Stratham yoeman decd. testate. WILL: Drawn 10/13/1786. Legatees: Wife-Sarah; Sons-Thomas of Darmascota, MA.ME, Joseph, Enoch, Elias (loses inheritance if he does not return), Wiggin, Paul, Levi and Samuel; Daus.-Susana Barker, Abagal Been, Ann Merril, Sarah Merril, Lydia Merril, Phebe Merril, Mehetable Merril, Betsey Merril and Mary Merril. Exec.- son Joseph. His sig. Witnesses: William Calley, Moses Thurston and Levi Giles. CERT. WILL (D29:106): 2/21/1787. Presented by Exec. and witnesses Calley and Thurston. INVY.: Appr. 3/21/1787. Comm.: Stephen Piper and Moses Clark. Value L432.3.7 1/2. Oaths 3/21/1787 Comm. and Exec. to judge. DOWER WARR.: 2/21/1787. Comm.: Samuel Lane, esq.; Jona. Wiggin, gent.; Moses Clark and Stephen Piper, all of Stratham and Capt. Theophilus Smith, Exeter esq. Of Widow Sarah Merril. Dower: 3/21/1787. Allowed. ACCOUNT: Of Exec. Allowed 4/16/1788. PETITION: Of Paul Merrill, Gilmanton, Strafford Co. yoeman. States he holds land in Stratham in common with his bros. Elias, Wiggin, Levi and Samuel. They hold in equal shares. As Levi and Samuel are minors, requests div. Wiggin Merrill and Elias Merrill for himself and as Gdn. of Levi and Samuel, consent. They have agreed on a Comm. of: Hubartus Neal of Newmarket and Jona. Piper of Stratham, gentlemen; Moses Clark, clothier; Jonathan Jewett, yoeman and Enos Hoag, blacksmith, all of Stratham. DIV. WARR.: 9/26/1788. Comm. as requested. To div. into equal shares the homestead of decd. DIV.: 9/30/1788. Divisees: Sons-Paul, Wiggin, Elias, Levi and Samuel (youngest). Oaths 10/15/1788 Neal and Clark, affirm. Hoag to W. Parker, JP. Allowed. ADDL. ACCOUNT: 3/17/1789. Of Exec. Allowed 3/18/1789. CITATION: 10/21/1789. To Exec. The judge has received a complaint from Exec.'s bro. Elias that Joseph's Addl. Account did not account for a yoke of oxen due decd. from Simon Pottle, which, Elias claims, the Exec. has received and other omissions. The Exec. is cited to appear and exhibit a further Account.

MERRIL. See also Merill, Merriel, Merrill

1738. MERRIL: CATHARINE, MARK & RUTH (1784) #5038
GDP. Of the children of Juba Merril, Newbury, Essex Co., MA yoeman decd. GDP.: 9/15/1784. Of: Catharine, Mark and Ruth of Exeter, minors under 14. Gdn. Ebenezer Thayer, Hampton clerk. Bond L1000.0.0. Sureties: Jonathan Moulton, Hampton esq. and Nathaniel Shannon of Moultonborough, Strafford Co. Witnesses: Nathl. Parker and W. Parker. See also #6010 Merrill: Catharine and Mark (1794) for later Gdp.

MERRILL. See also Merill, Merriel, Merril

1739. MERRILL, ABEL (1784) #4973
EST. Plaistow husbm. decd. testate. WILL: Drawn 10/31/1765. Legatees: Wife-Ruth; Sons-Abel, John, Stevens, Joshua, Caleb, Nathan and Nathaniel; Daus.-Abigail Knight and Sarah Knight. Execs.-sons Stevens and John. He notes that Abel, Stevens, Joshua, Caleb and his daus. have received their portions already, Abel "partly in learning." Nathaniel's portion is to have his college expenses, both in preparation and during, deducted. His sig. Witnesses: Thomas Merrill, William Searl Jr. and Thomas Merrill Jr. CERT. WILL (D27:379): 2/18/1784. Presented by Execs. and witnesses Searle and Wm. Merrill Jr. RENUN.: 1/17/1784. Stevens Merrill declines to administer the est. with his bro.

1740. MERRILL, BENJAMIN (1795) #6113
EST. Stratham yoeman decd. intestate. ADMIN.: 6/15/1795. Admx. Sarah Merrill, Stratham widow. Bond $3,000.00. Sureties: Ford Merrill, joiner and Joshua Lane, yoeman, both of Stratham. Witnesses: Mary S. Parker and Wm. Parker. INVY.: Appr. 7/13/1795. Comm.: Joshua Lane and Eliphalet Merrill. Value $1,458.82. Oaths 7/13/1795 Admx. and Comm. to W. Parker, JP. ACCOUNT: 10/1797. Of Admx. Allowed 10/16/1797 having been consented to by such heirs as attended. DOWER WARR.: 4/3/1798. Comm.: Moses Clark, clothier; Nicholas Rollins, esq.; Jonathan Wiggin, gent. Phinehas Merrill, yoeman, all of Stratham and Thomas Loveren, North Hampton gent. Of Widow Sarah Merrill. Dower: 4/13/1798. Oaths 8/11/1798 Rollins, Wiggin and Merrill to W. Parker, JP. Allowed. APPR. WARR.: 7/21/1798. Comm.: Nicholas Rollins, esq.; Jonathan Wiggin, gent. and Phinehas Merrill, yoeman, all of Stratham. To appr. 2/3 of the real est. at its present value in cash. Appr.: 8/11/1798. Appr. $876.13. Oaths 8/11/1798 Comm. to W. Parker, JP. DECREE SETTLM.: 8/11/1798. Joseph Merrill, oldest son, appearing and consenting, the real est. is settled on him, Joseph to pay each of his co-heirs $146.02: Anna Smith, Elezabeth Merrill and Abigail Merril within one year; Benjamin within 4 years; The heirs of Hannah Tilton, a dau. decd., 1/2 in 4 years and 1/2 in 9 years, with interest. BOND: 8/11/1798.

Of Joseph Merrill, Stratham yoeman. Bond $1,700.00. To pay his co-heirs per Decree Settlm. Sureties: Eliphalet Merrill and Phinehas Merrill, Stratham yoemen. Witnesses: Abm. Tilton and W. Parker. RELEASE: 2/5/1802. Of Abigail Merrill. To her bro. Joseph. She has received $146.02 as her share of the Decree Settlm. Witnesses: Benjamin Pottle and Salley Merrill. Oath 2/19/1802. Abigail Merrill to Josiah Bartlett, JP. RELEASE: 1/5/1802. Of Elezabeth Merrill. To her bro. Joseph. She has received of Joseph $146.02 as her share of Decree Settlm. Oath 2/9/1802 Elezabeth Merrill to Josiah Bartlett, JP. RELEASE: 1/22/1802. Of Abraham Tilton, Gdn. of the children of his decd. wife Hannah, dau. of Benjamin Merrill of Stratham decd. To Joseph Merrill. He has received of Joseph $146.02 as the children's share of Decree of Settlm. Witnesses: William Lane and Josiah Bartlett. Oath 7/22/1802 Tilton to Josiah Bartlett, JP.

1741. MERRILL: CATHARINE & MARK (1794) #6010
GDP. Of the children of Juba Merrill, Newbury, Essex Co., MA laborer decd. GDP.: 5/27/1794. Of Catharine, a minor over 14 and of Mark, a minor under 14. Gdn. George Odiorne, Exeter gent. Bond L1000.0.0. Sureties: Thomas Odiorne Jr. and Ebenezer Odiorne, yoeman, both of Exeter. Witnesses: Nathl. Parker and W. Parker. ACCOUNT: Of Rev. Ebenr. Thayer decd. of his Gdp. of Mark and Catharine, exhibited by Martha Thayer, Admx. Rev. Thayer's est. Allowed 7/23/1794, having been consented to by the present Gdn. See #5038 Merril: Catharine, Mark and Ruth (1784) for earlier Gdp.

1742. MERRILL, DANIEL No A# (1768) & (1782) #4847
GDP. Of a person of Atkinson naturally wanting of understanding. GDP.: From Archives but no # assigned. 1/7/1768. Of Daniel Merrill of Atkinson. Gdn. Dan. Poor. RECOMMENATION: 10/1/1782. Of Peter Clement and John Johnson, Atkinson Selectmen. In reply to a request, they recommend as Gdns. of the person and est. of Daniel, reputed to be n.c.m., either or both of Mrs. Ruth Parker, his mother, or James Merrill, his only bro. GDP.: 10/30/1782. Of Daniel, a person naturally wanting of understanding. Gdn. James Merrill, Atkinson husbm. Bond L1000.0.0. Sureties: Nathaniel Peabody, esq. and Peter Clement, gent., both of Atkinson. Witnesses: Moses Knight, Robt. Young and Benjamin Clement. ACCOUNT: 11/20/1782. Of Daniel Poor, Gdn. Allowed 11/20/1782 after hearing objections of James Merrill, the present Gdn. Oath 11/20/1782 of James Merrill, Gdn. He acknowledges that he has received of Daniel Poor the sum of L44.13.1, being the bal. of Poor's Account. Account includes Poor's statement of the agreement about Daniel's living with him. The orig. Archives Gdp. shows Daniel Poore as Gdn. Note: For Daniel's est. see #5371 Daniel Merrill (1788).

1743. MERRILL, DANIEL (1788) #5371
EST. Atkinson yoeman decd. ADMIN.: 9/17/1788. Admr. James Merrill, Atkinson husbm. Bond L1000.0.0. Sureties: Benjamin Emery Jr., Atkinson husbm. and Thomas Dow, Salem gent. Witnesses: Nat. Parker and W. Parker. INVY.: Comm.: Eliphalet Knight and Samuel Webster. Value L59.2.0. Oaths 3/31/1789 Comm. to Peter Clement, JP. Oath 5/20/1789 Admr. to W. Parker, Reg. PETITION: Dated by clerk 5/1789. Of Admr. For License. Gives list claims of L119.6.3. PETITION: 2/18/1791. Of Jeremiah Page, Dunbarton esq. in right of his wife, an heir to ests. Of Daniel and of Ruth Parker, late of Atkinson, widow decd. States that in 1784 Admin. of the est. of Ruth was granted to James Merrill of Atkinson, who has not settled or returned an Invy. of her est. James also neglects to settle est. of Daniel. Requests James be cited to account for both ests. CITATION: 2/18/1791. to James Merrill, Admr. ests. Of Ruth Parker, Atkinson widow, and Daniel Merrill, Atkinson yoeman. To appear and exhibit Accounts of both ests. for settlm. This file also includes an Account of Gdp. which belongs with #4847 Daniel Merrill (1782), the Gdp. of Daniel n.c.m., For est. of Ruth Parker see #5014 (1784).

1744. MERRILL, JAMES (1784) #4993
EST. Stratham joiner decd. intestate. RENUN.: 4/7/1784. Of Sarah Merrill, widow of James. Of Admr. Requests appointment of her oldest son, Ford Merrill. Witnesses: Theos. Smith and Phinehas Merrill. ADMIN.: 4/7/1784. Admr. Ford Merrill, Stratham joiner. Bond L2000.0.0. Sureties: Theophilus Smith, esq. and Nicholas Rollins, gent., both of Stratham. Witnesses: Nathl. Parker and John Parker. INVY. WARR.: 4/7/1784. Comm.: Theophilus Smith, esq.; Joshua Lane, yoeman and Nathaniel Wiggin Jr., all of Stratham. INVY.: Appr. 4/10/1784. Value L183.13.0. Oaths 4/21/1784 Smith, Lane and Admr. to judge.

1745. MERRILL, JAMES (1790) #5610
EST. Raymond gent. decd. testate. WILL: Drawn 7/8/1790. Legatees: Wife-Abegail; Sons-James, Nathaniel and Joseph; Daus.-Molly wife of Aaron Whittier, Abegail wife of Joseph True Jr., Betty Merrill, Sarah Merrill and Nanny Merrill. Exex.-wife Abegail. His sig. Witnesses: Jno. Swain, Benja. True Jr. and William Moor. Codicil: 11/6/1790. He resinds legacy of part of the household furniture to sons and gives it to his 5 daus. His sig. Witnesses: Jona. Swain, William Moor and Ebenezer Poor. CERT. WILL (D29:453): 12/15/1790. Presented by Exec. and all witness. Swain, esq. and Moor swore to Codicil. ADMIN.: 12/15/1790. Exex. Abigail Merrill, Raymond widow. Bond L1000.0.0. Sureties: William Moor, Raymond gent. and Benjamin True Jr., Chester yoeman. Witnesses: Jona. Swain and N. Parker. INVY.: Appr. 1/3/1791. Comm.: Joseph True and

Thomas Gordon. Value not tallied. Esti. L528.0.0+. Oaths 1/14/1791 Comm. and Exex. to Jona. Swain, JP.

1746. MERRILL, DEACON JOHN (1773) #4061
EST. Rumford yoeman decd. testate. WILL: Drawn 10/8/1765. Legatees: Wife-Lydia; Sons-Thomas, Moses, Nathaniel and Jonathan; Daus.-Lydia Foster, Hannah Merrill, Sarah Chandler, Ann Farnham and Abigail Merrill; Grandchildren-John and Rebecca children of his son John decd. Exec.-son Jonathan. His sig. Witnesses: Timothy Walker, Richard Eastman and William Haseltine. Codicil: 10/14/1773. As his son Moses has died, he orders Moses' portion be divided among his surviving children. He also gives his wife Lydia use of his ferry as long as she remains his widow. Witnesses: Timo. Walker, Jacob Shute and Ebenezer Harnden Goss. CERT. WILL (D22:342): 12/2/1773. Proved on oaths of witnesses Rev. Walker and Hazeltine to the Will, Walker and Shute to Codicil. PETITION: Dated by clerk 12/1773. Of Widow Lydia Merrill. She is content with what the Will provides for her, but explains that it is too difficult for her to repair and main. the ferry personally. Asks judge if she might not just have use of roads and ferry and some part of the meat fattened on the farm. Her mark. Witness Timo. Walker. The Exec. was present and consented to the Petition. Allowed 12/2/1773 "for the present." INVY.: Appr. 11/23/1773. Comm.: Thomas Stickney and Joshua Abbot. Value L637.2.0. Oaths 11/27/1773 Comm. to Peter Green, JP. Oath 3/17/1775 Exec. to judge. LIST OF DEBTS. Total L8.12.4 1/4. ACCOUNT: 3/17/1775. Of Exec. Allowed 3/17/1775.

1747. MERRILL, JOHN (1797) #6336
EST. Atkinson yoeman decd. ADMIN.: 4/24/1797. Admx. Mary Merril, Atkinson widow. Bond $3,000.00. Sureties: Moses Greenough, Atkinson gent. and Joshua Merrill, Kingston yoeman. Witnesses: Edward Mason and W. Parker. INVY.: Appr. 6/8/1797. Comm.: Peter Clement, Moses Greenough and Joseph Welch. Value $1,347.55. Oaths 11/3/1797 Greenough and Welch and on 12/9/1797 Admx. to Peter Clement, JP. PETITION: 12/18/1799. Of Joshua Poor on behalf Admx. For License. States that most of personal est. already used for claims and about $400.00 more claims remain. Granted. LICENSE (D33:181): 12/18/1799. To Admx. To sell real est. to amount of $400.00.

1748. MERRILL, JOSEPH (1771) #3830
EST. Pembroke gent. decd. ADDL. ACCOUNT: Of Timothy Walker, esq., Admr. Oath 8/17/1799 Admr. to William Parker, JP. Allowed. Note: It is probable that this Addl. Account does belong to the est. given, but the file for the est. is missing.

1749. MERRILL, JOSEPH (1772) #3974
EST. South Hampton yeoman decd. testate. WILL: Drawn 6/4/1766. Legatees: Wife-Mary; Children of his bro. Eliphalet- Eliphalet Merrill and Sarah Merrill; His negro Florency to have her freedom after wife's death. Exec.-nephew Joseph. His sig. Witnesses: Richd. Collins, Benjamin Quinby and Jonathan Quinby. Oath 12/29/1772 Collins to P. White, JP. CERT. WILL: 12/30/1772. Presented by Exec. and witness Benjamin Quimby, Collins too ill to attend court. DECLARATION: 12/29/1772. Of Joseph Merrill. He accepts the executorship of his uncle's Will. Mary Merrill, widow of Joseph, abides by his Will. Witnesses Parker Flandere and Benjamin Quinby. INVY. WARR.: 12/30/1772. Comm.: Enoch Page, gent. and Richard Collins, yoeman, both of South Hampton. Oaths 3/29/1773 Comm. and Exec. to P. White, JP. INVY.: Appr. 3/29/1773. Value L164.3.0, "A negro slave not appr. being now sick."

1750. MERRILL: LEVI & SAMUEL (1788) #5376
GDP. Of the sons of Enoch Merrill, Stratham yoeman decd. GDP.: 9/26/1788. Of: Levi, a minor over 14 and of Samuel, a minor under 14. Gdn. Elias Merrill, Stratham yoeman. Bond L500.0.0. Sureties: Moses Clark, clothier and Joseph Merrill, gent., both of Stratham. Witnesses: Wiggin Merrill and W. Parker.

1751. MERRILL, NATHANIEL (1791) #5725
EST. Salem yoeman decd. testate. WILL: Drawn 9/26/1789. Legatees: Wife-Judith; Sons-Joseph, Daniel Peasly Merrill, Perley and Nathaniel; Daus.-Betty wife of David Buswell, Sarah wife of Richard Messer and Hannah. Exec.- son Perley. Witnesses: Daniel Corlis, Edward Patee and Timothy Ladd. CERT. WILL (D30:158): 12/21/1791. Presented by Exec. and witnesses Corlis and Peaslee(sic.). ADMIN.: 12/21/1791. Exec. Perley Merrill, Salem yoeman. Bond L1000.0.0. Sureties: Daniel Corlis and Edward Patee, Salem yoemen. Witnesses: Nat Parker and Willm. White

1752. MERRILL, NATHANIEL (1793) #5891
EST. South Hampton yeoman decd. testate. WILL: Drawn 10/9/1792. Legatees: Bros.-Parker, John, Joseph, Eliphalet and Thomas; Sister-Mary Barnard wife of Isaac Barnard, Sarah Perkins wife of True Perkins and Lydia Tuxbury wife of Moses Tuxbury. Execs.-bros. Parker and John. His sig. Witnesses; Henry French, Israel Sawyer and John French. CERT. WILL (D30:428): 5/13/1793. Presented by Execs. and witnesses Sawyer and John French. ADMIN.: 5/13/1793. Execs.: John Merrill and Parker Merrill, both of South Hampton. Bond L500.0.0. Sureties: Israel Sawyer and John French, both of South Hampton. Witnesses: W. Parker and Thos. S. Ranney.

1753. MERRILL, PETER (1787) #5270
EST. Salem trader decd. ADMIN.: 5/16/1787. Admr. Joshua Heath, Salem yoeman. Bond L500.0.0. Sureties: William Duty, esq. and William Rogers, gent., both of Salem. Witnesses: Jer. Dow to sigs. Of Heath and Duty, Benja. Poor, Nancy Rogers and James Heath. INVY. WARR.: 5/16/1787. Comm.: Henry Little, gent.; William Duty and William Rogers. INVY.: Appr. 6/29/1787. Value L46.0.1. Oaths 1/14/1788 Duty and Rogers to Timothy Ladd, JP. Oath 2/26/1788 Admr. to W. Parker, JP. DOWER WARR.: 11/21/1787. Comm.: Joseph Wardwell, esq.; Jeremiah Dow, Henry Little, Silas Betton, and Jesse Webster, Salem gentlemen. Of Widow Judith Merrill. Dower: 11/23/1795. Signed by Dow, Wardwell, Little and Betton. PETITION: 3/19/1788. Of Admr. For License and Comm. Insolvency. Gives list claims of L61.11.0. PETITION: 12/15/1794. Of Admr. Requests a new Comm. Insolvency as Commissioner Poor moved to the eastern country and Commissioner Young to Cohoss before completing claims. Suggests for Comm. Ensign Henry Little, Capt. Joseph Wardwell and Silas Betton. Requests Warr. beleft with Esq. Thomas as he cannot attend court. Adds that he procured the papers from the old Comm. CLAIMS: 8/18/1795. Total $245.50. Oaths 8/18/1795 Little and Betton to Josiah Gage, JP. Also a bill from Betton, Wardwell and Little for services as Commissioners. Note: This paper is torn and badly damaged, but the above information was recoverable. LICENSE (D32:49): 9/25/1795. To Admr. To sell real est. to amount of $250.00. DOWER: Oaths 12/6/1795 Dow, Little and Betton to James Gilmore, JP. Allowed. ACCOUNT: 12/1795. Of Admr. Oath 12/8/1795. Of Admr. to Wm. Parker, JP. Allowed. Account includes main. 4 children.

1754. MERRILL, PHINEAS (1799) #6559
See #2169 Thomas Chase (1757)

1755. MERRILL, SAMUEL JR. (1758) A#2400
EST. Nottingham West, Hillsborough Co. yoeman decd. intestate. ADDL ACCOUNT (D21:345): Of Rebecca Merril, Admx. Allowed 5/7/1772 it being just as proved by the evidence. Account includes main. 2 children. Orig. Archives file includes Admin., Invy., Account of 1760 and Gdp. of son Abel 1760, Gdp. Abel 1763 and Gdp. of children of his son Samuel.

1756. MERRILL, SAMUEL GREENOUGH (1784) #4963 &
INCORRECTLY AS SAMUEL GREENOUGH (1791) #5637
EST. Salem yoeman decd. ADMIN. (#4963): 1/16/1784. Admr. John Dow Jr., Atkinson esq. Bond L500.0.0. Sureties: Nathaniel Peabody of Atkinson and Jonathan Blanchard of Dunstable, Hillsborough Co., esquires. Witnesses: Jona. Swain and James Thurston. INVY. (#5637):

Comm.: Danl. Richards, Enoch Knight and Jona. Poor. Value L4.5.6. Oaths 4/19/1791. Shown by John Dow, esq., Admr. Oaths 4/19/1791 Knight and Poor to Peter Clement, JP. ACCOUNT (#5637): 4/16/1791. Of John Dow, Admr. Allowed 4/16/1791. Account includes payment to Moses Merrill, father and only heir.

1757. MESERVE, GEORGE (1782) #4766 & (1789) #5404
EST. London, Great Britain esq. decd., intestate, formerly of Portsmouth, an absentee. BOND (#4766): 1/5/1782. Of John Parker, Portsmouth esq. Bond L500.0.0. To account for the sale of lands in Wolfeborough, Strafford Co. of George Meserve, esq., an absentee, as authorized by an Act passed by the NH General Court. Sureties: Ammi Ruhamah Cutter, esq. and James Sheafe, merchant, both of Portsmouth. Witnesses: Danl. R. Rogers and W(?). Haven. ADMIN. (#5404: 1/21/1789. Admr. James Sheafe, Portsmouth merchant. Bond L1000.0.0. Sureties: John Pickering of Portsmouth and Clement March of Greenland, esquires. Witnesses: Joseph Peirce and W.H.S.E. INVY.: 5/22/1789. Comm.: Thos. Martin, Jno. Parker and Danl. R. Rogers. Value L558.0.6. Shown by Admr. as property left in 1775 by Meserve in the hands and possession of his wife, Mrs. Esther Meserve decd., which property he, James Sheafe, found in possession of his wife Sarah Sheafe in 1783, which est., real and personal, remains in Sheafe's hands under the encumbrance of a deed of Wm. Parker, Danl. Peirce and Wm. Torrey, esquires, in trust in 1768 as security for his creditors, also under the demands and attachments of the Confiscating Act and other demands and attachments. Oaths 5/28/1790 Comm. and Admr. to W. Parker, JP. PETITION (#5404): 5/1789. Of Admr. For Comm. Insolvency. Gives list claims of L5450.10.10 1/2. CLAIMS: 1/22/1790. Comm.: Jno. Parker and Thos. Martin, esquires and Danl. R. Rogers. Total L1015.3.11. Oaths 1/22/1790 Comm. to Nathl. Adams, JP. LICENSE (D29:341): 2/17/1790. To Admr. To sell real est. to amount of L1015.0.0. ACCOUNT (#5404): 10/7/1796. Of Admr. Allowed 10/19/1796 heirs consenting. Cert. 9/23/1796. Of: Sarah Sheafe and Esther Meserve, heirs. They approve of Account of their father's est. ACCOUNT (#5404): 10/19/1796. Of Admr. Cert. 10/19/1796. Of: Sarah Sheafe and Esther Meserve, sole heirs to est. They approve Account. Allowed 10/10/1796 heirs consenting.

1758. MESSANARY, FRANCIS (1787) #5295
EST. Portsmouth mariner decd. intestate. ADMIN.: 10/4/1787. Admx. Alice Messanary, Newington widow. Bond L1000.0.0. Sureties: James Gooch, Portsmouth merchant and Nathaniel Hart, Newington yoeman. Witnesses: Nathl. Parker and W. Parker.

1759. MESSER, DAVID (1794) #6011
EST. Salem yoeman decd. testate. WILL: Drawn 5/20/1794. Legatees; Wife-Rachel; Son-David; Daus.-Rachel Messer, Elise Messer and Abigail Messer. Execs.-bros.-John Messer and Richard Messer. His sig. Witnesses: Samuel Webster, Seth Emerson and Ebenezer Barker. CERT. WILL (D31:318): 7/14/1794. Presented by Execs. And witnesses Webster and Emerson. ADMIN.: 7/14/1794. Execs.: John Messer and Richard Messer, Salem yoemen. Bond L1000.0.0. Sureties: Seth Messer, yoeman and Samuel Webster, gent., both of Salem. Witnesses: Jno. Parker and W. Parker. INVY.: Appr. 9/12/1794. Comm.: Benja. Town, Saml. Webster and Dudley Bixbey. Value L187.0.10. Oaths 9/13/1794 Comm. to Josiah Gage, JP. Oath 9/15/1794 John Messer, an Exec., to judge. PETITION: 4/15/1795. Of John Messer, an Exec. For License. Gives claims and legacies of L87.19.2. Granted. LICENSE (D31:518): 4/15/1795. To Execs. To sell real est. to the amount of L54.0.0. DOWER: 4/20/1795. Comm.: Benjamin Town, Dudley Bixbey, Seth Emerson, Samuel Webster and Edward Pettee. Of Widow Rachel Messer. Oaths 7/16/1796 Town, Bixbey and Emerson to Joseph Wardwell, JP. Allowed. ACCOUNT: 7/18/1796. Of Execs. Allowed 7/18/1796.

1760. MESSER, RICHARD (1779) #4570
EST. Salem husbm. decd. testate. WILL: Drawn 3/11/1779. Legatees: Wife-Abigail; Sons-David, John, Richard, Theodore, Moses and Frederick. Daus.-Hannah Messer, Olive Messer, Abigail Messer and Rhoda Messer. Exex.-wife Abigail. His sig. Witnesses: Benja. Woodbury, Ebenezer Eaton and Ebenezer Barker. Proved 9/29/1779 on oaths of Ebenezer Barker and Woodbury. ADMIN.: 9/29/1779. Exex. Abigail Messer, Salem widow. Bond L2000.0.0. Sureties: John Messer of Salem and Ebenezer Barker of Methuen, Essex Co., MA, yoemen. Witness Nathaniel Parker.

1761. MILLAR, MOSES (1778) #4437
EST. Portsmouth yoeman decd. intestate. RENUN.: 3/20/1778. Of Widow Temperance. Of Admin. Requests appointment of her oldest son Benjamin Millar. Witnesses: John Clark and Abraham Elliot. ADMIN. (D25:263): 3/27/1778. Admr. Benjamin Millar, Portsmouth yoeman. INVY.: Appr. 4/6/1778. Comm.: William Ham, John Dennett and Jeremiah Libbey. Value L446.1.0. Oaths 5/25/1778 Comm. to Saml. Penhallow, JP. Oath 5/27/1778 Admr. to judge. ACCOUNT: 3/27/1782. Of Admr. CLAIMS WARR.: 3/27/1792. Comm.: Thomas Bickford, Jeremiah Libbey and Nahum Ward, all of Portsmouth. CLAIMS: 12/12/1782. Total L81.15.3 3/4. Comm. also reports that they have examined the Administrator's Account, but because of want of vouchers, they cannot enter it with above

claims. Oaths 12/12/1782 Comm. to Saml. Penhallow, JP. APPR. WARR.: 2/26/1783. Comm.: William Thompson, Abraham Elliot, Gideon Walker, James Ayers and Nathaniel Jackson, all of Portsmouth. To appr. 2/3 of the real est. and see if it can be div. among his children. Div. or appr. Appr.: 7/3/1783. Value L181.10.0. Oaths 2/26/1783 Comm. to H. Wentworth, JP. PETITION: 7/30/1783. Of Admr. (sig. now Miller). For License. LICENSE (D27:271): 7/30/1783. To Admr. To sell sufficient real est. to pay debts. Note: The following Petition recorded as #5485 Jonathan Warner, et. al. (1789) belongs here. PETITION: 9/16/1789. Of Jonathan Warner, Portsmouth esq. States that he is owner of about 30 acres in Portsmouth with bldgs., one unsevered third of which is the lifetime Dower of Temperance Miller, widow of Moses. Requests div. Order: 9/16/1789. For hearing, Petitioner to notify Widow so she may object or join Warner in nominating a Div. Comm. DOWER: 9/18/1790. Comm.: Isaac Rindge and John Dennett, esquires; William Hart; Capt. Geo. Wentworth and Joseph Akerman. Of Widow Temperance Miller. Oaths 9/18/1790 Rindge, Wentworth and Dennett to George Gains, JP. Allowed. ACCOUNT: 10/20/1790. Of Jonathan Warner. Of the expense of setting off Dower.

1762. MILTIMORE, JAMES (1794) #5991
EST. Londonderry taylor decd. testate. WILL: Drawn 6/6/1793. Legatees: Sons-John, Daniel and James; Son-in-law-Robert Patterson. Exec.- son James. His sig. Witnesses: John Macfarland, John Gregg and James Gregg. CERT. WILL (D31:249): 4/16/1794.Presented By Exec. and Witnesses Macfarland and James Gregg. ADMIN.: 4/16/1794. Exec. James Miltimore, Strathamclerk.BondL3000.0.0. Sureties: James Macgregore, esq. and James Nesmith, yoeman, both of Londonderry. Witnesses: Joseph Blanchard and Nathl. Parker. INVY.: Comm.: James Macgregore, Benjamin Gregg and James Nesmith. Value L839.15.8. Oaths 8/20/1794 Comm. and Exec. to judge. MITCHEL. See also Mitchell

1763. MITCHEL, REV. DANIEL (1777) #4365
EST. Pembroke clerk decd. ADMIN.: 6/20/1777. Admx. Martha Mitchel, Pembroke widow. Bond L500.0.0. Sureties: Samuel McConnel, Pembroke gent. and John Bryent, Bow esq. Witnesses: Samuel Parker and Timo. Walker Jr. INVY.: Comm.: Timo. Walker Jr. and Samll. McConnel. Value L485.0.9. Oaths Comm. to judge. CAVEAT: 3/18/1783. Of Robert Moor, Pembroke yoeman. States that he has been informed that Samuel Parker of Pembroke is about to apply for Admin. D.B.N. He believes that Admin. D.B.N. is unnecessary as the heirs, being of full age since the death of the Admx., have settled the real and personal est. among themselves. However, if such admin. is necessary, he thinks it properly

belongs to him as he married the oldest dau. of Rev. Mitchel. Requests notification of a hearing before any Admin. D.B.N. is granted.

MITCHELL. See also Mitchel

1764. MITCHELL, JOSEPH (1796) #6201
GDP. Of the son of Thomas Mitchell of Londonderry decd. GDP.: 4/20/1796. Of Joseph, a minor over 14. Gdn. Moody Morse, Londonderry physician. Bond L1000.0.0. Sureties: John Morrison and Thomas Mitchel, Londonderry yoemen. Witnesses: Nathl. Parker and John Carr.

MOFFAT. See also Moffatt

1765. MOFFAT, THOMAS PHILIP (1797) #6343
EST. Portsmouth mariner decd. ADMIN.: 6/21/1797. Admr. Nathaniel A. Haven, Portsmouth physician. Bond $3,000.00. Sureties: Samuel Haven Jr., gent. and Henry Haven, merchant, both of Portsmouth. Witnesses: James Rundlet and Geo. Andrews. INVY.: Appr. 7/6/1797. Comm.: Geo. Gains, esq.; Nathaniel Dean and Saml. Elliot. Value $227.81 plus fee of Comm. $4.50. Oaths 7/6/1797 Comm. and Admr. to Saml. Penhallow, JP. ACCOUNT: 2/19/1799. Of Admr. Allowed 2/20/1797 having previously been approved by heirs. Cert.: Of: N. Rousselet, William Odiorne, Sarah Catherine Moffatt and Saml. R.C. Moffatt. They have examined Account and request its allowance. These were all heirs 1/6 of est. There were also payments to: John Moffatt, Mrs. M. T. Haven and Mrs. Lucy T. Odiorne, each of whom received the same amount.

MOFFATT. See also Moffat

1766. MOFFATT, JOHN (1786) #5173.
EST. Portsmouth esq. decd. testate. WILL: Drawn 2/23/1784. Legatees: Dau.-Catharine Whipple; Grandsons-Henry Sherburne, Samuel Sherburne, Robert Cutts Moffatt and Thomas Philip Moffatt and their male and female heirs; Granddaus.-Elizabeth Langdon, Elizabeth Moffatt and Mary Tufton Moffatt; Children of his son Samuel decd.; Oldest surviving dau. of his son Samuel and her heirs; Sons-in-law-John Sherburne, esq., William Knight and William Whipple, esq. Residual heirs in case of deaths of some above: male heirs then female heirs of, first, Robert Cutts Moffatt than Thomas Philip Moffatt and then to eldest surviving dau. of son Samuel Moffatt and her heirs, and also Martha Tufton Moffatt, sister of Elizabeth Knight. Execs.: William Knight and William Whipple. His sig. Witnesses: Noah Parker, David Folsom, John Pickering and George Libbey. Codicil: 1/16/1786. William Whipple has died. Appoints dau. Catharine Whipple

and Joshua Brackett, Portsmouth physician, executors instead of Knight and William Whipple. His sig. Witnesses: Saml. Cutts, Noah Parker and Jos. Whipple. CERT. WILL: 2/15/1786. Presented by Execs. and affirm of witness Parker, oath of witness Libbey to Will; oath of Cutts, esq., affirm. Parker to Codicil. INVY.: 6/14/1786. Comm.: Richard Hart, Noah Parker and Joseph Whipple, all of Portsmouth. Value L13457.13.2. Oaths: 8/31/1786 Execs. to George Gains, JP. Oaths: 6/14/1786 Hart and Whipple, affirm. Parker to W. Parker, JP.PETITION: 11/7/1788. Of Nathl. Appleton Haven, Portsmouth physician, husb. of Mary Tufton Moffatt granddau. of decd., and for other divisees of est. States License and Comm. Insolvency were obtained before debts were determined. Requests an appeal against Decree allowing License. Granted 11/19/1788. BOND: 11/20/1788. Of Nathaniel Appleton Haven, Portsmouth physician. Bond L100.0.0. To appeal Decree allowing License. Sureties: Samuel Haven, Jr., gent. and Joseph Haven, merchant, both of Portsmouth. Witnesses: John Haven and Henry Haven. PETITION: 12/19/1787. Of Joshua Brackett, an Exec. For Comm. Insolvency and License. Gives list claims already in of L7460.18.1. Also notes that all of the land in the Invy. in Mason's Patent is now claimed by the State of NH and rest of est. appr. at higher than it will sell for. Witnesses: John Parker, Danl. Rindge and Woodbury Langdon. LICENSE: 12/19/1787. To Execs. To sell sufficient real est. to pay debts. CLAIMS: 12/12/1788. Comm.: Woodbury Langdon, Daniel Rindge Rogers and John Parker. Total L2846.13.11 1/4. Oaths 12/12/1788 Comm. to Saml. Penhallow, JP. PETITION: 3/18/1789. Of Nathl. Appleton Haven, one of heirs in right of his wife. Requests appeal from the Decree allowing Comm. of Insolvency and their report. Granted. ACCOUNT: Of Execs. Exhibited3/18/1789 but was objected to by N.A. Haven. Decree:3/18/1789. Due to objections of N.A. Haven and because it was not properly vouched and proved, Account disallowed. Exec. Brackett requested an appeal from decision. BOND: 3/18/1789. Of Exec. Brackett. Bond L100.0.0. To appeal disallowance of Account. Sureties: John Pickering and Joseph Whipple, Portsmouth esquires. Witnesses: Hannah Pickering and Henry (S?) Langdon. BOND: 3/19/1789. Of Nathaniel Appleton Haven, Portsmouth physician. Bond L100.0.0. To appeal Decree allowing Comm. Insolvency and report. Surety Daniel Humphreys, Portsmouth esq. Witnesses: Benja. Butler and W. Parker. DECREE: 4th Tues. April, 1789. Of Supreme Court of Judicature. On Appeal of Dr. Haven against License. Court affirms License and orders following restrictions on how the sale of lands to be carried out: 1. Execs. to have License to sell sufficient real est. to pay debts remaining due at time of death of decd. and the charges of Admin., after the personal est. is appropriated therefore. 2. The Execs. are to sell first the residue of the real est. devised to dau. Catherine, not including any est. specifically devised to her. 3. If the proceeds should not be sufficient to discharge debts and charges, the Execs. to raise the remainder of the money by selling as much of the real est. devised to all the divisees named in Will, in proportion as near as possible to the value of the respective divisees, as will be sufficient to raise the remainder of the money due. 4. The Execs. are to govern themselves, when selling, by the rules and regulations of the law, accounting for the proceeds to the Judge of Probate. 5. the Judge of Probate is directed to grant the License and govern himself by this Decree. Copy of record examined by Nathl. Adams, clerk. LICENSE: 5/20/1789. To Execs. To sell real est. in manner ordered by Superior Court. DECREE ON APPEAL AGAINST DISALLOWANCE OF ACCOUNT OF ADMIN. 3d Tues. Sept. 1789. Of Superior Court of Judicature. The parties appeared before the court and agreed that the Account is to be audited by Hon. Charles Chauncy, Hon. John Calfe and Oliver Peabody, esquires, as Referees. They are to report to the court and the court's decree, based on the finding of the auditors, to be final. They further agreed that the Comm. is to appr. and add to the Invy. such articles as they may find were omitted and to deduct such items, if there are any, which were erroneously appr. The appr. of the real est. to be the true value, by which the devised ests. are to be estimated and apportioned in any sales of real est. made by Execs. pursuant to Licenses granted, or to be granted, by the Judge of Probate by Decree of this court the past term. It was further agreed that the devise to Catharine in the Will of a house and other real est. for the period of 16 years shall be considered as real est. and subject to sale as such by any License. The appraisers are to determine what part of the appraised value of the house and est. devised to Catharine was worth during the devised time and what part of the remainder was worth at the time of appraisement. Report: 7/1/1789 The Audit Comm. has heard the parties by themselves and their counsel, with their proofs and allegations. They have audited the Admin. Account. They report: 1. There be deducted from the Account L59.1.1. for overcharge in certificates for repairing the mansion house. 2. The Execs.'s allowance for articles erroniously inventoried as est. John Moffatt esq., said to have been given by him when alive to Elizabeth Moffatt, amounting to L130.3.8., be allowed and deducted from the Invy. This was agreed to by the parties. 3. The Execs.'s allowance for articles erroniously inventoried as Moffatt's est., said to belong to the est. of William Whipple, esq. decd., not to be allowed in Account and to remain in the Invy. and be accounted for by the Execs. as Moffatt's est. 4. They have added to the Invy. of Moffatt's est. the lands and personal est. mentioned in the annexed schedule, which they appr. at L143.2.0. 5. They have appr. the term of Catharine in the mansion house, wharfe and store at L2000.0.0 and the remainder or reversion at L3000.0.0. 6. If any of the divisees of Moffatt's est. have paid taxes or made repairs on parts of the est. devised to them and the est. is proved insolvent, that sum shall be allowed them in settlm. which may be made by the Judge of Probate. 7 The costs of the reference of L14.4.1., together with the court costs, are to be paid by the Execs. and charged by them in future Admin. Accounts and allowed out of est. 8. They agree that this Report will not affect the property in any dispute regarding certain Continental Certificates said by Haven to be part of the est. of Moffatt decd., which are now inventoried as the est. of William Whipple, esq. decd., and shall not affect any Accounts exhibited to the referees other than the Account of Admin. A formal Account of the charges is given and approved by the Superior Court with an Order that the bal. of L6.13.9 be charged by Execs. To future Admin. Accounts. Copy of record examined by Nathl. Adams, clerk. PETITION: 9/6/1791. Of Nathl. A. Haven of Portsmouth as heir in right of wife and atty. and agent for sundry heirs. Requests an accounting by Execs. at next court. He claims Brackett's list of claims was false, which Exec. conceded at Haven's appeal hearing, that Execs. have gone ahead and sold real est. according to license, raising even more than the L2846.13.11 reported by Comm. of Insolvency. Haven believes Comm. is out of order as Exec. admitted false list of claims. 2D ACCOUNT: 10/16/1793. Signed by Brackett. Allowed, objections of Nathl. A. Haven having been heard. 3D ACCOUNT: 2/18/1795. Of Execs. Signed by Brackett. PETITION: 4/6/1795. Of Nathl. Appleton Haven in right of Mary T. Haven his wife and other heirs. States the last Account shows a large bal. in hands of Execs. Requests distribution of bal. according to law and the Will. ORDER: 4/6/1795. For hearing, Petitioner to serve Execs. with copies of Petition and Order. ADDL. ACCOUNT: 8/6/1795. Of Execs. Allowed 8/6/1795 with Order to Execs. to distribute bal. in their hands to divisees according to the value of their respective legacies as appr. in Invy. and the sums taken from them for payment of debts of decd. Divisees: Elizabeth Langdon L9.3.0, Philip Moffatt L20.1.0., Robert Cutts Moffatt L220.15.3,Elizabeth Moffatt L96.4.0,Mary Tufton Moffatt L75.15.4, Lucy Moffatt L23.0.3 John Moffatt L23.0.3 and Catharine Whipple L267.18.3, being a total of L735.17.4. PETITION: 1/7/1811. Of: R.C. Moffatt by his atty Nathl. A. Haven and Samuel Robert Cutts Moffatt, Boston, Suffolk Co. mariner, a divisee. They state that Exec. Brackett has lately died. Request that Catherine Whipple, surviving Exec., be cited to account. Granted 1/71/1812 with order that Catherine to be cited. CITATION (copy): 1/7/1812(sic.) To Catherine Whipple, Portsmouth widow, surviving Exec. To appear and present addl. account. Cert.: Rockinghamss.1/9/1812. Of Timo. Gerrish, Dy. Sherf. He has delivered Citation. REPLY TO CITATION: 2/20/1812. Of Catharine Whipple. On oath declares that to the best of her recollection, excepting some small sums of money said to be paid or due her as a divisee by the will, and in consequence of a final decree of the Probate Court 8/1795, she has received no money due est. nor has she paid any money whatsoever and has no further Account to exhibit. The whole management was conducted by her co-Exec., Brackett, and other than signing papers, which she did not read, she never acted in fact as an Exec. She has never had in her possession papers, vouchers, receipts, etc. of the settlm. She believes they remain in Brackett's papers in possession of his rep. Joseph Whipple, Portsmouth esq. The charge exhibited against her for the value of the remainder of est. in (4th?) Street was conveyed to her in fee by Woodbury Langdon, esq., late of Portsmouth and she conceives the same to be her own proper est. and should not render an Account for the rent of profits. Oath: 2/20/1812 Catharine Whipple to Danl. Humphreys, JP. DECREE: 2/21/1812. At a hearing on Citation for Addl. Account, Samuel Robert Cutts Moffatt presented a list of US Certificates not yet accounted for. Value plus interest $53,366.42. At hearing Catharine repeated the information given in her reply to Citation. Decree: Catharine is not bound to account for any items as alleged and she is discharged as Exec., no relief being granted to Samuel. Samuel requested an appeal from Decree. Granted 2/21/1812. Appeal signed by his atty. N. A. Haven. BOND: 3/4/1812. Of Nathaniel A. Haven, Portsmouth merchant. Bond $100.00. For suit of Samuel R.C. Moffatt vs. Catharine Whipple. Witness: N.A. Haven, Jr.

1767. MOFFATT, ROBERT CUTTS (1795) #6128
GDP. Of the son of Sarah Catharine Moffatt, Portsmouth widow. GDP.: 8/17/1795. Of Robert Cutts Moffatt, a minor under 21. Gdn. Sarah Catharine Moffatt, Portsmouth widow, his mother. Bond $3,000.00. Sureties: Nathl. Appleton Haven and Samuel Haven Jr., Portsmouth merchants. Witnesses: Wm. Sowersby and Job Harris.

1768. MOFFATT, SARAH CATHARINE (1787) #5274
Bond of Portsmouth widow. BOND: 1/15/1787. Of Sarah Catharine Moffatt, Portsmouth widow. Bond L2000.0.0. To account for sale of land in Tuftonborough belonging to her children John Moffatt, Lucy Tenier Moffatt, Thomas Philip Moffatt and Robert Cutts Moffatt, for their main. and education, she having been so empowered by an Act of the N.H. General Court passed 6/19/1786. Sureties: Samuel Haven, clerk and Nathl. Appleton Haven, physician, both of Portsmouth. Witnesses: Leverett Hubbard and Nathl. Griffith.

1769. MONTGOMERY, ROBERT (1777) #4335
EST. Londonderry yeoman decd. testate. WILL: Drawn 2/24/1775. Legatees: Son-Hugh; Daus.-Mar. Montgomery (oldest dau.) and Margaret Steel; Grandchildren-John Steel and Rebeca Steel. Execs.-James Betton, Windham esq. and son Hugh. His mark. Witnesses: William Gregg, Ebenezer Gregg and Margaret Robinson. CERT. WILL: 3/26/1777. Presented by Execs. and witnesses Ebenezer Gregg and Robinson.

1770. MOODY, CHARLES (1795) #6140
See #6140 William Moody (1795)

1771. MOODY, REV. JOHN (1778) #4488
EST. Newmarket clerk decd. testate. WILL: Drawn 4//16/1774. Legatees: Wife-Elizabeth; Dau.-Mary Smith; Grandsons-John Moody Smith, Eliphalet Smith, Andrew Smith, Ezra Smith and Joseph Smith; Granddau.-Anna Smith. Execs.-wife Elizabeth, John Lowell and David Moody his bro.'s son. His sig. Witnesses: Richard Clark, John Bartlett and Edward Parsons. CERT. WILL (D24:384): 10/28/1778 Presented by David Moody, an Exec., the others refusing the trust, and witnesses Clark and Bartlett. RENUN.: 10/20/1778. Of John Lowell, esq., barrister. Of co-executorship as it will be inconvenient for him to execute trust. Dated at Newburyport, Essex Co., MA. RENUN.: 10/28/1778. Of Elizabeth Moody, widow of Rev. John. Of Admin., but fully accepts provision made for her in Will. INVY. WARR.: 10/28/1778. Comm.: Hubartus Neal, gent.; Philip Fowler, yoeman and Joseph Adams, esq., all of Newmarket. Invy.: Appr. 11/24/1778. Value L7015.11.1 1/2. Oaths11/25/1778 Comm. and Exec. to W. Parker, JP. & Reg. PETITION: 11/29/1780. Of: John Moody Smith, principal heir, and Nathl. Gilman on behalf of the widow. For her Dower per Will. They suggest a comm. of Ebenezer Thompson, esq. and John Smith, gent., both of Durham; Mark Wiggin, Stratham esq.; Philip Fowler of Newmarket and Eliphalet Hale, Exeter gent.

1772. MOODY, WILLIAM (1795) #6140
EST. Canterbury yoeman decd. ADMIN.: 9/29/1795. Admx. Sarah Moody, Canterbury widow. Bond $1,000.00. Sureties: John Kimball of Canterbury and Charles Moody of Newbury, Essex Co., MA, yoemen. Witnesses: Mary S. Parker and W. Parker. Note: This est. filed as Charles but the Admin. is clearly est. of William.

MOOERS. See also Moor, Moore

1773. MOOERS, SAMUEL (1793) #5939
EST. Candia esq. decd. RENUN.: 11/12/1793. Of Mehetibl Mooers, widow of Samuel. Requests appointment of Major Samuel Mooers. ADMIN.: 11/20/1793. Admr. Samuel Mooers, Candia esq. Bond L1000.0.0. Sureties: Walter Robie, esq. and Thomas Fowle, yoeman, both of Candia. Witnesses: W. Parker and Nathl. Parker. INVY.: Appr.11/22/1793. Comm.: Nathl. Emerson and Walter Robie, esquires and Abram. Fitts. Value L60.0.0. Oaths 1/6/1794 Robie, Fowle and Admr. to Nathl. Emerson, JP. PETITION: 1/13/1794. Of Admr. For Comm. Insolvency. Gives claims of L114.0.0. Requests Comm. of Walter Robie and Nathaniel Emerson, esquires and Abraham Fitts, gent., all of Candia. Granted. CLAIMS WARR.: 1/13/1794. Comm. as requested. CLAIMS: Total L81.17.5. Oaths 12/17/1794 Comm. to judge. ACCOUNT: 2/16/1795. Of Admr. Allowed 2/16/1795. PROP. & SETTLM.: Claims L81.17.5. Amount to be proportioned L25.0.0. Allowed 3/2/1795 with order to Admr. to pay.

MOOR. See also Moore, Mooers

1774. MOOR, JAMES (1773) #4004
EST. Of Pembroke decd. intestate. PETITION (D22:334): 3/25/1773. Of the heirs of James: Widow Agness Moor, William Moor, John Moor, James Moor, Ephraim Moor, Daniel Moor, Ephraim Foster and Robert Kellse. They request that the est. be settled in the following manner: The home place and part of what is known as the School Lot on Robert Moor; the remainder of the School Lot and land purchased of Ephraim Blunt on John Moor; the personal est., except their mother's dower, be divided among the rest, including Mary Kelsey and Hannah Foster. Along with their mother, they desire that their bro. Robert be Admr. Witnesses: Joseph Baker and Saml. McConnel. Oaths 4/8/1773 Daniel Moor and Robert Kellse to Saml. Leavitt, JP. Oaths 6/9/1773 William Moor, John Moor, James Moor and Ephraim Moor to Jno. Bryent, JP. Oath 11/26/1773 Agness Moor and Ephraim Foster to Jno. Bryent, JP. ADMIN.:4/7/1773. Admr. Robert Moor, Pembroke yoeman. Bond L500.0.0. Sureties: Samuel McConnel and Joseph Baker, Pembroke gentlemen. Witnesses: Samuel Hale Jr. and Nathl. Rogers.

1775. MOOR, ROBERT (1796) #6210
EST. Londonderry yoeman decd. testate. WILL: Drawn 6/27/1795. Legatees: Wife-unnamed, her legacy being for only 3 years "she being otherwise endowed in est. her late husb. Samuel Wallace decd.; Sons-John, Thomas, Jehoiada, Peter, Robert and Samuel; Daus.-Euphamy Ramsay wife of William Ramsay, Jannet, Jane and Mary. Exec.- son Peter.

His sig. Witnesses: Margret Macgregore, James Macgregore and David Macgregore. CERT. WILL (D32:133): 5/14/1796. Presented by Exec. and witnesses James Macgregore, esq. and Margret Macgregore. ADMIN.: 5/14/1796. Exec. Peter Moor, Londonderry yoeman. Bond $3,000.00. Sureties: James Macgregore, esq. and James Barnet, gent., both of Londonderry. Witnesses: Stephen H. Reid and Margret Macgregore. INVY.: Comm.: James Macgregore, John Nesmith Jr. and John Reid. Value L902.3.1. Oaths 8/4/1796 Comm. to Isaac Thom, JP. Oath 8/17/1796 Exec. to judge. PETITION: 12/18/1799. Of Robert Moor of Londonderry. Requests that Exec., who is also Admr. of est. of their bro. Josiah decd. and who refuses to settle, be cited to settle his Accounts. Granted. PETITION: 4/16/1800. Of Robert Moor. For permission to sue Bond of Admin. as Exec. still has not settled his Account though cited to do so. BOND: 4/16/1800. Of Robert Moor, Londonderry yoeman. Bond $1,000.00. To sue Bond of Admin. Sureties: John Morrison and John Nesmith, Londonderry esquires. Witnesses: John Dinsmore and N. Parker. ACCOUNT: 4/15/1801. Of Exec. Allowed 4/15/1801 having been consented to by Robert Moor, the principal heir.

MOORE. See also Moor, Mooer

1776. MOORE: ANN & WILLIAM (1782) #4819
GDP. Of the children of George Moore, Londonderry yoeman decd. GDP.: 7/4/1782. Of: William and Ann, minors over 14. Gdn. James Betton, Windham esq. Bond L1000.0.0. Sureties: Samuel Hobart, esq. and Hugh Johnson, yoeman, both of Exeter. Witnesses: Joseph Dudley and W. Parker. Note: This Gdp. is filed as Moore, George et. al., an error as above George is the children's father.

1777. MOORE: ARCHELAUS, HANNAH, JOHN, MARY, REUBEN, STEPHEN, SUSANNA & THOMAS (1777) #4362
GDP. Of the children of Samuel Moore, Canterbury gent. decd. GDP.: 2/15/1777. Of Reuben, Susanna and Stephen, minors under 14. Gdn. Susanna Moore, Canterbury widow. Bond L1000.0.0.Sureties:Stephen Webster, gent. and Thomas Clough, yoeman, both of Canterbury. Witness Eliza. Parker Jr. GDP.: 5/30/1777. Of Mary, a minor over 14 and of John, Archelaus and Hannah, minors under 14. Gdn. Archelaus Moore, Canterbury esq. Bond L1000.0.0. Sureties: John Moore Jr. of Canterbury and Henry Elkins, Hampton gent. Witnesses: Abraham Perkins and Wm. Parker. GDP.: 6/25/1777. Of Thomas, a minor over 14. Gdn. Henry Elkins, Hampton esq. Bond L500.0.0. Sureties: William Smith, Hampton joiner and Abraham Tilton of Stratham. Witnesses: Thomas Baker and Wm. Parker

1778. MOORE, DR. COFFIN (1784) #5054
EST. Candia physicien decd. ADMIN.: 11/17/1784. Admx. Comfort Moore, Candia widow. Bond L1000.0.0. Sureties: Samuel Mooers, Candia esq. and Joseph Brackett, Lee, Strafford Co. gent. INVY.: 1/6/1785. Comm.: Samuel Mooers and Walter Robie, esquires and Abram. Fitts, gent. Value L4.6.6. Oaths 1/6/1785 Robie, Fitts and Admr. to Saml. Mooers, JP. CLAIMS WARR.: 3/16/1785. Comm.: Samuel Mooers and Walter Robie, Candia esquires. CLAIMS: 9/13/1785. Total not tallied. Esti. L116.0.0+. Oaths 9/13/1785 Comm. to Robt. Wilson, JP. ACCOUNT: 11/16/1785. Of Simon French and Comfort his wife, Admx. Allowed 11/16/1785.

1779. MOORE, EPHRAIM (1791) #5704
EST. Bow gent. decd. RENUN.: 10/31/1791. Of Hannah Moor, widow of Ephraim. Of Admin. Requests appointment of her son Moses. ADMIN.: 11/2/1791. Admr. Moses Moor, Bow yoeman. Bond L1000.0.0. Sureties: Benjamin Noyes, Bow gent. and Arthur Livermore, Concord esq. Witnesses: Nathl. Parker and W. Parker. INVY.: Comm.: Benjamin Noyes, John Knox and Joseph Haseltine. Value L22.9.0.. Oaths 2/13/1792 Comm. to Jno. Bryent, JP. Oath 2/15/1792 Admr. to judge. PETITION: 2/15/1792. Of Admr. For Comm. Insolvency. Gives list claims of L180.0.0. with more to come. PETITION: 8/2/1792. Of Claims Comm. They have met one day in each of 6 months and still some claimants request more time.8/15/1792 3 more months allowed. Note: This Petition also includes a note by judge granting License which belongs with #5599 Saml. Webster (1790) and is recorded there. CLAIMS: Total L94.12.81/2. Oaths11/17/1792 Noyes and Knox to Jno. Bryent, JP. DOWER: 11/17/1792. Comm.: Benja. Noyes, Samuel Alexander and John Knox. Of Widow Hannah Moor. Oaths 11/17/1792 Comm. to Jno. Bryent, JP. Allowed. PETITION: 11/21/1792. Of Admr. For License to settle the bal. of L72.8.8. of Claims. Granted. LICENSE (D30:325): 11/21/1792. To Admr. To sell real est. to amount of L75.0.0. ACCOUNT: 12/1792. Of Admr. Allowed 12/19/1792. PROP. & SETTLM.: Claims L94.12.8 1/2. Amount to be proportioned L32.12.3. Allowed 1/14/1793 with order to Admr. to pay.

1780. MOORE, GEORGE (1782) #4834
EST. Londonderry yeoman decd. ADMIN.: 8/28/1782. Admx. Jane Moore, Londonderry widow. Bond L500.0.0. Sureties: Joseph Hodgkins, gent. and Daniel Hunter, yoeman, both of Londonderry. Witnesses: William Heard and Joanna Hodgkins. INVY.: Appr. 10/22/1782. Comm.: Thomas Christy, Robert Archabald and Daniel Hunter. Value not tallied. Esti. L1400.0.0+. Oaths11/19/1782 Comm. and Admx. to James Betton, JP.

1781. MOORE, HENRY (1786) #5210
EST. Portsmouth mariner decd. intestate. ADMIN.: 8/18/1786. Admx. Sarah Moore, Portsmouth widow. Bond L1000.0.0. Sureties: Thomas Odiorne, esq. and Simeon Ladd, gent., both of Exeter. Witnesses: Nathl. Parker and W. Parker. INVY. WARR.: 8/18/1786. Comm.: Peter Coues, Reuben Shapleigh and Edward Sargent, all of Portsmouth. INVY.: The Admx. returns Warr. with note, "There was no estate to be shown the within named appraisers, real or personal, except a Note from a David Meings late of Virginia decd. which was sent there to recover the money, being about the sum of L208.0.0. as liquidated by the Virginia Scale of Depreciation."

1782. MOORE, HENRY (1798) #6452
EST. Londonderry gent. decd. intestate. RENUN.: 4/17/1798. Of Willm. Moor. Of Admin., being advanced in age, of his son, who died leaving no wife or children. Requests appointment of his son James Moor. Petition: 4/18/1798. Of James Moor of Windham. For Admin. as requested by his father. ADMIN.:4/18/1798. Admr. James Moor, Windham yoeman. Bond $3,000.00. Sureties: James Betton, esq. and John McClary, yoeman, both of Windham. Witnesses: Robert Barnet and Nathl. Parker. INVY.: Appr. 5/16/1798. Comm.: John McClary, John Karr and Andrew Mack. Value $122.60. Oaths 5/19/1798 Karr and McClary to John Nesmith, JP. Oath 8/15/1798 Admr. to W. Parker, JP. ACCOUNT: 4/17/1799. Of Admr. Allowed 4/17/1799.

1783. MOORE, JANNET (1799) #6525
EST. Londonderry single woman decd. testate. WILL: Drawn 12/28/1798. Legatees: Bros.-Robert, John, Peter, Jehoiada, Thomas and Samuel; Sisters- Euphemy Ramsey, Jane and Mary; Lattice dau. of her bro. Thomas. Exec.-bro. Jehoiada. Her mark. Witnesses: John Barnet, Joseph Hovey and John Nesmith. CERT. WILL (D33:23): 1/8/1799. Presented by Exec. and witnesses Barnet and Nesmith, esq. INVY. (D33:167): Comm.: John Hughes, John Reid and John Nesmith. Value $664.68. Oaths 11/30/1799 Comm. and Exec. to John Dinsmore, JP.

1784. MOORE, JOHN (1777) #4318
EST. Candia yoeman decd. ADMIN.: 2/26/1777. Admx. Jane Moor, Candia widow. Bond L500.0.0. Sureties: Henry Moore, esq. and Charles Moore, yoeman, both of Chester. Witnesses: Theophilus Sargent and Saml. Mooers. INVY.: Appr. 4/7/1777. Comm.: William Baker and Theophilus Sargent. Value real est. L450.0.0, rest not tallied but esti. L199.0.0. Oaths 5/27/1777 Comm. and Admx. to Saml. Mooers, JP.

1785. MOORE, JOHN (1792) #5764
EST. Londonderry blacksmith decd. RENUN.: 4/18/1792. Of Mary Moore, widow. She employs Robert Moore to be Admr. Witnesses: William Parkinson and Saml. Allison. ADMIN.: 4/18/1792. Admr. Robert Moore, Londonderry yoeman. Bond L1000.0.0. Sureties: John McKeen Jr. and Robert Barnet, gent., both of Londonderry. Witnesses: John Morrison and W. Parker.

1786. MOORE, ENSIGN JOSIAH (1796) #6209
EST. Londonderry gent. decd. ADMIN.: 5/14/1796. Admr. Peter Moor, Londonderry yoeman. Bond $2,000.00. Sureties: James Macgregore, esq. and James Barnet, gent., both of Londonderry. Witnesses: Stephen H. Reid and Margaret Macgregore. INVY.: Comm.: James Macgregore, John Reid and Jno. Nesmith Jr. Value l14.1.6. Oaths 8/4/1796 Comm. to Isaac Thom, JP. Oath 8/17/1796 Admr. to judge. ACCOUNT: 4/1801. Of Admr. Allowed 4/15/1801 Robert Moor, an heir, consenting for himself and rest of heirs.

1787. MOORE, PARKER (1791) #5726
EST. Londonderry yoeman decd. RENUN.: 12/21/1791. Of James Bamford, husband of Judith, dau.; Ruth Moore and Solomon Moore, heirs. Of Admin. Request appointment of James Choate. Witness John Morrison. ADMIN.:12/21/1791.Admr.James Choate, Londonderry yoeman. Bond L2000.0.0. Sureties: Nathan Stinson and John Morrison, Londonderry yoemen. Witnesses: Jno. Nesmith Jr. and David Ela. INVY.: Appr. 12/29/1791. Comm.: Samll. Allison and John Cochran. Value L123.13.6. Oaths 3/3/1792 Comm. to Isaac Thom, JP. Oath 4/18/1792 Admr. to judge. PETITION: 12/19/1792. Of Admr. For license. Also requests judge to consider if selling part would be prejudicial to heirs. NOTICE: 12/19/1792. To heirs. Of hearing on Petition. Cert. 1/18/1793. Of Moses Kelly, Sheriff. He has notified John Adams of Sutan (Sutton?) by reading Petition and order to him. His receipt for L0.12.0 for notifying. LICENSE: 2/18/1793. To Admr. To sell all the real est. BOND.: 2/18/1793. Of Admr. Bond L300.0.0. To account for sale of real est. Sureties: James Adams Jr. and Amos Adams, Londonderry yoemen. Witnesses: W. Parker and Nathl. Parker. ACCOUNT: Of Admr. Allowed 12/18/1793.

1788. MOORE, PETER (1798) #6438
EST. Stratham yoeman decd. RENUN.: 3/27/1798. Of Mary Moore, widow of Peter. Of Admin. ADMIN.: 3/28/1798. Admr. Benjamin Moore, Stratham yoeman. Bond $3,000.00. Sureties: Jonathan Wiggin, gent. and Thomas Veasey, yoeman, both of Stratham. Witnesses: W. Parker and Saml. Parker. INVY. WARR.: 3/28/1798. Comm.: Paine Wingate. esq.;

Jonathan Wiggin, gent. and Phinehas Merrill, yoeman, all of Stratham. Invy.: Appr. 3/31/1798. Value $1,606.68. Oaths 6/14/1798 Comm. and on 6/19/1798 Admr. to judge. PETITION: 4/13/1813. Of John Moore, Stratham yoeman. For div. of land in Stratham of est. of decd. which he holds in common with Benjamin Moore and Peter Moore. Benjamin owns about 29 acres, Peter about 10 acres and heownsrest.Order:4/13/1813. For hearing, Petitioner to serve Benjamin and Peter with copies of Petition and Order. Petition granted 4/16/1813. Comm. appointed: Phinehas Merrill, esq.; Thomas Veasey, James Scammon and Benjamin Norris, yoemen, all of Stratham and Gideon Colcord, Newmarket yoeman. DIV. WARR.: 4/16/1798. Comm. as appointed. To make Div. as in Petition. Div.: 5/25/1813. Divisees: John Moore, Peter Moore and Benjamin Moore.Oaths5/25/1813 Veasey, Colcord, Scammon and Norris to Phinehas Merrill, JP. Allowed 8/19/1813.

1789. MOORE, COL. ROBERT (1779) #4581
EST. Londonderry esq. decd. testate. WILL: Drawn 5/8/1778. Legatees: Wife-Mary; Sons-John, William and Robert; Daus.-Martha Holmes, Janet Wallace, Mary, Elizabeth Moore, Ann Moore and Hannah Moore; Gives negro wench to wife. Specifies wife to be Gdn. of his children. Execs.-wife Mary and son John. His sig. Witnesses: Thomas Willson, John Ramsey and John Crombie. CERT.WILL: 10/27/1779. Presented by Execs. and witnesses Willson and Crombie. INVY.: Appr. 11/30/1779. Comm. John Crombie, John Clark and Moses Barnett. Value not tallied. Esti. L35500.0.0. Oaths 12/3/1779 Crombie and Clark to Moses Barnett, JP. Oaths. Execs. to Moses Barnett, JP.

1790. MOORE: RUTH & SOLOMON (1791) #5727
GDP. Of the children of Parker Moor, Londonderry yoeman decd. GDP.: 12/21/1791. Of: Solomon and Ruth, minors under14. Gdn. John Morrison, Londonderry yoeman. Bond L1000.0.0. Sureties: James Choate and Nathan Stinson, Londonderry yoemen. Witnesses: Jno. Nesmith Jr. and James Gibson.

1791. MOORE, CAPT. SAMUEL (1776) #4198
EST. Canterbury gent. decd. intestate. ADMIN.: 2/8/1776. Admx. Susanna Meer, Canterbury widow. Bond L1000.0.0. Sureties: Jeremiah Clough, Canterbury esq. and Stephen Webster, Boscawen, Hillsborough Co. gent. Witnesses: Elizabeth Parker and W. Parker. INVY.: Comm.: Stephen Gerrish, Nathan Bachelder and David Forster. Value L1684.1.11. Oath 2/15/1777 Admx. to Wm. Parker, JP. ADDL. INVY.: Value L10.13.1 1/2. Signed by Forster and Bachelder. CITATION: 3/28/1778. To David McCrillis, Canterbury, blacksmith and Susanna his wife, Admx.

Complaint has been made on behalf of heirs that Admrs. have not accounted for more than two years and heirs are left out of their share of the personal est. and the improvement of the real est. Order: The Admrs. are cited to appear and exhibit Account in order for distribution. ACCOUNT.: 4/28/1778. Allowed 4/28/1779 after a hearing on objections. ADDL. ACCOUNT: 4/28/1778. Allowed 4/28/1778 objections having been heard. ACCOUNT: 4/28/1779. Allowed 4/29/1779.Account includes main. 4 children and expense of Widow lying-in with a posthumous child. Also ref. to objections of Gdn. DOWER: 7/10/1779. Comm.: Timo. Walker Jr., George Jackman, John Hoit, Samuel Gerrish and David Forster. Of Susanna McCrillis in est. of Capt. Samuel Moore. Oaths 7/10/1779 Comm. to Archelaus Moore, JP. DIV.: 11/24/1779. Same Comm. as for Dower. To div. the real est. among his children, except oldest son who, during the lifetime of his father, received his full portion. Divisees: Sons-Elkins, Thomas, Archelaus, John, Reuben, and Stephen; Daus.-Joanna Mooney wife of Obadiah Mooney; Mary Moore, Hannah Moore and Susanna Moore. Oaths 11/24/1779 Comm. to Archelaus Moore, JP. Allowed. ADDL. ACCOUNT: 9/1781. Of Admrs. Allowed 9/26/1781. PETITION: 3/21/1822. Of: David McCrilles, Abiel Foster, Susanna Foster, Comfort Moor Admx. est. Thomas Moore and Gdn. of his minor heir; Stephen Moore son of Thomas Moore and Samuel Moore. Request div. among the heirs of the Dower of Susanna McCrillis of Canterbury, now decd., widow of Samuel Moore decd. Request a Comm. of Josiah Sanborn of Epsom; Jona. Clough of Loudon and Stephen Ambrose of Concord, esquires.; Jeremiah Pecker of Concord and Joseph Gerrish of Canterbury, gentlemen. ACCOUNT: 9/26/1781. Of David McCrillis. Allowed 9/5/1822 after a hearing and consideration of objections of some of heirs.

1792. MOORE, SUSANNA (1782) #4825
EST. Of Hampstead decd. ADMIN.:7/31/1782. Admr. Jonathan Roberts Hale, Hampstead yoeman. Bond L1000.0.0. Sureties: Jesse Johnson of Hampstead and James Little of Atkinson, gentlemen. Witnesses: Robert Young and W. Parker. INVY.: Appr. 3/24/1783. Comm.: Jesse Johnson and John Calfe. Value L213.0.0. Affirm. 3/24/1783 Johnson to John Calfe, JP. Oath 4/2/1783 Calfe, esq. and on4/5 Admr. to judge. APPR. WARR.: 4/3/1783. Comm.: Joseph French, Jona. Eastman, David Poor and Eliphalet Poor, gentlemen and John Bond, physician, all of Hampstead. To view the real est. to see if it can be div. among her children. Div. or appr. so it may be settled on oldest son. Appr.: 6/2/1783. Value L$24.00 per acre. Oaths 6/2/1783 French, Poor and Bond to Samuel Little, JP.

1793. MOORE, THOMAS (1791) #5669
EST. Stratham gent. decd. testate. WILL: Drawn 7/29/1780. Legatees: Wife-Rachel; Sons-Thomas and William; Daus.-Rachel Taylor, Agnis Robinson, Anna Stevens and Elizabeth Sinkler. Exec.-son Thomas. His sig. Witnesses: Saml. Lane, Sarah Lane and Jabez Lane. CERT. WILL (D30:80): 6/13/1791 on oaths of Samuel Lane and Sarah Lane and affirm. of Jabez Lane, who did not remember the transaction but believes that it was executed according to law and that he signed his name as a witness in presence of testator.

1794. MOORE, WILLIAM (1774) #4090
EST. Kingston mariner decd. ADMIN.: 3/11/1774. Admr. William Parker, Exeter esq. Bond L100.0.0. Sureties: Nathanael Folsom of Exeter and Samuel Hale Jr. of Portsmouth, esquires. Witnesses: John Lowell and Geo. King.

1795. MOORE, WILLIAM (1791) #5682
EST. Stratham esq. decd. testate. WILL: Drawn 4/13/1791. Legatees: Sons-Harvey and Peter; Daus.-Widow Abigail Gilman and Mary Colcord; Grandson-William Moore son of William Moore decd. Execs.-sons Harvey and Peter. His sig. Witnesses: Joseph Norris, Caleb Wiggin and Jabez Lane. CERT. WILL (D30:3): 8/15/1791. Presented by Execs. and witnesses Norris and Wiggin. ADMIN.: 8/15/1791. Execs.: Harvey Moore and Peter Moore, Stratham husbandmen. Bond L1000.0.0. Sureties: Joseph Norris and Caleb Wiggin, Stratham husbandmen. Witness Nathl. Parker. INVY. WARR.: 8/15/1791. Comm.: Joseph Norris and Caleb Wiggin, yoemen and Saml. Pottle, all of Stratham. INVY.: Value L1009.15.6. Oaths 11/16/1791 Comm. and "one of Execs." to W. Parker, JP.

1796. MORELAND, JOHN (1798) #6451
EST. Salem yoeman decd. testate. WILL: Drawn 3/12/1798. Legatees: Son-James; Daus.-Cathrine, Mary, Elizabeth and Margaret; Grandsons-William Moreland, Thomas Moreland, John Buckley and Wm. Addison Jr.; Granddaus.-Elisabeth Moreland and Linde Buckley; Servant girl-unnamed. Provides gravestones for self, wife and son Thomas. Exec.-Wm. Thom. His mark. Witnesses: Robert Kennedy, James Addison and John Kennedy. CERT. WILL (D32:468): 4/18/1798. Presented by Exec. and witnesses Addison and John Kennedy. ADMIN.: 4/18/1798. Exec. William Thom, Salem gent. Bond $3,000.00. Sureties: Thomas Dow, esq. and Jonathan Emerson, husbm., both of Salem. Witnesses: James Moorland and Nathl. Parker. INVY.: Appr. 4/30/1798. Comm.: Joseph Kitbridge, Samuel Cross and Elisha Woodbery. Value $638.03. Oaths 4/30/1798 Comm. to Josiah Gage, JP.Oath5/10/1798 Exec. to W. Parker.

Note: The following Petition recorded as #6447 William Thom (1798) but belongs here. PETITION: 4/18/1798. Of William Thom, Exec. est. John Moreland, Salem yoeman decd. For div. of land in Salem held in common by decd. with his son James Moorland, Salem yoeman, in order for settlm. Consent of James Moorland. Granted. PETITION: 5/10/1798. Of Exec. For License to sell personal est. DIV. WARR.: 4/18/1798. Comm.: Josiah Gage, esq.; Alexander Graham, gent., both of Pelham; Israel Woodbury and Robert Campbell, Salem yoemen and Ebenezer Barker, Methuen, Essex. Co., MA husbm. To div. land in Salem of which decd. owned 1/2 in common with his son James. DIV.: Divisees: Heirs of John Moreland and James Moorland. Oaths 4/25/1798 Gage, Graham, Woodbury and Campbell to John Dinsmore, JP. The Exec. and James Moorland represented the heirs. Allowed. PETITION: 8/15/1798. Of Exec. For Comm. Insolvency. Gives claims now more than $600.00. Granted. CLAIMS: 3/13/1799. Comm.: Josiah Gage, Samuel Armour and Silas Betton. Total $363.88. Oaths 3/13/1799 Comm. to Wm. Thom, JP. PETITION: 4/9/1799. Of Exec. For License. Granted. LICENSE (D33:64): 4/9/1799. To Exec. To sell real est. to amount of $420.00. ACCOUNT: 4/16/1800. Of Exec. Allowed 4/16/1800 a majority of heirs having examined it.

1797. MORGAN, JONATHAN (1771) #3840
GDP. Son of Jonathan Morgan, Pelham yoeman decd. GDP.: 4/5/1771. Of Jonathan, a minor over 14. Gdn. Joseph Butler, Pelham gent. Sureties: Joseph Wright of Salem and Samuel Greelee, Nottingham West, Hillsborough Co. gentlemen. Witnesses: Kimball Cotton and Nehemiah Butler.

1798. MORGAN, SIMEON (1784) #4974
EST. Brentwood tanner decd. ADMIN.: 2/10/1784. Admx. Lydia Morgan, Brentwood widow. Bond L500.0.0. Sureties: Jonathan Shaw, Brentwood yoeman and James Carruth, Kingston trader. Witnesses: Nathl. Parker and W. Parker. INVY. WARR.: 2/18/1784. Comm.: Ezekiel Godfrey, Poplin gent.; Joseph Johnson and Jonathan Shaw, Brentwood yoemen. INVY.: Appr. 2/27/1784. Value L223.15.6. Oaths 6/16/1784 Shaw, Godfrey and Admx. to Wm. Parker, JP. PETITION: 6/16/1784. Of Admx. For Comm. Insolvency. Gives list claims of L106.8.0. and more to come. LICENSE (D28:522): 6/15/1785. To Admx. To sell the real est. DOWER: 9/19/1785. Comm.: Abraham Sanborn, Jeremiah Rowe and Ezekl. Godfrey. Of Widow Lydia Morgan. Oaths 9/21/1785 Comm. to judge. Allowed. CLAIMS: 9/19/1785. Comm.: Abraham Sanborn and Ezekl. Godfrey. Total L151.0.6. Oaths 9/21/1785 Comm. to W. Parker, Reg. APPR.: 1/28/1786. Comm.: James Sinkler and Ezekl. Godfrey. At the request of

Admx., they assess the rent of 2/3 of the real est. for the years 1784 and 1785, allowing one half for carrying on same, at L6.3.0. ACCOUNT: 12/21/1785. Of Admx. Examined and vouched by Admx. 1/28/1785 before W. Parker, JP & Reg. Allowed 2/15/1786. Account includes maintenance of David, Theophilus and Abigail Caruth Morgan. PROP. & SETTLM.: Claims L151.0.6. Amount to be proportioned L75.4.0. Allowed 2/15/1786 with order to Admx. to pay.

Morril. See also Morrill

1799. MORRIL, BETTY (1776) #4295 & (1782) #4865
GDP. Of the dau. of Moses Morril, Kingston yoeman decd. GDP.(#4295): 12/25/1776. Of Betty, a minor under 14Gdn. Nathaniel Bachellor, Kingston esq. Bond L500.0.0. Surety John Prescott, Epping yoeman. Witnesses: Nowell Herley and Wm. Parker. ACCOUNT (#4295): Of Gdn. Allowed 3/29/1780. Note: Clerk calls Gdn. Batchelder "elder." GDP. (#4295): 3/29/1780. Of Betty, minor over 14. Gdn.: David Tilton, Kingston gent. Bond $5000.00(sic.). Sureties: Philip Tilton, gent. and John Morril, tanner, both of Kingston. Witnesses: Samuel Stevens and Eliphalet Webster. RECEIPT (#4295): 11/2/1779. From Nathl. Bachellor, Gdn. To John Prescut, Admr. est. Betty's father. Of L23.17.4. in full of bal. of Admr.s' Account due Betty from est. plus 1 year's income of her part of est., the other being accounted for. Acknowledged before the judge. GDP. (#4865). 12/5/1782. Of Betty, a minor over 14. Gdn. John Morril, Kingston tanner, her stepfather. Bond L1000.0.0. Sureties: David Tilton, gent. and Samuel Stevens, yoeman, both of Kingston. Witnesses: Philip Tilton and Daniel Tilton. ACCOUNT (#4865): 12/9/1782. Of David Tilton, former Gdn. Receipt: Of John Morril present Gdn. He has received of David Tilton L2.9.11. the bal. of his Account. Allowed 12/9/1782.
1800. MORRIL, DEACON DAVID (1799) #6611
EST. Canterbury yoeman decd. RENUN.: Of: Widow Abigail Morrill and Josiah Capeter. Of Admin. Request appointment of Asa Foster Jr. PETITION: 9/18/1799. Of Asa Foster Jr. of Canterbury. For Admin. at request of the widow and Capeter (called Carpenter), who married oldest dau., and oldest son who declines. Foster is husb. of the other dau. Granted. ADMIN.: 9/18/1799. Admr. Asa Foster Jr., Canterbury gent. Bond $3,000.00. Sureties: Samuel Sargent of Canterbury and Ephraim Carter of Concord, yoemen. Witnesses: David Stickney and Nathl. Parker. INVY.: Comm.: Abiel Foster, esq.; Samuel Gerrish and Leavitt Clough. Value $1,815.01. Oaths 9/28/1799 Comm. to Asa Forster, JP. Oath 5/21/1800 Admr. to judge. ACCOUNT (D34:135): Of Admr. Allowed 5/19/1802. PETITION: 8/20/1804. Of David L. Morril. Requests that Admr. be requested to apply for div. of real est. to heirs. They have agreed

on a Comm. of Major McClary, Capt. Babb and Capt. Sanborn. His sister Hannah joins him in request. As he is leaving for the Coos country, he cannot appear in person.

1801. MORRIL, SAMUEL (1798) #6463
GDP. of the son of Samuel Morrill, Epping gent. decd. GDP.: 5/16/1798. Of Samuel, a minor over 14. Gdn. David Lawrence Morril, Epsom physician. Bond $1,000.00. Sureties: Thomas Babb, Epsom gent. and George Wallis, Deerfield yoeman. Witnesses: Michl. McClary and Nathl. Parker.

Morrill. See also Morril

1802. MORRILL, AARON (1786) #5230
EST. Of Salisbury, Essex Co., MA decd. CERT.: 4/14/1786. Of Daniel Noyes, Reg. Probate, Essex Co., MA. There is a bal. of L71.1.9. due from est. of Aaron Morrill to the est. of Col. Henry Morrill, late of Salisbury, Essex Co., MA as appears in the Probate Office records. ADMIN.: 12/20/1786. Admr. Ezekiel Morril, Salisbury, Essex Co., MA blacksmith. Bond L500.0.0. Sureties: John Shaw, wheelwright and Samuel Gilman, taylor, both of Exeter. Witnesses: W. Parker and Nathl. Parker. INVY. WARR.: 12/20/1786. Comm.: Daniel Hoit, Increase Bachelder and Benja. Johnson, all of Northwood. INVY.: Appr. 4/18/1787. Value of 2/3 of a 156 acre lot in Northwood, 2/3 supposed to be 104 acres, at L187.4.0. Oaths 4/18/1787 Comm. to Joseph Demerit, JP. Oath 4/18/1787 Admr. to W. Parker. Reg. ACCOUNT: Of Admr. Allowed 7/16/1788.

1803. MORRILL, ELIJAH (1798) #6439
EST. Epping mariner decd. ADMIN.: 3/31/1798. Admr. William Morrill, Epping yoeman. Bond $3,000.00. Sureties: Jacob Morrill of Epping and David Rawlings of Northwood, yoemen. Witnesses: W. Parker and Jno. Parker.

1804. MORRILL, HENRY (1799) #6622
EST. Hawke husbm. decd. testate. WILL: Drawn 2/10/1792. Legatees: Wife-unnamed. They have a jointure between them; Son-Nathaniel; Daus.-Apphia, Miriam and Sarah; Grandchildren-Susanna Swett, Mary Nichols and Henry Morril Blake. Exec.- son Nathaniel. His sig. Witnesses: Samuel Ely, Elisha Bean and Saml. Eastman. CERT. WILL (D33:163): 11/11/1799. Presented by Exec. and witnesses Bean and Eastman. ADMIN.:11/11/1799.Exec. Nathaniel Morrill, Hawke husbm. Bond $2,000.00. Sureties: Samuel Eastman of Hawke and Elisha Bean of Sandown, husbandmen. Witnesses: Levi Healey and Nath. Parker.

1805. MORRILL, SAMUEL (1785) #5143
EST. Epping gent. decd. intestate. ADMIN.: 10/18/1785. Admx. Anna Morrill, Epping widow. Bond L2000.0.0. Sureties: David Lawrence Jr., yoeman and Benjamin Hoit, gent, both of Epping. Witness Nat Parker. INVY. WARR.: 10/19/1785. Comm.: Jeremiah Sanborn, gent.; Jonathan Clark, yoeman and Timothy Johnson, physician, all of Epping. INVY.: Appr. 3/14/1786. Value L266.18.11. Oaths 3/14/1786 Comm. and on 3/15/1786 Admx. to Abraham Perkins, JP. LICENSE (D29:193): 3/15/1788. To Admx. To sell sufficient real est. to pay debts. PETITION: 5/20/1788. Of Timo. Johnson. For Comm. Insolvency. Gives list claims of L268.14.1. Granted. CLAIMS WARR.: 5/21/1788. Comm.: Enoch Coffin and Seth Fogg, esquires and Reuben Osgood, yoeman, all of Epping. On 10/15/1788 Comm. allowed 6 months longer. Claims: Total L405.6.4. Oaths 5/15/1790 Comm. to Wm. Plumer, JP. RELEASE: Undated. Of Jona. Clark. He releases for the benefit of the creditors his claim of L65.18.11, having been otherwise satisfied. ACCOUNT: 5/19/1790. Of Timo. Johnson and his wife, Admx. Allowed 5/19/1790. Account includes main. Samuel and note that Anna gave up her Dower. ADDL. ACCOUNT: 7/21/1790. Of Admrs. Allowed 7/21/1790. ADDL. ACCOUNT: 5/13/1793. Of Admrs. Allowed 5/13/1793. PROP. & SETTLM. (D30:427): Claims L405.6.4. Amount to be proportioned L120.10.0. Allowed 5/13/1793 with order to Admrs. To pay.

1806. MORRILL, SAMUEL BARNARD (1789) #5483
GDP. Of the son of Abraham Morrill. GDP.: 9/16/1789. Of Samuel Barnard Morrill, a minor under 14. Gdn. Abraham Morrill, Brentwood gent. Bond L500.0.0. Sureties: Nathan Merrill, Poplin innholder and John Bartlet, Amesbury, Essex Co., MA yoeman. Witness Nathl. Parker.

MORISON. See also Morrison

1807. MORISON, ROBERT JR. (1794) #5967
EST. Londonderry husbm. decd. testate. WILL: Drawn 2/4/1794. Legatees: Sister-in-law-Widow Jean Morrison; Nephew-David Morrison; William Morrison son of his nephew David Morrison; Jean Luce wife of Moses Luce of Hartland, VT; Mary Shirley wife of William Shirley of Chester. He notes that he has already given portions to the other children of his bros. And sisters. Exec.-Isaac Thom and desires that Isaac Thom also be Exec. of est. his father Robert Morrison. His sig. Witnesses: John Betton, John Warner and Andrew Moor. CERT. WILL (D31:176): 2/17/1794. Presented by Exec. and witnesses Betton and Moor. ADMIN.: 2/17/1794. Exec. Isaac Thom, Londonderry esq. Bond L1000.0.0. Sureties: John Betton and Andrew Moor, Londonderry yoemen.

Witnesses: Jno. Parker and W. Parker. CLAIMS WARR.: 4/17/1794. Comm.: Daniel Runnels, esq.; John Hunter Jr. gent. and Robert McNeal, yoeman, all of Londonderry. CLAIMS: 4/15/1795. Total L200.0.0. Oaths 4/15/1795 McNael and Hunter to J. Macgregore, JP. PETITION: 4/15/1795. Of Exec. For License. He notes that decd. left no personal est. Granted to the amount of L200.0.0. ACCOUNT: 12/18/1799. Of Exec. Allowed 12/18/1799.

MORRISON. See also Morison

1808. MORRISON, JOHN (1758) A#2405
EST. Of Epping. Note: The following Addl. Account found in #4211 John Morrison of Londonderry (1776) belongs here. ADDL. ACCOUNT.: 1/1778. Of John Perkins an Admr. Allowed 1/1/1778. GDP. of the children of John Morrison of Epping decd. RELEASE (D23:558): 2/28/1778. Of John Morrison and Thomas Dearborn, yoemen and Mary his wife, all of Candia. Their brother David is decd. In consideration of L20.0.0. paid to them by Moses Baker, Candia esq., who was their Gdn., they release Baker from all claims they have or ought to have against his Gdp. All sigs. Witnesses; John Knowles and Saml. Emerson. Oaths 5/26/1778 John Morrison and Thomas and Mary Dearborn to Saml. Emerson, JP. Orig. Archives file includes Admin. with Widow Mary Morrison later Mrs. John Perkins of Epping as Admx., Invy., Account by John Perkins and Gdp. of Mary, John and David.

1809. MORRISON, JOHN (1776) #4211
EST. Londonderry yoeman decd. ADMIN.: 3/12/1776. Admx. Elizabeth Morrison, Londonderry widow. Bond L1000.0.0. Sureties: James Nesmith Jr. and Robert Wilson, Londonderry yoemen. Witnesses: James Nesmith and Gorg Corning. INVY. WARR.: 3/12/1776. Comm.: James Nesmith, Georg Corning and Robert Wilson, all of Londonderry. INVY.: Value L212.3.5.0. Oaths 4/2/1776 Comm. and Admx. to James Betton, JP. Note: This file also includes an Addl. Account which belongs with A#2405 John Morrison of Epping (1758) and is recorded there.

1810. MORRISON, MATTHEW (1777) #4397
GDP. Of a Londonderry adult n.c.m. REPETITION: 10/28/1777. Of John Moor, Selectmen's clerk. States that Matthew Morrison, by the death of friends, has been left a piece of land and some other things, but is not capable of caring for himself. His cousin, James Morison, has been with the Selectmen of Londonderry and says he will give bond for the main. of his "uncle" during life if the judge wishes to appoint James as Gdn. GDP.: 10/30/1777 Of Matthew Morrison of Londonderry, an adult adjudged

n.c.m. Gdn. James Morrison of Londonderry. Bond L500.0.0. Sureties: Robert Boyes, yoeman and William Wallace, gent., both of Londonderry. Witnesses: Elizabeth Parker Jr. and W. Parker. INVY.: Comm.: James Aiken, Robert Boyes and James Nesmith Jr. Value L119.15.0. Oaths 11/22/1777 Comm. to John Bell, JP. Oath 11/27/1777 Gdn. to Wm. Parker, Reg. & JP.

1811. MORRISON, ROBERT (1794) #5966
EST. Londonderry husbm. decd. ADMIN.: 2/17/1794. Admr. Isaac Thom, Londonderry esq. Bond L1000.0.0. Sureties: John Betton and Andrew Moore, Londonderry yoemen. Witnesses: Jno. Parker and W. Parker, Reg. INVY.: Appr. 3/20/1794. Comm.: Robert McNeill, Danl. Raynolds and John Hunter Jr. Value L127.10.0. Oaths 3/20/1794 Comm. to Isaac Thom, JP. Oath 4/17/1794 Admr. to judge. PETITION: Dated by clerk 4/16/1794. Of Admr. For Comm. Insolvency. Lists one claim of L200.0.0. Granted. LICENSE (D31:509): 4/15/1795. To Admr. To sell real est. to amount of L210.0.0. ACCOUNT: 12/18/1799. Of Admr. Allowed 12/18/1799 having been consented to by Atty. of residuary heir. Receipt: Of Atty. for David Morrison, residuary legatee of decd. He has received from Exec. of the Will of Isaac Thom, who was Admr., $24.83.

1812. MORRISON, SAMUEL (1776) #4243
EST. Londonderry weaver decd. testate. WILL: Drawn 2/15/1775. Legatees: Wife- Isabela; Sons-Samuel (oldest), Abraham (2d), Robert (3d), Jonathan (4th) and David (5th); Daus.-Jennet Morrison (oldest), Margaret (2d) and Isabella (3d). Exec. wife-Isabella. His mark. Witnesses: George Duncan Jr., Samuel Taggart and Joseph McFarland. CERT. WILL (D23:318): 6/19/1776. Presented by Exex. and witnesses Duncan and Taggart. INVY.: Comm.: Samuel Fisher, Geoge Duncan Jr. and Moses Watt. Value L90.12.7. Oaths 8/27/1776 Comm. to Matthew Thornton, JP. Oath 9/6/1776 Exex. to Wm. Parker, JP.

1813. MORRISON, WILLIAM (1781) #4724
GDP. Of the son of William Morrison, Portsmouth mariner decd. GDP.: 6/28/1781. Of William, a minor over 14. Gdn. Simeon Ladd, Exeter gent. Bond L20000.0.0. Sureties: Benjamin Lamson, innholder and Caleb Greenleaf Adams, physician, both of Exeter. Witness Nathl. Parker.

1814. MORROW, JOHN (1781) #4704
EST. Windham yoeman decd. testate. WILL: Drawn 3/3/1781. Legatees: Wife-Margret; Sons-Allexander and James; Servant-William Mcilvaine. Execs.-son Allexander and friend Gain Armour. His mark. Witnesses: Danl. Mcilvane, Robert Spear and John Armour. CERT. WILL (D26:48):

3/28/1781. Presented by Execs. and witnesses Spear and Armour. INVY.: Appr. 4/4/1781. Comm.: Danl. Mcilvane, Alexander Park and Benja. Thom. Value L43697.13.4. The Widow's part of the personal est. appr. at L1573.6.8. Oaths 5/4/1781 Comm. and Execs. to James Betton, JP. ACCOUNT: 3/31/1784. Of Gain Armour, an Exec. Allowed 3/31/1784.

1815. MORSE, HANNAH (1799) #6523
EST. Salem single woman (sic.) decd. testate. WILL: Drawn 1/25/1799. Legatees: Sons-Moody Morse, Daniel Peaslee Morse and Caleb Morse. Exec.- son Caleb. Her sig. Witnesses: Mitchel Whittier, Joseph Merrill and Samuel Kelley. No proving or cert.

1816. MORSE, PETER (1779) #4510
EST. Hampstead gent. decd. ADMIN. (D25:12): 1/7/1779. Admr. Edmund Morse, Hampstead gent. Sureties: Richard Jenness 3d of Rye and Jonathan Woodman of Deerfield, yoemen. INVY.: Appr. 2/22/1779. Comm.: John Harriman and Benjamin Pilsbury. Value L263.18.0. Oaths 4/7/1779 Comm. to Saml. Little, JP. Oath 6/30/1779 Admr. to judge.

1817. MOSES, AARON JR. (1771) #3846
EST. Of Portsmouth, decd. ADMIN.: 5/11/1771. Admx.: Elizabeth Moses, Portsmouth widow. Bond L100.0.0. Surety: Eliphalet Daniel, Portsmouth gent. Witnesses: Ephm. McFarland and Philip Fowler.

1818. MOSES, JAMES (1779) #4517
EST. Portsmouth yoeman decd. testate. WILL: Drawn 6/3/1772. Legatees: Sons-John and Aaron; Daus:-Mary Melcher wife of John Melcher, weaver; Sarah Wallace wife of Samuel Wallace, Rye yoeman; Martha Stavers wife of Bartholomew Stavers and Ruth Seavey wife of William Seavey, Rye yoeman; Grandson-Nadab Moses son of Aaron. Exec.-grandson Nadab. His sig. Witnesses: John Pickering Jr., George Libbey and Jona. M. Sewall. CERT. WILL (D25:35): 2/24/1779. Presented by Exec. and witnesses Pickering, esq. and Libbey. INVY. WARR.: 2/24/1779. Comm.: Joseph Tucker, Andrew Beck and Timothy Marden, all of Portsmouth. INVY.: Appr. 5/25/1779. Value L3118.0.0. Oaths 5/25/1779 Comm. to Saml. Penhallow, JP. Oath 5/26/1779 Exec. to judge.

1819. MOSES, NADAB (1794) #5746
EST. Portsmouth yoeman decd. testate. WILL: Drawn 1/17/1792. Legatees: Wife-Abigail; Sons-James, Aaron and Levi; Daus.-Martha Moses (called "James's sister"), Elizabeth Moses and Dorothy Moses; Execs.-wife Abigail, Joseph Tucker and a son when he arrives at 21. His

sig. Witnesses: George Gains, Andrew Beck and Levi Jenness. CERT. WILL (D30:202): 2/15/1792. Presented by Execs. and all witnesses. ADMIN.: 2/15/1792. Execs.: Abigail Moses, widow and Joseph Tucker, yoeman, both of Portsmouth. Bond L1000.0.0. Sureties: Andrew Beck of Portsmouth and Levi Jenness of Rye, yoemen. Witness Nathl. Adams. INVY: Comm.: Nathl. Gookins, Samuel Wallis and Levi Jenness. Appr. 4/25/1792. Value L344.1.0. Oaths 5/10/1792 Joseph Tucker, an Exec., and Comm. to George Gains, JP.

1820. MOSES. THEODORE (1777) #4380
EST. Portsmouth barber decd. testate. STATEMENT: 7/2/1777. Of Hannah Moses, widow of Theodore. She is content that the Execs. named in Will give bond and with the taking of an Invy. WILL: Drawn 4/29/1777. Legatees: Wife-Hannah; His bros. and sisters (unnamed); Bro. Samuel Moses. Execs.-bro. Samuel Moses and Joseph Walton. His sig. Witnesses: Samuel Bowles, Elisabeth Mills and Ales Beck. CERT. WILL (D24:81): 7/30/1777. Presented by Execs. and witnesses Bowles and Beck. ADMIN.: 7/2/1777. Execs.: Joseph Walton, Stratham cooper and Samuel Moses, Portsmouth barber. Bond L500.0.0. Sureties: Joseph Cotton, boatbuilder and Samuel Bowles, merchant, both of Portsmouth. Witnesses: Nathaniel Weare and Wm. Parker.

1821. MOSES, THOMAS (1793) #5863
EST. Portsmouth cordwainer decd. ADMIN.: 3/15/1793. Admr. Richard Jackson, Portsmouth joiner. Bond L1000.0.0. Sureties: Nathaniel Jackson, cordwainer and John March, saddler, both of Portsmouth. Witnesses: Ebenr. Wentworth and Nathl. Adams. INVY.: Appr. 3/16/1793. Comm.: Nathaniel Jackson, Jeremiah Libbey and John March. Value L89.0.2 1/2. Oaths 3/16/1793 Jackson, March and Admr. and affirm. Libbey to Nathl. Adams, JP. GDP. Of the children of Thomas Moses, Portsmouth cordwainer decd. GDP.: 4/24/1793. Of: Benja. and Polly, minors over 14 and of Thomas, William and John, minors under 14. Gdn. Richard Jackson, Portsmouth joiner. Bond L1000.0.0. Sureties: John Sheafe, merchant and Martin Parry, gent., both of Portsmouth. Witnesses: Nathl. Adams and Ebenr. Wentworth. ACCOUNT: 2/18/1795. Of Admr. Allowed 2/18/1795. Account includes main. John. APPR. WARR.: 2/6/1796. Comm.: Isaac Rindge, George Gains and Capt. George Wentworth, Portsmouth esquires. To appr. real est. for settlm., it appearing it cannot be div. Appr.: 2/15/1796. Value $600.00. Oaths 2/15/1796 Comm. to R. Cutts Shannon, JP. DECREE SETTLM.: 2/7/1796. Benja. Moses, oldest son appearing and consenting, real est. settled on him, Benjamin to pay his co-heirs $102.58 each, Mary Moses in 6 months, Thomas Moses in 3 years, William Moses in 4 years and John Moses in 11

years, with interest. ADDL. ACCOUNT: Of Admr. Allowed 2/17/1796 having been consented to by Gdn. of heirs and for himself. GDP.: 2/17/1796. Of: Thomas and William, minors over 14 and of John, a minor under 14. Gdn. Benjamin Moses, Portsmouth cordwainer. Bond $1000.00. Sureties: John Sherburne Jr., joiner and Joshua Deverson, boatbuilder, both of Portsmouth. Witnesses: Hall Jackson and W. Parker. BOND: 2/17/1796. Of Benjamin Moses, Portsmouth cordwainer. Bond $600.00. To pay his co-heirs per Decree Settlm. Sureties: John Sherburne Jr., joiner and Joshua Deverson, boatbuilder, both of Portsmouth. Witnesses: Hall Jackson and W. Parker.

1822. MOULTON, BENJAMIN (1782) #4857
EST. Hampton Falls gent. decd. intestate. RENUN.: 11/1/1782. Of Sarah Moulton, widow of Benjamin. Of Admin. being old and infirm. Requests appointment of her sons Benjamin and Thomas. ADMIN.: 11/1/1782. Admrs.: Benjamin Moulton of Kingston and Thomas Moulton of Hampton Falls, yoemen. Bond L1000.0.0. Surety Samuel Brooks, Exeter esq. Witnesses: Elizabeth Parker and W. Parker. INVY.: Appr. 11/29/1782. Comm.: Nehemiah Cram, James Prescut Jr. and Jere. Bachelder. Value L347.3.0 plus a long list of Notes of Hand not tallied and other Notes and Certificates. Oaths 12/25/1782 Comm. to W. Parker, JP. PETITION: 12/10/1782. Of Widow Sarah Moulton. States that she desires to obtain all the household furniture left by her husb., either over and above her Dower or included in them, as the judge deems proper. She feels the debts may easily be settled by the Notes of Hand without selling the movables. As Benjamin died intestate, she is in a difficult position. Signed by Sarah, Nehemiah Cram and James Prescut Jr. APPR. WARR.: 9/24/1783. Comm.: John Fogg, yoeman; John Taylor Jr., gent., both of Hampton; Joseph Cram of Exeter and Samuel Prescott of Hampton Falls, yoemen and Joseph Brown Jr., Kensington gent. To view 2/3 of the real est. to see if it can be div. among his children. Div. or appr., giving 2 shares to oldest son and one share to each of the others. APPR.: L1486.12.0. Oaths 1/21/1784 Comm. to judge. Accepted after hearing objections of Edward Melcher. DECREE SETTLM.: 1/21/1784. Benjamin Moulton of Kensington, oldest son, appearing and consenting, 2/3 of the real est. is settled on him, Benjamin to pay his co-heirs L371.13.0 each within 9 months, that being their proportions. Receipt: 1/19/1785. Of Edward Melcher and Jemima Melcher. The have received from Benjamin 1393.19.0 in full, plus interest, for one share as in Decree. Witnesses: Jerh. Bachelder and Joseph Cram. Oaths 1/26/1785. Of Jeremiah Bachelder and Joseph Cram. To W. Parker, JP. They saw Edward Melcher and his wife sign the Receipt. Cert. Of W. Parker, Reg. that this is a true copy of the Receipt and oaths. BOND: 1/21/1784. Of Benjamin Moulton, Kensington

yoeman. Bond L1500.0.0. To pay each of his co-heirs re Decree Settlm. Sureties: Jeremiah Bachelder, Kensington gent. And James Thurston, Exeter innholder. Witnesses: John Dean and W. Parker. DOWER: 12/25/1783. Comm.: Joseph Brown Jr., Samuel Prescot, John Taylor Jr., Jere. Fogg and Joseph Cram. Of Widow Sarah Moulton. Oaths 1/21/1784 Prescot, Taylor, Fogg and Cram to judge. Allowed all the heirs being present and making no objections. ACCOUNT: Of Benj. Moulton, an Admr. Allowed 11/17/1781 after hearing objections of Melcher and wife. ACCOUNT: 11/17/1784. Of Admrs. Allowed 11/17/1781 on oath of Thomas Moulton, an Admr. Account includes payment to Thomas for 7 1/2 years service on est. after reaching age 21 PETITION: 6/3/1791. Of Thomas Moulton, Hampton Falls yoeman. For div. of lands which were his mother's Dower, which he holds in common with his bro. Benjamin, Kensington yoeman, each owning 1/2. Order: 6/3/1791. For hearing, Petitioner to serve his bro. with copies of Petition and Order. Judge notes parties agreed on a Comm. and Warr. was issued. DIV. WARR.: 6/13/1791. Comm.: Jonathan Swain, Raymond esq.; Benjamin Pike, esq. and Stephen Caldwell, yoeman, both of Hampton Falls and Jeremiah Leavitt, Exeter hatter. To div. various lands which were the Dower into equal shares per Petition. DIV.: 6/25/1791. Divisees: Thomas Moulton and Benjamin Moulton. The Comm. divides some lands and orders Thomas to pay Benjamin L93.10.3. to equalize the shares. Oaths 6/25/1891 Comm. to W. Parker, JP. Allowed.

1823. MOULTON, BENJAMIN (1793) #5874
EST. Hampton cooper decd. testate. WILL: Drawn 6/11/1783. Legatees: Wife-Mary; Dau.-Sarah Quinby; Grandson-John Moulton Quinby; Eldest grandchild surviving his wife and dau. Execs.-wife Mary and Nehemiah Moulton. His sig. Witnesses: William Lane Jr., Jonathan Godfey Jr. and John Lane Jr. CERT. WILL (D30:396): Presented by Nehemiah Moulton, an Exec., the other refusing, and witnesses William Lane Jr. and Godfrey. RENUN.: 6/15/1792. Of Mary Moulton, widow of Benjamin. She does not accept the provision made for her in Will and wishes her dower instead. Witnesses: Nehemiah Moulton and Small Moulton. ADMIN.: 3/29/1793. Exec. Nehemiah Moulton, North Hampton yoeman. Bond L1000.0.0. Sureties: Joseph Moulton of North Hampton and Small Moulton of Hampton, yoemen. Witnesses: William Lane Jr. and William Parker. INVY.: Comm.: Philip Towle, John Fogg and William Lane Jr. Value L56.0.5. Oaths 4/9/1793 Comm. to Moses Leavitt, JP. Oath 4/29/1793 Exec. to W. Parker, Reg. PETITION: 4/29/1793. Of Exec. For Comm. Insolvency. Gives list claims of L73.11.0. Granted. CLAIMS WARR.: 4/29/1793. Comm.: Philip Towle, gent.; William Lane Jr., yoeman, both of Hampton and John Fogg, North Hampton physician. ADDL. INVY.:

Value L3.18.0. Oaths 12/11/1793 Comm. to Oliver Whipple, JP. CLAIMS: Total L149.10.0. Oaths 12/10/1793 Comm. to Oliver Whipple, JP. DOWER: 12/11/1793. Comm.: Danl. Weare, Jona. Blake, John Fogg, Philip Towle and William Lane Jr. Of Widow Mary Moulton. Oaths 12/11/1793 Fogg, Towle and Lane to Oliver Whipple, JP. Allowed. PETITION: 12/24/1793. Of Exec. For License. Granted. LICENSE (D31:145): 12/24/1793. To Exec. To sell real est. to amount of L150.0.0. Note: This file also contains a Petition which belongs with est. of Gen. Jonathan Moulton #5275 (1789) and is recorded there.

1824. MOULTON, BENJAMIN (1795) #6084
See #6014 Joseph Steel (1794)

1825. MOULTON, JEREMIAH (1795) #6122
EST. Hampton gent. decd. testate. WILL: Drawn 6/9/1795. Legatees: Mother-unnamed; Bros.-John, David and James; Sister-Dolly Moulton. Exec.-bro. James. His sig. Witnesses: Simon Marston, Nathaniel Johnson and Samuel Palmer. CERT. WILL (D32:21): 7/15/1795. Presented by Exec. and witnesses Marston and Johnson. ADMIN.: 7/15/1795. Exec. James Moulton, Hampton yoeman. Bond $3,000.00. Sureties: Simon Marston and Nathaniel Johnson, Hampton yoemen. Witnesses: Walter Robie and Wm. Parker.

1826. MOULTON, JOHN (1779) #4571
EST. Hampton joiner decd. testate. WILL: Drawn 5/21/1776. Legatees: Son-John; Daus.-Mary Palmer, Jane Porking (Perkins), Hannah Batchielder and Abigail Towle. Exec.-son John. His sig. Witnesses: John Dow, James Hobbs and Joseph Dow. CERT. WILL (D25:247): 9/29/1779. Presented by Exec. and witnesses Joseph Dow, esq. and John Dow. INVY.: Appr. 12/28/1779. Comm.: Samuel Dow, John Marston and Simon Nudd. Value L19378.0.0 or L518.18.0 "at allowing twenty for one." Oaths 12/28/1779 Comm. to Joseph Dow, JP. Oath 1/26/1780 Exec. to W. Parker, Reg.

1827. MOULTON, JOHN JR. (1794) #5984
EST. Hampton yoeman decd. intestate. ADMIN.: 3/24/1794. Admx. Hannah Moulton, Hampton widow. Bond L1000.0.0. Sureties: Abner Page and James Moulton, Hampton yoemen. Witnesses: W. Parker and Nathl. Parker. INVY.: Appr. 4/3/1794. Comm.: Morris Hobbs, Josiah Dearbon and Jonathan Garland. Value L1045.0.11. Oaths 6/1794 Comm. to Christo. Toppan, JP. Oath 6/19/1794 Admx. to judge. PETITION: 1/6/1795. Of: Jane Perkins, Hannah Bachelder, Joseph Palmer Jr., Saml. Palmer, Moses Perkins, John Blake and Abraham P. Towle, the heirs.

They are dissatisfied with the Admx.'s manner of occupying the land of est. and have paid the greater part of the Notes of decd. Request Dower be set off and rest divided among heirs. They are ready to give bond for payment of any debts which still may be due from est. Order: 1/8/1795. For hearing, Petitioners to serve copies of Petition and Order on Admx. BOND: 1/15/1795. Of: Widow Jane Perkins, Widow Hannah Bachelder, Joseph Palmer Jr., Samuel Palmer, Moses Perkins, John Blake and Abraham Perkins Towle, yoemen, heirs. Bond not given. Sureties: Joseph Dow, esq. and Jonathan Lock, gent., all of Hampton. To pay their ratable shares of debts and charges of admin. of decd. Witnesses: Simon Lane Jr. and Ashel Marston. RECEIPT: 6/2/1795. Of Jeremiah Moulton. To Admx. For various contents of est. APPR.: 7/6/1795. Comm.: Joseph Dow, esq.; Cotton Ward and Simon Nudd, gentlemen. To appr. income of 2/3 real est. for past year. Appr.: $84.50. Oaths 7/6/1795 Comm. to Christo. Toppan, JP. DIV.: 7/6/1796. Comm.: Joseph Dow, esq.; Jonathan Lock, Cotton Ward, Simon Nudd and Philip Towle, gentlemen. Divisees: Widow Hannah Moulton, her Dower; Widow Jane Perkins; Widow Hannah Batchelder; Abigail Towle wife of Abraham P. Towle; Heirs of Mary Palmer decd. late wife of Joseph Palmer. Oaths 7/6/1795 Comm. to Christo. Toppan, JP. Allowed 7/7/1795. CITATION: 7/7/1795. To Admx. To appear and exhibit Account for settlm. and so personal est. may be distributed among heirs, they having given bond for payment of debts remaining undischarged. ACCOUNT: 7/15/1795. Of Admx. Allowed 7/15/1795.

1828. MOULTON, JONATHAN (1771) #3873
EST. Chester yoeman decd. ADMIN.: 9/20/1771. Admx.: Sarah Moulton, Chester widow. Bond L500.0.0. Sureties: Samuel Emerson, esq. and Jonathan Browne, yoeman, both of Chester. Witnesses: Amos Merrill and Abigail Moulton. INVY.: Comm.: Nathan Webster and Benj. Hill. Value L504.17.0. Oaths 11/23/1771 Comm. and Admx. to Samuel Emerson, JP. Returned 11/12/1772. DOWER: 11/12/1793. Comm.: Josiah Flagg and Simon Towle, esquires; Edmund Sleeper, Saml. Wilson and Nathan Brown. Of Widow Sarah Moulton. Oaths 11/12/1793 Brown, Towle, Sleeper and Wilson to Josiah Flagg, JP. Allowed.

1829. MOULTON, GEN. JONATHAN (1787) #5275.
EST. Hampton esq. decd. testate. WILL: Drawn 6/16/1787. Legatees: Wife-Sarah; Sons-Josiah, Jonathan, Benning, William Pitts Moulton, Jacob Smith Moulton, Emery, Joseph and John Washington Moulton; Daus.-Anne wife of John Marston and Sally; Other children his wife may have by him; Children of his son Josiah specifically named-John Shackford Moulton, Jonathan, Josiah, Abigail and Dorothy; Any lawful

children of his son Jonathan; Bro.-John Moulton; Sisters-Sarah Knowles and Lydia Garland; Children of his bro. Nathan decd.; Nephew-Timothy son of his bro. John; Mehitabel wife of his bro. John and the children she has had by John; Sister-in-law-Theodate Batchelder wife of Deacon Josiah Batchelder; Bro.-in-law-Benjamin Smith; Kinsman-Edward B. Moulton and Anne his wife; Sons of Edward B. Moulton-Moses and Jonathan; Dorothy dau. of his sister-in-law Theodate Batchelder; Benjamin Batchelder; Abigail Choat; Dorothy Moulton, John Garland and Widow Yeaton who live with the family; John Crosby and his wife; Children of Bradbury Richardson, esq.; Fanny Towle wife of James Towle. Execs.-wife Sarah; John Pickering, esq.; Deacon Benjn. Smith; Jona. Garland, esq.; and Capt. Thomas Leavitt. His sig. Witnesses: John Moulton, Thomas Levitt and Benja. Batchelder. Oaths 10/17/1787 Leavit and Batchelder and on 11/21/1787 John Moulton esq. The acceptance of the Will was deferred at the request of the heirs to 12/19/1787, at which time it was allowed, there being no further objections. CERT. WILL (D29:162): 12/19/1787. Presented by Widow Sarah Moulton and Thomas Leavitt, two of Execs. RENUN.: Of John Pickering, one of Execs. named in Will. Of Admin. RENUN.: 8/19/1787. Of Jona. Garland, esq. named as an Exec. in will. Of Admin. INVY. WARR.: 12/19/1787. Comm.: Christopher Toppan of Hampton, Thomas Odiorne of Exeter and Nathaniel Rogers of Newmarket, esquires. INVY.: Appr. 3/13/1788. Value L7372.5.8 1/2. Oaths 3/13/1788 Comm. to Joseph Dow, JP. Oaths 3/19/1788 Execs. to W. Parker, Reg. PETITION: 4/16/1788. Of Execs. For License and Comm. Insolvency. Give list claims of L8121.16.6. Granted, with note of Reg. that both were issued that same day. LICENSE (D29:188): 4/16/1788. To Execs. To sell sufficient real est. to pay debts. PETITION: 7/16/1788. Of John Sullivan, Durham, Strafford Co. esq., a creditor. Requests an appeal from Decree accepting Invy. and granting of License and Comm. Insolvency. He states that the whole est. was not appraised and much undervalued, that the widow is not entitled to the dower for which she has applied as she had a jointure settled upon her before her marriage, all of which is injurious to the creditors. Granted 7/16/1788. BOND: 8/12/1788. Of John Sullivan, Durham, Strafford Co. esq. Bond L100.0.0. To appeal Decrees allowing Invy., Comm. Insolvency and Dower. Sureties: John Prentice of Londonderry and Noah Emery of Exeter, esquires. Witnesses: Jona. Rawson and W. Parker. ACT OF N. H. LEGISLATURE: Passed House 1/19/1789 and Senate 1/20/1789. Allowing the petition of Widow Sarah Moulton to have a single comm. to divide her Dower in lands throughout the state as the Judge of Probate of Rockingham Co. felt he was not authorized to act in other counties. The Comm. of Simon Wiggin, Jonathan Robinson and Moses Leavitt, esquires; Samuel Jenness and Joseph Cram, yoemen, as appointed for Rockingham Co., is empowered to set off the Dower and the Probate Judge of Rockingham Co. to receive and record their report. PETITION: 1/21/1789. Of Josiah Moulton, Hampton gent. For div. of land in Hampton which he holds in common with the est. of his father Jonathan decd. DIV. WARR.: 1/21/1789. Comm.: Joseph Cram, Exeter yoeman; John Dearborn, esq.; Cotton Ward and Philip Towle, gentlemen and Elisha S. Marston, husbm., all of Hampton. To div. the land held in common by Josiah Moulton and est. of his father Jonathan decd. DIV.: 3/5/1789. Divisees: Josiah Moulton and est. Jonathan Moulton, esq. decd. Oaths 3/5/1789 Comm. to Christo. Toppan, JP. Allowed 3/18/1789. PETITION: 3/7/1789. Of: Oliver Whipple and Samuel Sherburne Jr. of Portsmouth; John Prentice of Londonderry and Edward St. Loe Livermore of Concord, esquires and creditors of est. For an appeal against the Decrees allowing the Invy., Comm. Insolvency and Dower. They give the same arguments as Sullivan. Granted 3/18/1789. BOND: 3/18/1789. Of: Oliver Whipple and Samuel Sherburne Jr., esquires. To appeal Decrees allowing Invy., Comm. Insolvency and Dower. Bond L100.0.0. Sureties: John Prentice, Edward St. Loe Livermore, John Rawson and John Sullivan, esquires. Witness Daniel Peirce. DOWER: 12/16/1789. Oaths 12/16/1789 Comm. to Simon Jenness, JP. Allowed 1/20/1790, there being no objections. ADDL. INVY.: Appr. 5/5/1788. Value L74.1.9. Oaths 8/31/1790 Toppan and Rogers to Joseph Dow, JP. Returned 6/1790. ADDL. INVY.: Appr. 12/12/1789. Value L2225.13.6. Oaths 12/14/1789 Comm. to Moses Leavitt, JP. Noted by clerk as returned 6/1790. ADDL. INVY.: 12/12/1789. Value L975.14.2. Oaths 8/31/1789 Toppan and Rogers to Joseph Dow, JP. Noted by clerk as returned 6/1790. CLAIMS: 10/12/1790. Comm.: Jno. Parker, Ephm. Robinson and Nat. Rogers. Total L11077.19.10. Oaths 11/6/1790 Comm. to W. Parker, JP. ADDL. INVY.: Value L1923.1.6 1/2. Oaths 8/3/1791 Comm. to Moses Leavitt, JP. DOWER: 7/18/1791. In part of est. not before shown to Comm. Of Sarah Thurston in est. Jonathan Moulton. Oaths 7/18/1791 Wiggin, Robinson, Leavitt and Jenness to Levi Dearborn, JP. Allowed 12/5/1791. ACCOUNT: 3/5/1793. Of Thomas Leavitt and Sarah Moulton now Sarah Thurston, Execs. Exhibited by Leavitt. On 3/6/1793 judge notes the Account was exhibited on 11/20/1792 and that a notice was advertised of its examination on 12/14/1792, at which time the parties appeared and objections of creditors heard. Decree: The Execs. be charged with the articles on p.16 of Account amounting to L440.19.11, in addition to several articles charged by himself (the Exec.). The balance of L2934.11.1 be distributed to creditors. Note: The following Petition found in #5874 Benjamin Moulton (1793) belongs here. PETITION: 4/29/1793. Of Thomas Leavitt, an Exec. Requests appeal from Decree allowing Accounts as amended as he objects to several deductions made. Granted. BOND: 5/3/1793. Of Thomas Leavitt, North Hampton esq. To appeal Decree disallowing certain articles in the Account of both Execs, and his

Account since the remarriage of Sarah Moulton. Bond L100.0.0. Sureties: Benjamin Leavit, innholder and Moses Leavitt, esq., both of North Hampton. Witness Benja. Thurston. DECREE: 9/3rd Wed./1793. Of Superior Court of Rockingham Co. After hearing Execs. and creditors, they rule that the former Decree is affirmed. Signed by Nathl. Adams, clerk. PROP.& SETTLM.: Claims L11072.14.9. Amount to be proportioned L2934.11.1. Allowed 3/17/1794 with order to Exec. Leavitt to pay.

1830. MOULTON, JOSEPH (1787) #5306
EST. Portsmouth blacksmith decd. ADMIN.: 11/21/1787. Admr. Joseph Moulton, Portsmouth blacksmith. Bond L500.0.0. Sureties: Jonathan Shillaber, potter and Ezekiel Pitman, blacksmith, both of Portsmouth. Witnesses: Saml. Drowne and William Vaughan.

1831. MOULTON, JOSEPH (1793) #5872
EST. North Hampton yoeman decd. testate. WILL: Drawn 6/19/1789. Legatees: Wife-Abigail; Sons-Nehemiah, Joseph and Samuel; Daus.-Deborah Moulton and Bethia Smith. Exec.-son Joseph. His mark. Witnesses: Benjamin Moulton, Isaac Jenness and Samuel Moulton Jr. CERT. WILL (D30:394): Oath 2/25/1793 Samuel Moulton Jr. to judge. Presented on 3/25/1793 by Exec. and witness Jenness. ADMIN.: 3/25/1793. Exec. Joseph Moulton, North Hampton husbm. Bond L1000.0.0. Sureties: Isaac Jenness and Nehemiah Moulton, North Hampton husbandmen. Witnesses: Samll. Moulton and W. Parker. INVY.: Comm.: Dr. John Fogg, Isaac Jenness and Joseph Hobbs. Value L1166.4.0. Oaths 6/6/1793 Fogg and Jenness to Simon Jenness, JP. Oath 6/17/1793 Exec. to W. Parker, JP.

1832. MOULTON, DEACON JOSIAH (1776) #4296
EST. Of Hampton, decd. testate. WILL: Drawn 8/4/1769. Legatees: Wife-Mary; Bro.-Edward; Sister-Elizabeth Batchilder wife of John Batchilder; Mary Bracket dau. of Samuel Bracket of Rye; Rev. Mr. Ebenezer Thayer of Hampton; Love Gookins widow of Rev. Mr. Nathaniel Gookins late of North Hampton decd; Cousin(sic)-Josiah Moulton son of his bro. William Moulton decd. Exec.-cousin Josiah Moulton. His sig. Witnesses: John Lamprey, Simon Dow and Christo. Toppan, esq. CERT. WILL (D23:440): 12/25/1776. Presented by Exec. and witnesses Lamprey and Dow. ADMIN. 12/25/1776. Exec. Josiah Moulton, Hampton esq. Bond L1000.0.0. Sureties: John Lamprey and Simon Dow, Hampton yoemen. Witnesses: Jabez Hoit and Wm. Parker.

1833. MOULTON, JOSIAH (1784) #5021
EST. Hampton gent. decd. testate. WILL: Drawn 2/26/1784. Legatees: Wife-Abigail; Cousins-Elisha Moulton, Elizabeth Moulton and John Mobbs Moulton. Execs-Joseph Dow, esq. and John Mobbs Moulton. His sig. Witnesses: John Lamprey, Joshua Shaw and Joseph Redman. CERT. WILL: 7/21/1784. Presented by Execs. and witnesses Lamprey and Redman. INVY.: Appr. 11/10/1784. Comm.: Cotton Ward, Simon Nudd and Jona. Garland. Value L841.15.6. Oaths 11/10/1784 Comm. to Jona. Moulton, JP. Oath 12/15/1784 Execs. to W. Parker, Reg.

1834. MOULTON, NATHAN (1772) #3910
EST. Of Hampton decd. intestate. ADMIN.: 2/26/1771. Admrs. Christopher Toppan, esq. and Mary Moulton, widow, both of Hampton. Bond L5.0.0. Sureties: Samuel Nay, gent. and Simon Dow, husbm., both of Hampton. Witnesses: Saml. Hale Jr. and John Pickering Jr.

1835. MOULTON, RICHARD (1782) #4781
EST. Hampton Falls yoeman decd. testate. WILL: Drawn 12/26/1776. Legatees: Wife-Susanna; Sons-Redman, John, Josiah and James; Dorothy Moulton who now lives with him. His son Redman is to fulfill Richard's obligation to Redman's Aunt Hannah Bean as long as she remains a widow. Execs.-sons Redman and Josiah. His sig. Witnesses: James Prescut Jr., Aaron Wells and Jeremiah Lane. CERT. WILL: (D26:323): 3/13/1782. Presented by Execs. and witnesses Prescut and Wells. INVY.: Appr. 3/14/1782. Comm.: James Prescut Jr., Jonathan Burnham and Aaron Wells. Value L1327.4.0. Oaths 9/28/1782 Comm. to Saml. Weare, JP. ACCOUNT: 1792. Of Redman Moulton, an Exec. Allowed 4/16/1792. PETITION: 4/15/1793. Of Susanah Moulton. Requests her dower be set off. Suggests a comm. of Samuel Lane, Samuel Melcher Jr. and Jonathan Cram Jr., Hampton yoemen; Major John Taylor and Dearbun Taylor of Hampton. Witnesses; Jonathan Moulton and Joseph Melcher. Order: For hearing, John Moulton, Josiah Moulton and the other owners of some of the land to be notified.

1836. MOULTON, ROBERT (1778) #4489
EST. Hampton yoeman decd. testate. WILL: Drawn 5/12/1768. Legatees: Son-Robert; Daus.-Sarah Shaw wife of Ichabod Shaw esq. and Mary Sanborn wife of William Sanborn; Granddaus.-Mary Fogg and Deborah Fogg. daus. of Enoch Fogg. Exec.- son Robert. His sig. Witnesses: Daniel Philbrick, Morris Hobbs and Christo. Toppan. CERT. WILL: 10/28/1778. Presented by Exec. and witnesses Philbrick and Toppan, esq. ADMIN.: 10/28/1778. Exec. Robert Moulton, Hampton yoeman. Bond L500.0.0. Sureties: Daniel Philbrick, yoeman and Christopher Toppan, esq., both of Hampton. Witnesses: Nathl. Parker and Sam. Brooks Jr.

1837. MOULTON, ROBERT (1795) #6123
EST. Hampton yoeman decd. intestate. ADMIN.: 7/16/1795. Admx. Mary Moulton, his widow. Bond $2,000.00. Sureties: Simon Sanborn and James Leavitt, Hampton yoemen. Witnesses: Ebenezer Tilton and Nathl. Parker. INVY.: Comm.: Peter Tilton, Thomas Moulton and James Leavitt. Value L591.15.2. Oaths 10/31/1795 Comm. and Admx. to W. Parker, JP. APPR. WARR.: 4/5/1797. Comm.: Jonathan Marston, gent.; Simon Sanborn and Nathaniel Bachelder Jr., Hampton yoemen. To view the real est. and appr. its present value and to appr. neat income of est. since death of Robert. They are also to judge if the est. is better now than at the death as a result of the labor and expense of Ebenezer Tilton Jr. APPR.: 4/7/1797. Of the real est. under the encumbrance of the Dower $1,518.00. Of the income of 2/3 $80.00 and they think Tilton has bettered the est. by $100.00. Oaths 4/7/1797 Comm. to W. Parker, JP. DECREE SETTLM.: 4/10/1797. Ebenezer Tilton Jr., the only male grandchild, appearing and consenting, the real est. is settled on him, Ebenezer to pay his co-heirs, also grandchildren, Susanna Tilton and Nancy Tilton $486.00 each within 9 months, with interest. BOND: 4/10/1797. Of Ebenezer Tilton Jr., Hampton joiner. Bond $2,000.00. To pay his co-heirs per Decree Settlm. Sureties: Benjamin Shaw of Hampton and Stephen Tilton of Hampton Falls, gentlemen. Witness William P. Adams. ACCOUNT: 9/18/1797. Of Admx. Allowed 9/18/1797 those heirs attending consenting. Account includes an item for paying a legacy of decd.'s father to his granddaus. Mary and Deborah Fogg which decd. was ordered to pay but had not done.

1838. MOUNTFORD, TIMOTHY (1799) #6579
EST. Portsmouth mariner decd. testate. WILL: Drawn 5/28/1798. Legatees: Son-Timothy; Dau.-Polly Chadbourn Mountford. Requests that he be buried as near his wife and children as convenient. Execs.-Joshua Brackett and Thos. Martin, esq. Witnesses: James Shapley, Charles Neil and George Gains. CERT. WILL (D33:99): 6/19/1799. Presented by Timothy Mountford, the Execs. named refusing, and witnesses Shapley and Gains. RENUN.: 6/19/1799. Of: Brackett and Martin of Admin. Request appointment of the son of the decd. ADMIN.: 6/19/1799. Admr. Timothy Mountford, Portsmouth trader. Bond $3,000.00. Sureties: Samuel Storer and William Stanwood Jr., Portsmouth merchants. Witnesses: W. Parker and Willm. Appleton. INVY. (D33:109): 7/9/1799. Comm.: Nathl. Marshall, Wm. Stanwood Jr. and Edward Sargent. Value $2,329.20. Oaths 7/9/1799 Comm. and Admr. to Geo. Gains, JP. ACCOUNT: 6/18/1800. Of Admr. Allowed 6/18/1800 having been consented to by heirs.

1839. MOWATT, HENRY (1790) #5577
GDP.: 9/22/1790. Of Henry of Newmarket, a minor over 14. Gdn. Samuel Chapman, Newmarket yoeman. Bond L1000.0.0. Sureties: Moses Davis of Epping and Samuel Woodman of Deerfield, yoemen. Witnesses: W. Parker and N. Parker.

1840. MUDGET, NICHOLAS (1788) #5341
EST. Brentwood yoeman decd. ADMIN.: 3/19/1788. Admx. Mary Mudget, Brentwood widow. Bond L500.0.0. Sureties: Noah Dollof of Brentwood and James Gordon of Exeter, yoemen. Witnesses: Nathl. Parker and W. Parker. INVY.: Appr. 8/20/1788. Comm.: Winthrop Dudley and Nicholas Smith. Value L127.11.6. Oaths 8/20/1788. Comm. and Admx. to W. Parker, Reg. ACCOUNT: 3/17/1790. Of Molly Mudget, Admx. Allowed 3/17/1790. DOWER: 10/4/1790. Comm.: Thos. Stow Ranney, Winthrop Dudley and Gilman Leavitt. Of Widow Molley Mudgett. Oaths 11/27/1790 Comm. to W. Parker, JP. DIV.: 10/4/1790. Comm.: Same as for Dower. To div. 2/3 of the real est. Divisees: Nicholas Mudgett (oldest son, double share); Daus.-Esther Dolliff, Molley Ward and Abigail Robinson. Oaths 11/27/1790 Comm. to Wm. Parker, JP. Allowed. DIV. WARR.: 6/15/1805. Comm.: Thomas Stow Ranney, esq.; Richard York, mariner; Stephen Leavitt, gent. and Jonathan Veasey, yoeman, all of Brentwood and Ezekiel Godfrey, Poplin esq. To div. the widow's Dower plus 3 acres purchased by Molley, giving to John Thing, Brentwood yoeman 2/3 and to Andrew Ward of Brentwood in right of his wife Molley 1/3/ DIV.: 6/20/1805. Divisees as in Warr. Oaths 6/20/1805 York, Leavitt and Godfrey to Thos. Stow Ranney, JP.

1841. MUGGRIDGE, SAMUEL (1777) #4349
EST. Amesbury, Essex Co., Mass Bay shipwright decd. intestate. RENUN.: 4/28/1777. Dated at Haverhill, Essex Co., MA. Of Ruth Sawyer, widow of Samuel Morgeridge. Of Admin. Requests appointment of Thomas Clark. Cert.: Of Oliver Sawyer. That it is his desire that the petition be granted. RECOMMENDATION: 4/29/1777. Of: Thomas Rowell and Caleb Pilsberry, a Comm. appointed by the town of Amesbury to search for the est. of Samuel Margridge, one of whose children has become a charge to the town and the widow declines taking Admin. Samuel had a small est. in Canterbury, NH. The Comm. recommends that Lt. Thomas Clark, a member of the Comm., be granted Letter of Admin. ADMIN.: 4/30/1777. Admr. Thomas Clark, Amesbury, Essex Co., Mass Bay gent. Bond L500.0.0. Sureties: Joseph Welch, esq. and Ezekiel Gile, gent., both of Plaistow. Witness Nathl. Parker. INVY. WARR.: 4/30/1777. Comm.: Moses Ordway, housewright; Joseph Moulton, tanner and Capt.

Benjamin Sias, gent., all of Loudon. Oaths 6/13/1777 Comm. to Nathan Bachelder, JP. INVY.: Appr. 6/13/1777. Value L37.18.3. Mostly land in Canterbury in the Parish of Loudon. Oath 7/12/1777 Admr. to judge. PETITION: 9/30/1778. Of Admr. For License. States claims already amount to L50.0.0. LICENSE: 9/30/1778. To Admr. To sell sufficient real est. to pay debts. ACCOUNT: 2/24/1779. Of Admr. Allowed 2/24/1779.

1842, MURPHY, THOMAS (1780) #4621
EST. Island of Hispaniola merchant decd. ADMIN.: 5/5/1780. Admr. John Warmsley, Portsmouth merchant. Bond L10000.0.0. Sureties: John Parker, esq. and Noah Parker, gent., both of Portsmouth. Witnesses: John Adams and W. Parker. INVY.: Appr. 5/20/1780. Comm.: Jno Parker and Noah Parker. Value L518.9.7 1/2=L1728.0.1/4 Spanish milled dollars at 6/a pt. Oaths 7/24/1780 Comm. and Admr. to Geo. Gains, JP.

1843. MURRAY, TIMOTHY (1774) #4123
EST. Newmarket taylor decd. ADMIN.: 9/28/1774. Admx. Abigail Murray, Newmarket widow. Bond L1000.0.0. Sureties: Thomas Tash, esq. and Ede Hall Bergin, yoeman, both of Newmarket. Witness Richard Brown. INVY.: Appr. 10/25/1774. Comm.: James Cram and Edward Smith. Value L103.17.3. Oaths 10/26/1774 Admx. and Comm. to judge. PETITION: 3/13/1775. Of Admx. For Comm. Insolvency. Witness Bettey Wiggin. Allowed 3/15/1775 with Order to Hon. William Parker, esq., Reg. of Probate, to make out a Warr. to Wentworth Cheswill and Joshua Frost, both of Newmarket.

1844. NASON, ANN (1795) #6155
EST. Of Hampton Falls decd. testate. WILL: Drawn 9/13/1795. Legatees: Bro.-David Nason; Sister-Elizabeth Nason. Execs.-bro. David and sister Elizabeth. Her sig. Witnesses: Benja. Rowe, Jonathan Lane and Ebenr. Tilton. CERT. WILL (D32:61): 11/4/1795. Presented by Execs. and witnesses Rowe and Lane. ADMIN.: 11/4/1795. Admrs.: David Nason, yoeman and Elizabeth Nason, spinster, both of Hampton Falls. Bond $1,000.00. Sureties: Jonathan Lane, Hampton Falls gent. and Benjamin Rowe, Kensington physician. Witnesses: Thomas Page, W. Parker, James Sanborn and Richard Fifield.

1845. NASON, RICHARD (1795) #6064
EST. Hampton Falls esq. decd. testate. WILL: Drawn 6/21/1791. Legatees: Sons-Richard and David; Daus.-Elizebeth Nason, Ann Nason, Shuah Philbrick, Huldah Fifield, Deborah Rowel and Hannah Weare; Grandson-Richard Fifield; Granddaus.-Deborah Nason and Ann Nason. Exec.-son David. His sig. Witnesses: Benjamin Leavitt, Thomas Leavitt

and Elisha Brown. CERT. WILL (D31:444): 1/16/1795. Presented by Exec. and witnesses Benjamin Leavitt and Brown, esq. ADMIN.: 1/26/1795. Exec. David Nason, Hampton Falls yoeman. Bond L1000.0.0. Sureties: Benjamin Leavitt, Hampton Falls yoeman and Elisha Brown, Seabrook esq. Witnesses: Samuel Parker and W. Parker. INVY.: Appr. 2/17/1795. Comm.: Benja. Leavitt, Samll. Weare and Elisha Brown. Value L1639.0.3. Oaths 3/3/1795 Comm. to Caleb Tilton, JP. Oath 4/12/1795 Exec. to judge. PETITION: 2/23/1810. Of Jona. Nason and David Nason attys. to Richard Nason, Hampton Falls husbm. Request Exec. be cited to Account, which he has neglected to do though frequently requested, so est. may be distributed according to Will. Granted. CITATION: 2/23/1810. To Exec. To appear and exhibit Account in order for settlm. Cert.: Of (Name heavily blotted with ink.) He cited the Exec. to appear.

1846. NAY, JOHN (1779) #4527
EST. Hampton yoeman decd. testate. WILL: Drawn 10/4/1774. Legatees: Wife-Elizabeth; Sons-Samuel and Joseph; Dau.-Sarah Mace; Grandson-John Nay. Exec.-son Joseph. His mark. Witnesses: Jonathan Leavitt, Moses Elkins and Christo. Toppan. CERT. WILL (25:59): 3/31/1779. Presented by Exec. and witnesses Elkins and Toppan. INVY. WARR.: 6/31/1779. Comm.: John Dearborn and Philip Towle Jr., gentlemen and Elisha Marston, yoeman, all of Hampton. INVY.: Appr. 5/26/1799. Value L224.0.0. Oaths 5/26/1779 Comm. to Joseph Dow, JP. Oath 6/14/1779 Exec. To W. Parker, Reg. and JP.

NEAL. See also Neill

1847. NEAL, JOHN (1788) #5532)
EST. Londonderry esq. decd. ADMIN. (D29:232): 12/11/1788. Admx. Mary Neal, his widow and John Neal, son, of Londonderry. Sureties: David Patterson and William Danforth. INVY.: Comm.: John Prentice, James Macgregore and David Patterson. Value not tallied. Esti. L961.0.0+. Oaths 12/3/1789 Comm. to John Bell, JP. Oaths 4/21/1790 Admrs. to James Betton, JP. PETITION: Dated by clerk 12/15/1790. Of Admrs., For Comm. of Insolvency. CLAIMS: Comm.: Geo. Reid, esq. and John Prentice. Total L553.15.4 3/4. Oaths 4/15/1795 Comm. to W. Parker, Reg. PETITION: 4/15/1785. Of John Neal, an Admr. For License. Granted. LICENSE (D31:513): To Admrs. To sell real est. to amount of L600.0.0. DOWER: Comm.: Joseph Gregg, esq.; David Patterson, yoeman; M. Morse, John Morrison and Robt. Ramsey. Of Widow Mary Neal. Oaths 4/15/1795 Comm. to judge. Allowed. PETITION: 6/12/1795. Of James MacGregore, esq. for himself and others, creditors to est. They are aggrieved and dissatisfied with the Dower as approved as it sets off to the

Widow more than 1/2 of the improved est. Request appeal against the Decree allowing Dower. Granted. BOND: 6/12/1795. Of James MacGregore, Londonderry esq. Bond L50.0.0. To prosecute appeal against Decree allowing Dower. Surety James Rundlett, Exeter yoeman. Witnesses: N. Emery, and W. Parker. PETITION: 7/15/1801. Of Jonathan Poor, Atkinson gent., a creditor. Requests permission to sue Bond of Admin. as Admrs. have not paid creditors or given accounting. Order 7/15/1801. Surviving Admx. to be cited to appear and settle Account. Petition granted for surviving Admix. did not appear as cited. BOND: 7/15/1801. Of Jonathan Poor. Bond $500.00. To sue Bond of Admin. Witness Nathl. Parker. PETITION: 7/15/1801. Of Jonathan Poor. Note: This item appears to be a dupl. of previous.

1848. NEALY, JOSEPH (1799) #6632.
GDP. Nottingham adult adjudged n.c.m. PETITION: 12/25/1799. Of Matthew Nealey, Nottingham yoeman. For Gdp. of his father, Joseph Nealey, who is n.c.m. Order: To Nottingham Selectmen. Too make inquisition into condition of Joseph. Report: 12/25/1799. Of: Thos. Bartlett and Jon. Cilley, Selectmen. The major part of Selectmen have investigated and agree that Joseph is n.c.m. Recommend his son Matthew as Gdn. GDP.: Of Joseph, and adult adjudged n.c.m. Gdn. Matthew Nealey, Nottingham yoeman. Bond $3,000.00. Sureties: Jonathan Cilley and Greenleaf Cilley, Nottingham esquires. Witnesses: Saml. Blodget and W. Parker. INVY.: 3/6/1800. Comm.: Tho. Bartlett, John Ford and Henry Butler. Value $237.74. Oaths 1/20/1800 Ford and Butler to Tho. Bartlett, J.P. Oath: 3/6/1800 Gdn. to W. Parker, Reg. ACCOUNT; 1/27/1813. Of Gdn. Allowed after hearing witnesses and Decree regarding the money owed Gdn. PETITION: Of Gdn. For appeal against Decree allowing amended Account. BOND: 3/15/1813 Of Gdn. Bond $200.00. To appeal Decree allowing amended Account. Sureties: Ezra True and John Churchill, Deerfield yoemen. Witness John J. Parker. PETITION: 1/7/1815. Of: Jane Cilley, Benja. Nealley and Edward B. Nealley, heirs. They claim that: 1. Gdn. is not giving a comfortable main. to Joseph and his wife though there is sufficient income to do so; 2. Gdn. is not managing the est. to its best advantage; 3. Gdn. has no bondsmen. Order: 1/9/1815. For hearing, Gdn. to be notified so he can appear and post new bond, or, in default, to show cause why he should not have his Gdp. revoked. Cert.: 1/11/1815. Of Bradbury Bartlett, Nottingham Constable. He has notified Matthew Neally and read to him Citation. Postponement: 1/23/1815. Upon hearing the Petitioners, judge ordered further consideration. Postponed to 3/16/1815. Cert. of John J. Parker, Reg. Postponement 3/15/1815. By consent of parties, further consideration postponed to 3/30/1815. Cert. of John J. Parker, Reg. Decree: 3/30/1815.

Gdn. ordered to give new bond on 5/18/1815 at house of Capt. Bradbury Bartlett in Nottingham and there to exhibit his Account. If he defaults his Letter of Gpd. to be revoked. ADDL. ACCOUNT: 5/18/1815. Of Gdn. Allowed after hearing objections. Account includes ref. to main. of Joseph's wife Molley. GDP.: 5/18/1815. Of Joseph n.c.m. Gdn Matthew Nealey, yoeman. Bond $3,000.00. Sureties: John Simpson, yoeman and Bradbury Bartlett, gent., both of Nottingham. Witness John J. Parker. ADDL. ACCOUNT: Of Gdn. Allowed 6/16/1817 with consent of heirs.

1849. NEALEY, THOMAS (1777) #4305
EST. Exeter joiner decd. RENUN.: 1/27/1777. Of Joanne Nealey, widow of Thomas, and William Neele, oldest son. Of Admin. in favor of son Andrew Nealey of Exeter. Witnesses: Jonathan Call and Hannah Call. ADMIN.: 1/13/1777. Admr. Andrew Neele of Exeter. Bond L500.0.0. Sureties: James Folsom and Benjamin Safford, both of Exeter. Witnesses: Elizabeth Parker Jr. and W. Parker. INVY.: Appr. 2/3/1777. Comm.: Josiah Gilman Jr.; Jonathan Call, baker and Eliphalet Hale, gent., all of Exeter. Value L57.1.3. Oaths 2/3/1777 Comm. and Admr. to Wm. Parker, JP. PETITION: 1/1/1778. Of Admr. For license. Gives list of claims of L30.4.8. Granted. LICENSE; 1/1/1778. To Admr. To sell suffient real est. to pay debts. ACCOUNT: 1/27/1778. Of Admr. Allowed 1/29/1779.

NEILL. See also Neal

1850. NEILL, WILLIAM (1772) #3971
EST. Londonderry yeoman decd. intestate. ADMIN.: 12/17/1772. Admrs.: Margaret Neill, Londonderry widow and John Tolford, Chester esq. Bond L500.0.0. Sureties: Stephen Holland, Londonderry esq. and William Tolford, Chester gent. Witnesses: Hugh Tolford and John Tolford Jr. INVY. WARR.: 12/17/1772. Comm.: James Wallace and William Wallace, Londonderry gentlemen. INVY.: Appraised 12/23/1772. Value L56.11.9. Oaths 1/9/1773 Comm. to Stepham Holland, JP. Oath 1/15/1773 John Talford, an Admr., to judge. LICENSE: 1/15/1773. To Admrs. To sell sufficient real est. to pay debts. ACCOUNT: Of Admrs. Oath 12/30/1773 Admr. John Tolford to judge. Allowed.

1851. NELSON, JOHN (1795) #6098
EST. Greenland esq. decd. PETITION: 5/18/1795. Of Jonathan Warner, Portsmouth esq. States that John Nelson died at Greenland a year ago, was formerly a Portsmouth esq. He left no widow, bro. or sister, but Warner assumes he left real and personal est. Before leaving Portsmouth, Nelson made a Will but did not legally execute it, having only two witnesses, both now dead. Warner was named one exec. in Will and is probably the largest

creditor. Requests admin. ADMIN.: 5/18/1795. Admr. Jonathan Warner, Portsmouth esq. Bond L1000.0.0. Sureties: Nathaniel Folsom, of Portsmouth and George Sullivan of Exeter, esquires. Witness: W. Parker. CERT.: 2/24/1803. Of William Parker, Reg. Pro-bate for Rockingham Co. Certifies that on 5/18/1795 Admin. was granted to Warner, but that the records of the court do not show Warner has ever having returned an Invy. or submitted any matter relative to his Admin.

1852. NELSON, MARK (1787) #5246
EST. Portsmouth goldsmith decd. testate. WILL: Drawn 1/1/1787. Legatees: Wife-Mary; Sons- Mark, Thomas, John and Samuel; Daus.- Hannah Nelson and Elizabeth Nelson; Anna Thompson, "who is living with me and has lived with me from a child." Exex.-wife Mary. His sig. Witnesses: Saml. Pemhallow, Peter Man and Jacob Walden. Codicil; 1/1/1787. He gives dau. Hannah an addl. bequest and provides for mourning clothes for "Hannah" Thompson to be paid by est. His mark. Witnesses: Saml. Penhallow, Peter Man and Jacob Walden. CERT. WILL (D29: 102): 2/27/1787. Presented by Exex. and witnesses Man and Walden. INVY. Appr. 5/12/1787. Comm.: Noah Parker, Jacob Walden and Danl. Peirce. Value L938.9.0. Oaths Comm. to Geo. Gerrish, JP. Oath 5/16/1787 Exex. to W. Parker, Reg. PETITION: Dated by clerk 10/1788. Of Admx. For license. Gives list of both paid and unpaid debts. Unpaid total L56.15.10.

1853. NESMITH, JAMES (1796) #6202
EST. Londonderry husbm. decd. testate. WILL: Drawn 2/16/1796. Legatees: Wife-Jean; Sons-Isaac, Robert, William and James; Daus.- Martha Nesmith, Peggy Nesmith and Sally Nesmith. Exec.-Capt. Robert Nesmith. His sig. Witnesses: John Bell, James Morrison and Elisabeth Morrison. CERT. WILL (D32:120): 4/20/1796. Presented by Exec. and witnesses Bell, esq. and James Morrison. ADMIN.: 4/20/1796. Exec. Robert Nesmith, Londonderry gent. Bond $3,000.00. Sureties: Moody Morse, physician and James Morrison, yoeman, both of Londonderry. Witnesses: John Anderson and Nathl. Parker. INVY.: Appr. 4/23/1796. Comm.: Jonathan Griffin, Abraham Duncan and Jno. Dickey. Value $1792.49. Oaths 8/12/1796 Comm. and Exec. to John Bell, JP. ACCOUNT: 4/13/1807. Of Exec. Allowed 4/15/1807. ACCOUNT: Of Exec. Consent of David Morrison, William Nesmith and James Nesmith that Account be allowed. Allowed 12/18/1811.

1854. NESMITH, THOMAS (1789) #5503
EST. Londonderry gent. decd. intestate. RENUN.: 12/12/1789. Of Annes Nesmith, widow of Thomas. Of Admin. Requests appointment of her son John. ADMIN.: 12/16/1789. Admr. John Nesmith, Londonderry gent. Bond L500.0.0. Sureties: Thomas Patterson, Londonderry yoeman and James Betton, Windham esq. Witnesses: Nathl. Parker and W. Parker. ADDL. ACCOUNT (D30:168): 12/21/1791. Of Admr. Allowed 12/21/1791. Addl. Account refers to bal. of former account, but none found.

1855. NEWMARCH, BENJAMIN (1779) #4518
EST. Portsmouth blacksmith decd. Testate. WILL: Drawn 7/20/1775. Legatees: Sister-Mary Ley; Cousin-Benjamin Cutt. Exex.-Sister Mary Ley. His sig. Witnesses: Elizabeth Warner, Margaret Lear and H. Wentworth. Oaths 2/23/1779. Hunking Wentworth and Elizabeth Warner, being infirm and unable to travel, gave oaths to Geo. Gains, JP. CERT. WILL: 2/24/1779. Presented by Exex. and witness Margaret Neal, formerly Margaret Lear, witnesses Hunking Wentworth, esq. and Eliz. Warner having deposed to a justice of the peace. INVY.: Comm.: George Hart, Elisha Hill and John Furnald. Value L721.11.0. Oaths 10/26/1779 Comm. and Exex. to Saml. Penhallow, JP.

1856. NEWMARCH, JOHN (1776) #4238
EST. Portsmouth esq. decd. testate. WILL: Drawn 10/3/1771. Legatees: Daus.-Esther Meserve and Hannah Newmarch; Children of his dau. March; Grandchild-John March; Son-in-law Paul March. Exex.-dau. Hannah. Witnesses: Peter Man, Mark Nelson and John Thompson. CERT. WILL: 5/30/1776. Presented by Exex. and all witnesses. ADMIN.: 5/28/1776. Exex. Hannah Newmarch, Portsmouth single woman. Bond L1000.0.0. Sureties: Peter Man, barber and Mark Nelson, goldsmith, both of Portsmouth. Witnesses: Joseph Pearson and W. Parker.

1857. NICHOLAS. See #5773 Harvey Nichols (1792)

1858. NICHOLS, HARVEY (1792) #5773
EST. Exeter mariner decd. intestate. ADMIN.: 5/17/1792. Admx. Hannah Nichols, Exeter widow. Bond L100.0.0. Sureties: Simeon Ladd, esq. and Stephen Lamson, innholder, both of Exeter. Witnesses: Deborah Ladd and Nathl. Parker. INVY. Appr. 8/25/1792. Comm.: Simeon Ladd and Stephen Lamson. Value L12.5.0. Oaths 8/25/1792 Admx. and Comm. to W. Parker. Note: The Brentwood card file mistakenly lists this as Nicholas.

1859. NICHOLS, CAPT. SAMUEL (1797) #6311
EST. Portsmouth mariner decd. intestate. CITATION: 11/10/1796. To: Elizabeth Nichols, widow; David Nichols, Samuel Nichols and Daniel Furnald, mariners, all of Portsmouth. To appear so one or more of them may be granted admin. or admin. will be granted to a creditor, Samuel having died long since and his debts remain unpaid. Cert.: 12/27/1796. Of Edward Hart, Shrff. He has summoned Elizabeth Nicholls and Daniel Fernald by reading the Citation to them. David and Samuel Nicholls are out of state. The following Pet. recorded as #6310 Daniel Furnald (1797) belongs here. PETITION: 1/7/1797. Of Daniel Furnald in right of his wife Buler and on behalf of Samuel Nichols and David Nichols, all Portsmouth mariners. For div. of land on Pickering's Neck of which they own half in common with others. Order: 1/7/1796 (clerk's error). For hearing, Petitioner to advertise Petition and Order in newspaper. ADMIN.: 2/15/1797. Admr. Capt. Daniel Furnald, Portsmouth mariner. Bond $3,000.00. Sureties: Amos Furnald, cordwainer and John Melcher, blockmaker, both of Portsmouth. Witnesses: Richd. Pickering and W. Parker. INVY.: Appr. 5/16/1797. Comm.: Nathl. Marshall, Peter Coues and Samuel Hutchings. Value $670.15. Oaths 5/17/1797 Admr. and Comm. to Geo. Gains, JP. RECEIPT: 5/16/1797. Of Invy. Comm. For payment of Invy. fee. DIV. WARR.: 2/15/1797. Comm.: Isaac Rindge and George Gains, esquires; George Wentworth and Nathaniel Marshall, mariners and Samuel Hutchings, trader, all of Portsmouth. To div. land and bldgs. at Pickerings Neck. Div.: 4/18/1797. Divisees: Samuel Nichols, David Nichols and Daniel Furnald in right of his wife, 1/2 share. Oaths 4/18/1797 Rindge, Hutchings, Gains and Wentworth to Saml. Penhallow, JP. Allowed 6/20/1798. ACCOUNT: Of Admr. Allowed 6/17/1801 the heirs living out of U.S. PETITION: 6/17/1801. Of Admr. For License to sell all the real est. so as to settle the bal. of $127.67 due him. Selling part would be injurious. Order: 6/17/1801. For hearing, Petitioner to advertise Petition and Order. COPY OF AD AS RUN IN NEWSPAPER. LICENSE. 8/26/1801. To Admr. To sell all the real est.

1860. NOBLE, JOHN, ET. AL. (1794) #6040
PET. For div. of Jackson Island. PETITION: 10/25/1794. Of: Mark Noble Jr., Robert Noble, John Noble and Joseph Noble, all of Portsmoth. For div. of an island in Piscataqua River known as Jackson Island, which they hold as tenants in common with John Roach (sic.) and others unknown. They own 1/3. Order: For a hearing, Petitioners to advertise the Petition and hearing. 11/20/1794 hearing postponed to 2/1794. PETITION: 11/19/1794. Of John Noble on behalf of the Petitioners. States that after presenting the Petition, they were surprised to learn that Thomas(sic) Roach had received a return setting off to him one acre of Jackson's Island, which single acre is

worth more than any 2 acres of the rest. Request hearing. Order: For a hearing. NOTIFICATION: 11/20/1794. To Thomas Roach, Portsmouth mariner. Of hearing on Petition because the Div. Of the Comm. appointed 11/17/1792 to set off to Thomas one acre of the island known as Wallingford's or Jackson's Island was done without notice by Comm. to other owners concerned. DIV. WARR.: 2/18/1795. Comm.: George Gains, Supply Clap, Capt. George Wentworth and Isaac Rindge, esquires and William Hart, gent., all of Portsmouth. To div. Jackson's Island giving John Noble and his bros. 1/3, Nathaniel Ham and his bros. 1/3 and Thomas Roach and others 1/3. DIV.: 5/20/1795. Divisees as in Warr. Oaths 5/25/1795 Gains, Wentworth, Rindge and Hart to R. Cutts Shannon, JP. Allowed. Includes map.

1861. NOBLE, REV. OLIVER (1793) #5889
EST. New Castle clerk decd. intestate. ADMIN.: 5/8/1793. Admr. Habijah Weld Noble, Berwick, York Co., MA/ME gent. Bond L1000.0.0. Sureties: Benjamin Prescott, mariner and George Frost, esq., both of New Castle. Witnesses: Elias Tarlton and John White. INVY. WARR.: 5/8/1793. Comm.: Henry Prescott and George Frost, esquires and Capt. William Vennard, all of New Castle. Invy.: Appr. 5/27/1793. Value L418.12.3. Oaths 5/28/1793 Prescott and Vennard to Geo. Frost, JP. Oath 5/28/1793 Admr. to judge. ACCOUNT: 6/17/1795. Of Admr. Allowed 6/17/1795. APPR.: 6/17/1795. Comm.: Henry Prescott and George Frost, esquires; John Tarlton, yoeman; William Vennard and Thomas Bell, traders, all of New Castle. To view the real est. to see if it can be div. Among all his children. Div. or appr. Appr.: $875.00. Oaths 9/19/1795 Prescott, Vennard, Tarlton and Bell to Geo. Frost, JP. Follows a list of names which are same as heirs of Settlm. ACCOUNT: Of Admr. Allowed 9/21/1795. DECREE SETTLM.: 9/21/1792. Habijah Weld Noble, only son, appearing and consenting, the real est. is settled on him, Habijah to pay his co-heirs $109.37 1/2 each as follows: Lucy Collins, Tirzah Noble and Salley Allen in one year; Fanny Noble, Eunice Noble, Hannah Noble and Elizabeth Noble in 2 years, with interest. BOND: 9/21/1795. Of Habijah Weld Noble, New Castle gent. Bond $1,750.00. To pay his co-heirs per Decree Settlm. Sureties: William Vennard, mariner and John Tarlton, yoeman, both of New Castle. Witnesses: Henry Prescott and Thomas Bell. RECEIPT: 10/9/1790. Of David Thacher Jr. on behalf of Eunice W. Noble. To Admr. For $109.37. RECEIPT: 10/10/1790. Of Fanny Noble, at Newmarket. To Admr. For $109.37. RECEIPT: 10/12/1790. Of Hannah Noble, at Somersworth, Strafford Co. To Admr. For $109.36. RECEIPT: 11/8/1790. Of Tirzah Noble, at Newington. To Admr. For $109.36. RECEIPT: 11/12/1796. Of Sally Allen and William Allen. To Admr. For $109.36. ACCOUNT: 10/4/1798. Of H. Weld Noble,

as Gdn.? To Miss Elizabeth Noble. Account includes her $109.36. share. RECEIPT: 8/28/1801. Of Elizabeth Noble, at Barrington, Strafford Co. To Admr. For $109.37 1/2. LETTER: 1/7/1801, Brome, (MA/ME?). From Henry Collins and Lucia Collins. To Bro. H. Weld Noble. They ask him to pay or deliver to Ben Porter, esq. the money due them from est., Porter's receipt being their release to Admr. Receipt: 8/18/1801. From Moses Porter for his. bro. B. Porter. To Admr. For $109.37 1/2.

1862. NOLDRED, SAMUEL (1773) #4020
EST. Portsmouth mariner decd. intestate. ADMIN.: 5/26/1773. Admr. Robert Calder, Newburyport, Essex Co., MA innholder. Bond L500.0.0. Sureties: Stephen Hardy, taylor and Robert Harrold, cabinet maker, both of Portsmouth. Witnesses: Cotton Ward and Samuel Parker. INVY. WARR.: 5/26/1773. Comm.: Stephen Hardy, taylor and Robert Harrold, cabinet maker, both of Portsmouth. INVY.: Value L20.17.2. Oaths 5/26/1773 Comm. and Admr. to judge. INVY. WARR.: 6/8/1774. Comm.: Robert Traill and Thomas Martyn, esquires, both of Portsmouth. To invy. est. not already appr. Signed by Saml. Hale Jr., Reg, by order of the judge. CLAIMS: Comm.: Samuel Parker and Joseph Peirce. Total L13.2.3. Oaths 6/8/1774 Comm. to judge. ACCOUNT: Total income was L31.17.0 which included a pew inventoried by Traill and Martyn and the amount of the est. sold for over the Invy. estimate. Allowed 6/9/1774. PROP. & SETTLEMENT: 6/8/1777. Claims L13.2.3. Amount to be proportioned L11.13.0.0. Allowed with order to Admr. to pay.

1863. NORIE, JAMES (1795) #6076
EST. Portsmouth tinplate worker decd. testate. WILL: Drawn 9/25/1794. Legatees: Wife-unnamed; His children. His wife to be Gdn. of his children. Exec.-wife. Hissig. Witnesses: Stephn. Hardy, F. Hide and James Foster. CERT. WILL (D31:474): 2/18/1795. Presented by Katharine Norie, Exex. and witnesses Hardy and Foster. ADMIN.: 2/18/1796 (sic.) but by clerk 1795. Exex. Catharine Norie, Portsmouth widow. Bond L1000.0.0. Sureties: Stephen Hardy, taylor and James Foster, mariner, both of Portsmouth. Witnesses: W. Parker and Jacob Walden. GDP. Of the daus. of James Norie. GDP.: 2/16/1803. Of Mary and Margaret, minors over 14 and of Elizabeth and Jane, minors under 14. Gdn. Samuel Bowles, Portsmouth schoolmaster. Bond $4,000.00. Sureties: Samuel Hutchings, merchant and James Day, cooper, both of Portsmouth. Witnesses: William Greenough and Sally Greenough

1864. NORRIS: BENJAMIN, JAMES & SAMUEL (1771) #3878
GDP. Of the sons of Jonathan Norris, Exeter yoeman decd. GDP.: 10/2/1771. Of Benjamin, a minor over 14. Gdn. Caleb Robinson, Exeter innholder. Bond L500.0.0. Surety Jacob Tilton, Portsmouth innholder. GDP.: 3/23/1774. Of James and Samuel, minors under 14. Gdn. Jonathan Norris, Exeter yoeman, their bro. Bond L200.0.0. Sureties: Caleb Robinson, innholder and Josiah Baker, clothier, both of Exeter. Witnesses: Nathl. Parker and W. Parker Jr.

1865. NORRIS, BENJAMIN (1799) #6537
EST. Pembroke gent. decd. RENUN.: 2/13/1799. Of Sarah Norris, widow of Benjamin. Of Admin. due to age, reserving her right to any alimony the judge may provide. Requests appointment of her son David. ADMIN. (D33:47): 2/14/1799. Admr. David Norris, Pembroke yoeman. Sureties: Anthony Somersby Stickney, esq. and Solomon Whitehouse, gent., both of Pembroke. INVY. (D33:80): Comm.: Daniel Knox, esq.; Solomon Whitehouse and Joseph Swett Jr. Value $1,491.30. Oaths 5/10/1799 Comm. to Thos. Adams, JP. Oath 5/15/1799 Admr. to judge. PETITION: 5/15/1799. Of Admr. on his own behalf and as Admr. on behalf of heirs. For div. Of real est. in Pembroke held in common and in equal shares by himself and heirs. PETITION: 5//15/1799. Of Admr. For Comm. Insolvency. Gives list claims of $1,351.00. Granted. CLAIMS: Comm.: Solomon Whitehouse, Joseph Swett Jr. and John Knox Jr. Total $1,477.36. Oaths (date covered up). Comm. to Richard Bartlett, JP. PETITION: 1/15/1800. Of Admr. For License to sell all the real est. and reversion of Dower. LICENSE: 1/15/1800. To Admr. To sell all the real est and reversion of Dower. BOND: 1/15/1800. Of Admr., Pembroke gent. Bond $5,000.00. To account for proceeds of sale of real est. and Dower by License. Sureties: Anthony S. Stickney, esq. and John Knox Jr., both of Pembroke. DIV.: 11/19/1799. Comm.: James Cochran; Daniel Knox, esq.; Solomon Whitehouse, Joseph Swett Jr. and Asa Robinson. Divisees: Est. of Benjamin Norris decd. and David Norris. Oaths 11/19/1799 Knox, Whitehouse, Swett and Robinson to Richard Bartlett, JP. Allowed 1/15/1800. DOWER: 11/19/1800. Same Comm. as Div. Of Widow Sarah Norris. Oaths 11/19/1799 Comm. to Richard Bartlett, JP. Allowed 1/18/1800. ACCOUNT: 9/17/1800. Of Admr. Allowed 9/17/1800. PROP. & SETTLM.: Claims $1,477.36. Amount to be proportioned $1,022.80. Allowed 10/6/1800 with order to Admr. to pay.

1866. NORRIS, COFFIN DOLE (1789) #5437
GDP. Of the son of Josiah Norris, Epping yoeman decd. GDP.: 4/15/1789. Of Coffin Dole Norris, a minor over 14. Gdn. William Norris, Nottingham yoeman. Bond L500.0.0. Sureties: Benjamin Hoit, gent. and Joseph Blake, yoeman, both of Epping. Witnesses: Wm. (unreadable) and Nathl. Parker. RELEASE (D32:108): 4/1/1796. Of Coffin Dole Norris, Deerfield yoeman To William Norris, Nottingham gent. He has received from William $2.00 and releases him from all claims as his Gdn. Oath 4/1/1796 Coffin Dole Norris to Wm. Parker, JP.

1867. NORRIS: JAMES & SAMUEL (1774) No#
GDP. 3/23/1775. Of Samuel and James. Gdn. Jonathan Norris.

1868. NORRIS, JAMES (1780) #4635
EST. Epping husbm. decd. testate. WILL: Drawn 1/18/1775. Legatees: Wife-Johannah; Sons-James and Thomas; Daus.-Johannah Stevens, Mary Blake, Lydia Norris and Marcy Blake. Exec.-son Thomas. His sig. Witnesses: Daniel Gordon, Gordon Lawrence and Abraham Perkins. CERT. WILL (D25:352): 6/28/1780. Presented by Exec. and witnesses Perkins, esq. and Daniel Gordon. Note: The Cert. Will calls witness Gideon Lawrence but the sig. on Will is clearing Gordon. ADMIN.: 6/28/1780. Exec. Thomas Norris, Epping yoeman. Bond L10000.0.0. Sureties: Abraham Perkins, esq. and James Rundlet Jr., yoeman, both of Epping. Witnesses: Andrew Freese and W. Parker. PETITION: 6/23/1780. Of Johanah Norris and James Norris Jr. As James gave them his personal est. in his Will, they accept it without being inventoried and request est. be saved cost appr. DOWER WARR.: 9/17/1788. Comm.: Abraham Perkins, esq.; Jacob Rundlet, Judah Hackett, Simeon Norris and Andrew Hanson, yoemen, all of Epping. Of Widow Johannah Norris, her Dower according to Will. DOWER: 9/22/1788. Oaths 9/22/1788 Rundlet, Norris and Hanson to Abraham Perkins, JP. Order: 11/19/1788. When return was presented, Theops. Blake, on behalf of Widow, made objection and the return disallowed. DOWER: 12/5/1788. Comm.: Seth Fogg, Enoch Coffin, Benja. Hoit and Gordon Lawrence. Of Widow Johannah Norris. Oaths 12/5/1788 Fogg, Hoit and Lawrence to Enoch Coffin, JP. Allowed 12/17/1788.

1869. NORRIS, JOHANNAH (1790) #5561
EST. Epping widow decd. testate. WILL: Drawn 9/5/1789. Legatees: Sons-Thomas Norris and James Norris; Daus.-Johannah and Lydia; Children of her dau. Mercy decd.; Son-in-law Theophilus Blake with whom she now lives. Exec.-Theophilus Blake. Her mark. Witnesses: Joseph Blake, Joseph Blake Jr. and Wm. Plumer. CERT. WILL

(D29:397): 7/21/1790. Presented by Exec. and witnesses Joseph Blake (oath) and Plumer, esq. (affirm.) ADMIN.: 7/21/1790. Exec. Theophilus Blake, Epping yoeman. Bond L1000.0.0. Sureties: Joseph Blake, yoeman and William Plumer, esq., both of Epping. Witnesses: W. Parker and N. Parker. INVY.: Appr. 10/14/1790. Comm.: Stephen Clifford, Daniel Tilton and John Piper. Value L21.17.6. Oaths 10/14/1790 Comm. to Wm. Plumer, JP. Oath 10/20/1790 Exec. to W. Parker, Reg. PETITION: 10/20/1790. Of Exec. For Comm. Insolvency. Gives claims as L117.7.2. CLAIMS WARR.: 10/20/1790. Comm.: William Plumer, esq. and Abraham Tilton, blacksmith, both of Epping. Claims: 4/16.1791. Total not tallied. Esti. L119.0.0+. Oaths 4/16/1791 Tilton to Wm. Plumer, JP. Affirm. 4/18/1791 Plumer to judge.

1870. NORRIS, JONATHAN (1773) #4050
EST. Epping husbm. decd. intestate. ADMIN.: 10/21/1773. Admr. David Norris, Epping husbm. Bond L500.0.0. Sureties: William Dowling and Israel Norris, Epping husbandmen. INVY. WARR.: 10/21/1773. Comm.: David Lawrence, esq. and Jeremiah Prescott, husbm., both of Epping. Appr. 12/20/1773. Value L165.13.6. Oaths 12/21/1773 Comm. to Noah Emery, JP. Oath 12/26/1773 Admr. to judge. PETITION & RECEIPTS: 12/6/1773. Of Admr. For License. The receipts are for payments made by Admr. Allowed. LICENSE (D22:386): 12/29/1773. To Admr. To sell real est. to amount of L100.0.0 at a reasonable rate. ACCOUNT: Of Admr. Allowed 12/19/1787.

1871. NORRIS, JOSEPH (1786) #5199
GDP. Of the son of Joseph Partridge Norris, Kingston hatter decd. GDP.: 5/17/1786. Of Joseph, a minor over 14. Gdn. Joseph Chase Smith, Brentwood yoeman. Bond L1000.0.0. Surety Chase Smith, Brentwood yoeman. Witnesses: John Pinkerton and Wm. Parker.

1872. NORRIS, JOSEPH (1796) #6277
EST. Brentwood cooper decd. ADMIN.: 11/19/1796. Admrs.: Jonathan Marston, yoeman and Elizabeth Norris, widow, both of Brentwood. Bond $2,000.00. Sureties: John Tucke and Charles Sanborn, Brentwood yoemen. Witnesses: W. Parker and Saml. Parker. INVY.: Appr. 12/5/1796. Comm.: Ezekl. Godfrey, Benjamin Cram and Benj. Shephard. Value $126.18. Oaths 12/10/1796 Godfrey and Cram to Thos. S. Ranney, JP. Affirms. 12/15/1796 Admrs. to judge.

1873. NORRIS, JOSEPH (1798) #6412
EST. Stratham gent. decd. testate. WILL: Drawn 10/16/1797. Legatees: Wife-Comfort; Sons-James, Joseph, Benjamin, Charles, Nathaniel and Caleb; Daus.-Mehitable Norris, Mary Norris and Anna Norris. Execs.-wife Comfort and oldest son James. His sig. Witnesses: Samuel Pottle, Henry Pottle and Jabez Lane. CERT. WILL (D32:423): 1/15/1798. Presented by Comfort Norris, an Exec. and witnesses Saml. Pottle and Lane. ADMIN.: 1/15/1798. Exex. Comfort Norris, Stratham widow. Bond $3,000.00. Sureties: Jonathan Piper, gent. and Samuel Pottle, yoeman, both of Stratham. Witnesses: W. Parker and Nathl. Parker. INVY. WARR.: 1/15/1798. Comm.: Jonathan Wiggin, gent.; Phinehas Merrill and Thomas Veasey, yoemen, all of Stratham. Invy.: Appr. 3/1/1798. Value $3,866.67. Oaths 3/10/1798 Wiggin, Merrill and Exex. To W. Parker.

1874. NORRIS, JOSIAH (1786) #5188
EST. Epping husbm. decd. testate. WILL: Drawn 3/8/1786. Legatees: Wife-unnamed; Sons-Josiah, William, Moses and Coffin Dole Norris; Daus.-Sarah Baker, Anna Norris and Eunice Norris. Ref. to the mother of Eunice decd. and dau. Catharine decd. Appoints son Josiah Gdn. of Moses, son William Gdn. of Coffin Dole and his wife Gdn. of Eunice. Execs.-sons Josiah and William. His sig. Witnesses: Abraham Tilton, Benjamin Hoit and William Plumer. CERT. WILL (D28:513): 4/19/1786. Presented by Execs. and witnesses Tilton and Hoit. ACCEPTANCE: 4/18/1786. Of Anna Norris, widow of Josiah. She accepts the provision made for her in Will and relinquishes to the legatees her right of dower in the real est. devised to them. Witnesses: Abraham Tilton and Benja. Hoit. INVY.: Appr. 6/15/1786. Comm.: Thos. Bartlet, esq.; Jonathan Winslow and David Lawrence Jr. Value L1694.5.1. Oaths 6/15/1786 Winslow and Norris to Thos. Bartlet, JP. Oaths 6/21/1786 Execs. to Abraham Perkins, JP. DIV.: 12/6/1787. Comm.: Simon Marston; Andrew Freese; Jona. Swain, esq.; Jona. Eliot and Rice Rowell. To div. 2 lots, about 206 acres in Deerfield and about 6 acres in Nottingham between Josiah Norris of Epping, William Norris of Nottingham and their bro. Coffin Dole Norris, giving Josiah 1/3 of the Deerfield lot and 1/2 of the Nottingham lot, their bro. Coffin Dole Norris 1/4 of both lots and William Norris the remainder. Divisees as stated. Oaths 12/17/1787 Swain, Eliot and Rowell to Abraham Perkins, JP. Allowed 6/2/1794. See #5226 William Norris et. al. (1786) for Petition for this Div. and Addl. Petition and Div. between William and Coffin.

1875. NORRIS, LYDIA (1789) #5464
GDP. Epping spinster adjudged n.c.m. PETITION: 2/23/1789. Of Thomas Norris. Requests inquisition into the state of his sister, a spinster over 21, n.c.m., incapable of caring for herself or est. and in need of a Gdn. Order: 2/23/1789. To Epping Selectmen. To make inquisition into state of Lydia's mind. Report: 3/7/1789. Of: Joseph Shepard and David Lawrence Jr., Epping Selectmen. After examing Lydia's neighbors and from what they know of her themselves, they think she needs a Gdn. and recommend Capt. Benjamin Hoit of Epping. Order: 3/18/1789. The Report of the Selectmen having been considered, witnesses in support of the Petition examined and the parties heard by their council, at request of Lydia's atty. a further hearing deferred to next court. Decree: 4/15/1789. The council for the parties having been heard again, and their witnesses examined, the judge rules that Lydia does not need a Gdn. and Petition dismissed. PETITION: 6/3/1789. Of Thomas Norris, Epping yoeman. Requests inquisition into the state of Lydia's mind, saying she is n.c.m. Order: 6/3/1789. To Epping Selectmen. To make inquisition concerning the state of Lydia's mind. Report: 6/8/1789. Of: Seth Fogg and Samuel Morrill, Epping Selectmen., They have discoursed with Lydia and find her not capable of caring for herself and est. Recommend Capt. Benjamin Hoit of Epping to be her Gdn. GDP.: 6/17/1789. Of Lydia, an adult adjudged n.c.m. Gdn. Benjamin Hoit, Epping gent. Bond L500.0.0. Sureties: Theophilus Stevens and Thomas Norris, Epping yoemen. Witnesses: John Hale and Nathl. Parker. INVY.: Appr. 10/20/1789. Comm.: Jonathan Clark and Jacob Rundlet. Value L51.8.1. Oaths 10/20/1789 Comm. to Wm. Plumer, JP. Oath 10/21/1789 Gdn. To W. Parker, JP. ACCOUNT: 3/1800. Of Gdn. Allowed 3/7/1800.

1876. NORRIS, MOLLY (1799) #6568
GDP. Of the dau. of Benja. Norris, Pembroke gent. decd. GDP.: 5/15/1799. Of Molly, a minor over 14. Gdn. Daniel Knox, Pembroke esq. Bond $1,000.00. Sureties: David Norris, yoeman and Anthony S. Stickeny, esq., both of Pembroke. Witnesses: Joseph Emery Jr. and N. Parker.

1877. NORRIS, MOSES (1776) #4239
EST. Nottingham yoeman decd. ADMIN.: 5/29/1776. Admx. Susanner Norris, Nottingham widow. Bond L1000.0.0. Sureties: Ithiel Gordon of Raymond and John Carr Jr. of Epping, yoemen. Witnesses: Joseph Pearson and W. Parker. INVY. WARR.: 5/29/1776. Comm.: Jonathan Swain of Raymond; Joseph Shepherd and John Carr Jr., Epping, yoemen. INVY.: Appr. 6/24/1776. Value L286.10.9. Oaths 6/26/1776 Comm. and Admx. to judge. ACCOUNT: 9/1777. Of Nathan White and Susanna his wife, Admx. Allowed 9/24/1777. Account includes maintenance of one child.

1878. NORRIS: WILLIAM & JOSIAH (1786) #5226
PET. Div. PETITION: 8/16/1786. Of: William Norris of Nottingham. States he and his bro. Coffin Dole Norris are tenants in common of land in Nottingham. Coffin is a minor. Requests div. DIV. WARR. 8/16/1786. Comm.: Thomas Bartlet, esq.; Rice Rowell and Francis Harvey Jr. of Nottingham; Josiah Tilton, Deerfield gent. and Theophilus Stevens of Epping. To div. Lot No. 35 in Nottingham in equal shares between William Norris and his bro. Coffin Dole Norris. As Coffin is a minor and William is his Gdn., Josiah, their bro., is appointed agent for Coffin. DIV. 8/24/1786. Divisees as in Petition. Oaths 8/25/1786 Bartlett, Rowell and Harvey to Benjamin Butler, JP. Allowed. AGREEMENT: 8/24/1785. Of Josiah Norris, agent for Coffin Dole Norris. He has no objection to the Div. as returned by Comm. PETITION: 11/16/1786. Of William Norris of Nottingham and Josiah Norris of Epping, husbandmen. They, with their bro. Coffin Dole Norris, are tenants in common of land in Deerfield Parish of Nottingham Twp. Josiah owns 1/3, Coffin 1/4 and William the residue. Request div. as Coffin is a minor. For this Div. see File #5888 Josiah Norris (1786), their father.

1879. NORTON, DANIEL (1777) #4341
GDP. Of the son of Nathan Norton, Chester yoeman decd. GDP.: 4/10/1777. Of Daniel, a minor under 14. Gdn. Joshua Johnson, Greenland yoeman. Bond L500.0.0. Sureties: Joshua Haynes, Greenland gent. and Simeon Dearborn, Wakefield, Strafford Co., esq. Witnesses: Josiah Fogg and W. Parker.

1880. NORTON, DANIEL JOHNSON (1794) #5996
PET. DIV. No information given except for abuttors. PETITION: 4/1794. Of Daniel Johnson Norton. For div. of land in Greenland of which he owns 1/8. Order: 4/1794. For hearing, Petitioner to notify others concerned.

1881. NORTON, ENOCH (1796) #6240
PET. DIV. Of est. of James Norton of Seabrook decd. PETITION: 8/16/1796. Of Enoch Norton of Seabrook. For div. of land in Seabrook, late the est. of his father James Norton of Seabrook decd., which he holds in common with his two sisters. He owns 1/3. Order: 8/6/1796. For hearing, Petitioner to serve Gdn. of his sisters with copies of Petition and Order. Note: No est. for a James of Seabrook found.

1882. NORTON: HANNAH, JUDITH & MOSES (1778) #4449
GDP. Of the children of John Norton, South Hampton husbm. GDP.: 1/3/1778. Of: Hannah, Judith and Moses, minors under 14. Gdn. John

Norton, their father. Bond L500.0.0. Sureties: James Hadlock, cordwainer and Moses French, joiner, both of South Hampton. Witnesses: Isaiah Dole and Nathl. White.

1883. NORTON, JOHN SR. (1774) #4140
EST. South Hampton yoeman decd. testate. WILL: Drawn 3/24/1773. Legatees: Wife-Mehitabel; Son-John; Daus.-Mehitabel Clough wife of David Clough; Jane Flanders wife of Timothy Flanders; Sarah Eastman wife of Moses Eastman and Hannah Tuxbury wife of Jacob Tuxbury. Exec.-son John. His sig. Witnesses: Daniel Page, Richd. Collins and Daniel Page Jr. CERT. WILL (23:87): 12/27/1774. Presented by Exec. and witnesses Daniel Page and Daniel Page Jr. INVY. WARR.: 12/27/1774. Comm.: Daniel Page, husbm. and Benjamin Brown, gent., both of South Hampton. INVY.: Appr. 1/3/1775. Value L172.15.0. Oaths 2/21/1775 Admr. and Comm. to judge.

1884. NORTON, JONATHAN (1791) #5685
EST. Chester yoeman decd. ADMIN.: 8/17/1791. Admr. Simon Norton, Deerfield yoeman. Bond L1000.0.0. Sureties: Richard Jenness, Deerfield esq. and Moses Leavitt Neal, Londonderry gent. Witnesses: John Taylor and Nathl. Parker. INVY.: Appr. 8/31/1791. Comm.: Jona. Swain and Jacob Chase. Value L270.17.0. Oaths 9/17/1791 Comm. and Admr. to Josiah Flagg, JP. DOWER: 10/5/1791. Comm.: Stephen Chase, John Butterfield, Moses Hall "and others." Of Susanna Lufkin in est. Jonathan Norton. Oaths 10/5/1791 Chase, Butterfield and Hall to Jabez Hoit, JP. Allowed 4/20/1796. ACCOUNT: 5/20/1795. Of Admr. Allowed 4/20/1796. Cert.: Of John Norton. That he and rest of heirs have seen the Account and are content with it.

1885. NORTON, MOSES (1795) #6099
EST. Seabrook yoeman decd. intestate. RENUN.: 5/15/1795. Of Hannah Norton, Seabrook single woman. Of admin. of her bro.'s est. Requests appointment of Lt. John Smith. Witnesses: Elisha Brown and Jacob _____(sic.) ADMIN.: 5/18/1795. Admr. John Smith, Seabrook gent. Bond L1000.0.0. Sureties: Elisha Brown, esq. and Edmund Noyes, gent., both of Seabrook. Witnesses: Enoch Smith and W. Parker. INVY.: 5/25/1795. Comm.: Elisha Brown, Robert Collins and Belcher Dole. Value $1,861.45. Oaths 10/22/1795 Collins and Dole to Elisha Brown, JP. RECEIPT: 1/3/1797. Of Barnet Thorne. To Admr. He has received $88.82 of the personal est. ACCOUNT: 9/14/1801. Of Admr. Allowed 9/14/1801 heirs having been notified. Admr. ordered to distribute bal. of $107.60. DIV.: 11/8/1796. Comm.: Jeremiah Lane, Robert Collins, Belcher Dole, Winthrop Eaton and Eliash Brown. To div. the est. Divisees: Heirs of

James Norton decd.; Barnard Thorn in right of his wife and Hannah. Oaths 11/8/1796 Lane, Collins, Dole and Eaton to Elisha Brown, JP. Allowed 9/14/1801 there being no objections. RECEIPT: 4/12/1825. Of Enoch Norton. To Admr. He has received $83.41 in full of personal est. Witness Robert Greely. PETITION: 6/22/1825. Of Simeon Choate of Salisbury, Essex Co., MA and Hannah Choate his wife and a sister of decd. who is due 1/3 of est. They state that when Account was settled, Admr. was to pay the bal. to heirs, but he has not paid Hannah. Request permission to sue Bond of Admin. Order: 6/22/1826. For hearing, Petitioners to notify Admr. and serve him with copies of Petition and Order. Cert.: 6/26/1825. Of Samuel George, Seabrook Constable. He served the Admr. with the copies. Order: 7/13/1826. The report of the referees having been submitted, the Petition is dismissed. CERT.: Isaac Parker, Chief Justice of the Supreme Judicial Court of MA, certs. that Ichabod Tucker is clerk of the court and for all judicial courts of Essex Co. and his cert. of the attached record and proceedings is in due form. Demands (copy): Of Simeon Choate of Salisbury, Essex Co., MA. He claims that John Smith, Admr., owes Hannah Choate, his wife and an heir to est. of Moses Norton, $100.00. Agreement (copy): Simeon Choate and Admr. agree to submit the demand to determination of Benjamin Evans, Winthrop Eaton and Benjamin Joy and to accept their decision as final. Oaths 6/12/1826 Choate and Eaton to Samuel Nye, JP. Return: 6/19/1826. The Referees rule that Simeon and Hannah Choate have no equitable demand against Admr. and they are to pay the cost of $5.00 for reference. DECREE: 6/19/1826. Of Court of Common Pleas for Essex Co., MA. The Report is accepted and Admr. to recover from Simeon Choate costs of $12.13. Cert.: 7/13/1826. Of Ichabod Tucker.

1886. NORTON, NATHAN (1776) #4259
EST. Chester tanner decd. ADMIN.: 8/28/1776. Admx. Hannah Norton, Chester widow. Bond L500.0.0. Sureties: Reuben Hills, Chester tanner and Joseph Wadleigh, Brintwood yoeman. Witnesses: Joseph Wadleigh Jr. and Josiah Hills. INVY.: Appr. 11/22/1776. Comm.: Saml. Robie, Robt. Wilson and Benjn. Hills. Value L298.5.0. Oaths 11/25/1776 Comm. to Saml. Emerson, JP. ACCOUNT: 3/25/1778. Of Admx. Allowed 3/25/1778. Account includes main. of youngest child. DIV.: 12/7/1778. Comm.: Simon Towle; Jona. Berry; Jona. Swain, esq.; John Knowles and Joseph Knowles. To div. the real est., giving the Widow her Dower, a double share to son and a single share to other child. Divisees: Hannah, the widow; Son- Daniel Johnson Norton and Dau.- Hannah Norton. Oaths 3/16/1791. Swain, John Knowles and Joseph Knowles to Robt. Wilson, JP. Allowed 3/16/1791. ADDL. ACCOUNT: 3/17/1791. Of Nathl. Maxfield and Hannah his wife, Admx. Allowed 3/16/1791.

1887. NOURSE, NATHANIEL ET. ALS. (1784) #5051
See #A1514 John Karr (1750)

1888. NOWELL, SILAS (1794) #5978
EST. Ralph Cross of Newburyport, Essex Co., MA decd. BOND: 3/10/1794. Of Silas Nowell, Newburyport, Essex. Co., MA, mariner. Bond L500.0.0. To account for the sale of land in N. H. of his children devised to them by their grandfather, Robert Cross of Newburyport, Essex Co., MA decd., now held in common with the other divisees and which Nowell is authorized to sell by an Act of the NH General Court passed 12/7/1792. Sureties: Stephen Cross and Ralph Cross, esq., both of Newburyport, Essex Co., MA. Witnesses: Peter Herrick and Abrm. Moor.

1889. NOYES, BENJAMIN (1783) #4876
EST. Plaistow yeoman decd. testate. WILL: Drawn 2/15/1770. Legates: Wife-Sarah; Sons-Benjamin, Philip, James and Joseph; Daus.-Mary Smith, Elizabeth Huntington, Lydia Noyes and Sarah Noyes. He notes that Benjamin has already received his portion. Execs.-wife Sarah and friend John Knight. His mark. Witnesses: Thomas Johnson, Ebenezer Noyes and Enoch Johnson. CERT. WILL (D27:170): Presented by Sarah Noyes, Exex. and witnesses Noyes and Enoch Johnson. INVY. WARR.: 2/19/1783. Comm.: Ebenezer Noyes and Josiah Johnson, yoemen and Nathaniel Little, gent., all of Plaistow. INVY.: Appr. 5/9/1783. Value L222.11.0. Oaths 5/9/1783 Noyes and Little to Peter Clement, JP. Oath 5/28/1783 Exex. to W. Parker, Reg.

1890. NOYES: CLARK, MARTHA & THOMAS (1772) #4572
GDP. of the children of Thomas Noyes, Atkinson gent. decd. GDP.: 9/29/1779. Of: Clark and Thomas, minors over 14 and of Martha, a minor under 14. Gdn. Peter Clement, Atkinson blacksmith. Bond L2000.0.0. Sureties: Joseph Knight of Atkinson and Joseph Noyes of Hampstead, yoemen.

1891. NOYES, CLARK (1785) #5099
EST. Atkinson yoeman decd. PETITION: 5/12/1785. Of: Caleb Noyes, Joshua Hale Noyes, Annah Noyes and Sarah Noyes. They request appointment of Peter Clement, esq. as Admr. the est. their bro. ADMIN.: 5/18/1785. Admr. Peter Clement, Atkinson esq. Bond L1000.0.0. Sureties: Jesse Johnson, Hampstead gent. and John White, Plaistow yoeman. Witnesses: Stepn. Lamson and Nat Parker.

1892. NOYES, ENOCH (1797) #6307
EST. Atkinson gent. decd. testate. WILL: Drawn 7/16/1790. Legatees: Wife-Mehetabel; Son-James Jr.; Daus.-Eunice wife of Joseph Harriman, Judith Noyes, Phebe wife of John Bassett and Sarah wife of Peter Noyes. Exec.-son James Jr. His sig. Witnesses: John Dow, James Noyes, Joseph Knight Jr., James Dow and Nathl. Peabody. CERT. WILL (D32:254): 2/13/1797. Presented by Exec. and witnesses John Dow, James Dow and Knight. ACCEPTANCE: 2/13/1797. Of Mehetabel Noyes, widow of Enoch. She accepts provision made for her in Will in lieu of Dower. Witnesses: John Dow and James Noyes. Requests no Invy. be taken. ADMIN.: 2/13/1797. Exec. James Noyes Jr., Atkinson gent. Bond $3,000.00. Sureties: John Dow, esq. and James Noyes, gent., both of Atkinson. Witnesses: W. Parker and Saml. Parker. INVY.: Comm.: Humphrey Noyes, John Dow and Samuel N. Little. Value $2,852.51. Oaths 3/14/1797 Comm. to William Cogswell, JP. Oath 3/22/1797 Exec. to W. Parker.

1893. NOYES: EPHRAIM & HANNAH (1793) #5868
GDP. Of the children of Stephen Noyes of Atkinson decd. PETITION: 3/16/1793. Of Lydia Noyes. Requests appointment of Peter Clement, esq. as Gdn. of her dau. Hannah. GDP.: 3/19/1793. Of: Ephraim, a minor over 14 and of Hannah, a minor under 14. Gdn. Peter Clement, Atkinson esq. Bond L1000.0.0. Sureties: Joseph Noyes and Amos Noyes, both of Atkinson.

1894. NOYES, HUMPHREY (1790) #5562
EST. Atkinson yeoman decd. testate. WILL: Drawn 5/21/1790. Legatees: Wife-Elizabeth; Sons-Humphrey, Joseph, Samuel, Peter and John; Daus.-Sarah wife of Daniel Poor Jr and Jane wife of Moses Bartlet. Execs.-sons Joseph and Peter. His sig. Witnesses: Peter Clement, Moses Greenough and Stephen Peabody. CERT. WILL (D29:405): 7/21/1790. Presented by Execs. and witnesses Clement, esq. And Greenough. ADMIN.: 7/21/1790. Execs. Joseph Noyes and Peter Noyes, Atkinson husbandmen. Bond L1000.0.0. Sureties: Peter Clement, esq. and Moses Greenough, gent., both of Atkinson. Witness W. Parker.

1895. NOYES, JAMES (1790) #5568
EST. Kingston yoeman decd. intestate. ADMIN.: 8/12/1790. Admr. James Noyes, Kingston cordwainer. Bond L1000.0.0. Sureties: Nathl. Peabody, Atkinson esq. and Jonathan Pollard, Kingston yoeman. Witnesses: Nathl. Kimball and Jona. Cass. RENUN.: 8/13/1790. Of Mary Noyes, widow of James. Of Admin. Requests appointment of her son James. INVY.: Comm.: Jos. Smith, Amos Sawyer and Jacob Peaslee. Value L312.14.11.

Oath 8/3/1790 Smith, affirm. Sawyer to John White, JP. Clerk notes Admr. sworn 9/22/1790, presumably to judge. GDP.: Of the sons of James Noyes of Kingston decd. GDP.: 3/4/1791. Of: Daniel and Caleb, minors over 14 and of Johnson, a minor under 14. Gdn. Mary Noyes, Kingston widow. Bond L500.0.0. Sureties: Jacob Peaslee, esq. and James Noyes, yoeman, both of Kingston. Witnesses: Sarah Toppan and W. Parker. DOWER: 4/12/1791. Comm.: Simmons Seccombe, Jos. Smith, Amos Sawyer, Nehh. Sleeper and Jacob Peaslee. Of Widow Mary Noyes. Oaths 4/12/1791 Smith, Sawyer, Sleeper and Peaslee to Matthias Bartlet, JP. Allowed. APPR. WARR.: 3/4/1791. Comm.: Jacob Peaslee and Simmons Seccombe, Kingston esquires; Amos Sawyer, yoeman and Joseph Smith, gent., both of Plaistow and Nehemiah Sleeper, Hawke gent. To view 2/3 of real est. and see if it can be div. among all his children. Div. or appr. Appr.: 4/12/1791. Value L169.10.0. Oaths 4/12/1791 Sleeper, Sawyer, Smith and Peaslee to Matthias Bartlet, JP. ACCOUNT: 8/15/1791. Of Admr. Allowed 8/15/1791. DECREE SETTLM.: 8/15/1791. James Noyes, 2d son, appearing and consenting, the real est. settled on him, James to pay each of his co-heirs L28.5.0 within one year, with interest. BOND: 8/15/1791. Of James Noyes, Kingston yoeman. Bond L500.0.0. To pay his co-heirs per Decree Settlm. Sureties: Jacob Peaslee, esq. and Daniel Noyes, yoeman, both of Kingston. Witnesses: Nathl. Parker and Wm. Parker.

1896. NOYES, MARY (1782) #4821 & (1782) #4947
EST. Atkinson & Hampstead widow decd. Note: #4821 gives her res. as Hampstead; #4957 as Atkinson. ADMIN. (#4821): 7/12/1782. Admr. Joshua Hale Noyes, Hampstead yeoman. Bond L1000.0.0. Sureties: Caleb Johnson and John Calfe, esq., both of Hampstead. Witnesses: Moses Johnson and Caleb Johnson Jr. INVY. WARR. (#4957): 7/31/1782. Mary of Atkinson. Comm.: James Huse, Andrew Bryant and Timothy Stevens, all of Hampstead. INVY. (#4957): Value L7.14.10. Oaths 6/26/1783 Comm. to Saml. Little, JP. Oath 12/17/1783 Joshua Hale Noyes, Admr. to W. Parker, Reg. ACCOUNT (#4957): 12/17/1783. Of Admr. Allowed 12/17/1783, plus a note that since settling Account the Admr. acknowledges receiving L21.18.0. more.

1897. NOYES, STEPHEN (1793) #5869
EST. Atkinson husbm. decd. testate. WILL: Drawn 8/7/1792. Legatees: Wife-Lydia; Sons-Moses, David, Ephraim and Amos; Daus.-Lydia wife of Samuel Noyes, Bette wife of Jonathan Kimball, Dolle Noyes, Sarah Noyes and Hannah Noyes. Exec.-son Amos. His sig. Witnesses: Peter Clement, Joseph Noyes and Benjamin Clement. CERT. WILL(D30:376): 3/20/1793. Presented by Exec. and witnesses Peter Clement, esq. and Noyes.

ADMIN.: 3/20/1793. Exec. Amos Noyes, Atkinson yoeman. Bond L1000.0.0. Sureties: Joseph Noyes, yoeman and Peter Clement, esq., both of Atkinson. INVY.: Comm.: Peter Clement, esq.; Moses Greenough and Joseph Noyes. Value L696.18.6 Oaths 1/27/1794 Greenough and Noyes to Peter Clement, JP. Oath 4/16/1794 Exec. to judge.

1898. NOYES, CAPT. THOMAS (1779) #4562
EST. Atkinson gent. decd. intestate. ADMIN.: 8/25/1779. Admrs.: Mary Noyes, Atkinson widow and Caleb Noyes, Hampstead yoeman. Bond L2000.0.0. Sureties: Benjamin Hale, gent. and Peter Clement, blacksmith, both of Atkinson. Witnesses: Jona. Blake and W. Parker. INVY.: Comm.: Jesse Page, Peter Clement and Moses Greenough. Value L17108.3.9. Oaths 11/18/1779 Comm. to Saml. Little, JP. Oath 11/24/1779 Caleb Noyes, an Admr., to judge. DOWER: 4/13/1780. Comm.: John Knight, Moses Greenough, James Little, Asa Page and Jesse Page. Of Widow Mary Noyes. Oaths 10/2/1780 Comm.: to Samuel Little, JP. Allowed 10/25/1780. DIV. WARR.: 11/24/1779. Comm. Same as for Dower. To view 2/3 of the real est. and see if it can be div. among his children. Div. or appr. Appr.: 10/2/1780.1,162.00 dollars. Oaths 10/2/1780 Little, Jesse Page and Asa Page to Samuel Little, JP. APPR. WARR.: Comm.: Jonathan Webster, John Knight, Joseph Knight, Daniel Richards and Jona. Poor. To view 2/3 of the real est. and appr. at its present value in silver money, excluding the land in Perrys Town, Hillsborough Co. Appr. also includes several pews in meeting house. Appr. 1,718.00 dollars. Oaths 12/4/1780 Joseph Knight, Poor and Richards to Saml. Little, JP. DECREE SETTLM.: 3/22/1781. Caleb Noyes, oldest son, appearing and consenting, the real est. is settled on him, Caleb to pay each of his co-heirs of age within 6 months and those under 21 within 2 years, $214.00 & 3/4 of Spanish milled dollars or other current money equal thereto, with interest. Cert.: Of W. Parker, Reg. that Caleb gave bond. BOND: 3/22/1781. Of Caleb Noyes, Hampstead yeoman. Bond L80000.0.0. Sureties: Nathaniel Peabody, esq.; Enoch Noyes, gent. and James Noyes, yoeman, all of Atkinson. Witnesses: Benaiah Clement and William Cogswell. APPR. WARR.: 8/28/1781. Comm.: Benjamin Stone, gent.; Daniel Richards, Jesse Sawyer, Humphrey Noyes Jr. and Joseph French, Atkinson yoemen. To appr. the value of Dower since death of widow at the present value in silver at 0.6.8 an ounce. Appr.: 10/22/1781. L270.14.3. Oaths 10/22/1781 Comm. to Nathl. Peabody, JP. DECREE SETTLM.: 4/24/1782. Caleb Noyes, oldest son, appearing and consenting, the Dower is settled on him, Caleb to pay each of his co-heirs L33.16.9.1 1/2, those of age within 6 months and those under 21 within 8 months, with interest. BOND: 4/24/1782. Of Caleb Noyes, Atkinson yoeman. Bond L600.0.0. Sureties: Enoch Noyes, gent. and James Noyes, yoeman, both of Atkinson.

Witnesses: Nathl. Parker and Saml. Pilsbury. ACCOUNT: 1/30/1783. Of Caleb Noyes, surviving Admr. As in his Account, the heirs have neglected to pay him the bal. of $39.34 due him. Requests License to sell real est. to that amount. ADDL. ACCOUNT: 6/1/1797. Of Admr. Allowed 6/28/1797, the majority of heirs having been notified. LICENSE: 8/21/1799. To Admr. Cert.: Of Wm. Parker, Reg. Upon settlm. of the Addl. Account, there is a bal. due Admr. of L11.16.1=$39.34. License allowed for $60.00. The Account includes the shares of bal. due from Mary Noyes decd., Thomas Noyes, Martha Noyes, Anna Noyes, Caleb Noyes and Peter Clement, esq. as Admr. est. Clark Noyes decd.

1899. NUDD, THOMAS (1780) #4610
EST. Hampton gent. decd. testate. WILL: Drawn 6/29/1776. Legatees: Wife-Deborah; Son-Simon; Daus.-Hannah Ward, Sarah Towle and Molley Marston. Exec.-son Simon. His sig. Witnesses: James Philbrick. John Moulton 5th and Joseph Dow. CERT. WILL (D25:329): 3/26/1780. Presented by Exec. and witnesses Moulton and Dow. ADMIN.: 3/26/1780 Exec. Simon Nudd, Hampton gent. Bond L5000.0.0. Sureties: Joseph Dow, esq. and John Moulton, yoeman, both of Hampton. Witnesses: Nathl. Bachellor and W. Parker.

1900. NUTE, WILLIAM (1791) #5712
Incorrect name. See File #5670 WILLIAM SHUTE (1791). This file originally contained the Invy., which was moved to #5670.

1901. NUTTER, JOHN (1777) #4383
EST. Newington esq. decd. ADMIN.: 8/27/1777. Admrs.: Ann Nutter, widow and Hatevil Nutter, yoeman, both of Newington. Bond L500.0.0. Sureties: William Furber, gent. and Josph Dodge, yoeman, both of Newington. Witness John Cram. INVY. WARR.: 11/24/1777. Comm.: Richd. Downing, Samll. Shackford, gent. and John Colman, yoeman. Invy.: Value 313.19.0. Oaths 11/25/1777 Comm. to H. Wentworth, JP. Oath 11/26/1777 Hatevil Nutter, an Admr., to W. Parker, Reg. & JP with a note that the other Admr. was sworn by H. Wentworth, esq.

1902. NUTTER, CAPT. SAMUEL (1771) #3857
EST. Newington gent. decd. intestate. ADMIN.: 7/10/1771. Admx. Sarah Nutter, Newington widow. Bond L500.0.0. Sureties: Joseph Adams, gent. and Joseph Dam, yoeman, both of Newington. INVY.: Appr. 9/23/1771. Comm.: Benjamin Adams and Ephraim Pickering. Value L426.15.6. Returned 9/24/1771. PETITION: 3/29/1775. Of Joseph Pevey and Arabella his wife and Daniel Walker and Betty his wife, daus. of decd. For Div. of real est., which, they claim, Admx. has been holding for her own

benefit without settling est. ORDER: For hearing on the Pet. and for Admx. to exhibit Account.

1903. OAKES, SAMUEL (1794) #5970
EST. Portsmouth husbm. decd. testate. WILL: Drawn 1/29/1794. Legatees: Wife-Hannah; His wife's nephew Thomas Beck. Exec.-Thomas Beck Jr. His sig. Witnesses: Tobias Banfill, Samuel Whidden and Thomas Cotton. CERT. WILL (D31:183): 2/19/1794. Presented by Exec. and witnesses Banfill and Whidden. INVY.: Appr. 5/10/1794. Comm.: Nathaniel Banfill and Phinehas Hodgdon. Value (torn). Rough esti. L95.0.0+. Oaths 5/10/1794 Exec. and Comm. to Geo. Gains, JP. Note: The Invy. is partially destroyed and no D. record found.

1904. O'BRIEN, DANIEL (1778) #4481
EST. Portsmouth mariner and yoeman decd. intestate. ADMIN.: 10/22/1778. Admrs.: Hunking Wentworth, esq. and George Wentworth, merchant, both of Portsmouth. Bond L500.0.0. Sureties: Nahum Ward, merchant and Capt. John Mendum, both of Portsmouth. Witnesses: John Greenleaf and Andrew Clark. INVY.: Appr. 12/29/1778. Comm.: H. Wentworth and Geo. Wentworth. Value L270.0.0, all cash in possession of the Wentworths. Oaths 12/29/1778 Hunking Wentworth to Saml. Penhallow, JP. Oath 3/29/1779 Geo. Wentworth to George Gains, JP.

1905. ODEL, THOMAS (1781) #4742
EST. Stratham yoeman decd. testate. WILL: Drawn 12/20/1779. Legatees: Wife-Mary; Sons-Thomas and James; Daus.-Mary Wiggin and Hannah Kennison; Grandson-Daniel French. Execs.-sons Thomas and James. His sig. Witnesses: Thomas Moore Jr., Martha Moore and Saml. Lane. CERT. WILL (D26:188): 9/26/1781. Presented by Execs. and witnesses Thomas Moore Jr. and Martha Moore. INVY. WARR.: 9/26/1781. Comm.: Thomas Moore Jr., Jacob Low and John Taylor, all of Stratham. INVY.: Value L1419.3.6. Oaths 11/28/1781 Comm. and Execs. to W. Parker, Reg.

1906. ODIORNE, DANIEL, ET. ALS. (1792) #5789
See A#1578 1/2 Jotham Odiorne (1751)

1907. ODIORNE, EBENEZER (1772) #3911
EST. Portsmouth chaisemaker decd. intestate. ADMIN.: 3/5/1772. Admx. Sarah Odiorne, Portsmouth widow. Bond L500.0.0. Sureties: Saml. Sherburne and Thomas Chadbourn, Portsmouth yoemen. Witnesses: Saml. (Walton?) and Sarah Wentworth. INVY.: Appr. 5/8/1772. Comm.: Temple Knight and Thomas Chadbourn. Value L215.4.0. Oaths 5/9/1772 Admx. and Comm. to judge.

1908. ODIORNE, JOHN (1779) #4549
EST. New Castle yoeman decd. intestate. ADMIN. (D25:154): 5/12/1779. Admr. Benjamin Odiorne. Sureties: Daniel Tilton, esq. and Minor Daniels, yoeman, both of Exeter. INVY. (D25:158): Appr. 6/12/1779. Comm.: John Blunt, Thomas Seavy and Samuel Wallace. Value L2863.14.0. Oaths 6/18/1779 Blunt and Wallace to Samuel Penhallow, JP. Oath 6/21/1779 Admr. to W. Parker, JP & Reg. APPR. WARR.: 1/1/1783. Comm.: John Blunt, esq. and Abraham Trefethen, miller, both of New Castle; Amos Sevey, esq. and Jeremiah Berry, yoemen, both of Rye and Joseph Banfill, Portsmouth yoeman. To view the real est. and see if it can be div. among his children and the legal reps. of those dead. Div, giving double share to oldest son and single share to each of others or appr. They are also to appr. the annual income, exclusive of taxes and labor. APPR.: 1/21/1783. Value of 2/3 of the real est. L240.16.6. Oaths 2/1/1783 Blunt, esq. and Banfill and on 3/6/1783 Berry to Saml. Penhallow, JP. ORDER: To: John Blunt and Amos Sevey, esquires and James Randall, yoeman. They are requested to consider the enclosed bill of L134.19.6 from Benjamin Odiorne to the est. and report to the judge whether the whole or how much of it is due Benjamin. Report: 4/15/1783. The Comm. reports that they examined Benjamin and also Lydia and Abigail Odiorne, found John lived with their father and worked on the farm during the time for which he has billed. Because he has been without the use of his money so long a time, he should be allowed the sum charged. ACCOUNT: 5/28/1783. Of Admr. Allowed 5/28/1783. ADDL. ACCOUNT: 6/1783. DECREE SETTLM.: 6/6/1783. Benjamin Odiorne, only surviving son, appearing and consenting, the real est. is settled on him. Deducting what is still owed to Benjamin by the est. and there being 9 shares, Benjamin is to pay each of his 5 sisters L21.5.5.3 and the heirs of his oldest bro. decd. L42.10.11.2, being 2 shares, and the child of his other bro. L21.5.5.3 within 12 months, with interest. BOND: 6/16/1783. Of Benjamin Odiorne, New Castle yoeman. Bond L500.0.0. To pay his co-heirs per Decree Settlm. Sureties: Richard Brown, gent. And Jonathan Lock, yoeman, both of Rye. Witnesses: Nathl. Parker and W. Parker. ADDL. ACCOUNT (D33:359): 11/1800. Of Admr. Allowed 11/14/1800. PETITION: 11/30/1802. Of Samuel Odiorne of Rye, one of the heirs. States that Benjamin has not paid his co-heirs as ordered and requests permission to sue Bond of Admin. Decree: 12/13/1802. Benjamin appearing and showing no cause why Petition should not be granted, Petition granted.

1909. ODIORNE, JOSEPH (1778) #4458
EST. New Castle mariner decd. ADMIN.: 6/9/1778. Admr. John Odiorne, New Castle yoeman. Bond L500.0.0. Sureties: Jedediah Jewett, merchant and Minos Daniels, yoeman, both of Exeter. Witnesses: Jeremiah Parker and Wm. Parker.

1910. ODIORNE, JOTHAM (1751) A#1578 1/2
EST. Portsmouth esq. decd. Note: The following Petition found in #4093 Jotham Odiorne (1774) belongs here. PETITION: 8/20/1788. Of Peter Pearse, Portsmouth merchant, in right of his wife, an heir of Jotham Odiorne, Portsmouth esq. decd. States that Jotham died possessed of a large real and personal est. and had a Will which div. his est. between his wife and children as if he died intestatate. Execs. Nathaniel Meserve and Mark Hunking Wentworth have both died and never rendered an Account. Requests Wentworth's Exec. be cited to Account as the Exec. of Meserve is not in US. Note: The following Petition, Warrs. and Divs. recorded as #5789 Daniel Odiorne et. als. (1792) belong here. PETITION: 8/1/1792. Of: Daniel Odiorne; Peter Pearse and Mary his wife in her right; Samuel Penhallow Exec. of Will of Mehitable Odiorne; Sarah Hart; Sarah Preston; Mehitable Treadwell by her Gdn. Robert Odiorne Treadwell and Robert Odiorne Treadwell. For div. of land held in common which was part of the Dower of Mehitable Odiorne in est. her husb. Jotham Odiorne, Portsmouth esq. decd. Daniel Odiorne owns 1/8, Mary Pearse 1/8, Est. of Mehitable Odiorne 1/8 and 2/3 of 1/8, Sarah Hart 1/8, Sarah Preston 1/3 of 1/8, Mehitable Treadwell 1/8 and Robert Odiorne Treadwell 2/8. COPY OF PET. DIV. WARR.: 9/12/1792. Comm.: Isaac Rindge, esq.; William Hart, gent.; Nathaniel Marshall and George Wentworth, merchants and Nathaniel Appleton Haven, physician, all of Portsmouth. To div. part of Dower as in Petition. DUPL. OF DIV. WARR. DIV.: 10/5/1792. Divisees as in Petition. Oaths 10/5/1792 Rindge, Hart and Haven to Saml. Penhallow, JP. Allowed. Orig. Archives file includes Will, Admin., Account, Div. 1755 and Gdp. of children Samuel, Daniel, Mary and Sarah. Includes Map.

1911. ODIORNE, JOTHAM (1765) A#3168
EST. Portsmouth mariner decd. LICENSE (D23:134): 2/20/1775. To Admrs. Samuel Penhallow and Wyseman Claggett, esquires. To sell sufficient real est. to pay debts. Orig. Archives file includes Admin., Invy., Account 1769, Div. 1771, Account 1777, License 1789 and 2 Gdps. son Jotham.

1912. ODIORNE, JOTHAM (1774) #4093
EST. Portsmouth mariner decd. intestate. RENUN.: 3/10/1774. Of Mary Odiorne, widow of Jotham. Of Admin. Requests appointment of Peter Pearse. Allowed. ADMIN.: 3/22/1774. Admr. Peter Pearse, Portmouth merchant. Bond L1000.0.0. Sureties: George Meserve, esq. and Benjamin Mackay, saddler, both of Portsmouth. Witnesses: John Parker Jr. and Samuel Hale Jr. INVY.: Appr. 3/26/1774. Comm.: Richard Hart and John Sparhawk. Value L364.17.0. Oaths 3/26/1774 Admr. And Comm. to

judge. PETITION: 4/15/1774. Of Admr. For License. Allowed. LICENSE (D29:249): 2/3/1789. To Admr. To sell sufficient real est. to pay debts. ACCOUNT: Of Admr. Allowed 4/29/1775. 2D ACCOUNT 2/1793. Of Admr. Allowed 5/29/1793. There is a note which says Admr. cited by request of heirs to settle Account.

1913. ODIORNE, MEHITABLE (1789) #5412
EST. Portsmouth widow decd. testate. WILL: Drawn 12/9/1785. Legatees: Son-Daniel of Kittery, York Co., MA/ME. Reference to sons Jotham and Robert, both decd. Daus.- Mehetabel Treadwell wife of William Earl Treadwell, Mary Pearse wife of Peter Pearse Portsmouth merchant and Sarah Appleton widow of William Appleton. Grandsons-Samuel Pearse, Peter Pearse, Stephen Pearse and William Pearse sons of her dau. Mary and Peter Pearse, Robert Odiorne Treadwell son of William Earl Treadwell, Daniel Odiorne, and William Storer Elliot Appleton son of her dau. Widow Sarah Appleton; Grand-daus.-Sarah Preston dau. of her son Jotham decd. and Sarah's daus.-Sarah Hains and Hannah Hains; Margaret Gibbs Appleton dau. of her dau. Widow Sarah Appleton, Mary Pearse and Anna Stocker Pearse daus. of her dau. Mary and Peter Pearse; Samuel Odiorne grandson of William Deering. Execs.-Samuel Penhallow and son Daniel. Her sig. Witnesses: James Grouard, Danl. Peirce and John Barns. CERT. WILL (D29:245): 2/3/1789. Presented by Execs. and witnesses Grouard and Peirce. Note: All of the following items relating to a Petition of Sarah Appleton for a div. are recorded as #5422 Sarah Appleton (1789) but belong here. PETITION (#5422): 3/2/1789. Of Sarah Appleton. For div. of a house and land in Portsmouth and other buildings which Mehetabel Odiorne, Portsmouth widow decd. occupied and of which Sarah is seized of 3/8 in fee with others. PETITION (#5422): Dated by clerk 3/1789. Same as previous but with addition of 2/3 of 1/8 of another lot, 1/8 of a 3d lot and 1/8 of a lot at Pickering's Neck, all lately in occupation of Mehitabel Odiorne decd. ORDER: 3/19/1789. For hearing, Petitioner to advertise in N. H. newspapers. INVY.: Appr. 4/13/1789. Comm.: Richard Hart, Isaac Rindge and Joseph Whipple, esquires. Value L2930.13.3. Oath 4/14/1789 Samuel Penhallow, esq., an Exec., and Comm. to George Gains, JP. DIV. WARR. (#5422): 4/15/1789. Comm.: Samuel Hale, Joseph Whipple, Isaac Rindge and Jeremiah Libbey, esquires and William Hart, gent., all of Portsmouth. To set off to Sarah Appleton her share of land and bldgs. as in the 2d Petition, the Comm. to notify all concerned or their Gdns. DIV. (#5422): 4/27/1789. Comm. reports the Warr. not set off, the parties agreeing to defer it until a Div. Made between all those concerned. Oaths 6/4/1789 Hale, Whipple, Rindge and Hart and affirm. Libbey to Nathl. Adams, JP. NOTIFICATION (#5422): 5/20/1789. To Sarah Appleton. She is notified that Peter Pearse of Portsmouth and Mary his

wife; and Samuel Penhallow and A. R. Cutter, esquires, Gdns. of Mehetabel Treadwell, have petitioned the judge representing that they, with Sarah Appleton, Portsmouth widow are tenants in common of the mansion house of the late Mehetable Odiorne decd., Peter and Mary in her right owning 2/8, Mehetable Treadwell 3/8 and Sarah Appleton 3/8. They have requested div. Order: Sarah Appleton to be served with copy of Petition so she may appear at a hearing. Cert.: 6/2/1789. Of Edw. Hart, Dup. Sher. He has summoned Sarah by reading Petition to her. PETITION (#5422): 11/16/1789. Of: Widow Sarah Appleton; Peter Pease, merchant, and Mary his wife; Peter Pearse Jr., merchant; and Samuel Penhallow and Ammi Ruhamah Cutter, esquires, Gdns. of Mehetabel Treadwell, wife of William Earl Treadwell. For div. of the mansion house. They recommend a Comm. to George Gains, esq.; Thos. Sheafe, Peter Coues, Alexander Ewen and Jacob Walden. DIV. WARR.: 11/18/1789. Comm. as requested. To div. the mansion house with its land. Divisees: Sarah Appleton, Peter Pearse and Mary his wife, Mehetabel Treadwell and Peter Pearse Jr. PETITION: 7/21/1790. Of Saml. Penhallow, an Exec. For License. Gives known claims of L488.12.1. Granted. LICENSE (D29:397): 7/21/1790. To Execs. To sell real est. to amount of L300.0.0. PETITION: 10/20/1790. Of Samuel Penhallow, an Exec. For Comm. Insolvency. Gives income from sales and notes as L1086.18.1 and claims of L991.6.1. CLAIMS: 11/20/1791. Comm.: Supply Clap, James Sheafe and Danl. R. Rogers. Total L425.6.4 3/4. Oaths 8/16/1791 Comm. to Nathl. Adams, JP. Addl. Claims: 11/20/1791 bringing total to L468.7.10 3/4. Oaths 11/30/1791 Comm. to Nathl. Adams, JP. PETITION: 2/15/1792. Of Saml. Penhallow, an Exec. He still needs L149.6.11 to discharge claims. Requests judge decide how to raise the money. LICENSE (D30:204): 2/15/1792. To Saml. Penhallow, an Exec. To sell real est. to amount of L150.0.0. ACCOUNT: Of Samuel Penhallow, an Exec. Allowed 5/20/1793. ADDL. ACCOUNT: 10/21/1795. Of Samuel Penhallow, esq., an Exec. Allowed 10/21/1795. DIV.: 1/30/1790. Comm. and Divisees as in Warr. Allowed 2/17/1790. Includes Map. ADDL. ACCOUNT: Of Samuel Penhallow, esq., an Exec. decd. Receipt: 6/3/1797. Of Peter Pearse. He has received from Execs. L20.10.10.3 on behalf of himself and the rest of the heirs in full bal. of the Execs. Account and dischanges them. Allowed 6/21/1797.

1914. ODIORNE, ROBERT (1762) A#2946
EST. Portsmouth merchant decd. testate. LICENSE (D29:417): 8/24/1790. To Admr. d.b.n. Robert Odiorne Treadwell. To sell real est. to amount of L740.0.0. Orig. Archives file includes Will, Invy., Bond, License (1764), Account, Prop. & Settlm. (1765), Addl. Prop. & Settlm. (1770), Addl. Prop. & Settlm. (1770), Admin. d.b.n. and Addl. Invy.

1915. ODIORNE, SAMUEL (1783) #4905
EST. Portsmouth mariner decd. intestate. ADMIN.: 6/17/1783. Admr. Benjamin Odiorne, New Castle yoeman. Bond L2000.0.0. Sureties: Jonathan Lock, yoeman and Richard Brown, gent., both of Rye. Witness Nathl. Parker. INVY.: Appr. 6/23/1783. Comm.: Jno. Blunt and Pierce Long, esquires and John Salter. Value L498.5.8. Oaths 6/23/1783 Comm. to Saml. Penhallow, JP. Oath 4/25/1783 Admr. to W. Parker, JP. GDP. Of the son of Samuel Odiorne, Portsmouth mariner decd. GDP.: 6/26/1783. Of Samuel, a minor under 14. Gdn. Joseph Holbrook, Portsmouth mariner. Bond L1000.0.0. Sureties: Ephraim Ham, blockmaker and William Blunt, boatbuilder, both of Portsmouth. Witnesses: Pierce Long and Saml. Ham. PETITION: 12/23/1800. Of Samuel Odiorne, Portsmouth mariner. Requests permission to sue Bond of Admin. of his uncle Benjamin Odiorne, who has never submitted an accounting of his admin. Order: 12/23/1800. Admr. to be to be cited to appear and exhibit his Account or in default his Bond of Admin. will be put in suit.

1916. ODLIN: ABIGAIL, CHARLOTTE, JOHN, MARYANN, PETER & WOODBRIDGE (1779) #4573
GDP. of the children of Rev. Woodbridge Odlin of Exeter, decd, intestate. GDP.: 9/27/1779. Of: Woodbridge and Peter, minors over 14 and of Abigail, John, Maryann and Charlotte, minors under 14. Gdn. Abigail Odlin, Exeter widow. Bond L2000.0.0. Sureties: Daniel Tilton, esq. and Dudley Odlin, gent., both of Exeter. Witnesses: Elizabeth Parker and W. Parker.

1917. ODLIN, ABIGAIL (1790) #5612
EST. Exeter widow decd. ADMIN.: 12/17/1790. Admr. Eliphalet Hale, Exeter gent. Bond L1000.0.0. Sureties: John Taylor Gilman and Nathaniel Gilman, Exeter esquires. Witnesses: Jotham Rollins and W. Parker. INVY.: Appr. 7/7/1791. Comm.: B. Lamson, Wm. Parker Jr. and Jona. Cass. Value L23.5.0. Oaths 7/7/1791 Parker and Cass to W. Parker, JP. PETITION: 3/12/1792. Of Admr. For Comm. Insolvency. Gives list claims of L153.19.6. Also notes that Invy. was L108.18.6. Invy. On file includes only land and he suggests perhaps Invy. of personal est is missing. BOND: 3/18/1793. Of Nathl. Gilman, Exeter esq. Bond L160.0.0. By an Act of NH General Court, Gilman is allowed to sell all the undivided right or share Charlotte Odlin has in est. of Hon. Peter Gilman, Exeter esq. decd., which descended to her mother Abigail Odlin decd. and all the real est. unsold which descended to her from est. her father Woodbridge Odlin, Exeter clerk decd. Gilman to account for proceeds and interest to Charlotte when she comes of age or with her heirs. Sureties: Samuel Gilman, Exeter merchant and Ebenezer Clifford, Kensington esq.

Witnesses: W. Parker and Huard Lanoiraix. CLAIMS: 11/7/1792. Comm.: John Haven, Saml. Tenney and Wm. Parker Jr. Total L25.4.10. Oaths 5/13/1793 Comm. to W. Parker, JP. ACCOUNT: 5/1793. Of Admr. Allowed 6/3/1793.

1918. ODLIN, CHARLOTTE (1788) #5335
GDP. Of the dau. of Rev. Woodbridge Odlin, Exeter clerk decd. GDP.: 3/6/1788. Of Charlotte, a minor under 14. Gdn. Nathl. Gilman, Exeter esq. Bond L500.0.0. Sureties: Dudley Odlin, esq. and Woodbridge Odlin, trader, both of Exeter. Witnesses: Nathl. Parker and W. Parker.

1919. ODLIN, CHARLOTTE, JOHN & MARYANN (1788) #5336
GDP. Of the children of Rev. Woodbridge Odlin, Exeter clerk decd. GDP.: 3/6/1788. Of: John and Maryann, minors over 14. Gdn. Dudley Odlin, Exeter esq. Bond L500.0.0. Sureties: Nathaniel Gilman, esq. and Woodbridge Odlin, trader, both of Exeter. Witnesses: N. Parker and W. Parker. GDP.: 12/2/1791. Of Maryann and Charlotte, minors over 14. Gdn. Nathl. Gilman, Exeter esq. Bond L2000.0.0. Sureties: Samuel Gilman 3d, gent. and Benjamin Lamson, innholder, both of Exeter. Witnesses: Nathl. Parker and John Parker. BOND: 1/10/1792. Of Nathaniel Gilman, Exeter esq., Gdn. of Maryann Odlin and Charlotte Odlin. Bond L1000.0.0. By an Act of the N. H. General Court the Gdn. is permitted to sell all of the share of Maryann and Charlotte in the est. of their father lying in Brentwood and account to the minors when they reach full age or as directed by judge. Sureties: John Taylor Gilman, esq. And Benjamin Connor Jr., yoeman, both of Exeter. Witnesses: Gideon Lamson and Sam. Gilman.

1920. ODLIN, CAPT. JOHN (1783) #4871
EST. Exeter gent. decd. intestate. RENUN.: 1/29/1783. Of Alice Odlin, widow of John. Of Admin. Requests appointment of her son Saml. Odlin. ADMIN.: 1/29/1783. Admr. Samuel Odlin, Exeter gent. Bond L4000.0.0. Sureties: Stephen Thing, yoeman and James Leavitt Jr., gent., both of Exeter. Witnesses: Paul Jewett and Nathl. Parker. INVY.: Appr. 4/29/1783. Comm.: Stephen Thing, Saml. Brooks and Eliphalet Hale. Value L4014.11.4. Oaths 4/30/1783 Brooks, Hale and Admr. to judge. DIV.: 3/21/1785. Comm.: Deacon Saml. Brooks, Stephen Thing, Capt. Trueworthy Gilman, Elipht. Hale and Joseph Cram. To div. 2/3 of the real est., giving oldest son 2 shares. Divisees: Sons-Samuel (oldest); Daus.-Elizabeth Lamson, Alice Odlin, Abigail Page and Sarah Fowl. Oaths 3/21/1785 Brooks, Gilman and Cram to W. Parker, Reg. & JP. Allowed 5/17/1790. ACCOUNT: Of Admr. Judge notes 2 postponements of consideration of Account. No oath or allowance. PETITION: 10/18/1792. Of: Saml. Odlin, Benja. Page, Robert Fowler (sic.), Alice Odlin and

Elizabeth Lamson. For div. of the Dower lands, Samuel owning 2 shares and each of others one share. DIV. WARR.: 10/18/1792. Comm.: Jeremiah Leavitt and Benjamin Lamson, innholders; Trueworthy Gilman, gent.; William Parker Jr., physician and Daniel Clark, clothier, all of Exeter. To div. the Dower. DIV.: Divisees: Samuel Odline (only surviving son, 2 shares), Elizabeth Lamson, Alis Odlin, Abigail Page and Sarah Fowler. Signed by Gilman, Lamson, Leavitt and Clark. DOWER: 3/21/1785. Comm. same as 1st Div. Of Widow Alice Odlin. No oaths, no allowance and noted by clerk as "returned 9/10/1799." Note: This file jacket is dated incorrectly as 1783.

1921. ODLIN, JUDITH (1796) #6174
EST. Exeter widow decd. ADMIN.: 1/18/1796. Admr. William Odlin, Exeter saddler. Bond $2,000.00. Sureties: Saml. Gilman, taylor and James Leavitt, gent., both of Exeter. Witness W. Parker. INVY.: Appr. 2/8/1796. Comm.: Benja. Boardman, Saml. Gilman and James Rundlett. Value L183.17.3. Oaths 5/2/1796 Comm. and Admr. to judge.

1922. ODLIN, REV. WOODBRIDGE (1778) #4498
EST. Exeter clerk decd. intestate. ADMIN.: 11/23/1778. Admx. Abigail Odlin, Exeter widow. Bond L1000.0.0. Sureties: John Giddinge and Daniel Tilton, Exeter esquires. Witnesses: Dudley Odlin and W. Parker. INVY.: Appr. 1/7/1779. Comm.: John Rice, Saml. Brooks and Eliphalet Hale. Value L10655.8.0. Note of several items omitted but no value given. Oaths 1/1779 Comm. to W. Parker, JP. Oath Admx. to W. Parker, Reg. & JP. DIV. WARR.: 10/27/1779. Comm.: Ebenezer Smith, Meredith, Strafford Co. esq.; Samuel Brooks, esq.; Eliphalet Giddinge and Elipht. Hale, gentlemen and Joseph Cram, yoeman, all of Exeter. To div. The real est., giving two shares to oldest son and one share to each of other children, having respect for any advanced settlm. or proportion any may have had during decd.'s lifetime and giving widow her Dower. Petition: 10/27/1779. Of Dudley Odlin, oldest son. States that in his education he has received much more than any of the other children. Requests in Div. he be given only one share as his full proportion. DOWER & DIV.: 11/5/1779. Divisees: Widow Abigail Odlin, her dower; Sons Dudley, Woodbridge, Peter and John; Daus.-Mary-Ann, Abigail and Charlotte (youngest dau.). Oaths 11/5/1779 Smith, Brooks and Cram to Wm. Parker, JP. Allowed 11/25/1779, there being no objections. ADMIN. D.B.N.: 1/1/1788. Admr. d.b.n Dudley Odlin, Exeter gent. Bond L1000.0.0. Sureties: Woodbridge Odlin, yoeman and Nathaniel Gilman, esq., both of Exeter. Witnesses: Nathl. Parker and W. Parker. INVY.: Comm.: Saml. Brooks, Joseph Cram and Saml. Odlin. Value not tallied. Esti. L725.0.0+. Oaths 3/6/1788 Comm. to W. Parker, JP. PETITION: 12/17/1790. Of:

Woodbridge Odlin, Peter Odlin and Nat. Gilman, heirs. They are heirs of ests. of both Rev. Woodbridge Odlin and Abigail Odlin, both decd. Request div. where it has not already been made and final settlm. Request appointment of Eliphalet Hale of Exeter as Admr. d.b.n. ADMIN. D.B.N.: 12/17/1790. Admr. d.b.n. Eliphalet Hale, Exeter gent. Bond L1000.0.0. Sureties: John Taylor Gilman and Nathl. Gilman, Exeter esquires. Witnesses: Jonathan Kollins and W. Parker. INVY.: Comm.: Benjamin Lamson, Wm. Parker Jr. and Jona. Cass. Value L554.13.10. Oaths 4/1791 Comm. and Admr. d.b.n. to W. Parker, JP. DIV.: 8/1/1788. Comm.: Eliphalet Hale, Samuel Odlin, Joseph Cram, Wm. Parker Jr. and Benj. Lamson. To div. the real est. of Rev. Odlin and Abigail his wife. Divisees: sons-Dudley (oldest, double share), Woodbridge, Peter and John; Daus.-Abigail Gilman, Mary Ann Odlin and Charlotte Odlin. Oaths 8/13/1793 Hale and Lamson to Wm. Parker, JP. Allowed. ACCOUNT: 5/13/1793. Of Admr. d.b.n. Allowed 5/12/1793 the heirs having been notified and no objections.

1923. ORDWAY: ANNA, DOLLY, EDWARD & NEHEMIAH (1792) #5755
GDP. Of the children of Thomas Ordway, South Hampton yoeman decd. GDP. (D27:185): 2/28/1783. Of: Hannah and Nehemiah, minors over 14 and of Edward a minor under 14. Gdn. Edward Robie of Candia. Sureties: Nathaniel Emerson, Candia esq. and Daniel Gordon, Epping gent. GDP.: 4/3/1792. Of: Anna, Nehemiah and Dolly, minors under 14. Gdn. John Bartlet, Amesbury, Essex Co., MA tanner. Bond L1000.0.0. Sureties: Israel Sawyer, yoeman and Joseph Merrill, esq. both of South Hampton. Witnesses: Benjn. Barnard Jr. and Hannah Barnard.

1924. ORDWAY, DAVID (1783) NO#
GDP. Of the son of Samuel Ordway, Goffstown, Hillsborough Co. yoeman decd. GDP. (D27:201): 3/14/1783. Of David, a minor over 14. Gdn. Ebenezer Parker, Atkinson husbm. Sureties: Nathaniel Peabody and Benjamin Stone, Atkinson esquires.

1925. ORDWAY, EDWARD (1789) #5484
GDP. Of the son of John Ordway, Chester physician decd. GDP.: 9/16/1789. Of Edward, a minor over 14. Gdn. Bradbury Cilley, Nottingham esq. Bond L500.0.0. Sureties: Thomas Bartlett, esq. and John Pingrey Williams, trader, both of Nottingham. Witnesses: W. Parker and Nathl. Parker.

1926. ORDWAY, JOHN (1773) #4045
EST. South Hampton cordwainer decd. testate. WILL: Drawn 10/31/1765. Legatees: Wife-Sarah; Son-Nehemiah; Dau.-Mary Sawyer; Grandson-Richard Ordway son of his son Nehemiah. Exec.-Son Nehemiah. His sig. Witnesses: Abraham Rowell, Samuel Stuart and Elijah Rowell. CERT. WILL: 9/29/1773. Presented by Exec. and witnesses Abraham Rowell and Elijah Rowell. ADMIN.: 9/29/1773. Exec. Nehemiah Ordway, Amesbury, Essex Co., Mass. Bay physician. Bond L500.0.0. Sureties: Elijah Rowell and James Hadlock, both of South Hampton. Witnesses: Samuel Parker and Abraham Rowell.

1927. ORDWAY, DR. JOHN (1775) #4183
EST. Chester physician decd. intestate. RENUN.: 11/8/1775. Of Sarah Ordway, widow of John. Of Admin. Requests appointment of her father, Capt. Saml. Robie. Witnesses: Jabez Robie and Edward Robie. ADMIN.: 11/10/1775. Admr.: Samuel Robie, Chester gent. Bond L1000.0.0. Sureties: Robert Wilson, of Chester and Samuel Moore of Candia, esquires. Witnesses: Nathl. Parker and Wm. Parker Jr. INVY. WARR.: 11/10/1775. Comm.: Samuel Emerson, esq. and Stephen Morse both of Chester. INVY.: Appr. 1/20/1776. Value not tallied. Esti. L272.0.0+. Oaths 4/20/1776 Comm. to Robt. Wilson, JP. Oath 4/24/1776 Admr. to judge. ACCOUNT: 11/10/1775. Of Admr. Allowed 10/29/1778. GDP. Of the children of John Ordway, Chester physician decd. GDP.: 2/28/1783. Of: Hannah and Nehemiah, minors over 14 and of Edward, a minor under 14. Gdn. Edward Robie, Candia gent. Bond L1000.0.0. Sureties: Nathaniel Emerson, Candia esq. and Daniel Gordon, Epping gent. Witness Nathl. Parker. DIV.: Comm.: John Webster, Jabez French, Isaac Blaydel and Jonathan Dearborn. To set off Dower of Sarah Gordon, in est. of Dr. John Ordway and div. remaining among his surviving children. Divisees: Sarah Gordon, her Dower; Sons-Nehemiah and Edward; Daus.-Sarah Thirsten (oldest dau.) and Hannah Ordway. Oaths 4/4/1783 Comm. to Saml. Emerson, JP. Allowed.

1928. ORDWAY, MOSES (1792) #5775
EST Plaistow yoeman decd. ADMIN.: 5/28/1792. Admr. John Ordway, Lyndeborough, Hillsborough Co. yoeman. Bond L1000.0.0. Sureties: Benjamin Bly, cordwainer and Moses Bly, yoeman, both of Plaistow. Witnesses: Dustin Cheney and Josiah Gains Peabody. INVY.: Appr. 8/16/1792. Comm.: John White, Joshua Dow and Moses Harriman. Value L35.12.6. Oaths 8/16/1792 Dow and Harriman to John White, JP. Oath 8/17/1792 Admr. to W. Parker, JP. PETITION: 4/12/1793. Of Admr. For Comm. Insolvency. States claims already L40.0.0. Granted. CLAIMS WARR.: 4/12/1793. Comm.: John White, esq.; Dustin Cheney and Moses

Harriman, yoemen, all of Plaistow. Cert.: Of Comm. that they had advertised the times and place of their meetings to receive claims. ACCOUNT: 3/15/1794. Of Admr. Allowed 3/15/1792. CLAIMS: Total L49.7.0. Oaths 12/3/1793 Cheney and Harriman to John White, JP. PROP. & SETTLM.: Claims L49.7.9. Amount to be proportioned L13.16.9. Allowed 4/16/1794 with order to Admr. to pay. DUPL. COPY OF PROP. & SETTLM.

1929. ORDWAY, THOMAS (1789) #5409
EST. Of South Hampton decd. INVY.: Comm.: Benja. Clough, Jacob Collins and John Currier. Value L381.1.5. Oath 11/17/1789 Currier and affirms. Clough, Collins and Admr. Joseph Merril, esq. To judge. LIST. CLAIMS: Total L64.12.6. LIST CLAIMS: 5/17/1790. Signed by Admr. Total L65.10.0. Some are included in previous list. ACCOUNT: Of Admr. Allowed 5/17/1790. Account includes main. 2 children. ACCOUNT: Dated by clerk 9/1790. Of Admr. With request for License. Granted. LICENSE (D29:422): 9/17/1790. To Admr. To sell real est. to L45.0.0. DOWER: 11/5/1790. Comm.: Jacob Collins, Henry French, Israel Sawyer and Benjamin Clough. Of Widow Prudence Ordway. They also appr. the neat income of 2/3 of real est. at L9.17.9. Oaths 11/5/1790 Collins, French and Clough to Nathl. Bacheller, JP. Allowed 11/17/1790. ACCOUNT: Of Admr. Allowed 6/18/1792.

1930. ORNE, THERESA (1793) #5877
GDP. Of the dau. of Joseph Orne, Salem, Essex Co., MA physician decd. GDP.: 4/8/1793. Of Teresa, a minor under 14. Gdn. Theresa Orne, Exeter widow. Bond L1000.0.0. Sureties: Noah Emery, esq. and Benjamin Abbot, gent., both of Exeter. Witnesses: Nathl. Emery and Nat Parker. RELEASE GDP. (D35:161): 3/10/1804. Of Theresa Orne, Exeter single woman. To Theresa Orne, Exeter widow, her Gdn. For receipt of $20.00 she discharges Gdn. Oath 3/10/1804 Theresa Orne to Wm. Parker, JP.

1931. ORR, ANDREW (1784) #5002
EST. Portsmouth merchant decd. intestate. ADMIN.: 4/24/1784. Admr. Jacob Sheafe Jr., Portsmouth merchant. Bond L2000.0.0. Sureties: Thomas Sheafe and William Sheafe, Portsmouth merchants. Witnesses: Martin Parry and Edmund Quincy. INVY. WARR.: 4/24/1784. Comm.: John Parker, esq.; Daniel Rindge Rogers and William Dame, Portsmouth merchants. INVY.: Appr. 4/29/1784. Value L58.8.1 1/2. Oaths 6/10/1784 Admr. And Comm. to Saml. Penhallow, JP. PETITION: 12/1787. Of Admr. For Comm. Insolvency. Shows claims of L174.11.0. CLAIMS WARR.: 12/19/1787. Comm.: Samuel Hale and Isaac Rindge, esquires and Danl. Rindge Rogers, merchant, all of Portsmouth. CLAIMS: 7/28/1778.

Total L169.15.10 1/4. Oaths 7/29/1788 Comm. to Oliver Whipple, JP. ACCOUNT: 7/29/1788. Of Admr. Allowed 6/17/1789. PROP. & SETTLM.: Claims L169.15.10. Amount to be proportioned L112.18.5. Allowed 7/15/1789 with order to Admr. to pay.

1932. ORR, GEORGE (1779) #4519
EST. Londonderry yoeman decd. ADMIN.: 2/4/1779. Admr. Timothy Carr, Chester yoeman. Bond L1000.0.0. Sureties: William Gregg, esq. and Robert Smith, gent., both of Londonderry. Witnesses: Simeon Ladd "to R. Smith" and W. Parker (Jr.?)

1933. ORR, JAMES (1778) #4450
GDP. Of the son of William Orr, Londonderry yoeman decd. PETITION: 3/3/1778. Of James Orr. He chooses John McKeen as his Gdn. GDP.: 4/29/1778. Of James, a minor over 14. Gdn. John McKeen Jr., Londonderry yoeman. Bond L500.0.0. Sureties: Abram. Reid, gent. and James Cochran, both of Windham. Witnesses: Nathl. Parker and Wm. Parker.

1934. ORR, JAMES (1797) #6334
EST. Londonderry yoeman decd. testate. WILL: Drawn 3/24/1797. Legatees: Wife-Lucy; Son-John; Daus.-Susannah, Anne and Eliza; Mother-Jean Orr. Execs.-wife Lucy and friend Daniel McKeen. His sig. Witnesses: Geo. Reid, William Boyd and Samuel McKeen. CERT. WILL (D32:291): 4/19/1797. Presented by Execs. and all witnesses. ADMIN.: 4/19/1797. Execs.: Lucy Orr, widow and Daniel McKeen, yoeman, both of Londonderry. Bond $2,000.00. Sureties: George Reid, esq. and John Adams, yoeman, both of Londonderry. Witnesses: John Morrison and Nathl. Parker. INVY.: Appr. 4/22/1797. Comm.: Wm. Boyd, Geo. Reid and Samuel McKeen. Value $2,811.43 plus notes not tallied. Oaths 8/16/1797 Reid, McKeen and Execs. to judge. PETITION: 12/20/1797. Of Execs. For License. Give claims as about $550.00. Granted. LICENSE (D32:412): 12/20/1797. To Execs. To sell real est. to amount of $375.00. ACCOUNT: 4/1803. Of Execs. Allowed 4/20/1803 the objections of the Gdn. of the children having been considered. Account includes main. 3 children. DOWER WARR.: 8/17/1803. Comm.: Georg Reid, esq.; William Choate, Aaron Choate and John Moore, gent., all of Londonderry and John Dinsmoor, Windham esq. Of Lucy Shute in est. of James Orr. ADDL. ACCOUNT: 8/17/1803. Of Daniel McKeen, an Exec. Allowed 8/17/1803 having been consented to by Gdn. DOWER: 8/15/1804. Oaths 8/15/1804 William Choate, Aaron Choate and Moor to Isaac Thom, JP. Allowed. ADDL ACCOUNT: 12/18/1805. Of Daniel McKeen, an Exec. Allowed 12/18/1805. Account includes an item for payment of board for children to

Benjamin Shute and wife and the bal. of account as being paid to Wm. Boyd, Gdn. of the children. Note: This file also contains a Cert. 12/16/1797. Of Elijah Dwinell Jr. and Mary Ann Dwinell. They have examined the Account of John Bell of his Gdp. of Mary Ann's est., are satisfied and willing that it be allowed. Witnesses: J. Bell Jr. and Elisha Dwinel. No identification of Mary Ann has been found, unless she is the dau. Ann in Will.

1935. ORR, WILLIAM (1776) #4234
EST. Londonderry husbm. decd. testate. WILL: Drawn 5/24/1775. Legatees: Wife-Jean; Sons-George and James; Daus.-Jean Carr alias Orr and Annas Orr. Execs.-Friend John Mackeen and son George. His sig. Witnesses: John Moor, John Cochran and Joseph Mackeen. CERT. WILL: 5/29/1776. Presented by Execs. and witnesses Moore and Cochran. INVY.: Comm.: John Moor and John Cochran. Value L377.18.10. Oaths 8/27/1776 Comm. to Matthew Thornton, JP. Oath 8/28/1776 George Orr, an Exec., to judge.

1936. OSGOOD, HANNAH (1775) #4143
GDP. Of the dau. of James Osgood of Rumford. GDP.: 6/8/1763 (sic) Note on back says "Bond 1775." Of Hannah. Gdn. Hannah Osgood, Rumford widow. Bond L500.0.0. Surety John Noyes, Pembroke esq. Witness: W. Parker Jr. Note: Hannah is referred to in the Will of her father James probated in 1757.

1937. OSGOOD, HANNAH (1783) #4898
EST. Concord widow decd. testate. WILL: Drawn 5/4/1783. Legatees: Sons-Samuel, James, Benjamin, John, and Richard Hazen Osgood; Daus.-Anna Stickney and Elizabeth Webster; Negro woman Lucy. Exec.-son-in-law Thomas Stickney. Her sig. Witnesses: Timo. Walker, John Kimball and William Duncan. CERT. WILL (D27:231): 5/28/1783. Presented by Exec. and witnesses Walker, esq. and Kimball.

1938. OSGOOD, REUBEN (1798) #6493
EST. Epping husbm. decd. testate. WILL: Drawn 8/20/1798. Legatees: Wife-Mary; Sons-Samuel, Joseph, Reuben and William; Grandsons-Reuben Page, Israel Page and Ebenezer Page; Granddau.- Molley Page. Exec.-son William; His sig. Witnesses: Enoch Coffin, Aaron Smith and Wm. Stearns. CERT. WILL (D32:523): 9/13/1798. Presented by Exec. and witnesses Coffin and Smith.

1939. OTIS, ANDREW (1787) #5298
EST. Deerfield weaver decd. ADMIN.: 10/31/1787. Admx. Betty Otis, Deerfield widow. Bond L500.0.0. Sureties: Samuel McCluer and Chase Prescott, Deerfield yoemen. Witnesses: John Parker and W. Parker. INVY.: Appr. 1/10/1788. Comm.: George Evens and Benjamin Fellows. Value not tallied. Est. L9.0.0+. Oaths 1/10/1788 Comm. and Admx. to Jeremiah Eastman, JP.

PAAGE. See also Page

1940. PAAGE, NATHANIEL (1778) #4502
EST. Atkinson yoeman decd. testate. WILL: Drawn 3/25/1777. Legatees: Sons Samuel and John who have received their shares. Daus.-Ruth wife of Benjamin Honeyford, Phebe wife of Micah Rice and Sarah wife of Joseph Grover; Children of his dau. Phebe; Son-in-law Joseph Grover. Exec.-son-in-law Joseph Grover. His sig. Witnesses: Benjamin Emery, Moses Emery and John Knight. CERT. WILL: 11/25/1778. Presented by Exec. and witnesses Knight and Benjamin Emery. ADMIN.: 11/25/1778. Exec. Joseph Grover of Atkinson. Bond L1000.0.0. Sureties: Benjamin Emery and John Knight, both of Atkinson. Witnesses: Nathl. Gilman and W. Parker.

1941. PACKER, MARTHA (1790) #5604
EST. Portsmouth widow decd. testate. WILL: Drawn 1/28/1783. Legatees: Friends-Eleazer Russell, esq. and Ann Russell; John Sparhawk Jr. son of John and Abigail Sparhawk; Martha Wentworth dau. of Michael and Martha Wentworth; Amy Odling wife of Winthrop Odling of Exeter; The servant maid who is living with her at her death; Eunice Butler wife of Alford Butler; Abigail Sparhawk wife of John Sparhawk; Martha Russell; Mary Cotton and Susanna Davis, both of Boston, MA; Martha Creighton of Newmarket; Ann Pearson Odling dau. of Winthrop Odling of Exeter; The poor "without distinction" as decided by Execs. Execs.-John Sparhawk esq. and Jeremiah Libbey. Her sig. Witnesses: William Hart, Isaac Rindge, John Peirce and Thos. R. Rogers. CERT. WILL (D29:450): 12/8/1790. Presented by Jeremiah Libbey, surviving Exec. and witnesses Hart, Rindge and Peirce. ADMIN.: 12/8/1790. Exec. Jeremiah Libbey, Portsmouth esq. Bond L1000.0.0. Sureties: Isaac Rindge, esq. and John Peirce, merchant, both of Portsmouth. Witnesses: W. Parker and Nathl. Parker. INVY.: Appr. 12/10/1790. Comm.: John Furnald and Danl. R. Rogers. Value L132.15.3. Oaths 1/15/1791 Comm. and affirm. Exec. to Nathl. Adams, JP. ACCOUNT: 2/16/1791. Of Exec. Allowed 2/16/1791. ADDL. ACCOUNT: 3/16/1791. Of Exec. Allowed 3/16/1791. Account notes payment of legacies to Martha Creighton now wife of Walter Neal and Woodbridge Odlin for his dau. Winthrop Odling incorrect.

1942. PACKER, REBECCA (1782) #4791
EST. Of Portsmouth decd. ADMIN.: 4/5/1782. Admr. Thomas Packer, Greenland husbm. of est. his mother. Bond L1000.0.0. Sureties: Joshua Haines, gent. and George Philbrook, yoeman, both of Greenland. Witnesses: William Jenkins Jr. and Joseph (Harress?-sp. uncer.)

1943. PACKER, SHERIFF THOMAS (1771) #3856
EST. Portsmouth esq. decd. testate. WILL: Drawn 6/22/1771. Legatees: Wife-Martha; Son-Thomas; Grandson-Oldest son of his son Thomas; His Excellency John Wentworth, Gov., to give what he feels needed to his, Thomas', poor relations. Exec.: Gov. John Wentworth. His mark. Witnesses: Clement Jackson, Hall Jackson, Clement March and William Parker. CERT. WILL (D21:105): 6/27/1771. Presented by Exec. and all witnesses. ADMIN.: 6/27/1771. Exec. John Wentworth, Portsmouth esq., Gov., Commander-in-Chief over His Majesty's Province of NH. Bond L2000.0.0. Surety John Hurd of Portsmouth. Witnesses: Samuel Brewster and David Brewster.

1944. PACKER, THOMAS (1781) #4718
EST. Portsmouth esq. decd. ADMIN.: 6/19/1781. Admr. Thomas Packer, Greenland husbm. Bond L40000.0.0. Sureties: Noah Emery of Exeter and Ephraim Pickering of Newington, esquires. Witnesses: Nathl. Parker and W. Parker. INVY.: Appr. 7/24/1781. Comm.: Joshua Brackett, esq.; Capt. Geo. Wentworth and Capt. John Blunt. Value L17560.0.0. Oath 7/27/1781 Brackett and Blunt on 8/17/1781 Wentworth and on 8/29/1781 Admr. to Saml. Penhallow, JP.

1945. PACKER, THOMAS (1794) #5971
EST. Portsmouth husbm. decd. intestate. CAVEAT: 1/20/1794. Of Hall Jackson, Portsmouth physician. States that in a pre-nuptial agreement Molly Packer released all her right of dower. Asa creditor and on behalf of heirs of Thomas Packer, Portsmouth gent. decd. requests she may not be granted admin. ADMIN.: 2/19/1794. Admx. Molly Packer, Portsmouth widow. Bond L1000.0.0. Sureties: Walter Akerman,, tanner and Isaac Rindge, esq., both of Portsmouth. Witnesses: W. Parker and Jona. M. Sewall. CONTRACT: 12/25/1779. Between Thomas Packer, Greenland husbm. and Molly Tarlton, Greenland spinster. A pre-marital agreement. Gives Molly an annual annuity of $12.0.0 plus use of part of the mansion house and bldgs., all the household goods she brings to the marriage, provisions of food, etc., all at no expense to her, as long as she remains Thomas' widow. Molly gives up all rights of dower in exchange. The parties mutually bind themselves in the penal sum of L6000000.0.0. Thomas' sig. and Molly's mark. Witnesses: (Thos.?) Haines, Jacob Haness

and Saml. Hutchings. Marked by clerk as filed by Hall Jackson 2/19/1794. INVY.: Appr. 3/15/1794. Comm.: Supply Clap, William Hart and Clement March. Value L9241.6.0. Oaths 3/15/1794 Comm. and Admx. to Saml. Penhallow, JP. PETITION:3/18/1794. Of Admx. Her son Mathew Bramble Packer has just reached age 14 and has chosen her as his Gdn. Requests gdp. PETITION: 3/18/1794. Of Admx. For License. Gives claims of L998.5.4. Granted. LICENSE: 3/19/1794. To Admx. To sell real est. to amount ofL800.0.0. PETITION: 9/8/1794. Of Admx. For License. Former License was insufficient as claims already exhibited plus others not yet in will be nearly L2000.0.0. Granted. LICENSE (D31:342): 9/10/1794. To Admx. To sell real est. to amount of L400.0.0. ACCOUNT: 2/17/1795. Of Danl. R. Rogers atty. to Admx. Allowed 2/18/1795. PETITION: 2/18/1795. Of Danl. R. Rogers atty. to Admx. For License. States that income from previous sales insufficient to discharge claims. Granted. LICENSE (D31:477): 2/18/1795. To Admx. To sell real est. to amount of $6,000.00. ADDL. ACCOUNT: 3/2/1796. Of Danl. R. Rogers atty. to Admx. Allowed 3/4/1796. ADDL. ACCOUNT: 10/19/1796. Of Danl. R. Rogers atty. to Admx. Allowed 10/19/1796. APPR. WARR.: 10/19/1796. Comm.: Jeremiah Libbey, esq.; Jacob Walden, innholder, both of Portsmouth and Clement March, Greenland esq. To appr. neat yearly income of est. Appr.: 1/9/1797. Value $350.00. Oaths 1/12/1797 Comm. to Geo. Gains, JP. RECEIPT: 1/16/1797. Of Jeremiah Libbey for Appraisal Comm. He received $3.87 for services and expenses. ADDL. ACCOUNT: 2/15/1797. Of Danl. R. Rogers atty to Admx. Allowed 2/15/1797. PETITION: 3/7/1798. Of Danl. R. Rogers for Admx. For License for $1,400.00. There is a bal. due Admx. of $400.00 and the referees for Jonah Minot's account have awarded him $600.00, plus several other demands. LICENSE (D32:456): 3/12/18. To Admx. To sell real est. to amount of $1,400.00. LIST CLAIMS: Total L848.5.4 1/2. CERT.: 10/17/1798. Of Ebenezer Belknap. That during his lifetime, through his atty. Jonas Minot, the decd. contracted to sell Belknap all of his right in Lot #86 in Marlborough, Cheshire Co. Ebenezer paid part of the sale price and since Thomas' death has constantly applied to pay the rest and receive a deed. His dwelling house on the lot was consumed by fire and the contract lost in fire. Oath 10/17/1798 Belknap to Saml. Grffin, JP. License: 10/25/1798. to Admx. To sell the lot to Belknap according to the contract and convey the deed. CONTRACT: 11/29/1792. Of Thomas Packer, Greenland husbm. Appoints Jonas Minot, Concord, Middlesex Co., MA gent., his atty. in all causes representing his lands in NH, lands west of Connecticut River, in any NH grants in NY and VT. To ascertain the lands belonging to Packer, the value of them and to inquire into every sale which has been made for taxes to see if the sales were legal and can be recovered. To sell 2 lots in Packersfield, lots in Richmond, Fishersfield,

Alexandria, (this town not identifiable, possibly Perry's Town?), Campbell Gore, New Bradford, (unreadable, may be Kearsarge), New London, New Chester, Marlborough and Sliptown. Witnesses: Richard Brown and George Packer. Cert.: Of Jonas Minot, Stephen Minott and George Packer. That this is a true copy. CERT.: 10/24/1798. Of Jonas Minot. He has taken the Cert. of Ebenezer Belknap concerning the bargain for sale of land in Marlborough, Cheshire Co., knows it to be the truth and from hearsay of all the people of his acquaintance that the house was burnt. He has examined the Power of Atty. sent on by his son Stephen Minot, but he is not well and will be going abroad so requests License to be granted to Admx. to sell the land contracted to Belknap. PETITION: 12/3/1798. Of Admx. For License to convey a deed to Ebenezer Eaton of Bradford, Hillsborough Co. for land in Bradford which decd. contracted on 7/11/1791 to sell to Eaton and on which Eaton has paid the greater part and is ready to pay bal. Order: 12/3/1798. For hearing. LICENSE: 2/4/1799. To Admx. To sell land in Bradford, Hillsborough Co. to Ebenezer Eaton and convey deed. ADDL. ACCOUNT: 2/20/1799. Of Danl. R. Rogers atty. to Admx. Allowed 2/20/1799. PETITION: 11/15/1802. Of Admx. For Dower as her son, Matthew B. Packer heir of her husband's est., arbitrarily withholds her right and refuses to provide a decent and comfortable support for her.

PAGE. See also Paage

1946. PAGE: CALEB, DAVID, HANNAH, JESSE, JOSHUA, LYDIA & NABBY (1789) #5488

GDP. Of the children of Jesse Page, Atkinson gent. decd. GDP.: 10/21/1789. Of: Jesse, Lydia and Caleb, minors over 14 and of Nabby, Hannah, David and Joshua, minors under 14. Gdn. Peter Clement, Atkinson esq. Bond L1000.0.0. Sureties: William Page, Atkinson yoeman and James Thurston, Exeter gent. Witnesses: Obadiah Page and Eliza Thurston. ACCOUNT: 4/16/1794. Of Gdn. Of his Gdp. of Caleb, decd. Allowed 4/16/1794, the bros. of Caleb being present and having no objections. RECEIPT: 3/29/1794. Of Peter Clement, Gdn. To William Page, Admr. est. Jesse Page. The Gdn. has received L17.2.10.1 in full of Caleb's proportion in 2/3 of real est. of his father, Jesse Page, and also L9.4.6 1/2 for Caleb's share in 1/3 of his mother's Dower, as decreed by Judge of Probate. He discharges Exec. of all demands. Witnesses: Nathl. Parker and Amos Noyes. Oath 4/16/1794 Clement to Joseph Blanchard, JP.

1947. PAGE, CHRISTOPHER (1796) #6258
EST. Chichester yoeman decd. testate. WILL: Drawn 4/15/1796. Legatees: His parents; Bro.-Benjamin; Sisters-Ruth Page and Anna Page; Mary Masten and Abigail Shaw; David Sanborn. Exec.-Deacon Abraham True. His sig. Witnesses: Saml. Gile, Daniel Tilton, Thomas Lake and Josiah Carpenter. CERT. WILL (D32:188):9/21/1796. Presented by Exec. and witnesses Tilton and Carpenter. ADMIN.: 9/21/1796. Exec. Abraham True, Chichester yoeman. Bond $3,000.00. Sureties: Edmund Leavitt, gent. and Daniel Tilton, yoeman, both of Chichester. Witnesses: Josiah Carpenter and W. Parker. INVY.: Comm.: Asa Lane, Daniel Tilton and Edmund Leavitt. Value $800.00. Oaths 1/10/1797 Lane and Leavitt to Jonathan Leavitt, JP. Oath 1/19/1797 Exec. to judge.

1948. PAGE, COFFIN (1797) #6390
DIV. land in North Hampton. PETITION: 10/19/1797. Of Coffin Page, Effingham, Strafford Co. husbm. For div. of land in North Hampton which he holds in common with Francis Page of North Hampton, each owning half. Order: 10/21/1797. For hearing, Petitioner to serve Francis with copies of Petition and Order. Cert.: 10/23/1797. Of Simon Ward, Constable. He left copies at Francis Page's house. PETITION: 3/22/1799. Of Coffin Page, Effingham yoeman. For div. of land in North Hampton held common with his bros. John Page and Noah Page, both of North Hampton. Coffin owns 1/2/ Order: 3/22/1799. For hearing, Petitioner to serve others with copies of Petition and Order. Cert.: 3/23/1799. Of Simon Ward, North Hampton Constable. He served copies to both Noah and John Page. DIV.: Comm.: Moses Leavitt, esq.; Simon Ward, Nehemiah Moulton, Samuel Fogg Leavitt and Joseph Hobbs Jr. To div. land in North Hampton, late the est. of Francis Page, setting off to Coffin 1/2 and to John and Noah the other half. Oaths 4/18/1799 Comm. to John Fogg, JP. Allowed.

1949. PAGE, DANIEL (1783) #4901
EST. South Hampton yoeman decd. testate. WILL: Drawn 6/5/1777.Legatees: Wife-Judith, Sons-Onesiphorus and Daniel; Daus.-Jenne wife of Moses Thompson; Hannah, wife John Bartlet and Ruth Page; Grandson-William Page; Granddau.-Anne Clough. Execs.-wife Judith and son Daniel. His sig. Witnesses: Moses French, Josiah Dole and Enoch Page. CERT. WILL (D27:229): 5/28/1783. Presented by Execs. and witnesses French and Dole.

1950. PAGE, DAVID (1777) #4384
EST. Of Northwood decd. ADMIN.: 8/27/1777. Admr. Thomas Peabody, Brentwood esq. Bond L500.0.0. Sureties: Joseph Greely and Jonathan Shaw, yoemen, both of Brentwood. Witness Jeremiah Parker.

1951. PAGE, DAVID (1785) #5114
EST. North Hampton husbm. decd. testate. WILL: Drawn 2/19/1783. Legatees: Sons-John, Robert, Benjamin, Josiah and David; Daus.-Abigail wife of Benjamin Perkins and Ruth Page. Exec.-son David. His sig. Witnesses: Reuben Gove Dearborn, Jonathan Page and Philip Smith. CERT. WILL (D28:204): 6/15/1785. Presented by Exec. and witnesses Dearborn and Page.

1952. PAGE: EBENEZER, JOHN & MEHITABLE (1779) #4550
GDP. Of the children of Timothy Page, Atkinson yoeman decd. PETITION: 6/28/1779. Of Moses Page of Londonderry. He states that his bro. Timothy Page decd. left children Ebenezer, John and Mehitable Page who are not capable of caring for themselves or their ests. Requests appointment of Daniel Poor and Daniel Richards as Gdns. Cert.: 6/28/1779 Jereh. Poor and Joseph Little, Atkinson Selectmen, consider Poor and Richards to be suitable Gdns. GDP. (D25:203): 6/30/1779. Of: Ebenezer, John and Mehetabel, adults adjudged n.c.m. Gdn. Daniel Poor. Sureties: Jonathan Webster and Joseph Little, Atkinson gentlemen. ACCOUNT: Of Lt. Daniel Poor of his Gdp. of John Page. (If there are others mentioned, document torn off.) Oath 8/12/1783 Gdn. to Peter Clement, JP. Receipt 8/26/1783. Of Robert Young. He has received of Lt. Daniel Poor on behalf of John Page L24.16.11, the bal. of the Account. Allowed 6/15/1785 after being adjusted by arbitrators, sworn to by Gdn. and agreed to by Robert Young, atty. to John Page. Note: the following Bond and Release recorded as #5382 Page: Ebenezer, and Methitabel (1788) are put here because they concern the wards. BOND: 10/15/1788. Of: Peter Clement, esq.; James Noyes, gent. and Enoch Knight, yoemen, Atkinson Selectmen and Overseers of the Poor of Atkinson for the present year. By an Act of the NH General Court, the Selectmen and Overseers of the Poor are empowered to sell the estates of Ebenezer Page and Mehetabel Page, both of Atkinson, and apply the monies from the sale of the land to reimburse the town the sums advanced by them for the future main. of Ebenezer and Mehetabel Page. They are to account to the heirs of the Pages for any monies remaining in the hands of the Selectmen at the deaths of Ebenezer and Mehitabel, or of whichever lives longest. Sureties: John Dow, esq. and John Gilbert, cordwainer, both of Atkinson. Witnesses: John Atwood and Ebenr. Green. RELEASE: 4/23/1793. Of John Page, Salem husbm., son of Timothy Page late of Atkinsons and bro. and heir of both ests. He has settled with the Atkinson Selectmen, Peter Clement, Samuel N. Little and John Knight, receiving L55.15.0 in full of the ests. and acquits the Selectmen and Overseers of the Poor of any further demands affecting the ests. of Ebenezer and Mehetabel Page. Oath 4/23/1793 John Page to Joseph Welch, JP. Witnesses: Josh. Tenney and

David Allen. See also #4706 for John, #4707 for Mehitable and #4710 for Ebenezer.

1953. PAGE: EBENEZER & MEHITABLE (1788)#5382.
See #4550 Page: Ebenezer, John & Mehitable (1779).

1954. PAGE, EBENEZER (1781) #4710
GDP. Of Atkinson yoeman decd., an adult adjudged n.c.m. INVY. WARR.: 6/30/1779. Comm.: Josph Little, Jonathan Webster and Jesse Page, all of Atkinson. INVY.: Appr. 4/23/1781. Value 99.15.3 plus Notes held with his bro. John and sister Mehetabel. Oath 4/24/1781 Comm. to Nathl. Peabody, JP. Oath 4/25/1781 Gdn. to judge. See #4706 John Page (1781) for his Invy. which includes information for this est. ACCOUNT: Of Gdn. Oath 8/26/1783 Gdn. to Peter Clement, JP. Allowed 9/25/1784 having been sworn to by Gdn. and balanced by Atkinson Selectmen. See also #4550 Ebenezer, John& Mehitabel Page (1779) for orig. Gdp., etc.

1955. PAGE, ELISHA (1775) #4144
EST. Epping yoeman decd. intestate. ADMIN.: 1/8/1775. Admrs.: Meribah Page and John Towle, yoeman, both of Epping. Bond L1000.0.0. Sureties: Jeremiah Sanborn and Edmund Chapman, Epping yoemen. Witnesses: Saml. Hale Jr. and Josiah Clark. INVY.: Appr.2/1775.Comm.:Enoch Coffin and Josiah Tilton. Value L604.6.10. Oaths 4/11/1775 Admrs. and Comm. to judge. PETITION: 6/28/1777. Of Meribah Page, widow of Elisha. To have her Dower set off as John Towle, the co-admr. who married the only heir, refuses to do so. Judge's note that he appoints a Comm. of Timy. Jones; James Sanborn; Stephen Clark, esq.; and Abra. Perkins and Simon Dearborn, gentlemen.

1956. PAGE, ELIZABETH (1787) #5276
EST. Exeter widow decd. testate. WILL: Drawn 4/6/1787. Legatees: Sons-Josiah Clark Page and Nathaniel Page; Dau.- Elizabeth Page; Dau.-in-law-Elizabeth Page. Execs.-bros.-in-law John Page and Richard Langdon. Her sig. Witnesses: Elipt. Ladd, Wm. Parker Jr. and Joseph Tilton. Proved 6/20/1787 on oaths of witnesses Parker and Tilton, physicians. INVY.: Value L230.5.0. Noted the Exec. sworn 9/1792. ACCOUNT: 9/5/1792. Of Execs. Allowed 9/5/1792.

1957.PAGE, ISAAC (1788) #5344
See #5404 1/2 Capt. Jesse Page

1958. PAGE, JABEZ (1782) #4809
EST. Hawke yoeman decd. testate. WILL: Drawn 11/10/1773. Legatees: Wife-Abigail; Sons-Thomas and Henry; Dau.-Ruth. Exec.-son Thomas. Witnesses: Josiah Bartlett, Joshua Woodman Jr. and John Hills. CERT. WILL (D26:390): Presented by Exec. and witnesses Bartlett, esq. and Woodman. INVY. WARR.: 5/30/1782. Comm.: Benjamin Sweat of Kingston, William Busel of Hawke, yoemen and John Calfe, Hampstead esq. INVY.: Value L1225.19.0. Oaths 6/5/1782 Sweat and Busel and on 4/17/1784 Exec. to John Calfe, JP.
1959. PAGE, CAPT. JESSE (1788) #5344 & (1789) #5404 1/2 (#5344 is incorrectly registered as Isaac Page)
EST. Atkinson gent. decd. intestate. RENUN. (#5344): 3/31/1788. Of Sarah Page, widow of Jesse. Of Admin. Requests appointment of oldest son William. Witnesses: David Page and (unreadable). ADMIN. (#5344): 4/10/1788. Admr. William Page, Atkinson yoeman. Bond L1000.0.0. Sureties: James Dow, yoeman and Nathaniel Peabody, esq., both of Atkinson. Witnesses: Abraham Dow and Abigail Peabody. INVY. (#5344): Comm.: Peter Clement, Eliphalet Knight and Daniel Page. Value L66.19.11 and Comm. notes 100 acres land in Sutton, Hillsborough Co. omitted. Oaths 7/15/1788 Page and Knight to Peter Clement, JP. Oath 8/20/1788 Admr. to W. Parker, Reg. Note: All of the above papers call it est. Capt. Jesse Page. APPR. WARR. (#5404 1/2): 10/21/1789. Comm.: James Noyes, Jesse Sawyer, Ezekiel Belknap and Jonathan Poor, gentlemen and Daniel Page, Atkinson yoeman. To view 2/3 real est. to see if it can be div. among all his children. Divide or appr. PETITION (#5404 1/2): 1/19/1790. Of: William Page, Edmund Page and Sarah Page, heirs. State that a Comm. was appointed to div. est. among children and objections made to Comm. members Eliphalet Knight and Capt. Jeremiah Poor. Request that Jonathan Poor and Lt. Jesse Sawyer, both of Atkinson, be appointed instead and they will all agree on the Comm. DOWER (#5404 1/2): 4/13/1790. Comm.: Eliphalet Knight, Jeremiah Poor, James Noyes, Ezekiel Belknap and Daniel Page. Of Widow Sarah Page. Oaths 4/13/1790 Comm. to Peter Clement, JP. Allowed 4/2/1790. APPR. (#5404 1/2): Of 2/3 of real est. Value L188.11.6. Oaths 4/13/1790 Comm. to Peter Clement, JP. DECREE SETTLM. (#5404 1/2): 5/17/1790. William Page, oldest son, appearing and consenting, real est. settled on him, William to pay each of his co-heirs L17.2.10 1/4 within one year, with interest. BOND (5404 1/2): 5/17/1790. Of William Page, Atkinson husbm. Bond L300.0.0. To pay his co-heirs per Decree Settlm. Sureties: Peter Clement, Atkinson esq. and Jona. Poor, gent., both of Atkinson. Witnesses: N. Parker and O. Peabody. APPR. (#5404 1/2) :12/4/1792. Comm.: Jeremiah Poor, Exekiel Belknap, Moses Emery, John Dow and Daniel Page. To appr. widow's dower to see if it can be div. among all the children. Div. or

appr. Value L101.10.0. Oaths 12/4/1792 Comm. to Peter Clement, JP. DECREE SETTLM. (#5404 1/2): 3/20/1793. William Page, oldest son, appearing and consenting, Dower settled on him, William to pay each of his co-heirs L9.4.6.2, to those of age within one month and those not of age in one year, plus interest. BOND: (#5404 1/2) 3/20/1793. Of William Page, Atkinson yoeman. Bond L203.0.0. To pay his co-heirs per Decree Settlm. Sureties: Peter Clement, esq. and Amos Noyes, yoeman, both of Atkinson. Witnesses: Nat. Rogers and Josiah Adams. ACCOUNT (#5404 1/2): Of Admr. Allowed 5/14/1792. Account includes main. one child.

1960. PAGE, JOHN (1781) #4706
EST.: Atkinson adult n.c.m. GDP. INVY. WARR.: 6/30/1779. Comm.: Jonathan Webster, Jesse Page and Joseph Little, all of Atkinson. INVY.: Appr. 4/23/1781. Value L43.17.7 1/2 plus Notes of L8.5.7 and L9.7.10. The Comm. was also shown 3 Notes of Hand part of est. of John's bro. Timothy decd., all for considerable sums and of long standing, on interest. Some have partial payments plus other conditions which make it impossible to ascertain at this time their value. John is also heir to some articles from his decd. father's est. which were sold at vendue and the amount not yet settled. Therefore, these items omitted. Oaths 4/24/1781 Comm. to Nathl. Peabody, JP. Oath 4/25/1781 Gdn. to judge. See also #4550 Page: Ebenezer, John & Mehitable (1779) for orig. Gdp., etc.

1961. PAGE, REV. JOHN (1782) #4789
EST. Hawke clerk decd. testate. WILL: Drawn 1/19/1782. Legatees: Wife-Mary; His 9 children-unnamed. Exex.-wife Mary. His sig. Witnesses: David Quimby, Joseph Williams and Anne (pos. Annes) Campbell. CERT. WILL (D26.311): Presented by Exex. and witnesses Quimby and Williams. ADMIN.: 3/27/1782. Exec. Mary Page, Hawke widow. Bond L500.0.0. Sureties: David Quimby and Joseph Williams, Hawke gentlemen. Witnesses: Peter Emerson and Hitty (?) French. NOTE: In this file there is also a fragment of the Will, probably a copy, on back of which the clerk has written "Will of Ebenezer Janvrin late of Portsmouth decd., proved July 30, 1783 and is referenced with Janvrin's est.

1962. PAGE, JOHN (1787) #5307
EST. Kensington yoeman decd. testate. WILL: Drawn 4/18/1787. Legatees: Sons-John, Aaron, James, Daniel and Benjamin. Daus.-Mary Page, Rachel Pervere, Abigail Gove and Sarah Kendrick. Execs.-sons John and Aaron. His sig. Witnesses: Benjamin Moulton, Levi Batchelder and Jere. Bachelder. CERT. WILL (D29:151): 11/21/1787. Presented by Execs. and witnesses Moulton and Jere. Bachelder. INVY.: Appr. 11/26/1787. Comm.: Jere. Bachelder and Benja. Moulton. Value not

tallied. Esti. L468.0.0.+. Oaths 11/26/1787 Comm. and Execs. to Jere. Fogg, JP.

1963. PAGE, JOHN (1790) #5559
EST. Kensington yoeman decd. ADMIN.: 7/21/1790. Admx. Elizabeth Page, Kensington widow. Bond L500.0.0. Sureties: Jeremiah Fogg of Kensington and Jonathan Cass of Exeter, esquires. Witnesses: N. Parker and W. Parker. INVY.: Appr. 8/25/1790. Comm.: Benjamin Moulton, Jere. Bachelder and Benjamin James Jr. Value L249.1.4. Oaths 11/8/1790 Bachelder, James and Admx. to Jere. Fogg, JP. DUPL. INVY.: Shows a total of L248.11.4. and oaths on 8/25/1790. LICENSE (D30:150): 11/16/1791. To Admx. To sell real est. to amount of L90.0.0. DOWER: Comm.: John Lane, esq.; Jere. Bachelder, Benja. Moulton, Benja. James Jr. and Jere. Fellows. Of Widow Elizabeth Page. Oaths 12/20/1791 Comm. to Jere. Fogg, JP. Allowed. ACCOUNT: Of Admx. Allowed 9/15/1794 the heirs being notified but not attending.

1964. PAGE, JOHN (1790) #5596
EST. Epping husbm. decd. testate. WILL: Drawn 8/31/1790. Legatees: Wife-Lydia; Sons-David, John, Reuben, Moses and Aaron; Daus.-Deborah Kelley, Molley Kelley, Margaret Clough, Ruth Sanders and Lydia Page. Ref. to his bro. David. Execs.-bro. Robert and wife Lydia. His sig. Witnesses: Enoch Coffin, Benjamin Page and Samuel French. CERT. WILL (D29:435): Presented by Lydia Page, widow, the only Exec. accepting trust, and witnesses Coffin and Page. Note: The proving of Will also includes affirm. of French. RENUN.: 11/17/1790. Of Lydia Page, widow of John. Of all that is devised to her in Will and claims her right of dower. She accepts the executorship as in Will. Witness W. Parker. ADMIN.: 11/17/1790. Exex. Lydia Page, Epping widow. Bond L1000.0.0. Sureties: Enoch Coffin, esq. and Benjamin Page, husbm., both of Epping. Witnesses: Samuel Parker and W. Parker. INVY. WARR.: 11/17/1790. Comm.: David Lawrence, Ebenr. Straw and Levi Towle, all of Epping. Invy.: Appr. 5/11/1791. Value L362.15.6. Oaths 12/6/1796 Lawrence and Towle to Wm. Plumer, JP.

1965. PAGE, JONATHAN (1774) #4127
EST. North Hampton yeoman decd. testate. WILL: Drawn 12/15/1769. Legatees: Wife-Mary; Sons-Simon, Joseph ("distracted"), Stephen and Jonathan; Dau.-Mary Fogg. Execs.-sons Jonathan and Stephen. His sig. Witnesses: Samuel Chapman, Christopher Smith and Joseph Palmer. Proved 10/21/1774. Presented by Execs. and witnesses Smith and Palmer. ADMIN.: 10/20/1774. Execs.: Jonathan Page and Stephen Page, North Hampton husbandmen. Bond L1000.0.0. Sureties: Christopher Smith and

Joseph Palmer, North Hampton yoemen. Witnesses: Benja. Mackay and Saml. Hale Jr.

1966. PAGE, JOSIAH (1775) #4151
EST. Epping yoeman decd. intestate. ADMIN.: 2/9/1775. Admr. Joseph Mason, Epping yeoman. Bond L1000.0.0. Sureties: Timothy Jones and James Sanborn, Epping yeomen. Witnesses: Samuel Blodget and William Seaward.

1967. PAGE, MEHITABLE (1781) #4707
GDP. Atkinson adult n.c.m. INVY. WARR.: 9/13/1779. Comm.: Jesse Page, Joseph Little and Jonathan Webster, all of Atkinson. INVY.: 4/23/1781. Value L43.17.7 1/2 plus Notes of Hand belonging to Mehitable's share and part of six Notes belonging to the est. of her bro. Timothy decd. The Comm. cannot assess these at this time. The land she owns is the real est. of her father Timothy Page decd., formerly of Plaistow, and is held in common and undivided by Mehitable and her co-heirs of father's est. Oaths 4/24/1781 Comm. to Nathl. Peabody, JP. Oath 4/25/1781 Gdn. to judge. ACCOUNT: 8/26/1783. Of Gdn. Oath 8/26/1783 Gdn. to Peter Clement, JP. Allowed 9/15/1784 having been sworn to by Gdn. and balanced by Atkinson Selectmen. See also #4550 Page: Ebenezer, John & Mehitable (1779) for orig. Gdp., etc. and #4706 John Page (1781) for details of the Invys. of the 3 siblings.

1968. PAGE, PATIENCE (1760) A#2480
GDP. Of the dau. of Samuel Page of Kensington. RELEASE (D26:287): 9/29/1778. Of Patience Page of Kensington. She releases her Gdn., her grandfather Theophilus Page, as her Gdn., having received what he had of hers in his care and on this date L20.0.0 in full for rent of her premises. Witnesses: Nathan Dow and Ebenr. Loveren. Oath 11/15/1782 Patience to Wm. Parker, JP. Orig. Archives file includes Gdp. of 2/14/1760 with Samuel Page, her father, as Gdn. and Gdp. of 4/13/1770 with Theophilus Page, her grandfather, as Gdn.

1969. PAGE, SAMUEL (1774) #4124
EST. Kensington gent. decd. testate. WILL: Drawn 7/23/1774. Legatees: Wife-Mary; Sons-Stephen, Simon, Enoch and Robert of Deerfield; Daus.-Elisabeth Lock, Anna Rowe, Mary Hobbs, Marcy Longfellow and Sarah Bachelder; Grandson-Samuel Page son of his son Simon; Church of Christ in Kensington. Execs.-Sons Stephen and Simon. His sig. Witnesses: Meshech Weare, Samuel Lamprey and Stephen Green. CERT. WILL (D23:52): 9/28/1774. Presented by Execs. and witnesses Lamprey (oath) and Green (affirm.) ADMIN.: 9/28/1774. Execs. Stephen Page, gent. and

Simon Page, yoeman, both of Kensington. Bond L3000.0.0. Sureties: Nathanael Healy, esq. and Samuel Lamprey, yoeman, both of Kensington. Witnesses: Simon Page, yoeman; Henry Prescott and Saml. Hale Jr. APPR. WARR. (D27:138): Comm.: Jona. Purington, Ebenr. Loveren, Jeremiah Bachelder, Joseph Clifford and Nathan Dow. To view the real est. and see if it can be div. Div. or appr. Appr.: Value L419.5.0. Oaths 12/16/1782 Purington, Loveren and Dow to Nathl. Bachelder, JP. DECREE SETTLM. (D27:139): 12/18/1782. Eliphalet Page, oldest son, appearing and consenting, the real est. is settled on him, Eliphalet to pay each of his co-heirs L59.17.9 within 6 months, with interest.

1970. PAGE, SAMUEL (1797) #6305
EST. Hampstead yoeman decd. ADMIN.: 2/8/1797. Admx. Dolly Page, Hampstead widow. Bond $3,000.00. Sureties: Daniel Nichols, yoeman and Joseph French, gent., both of Hampstead. Witnesses: W. Parker and Saml. Parker. INVY.: Comm.: John Calfe, esq.; David Poor and John True. Value $1,534.44 plus Notes of $78.10, less a brindle cow which died after appr. Oaths 3/31/1797 Poor and True and on 5/11/1797 Admx. to John Calfe, JP. PETITION: 4/15/1797. Of David Nichols on behalf of Admx. For Comm. Insolvency. Gives list claims of $1,062.07 plus another large claim not yet in and others from the East Parish of Haverhill, Essex Co., MA were decd. formerly lived. Granted. CLAIMS: 10/28/1797. Comm.: John Calfe, Edmund Morse and John True. Total $230.12. Affirms. 10/28/1797 Morse and True to John Calfe, JP. LETTER: From John Calfe. To judge. He encloses the Account requested for Comm. Insolvency. Also, he does not know the fees of Nicholas and Capt. French for setting off Dower or Morse and True for Comm. Insolvency, which he supposes were about half a dollar. His was $1.00 each. DOWER: 10/28/1797. Comm.: John Calfe, esq.; Daniel Nichols, Edmund Morse, John True and Joseph French. Of Widow Dolly Page. Affirms. 10/28/1797 Morse and True and oath 11/2/1797 French to John Calfe, JP. Allowed. CITATION: 4/18/1798. To Admx. To appear and exhibit her Account for settlm. She is also to notify heirs and advertise same in newspaper. ACCOUNT: Of Admx. Allowed 9/17/1798 heirs not appearing. Account includes main. 2 children. PETITION: Of Admx. For License. Gives claims of $548.51 plus others not before exhibited. Order: For hearing, Admx. to notify heirs. LICENSE (D32:528): 9/17/1798. To Admx. To sell real est. to amount of $140.00. BOND: 9/17/1798. Of Admx. Bond $400.00. To account for proceeds of sale of real est. by License. Surety Jesse Davis, Hampstead yoeman. Witnesses: W. Parker and Wm. P. Adams. PETITION: 9/28/1798. Of Admx. and heirs. Samuel Page, Paul Page and Job Page, heirs, are dissatisfied with the Commissioners' processing and the widow is dissatisfied with setting off of the real est. They desire to leave the

matters to a Rule and have agreed on Thomas Hoat of Sandown, Nathaniel Brown of Hawk and Robert Emerson of Hampstead. Witness Jesse Davis. Allowed and the judge requests Judge Parker to make out a Rule. DOWER WARR.: 2/8/1799. Comm.: Oliver Warren and David Poor of Hampstead; Nathaniel Brown of Hawke; Thomas Cotton and Benjamin Pillsbury of Sandown, husbandmen. Of Widow Dolly Page. DOWER: 7/16/1799. Oaths 8/12/1799 Pillsbury, Poor and Cotton to Thomas Muzzey, JP. Allowed. PETITION: 9/20/1802. Of Stephen Wheeler Page, Hampstead yoeman. For div. of lands in Hampstead and Sandown of the est. not set off to widow, which he holds in common with Paul Page Londonderry yoeman and John Page and Stephen Page, minors under the gdp. of John True, Hampstead esq. He owns 7/10, the minors 2/10 and Paul 1/10. Order: 9/20/1802. For hearing, Petitioner to serve others with copies of Petition and Order. CERT.: 10/16/1802. Of John True and Paul Page. That Stephen W. Page was notified of hearing. They consent to a Comm. of Capt. William Marshall, Benjamin Pilsbury, Lt. David Poor, James Atwood and Jonathan Eastman. DIV. WARR.: 10/18/1802. Comm. As requested. To make div. per Petition of Stephen Wheeler Page. AGREEMENT: 2/9/1799. Of: Paul Page; Nathaniel Page, Job Page and Dolly Page, Admx. and heirs. They have agreed on the following settlm.: The widow is to have all the personal est. except the wearing apparel, Notes and book accounts; all that she has given to the heirs since appr. She is to pay all debts, suits and funeral charges. She is to keep the children for 2 years from appr. and to have the income for 2 years from appr. of the appr. The heirs are to provide for the children until they are 7 years old. Allowed as full settlm. 1/17/1803 the parties having appeared and Stephen Wheeler Page, a purchaser of the greater part of the est., consenting. DIV.: 1/20/1803. Divisees: Stephen Wheeler Page; Paul Page, John Page and Stephen Gale Page, children of decd., John and Stephen being minors. Oaths 1/20/1803 Comm. to John True, JP. Allowed 5/16/1803.

1971. PAGE, SHUBEL (1791) #5674
EST. Hampton husbm. decd. testate. WILL: Drawn 3/26/1778. Legatees: Wife-Hannah; Sons-Samuel, Nathaniel and Abner; Daus.-Abigail Hobbs, Sarah Philbrick and Mary Smith. Exec.-son Abner. His mark. Witnesses: Jereh. Marston Jr., James Hobbs and Joseph Dow. CERT. WILL (D30:94): 7/11/1791. Presented by Exec. and witnesses Hobbs and Dow, esq. ADMIN.: 7/11/1791. Exec. Abner Page, Hampton yoeman. Bond L1000.0.0. Sureties: Joseph Dow, Hampton esq. and James Hobbs of Parsonsfield, York Co., MA/ME. Witness W. Parker.

1972. PAGE, STEPHEN JR. (1793) #6393
GDP. Of South Hampton yeoman, an adult adjudged n.c.m. PETITION: 11/8/1797. Of Reuben Jenness, Hampton yoeman. States his bro-in-law Stephen Page Jr. is n.c.m. Requests appointment of a Gdn. Order: 11/8/1797. To Hampton Selectmen. To make inquisition into state of Stephen Page Jr. Report: 11/13/1797. Of Simeon Ladd, Philip Towle and Stephen Coffin, Hampton Selectmen. They judge Stephen to be n.c.m. and recommend Lt. Cotton Ward and Capt. Jonathan Marston to be his Gdns. GDP.: 11/14/1797. Of Stephen, an adult adjudged n.c.m. Gdns.: Cotton Ward and Jonathan Marston, Hampton gentlemen. Bond $3,000.00. Sureties: John Fogg, yoeman and Simon Nudd, gent., both of Hampton. Witnesses: Benja. Lamson and W. Parker.

1973. PAGE, THEOPHILUS (1782) #4816
EST. Kensington husbm. decd. testate. WILL: Drawn 5/28/1781. Legatees: Wife-Hannah; Sons-Daniel, Enoch and Nathan; Grandchildren-heirs of his son Samuel decd. Exec.-son Nathan. His sig. Witnesses: Samuel Clifford, Stephen Brown Jr. and Ebenezer Loveren. CERT. WILL: 6/26/1782. Presented by Exec. and witnesses Brown and Loveren. ADMIN.: 6/26/1782. Exec. Nathan Page of Kensington. Bond L1000.0.0. Sureties: Ebenezer Loveren and Stephen Brown Jr., both of Kensington. Witnesses: Nathl. Parker and W. Parker.

1974. PAGE, THOMAS (1780) #4648
EST. Hampton husbm. decd., testate. WILL: Drawn 6/17/1780. Legatees: Wife-Mary; Son-Benjamin; Daus.-Sarah Vittum, Hannah Atkinson and Tabitha Page; Grandson-Jose Page; Granddau.-Marcy Page. Exec.- son Benjamin. His mark. Witnesses: Cotton Ward, Joshua Towle Jr. and Samuel Drake Jr. CERT. WILL (D25:365): 8/30/1780. Presented by Exec. and witnesses Ward and Towle. INVY.: Appr. 11/6/1780. Comm.: Cotton Ward, Philip Towle Jr. and Joshua James. Value L223.14.0. Appr. at price of Indian corn at 4 shil./bu. Oaths 11/20/1780 Comm. to Lyford Dow, JP.

1975. PAGE, TIMOTHY (1779) #4575
EST. Atkinson yoeman decd. ADMIN. (D25:154): 5/27/1779. Admr. Robert Young, Salem yoeman. Sureties: John Allen and Elisha Woodbury, gent., both of Salem. INVY.: Comm.: John Webster, Jesse Page and John Ingalls. Value L1620. Oaths 8/23/1779 Comm. to Saml. Little, JP. Oath 9/29/1779 Admr. to W. Parker, Reg. & JP. ACCOUNT: 4/27/1780. Of Admr. Allowed 4/27/1780 after hearing objections of Danl. Poor, Gdn. of the heirs. NOTE: Though the Brentwood card Index gives his res. as Salem, all the papers say Atkinson.

1976. PALMER, ELIZABETH (1773) #4028
EST. Hampton spinster decd. testate. WILL: Drawn 5/8/1773. Legatees: Cousin-Daniel Lamprey; Dudley Lamprey minor son of her cousin Daniel Lamprey. Exec.-Cousin Daniel Lamprey. Her mark. Witnesses: Joseph Dow, Nathan Brown and James Hobbs. CERT. WILL: 6/30/1773. Presented by Exec. and witnesses Dow and Brown. ADMIN.: 6/30/1773. Exec.: Daniel Lamprey of Hampton. Bond L100.0.0. Sureties: Joseph Dow and Nathan Brown, both of Hampton. Witnesses: Philip Tilton and Samuel Parker. Note: The file jacket says Will missing, but it is there, mistakenly marked on back by the clerk "Will of Elizabeth Sanborn." The jacket for the est. of Elizabeth Sanborn is empty and does not contain the Will supposed to be there.

1977. PARK, ROBERT (1788) #5360
EST. Windham yoeman decd. testate. WILL: Drawn 12/17/1787. Legatees: Wife-Jane; Sons-Andrew, Alexander and Joseph; Daus.-Jane Park, Agnys wife of Nathaniel Hemphill, Margret wife of William Thom, Sarah wife of Saml. Morrison and Mary wife of Robert Dinsmore. Execs.-wife Jane and son Andrew. His sig. Witnesses: John Morison, Robert Morison and James Betton. CERT. WILL (D29:194): 6/18/1788. Presented by Execs. and witnesses John Morison and Robert Morison. INVY.: Appr. 12/4/1788. Comm.: Gain Armour, John Morison and Benjn. Thom. Value L245.1.1 1/2. Oaths 12/24/1788 Comm. to James Betton, JP. ACCOUNT: 4/19/1797. Of Execs. by their atty. Allowed 4/19/1797 with order for distribution of bal. of L32.12.9 to 5 of heirs per Will.

1978. PARKE, MARY (1772) #3860
GDP. Of the dau. of Joseph Parke of Windham decd. GDP.: 8/18/1772. Of Mary, a minor over 14. Gdn. Robert Parke, Windham husbm. Bond L500.0.0.Sureties: Saml. Morison and John Cochran, Windham husbandmen. Witnesses: Saml. Morison Jr. and John Cochran, Windham husbandmen. Witnesses: Saml. Morison Jr. and Andrew Park. RELEASE OF GDP. (D23:225): 2/26/1778. Of Mary Park, Windham single woman and spinster. For payment of L255.0.0. she discharges her Gdn, Robert Park, from all demands as Gdn. and also releases Robert Park and Alexander Park from demands against them as Execs. of the Will of her father, Joseph Park, Windham yoeman decd. Witnesses: Matthew Thornton and James Betton. Oath 2/26/1778 Mary to judge.

1979. PARKER, CATHARINE (1793) #5908
GDP. Portsmouth spinster adjudged n.c.m. PETITION: 7/11/1793. Of Samuel Parker. States that Catharine Parker, an adult person, dau. of the late Hon. Wm. Parker, for some years has been n.c.m. As she is a divisee

in the property of her father, it is necessary for a Gdn. to be appointed to take care of her and her est. ORDER: 7/11/1793. To Portsmouth Selectmen. To make inquisition into the claim that Catharine is n.c.m. and see if she is in need of gdp.. of her person and property. Report: 1/11/1793. Of Geo. Gains, Thomas Sheafe and Nathl. A. Haven, Selectmen. They have made inquiry and the representation is true. GDP.: 7/11/1793. Of Catharine, an adult adjudged to be n.c.m. Gdn. Nathaniel Adams, Portsmouth esq. Bond L1000.0.0. Sureties: William Parker, Exeter esq. and Samuel Parker, Boston, Suffolk Co., MA Dr. of Divinity. Witnesses: David Sewall and John P. Hale. ACCOUNT: 6/20/1804. Of Gdn. Allowed 6/20/1804 with consent of S. Parker and Christo. Toppan. "I also W. Parker."

1980. PARKER, JOHN (1791) #5697
EST. Portsmouth esq. decd. intestate. ADMIN.: 10/10/1791. Admrs. Samuel Parker, Boston, Suffolk Co., MA clerk and Nathaniel Adams, Portsmouth esq. Bond L1000.0.0. Sureties: Ammi R. Cutter, Portsmouth physician and Joseph Peirce, New Durham Gore, Strafford Co. esq. Witnesses: Moses Woodward Jr. and Matthew S. Parker. INVY.:Appr.10/19/1791. Comm.: John Peirce and James Sheafe, esquires. Value L303.4.9. Oaths 10/19/1791 Comm. to George Gains, JP. Oath 2/15/1792 Admrs. to judge. PETITION: 2/15/1792. Of Admrs. For Comm. Insolvency and License. Give list claims of L2406.5.8 1/2. Granted. LICENSE (D30:204): 2/15/1792. to Admrs. To sell real est. to the amount of L300.0.0. CLAIMS WARR.: 2/15/1792. Comm.: Thomas Martin, Ammi R. Cutter and John Hale, esquires. Comm. was allowed 5 months longer. CLAIMS: Total L134.1.3. Oaths 2/28/1793 Comm. to Geo. Gains, JP. ACCOUNT: 1/26(sic.)/1795. Of Admrs. Allowed 1/16(sic.)/1795. Christo. Toppan, Eliz. Adams, W. Parker for himself and as Gdn. to John Hale, heirs, consent to acceptance of Account. APPR. WARR.: 1/27/1795. Comm.: James Sheafe, Thomas Thompson, John Goddard, A.R. Cutter and William Smith, Portsmouth esquires. To view the real est. to see if it can be div. among his bros., sisters and legal reps. of those decd. Div. or appr. Appr.: The land at Portsmouth at L300.0.0. Other Portsmouth land and part of bldgs. at L30.0.0. Part of a house and land in Kingston at L6.0.0. Oaths 2/10/1795 Sheafe, Goddard, Cutter and Smith to Nathl. Adams, JP. ADDL. ACCOUNT: Of Admrs. Allowed 12/31/1795. DECREE SETTLM.:8/5/1799.WilliamParker, Exeter esq., an heir, appearing and consenting, the real est. is settled on him, William to pay Elizabeth Adams, Samuel Parker, Sarah Toppan, Catharine Parker and the reps. of Lydia Hale and Matthew Parker, his co-heirs, $106.00 each within 12 months, with interest. William gave bond. This file also includes an Account for the est. of Daniel Potter of Ipswich, MA decd.

1981. PARKER: MATTHEW STANLEY, NANCY RUST, NATHANIEL ADAMS & SAML. HALE (1793) #5909
GDP. Of the children of Matthew Stanley Parker, Wolfeborough, Strafford Co. esq. decd. GDP.: 7/11/1793. Of: Matthew Stanley Parker and Nathaniel Adams Parker, minors under 14. Gdn. Nathaniel Adams, Portsmouth esq. Bond L1000.0.0. Sureties: William Parker, Exeter esq. and Samuel Parker, Boston, Suffolk Co., MA Dr. Divinity. Witnesses: David Sewall and John P. Hale. GDP.: 7/11/1793. Of Nancy Rust Parker, a minor under 14. Gdn. Christopher Toppan, Hampton esq. Bond L200.0.0. Sureties: William Parker of Exeter and Nathaniel Adams of Portsmouth, esquires. Witnesses: David Sewwall and Samuel Parker. GDP.: 7/11/1793. Of Samuel Hale Parker, a minor under 14. Gdn. Samuel Parker, Boston, Suffolk Co., MA. Dr. Divinity. Bond L1000.0.0. Sureties: David Sewall of York, York Co., MA/ME and Nathaniel Adams of Portsmouth, esquires. Witnesses: W. Parker and Jno. P. Hale.

1982. PARKER, NATHANIEL (1797) #6332
See #6238 Elizabeth Lamson (1796).

1983. PARKER, NOAH (1787) #5288
EST. Portsmouth blacksmith decd. intestate. ADMIN.: 8/30/1787. Admx. Rebeckah Parker, Portsmouth widow. Bond L2000.0.0. Sureties: Jeremiah Libbey, esq. and Thomas Simes, chaisemaker, both of Portsmouth. Witnesses: Nathl. Adams and John Goddard. INVY.: Appr. 10/30/1787. Comm.: Jeremiah Libbey, George Wentworth and Thomas Simes. Value L295.12.0. Oaths and affirm. 11/20/1787Comm.andAdmx. to Geo. Gains, JP. PETITION: Dated by clerk 11/1787. Of Admx. For Comm. Insolvency. Gives list claims of L388.4.0. Admx. was told Pell & Co. drew an order while Noah was sick for L400.0.0. She is certain there will be more claims. CLAIMS WARR.: 11/21/1787. Comm.: John Goddard, physician; John Furnald, brazier and Daniel Rindge Rogers, merchant, all of Portsmouth. CLAIMS: 2/15/1790. Total L1516.13.4 1/4. Oaths 2/15/1790 Furnald and Rogers to Nathl. Adams, JP. ACCOUNT: 2/17/1790. Of Admx., presented by Jeremiah Libbey, her atty. Allowed 3/17/1790. PROP. & SETTLM.: Claims L1516.13.4 1/4. Amount to be proportioned L120.4.8. Allowed 3/17/1790 with order to Admx. to pay.

1984. PARKER, RUTH (1784) #5014
EST. Atkinson widow decd. intestate. ADMIN.: 6/16/1784. Admr. James Merrill, Atkinson yoeman. Bond L2000.0.0. Sureties: Nathaniel Peabody, Atkinson esq. and John Allen, Salem gent. Witnesses: Benja. Adams and Nathl. Parker. See #5371 Daniel Merril (1788) for Citation Admr. to account for ests. both Ruth and Daniel.

1985. PARKER, HON. WILLIAM (1781) #4736
EST. Portsmouth esq. decd. intestate. ADMIN.: 9/7/1781. Admr. John Parker, Portsmouth esq. Bond L2000.0.0. Sureties: Oliver Whipple of Portsmouth and Peter Green of Concord, esquires. Witnesses: Nathl. Healey Jr. and W. Parker. INVY.: Appr. 5/10/1782. Comm.: Thomas Martin, Ammi Ruhami Cutter and John Pickering. Value L1067.0.0. Oath 5/20/1782 Admr. and Comm. to Geo. Gains, JP. PETITION: 5/29/1782. Of Admr. For License. Allowed. LICENSE: 5/29/1782. To Admr. To sell sufficient real est. to pay debts. ADMIN. D.B.N.(D30:178): 1/26/1792. Admr. d.b.n. William Parker, Exeter esq. Sureties: Nathl. Parker of Exeter and Nathl. Adams of Portsmouth, esquires. INVY. (D30:280): Comm. A.R. Cutter, James Sheafe and John Hale. Value L896.0.0. Oaths 8/17/1792 Comm. to N. Adams, JP. LICENSE (D30:284): 8/17/1792. To Admr. d.b.n. To sell real est. to the amount of L300.0.0. ACCOUNT (D31:6): Of John Parker, Admr. decd., and Nathl. Adams, esq., Admr. (prob. of est. of John Parker decd.) Allowed7/11/1793 having been consented to by majority of the heirs. APPR. (D31:8): Comm.: Daniel Rindge, Joshua Brackett and Jeremiah Libbey, esquires; Jacob Sheafe, merchant and John Goddard, physician. To view the real est. and see if it can be div. Div. or appr. Appr.: 7/12/1793. Value L950.0.0. Oaths 7/12/1793 Rindge, Brackett, Sheafe and Goddard to Nathl. Adams, JP. ACCOUNT: 7/15/1793. Of Admr. d.b.n. Allowed, being consented to by majority of the heirs. Account shows support of Catherine Parker, an adult n.c.m., with consent of heirs. DECREE SETTLM. (D31: 11): 7/15/1793. William Parker, esq., oldest son and Admr. d.b.n., appearing and consenting, the real est. settled on him, William to pay each of his co-heirs and reps. of those decd.-Elizabeth Adams, Samuel Parker, Sarah Toppan, Catharine Parker, Reps. of John Parker, Mary Sewall, Lydia Hale and Matthew Stanley Parker, L83.3.0.3 within 6 months, with interest. Note: The file also contains a fragment marked on back, "Invy. of est. of Wm. Parker late of Portsmouth 5/1782." However, it appears to be an Account rather than an Invy. Note: The following Div. Warr. and Div. found in #6168 William Parker Jr. (1795) belong here. DIV. WARR. 7/1/1795. Comm.: William Parker, John Pierce, James Sheafe and John Hale, esquires; Nathaniel Appleton Haven, physician and Daniel R. Rogers, merchant, all of Portsmouth. To div. the real est. in N.H., exclusive of that in Rockingham Co., of William Parker, Portsmouth esq., decd., giving oldest son double share and single share to each of others or reps. of those decd. DIV.: 7/27/1796. Divisees: William Parker, esq., oldest son; Rev. Samuel Parker. D.D.; Mrs. Elizabeth Adams; John P. Hale, esq.; Mrs. Sarah Toppan; Catharine Parker and Heirs of Matthew Stanley Parker, esq. Oaths 7/28/1796 Peirce, Sheafe, Haven and Rogers to George Gains, JP. Allowed.

1986. PARKER, WILLIAM JR. (1786) #5201
GDP. Of the son of William Parker, Jr., Portsmouth mariner. GDP.: 6/6/1786. Of William Jr. Gdn. William Parker, Portsmouth mariner, his father. Bond L1000.0.0. Sureties: Robert Parker, mariner and John Furnald, brazier, both of Portsmouth. Witnesses: John Goddard and Jeremiah Libbey.

1987. PARKER, WILLIAM JR. (1795) #6168
EST. Portsmouth mariner decd. ADMIN.: 12/19/1795. Admr. William Parker, Portsmouth mariner, his father. Bond $3,000.00. Sureties: Samuel Fernald and Jeremiah Libbey, Portsmouth merchants. Witnesses: George W. Wendell and Mark Simes. Note: This file includes a Div. Warr. and Div. which belong with #4736 William Parker, esq. (1781) and are recorded there.

1988. PARKER, WILLIAM BENNETT (1797) #6353
GDP. Of the son of John Parker of Portsmouth decd. GDP.: 6/21/1797. Of William Bennett Parker, a minor under 14. Gdn. Elizabeth Parker, Portsmouth widow. Bond $1,000.00. Sureties: Nathaniel White, esq. and Niel McIntire, merchant, both of Portsmouth. Witnesses: Jona. M. Sewall and Nathl. Adams.

1989. PARROT, CAPT. JOHN (1790) #5518
EST. Portsmouth mariner decd. All items except final Div. are in #5518. ADMIN.: 2/17/1790. Admx.: Martha Parrott, Portsmouth widow. Bond L1000.0.0. Sureties: Joshua Brackett and Nathaniel Adams, Portsmouth esquires. Witness Nathl. Parker. INVY.: Appr. 4/8/1790. Comm.: Joshua Brackett, Jeremiah Libbey and Nathl. Adams. Value L961.17.11. Oaths 4/12/1790 Brackett and Adams, affirm. Libbey to George Gains, JP. Oath 10/20/1790 Admx. to judge. PETITION: 2/15/1792. Of Admx. For div. of land and bldgs. in Greenland of which she, as Admx., and William Pickering, Greenland tanner, are tenants in common, in order for the court to assign her dower. NOTIFICATION: 2/16/1792. To William Pickering, Greenland tanner. Of hearing on the Petition. Cert.: 3/19/1792. Of Edward Hart. He has read the notification to William Pickering. LETTER: 3/19/1792. From Admx. To judge. Notifies judge that since seeing him she has seen Saml. Cate who also agrees to a div. of land held in common. Requests same Comm. be appointed for both divisions. Because of the season of the year it is not convenient for her to attend court, so she has appointed Mr. Pickering to act for her. She supposes Mr. Cate will attend. Allowed. PETITION: 3/21/1792. Of Samuel Cate, Greenland yoeman. For div. of land in Greenland which he holds in equal shares with Martha Parrott as Admx. DIV. WARR.: 3/21/1792. Comm.: Stephen March and

Joshua Weeks, esquires; George Brackett, gent. and Josiah Haines, yoeman, all of Greenland and Samuel Sherburne, Portsmouth yoeman. To div. land in Greenland held in common by Cate and est. of Parrott. DIV.: 5/6/1792. Divisees: Samuel Cate and Martha Parrott as Admx. Oaths 6/5/1792 Weeks, Haines and Sherburne to Stephn. March, JP. Allowed. The following Div. is recorded as #6358 Parrot & Pickering (1797), but belongs here. DIV.: 10/13/1794. Comm. same as for previous Div. Divisees: William Pickering, Greenland tanner and Martha Parrott, Admx. est. John Parrott. Oaths 5/8/1797 Comm. to Ephraim Pickering, JP. Allowed 7/15/1797.

1990. PARROT & PICKERING (1797) #6358
See #5518 Capt. John Parrot (1790)
1991. PARRY, MARTYN (1773) #4062
GDP. Of the son of John Parry of Portsmouth (?-sic) decd. GDP.: 12/2/1773. Of Martyn, a minor over 14. Gdn.: George King, Portsmouth mariner. Bond L1000.0.0. Sureties: Benjamin Mackay, saddler and George King Jr., yoeman, both of Portsmouth. Witnesses: Saml. Hale Jr. and Richd. Jenness 3d.

1992. PARSONS, ________. (17__) #3941.
Incorrectly recorded by clerk. See Joseph Pearson (1772) #3941. There is no card file for ______ Parsons.

1993. PARSONS, EDWARD (1776) #4288
EST. Newmarket esq. decd. ADMIN.: 12/4/1776. Admr. William Parsons, Sanford, York Co., MA/ME joiner. Bond L500.0.0. Sureties: Samuel Baker, gent. and Josiah Adams, trader, both of Newmarket. Witnesses: Nathl. Parker and Wm. Parker. INVY.: Appr. 4/30/1777. Comm.: Saml. Baker, Josiah Adams and W. Cheswill. Value L353.0.0+. Oaths 4/30/1777 Comm. and Admr. to judge. PETITION: 12/25/1782. Of Admr. For Comm. Insolvency. Gives list claims of L307.0.0. and expects more. CLAIMS WARR.: 12/25/1782. Comm.: Nathaniel Rogers, esq.; Saml. Baker, gent. and John Shute, innholder, all of Newmarket. Claims: 9/24/1783. Total L378.5.9 1/2. Oaths Rogers and Shute to Josiah Adams.

1994. PARSONS, REV. SAMUEL (1789) #5429
EST. Rye clerk decd. testate. WILL: Drawn 4/10/1783. Legatees: Wife Mary; Son-Joseph; Daus.-Mary Tuck, Elizabeth Wallis and Hannah Parsons; Grandson Amos Sevey Parsons son of Capt. Joseph Parsons. Exex. Wife Mary. His sig. Witnesses: William Trefthen, Joseph Marden and Samuel Douse Foss. CERT. WILL (D29:258): 3/18/1789. Presented by Exex. and witnesses Trefethen and Foss.

1995. PARTRIDGE, BENJAMIN (1796) #6252
EST. Portsmouth mariner decd. PETITION: 9/5/1796. Of Lois Partridge and Daniel Lang. Request appointment of Jere. Libbey, esq. as Admr., or, if he refuses, Saml. Drowne. ADMIN.: 9/6/1796. Admr. Jeremiah Libbey, Portsmouth esq. Bond $3,000.00. Sureties: Nathl. Adams, esq. and Thomas Manning, merchant, both of Portsmouth. Witnesses: Mary Woodward and W.Parker.INVY.:Appr.9/10/1796. Comm.: Edward Sargent, Thos. Manning and Saml. Drowne. Value $4,800.90. Oaths 9/12/1796 Lois Partidge, the widow and Comm. to Isaac Rindge, JP. DOWER WARR.: 9/20/1796. Comm.: Isaac Rindge, esq.; William Hart, gent.; Edward Sargent and Thomas Manning, mariners and Samuel Drowne, goldsmith, all of Portsmouth. Of Widow Lois Partridge. In consider of this Dower, she relinquishes all her right of Dower in the house and land sold by her husb. decd. to Daniel Lang and land sold to Benjamin Yeaton. Oath 9/27/1796 Lois Partridge to Geo. Gains, JP. PETITION: 10/19/1796. Of Admr. For License. Gives list claims of $235.75. Granted. LICENSE (D32:200): 10/19/1796. To Admr. To sell real est. to amount of $270.00. ACCOUNT: 5/27/1799. Of Admr. Allowed 5/27/1799 the heirs having previously consented.Cert.:5/18/1799. Of Capt. James Drisco, owner of 1/2 of est. by purchase from heirs and as Gdn. Of Polly Goodwin, a minor, heir to 1/4 of the est. He has examined Account and re- quests allowance. Cert.: Of Betty Akarman, mother of Patty Partridge, heir of remaining 1/4/ She has no objections to allowance. Capt. James Drisco agrees to take several obligations owing to est. and to pay Admr. the bal. of $949.33 in order to discharge admin.

1996. PARTRIDGE, PATTY (1797) #6312
GDP. Of the dau. of Benjamin Partridge Jr., Portsmouth mariner decd. GDP.: 2/16/1797. Of Patty, a minor under 14. Gdn. Betsy Partridge, Portsmouth widow. Bond $2,000.00. Sureties: Josiah Akarman and Mark Akarman, Portsmouth baers. Witnesses: Thos. Bateman and W. Parker. GDP.: 3/25/1803. Of Patty, a minor under 14. Gdn. Arthur Melcher, Portsmouth blockmaker. Bond $3,000.00. Sureties: John Melcher, blockmaker and John Melcher 3d, mariner, both of Portsmouth. Witnesses: James Marden and Isaac Rindge. LETTER: 3/29/1803.From Isaac Rindge. To judge. He encloses the new Bond of Gdp., noting that the bondsmen are possessed of enough property and requesting the judge to send the Letter of Gdp. and his fees and he will give them to Hutchins.

1997. PASCAL, ELIZABETH (1794) #6035
EST. Portsmouth widow decd. testate. WILL: Drawn 10/30/1792. Legatees: Sons-Capt. George Wentworth and Joshua Wentworth. Execs.: Sons-George and Joshua. Her mark. Witnesses: Samuel Tappan, Tobias Walker and Aurelia Tappan. CERT. WILL (D31:369): 10/15/1794 Presented by Execs. and Walker, the other witnesses having moved out of state. ADMIN.: 10/15/1794. Admrs.: George Wentworth and Joshua Wentworth, Portsmouth esquires. Bond L1000.0.0. Sureties: Jotham Rindge and John Raynes, both of Portsmouth. Witnesses: Jacob Walden and Mark Simes. INVY. WARR.: 10/15/1794. Comm.: Isaac Rindge, esq.; Daniel Warner and Samuel Drowne, gentlemen, all of Portsmouth. INVY.: Appr. 10/30/1794. Value: L90.13.0. Oaths 10/30/1794 Comm. and on 10/31/1794 Capt. George Wentworth, an Exec., to R. Cutts Shannon, JP.

PASCHAL. See Pascal.

PATEE. See also Pettee
1998. PATEE, LAOMI (1782) #4785
GDP. Of the dau. of Richard Pettee of Salem decd. PETITION: 3/25/1782. Of Loammi Patee. She chooses James Paul, Londonderry gent. as her Gdn. Witnesses: Edward Patee and Thads. Butler. GDP.: 3/27/1782. Of Laomi, a minor over 14. Gdn. James Paul, Londonderry gent. Bond L500.0.0. Sureties: Stephen Duston, Salem yoeman and James Leavitt Jr., Exeter gent.

PATTEE. See also Patee, Pettee

1999. PATTEE: HANNAH ET. AL. (1780) #4611
Clerk's error. No Hannah in file. See John Pattee (1780) #4611 and for Gdp. of Hannah her father's file #4440 Richard Pettee (1778).

2000. PATTEE, JOHN (1780) #4611
GDP. of the son of Richard Pettee, Salem yoeman decd. GDP.: (8/23/1781. Of John, a minor over 14. Gdn. Moody Morse, Salem physician. Bond L1000.0.0 silver money. Sureties: Stephen Gage, cordwainer and James Webster, gent., both of Salem. Witnesses: Timo. Ladd and Silus Wheeler Note: See #4440 Richard Pettee (1778), father, for earlier Gdp. of Richard.

2001. PATTEN, JOHN (1786) #5217
EST. Of Londonderry decd. testate. WILL: Drawn 6/9/1786. Legatees: Wife-Jean; Sons-Samuel, John, Robert and Cochran; Daus.-Christian Caldwell, Mary McAdams, Elizabeth Shearer and Jean Patton. Execs.-son

Samuel and George Reid, esq. His sig. Witnesses: James Miltimor, John Pray and John Miltimor. CERT. WILL (D29:77): Presented by Execs. and witnesses James Miltimor and John Miltimore. INVY.: Appr. 11/14/1786. Comm.: John Cochran, John Miltimor and John Nesmith. Value L493.9.2. Oaths 12/1786 Comm. to Geo. Reid, JP. Oath 1/25/1787 Geo. Reid, esq., an Exec., to W. Parker, Reg.

2002. PATTERSON, GAVEN (1794) #6021
EST. Greenland trader decd. testate. WILL: Drawn 4/3/1794. Legates: Wife-Mary; Dau.-Mary Ayres. Exex.-wife Mary. His sig. Witnesses: Saml. Pickering, Nahum Ward and Clemt. Weeks. CERT. WILL (D31:340): 9/1/1794. Presented by Exex. and all witnesses. ADMIN.: 9/1/1794. Exex. Mary Patterson, Greenland widow. Bond L1000.0.0. Sureties: Clement Weeks, Greenland gent. and William Bell, Chester innholder. Witnesses: Nahum Ward and Wm. Parker. INVY.: Appr. 10/21/1794. Comm.: Josiah Adams, Wentworth Cheswill and Sam. Pickering. Value L1575.12.0. Oaths 10/6/1794 Cheswill and Pickering to Josiah Adams, JP. Oath 10/13/1794 Admx. to judge, except for sundry things omitted which she presented. Note: This file also contains a Div. which belongs with #6022 Capt. Edward Hilton (1794) and is recorded there.

2003. PATTERSON, JOHN (1793) #5950
EST. Londonderry husbm. decd. testate. WILL: Drawn 3/2/1793. Legatees: Wife-Jean; Son-Peter. Execs.-wife Jean and Samuel Willson. His sig. Witnesses: John Bell, Mary Ann Bell and Elisabeth Willson. CERT. WILL (D31:127): 12/18/1793. Presented by Execs. and witnesses Bell, esq. and Willson. ADMIN.: 12/18/1793. Execs.: Jane Patterson (sig.), widow and Samuel Willson, yoeman, both of Londonderry. Sureties: John Bell, esq. and James Alexander, yoeman, both of Londonderry. Witnesses: John Morrison and N. Parker.

2004. PATTERSON, JOSEPH (1790) #5585
EST. Newington yoeman decd. ADMIN.: 10/20/1790. Admx. Temperance Patterson, Newington widow. Bond: L1000.0.0. Sureties: Paul Rawlings, Newington yoeman and Samuel Moses, Portsmouth barber. Witnesses: W. Parker and Sam. Drowne. INVY.: Comm.: John Fabyan, Richd. Pickering and Wm. Stoodley. Value L140.7.3. Oaths 12/1/1790 Comm. and Admx. to Ephraim Pickering, JP. PETITION: 12/13/1790. Of Paul Rawlings on behalf of Admx. For Comm. Insolvency. Also indicates that the est. is encumbered with an old negro woman unable to help herself. Includes an untallied list of debts. CLAIMS: 7/9/1791. Comm.: Timy. Dame and Richd. Pickering. Total L179.4.11. Oaths 9/3/1791 Comm. to W. Parker,

JP. DOWER: 10/26/1791. Comm.: John Fabyan, Paul Rawlings, Benjamin Miller, John Shackford and Wm. Stoodly. Of Widow Temperance Patterson. Oaths 10/26/1791 Comm. to Ephraim Pickering, JP. Allowed. ACCOUNT: Of Admx. Allowed 6/20/1792. Account includes main. and funeral changes for negro woman. PROP. & SETTLM.: Claims L179.4.1. Amount to be proportioned L36.1.9. Allowed 8/30/1792 with order to Admx. to pay.

2005. PAUL, JAMES (1799) #6555
EST. Of Londonderry decd. PETITION: 4/17/1799. Of David Paul, Londonderry gent. For Admin., he being the only child and his mother, aged and infirm, refusing. Allowed 4/1799. ADMIN.: 4/17/1799. Admr. David Paul, Londonderry husbm. Bond $3,000.00. Sureties: John Morrison, Londonderry husbm. and Thomas Dow, Salem esq. Witnesses: Joseph Blanchard and Nath. Parker. INVY. (D33:218): 12/18/1799. Comm.: George Reid, John Moors Bayley and John Taylor. Value $1,342.52 plus notes not tallied. Oaths 12/18/1799 Comm. to judge. Oath 12/20/1799 Admr. to James Gilmore, JP. PETITION: 4/15/1800. Of Jona. Gove, atty. to Widow Sarah Paul of New Boston, Hillsborough Co. For Sarah's Dower. Hearing on Petition postponed by consent of the parties. Note: This file also contains the following Release which is hard to reconcile with the rest of the est., the 1785 being much earlier, but no other Paul est. found and none is given in the Index of the Hillsborough Co. Reg. Probate. RELEASE: 12/21/1785. Of Sarah McNeal, New Boston, Hillsborough Co. widow. By virtue of marriage she gives up all right of dower and power of thirds in all the real and personal est. of James Paul to James Paul, gent., his heirs and assigns. Witnesses: Thomas Willson and Moody Morse. Oaths 12/3/1785 Sarah McNielle and James Paul to Moody Morse, JP. A true copy.

2006. PEABODY, DR. THOMAS (1777) #4405
EST. Brentwood physician decd. intestate ADMIN.: 12/30/1777. Admx. Elizabeth Peabody, Brentwood widow. Bond L500.0.0. Sureties: Samuel Shaw and Jonathan Shaw, Brentwood yoemen. Witnesses: Jere. Parker and W. Parker. INVY.: Appr. 1/16/1778. Comm.: Joseph Shaw and Joseph Greely. Value L605.2.6. Oaths 1/29/1778 Comm. and Admx. to judge. PETITION: Of Admx. For License. Includes a list called "what subscriber has paid" at the beginning of the list, but at the end says, "claims against est." LICENSE: 11/21/1787. To Admx. To sell sufficient real est. to pay debts.

2007. PEARNE, MARY (1788) #5364
EST. Of Portsmouth decd. testate, wife of Capt. William Pearne, Portsmouth merchant. WILL: Drawn 11/15/1787. Legatees: Husb.-William Pearne; Son-William Pearne; Daus.-Mary Roach wife of Capt. Thomas Roach; Ann Pearne, Elizabeth Pearne and Phebe Pearne. Exec.-husb. William, or, if he is decd., friends Richard Hart and Isaac Rindge, esquires. Her sig. Witnesses: Joseph Low, Abner Blasdel and Nathl. Marshall. William Pearne consents to Will. CERT. WILL D29:204): 8/28/1788. Presented by Exec. William Pearne and all witnesses, William also swearing to his consent. ADMIN.: 8/20/1788. Exec. William Pearne, Portsmouth merchant. Bond L1000.0.0. Sureties: Peter Peirce, Portsmouth merchant and Joseph Hoit, Stratham esq. Witnesses: Jere. Fogg and Nat. Parker.

2008. PEARNE, CAPT. WILLIAM (1790) #5542
EST. Portsmouth mariner and merchant decd. testate. WILL: Drawn 9/26/1789. Legatees: Son-William; Daus.-Phebe Pearne and Elizabeth. Execs.-daus. Phebe and Elizabeth and friend Joseph Akerman, Portsmouth cordwainer. His sig. Witnesses: Joseph Low, Abner Blasdel and Jno. Jackson. CERT. WILL (D29:378): Presented by Phebe Pearne and Akerman, two of Execs. and witnesses Low and Blasdel. Will devises to Phebe William's share in the dwelling house that was the dower of Elizabeth Wallingford wife of Thomas Wallingford of Somersworth. INVY.: Appr. 9/3/1790. Comm.: Abner Blasdel and Joseph Low. Value L385.2.7. Oaths 9/3/1790 Comm. to George Gains, JP. Oath 9/3/1790 Joseph Akerman, an Exec., to W. Parker, JP. PETITION: 5/16/1791. Of Akerman, an Exec. For Comm. Insolvency. Gives list claims of L647.0.5. Granted with judge's note Comm. to be Jere. Libbey, John Evans and Jacob Walden. PETITION: 10/4/1792. Of Akerman, an Exec. For License. Gives claims allowed by Comm. as L845.10.3 1/2. Granted. LICENSE (D30:315): 10/4/1792. To Execs. To sell real est. to amount of L220.0.0. ADDL. ACCOUNT: 2/17/1802. Of Phebe Pearne and Joseph Akerman, two of the Execs. Allowed 2/17/1802 having been consented to by "the" heir.

PEARSE. See also Peirce

2009. PEARSE, JAMES (1796) #6255
EST. Chester cordwainer and yoeman decd. ADMIN.: 9/19/1796. Admx. Molly Pearse, Chester widow. Bond L1000.0.0. Sureties: Moses Underhill Jr. and Josiah Chase, Chester yoemen. Witnesses: Benja. Fitts and Stephen Chase. INVY.: Appr. 10/20/1796. Comm.: Stephen Chase, Jacob Elliot and Benja. Fitts. Value $103.18. Oaths 10/22/1796 Comm. and Admx. to

Josiah Flagg, JP. PETITION: 10/24/1796. Of Stephen Chase on behalf of Admx. For Comm. Insolvency. Gives claims already in of $164.00. Allowed. CLAIMS WARR.: 10/24/1796. Comm.: William White and Stephen Chase, esquires and Jacob Elliot, gent., all of Chester. 4/19/1797 one month more allowed Comm. PETITION: 10/24/1796. Of Stephen Chase on behalf of Admx. For License. Granted. LICENSE (D32:203): 10/24/1796. To Admx. To sell real est. to amount of $175.00. DOWER: 12/28/1796. Comm.: Josiah Flagg, Stephen Chase, Jacob Elliot and Benja. Fitts. Of Widow Molly Pearse. Oaths 12/28/1796 Comm. to Willm. White, JP. Allowed. CLAIMS: 4/18/1797. Total $138.37. Oaths 4/18/1797 Comm. to Josiah Flagg, JP. ACCOUNT: 4/18/1797. Of Admx. Oath 4/18/1797 Admx. to Josiah Flagg, JP. Allowed 4/19/1797 on oath atty. to Admx. ADDL. ACCOUNT: ADDL. CLAIMS: 5/9/1797. Total $24.03. Oaths Comm. to Josiah Flagg, JP. ADDL. ACCOUNT: 5/9/1797. Of Admx. Oath 5/9/1797 Admx. to Willm. White, JP. Allowed 5/15/1797. PROP. & SETTLM.: Claims $162.40. Amount to be proportioned $34.00.Allowed 5/29/1797 with order to Admx. to pay. COPY PROP. & SETTLM.

2010. PEARSON, JETHRO (1772) #3970.
EST. Exeter yoeman and gent. decd. testate. WILL: Drawn 10/12/1772. Legatees: Wife-Sarah; Sons-Dole and Edmund. Dau.-Abigail Grant. Grandsons-John Pearson, Taylor Pearson and Joseph Pearson; Granddau.-Sarah Norris. Dau.-in-law-Rachel Pearson. Exec.- son Dole. His sig. Witnesses: John Lamson, Thomas Folsom and Saml. Brooks. CERT. WILL: 12/12/1772. Presented by Exec. and witnesses Lamson and Samuel Brooks. DECLARATION: Of Sarah Pearson, widow of Jethro. States she has no objection to probate of his Will and accepts the provision made for her. Witnesses: Josiah Folsom and Thomas Folsom. INVY. WARR.: 12/4/1772. Comm.: Samuel Brooks, esq. and Thomas Folsom, gent., both of Exeter. INVY.: Appr. 12/25/1772. Value L929.6.2. Oaths 1/4/1773 Exec. and Comm. to Wm. Parker, JP. DIV. WARR.: 1/5/1773. Comm.: Samuel Lane, esq.; Daniel Clark and William Chase, yoeman, all of Stratham; Josiah Robinson and Thomas Folsom, Exeter gent. To div. farm in Stratham and Exeter in equal shares per Will. DIV.: 1/14/1773. Divisees: Dole Pearson, Taylor Pearson and Joseph Pearson. Oaths 1/27/1773 Lane, Clark and Chase to judge. Includes map.

2011. PEARSON: JETHRO, JONATHAN, JOSEPH, MARTHA, MOLLY, RACHEL, SARAH & TAYLOR (1772) #3975
GDP. Of the children of Joseph Pearson of Exeter decd. GDP.: 12/30/1772. Of: Jethro, Jonathan, Joseph, Martha, Molly, Rachel, Sarah and Taylor Pearson. Gdn. John Taylor, Stratham gent. Bond L1000.0.0.

Sureties: William Chase and Nicholas Rowlings, Stratham yoemen. Witnesses: Greenleaf Clark and Samuel Parker.

2012. PEARSON, JOHN (1793) #5896
EST. Deerfield yoeman decd. testate. WILL: Drawn 6/2/1792. Legatees: Wife-Hannah; Sons-Timothy Morse Pearson and John; Daus.-Dorothy Davis, Lydia, Hannah Colbey, Elizabeth Goodhugh, Sarah Woodbury, Molley Colbey, Eunis Morrill and Rhoda. Exec.-son Timothy. His sig. Witnesses; Enoch Robie, Noah Lane and Jeremiah Eastman. CERT. WILL (D30:432): 5/15/1793. Presented by Exec. and witnesses Lane and Eastman, esq. ADMIN.: 5/15/1793. Exec. Timothy Morse Pearson, Deerfield husbm. Bond L1000.0.0. Sureties: Jeremiah Eastman, esq. and Noah Lane, yoeman, both of Deerfield. Witnesses: Nichl. McClary and Nathl. Parker. INVY.: Appr. 6/13/1793. Comm.: Jeremiah Eastman, Edmund Chadwick and Samuel Goodhue. Value L297.18.4. Oaths 6/13/1793 Chadwick and Goodhue to Jeremiah Eastman, JP. Oath 7/15/1793 Eastman to Joseph March, JP. ACCOUNT: 1/19/1802. Of Exec. Allowed 9/13/1802 heirs not appearing. Account legacy payments show Rhoda now Rhoda Bailey.

2013. PEARSON, JOSEPH (1772) #3941
EST. Exeter yoeman decd. intestate. ADMIN.: 6/24/1772. Admr. John Taylor, Stratham gent. Bond L500.0.0. Sureties: Jacob Tilton, Portsmouth innholder and Joseph Cram, Exeter yoeman. Witnesses: Oliver Whipple and Samuel Parker. INVY. WARR.: 6/25/1772. Comm.: Josiah Robertson, gent. and Josiah Sanborn, yoeman, both of Exeter. INVY.: Appr. 3/30/1772. Value L203.14.11. Oaths 9/30/1772 Admr. and Comm. to judge. LICENSE: 11/12/1772. To Admr. To sell 5 acres of land, part of est. which lays detached from rest. DOWER WARR.:1/5/1773. Comm.: Samuel Lane, esq.; Daniel Clark and William Chase, yoemen, all of Stratham. Of Widow Rachel Pearson. DOWER: 1/14/1773. Oaths 1/27/1773 Comm. to judge. Allowed. LICENSE: 1/28/1773. To Admr. To sell all the real est., it being supposed that est. is probably insolvent. CLAIMS WARR.: 1/28/1773. Comm.: William Parker of Exeter and Samuel Lane of Stratham, esquires. At bottom is an undated note by judge that the Comm. is continued for two months longer. CLAIMS: 8/23/1773. Total L109.14.3. Oaths 8/23/1773 Comm. to Noah Emery, JP. ACCOUNT.: 10/27/1773. Of Admr. Allowed.CLAIMS:10/27/1773. Total L108.5.7. Oaths 10/7/1773 Comm. to Peter Gilman, JP. PROP. & SETTLM.: 11/ 30/1773. Claims L108.5.7. Amount to be proportioned L49.2.0. Allowed 11/30/1773 with order to Admr. to pay. Note: There is no card in the card file for this est. It was incorrectly listed as "Parsons" by the clerk in the Admin., but later papers are all correctly Pearson.

2014. PEASE, SEBA (1794) #6058
EST. Portsmouth mariner decd. intestate. ADMIN.: 12/26/1794. Admr. Thomas Chadbourn, Portsmouth trader. Bond L200.0.0. Sureties: Samuel Fernald, shopkeeper and Jeremiah Stickney, cardmaker, both of Portsmouth. Witnesses: (Mark?) Yeaton and John Adams. INVY.: Appr. 2/14/1795. Comm.: Samuel Fernald and John Noble. Value L19.12.0. Oath 2/14/1795 Admr. and Comm. to R. Cutts Shannon, JP. ACCOUNT: 2/16/1796. Of Admr. Allowed 2/17/1796.

2015. PEASLEE, DANIEL (1778) #4478
EST. Salem esq. decd. testate. WILL: Drawn 4/2/1776. Legatees: Wife-Rebekah; Dau.-Hannah wife of Dr. Moody Morse; Joseph, Pearly, Elizabeth Merril, Daniel Peasly Merril, Nathanl., Hannah Merril and Sarah Merril, children of his dau. Sarah who was wife of Nathl. Merril; Ebenezer, Mehetabel Eaton, Nathl., Daniel, John and Joshua, children of his dau. Abigail who was wife of John Eaton; Granddaus.- Zilla Woodbury wife of Benjamin Woodbury, dau. of his dau. Rebekah wife of Daniel Dow; Grandson-Piercy Dow, son of Rebekah the wife of Daniel Dow. Execs.-Dr. Moody Morse and Piercy Dow. His sig. Witnesses: John Kelly, Benja. Bixby, Phinehas Swan and Wm. Hall. CERT. WILL (D24:343): 9/30/1778. Presented by Execs. and witnesses Bixby and Swan. INVY. WARR.: 9/30/1778. Comm.: Benjamin Bixby, Jeremiah Dow and Evan Jones, Salem gentlemen. INVY.:Appr.2/15/1778. Value not tallied. Esti. L4936.0.0+. Oaths 12/15/1778 Comm. and on 12/16/1778 Execs. to Timothy Ladd, JP.

2016. PEASLEE, JAMES (1771) #3816
EST. Newton yoeman decd. APPR. WARR. (D34:73):11/30/1801. Comm.: Levi Bartlett, Eliphalet Bartlett and John Peaslee. To appr. that part of the real est. that was the Dower. Orig. Archives file includes Invy., Account, Addl. Acct., Dower, Decree, Appr. of Dower, Decree Settlm. and Addl. Account.

2017. PEASLEE: JOHN, JOSEPH & SAMUEL (1794) #6048
GDP. Of the sons of Micajah Peaslee, Newton yoeman decd. GDP.: 11/21/1794. Of: Joseph, Samuel and John, minors under 14. Gdn. Jenny Peaslee, Newton widow. Bond L1000.0.0. Sureties: John Peaslee of Newton and Joseph Philbrick of Seabrook, yoemen. Witnesses: Aaron Whittomore and W. Parker.

2018. PEASLEE, JOSEPH (1790) #5521

EST. Newton yoeman decd. intestate. RENUN.: Of Lydia Peasley, widow of Joseph. Of Admin. Requests appointment of her son John Peaslee. Consent: 2/25/1790. Of Nathaniel Peaslee, Joseph Peaslee, Stephen Peaslee and Micajah Peaslee that their bro. John be Admr. of their father's est. ADMIN.: 3/8/1790. Admr. John Peaslee, Newton yoeman. Bond L1000.0.0. Sureties: Timothy Peaslee of Kingston and James Peaslee of Newton, yoemen. Witnesses: Gilman White and Richard White. INVY.: Appr. 3/12/1790. Comm.: Timothy Peaslee and Robert Stuart. Value L107.4.0. Oath 3/12/1790 Stuart and affirms. Peaselee and Admr. to judge. PETITION: Dated by clerk 8/1790. Of Widow Lydia Peaslee. To have her Dower set off. Suggests Comm. of Capt. Robert Stuart, James Peaslee and Timothy Peaslee. Witnesses: Samuel Morrison and Micajah Peaslee. CONSENT.: 1/25/1791. Of: Enoch Page, Joseph Peaslee, Joseph Rowell, Enoch Peaslee, Stephen Peaslee, Micajah Peaslee and Nathaniel Peaslee. They agree with the Admr. that their mother should receive L4.14.0. from the personal est. over and above what the judge gave her. CITATION: 5/7/1791. To Admr. To appear and answer the Petition of Morris Whittier, an heir of Abner Whittier decd., to sue the Bond of Admin. of Abner for whom Joseph Peaslee decd. and Moses Peaslee were Sureties. Petition requests that the heirs of his father Abner Whittier decd. be paid certain sums which have not been paid. Order: 6/13/1791. The Admr. appeared and requested time to find the Principal, who lives in VT., and discover what he had done relating to the sums. This appearing reasonable, hearing postponed to November. DOWER: 9/18/1790. Comm.: Robert Stuart, Timothy Peaslee, James Peaslee, Francis Chase Jr. and Richard Bartlett. Of Widow Lydia Peaslee. Oaths 5/14/1791 Stuart, Timothy Peaslee and James Peaslee to Matthias Bartlet, JP. Allowed 5/16/1791. CONSENT: Dated by clerk 5/16/1791. Of: Joseph Peaslee, Enoch Peaslee, Micajah Peaslee, Nathaniel Peaslee and Stephen Peaslee. They have agreed that it is best to settle the est. on the Admr. APPR. WARR.: 5/16/1791. Comm.: Matthias Bartlett, esq.; Daniel Chase, gent.; Moses Peaslee and Jacob Colby, yoemen and Timothy Whittier, tanner, all of Newton. To appr. at its current value 2/3 of the real est. Cert.: 5/24/1791. Of Comm. They have appr. the real est. to the best of their judgment. APPR.: 5/24/1791. Value $59.14.0. Oaths 5/24/1791 Chase, Colby and Whittier and affirm. Peaslee to Matthias Bartlett, JP. DECREE SETTLM.: 7/20/1791. John Peaslee, one of sons, appearing and consenting, the real est. settled on him, at the request of oldest son. John is to pay each of his co-heirs and the legal reps. of those decd. L6.13.4 1/2 in 6 months, with interest. BOND: 7/20/1791. Of John Peaslee, Newton yoeman. Bond L200.0.0. Sureties: Paul Peaslee of Newton and Timothy Peaslee of Kingston, yoemen. Witnesses: W. Parker and W. Plumer. ACCOUNT: 7/20/1791. Of Admr. Allowed

7/20/1791. PETITION: Dated by clerk 3/31/1800. Of John Peaslee. The Widow has died. Requests comm. be appointed to appr. her Dower so it may be settled on him in accordance with the Decree Settlm. Granted. APPR. WARR.: 3/31/1800. Comm.: Matthias Bartlett, esq., Robert Stuart, gent.; Obadiah Peaslee, Francis Chase Jr. and Joshua Bagley, yoemen, all of Newton. To appr. the Dower. APPR.: 10/30/1800. Value $160.00. Oaths 10/30/1800 Stuart, Bagley and Peaslee to Matthias Bartlett, JP. DECREE SETTLM.: 11/4/1800. John Peaslee, oldest son now living, appearing and consenting, Dower is settled on him, John to pay each of his co-heirs and the legal reps. of those decd. $16.66, viz. Joseph Peaslee, Enoch Peaslee, Heirs of Stephen Peaslee, Heirs of Nathl. Peaslee, Heirs of Micajah Peaslee, Heirs of Mary Page, Ruth Page and Hannah Rowell, all in 6 months, with interest. BOND: 11/4/1800. Of John Peaslee, Newton yoeman. Bond $320.00. To pay his co-heirs per Decree Settlm. Sureties: Moses Peaslee of Newton and Benjamin Folsom of Epping, yoemen. Witness W. Parker.

2019. PEASLEE, MICAJAH (1794) #6049
EST. Newton yoeman decd. ADMIN.: 11/21/1794. Admrs. Jenney (sig.) Peaseley, widow and John Peaslee, yoeman, both of Newton. Bond L1000.0.0. Sureties: Joseph Peaslee of Epping and Joseph Philbrick of Seabrook, yoemen. Witness W. Parker. INVY.: Appr. 12/2/1794. Comm.: Benj. Folsom, Timothy Peaselee and Edmund Peaslee. Value L402.10.6. Affirms. 12/27/1794 Timothy Peaslee and Edmund Peaslee to Matthias Bartlett, JP. Affirm. 12/31/1794 John Peaslee, an Admr., to judge. APPR.: 12/9/1800. Comm.: Francis Chase Jr. and Moses Peaslee, at request of Admrs. to appr. yearly income of est. Appr.: Value $73.50 per year or $441.00 for 6 years. Affirms. 12/10/1800 Comm. to Matthias Bartlett, JP. ACCOUNT: 12/1800. Of Admrs. (Jane-sig.). Allowed 12/15/1800. Account includes main. 2 children.

2020. PEASLEE: PAUL & TIMOTHY (1791) #5655
DIV. PETITION: 5/2/1791. Of Timothy Peaslee, Kingston yoeman. For div. of land partly in Newton and partly in Kingston which he holds in common and in equal shares with Paul Peaslee, Newton yoeman. Order: Paul Peaslee to be notified of hearing. CITATION: 5/2/1791. To Paul Peaslee, Newton yoeman. To appear for hearing on Petition. Cert.: 5/4/1791. Of Samuel Huse, Dept. Sheriff. He read Citation to Paul Peaslee. DIV.: 5/27/1791. Comm.: Jos. Smith, David Bagley, John Webster, Asa Whittier and Nehh. Sleeper. Divisees: Timothy Peaslee and Paul Peaslee. Oaths 5/27/1791 Comm. to Matthias Bartlett, JP. Includes Map. Allowed 6/13/1791. ACCOUNT: Of Timothy Peaslee. Of Expenses of Div. Allowed 7/20/1791 Paul Peaslee present and having no objections. Order:

That Paul Peaslee pay half of the expenses. Receipt: Of Timothy Peaslee. He has received L2.12.8 from Paul Peaslee.

2021. PEASLEE, RUTH (1772) #3899
GDP. Of the dau. Nathan Peaslee of Newton decd. GDP.: 1/3/1772. Of Ruth, a minor over 14. Gdn. Reuben Peaslee, Newton yoeman. Bond L500. Sureties: John Peaslee and Paul Peaslee, Newton yoemen. Witnesses: Silas Peaslee and Daniel Peaslee.

2022. PEASLEE, STEPHEN (1798) #6505
EST. Amesbury, Essex Co., MA yoeman decd. testate. WILL: Drawn 3/10/1798. Legatees: Wife-Miriam; Bro.-Enoch Peaslee of Wells, York Co., MA/ME; Heirs of his sister Hannah Rowell-Joseph Rowell and Elizabeth Huntington wife of Elijah Huntington; Heirs of his bro. Nathaniel decd.; Heirs of his bro. Micajah decd. Exec.- Ezekiel Jones Jr. His sig. Witnesses: Robert Quinby, Moses Hoyt and Jacob Brown. CERT. WILL: 8/8/1798. Presented by Exec. and witnesses Brown, esq. and Quinby before S. Holton Judge of Probate, Essex Co., MA. Cert.: As a true copy by Daniel Noyes, Reg. PETITON: 10/23/1798. Of Ezekiel Jones Jr., Exec. of Will. Requests Will already probated in MA be accepted so real est. in Rockingham Co. may be probated. Order: 10/23/1789. For hearing, Exec. to advertise Order in newspaper. LETTER ADMIN. (D:33:4): 12/15/1798. To Exekiel Jones Jr. INVY. (D33:61): Comm.: Danl. Chase, Edmd. Peaslee and Moses Peaslee. Value $744.72. Oaths 2/7/1799 Edmd. Peaslee and Chase to Mr. Bartlett, JP. Oath 3/25/1799 Exec. to W. Parker, JP. CERT.: 3/5/1799. Of Daniel Noyes, Reg. Probate, Essex Co., MA. That the claims of persons living in Essex Co. amount to $244.37 more than debts due to est. PETITION: 3/25/1799. Of Exec. For License, the decd.'s Will having provided for sale of his NH real est. if needed. Granted. LICENSE (D33:61): 3/25/1799. To Exec. To sell real est. to the amount of $520.00. ACCOUNT: 8/2/1800. Of Exec. Allowed 8/2/1800. Note: This file also contains a Petition which belongs with #6300 Jacob Butler (1797) and a Prop. & Settlm. which belongs with #6595 Stephen Prescott (1799). Each is recorded in its proper place.

2023. PEASLEE, WILLIAM (1794) #5997
EST. Newton yoeman decd. ADMIN.: 5/19/1794. Admx. Hannah Peaslee, Newton widow. Bond L500.0.0. Sureties: James Peaslee of Newton and James Hadlock of South Hampton, yoemen. Witnesses: Isaac Hunkins and Wm. Parker. INVY.: 6/5/1794. Comm.: Abraham Kimball, Charles Collins and Joseph Merrill. Value L12.18.0. Oath 6/5/1794 Admx., Kimball and Collins to Joseph Merrill, JP.

PEAVEY. See also Peavy

2024. PEAVEY, HUDSON (1785) #5153
EST. Newington yoeman decd. testate. WILL: Drawn 6/4/1783. Legatees: Wife-unnamed; Sons-Joseph, John and James. Daus.-Widow Elinor Rimes, Sarah Peavey, Elizabeth Wigain, Massy Gotham, Mary Neal and Temperance Peavey; Grandson-Charles Hodgedon son of his dau. Sarah Peavey. He bequesths his negro man King to son James. Exec.- son James. His mark. Witnesses: Benjamin Adams, John Marshall, Nathan Webb Adams and Mary Adams. CERT. WILL (D28:343): Presented by Exec. and witnesses Bejamin Adams, esq. and Nathan Webb Adams. INVY.: Appr. 1/19/1786. Comm.: Ephraim Pickering and Benjamin Adams, esquires and Saml. Shackford, gent., all of Newington. Value not tallied. Esti. L667.0.0.+. Note: This file includes the report of Christo. Toppan, Speaker of N.H. House Reps., of a bill allowing judges of probate to grant up to six more months time to the creditors of confiscated estates of Absentees.

2025. PEAVEY, PRISCILLA (1784) #5057
EST. Portsmouth widow decd. testate. WILL: Drawn 9/20/1784. Legatee: Rebecca Appleton, Portsmouth single woman, dau. of Mrs. Mary Clapham of Portsmouth. No Exec. named. Her mark. Witnesses: Sarah Purcell and Saml. Drowne. CERT. WILL: (D28:24): Presented by Mary Clapham, named as Exex., and both witnesses.

PEAVY. See also Peavey

2026. PEAVY, JOHN (1773) #4046
EST. Portsmouth(?) shipwright and ship carpenter decd. intestate. ADMIN.: 9/29/1773. Admx.: Dorcas Peavy, Portsmoth widow. Bond L100.0.0. Sureties: George Jerry Osborne, school master and Edmund Coffin, mariner, both of Portsmouth. Witnesses: Samuel Parker and John Parker. INVY. WARR.: 12/29/1773. Comm.: George Jerry Osborne and John Marshall, Portsmouth yeomen. INVY.: Value L28.12.0. Oaths 7/11/1774 Admx. and Comm. to judge.

2027. PEIRCE, DANIEL (1773) #4067
EST. Portsmouth esq. decd. intestate. ADMIN.: 12/21/1773. Admrs.: John Peirce and Joseph Peirce, Portsmouth merchants. Bond L2000.0.0. Sureties: Isaac Rindge, esq. and Jacob Treadwell, merchant, both of Portsmouth. Witnesses: Saml. Hale Jr. and John Parker. INVY. WARR.: 12/21/1774. Comm.: Amm. Ruhami Cutter and John Parker, esquires. INVY.: Value L3276.12.9. Oaths 12/30/1775 Admrs. and Comm. to Wm. Parker, Reg. Invy. includes negro man named Portsmouth.

2028. PEIRCE, JAMES
See James Pearse (1796) #6255

2029. PEIRCE, JOHN (1773) #4054
EST. Portsmouth cordwainer decd. testate. WILL.: Drawn 8/24/1773. Legatees: Children-John, Thomas, Lydia and Amy; Son-in-law-Peter Babb. Grandchildren-Peter Babb and Mehitabel Babb. Execs.: sons John and Thomas. Witnesses: Saml. Penhallow, Saml. Jackson and Sarah Parry. CERT. WILL: 11/8/1773. Presented by Execs., and witnesses Jackson and Penhallow, esq. ADMIN.:12/21/1773. Execs.: John Peirce and Thomas Peirce, Portsmouth merchants. Bond L1000.0.0. Sureties: Isaac Rindge, esq. and Jacob Treadwell, merchant, both of Portsmouth. Witnesses: Saml. Hale Jr. and John Parker. INVY. WARR.: 11/8/1773. Comm.: Samuel Penhallow and Joshua Brackett, Portsmouth esquires. INVY.: Appr. 1/11/1774. Value L290.0.0. Oath 1/28/1774 Thomas Peirce, an Exec., and 1/29/1774 Comm. to judge.

2030. PEIRCE, JOSEPH (1785) #5142
EST. Atkinson yoeman and gent. decd. intestate. ADMIN.: 10/10/1785. Admr. Peter Clement, Atkinson esq. Bond L1000.0.0. Sureties: Stephen Dole and James Dow, both of Atkinson. Witness Nat Parker. INVY. Comm.: Benja. Stone, Stephen Dole and James Dow. Value L43.2.4. Oaths 2/12/1790 Comm. to Peter Clement, JP. Oath 4/21/1790 Admr. to judge. PETITION: 5/17/1790. Of Admr. For Comm. Insolvency. Gives list claims already exhibited of L77.2.0. CLAIMS WARR.: 5/17/1790. Comm.: James Noyes, Ezekiel Belknap and James Dow, Atkinson gentlemen. CLAIMS: Dated by clerk 6/13/1791. Total L152.7.11 1/2. Oaths 5/27/1791 Comm. to Peter Clement, JP. ACCOUNT: 6/13/1791. Of Admr. Allowed 6/13/1791. Account includes main. 2 children. PROP. & SETTLM.: Claims L152.7.11 1/2. Amount to be proportioned L102.7.11. Allowed 6/30/1791 with order to Admr. to pay. Note: This file includes a Citation which belongs with #4835 Samuel Peirce (1782) and is recorded there.

2031. PEIRCE, JOSHUA (1767) A#3060
EST. Of Portsmouth decd. LICENSE (D26:294): 2/27/1782. To Leveret Hubbard, esq. and Ann his wife, Admx. d.b.n. with Will attached. To sell sufficient real est. to pay debts as the lands ordered sold are not enough. The jacket of the orig. Archives file is empty but indicates a Will, Admin., Invy. and Lic. As the License above is the only item found in the Docket books, it is probable that it is not the License listed on jacket.

2032. PEIRCE, MOSES (1787) #5266
EST. South Hampton yoeman decd. ADMIN.: 5/3/1787. Admr. Josiah Rogers, South Hampton gent. Bond L500.0.0. Sureties: Benja. Clough, gent. and David Graves, yoeman, both of South Hampton. Witnesses: Thomas White and William White. INVY.: Appr. 5/5/1787. Comm.: Joseph Merrill and Barnard Currier. Value not tallied. Esti. L79.18.11. Oath 4/12/1790 Merrill, affirms. Deacon Currier and Admr. to judge.

2033. PEIRCE, NATHANIEL (1762) A#2953
EST. Portsmouth esq. decd. ACCOUNT: Of Leverett Hubbard, esq. and Ann Hubbard his wife, formerly Ann Peirce. Includes a memorandum re the Invy. taken 11/19/1762 by John Wentworth and Samuel Penhallow, esquires and returned as L13627.8.0. But on 4/26/1767 Samuel Penhallow and John Wendell, esquires, were appointed to Inventory the est. of Joshua Pierce, esq. and it was found that L8122.0.9. of Joshua's est. was included with Nathaniel's and the Invy. was so recorded. The real Invy. of Nathaniel's est. amounts to L5506.7.3 old tenor, L700 of which is a piece of land appraised and recorded as the est. by heirs of Peter Greely decd. and L1100.0.0 old tenor, being his part of a farm in Greenland, was, and still is, claimed by the heirs of Dr. Joseph Peirce decd. and is now in dispute. The rest of the Invy. is accounted for by Ann Hubbard, formerly Ann Peirce, Admx. Allowed 10/12/1773. The Account includes main. of Sally and George. Orig. Archives file includes Admin., Invy., Act. of NH General Court, List Claims, Claims Warr., Claims and Prop. & Settlm.

2034. PEIRCE, SAMUEL (1782) #4835
EST. Atkinson gent. decd. testate. WILL: Drawn 5/3/1782. Legatees; Wife-Mary; Nephew-Joseph Peirce of Newbury, Essex Co., MA son of his bro. Thomas Pirce; Relative-Silas Brown son of John Brown of Newbury, Essex Co. Ma decd. Exec.-Joseph Pirce. His sig. Witnesss; Bradley Richards, Moses Belknap and Saml. Little. CERT. WILL (D27:20): 8/28/1782. Presented by Exec. and witnesses Belknap and Little. INVY.: Appr. 10/17/1782. Comm.: Samuel Little, esq.; Moses Belknap and Stephen Dole. Value L849.5.2. Oaths 10/19/1782 Comm. to Nathl. Peabody, JP. Oath 10/30/1782 Exec. to judge. Note: The following Citation found in #5142 Joseph Peirce (1785) belongs here. CITATION: 10/19/1785. To Rebecca Pierce of Atkinson, widow of Joseph and to any heirs of Joseph. The judge has received an application on behalf of Mary Pierce, relict to Samuel, for Admin. of his est. with Will attached to be granted to Mary. The request has been deferred so those cited may appear and show any cause they may have why Admin. should not be granted to Mary. Oath 1/13/1786. Of Sarah White of Essex Co., MA. She read the Citation to Samuel Pierce of Chester, he being at her father's house in

Haverhill, (MA or NH?), sometime in Oct. or Nov. 1785. Samuel took the Citation in his own hands and read it himself. On 10/19/1785 she also saw Rebecca Pierce have the Citation in her hands and heard Rebecca say she had read it and that she, Rebecca, did not feel she was fit to admin. the est., but she did remember that she was to appear at the Probate Office in Exeter the following Wednesday Oath to Samuel Phillips, Jr., JP. DECREE: 4th Tues. April 1786. Of Superior Court of Judicature of Rockingham Co., Samuel Livermore, esq., Chief Justice and Josiah Bartlett, John Dudley and Woodbury Langdon, esquires, justices. On 2/15/1786 the Judge of Probate, after a hearing on the application of Rebekah Pierce, Atkinson widow, that she be granted Admin. of est. of Samuel, it was decreed that the Admin. did not belong to her, upon which decree she applied to the Superior Court. The Superior Court, following a hearing, decrees that Rebecca is entitled to Admin., the est. not now being administered, and orders the Decree of the Probate judge reversed and that he grant admin. to Rebehah. ADMIN. D.B.N.: 5/5/1786. Admx. d.b.n. Rebekah Peirce, Atkinson widow, Joseph Peirce, Exec., being decd. Bond L1000.0.0. Sureties: Ebenr. Parker and Parker Dole, Atkinson husbandmen. Witnesses: Peter Clement, Hannah Parker and Elizabeth Clement. LETTER ADMIN.: 5/17/1786. In pursuance of the Decree of the Superior Court, the Judge of Probate appoints as Exex. Rebekah Peirce of Atkinson, widow of Joseph Peirce, Atkinson yoeman decd., who was Exec. of the Will of Samuel Peirce but died before having fully executed the same. There is also a rough copy of the Letter. INVY.: Appr.2/12/1790. Comm.: Joseph Little, James Noyes and James Dow. Value L441.16.0. Oaths 2/12/1790 Comm. to Peter Clement, JP. Oath 5/15/1790 Exex. to Nathl. Peabody, JP. PETITION: Dated by clerk 5/1790. Of Peter Clement on behalf of Exex. d.b.n. For Comm. Insolvency. Gives list claims of L308.6.10 and expects more. CLAIMS WARR.: 5/17/1790. Comm.: Asa Page and William Cogswell, esquires and Samuel Noyes Little, yoeman, all of Atkinson. An extenson of 2 months granted Comm. from 1/20/1791. PETITION: 12/29/1790. Of Admx. d.b.n. by her atty. Peter Clement. For License. Allowed. LICENSE (D29:456): 12/29/1790. To Admx. d.b.n. To sell real est. to amount of L290.0.0. OATH: 3/26/1791. Of Admx. d.b.n. To Peter Clement, JP. She will carry out the sale of real est. by License in a manner which will be of the greatest advantage to heirs. CLAIMS: Total L347.10.10 1/4. Oaths 3/18/1791 Comm. to Peter Clement, JP. APPR.: Comm.: James Noyes, Enoch Knight and James Dow. At request of Admx. d.b.n. they have appr. the income of the real est. since it came into her hands at L15.0.0 besides taxes. Oaths 6/10/1791 Comm. to Peter Clement, JP. ACCOUNT: 6/13/1791. Of Admx. d.b.n. Oath 5/21/1791 Admx. d.b.n. to Nathl. Peabody, JP. PROP. & SETTLM.: Claims L347.10.10. Amount to be proportioned L259.10.7. Allowed 6/30/1791 with order to Admx. d.b.n. to pay.

2035. PEIRCE, THOMAS (1798) #6472
EST. Portsmouth gent. decd. PETITION: 6/20/1798. Of Thomas Peirce, Portsmouth sailmaker, nephew of Thomas and nearest of kin. For Admin. ADMIN.: 6/20/1798. Admr. Thomas Peirce, Portsmouth sailmaker. Bond $3,000.00. Sureties: Samuel Penhallow, esq. and Edward John Peirce, trader, both of Portsmouth. Witnesses: William Lang and Saml. (Slade?). INVY.: (D32:506): Comm.: Joshua Brackett, Nathl. Treadwell and Nathl. Marshall. Value $401.50. Oaths 6/30/1798 Comm. and Admr. to George Gains, JP. PETITION: 6/19/1799. Of Admr. For Comm. Insolvency. Gives list claims of $1,171.00. Granted 6/19/1799. LICENSE (D33:101): 6/19/1799. To Admr. To sell real est. to the amount of $1,200.00. BOND: 6/1799. Of Admr. Bond $3,000.00. To account for proceeds from sale of real est. by License. Surety Edward John Peirce, Portsmouth trader. Witnesses; Samll. Fabyan and W. Parker. ACCOUNT: 2/7/1800. Of Edward John Peirce atty. to Admr. Allowed 2/7/1800. CLAIMS WARR.: 6/19/1799. Comm.: Joshua Brackett, esq.; Nathanl. Marshall and Nathaniel Treadwell, merchants, all of Portsmouth. Claims: 12/10/1799. Total $1,402.14. Oaths 1/20/1800 Comm. to R. Cutts Shannon, JP. PROP. & SETTLM.: Claims $1,402.14. Amount to be proportioned $352.44. Allowed 2/7/1800 with order to Admr. to pay.

2036. PELTIER, FRANCOIS JOSEPH (1779) #4539
EST. "now of" Portsmouth, mariner decd. testate. WILL: Drawn 8/1/1778. Legatees: Miss Frances Gardner dau. of John Gardner, Portsmouth taylor. Exex. Frances Gardner. Witnesses: Thos. Rindge Rogers, Danl. Rogers and H. Wentworth. Oaths 5/6/1779 Thomas Rindge Rogers and Hunking Wentworth, esq. to W. Parker, JP & Reg. CERT. WILL: 5/6/1779. Presented by Exex., witnesses Thomas Rindge Rogers and Wentworth having been sworn before a justice. CITATION: 5/18/1779. To Stephen Mead, mariner; Samuel Stover, merchant and Seth Walker, taylor, all of Portsmouth. To appear and give evidence under oath of what they know about the concealment, embezzlement and conveying away of money, goods of chattels of Francois' est. INVY.: Appr. 9/10/1779. Comm.: Jno. Parker, Jeremiah Libbey, esquires and Joseph Seaward. Value L3868.2.8. Oaths 10/23/1779 Parker and Libbey to George Gain, JP. Oath 10/27/1779 Exex. to W. Parker, JP & Reg.

2037. PENHALLOW, THOMAS (1784) #5047
EST. Portsmouth merchant decd. intestate. ADMIN.: 10/20/1784. Admr. John Penhallow, Portsmouth esq. Bond L5000.0.0. Sureties: Samuel Penhallow and Joshua Brackett, Portsmouth esquires. Witnesses: Nathl. Parker and W. Parker. INVY.: Appr. 12/14/1784. Comm.: Joshua Brackett, Joseph Bass and Jeremiah Libbey. Value L146.10.4 1/2. Oaths 12/14/1784 Comm. to Saml. Penhallow, JP. Oath 12/15/1784 Admr. to judge. PETITION: 12/15/1784. Of Admr. For License and Comm. Insolvency. LICENSE (D27:546): 12/15/1784. To Admr. To sell sufficient real est. to pay debts. CLAIMS WARR.: 12/15/1784. Comm.: Joshua Brackett, Joseph Bass and Jeremiah Libbey, Portsmouth esquires. Claims: 7/7/1785. total L206.19.7 1/2. Oaths 7/13/1785 Comm. to Saml. Penhallow, JP. ACCOUNT: 2/15/1786. Of Admr. Allowed 2/15/1786. Account includes boarding of "children." PROP. & SETTLM.: Claims L206.19.7 1/2. Amount to be proportioned L63.18.5. Allowed 3/15/1786 with order to Admr. to pay. GDP.: 12/16/1801. Does not name father. Of: Thomas Penhallow and Sarah Ann Penhallow, Portsmouth minors over 14. Gdn. Daniel Austin, Portsmouth merchant. Bond $2,000.00. Sureties: Hunking Penhallow and Benjamin Penhallow, Portsmouth merchants. Witnesses: Ann W. Penhallow and Sarah W. Austin.

2038. PERKINS, DANIEL (1783) #4958
EST. Of Seabrook decd. intestate. ADMIN. D.B.N.: (D26:26): 2/28/1781. Admr. d.b.n. Daniel Perkins. Sureties: Ebenr. Fogg, gent. and Joseph Hook, cordwainer, all of Seabrook. INVY.: Appr. 11/20/1783. Comm.: Winthrop Gove, Ebenezer Fogg and John Brown. Value L48.12.0. Oaths 11/25/1783 Fogg and Brown to Winthrop Gove, JP. Oath 12/17/1783 Admr. d.b.n .to W. Parker, Reg. LICENSE (D27:348): 12/16/1783. To Admr. d.b.n. To sell sufficient real est. to pay debts. ACCOUNT: 4/21/1784. Of Admr. d.b.n. Allowed 4/21/1784.

2039. PERKINS, JAMES (1774) #4097
EST. Rye gent. decd. testate. WILL: Drawn 3/13/1774. Legatees: Wife-Huldah; Sons-John, James and Abraham; Daus.-Huldah Lock and Martha Dow; Children of his dau. Ann Page, decd. Exec.- son James. His sig. Witnesses: Jonathan Tuck, Benjamin Tucke and John Smith. CERT. WILL (D22:448). 4/27/1774. Presented by Exec. and witnesses Jonathan Tuck and Benjamin Tucke. ADMIN.: 4/27/1774. Exec. James Perkins, Rye yoeman. Bond L1000.0.0. Sureties: Josiah Haynes of Greenland and Benjamin Tucke of Hampton, yoemen. Witnesses: Benjamin Barker and Saml Hale Jr.

2040. PERKINS, JAMES (1776) #4275
EST. Hampton gent. decd. ADMIN.: 10/30/1776. Admx. Jenny Perkins, Hampton widow. Bond L1000.0.0. Sureties: Jeremiah Knowles, esq. and John Moulton, yeoman, both of Hampton. Witnesses: W. Parker and Nathl. Parker. INVY.: Appr. 12/20/1776. Comm.: Joseph Dow, Cotton Ward and Jona. Garland. Value L780.10.0. Oaths 12/24/1776 Comm. to Jona. Moulton, JP. Oath 12/25/1776 Admx. to judge. ACCOUNT: 2/1778. Of Admx. (sig. Jane). Allowed 2/25/1778. PETITION: 2/9/1793. Of James Perkins, Molley Perkins, Moses Perkins and John Perkins. For div. and Dower.

2041. PERKINS, JOHN (1771) #3853
EST. John Perkins Jr., Dover yoeman decd. intestate. ADMIN.: 6/14/1771. Admx. Patience Perkins, Somersworth widow. Bond L1000.0.0. Sureties: Alexander Caldwell and Wm. Willee, Somersworth yoemen. Witnesses: Wm. Parker and Matthew Stanley Parker. INVY. WARR.: 6/14/1771. Comm.: Howard Henderson and Timothy Robinson, Dover yoeman. INVY.: Appr. 7/3/1771. Value L116.1.10. Oaths 4/29/1772 Admx. and Henderson, Affirm. Robinson.

2042. PERKINS, JOHN (1772) #3969
EST. Portsmouth mariner decd. intestate. ADMIN.: 11/25/1772. Admr. Joshua Brackett, physician. Bond L100.0.0. Sureties: Jacob Tilton and Samuel Parker, Portsmouth gentlemen. Witnesses: Thomas Ransom and Archd. Achincloss. CLAIMS WARR.: 8/23/1773. Comm.: Joseph Whipple, merchant and Joseph Peirce, gent., both of Portsmouth. CLAIMS: 2/23/1774. Total L3.12.0. Oaths 2/23/1774 Comm. to judge.

2043. PERKINS, JONATHAN (1776) #4276
EST. Kensington yoeman decd. testate. WILL: Drawn 7/20/1776. Legatees: Wife-Abigail; Sons-Jonathan and Darbon; Daus.-Mary Perkins, Betty Perkins, Olive Perkins, Abigail Perkins and Lucy Perkins. Admx.-wife Abigail. His sig. Witnesses: Obadiah Gove, Nathan Dearbon and Joseph Tilton. CERT. WILL.: 10/30/1776. Presented by Exex. and witnesses Dearbon and Tilton. INVY.: Comm.: Chase Willard, Nathan Dearbon and Joseph Tilton. INVY.: Appr. 11/4/1776. Value not tallied. Esti. L400.0.0+. Oaths 11/27/1776 Exex., Tilton and Dearbon to judge.

2044. PERKINS, MOSES (1777) #4309
EST. Kensington taylor decd. ADMIN.: 2/18/1777. Admx. Betty Perkins, Kensington widow. Bond L500.0.0. Sureties: Joseph Tilton, esq. and Benjamin Tilton, yoeman, both of Kensington. Witnesses: Joseph Fogg and W. Parker. INVY.: Appr. 2/25/1777. Comm.: Joseph Tilton and

Benjamin Tilton. Value L71.6.6. Oaths 2/26/1777 Comm. and Admr. to judge.

2045. PERKINS, SAMUEL (1771) #3892
EST. Seabrook husbm. decd. intestate. ADMIN.: 11/27/1771. Admx. Patience Pearkins, Seabrook widow. Bond L500.0.0. Sureties: Winthrop Gove and Ebenezer Fogg, Seabrook husbandmen. Witnesses: Ezekiel Carr and (Wad?) Stickney. INVY.: Appr. 1/23/1772. Comm.: Elisha Brown and Winthrop Gove. Value L119.16.0. Oaths 1/23/1772 Comm. to Jona. Fifield, JP. Oath 3/23/1772 Admx. to Meshech Weare, JP. LICENSE: 7/17/1773. To Admx. To sell 5 acres of land.

2046. PERLEY, DR. ABRAHAM (1776) #4235
EST. New Gloucester, Cumberland Co., MA/ME physician decd. testate. WILL: Drawn 8/25/1775. Legatee: Samuel Perley Jr. of Seabrook. Exec.: Samuel Perley. His sig. Witnesses: Gershom Griffith, Jacob Green and Samuel Perley. CERT. WILL: 5/29/1776. Presented by Exec. and all witnesses. ADMIN.: 4/29/1776. Exec.: Samuel Perley, Seabrook clerk. Bond L1000.0.0. Sureties: Ebenezer Fogg and Elisha Brown, Seabrook gentlemen. Witnesses: Elizabeth Parker and W. Parker.

PETTEE. See also Patee, Pattee

2047. PETTEE, JOHN (1781) No#
GDP. Of the son of Richard Pettee, Salem yoeman decd. GDP. (D26:192): 8/23/1781. Of John, a minor over 14. Gdn. Moody Morse. Sureties: Stephen Gage, cordwainer and James Webster, gent. Note: See also #4266 Richard Pettee (1776), est. of John's father, for a 1780 Gdp.

2048. PETTEE, RICHARD (1776) #4266 & (1778) #4440
EST. Salem yoeman decd. ADMIN. (#4266): 9/25/1776. Admr. Edward Pattee, Salem yoeman. Bond L500.0.0. Sureties: Alexander Gordon of Salem and James Paul, Londonderry gent. Witnesses: Saml. Briard and W. Parker. INVY. (#4440): Appr. 11/26/1778. Comm.: James Paul, Daniel Gordon and Caleb Duston. Value L596.0.6. Oaths 3/23/1778 Comm. to Timothy Ladd, JP. Oath 3/26/1778 Admr. to judge. GDP. (#4440): Of the children of Richard. GDP. (#4266): 3/29/1780, Of: Hannah, a minor over 14, and of John, a minor under 14. Gdn. Thomas Dow, Salem yoeman. Bond L5000.0.0. Sureties: Nathaniel Belknap and Richard Dusten, Salem yoemen. APPR. WARR. (#4440): 7/17/1780. Comm.: Daniel Gordon, Robert Young, Caleb Duston, Nathaniel Woodman and Timothy Ladd, esq. To view the real est. and see if it can be div. among all his children. Appr.: 7/17/1780. Value L36540.0.0. Oaths 7/17/1780 Duston and

Woodman to Timothy Ladd, JP. ACCOUNT (#4440): 10/25/1780. Of Admr. Allowed 10/25/1780. JUDGEMENT (#4440): 2/27/1781. Of Nathaniel Woodman and Daniel Gordon. At the request of the Admr. and Thomas Dow, Gdn. of 2 of the minor children, they judge that the share of the minor children should be 1/7 part each of all the est., exclusive of the interest the decd. had in the town of Thornton. ADDL. ACCOUNT (#4440): 2/28/1781. Of Admr. Shows a bal. of L125.9.11. to be divided among the heirs. Allowed 2/28/1781. DECREE SETTLM. (#4440): 2/28/1781. Edward Pattee, oldest son, appearing and consenting, the real est. settled on him. Edward releases his right to a double share, taking only one. There are 7 children, two of whose rights Edward has purchased. Edward to pay James Paul Pettee, John Pettee, Laomi Pettee, Hannah Pettee and John Pettee L5220.0.0 each within 6 months, plus interest. BOND. (#4440): 2/28/1781. Of Edward Pattee, Salem gent. Bond L60000.0.0. To pay his co-heirs per Decree Settlm. Sureties: John Moors Bayley and James Paul Pettee, Salem yoemen. Witnesses: O. Peabody and Nathl. Parker. DEED (#4440): 5/16/1780. Grantors: Edward Pattee, Peter Pattee, Richard Pattee, William Pattee and Jacob Sargent, Thornton, Grafton Co. yoemen and Mary Sargent, "and the women spinsters." Grantee: Edward Pattee of Salem. For L100.0.0 paid to each of them, they sell all right and title in a tract of land in Salem of 240acres+/-,with bldgs., being the home farm their father Richard Pettee lived on. Witnesses: Richd. Dustin and Alexander Long. Signed by all but Edward, which name was added and must to be an error as a Grantor. Oaths 5/19/1780 Grantors to Moses Baker, JP.

2049. PETTEE, RICHARD (1778) #4440
See #4266 Richard Pettee (1776)

2050. PETTEE, SETH (1776) 4203
EST. Salem yoeman decd. intestate. RENUN.: 1/30/1776. Of Dorcas Petee, widow of Seth. Of Admin. Requests appointment of her son Seth Patee. Witness: Obadiah Eastman. RENUN.: 2/3/1776. Of Jedediah Patee. Of Admin. of est. his father. Requests appointment of his bro. Seth Patee. Witnesses: Caleb Duston and Peter Duston. ADMIN.: 2/28/1776. Admr. Seth Patee, Salem yoeman. bond L1000.0.0. Sureties: Nathaniel Woodman, yoeman and Abraham Dow, esq., both of Salem. Witnesses: Saml. Jenness and Wm. Parker Jr. INVY. WARR.: 2/28/1776. Comm.: Abraham Dow, esq.; Nathaniel Woodman and Obadiah Eastman, all of Salem. INVY.: Appr. 5/28/1776 Value L64.19.10. OATHS 5/28/1776 Comm. to James Betton, JP. Oath 5/29/1776 Admr. to judge. ACCOUNT: Of Admr. Allowed 5/28/1777. DOWER WARR.: 3/29/1780. Comm.: Caleb Duston; Nathaniel Belknap; Thomas Dow; Nathaniel Woodman,

yoeman and Daniel Gordon, gent. Of Widow Dorcas Pettee. Note: The following Dower found in #4612 Seth Pettee 91780 belongs here. DOWER: Comm.: Caleb Duston, Daniel Gordon and Nathl. Belknap. Of Dorcas Patee. Oaths 3/26/1783 Comm. to Timothy Ladd, JP. Allowed 3/17/1784.

2051. PETTEE, SETH (1780) #4612
EST. Salem yoeman decd. RENUN.: 11/30/1779. Of Susanna Patee and Jedediah Patee, widow and bro. of Seth. Of Admin. Request appointment of Odadiah Eastman. ADMIN.: 3/29/1780. Admr. Odabiah Eastman, Salem esq. Bond L5000.0.0. Sureties: Nathaniel Belknap and Thomas Dow, Salem yoemen. Witnesses: Nathl. Parker and W. Parker. INVY.: Appr. 4/20/1780. Comm.: Caleb Duston, Nathaniel Woodman and Daniel Gordon. Value L17980.9.0. Oaths 7/17/1780 Comm. to Timothy Ladd, JP. Oath 8/1/1780 Admr. to W. Parker, Reg. ACCOUNT: 3/9/1784. Of Admr. Allowed 3/10/1784. Account includes main. the 4 children, the "2d and 3d" pos. twins. DOWER: 3/18/1784. Comm.: Caleb Duston, Nathl. Belknap and Daniel Gordon. Of Susanna Corliss in est. of Seth Patee. Oaths 3/31/1784 Comm. to Timothy Ladd, JP. Allowed 10/18/1791. APPR. WARR.: 10/18/1791. Comm.: Caleb Duston and Nathaniel Belknap, yoemen and Daniel Gordon, gent., all of Salem. To appr. the income of est., exclusive of the 2 dowers taken off it, since death so it may be accounted for by Admr. APPR.: 11/1791. Of 2/3 of the real est. exclusive of the 2 Dowers. Value $8.50. Oaths 9/27/1798 Comm. to Jos. Wardwell, JP. APPR. WARR.: 8/27/1798. Comm.: Thomas Dow, esq.; Daniel Gordon and Benjamin Gordon, gentlemen, all of Salem. To appr. 2/3 of real est. and reversion of Dower set off to Susanna Corliss for settlm. APPR.: 9/16/1798. Of Dower of Susanna Corliss. Value $170.67. Oaths 9/27/1798 Daniel Gordon and Benjamin Gordon to Jos. Wardwell, JP. DECREE SETTLM.: 10/3/1798. Jonathan Patee, oldest son, appearing and consenting, the real est. settled on him, Jonathan to pay Eliphalet, Stephen and Susanna, his co-heirs, $187.73 each in 6 months, with interest. BOND: 10/3/1798. Of Jonathan Patee, yoeman. Bond $1,000.00. To pay his co-heirs per Decree Settlm. Sureties: Daniel Corliss, gent. and Eliphalet Patee, yoeman, both of Salem. Witnesses: Saml. Parker and W, Parker.

2052. PEVERLY, NATHANIEL (1799) #6619
EST. Canterbury yoeman decd. testate. WILL: Drawn 5/20/1799. Legatees: Sons-Nathaniel Jr., James and Benjamin. Exec.- son James. His sig. Witnesses: Leavitt Clough, Henry Beck and William Tirrell. CERT. WILL (D33:160): 10/22/1799. Presented by Exec. and witnesses Beck and Tirrell. INVY. (D33:479): On Warr. of 10/22/1799. Comm.: Leavitt

Clough, Henry Beck and Henry Tibbets. Value $1,966.46. Oaths 5/19/1801 Comm. to Saml. Piper, JP. Oath 5/20/1801 Exec. to judge.

2053. PHELPS, JOSHUA (1784) #5028
EST. Pembroke yoeman decd. RENUN.: 8/17/1784. Of Margaret Phelps, widow of Joshua. Of Admin. Requests appointment of her son Samuel Phelps. Witnesses: Richd. Bartlet and John Whittier. ADMIN.: 8/18/1784. Admr. Samuel Phelps, Pembroke yoeman. Bond L500.0.0. Sureties: Richard Bartlet, esq. and Samuel Kimball, yoeman, both of Pembroke. Witnesses: W. Parker and Nat Parker. INVY. WARR.: 8/18/1784. Comm.: Nathaniel Lakeman, Frederic McCutchon and Stephen Bartlet, all of Pembroke. INVY.: Appr. 11/13/1784. Value L190.15.10. Oaths 11/15/1784 Admr. and Comm. to Richd. Bartlet, JP.

2054. PHILBRICK, ABNER (1790) #5560
EST. Seabrook husbm. decd. testate. WILL: Drawn 9/24/1788. Legatees: Wife-Hannah; Sons-Samuel and Joseph; Daus.-Hannah Cram, Mary Cram and Mehetibel Gove. Grandsons-Abner Cram and Abner Gove. Exec.-son Joseph. His sig. Witnesses: Jonathan Marble, Abner Dow Jr. and Benjamin Dow. CERT. WILL (D29:400): 7/21/1790. Presented by Exec. and affirms. of witnesses Abner Dow Jr. and Benjamin Dow. ADMIN.: 7/21/1790. Exec. Joseph Philbrick, Seabrook yoeman. Bond L1000.0.0. Sureties: Abraham Dow and Benjamin Dow, Seabrook yoemen. Witnesses: W. Parker and N. Parker. INVY.: Appr. 10/9/1790. Comm.: Elisha Brown, Abraham Dow and Moses Gove. Value L975.10.0. Affirms. Dow and Gove to Elisha Brown, JP. Oath 11/17/1790 Exec. to judge.

2055. PHILBRICK, DANIEL (1767) A#3497
EST. Rye yeoman decd. DOWER (D25:387): Comm.: Richd. Jenness Jr., esq.; Saml. Knowles, Peter Garland, Henry Elkins and Nathl. Jenness. Of Abigail Davison in est. her former husband Daniel Philbrick of Rye decd. Oaths 11/21/1780 Comm. to Saml. Jenness, JP. ACCOUNT (D28:440): 2/15/1786. Of Reuben Philbrick, William Davison and Abigail his wife, Admrs. Allowed 2/15/1786. Orig. Archives file includes License and Invy.

2056. PHILBRICK: EDWARD, JOHN, MARY, MEHETABEL AND SAMUEL (1778) #4417
GDP. Of the children of Benjamin Philbrick, Exeter blacksmith decd. GDP.: 1/29/1778. Of: Samuel and John, minors over 14. Gdn. Jabez Dodge, Exeter potter. Bond L500.0.0. Sureties: Samuel Brooks, esq. and Nicholas Gilman Jr., cordwainer, both of Exeter. Witnesses: Nathl. Folsom and Wm. Parker. GDP.: 1/29/1778. Of: Mary, a minor over 14 and of

Mehetabel and Edward, minors under 14.Gdn. Benjamin Stevens, Kingston yoeman. Bond L500.0.0. Sureties: Samuel Brooks, esq. and Nicholas Gilman Jr., cordwainer, both of Exeter. Witnesses: John Turner (? sic.) and W. Parker.

2057. PHILBRICK, JAMES (1796) #6288
Error. See James Pickering (1796) #6288

2058. PHILBRICK, JAMES (1798) #6476
Error. See James Pickering (1798) #6476

2059. PHILBRICK, JEDEDIAH (1790) #5549
EST. Hawke gent. decd. ADMIN.: 5/27/1790. Admx. Mary Philbrick, Hawke widow. Bond L1000.0.0. Sureties: Jethro Sanborn and Jonathan Sanborn, Hawke yoemen. Witnesses: Thomas Page and Daniel Davis. INVY.: Comm.: Thomas Page, Daniel Davis and James Sawyer. Value L337.3.9. Oaths 7/21/1790 Admx., Davis and Sawyer to Thos. Page, JP. ACCOUNT: 10/3/1793. Of Admx. Allowed 10/3/1793. Account includes main. 3 children. PETITION: 10/3/1793. Of Admx. For License. LICENSE (D31:79): 10/31/1793. To Admx. To sell real est. to amount of L78.0.0.

2060. PHILBRICK, JEREMIAH (1791) #5687
EST. Kingston yoeman decd. testate. WILL: Drawn 3/5/1791. Legatees: Mother unnamed; Bros.-Abraham, Jedediah and John; Sister-Sarah Philbrick. Execs.-bros. Jedediah and Abraham. His sig. Witnesses: Abraham French, Joseph Judkins and Robert S. French. CERT. WILL (D30:111): 8/23/1791. Presented by Execs. and witnesses Abraham French and Judkins. ADMIN.: 8/23/1791. Execs.: Jedediah Philbrick of Protectworth, Cheshire Co. and Abraham Philbrick, Kingston yoeman. Bond L500.0.0.Sureties: Abraham French, esq. and Joseph Judkins, yoeman, both of Kingston. Witnesses: Nathl. Herrick and W. Parker. INVY.: Appr. 8/26/1791. Comm.: Amos Gale and Joseph Judkins. Value L216.17.0. Oaths 8/26/1791 Comm. to Simmons Seccombe, JP. Oaths 9/2/1791 Execs. to W. Parker, JP.

2061. PHILBRICK, JOHN (1780) #4593
EST. Deerfield husbm. decd,. testate. WILL: Drawn 7/29/1779. Legatees: Wife-Sarah, pos. former wife of Jacob Doe and also refers to a bond which he has given to John Guile assuring her of a comfortable maintenance; Sons-Caleb, Nathaniel and John; Dau.-Mary Philbrick. Execs.-sons Caleb and Nathaniel. His sig. Witnesses: Samuel Prescott, Stephen Prescott and Cotton Haines. CERT. WILL (D25:322): Presented by Execs. and

witnesses Samuel Prescott and Stephen Prescott. INVY.: Appr. 3/18/1780. Comm.: Nathan Sanborn, Benjamin Sanborn and Samuel Prescott, all of Deerfield. Value not tallied. Esti. L3477+. Oaths 3/21/1780 Comm. to Jeremiah Eastman, JP. Oath 4/27/1780 Caleb Philbrick, acting Exec., to W. Parker, Reg. & JP.

2062. PHILBRICK, JOHN (1791) #5715
EST. Newmarket cabinetmaker decd. ADMIN.: 11/21/1791. Admr. Samuel Philbrook, Greenland cabinetmaker. Bond L1000.0.0. Sureties: Joseph Clark, cabinetmaker and George Philbrick, yoeman, both of Greenland. Witnesses: N. Parker and W. Parker, Reg. INVY.: Appr. 2/8/1792. Comm.: Enoch Clark, Job Chapman and Joseph Clark. Value L8.5.5. Oaths 1 (sic.)/8/1792 Comm. to Stephn March, JP. Oath 2/9/1792 Admr. to W. Parker, JP. PETITION: 4/16/1792. Of Admr. For Comm. Insolvency. CLAIMS WARR.: 4/16/1792. Comm.: Enoch Clark and Job Chapman, Greenland husbandmen. Claims: 11/28/1792. Total L36.17.1. Oaths 11/28/1792 Comm. to Stephn. March, JP. ACCOUNT.: Of Admr. Allowed 5/13/1793.

2063. PHILBRICK, JOHN (1794) #6024
GDP. Of the son of John Philbrick, Deerfield yoeman decd. GDP.: 9/17/1794. Of John, a minor over 14. Gdn. Jonathan Philbrick, Deerfield yoeman. Bond L1000.0.0. Sureties: Edward Smith and Noah Lane, yoemen, both of Deerfield. Witnesses: Michl. McClary and W. Parker.

2064. PHILBRICK, JOSEPH (1788) #5372
EST. Rye blacksmith decd. testate. WILL: Drawn 8/25/1788. Legatees: Wife-Anna; Sons- Joses, Daniel, Levi, James, Joseph and Jonathan; Daus.- Anna Philbrook, Abigail Philbrook and Hannah Philbrook; Child with whom his wife is pregnant. Execs.-wife Anna and David Lock. His sig. Witnesses: Levi Dearborn, Huntington Porter and David Lock Jr. CERT. WILL (D29:209): 9/17/1788. Presented by Execs. and witnesses Porter and Lock. INVY.: Comm.: James Perkins, Nathan Goss and Samuel Walls Jr. Value L305.1.0. Oaths 12/11/1788 Execs. and Comm. to Simon Jenness, JP. Note: The following License found in file #5221 Joseph Pilsbury (1786) belongs here. LICENSE: 6/17/1789. To David Lock, an Exec. To sell real est. to amount of L20.0.0. ACCOUNT: 12/24/1788. Of David Lock, an Exec. Cert.: 6/15/1796 Of Jonathan Philbrick, residuary legatee. He has seen Account and is satisfied with it. Allowed 6/15/1796.

2065. PHILBRICK: JOSES & SARAH (1780) #4642
GDP. Of the children of Daniel Philbrick, Rye yoeman decd. GDP.: 7/26/1780. Of Joses and Sarah, minors over 14. Gdn. Joseph Jenness, Rye gent. Bond L5000. Sureties: Richard Jenness, esq. and Michael Dalton, cordwainer, both of Rye. Witnesses: Wm. Parker and Jno. Parker.

2066. PHILBRICK, LYDIA (1777) #4339
EST. Exeter widow decd. ADMIN.: 3/27/1777. Admr. Jabez Dodge, Exeter potter. Bond L500. Sureties: Trueworthy Gilman, gent. and Stephen Thing, yoeman, both of Exeter. Witness Nathl. Parker. INVY. WARR.: 3/27/1777. Comm.: Trueworthy Gilman, gent.; Stephen Thing and Jeremiah Leavitt, yoeman, both of Exeter. INVY.: Appr. 4/1777. Value L370.17.7. Oaths 9/29/1777 Thing and Gilman to W. Parker, JP. ACCOUNT: 12/30/1778. Of Admr. Allowed 12/31/1778.

2067. PHILBRICK, NATHANIEL (1780) #4594
GDP. Of the son of John Philbrick, Deerfield yoeman decd. GDP.: 1/26/1780. Of Nathaniel, a minor over 14. Gdn. Jonathan Philbrick, Deerfield yoeman. Bond L2000.0.0. Sureties: Seth Fogg of Epping and Jonathan Gove of Nottingham, gentlemen. Witnesses: Nathl. Parker and W. Parker.

2068. PHILBRICK, SAMUEL (1779) #4536
EST. Kingston esq. decd. testate. WILL: Drawn 3/29/1779. Legatees: Wife-Sarah; Sons-Jedediah, Jeremiah, Abraham, John and Samuel; Dau.-Sarah Philbrick. Exex.-wife Sarah. Hs sig. Witnesses: Abraham French, Joseph Judkins and Henry French. CERT. WILL (D25:86): 4/28/1779. Presented by Exex. and witnesses Abraham French and Judkins. INVY.: Comm.: Amos Gale, Abraham French and Joseph Judkins. Value L8900.02.0. plus a list of Notes not tallied. Esti. L31.0.0+. Oaths 7/27/1779 Comm. to Josiah Bartlett, JP. Oath 7/28/1779 Admx. to judge.

2069. PHILLIPS, HON. JOHN (1795) #6095
EST. Exeter esq. decd. testate. WILL: Drawn 9/7/1789. Legatees; Wife-Elizabeth; Kinsmen-Samuel Phillips Jr., esq. of Andover and his son John Phillips; Four children of his bro. William Phillips esq. who are living one year after his death; Children of his sister Lydia Clark decd. who are living one year after his death; John Phillips Gilman; John Phillips Thurston; His manservant ("slave I have none"); Trustees of Phillips Exeter Academy and Trustees of Phillips Academy in Andover, Ma. Exec.-Hon. Samuel Phillips Jr. esq. His sig. Witnesses: Gideon Lamson, Oliver Peabody, Nat. Gilman and John Lamson. CERT. WILL (D31:520): 4/28/1795. Presented by Exec. and witnesses Gilman, esq. and John Lamson. ADMIN.:

4/28/1795. Exec. Samuel Phillips, Andover, Essex Co., MA esq. Bond L2000.0.0. Sureties: John Taylor Gilman and Oliver Peabody, Exeter esquires. Witnesses: W. Parker and Nath. Parker. INVY.: Appr. 8/1/1795. Comm.: John Haven, John W. Gilman and Gideon Lamson. Value L5783.15.11 1/2 plus books at L23.5.2 = Esti. L5806.0.0+. ACCOUNT: 3/24/1803. Of Exec. Allowed 4/18/1803 having been examined by those interested in est. Cert.: 3/25/1803. Of J.T. Gilman and Oliver Peabody. By authorization of the Trustees of Phillips Exeter Academy they have examined and approve of Account. ADMIN. D.B.N.: 8/3/1807. Admr. d.b.n. Oliver Peabody, Exeter esq. Bond $4,000.00. Sureties: John Taylor Gilman, esq. and Gideon Lamson, merchant, both of Exeter. Witness Wm. Parker. PETITION: 6/19/1837. Of Jeremiah Smith, Treasurer of Phillips Exeter Academy. States that both Admrs. appointed are dead and since their deaths a dividend due Phillips Exeter Academy and Phillips Academy has not been paid, the Admr. of the est. of John Parker, of Litchfield decd., declining to pay anyone but a legal rep. of the est. Requests that he be appointed Admr. D.B.N. ADMIN. D.B.N.: 7/12/1738. Admr. d.b.n. Jeremiah Smith, Exeter esq. Bond $1,000.00. Sureties: Joseph Tilton and Timothy Farrar, Exeter esquires. Witness John Kelly.

2070. PHILLIPS, THOMAS (1779) No#
EST. Portsmouth mariner decd. ADMIN. (D25:154): 5/14/1779. Admr. John Wendell Jr., merchant. Sureties: John Wendell, esq. and Daniel Wentworth Wendell, all of Portsmouth.

2071. PICKERING: ANNA, ELIZABETH, GEORGE & MARY (1772) #3948
GDP. Of the children of Joshua Pickering of Greenland decd. GDP.: 6/29/1772. Of: Anna, Elizabeth, George and Mary Pickering, minors under 14. Gdn. Joshua Brackett, Portsmouth physician. Bond L500. Sureties: Samuel Hale Jr. and Samuel Parker, Portsmouth gentlemen. Witnesses: Wyseman Clagett and John Folsom.

2072. PICKERING, ANTHONY (1786) #5220
EST. Newmarket yoeman decd. RENUN.: 10/18/1786. Of Abigail Pickering, widow of Anthony and Anthony Pickering, oldest son. Of Admin. Request appointment of Samuel Pickering, a younger son. James Pickering, a younger son, joins in the request. ADMIN.: 10/18/1786. Admr. Samuel Pickering, Newmarket yoeman. Bond L1000.0.0. Sureties: Nathl. Rogers and Josiah Adams, Newmarket esquires. Witness W. Parker. INVY.: Appr. 11/15/1786. Comm.: James Hill, Nat. Rogers and Josiah Admas. Value L1185.5.0. Oaths 11/15/1786 Comm. and Admr. to W. Parker, Reg. ADDL. INVY.: 1/5/1787. Value L21.9.0. CITATION:

8/26/1791. To Admr. To appear and exhibit his Account for settlm. Cert. Of Richd. Hilton, Newmarket Constable. He read the Citation to Samuel Pickering. CITATION: 8/26/1791. To Elizabeth or Betty Tufts, single woman. To appear and give evidence of what she knows relating to the embezzling or concealing of any personal effects belonging to est. and to the Account of the Admr. Cert. of Richd. Hilton, Newmarket Constable. He read Citation to Elizabeth or Betty Tufts and gave her L0.1.6. ACCOUNT: The judge notes that the hearing postponed to Nov. Again postponed to 10/17/1791.

2073. PICKERING, BENJAMIN (1794) #6008
EST. Newington yoeman decd. testate. WILL: Drawn 3/26/1794. Legatees: Wife-Martha; Son-Thomas. Exex.-wife Martha. His sig. Witnesses: Benjamin Adams, Ephraim Pickering and Volintine Pickering. CERT. WILL (D32:310): 6/18/1794. Presented by Exex. and witnesses Volentine Pickering and Adams. ADMIN.: 6/18/1794. Exec. Martha Pickering, Newington widow. Bond L1000.0.0. Sureties: Benjamin Adams, esq. and Volintine Pickering. Witnesses: Jno. Parker and W. Parker. PETITION: 4/17/1813. Of Thomas Pickering of Newington. For div. of his 2/3 share of the real est. willed to him. Granted and Comm. named. DIV. WARR.: 4/17/1813. Comm.: Cyrus Frink, gent.; Richard D. Hart, Ephraim Coleman and Samuel Adams, husbandmen, all of Newington and Tobias Tuttle, Dover, Strafford Co. yoeman. To set off to Thomas Pickering 2/3 of the real est. Comm. to notify William Drew, owner of the other third in right of his wife during her life, so he may be present. DIV.: 5/15/1813. Divisees: William Pickering 3d and William Drew in right of his wife. Oaths 6/9/1813 Frink, Hart and Coleman to N.W. Adams, JP. Allowed 6/16/1813.

2074. PICKERING, CAPT. DANIEL (1765) #3170 & (1786) #6174 1/2
EST. Portsmouth mariner decd. Note: All of the following items are in #6174 1/2. PETITION: 4/27/2797. Of Jonathan Sherburne atty. to Dr. Titus Salter, Admr. For License. Gives personal est. as only L4.13.0 and list claims of L299.11.8. Allowed. LICENSE (D32:298): To Admr. Salter. To sell real est. to amount of $1100.00. ACCOUNT: Dated by clerk 1797. Of Admr. Dr. Titus Salter submitted by Jona. Sherburne his atty. especially appointed for the year 2/17/1798. Titus' claim against est. Total L50.9.2.0=$140.67 plus several items added without total. CLAIMS: Comm. George Wentworth and Nathl. Marshall, mariners and Samuel Hutchings, trader, all of Portsmouth. Total $1,141.24. Oaths 8/4/1797 Comm. to R. Cutts Shannon, JP. ACCOUNT: Of Admr. Allowed 10/18/1797. PROP. & SETTLM.: Claims $1,140.07. Amount to be proportioned $533.00. Allowed 10/30/1797 with order to Admr. to pay.

PETITION: 9/3/1807. Of John Saml. Sherburne, esq., Admr. of est. of Jno. Sherburne, Portsmouth esq. decd. For permission to sue Bond of Admin. as Admr., now decd., never paid Sherburne his proportion as allowed. Order: 9/3/1807. For hearing, Daniel Hart, Portsmouth, merchant, the only surviving person who signed the Bond, to be notified to appear. Note: The file also contains a newspaper ad from the N.H. GAZETTE for this est. by Dorothy Pickering, Admx. dated Oct. 1786. Orig. Archives file includes Admin. with Dorothy Pickering and Titus Salter Admrs. (Dorothy was Daniel's mother), Invy., License (1765), List Claims (1767), License (1767), Citation to Salter (1796) and Claims Warr. (1796).

2075. PICKERING, DEBORAH (1797) #6313
EST. Newington widow decd. ADMIN.: 2/15/1797. Admr. Richard Pickering, Newington gent. Bond $2,000.00. Sureties: Ephm. Pickering, esq. and Richard Downing Hart, yoeman, both of Newington. Witnesses: Geo. Gains and W. Parker. INVY.: Comm.: Ephraim Pickering and Stephen March. Appr. 3/7/1797. Value $1,984.04. Oaths 4/21/1797 Comm. to Thomas Leavitt, JP. Oath 7/31/1797 Admr. to Wm. Parker, JP. ACCOUNT: 3/17/1806. Of Admr. Allowed 3/19/1806 as there were no objections. GDP. ACCOUNT: Of Richard D. Hart against the est. of Deborah Pickering decd. 1/11/1820. Allowed 1/16/1820 as heirs were notified and those present made no objection. Also see file #10344 Deborah Pickering 1821. A partition between the heirs of Deborah Pickering in the est. formerly of Valentine Pickering. DIV. WARR.: 1/11/1820. Comm.: Benjamin Akerman of Portsmouth; Cyrus Frink, Richard D. Hart, Ephraim Colman and Hanson Hoit, all of Newington. To divide lands in Newington, part of the land formerly property of Volentine Pickering decd. which was set off from said est. to Deborah Pickering, one of the heirs of the est. of Valentine Pickering decd. DIVISEES: Isaac Dow and wife 3/6; Sally Hodgdon wife of Charles Hodgdon 1/6; Eliza Pickering 1/6 and Volentine Pickering 1/6. Oaths and affim. Akerman 5/15/1820 to Ephm. Colman, JP. Allowed 9/11/1821.

2076. PICKERING, DOROTHY (1790) #5571
EST. Portsmouth widow decd. testate. WILL: Drawn 9/28/1781.Legatees:Five daus.-Elizabeth Prowse, Abigail Janvrin, Dorothy Nelson, Lydia Underwood and Mary Drowne; Grandchildren-Alice Williams and George Jery Osborne. Execs.-dau. Dorothy Nelson and son-in-law Samuel Drowne. Her sig. Witnesses: John Pickering, Thomas Bickford and Abigail Pickering. CERT. WILL (D29:421): 9/3/1790. Presented by Execs. and witnesses John Pickering, Esq. and Abigail Pickering. ADMIN.: 9/3/1790. Execs.: Dorothy Nelson, widow and Samuel Drowne, goldsmith, both of Portsmouth. Bond L1000.0.0.

Sureties: Samuel Hutchings and George Jerry Osborne Jr., both of Portsmouth. Witnesses: John Salter and Nathl. Marshall. INVY. WARR.: 10/20/1790. Comm.: John Evans, Samuel Hutchings, trader and Nathaniel Marshall, mariner, all of Portsmouth. "and likewise an Invy. of the est. not already inventoried of William Pickering, late of Portsmouth, mariner decd. to be shown by Samuel Drowne. INVY.: Appr. 5/25/1791. Value L91.1.11. Oaths 5/25/1791 Hutchings, Marshall and Admr. Drowne to W. Parker, JP. There is a note added to Invy.: "not withstanding the Invy. org. not returned Oct. 15th (now?) following (Williams?)

2077. PICKERING, JAMES (1796) #6288
EST. Exeter yoeman decd. testate. WILL: Drawn 10/12/1796. Legatees: Son-James; Dau.-Mary Smith wife of Daniel Smith of Meredith, Strafford Co. Exec.- son James. His sig. Witnesses: Thos. S. Ranney, Wm. Parker Jr. and Joseph Perkins. Codicil: 11/26/1796. Gives dau. Mary addl. legacy. His sig. Witnesses: John Batchelder, Joseph Perkins and Wm. Parker Jr. CERT. WILL (D32:226): 12/16/1796. Presented by Exec. and witnesses Parker and Perkins. ADMIN.: 12/16/1796. Admr. James Pickering, Exeter yoeman. Bond $2,000.00. Sureties: Gideon Lamson, merchant and William Parker Jr., physician, both of Exeter. Witnesses: Wm. Parker Adams and W. Parker. The following Petition found in #6191 James Pickering (1796) belongs here. PETITION: 3/20/1799. Of Exec. For License. He notes est. owes him $102.51 and he has already paid the bal. of his former Account to the Gdn. of heirs. Order: 3/20/1799. For hearing, Petition to notify the heir. LETTER ADMIN.: 7/10/1799. To Daniel Smith, Meredith, Strafford Co. gent. To administer est. of James Pickering, Exeter yoeman, the Exec. of whose Will was his son James now decd. Note: This file also contains an Admin., Renun. and Admin. D.B.N. which belong with #6476 James Pickering (1798) and a Release which belongs with #5527 John Pickering (1790). They are recorded in the proper places.

2078. PICKERING, JAMES (1798) #6476
EST. Of Exeter decd. testate. WILL: Drawn 6/16/1798. Legatees: Wife-Roseymond; Sister-Mary Smith wife of Daniel Smith Jr. of Meredith, Strafford Co. Exec.-wife Roseymond. His sig. Witnesses: Gee Pickering, John Batchelder and Thos. S. Ranney. CERT. WILL (D32:508): 7/17/1787. Presented by Exex. and witnesses Pickering and Batchelder. Note: The following Admin., Renun. and Admin. D.B.N. found in #6288 James Pickering (1796) belong here: ADMIN.: 7/17/1798. Exex. Rosamond Pickering, Exeter widow. Bond $3,000.00. Sureties: John Fabyan of Newington and Joshua Pickering of Greenland, esquires. Witnesses: John Batchelder and W. Parker. RENUN.: 7/9/1799. Of

Rosamond Pickering, widow of James and Exex. States that there is little business to transact for est., mostly to effect transfer of stock bequeathed to wife of Daniel Smith. Requests appointment of Smith. ADMIN. D.B.N.: 7/10/1799. Admr. d.b.n. Daniel Smith, Meredith, Strafford Co. gent. Bond $2,000.00. Sureties: Daniel Smith and Jeremiah Leavitt, both of Exeter. Witnesses: Nathl. Parker and W. Parker.

2079. PICKERING, JOHN JR. (1790) #5527 & #5528 1790
EST. Newington husbm. decd. testate. INVY.: Appr. 4/8/1790. Comm.: Benjamin Adams, Saml. Shackford and Richd. Pickering. Value L85.2.4. Oaths 4/8/1790 Shackford and Pickering to Benjamin Adams, JP. Oath 4/9/1790 James Pickering, Admr., to W. Parker, JP. ADDL. INVY.: 11/26/1791. Total $25.5.0. Signed by Pickering and Adams. ACCOUNT: 3/21/1792. Of Admr. Allowed 3/22/1791.

2080. PICKERING, JOHN (1790) #5528
EST. Newington husbm. decd. testate. WILL: Drawn 1/4/1790. Legatees: Wife-Mary; Sons-Stephen, James, John, Volentine and William; Daus.-Temperance Hodgedon, Sarah Tasker, Polly Pickering and Abigail Huntress; Granddaus.-Mary Nutter and Mary Knight; Abigail Nutter and John Nutter. Execs.-sons Volentine and William. His sig. Witnesses: Ephraim Pickering, Joseph Pickering, James Grant and John Fabyan. Proved: 3/17/1790 on oaths of witnesses Ephraim Pickering, esq.; Joseph Pickering and Grant. Fabyan swore that about a fortnight after the signing, he saw decd. sign the instrument again and decale it to be his last Will. At that time, to the best of Fabyan's knowledge, the decd. was of sound mind and that he, Fabyan, had witnesses the Will. Will allowed. James Pickering, a son, petitioned for appeal against allowance. Granted. ADMIN.: 3/17/1790. Execs.: William Pickering, yoeman and Volentine Pickering, gent., both of Newington. Bond L1000.0.0. Sureties: Ephraim Pickering and John Fabyan, Newington esquires. Witness W. Parker. The following Invy. found in #5527 John Pickering Jr. (1790) belongs here. INVY.: 3/24/1790. Comm.: Ephraim Pickering, John Fabyan and Dennis Hight. Value L125.16.6. Oath 1790 Fabyan and on 3/24/1790 Volentine Pickering, an Exec., to Ephraim Pickering, JP. The following Bond found in #5527 John Pickering Jr. (1790) belongs here. BOND: 4/9/1790. Of James Pickering, Newington husbm. Bond L50.0.0. To sue Decree allowing Will. Sureties: Noah Huntress and Nehemiah Pickering, Newington husbandmen. Witnesses: Mary S. Parker and W. Parker. The following Account found in #6191 John Pickering (1796) belongs here. ACCOUNT: 3/20/1796. Of Volentine Pickering, an Exec. Allowed 3/20/1796 the objections of W. P. Pickering, Co-Exec., having been considered. The following Pet., Notification and copy of same, Div.,

Account and Warr. of Distress recorded as #5747 Volentine Pickering, et. al (1792) belong here. PETITION: 1/12/1792. Of Volentine Pickering, Newington gent. For div. of land in Newington which he holds as tenant in common with his bo. William Pepperell Pickering, who refuses to div. though requested and of age and understanding to do so. Order: 1/16/1792. For hearing, W. P. Pickering to be notified to appear. NOTIFICATION: 1/16/1792. To William Pepperell Pickering, Newington yoeman. Of hearing on Petition. Cert.: 2/3/1792. Of Joshua Pickering, Constable(?). He has received (sic.) the orig. Notice to William. COPY OF NOTIFICATION: Cert.: 7/12/1792. Of Ebenr. Chadwick, Dept. Shff. He has notified William of Notification. DIV.: 3/21/1792. Comm.: Saml. Langdon, Joseph Tucker, Sam. Sherburne, Joseph Whidden and George Brackett. Divisees as in Petition. Oaths 3/31/1792 Comm. to Ephraim Pickering, JP. Allowed 6/20/1792. Includes particularly fine Map. ACCOUNT: Of Volentine Pickering. Of expensew of Div. William P. Pickering was notified of exhibit of Account. He appeared and hearing postponed from time to time, William not appearing. On 11/21/1792 the Account allowed and Decreed that William pay to Volentine L8.10.6, half the cost of Div. William being in default, a Warr. of Distress ordered issued. WARR. OF DISTRESS: 1/30/1795. To Sheriff of Rockingham Co. or his Depy. They are to collect the sum due Volentine by William in money, goods or chattels plus an addl. L0.3.0 for the writ and the Sheriff's fees. For want to money, goods or chattels, he is to take the body of William and commit him to jail in Portsmouth. Receipt: 2/7/1795. Of Volentine Pickering. For full satisfaction of the debt. The following Account found in #6191 John Pickering (1796) belongs here. ACCOUNT: 3/20/1800. Of William Pepperell Pickering, an Exec. Allowed 3/20/1800 the objections of Volentine Pickering, Co-Exec., having been considered. Receipt: Of William P. Pickering. To Volentine Pickering. For the bal. of $267.83.

2081. PICKERING, JOHN (1796) #6191
EST. Portsmouth miller decd. intestate. ADMIN.: 3/26/1796. Admx. Elizabeth Pickering, Portsmouth widow. Bond $2,000.00. Sureties: James Sheafe, esq. and Matthew S. Marsh, merchant, both of Portsmouth. Witnesses: Augustus Willard and Robt. Price. INVY. WARR.: 3/26/1796. Comm.: George Gains, Isaac Rindge and Daniel R. Rogers, Portsmouth esquires. INVY.: Appr. 6/6/1796. Value $459.25. Oaths 6/7/1796 Gains and Rindge and on 6/29/1796 Admx. to Saml. Penhallow, JP. PETITION: 6/28/1796. Of Admx. For license. Granted 6/1/1796 to amount of L50.0.0. LICENSE (D32:157): 7/1/1796. To Admx. To sell real est. to amount of $166.66. Note: This file also includes 2 Accounts which belong with#5528 John Pickering(1790) and a Petition which belongs to #6288 John Pickering (1796). They are recorded in their proper places.

2082. PICKERING, JOHN GEE (1796) #6178
EST. Newington husbm. decd. testate. WILL: Drawn 8/8/1795. Legatees: Wife-Deborah; Sons-Gee and Thomas; Daus.-Mary Thompson, Temperance Pickering and Sarah Pickering. Execs.-wife Deborah, son Gee and bro. Richard. His sig. Witnesses: Samuel Fabyan, James Nutter and Absalom Pickering. CERT.WILL(D32:92): 2/17/1796. Presented by Execs. and all witnesses. ADMIN.: 2/17/1796. Execs.: Deborah Pickering, widow; Gee Pickering, yoeman and Richard Pickering, esq., all of Newington. Bond $4,000.00. Sureties: Ephraim Pickering, esq. and Samuel Fabyan, yoeman, both of Newington. Witnesses: Nathl. Treadwell and W. Parker. INVY.: Appr. 3/1/1796. Comm.: Stephen March, George Brackett and Ephraim Pickering. Value $13,373.16. Oaths 3/1/1796 Brackett and March to Ephraim Pickering, JP. Oath 10/19/1796 Richard Pickering, an Exec., to judge. ACCOUNT: 3/17/1806. Of Richard Pickering and Gee Pickering, Execs. Cert.: 3/17/1806. Of Gee Pickering and Thomas Pickering. They have received from Rickard Pickering, esq., an Exec., all of the real and personal est. in his hands and discharge him from any further demands against est. Allowed 3/19/1806 having been consented to by heirs.

2083. PICKERING, JOSHUA (1771) #3885
EST. Greenland gent. and blacksmith decd. intestate. INVY. WARR.: 7/17/1771. Comm.: John Haven, gent. and Enoch Clarke, esq., both of Greenland. ADMIN.: 10/20/1771. Admx. Mary Pickering, Greenland widow. Bond L500.0.0. Sureties: Joshua Brackett, physician and John Pickering Jr., both of Portsmouth. Witnesses: Saml. Hale Jr. and Job Jenness. INVY.: Appr. 9/6/1771. Oath 4/29/1774 Admx. to judge. LICENSE: 4/29/1772. To Admx. To sell enough real est. to raise L50. CLAIMS WARR.: 5/27/1772. Comm.: Samuel Penhallow, Portsmouth esq. and Greenleaf Clark, Greenland joiner. PETITION: Of Admx. Notes that Samuel Pickering, Greenland gent., has obtained by false presentation the Gdp. of four of her children under 14, who she had by Joshua, her husband decd. She is apprehensive that Samuel has some sinister end in mind in being appointed Gdn., seemingly to get into his hands Joshua's whole est. and defraud her and her children. Requests revocation of Samuel's Gdp. and that she, or some other suitable person, be appointed. Order: 6/16/1772. For hearing, Petitioner to notify Samuel Pickering. Order: 6/25/1772 Hearing adjourned to 6/29. Order: 6/29/1772. That Samuel Pickering's appointment as Gdn. be revoked and disannulled. Joshua Brackett, Portsmouth physician, to be appointed Gdn. of the children. DOWER WARR.: 6/29/1772. Comm.: Samuel Penhallow of Portsmouth and Samuel Lane of Stratham, esquires and Greenleaf Clark, Greenland joiner. Of Widow Mary Pickering. Dower: 8/26/1772. Oaths

Lane and Clark and on 9/5/1772 Penhallow to judge. Allowed. LICENSE: 11/2/1772. To Admx. To sell sufficient land to pay debts. PETITION: 11/30/1772. Of: Joshua Brackett and John Pickering Jr., Portsmouth gentlemen. They note that since the granting of Admin. to Mary, to which they were sureties, Mary has married Philip Johnson, Greenland gent., who therefore became Admr. in her riht. They feel the new Admr. may waste the est. and they, as bondsmen, will be requested to pay the debts. Request a new bond be given or the Admin. revoked and granted to John Pickering, bro. of Joshua decd. Order: 11/30/1772. For hearing, Petitioners to serve the Admrs. with notice. Ruling: 12/18/1772. After a hearing, and citing several legal references, the judge rules that the law does not allow him to revoke an admin. for arbitrary reasons and so denies petition. PETITION: 12/26/1772. Of Jonathan Moulton, Hampton esq. States that he had several large accounts open and unsettled with Joshua during his lifetime, that Pickering induced Moulton to settle by producing an Account against Moulton much larger than expected and so deceived him, with the stipulation on settlm. that if any mistakes were to be found, they would be rectified. Upon examination of Pickering's books, the orig. accounts were found to have been altered, the sums greatly augmented in Pickering's favor and Pickering refused to resettle. During Joshua's life, Moulton brought suit, and Pickering agreed to arbitration. Pickering died before the arbiters made a judgment. The Claims Comm. for Pickering's est. refused to admit Moulton's claim without knowing the evidence. Moulton requests court to appoint an impersonal person to examine his claim. Order: 12/30/1772. The List of Claims received by the court, compared with the Invy., shows that the est. is not insolvent so the Petition is ordered to lay on file until the Admrs. render an account. CLAIMS: 12/29/1772. Total L116.3.2. Oaths 12/30/1772 Comm. to judge.

2084. PICKERING, NICHOLAS (1799) #6526
GDP. Of the son of Anthony Pickering, Newmarket yoeman decd. GDP.: 1/17/1799. Of Nicholas, a minor over 14. Gdn. Samuel Pickering, Newmarket yoeman. Bond $1,000.00. Sureties: James Pickering, Newmarket yoeman and Levi Langly, Lee, Strafford Co. gent. Witnesses: John S. Durrell and W. Parker.

2085. PICKERING, SALLY F. (1791) #5633
GDP. Of the dau. of John Pickering, Newington husbm. decd. GDP.: 3/31/1791. Of Sally, a minor over 14. Gdn. Thomas Vincent, New Castle yoeman. Bond L1000.0.0. Sureties: Richard Dame and Levi Furber, Newington yoemen. Witnesses: Nathl. Parker and W. Parker. RELEASE: 8/27/1795. Of Sally F. Pickering, formerly of Newington, and her husband William Skriggn of Durham, Strafford Co. They have received from

Thomas Vincent, Rye husbm., a settlm. of his Account of Gdp. and all demands to date. They release Vincent and his atty. Richd. Dame and request judge to cancel his Gdp. and bond. Witnesses: Ephraim Pickering and Joel Leighton. Oaths 8/20/1795 William and Sally F. Skriggn to Ephraim Pickering, JP. See #6288 for Release of Sally and husband to est. James Pickering of Exeter.

2086. PICKERING, SAMUEL (1797) #6325
EST. Greenland gent. decd. testate. WILL: Drawn 2/13/1797. Legatees: Wife-Elizabeth; Sons-Benning and Joshua; Daus.-Mary Marston, Elizabeth Pingree and Sarah Dearborn. Execs.-wife Elizabeth and son Benning. His sig. Witnesses: Samll. Fabyan, Richd. Dame and Clemt. Weeks. CERT. WILL (D32;270): 3/15/1797. Presented by Execs. and all witnesses: ADMIN.: 3/15/1797. Execs.:Elizabeth Pickiring. widow and Benning Pickering, trader, both of Greenland. Bond $3,000.00. Sureties: Elijah Marston, gent. and Jonathan Bailey, both of Greenland. Witnesses: Ephraim Pickering and John Peverley. INVY.: Appr. 4/27/1797. Comm.: Clement Weeks, Samll. Fabyan and Richd. Dame. Value $516.72. Oaths 12/6/1797 Comm. to Ephraim Pickering, JP. Oath 12/18/1797 Elizabeth Pickiring, an Exec., to judge. PETITION: 2/2/1798. Of Benning Pickering, an Exec. For Comm. Insolvency. Gives claims already presented as L502.8.3. Granted. CLAIMS WARR.: 2/2/1798. Comm.: Samuel Fabyan, yoeman; Joshua Pickering, esq., both of Newington and Clement Weeks, Greenland csq. On7/3/1798Comm.allowed 6 months more. CLAIMS: 1/26/1799. Total $1,207.03 plus bills of the fees of appraisers, atty., Claims Comm. and Execs. not talled. Esti. $92.01. Oaths 5/16/1799 Fabyan and Pickering to Clement Weeks, JP. PETITION: 8/17/1801. Of John Pingree, Methuen, Essex Co., MA gent. by Jere. Mason, his atty. Claims he has a Note signed by decd. for $1,000.00, plus interest. which has not been exhibited to Claims Comm. and still due him. Also, he has discovered one piece of land and bldgs. and another piece of land belonging to Samuel's est., neither of which have ever been inventoried. Requests that his claim be examined by Comm. Insolvency and that the Execs. be given License to sell the real est. so he may be paid his Note or his due proportion. Order: 8/18/1801. For hearing, Petitioner to serve Execs. with copies of Order and Petition. On 9/18/1801 hearing postponed and on 9/26/1801 postponed again. Decree: 10/2/1801. The Execs. are to admin. est. according to law and Edward St. Loe Livermore, Jeremiah Libbey and Isaac Ringe, esquires, are appointed Commissioners to examine Petitioner's claim, at expense of Petitioner. Bond: 10/2/1801. Of Execs. Bond $1,000.00. To appeal Decree on Petition Sureties; Samuel Doe, Portsmouth joiner and Benjamin Dearborn, North Hampton gent. Witness John Blasdel. CLAIMS WARR.: 10/2/1801. A Comm. of

Edward St. Loe Livermore, Isaac Rindge and Jeremiah Libbey, Portsmouth esquires, is to examine and adjust the claims of John Pingree against the insolvent est. of decd. Return: 10/20/1801. The Comm. met with Pingree and Exec. Benning Pickering, who showed the Comm. the Executors' copy of the Petition and Bond to appeal Decree allowing Petition. But Execs. made no defense on the merit of Pingree's claim. They rule that there is still due to Pingree $871.07 on his Note. Pingree has paid the $10.50 charges of the Comm. Oaths 10/28/1801 Comm. to Jonathan Warner, JP. Also includes Notification 10/12/1801 of the Comm. to Pingree and Execs. Of time and place of their meeting to examine Pingree's claim. Cert.: 10/13/1801. of Richard Low, D. Sherf. He has notified Execs. of hearing by reading Notification to them. Oath 10/28/1801 Low to E. S. Livermore, JP. PETITION: 10/22/1801. Of Execs. To appeal Decree on Pingree Petition. Allowed. Cert.: Of W. Parker, Reg. The Execs. have given security. COPY OF PETITION: Of Execs. To appeal Decree allowing Petition. PETITION: 2/18/1802. Of Charles Walker atty. to Eliza Pickiring, widow. Requests Dower be set off and License. PETITION: 4/11/1803. Of Eliza Pickiring, an Exec. States that the Will left use of all the real est. to her during her life, but the est. was declared insolvent and there was a mortgage on the real est., so she holds nothing by the Will. Requests her Dower. DOWER WARR.: 4/11/1803. Comm.: Joshua Weeks and Enoch Clark, esquires; Samuel Hatch, innholder and James Wedgwood, gent., all of Greenland and Daniel Gookin, North Hampton esq. Of Widow Elizabeth Pickiring. DOWER: 4/23/1803. Oaths 4/23/1803 Weeks, Hatch, Wedgwood and Gookin to Enoch Clark, JP. LICENSE (D34:343): 5/16/1803. To Execs. To sell real est. to amount of $1,200.00. ANSWER TO PETITION: 7/18/1803. Of Execs. by Danl. Humphreys their atty. In answer to Pingree's Petition to sue their Bond of Admin., they claim: 1. Pingree did not present his claim within 3 years after proving of Will as provided by law, so he is barred from recovery; 2. If his claim is valid, the sale of the uninventoried real est. can satisfy his claim and Bond need not be sued; 3. Pingree in his own Petition pointed out the course of selling real est. and the judge has sanctioned the mode by appointing a new Comm. If their proceedings are not legal, another new Comm. can be appointed; 4. The Execs. should be compelled to settle their Account and pay any claims due. Only if the Execs. refuse, are the bondsmen liable; 5. The omission of the missing est. in the Invy. was an error in judgment by Execs. They are now ready to Invy. and request a License; 6. Suing the Bond of Admin. would be highly injurious to both the principals and bondsmen and should be resorted to only when the Judge of Probate cannot enfore his Decrees. ADDL. INVY.: 7/17/1803. Exhibited by Execs. Lists house and land in Greenland incumbered with a mortgage, the widow's Dower, 1/3 of a house belonging to Mary Pickering and a cedar swamp. No values given. Signed by Elisa. Pickering. CITATION: 5/22/1804. To Execs. Complaint having been made that they have not fully accounted for est., they are cited to appear and exhibit an Addl. Account in order for settlm. Cert.: 5/22/1804. Of H.B. Eastham(?), Depy, Shef. He left a copy of Citation at the dwelling house of Execs. CITATION: 5/22/1804. To: Execs., Elijah Marston and Jona. Bayley, Greenland gentlemen. To appear at a hearing on Petition of John Pingree stating that they have neglected to inventory all the real est. and requesting to sue Bond of Admin. Cert.: 5/22/1804. Of H.B. Eastham(?), Depy. Shef. He left a copy of Citation at residences of Execs., Marston and Bayley. PETITION: 5/15/1804. Of Jere. Mason of John Pingree of Methuen, Essex Co., MA. For permission to sue Bond of Admin. as Execs. have not settled Account or paid claims. Order: 5/15/1804. For hearing, Petitioner to cite Execs. and their bondsmen to appear. On 6/20/1804 hearing postponed. Decree: 7/18/1804. Elizabeth Pickering, an Exec. and one bondsman appeared but did not offer sufficient reason for their neglect and presented no Addl. Account. Petition to sue Bond Admin. granted. PETITION: 9/12/1804. Of Elisa Pickering, an Exec. For License to pay the claim due Pingree. Granted. LICENSE (D35:387): 9/17/1804. To Execs. To sell real est. to amount of $890.00. ACCOUNT: 11/15/1809. Of Elisa Pickering, an Exec. Allowed 11/15/1809 no objections having been made. BOND: 1/12/1810. Of Nancy Pickering, Newport, Newport Co., RI widow. Bond $150.00. To appeal Decree of 11/15/1809 allowing Addl. Account of Elisa Pickering, an Exec., on Sureties: Thomas Pickering, husbm. and Brackett Weeks, innholder, both of Greenland. Witnesses: John Pickering and David Pickering.

2087. PICKERING, CAPT. THOMAS (1779) #4540
EST. Portsmouth mariner decd. intestate. ADMIN.: 5/12/1779. Admx. Dorothy Pickerin, Portsmouth widow. Bond L5000.0.0. Sureties: John Pickering and George Jerry Osborne, both of Portsmouth. Witnesses: Saml. Drowne and Tho. Bickford. INVY.: Appr. 9/16/1779. Comm.: John Wendell, Peirce Long and Thos. Bickford. Value L570.10.0. Appr. at rate of dollars at 6 shillings each or silver at 6 shillings 8 pence pound. Oath 11/2/1779 Admx. and Comm. to H. Wentworth, JP. ADDL. INVY.:4/19/1781. Shown by Josiah Pickering atty. to Admx. Value L327.1.1 1/2. Oaths 4/20/1781 Long and Bickford to H. Wentworth, JP. PETITION: Dated by clerk 4/1781. Of John Hooker on behalf of Admx. For Comm. Insolvency. Gives list claims of L12269.0.0 but this was crossed out and changed to L57016.0.0. CLAIMS: 5/9/1782. Comm.: Thos. Martin, Peirce Long and John Sparhawk. Total L353.19.10 1/2. Oaths 5/9/1782 Comm. to Wm. Parker, JP. ACCOUNT: 4/9/1783. Of Admx. Allowed 4/9/1783. She notes the 2d Invy. is in dispute and cannot

be accounted for now. The following Petition found in #5241 Thomas Pickering (1787) belongs here. PETITION: Dated by clerk 10/20/1790. Of: Elizabeth Prowss, Abigail Janvrin and Dorothy Nelson, sisters of Capt. Thomas Pickering of Portsmouth decd. Request that Admin. D.B.N. be granted to their "bro." Samuel Drowne of Portsmouth. ADMIN. D.B.N. (D29:423): 10/20/1790. Admr. d.b.n. Samuel Drowne, Portsmouth goldsmith. Sureties: Samuel Hutchins, trader and George Jerry Osborne, printer, both of Portsmouth. INVY.: 5/25/1791. Comm.: Saml. Hutchings, and Nathl. Marshall. Value L47.14.3 plus the Invy. of est. of Mrs. Dorothy Pickering late of Portsmouth decd. shown by Dorothy Nelson and Saml. Drowne, Execs., value L47.14.3. Signed by Saml. Hutchings and Nathl. Marshall. S.D. adds, "The personal est. of Dorothy the heirs div. among themselves without any intereference of mine." Oaths 1/6/1810 Drowne, as Admr. and Exec. of Dorothy, Hutchings and Marshall to Nathl. Parker, JP. PETITION: 6/15/1808. Of Richard Low and Isaac Nelson. State that Drowne was granted Admin. D.B.N in 1790 and though twice cited to account has not done so. Request permission to sue his Bond of Admin. BOND: 7/27/1808. Of: Richard Low, trader and Isaac Nelson, boatbuilder, both of Portsmouth. Bond $100.00. To sue Bond of Admin. D.B.N. Sureties: James Shapley, merchant and William Varrell, trader, both of Portsmouth. Witnesses: Ephraim Blasdel and Geo. Melcher.

2088. PICKERING, THOMAS (1787) #5241
EST. Newington gent. decd. testate. WILL: Drawn 4/4/1782. Legatees: Sons-Nicolas, John Gee Pickering, James, William, Benjamin and Richard. He notes the last three as "children of my last wife;" Daus.-Temperance Knight, Elizabeth Dam, Mary Langdon, Sarah Pickering, Alice Brackett and Patience Pickering. He bequeaths his negro woman Rose to son John Gee. Execs.-sons Nichlas and John Gee. His sig. Witnesses: John Fabyan, James Nutter and John Pickering. CERT. WILL (29:93): 1/17/1787. Presented by Execs. and witnesses Fabyan and Nutter. INVY.: Appr. 2/27/1787. Comm.: George Brackett, Ephraim Pickering and Thomas Bickford. Value L4514.11.9. Oaths 2/27/1787 Comm. to Ephm. Pickering, JP. Oath 4/21/1787 John Gee Pickering, an Exec., to W. Parker, JP and RR. Note: This file includes a Petition which belongs with #4540 Capt. Thomas Pickering (1779) and is recorded there.

2089. PICKERING, VOLENTINE (1792) #5747
See #5528 John Pickering (1790)

2090. PICKERING, COL. WILLIAM (1795) #6150
EST. Greenland esq. decd. intestate. ADMIN.: 2/21/1795. Admx.: Abigail Pickering, Greenland widow. Bond $3,000.00. Sureties: John Fabyan, yoeman and Samuel Fabyan, esq., both of Newington. INVY.: Appr. 1/28/1796. Comm.: Stephen March, Ichabod Weeks and Ephraim Pickering. Value not tallied. Esti. $10,000.00+. Oaths 1/28/1796 March and Weeks to Ephraim Pickering, JP. Oath 2/10/1796 Ephraim Pickering to W. Parker, JP. DOWER WARR.: 10/28/1806. Comm.: Joshua Weeks, esq. and Shadrach Robinson, yoeman, both of Greenland; Daniel Gookin, North Hampton esq.; Thomas Boardman, Stratham yoeman and Richard Dame, Newington gent. Of Widow Abigail Pickering. CITATION: 12/15/1806. To Admx. To appear and settle Account. Agreement was reached between Admx. and heir who petitioned that Admx. to have further time to exhibit Account. DOWER: 4/8/1807. Oaths 4/18/1807 Weeks, Robinson, Boardman and Dame to Wm. Pickering, JP. APPR.: Comm. same as Dower. to view 2/3 of the real est. to see if it can be div. into 8 shares. Div. or appr. Appr.: Value $7,915.12 1/2. Oaths 4/18/1807 Weeks, Robinson, Boardman and Dame to Wm. Pickering, JP. STATEMENT: 4/20/1807. Of Wm. Pickering, oldest heir. He rejects all privileges of seniority in settlm. of est. DECREE SETTLM.: 5/1/1807. John Pickering and Thomas Pickering, two of the sons, appearing and consenting, 2/3 of the real est. settled on them, John and Thomas to pay their co-heirs William Pickering, Sally Weeks, Samuel Pickering, Mary Pickering, Stephen Pickering and Daniel Pickering $989.39 each within 6 months, with interest. BOND: 5/1/1807. Of: John Pickering and Thomas Pickering, Greenland yoemen. Bond $16,000.00. Sureties: Brackett Weeks, Greenland gent. and Samuel Fabyan, Newington yoeman. Witness W. Parker. PETITION: 7/12/1831. Of: Stephen Pickering, Daniel Pickering, Brackett Weeks, Sarah Weeks and Mary Haines by Samuel Cushing their attorney. For Admin. D.B.N. and request appointment of John Pickering, Greenland yoeman, one of the children and next of kin to decd. ADMIN. D.B.N.: 7/21/1831. Admr. d.b.n. John Pickering. Bond $500.00. Sureties: Daniel Pickering and Stephen Pickering, all of Greenland. Witnesses: Joseph Farrar, James Downs and John G. Pickering. INVY. WARR.: 8/10/1831. Comm.: Enoch Clark, esq.; John R. Hatch and Joseph Weeks, all of Greenland. Value $96.60. Oaths 11/14/1831 Hatch and Weeks to Enoch Clark, JP. Oath 11/30/1831 Admr. d.b.n. to John Kelly, JP.

2091. PICKERING, WINTHROP (1783) #4925
EST. Newington gent. decd. testate. WILL: Drawn 1/22/1780. Legatees: Wife-Phebe; Sons-Absolam, James and Gilbert; Daus.-Temperance, Charlotte, Hetteberry, Hannah, Elizabeth, Phebe and Rosamond, all

unmarried. Execs.-Ephraim Pickering and Samuel Fabens, both of Newington. His sig. Witnesses; Titus Salter, John Fabyan and Thomas Bickford. CERT. WILL: 8/26/1783. Presented on 8/5/1783 by Ephraim Pickering, one of Execs., the other refusing. Oath of witness Salter was given on 8/5 and on 8/7 of witness Bickford. INVY. WARR.: 7/30/1783. Comm.: Dennis Hight of Newington; Thomas Bickford and Samuel Nutter, both of Portsmouth. INVY.: Appr. 10/24/1783. Value not tallied. Esti. L1239.0.0. Oaths 10/25/1783 Bickford and Hight to George Gains, JP. Oath 10/26/1783 Exec. to Wm. Parker, JP. ACCOUNT: 2/20/1799. Of Exec., esq. Allowed 2/20/1799 having been approved by such of the heirs as attended. PETITION: 2/9/1802. Of Gilbert Pickering, husbm. For div. of 1/3 of the land in Newington devised to him in Will and which he holds in common with his bros. Absolom and James. Order: 3/30/1802. For hearing, Petitioner to notify the others. Cert.: Of James Pickering. He has chosen 2 and this bros. 2 of the following Comm.: Ephrm. Pickering, esq.; Richd. Dame, William Walker, George Colbeth and John Fabyan, esq. Order: 4/20/1802. The Widow having obtained a Dower Warr. and no one making objections, the Comm. to set of the Dower and div. what remains. PETITION: 4/17/1802. Of Widow Phebe Pickering. Requests Dower be set off per Will. Witnesses; Saml. Fabyan Jr. and William Fabyan. 4/20/1802. The agent of 2 of heirs of persons interested and the remaining person being present and having no objections, Petition granted. DOWER WARR.: 4/20/1802. Comm.: Ephraim Pickering and John Fabyan, esquires; Dennis Hight Jr. and Richard Dame, gentlemen, all of Newington and Joel Leighton, Exeter yoeman. Of Widow Phebe Pickering. Dower: 5/20/1802. Oaths 4/23/1803 Fabyan, Hight and Dame to Enoch Clark, JP. Oath 5/4/1803 Leighton to Wm. Parker, JP. Allowed 5/4/1803. DIV. WARR.: 4/20/1802. Same Comm. as Dower. To div. 2/3 of the real est. giving each son 1/3/ Div.: 8/6/1803. Divisees: Absolom Pickering, Gilbert Pickering and James Pickering. Oaths 8/6/1803 Fabyan, Hight and Dame to Nathan W. Adams, JP.

PIERCE. See also Pearse, Peirce

2092. PIERCE, GEORGE (1785) #5103

EST. Portsmouth mariner decd. RENUN.: 5/13/1785. Of Abigail Peirice, widow of George. Of Admin. Requests appointment of her "bro." Daniel Peirce. ADMIN.: 5/15/1785. Admr. Daniel Peirce, Portsmouth merchant. Witness W. Parker, Reg. ADMIN. BOND: 5/18/1785. Admr. Daniel Peirce, Portsmouth merchant. Bond L1000.0.0. Sureties: Jeremiah Hill and Israel True, Portsmouth joiners. Witnesses: Mich. Hooker and Saml. Rymes. INVY.: Comm.: Jacob Walden and Jeremiah Hill, Portsmouth gentlemen. Value L13.17.0. Oaths 6/4/1785 Admr. and Comm. to George Gains, JP.

2093. PILLAR, WILLIAM (1788) #5386
GDP. Of the son of _____ (sic.) Pillar, Kittery, York Co., MA/ME mariner decd. GDP.: 11/6/1788. Of William, a minor over 14. Gdn. Daniel Humphreys, Portsmouth esq. Bond L500.0.0. Sureties: John Pickering, Portsmouth esq. and Jona. Rawson, Dover, Strafford Co., esq. Witnesses: N. Emery and W. Parker.

PILSBURY. See also Pillsbury

2094. PILSBURY: CALEB, EBENEZER, HANNAH, JOHN, MARY & RUTH (1789) #5497
GDP. Of the children of Joseph Pilsbury. GDP.: 11/30/1789. Of: Ebenezer, John, Mary and Ruth, Hampstead minors. Gdn. Mary Pilsbury, Hampstead widow. Bond L1000.0.0. Sureties: Timothy Goodwin, yoeman and Caleb Webster, gent., both of Hampstead. Witnesses; Thomas Shannon and Benja. Pilsbury. GDP.: 12/4/1789. Of: Hannah and Caleb, minors under 14. Gdn. Mary Pilsbury, Hampstead widow. Bond L1000.0.0. Sureties: Caleb Webster, gent., and Timothy Goodwin, yoeman, both of Hampstead. Witnesses: Benja. Pilsbury and Edmd. Morss. RECEIPT: 4/1/1813 at Northwood. Of John Pilsbury. He received that day $1,200.00 from John Furber in full of all the property entrusted to him as John's Gdn. Witness Thomas Furber. Oath John Pilsbury to John Harvey, JP.

2095. PILSBURY, ENOCH (1796) #6267
EST. Northwood yoeman decd. testate. WILL: Drawn 4/8/1796. Legatees: Wife-Abigail; Children-John and Betty. Exec.-wife Abigail. His sig. Witnesses; Increase Batchelder, James Pilsbury and James Batchelder. CERT. WILL (D32:196):10/17/1796. Presented by Exec. and witnesses Pilsbury and James Batchelder. ADMIN.: 10/17/1796. Exex. Abigail Pillsbury, Northwood widow. Bond $2,000.00. Sureties: Abraham Batchelder and James Batchelder, Northwood yoemen. Witnesses: James Pilsbury and Wm. Parker. INVY.: 12/9/1796. Comm.: William Wallais, Jonathan Knowlton and Samuel Woodman. Value $1,104.81. Oath 12/9/1796 Admx. to Jona. Cilley, JP. Oaths 12/9/1796 Comm. to Jona. Cilley, JP. ACCOUNT: 9/10/1798. Of Thomas Furber and Abigail Furber his wife, Admx. Allowed 9/10/1798.

2096. PILSBURY, JOSEPH (1786) #5221
EST. Hampstead yoeman decd. intestate. RENUN.: Dated by clerk 10/1786. Of Widow Mary Pilsbery. Of Admin. Requests appointment of her husband's bro. Benjamin Pilsbury. ADMIN.: 10/18/1786. Admr. Benjamin Pilsbury, Sandown gent. Bond L500.0.0. Sureties: William Marshall and Edmund Morse, Hampstead gentlemen. Witnesses: Ichabod

Shaw and Rebeckah Currier. INVY.: Appr. 2/19/1787. Comm.: Edmund Morse, Caleb Webster and William Marshall. Value L231.9.7. Oaths 2/19/1787 Comm. to Elipht. Poor, JP. Oath 2/21/1787 Admr. to W. Parker, Reg. PETITION: 11/17/1789. Of Widow Mary Pilsbery. Requests something out of est. to support the family as two of her children were born cripples and are not able to do anything toward their support. Her own health is weak and she cannot do much labor or support for family. DOWER WARR.: 10/19/1789. Comm.: William Marshall, Edmund Morse and Caleb Webster of Hampstead, Nehemiah Sleeper of Hawke and Thomas Cotton of Sandown, all gentlemen. Of Widow Mary Pilsbery. DOWER: 10/28/1789. Affirms. of Marshall and Morse and oaths of Webster and Cotton to John Calfe, JP. Allowed. ACCOUNT: 5/30/1787. Of Admr. Allowed 12/16/1789. 12/2/1789 Mary Pilsbury, Sarah Shannon and Elisebeth Pilsbury have viewed the Account and find it just and right. Witnesses: Thomas Shannon and Amos Clark. Account includes maintenance of one child and also indicated all the income of the real est. allowed family. ADDL. ACCOUNT: 4/12/1793. Of Admr. Allowed 4/12/1793. Note: This file also includes a License which belongs with File #5372 Joseph Philbrick (1788) and is recorded there.

2097. PINKERTON, JOHN (1780) #4613
EST. Londonderry yoeman decd. testate. WILL: Drawn 2/19/1779. Legatees: Wife-Elizabeth ; Sons-David, John, Matthew, James and Samuel; Daus.-Mary Pinkerton, Jennet Pinkerton and Rachel Pinkerton; Son-in-law-James Aiken and Elizabeth his wife. Execs.-sons John and James. His mark. Witnesses: Isaac Brewster, Archibald McMurphy and John Bell. CERT. WILL (D25:328): 3/29/1780. Presented by Execs. and witnesses Brewster and Bell. INVY.: Comm.: John Bell, William Duncan and Archibald McMurphy. Value not tallied. Esti. L23000.0.0+. ACCOUNT: Of Execs. Allowed 5/17/1786 with order to Execs. to pay balance to heirs.

2098. PIPER, BENJAMIN (1778) #4507
EST. Stratham yoeman decd. intestate. ADMIN.: 12/31/1778. Admx. Sarah Piper, Stratham widow. Bond L500.0.0. Sureties: John Stockbridge and Israel Stockbridge, Stratham yoeman. Witnesses: Theophilus Smith and W. Parker. INVY. WARR.: 12/31/1778. Comm.: Moses Clark, clothier; Stephen Piper, yoeman and Theos. Smith, esq., all of Stratham. Invy.: Appr. 1/8/1779. Value L2587.17.6. Oaths 2/24/1779 Comm. and Admx. to judge. ACCOUNT: Of William and Sarah Rundlett, Admx. Allowed 2/15/178 with order to Admx. to pay balance to the Gdn. of children. Account includes main. 2 children.

2099. PIPER, HANNAH (1780) #4595
EST. Pembroke widow decd. testate. WILL: Drawn 12/8/1779. Legatees: Sons-Thomas, Gideon, William and Nathaniel; Daus.-Martha Thurstin and Hannah Goss; Heirs of her son Benjamin. Exec. son- Nathaniel. Her mark. Witnesses: Richard Bartlet, Pelatiah Bartlett and Abigail Gilman. CERT. WILL (D23:333): 1/26/1780. Presented by Exec. and witnesses Richard Bartlet and Pelatiah Bartlett. INVY. WARR.: 4/26/1780. Comm.: David Conner, Nathaniel Gilman and David Dexter, Pembroke yoemen. INVY.: Appr. 3/22/1780. Value L1021.6.0. Oaths 3/23/1780 Comm. to David Gilman, JP. Oath 3/29/1780 Exec. to W. Parker, JP. Note: The bottom of the Invy. is fragmented and the subtotal partly worn away, resulting in an error in the final total as given in the Docket book.

2100. PIPER, JOSIAH (1796) #6215
GDP. Of the son of Nathaniel Piper, Pembroke yoeman decd. GDP.: 5/18/1796. Of Josiah, a minor over 14. Gdn. Samuel Daniell, Pembroke esq. Bond $1,000.00. Sureties: William Cochran, gent. and Noah Dow Piper, husbm., both of Pembroke. Witnesses: James Gray and W. Parker.

2101. PIPER, NATHANIEL (1779) #4508
EST. Stratham yoeman decd. ADMIN. (D25:11): 1/12/1779. Admr. Nathan Piper, Pembroke yoeman. Sureties: Jesse Wiggin and Sargent Whitcher, Stratham yoemen. INVY. WARR.: 1/12/1779. Comm.: Theophilus Smith, esq.; Moses Clark, clothier and Stephen Piper, yoeman, all of Stratham. INVY.: Appr. 1/13/1779. Value note tallied. Esti. L441.0.0+. Oaths 1/14/1779 Comm. and Admr. to W. Parker, JP & Reg. ACCOUNT: 1/26/1780. Of Admr.

2102. PIPER, NATHANIEL (1788) #5328
EST. Pembroke husbm. decd. ADMIN.: 2/21/1788. Admx. Rachel Piper, Pembroke widow. Bond L1000.0.0. Sureties: Joseph Emery, gent. and William Cochran, husbm., both of Pembroke. Witnesses; William Holt and Nathl. Gilman. INVY.: Appr. 9/16/1788. Comm.: William Cochran, Joseph Emery and Thomas Robinson. Value L314.19.0. Oaths Emery and Robinson to Richard Bartlet, JP. Oaths 9/22/1788 Admx. to Joseph Sias, JP. APPR.: 9/19/1796. Comm.: Joseph Emery, William Cochran and Thomas Robinson. They appr. the neat annual income of real est. for 6 years and 8 months at L122.10.0. Oaths 9/19/1796 Comm. to Daniel Knox, JP. APPR.: 2/17/1797. Comm.: Joseph Emery, John Ayer and Daniel Knox. They appr. the real est. at $860.00, the Dower duly considered. Oaths 2/17/1797 Comm. to Thomas Adams, JP. ACCOUNT: Of Stephen Hoit and Rachel his wife, Admx. Allowed 9/21/1796, having been consented to by a majority of heirs of age. Account includes main. of

2 children. DECREE SETTLM.: 3/15/1797. Benjamin Piper, one of sons, appearing and consenting, the real est. is settled on him, Benjamin to pay each of his co-heirs $95.77, Noah, two shares in 6 months, Daniel in 9 months, Betsey in one year, Josiah and Polly in 4 years and Nathaniel in 8 years, with interest. BOND: 3/15/1797. Of Benjamin Piper, Pembroke yoeman. Bond $1,600.00. To pay his co-heirs per Decree Settlm. Sureties: Samuel Emery of Pembroke and Stephen Hoit of Northwood, yoemen. Witnesses: Saml. Parker and W. Parker. ADDL. ACCOUNT: 9/21/1796. Of Admx. Allowed 3/15/1797, having been consented to by heirs. Account includes main. of decd.'s mother who was entitled to her Dower.

2103. PIPER, SAMUEL (1771) #3886
EST. Stratham yoeman decd. intestate. ADMIN.: 11/2/1771. Admr. Jonathan Piper Jr., Stratham yeoman. Bond L500.0.0. Sureties: Joseph Hoit, Stratham gent. and Jonathan Cram, Hampton Falls, yoeman. Witnesses: Wm. Parker and Samuel Parker. INVY.: Comm.: Mark Wiggin and Jonathan Wiggin. Total L45.6.9. Oaths 5/28/1772 Comm. to Andrew Wiggin, JP. ACCOUNT: 12/10/1772. Of Admr. Bal. in hands of Admr. L83.6.9. The Admr. requests to be allowed to hold the bal. as during his lifetime Samuel bonded himself to the Selectmen of Stratham to be responsible for Josiah Piper, his wife and family if they moved from Greenland, as Josiah is incapable of supporting himself and family. Order: Admr. to use the bal. for the support of Josiah and his family unless the heirs will bind themselves to do so and indemnify the Admr..

2104. PIPER, STEPHEN (1799) #6337
EST. Stratham yoeman decd. testate. WILL: Drawn 3/26/1796. Legatees; Wife-Abigail; Sons-Stephen, Nathaniel, Thomas and Isareil; Daus.-Patience Buzel, Abigail Cate, Elizabeth Sanborn, Tabitha Chase, Hepzebath Piper, Susanna Piper and Nancy Piper; Grandchildren-Polley Gale, Joseph Jewett, Salley Jewett, Abigail Jewett, Nancy Jewett, Phebe Jewett and Mark Jewett. Appoints Isarel Piper Gdn. of his son Thomas. Exec.- son, Isareil to admin. until his son Thomas is 21. Note: The wording here is a bit confusing. His sig. Witnesses: Nathl. Stevens, Thomas Marston Jr. and Thomas Chase. CERT. WILL (D32:302): 5/1/1797. Presented by Thomas Piper, Exec. and witnesses Stevens and Marston. ADMIN.: 5/1/1797. Exec. Thomas Piper, Stratham yoeman. Bond $3,000.00. Sureties: Israel Piper and Nathaniel Wiggin of Stratham and Thomas Marston Jr. of North Hampton, yoemen. Witnesses: Nathl. Stevens and W. Parker. RECEIPT: 6/11/1798. From Stephen Piper. To Exec. For $5.00, his legacy. RECEIPT: 1/24/1799. From Tabitha Chase. To Exec. For $5.00, her legacy. RECEIPT: 7/8/1799. From Israel Piper. To Exec. For $5.00, his legacy. RECEIPT: 9/21/1799. From Elizabeth

Sanborn. To Exec. For $5.00, her legacy. RECEIPT: 9/21/1799. Of Patience Busel. To Exec. For $5.00, her legacy. RECEIPT: 3/8/1800. From Abigail Cate. To Exec. For $5.00, her legacy. RECEIPT: 6/28/1800 Of Hephzibah Piper. To Exec. For $102.50, her legacy. Witness Isrl. Piper. RECEIPT: 12/13/1800. From Andrew Jewett. To Exec. For $6.50, his legacy. RECEIPT: 12/18/1800. From Dolley Gale. To Exec. For $1.00, her legacy. RECEIPT: 6/10/1801 (pos. 1807?). From Nathaniel Piper. To Exec. For $5.00, his legacy. RECEIPT: 7/10/1802. From Nancy Colman and James Colman. To Exec. For $100.00 in full of her legacy "before my mother's decease." RECEIPT: 5/25/1821. From Nancy Colman and James Colman. To Exec. For household goods bequeathed to her in Will. Witnesses: Levi Barker and Theos. Smith. RECEIPT:5/25/1821. Of Susanna Trefethen and William Trefethen Jr. To Exec. For all the household goods given to her in Will. Witnesses: Theos. Smith and Levi Barker.

2105. PIPER, THOMAS (1791) #5671
EST. Northwood yoeman decd. Note: The following Renun. found in #5621 Rev. Joseph Prince (1791) belongs here. RENUN.: 6/27/1791. Of Elizabeth Piper, widow of Thomas. Of Admin. as neither she nor children are capable. Requests appointment of Jonathan Clark, esq. She also notes that est. must be represented as insolvent. Witnesses: Benja. Hill and Lydia Hill. ADMIN.: 6/24/1791. Admr. Jonathan Clark, Northwood esq. Bond L1000.0.0. Sureties: Levi Mead and Benjamin Colcord, Northwood yoemen. Witnesses: Sherbun Blake and Joshua Thurber. PETITION: 10/16/1792. Of Admr. For Comm. Insolvency. Recommends Levi Mead, Benj. Kelley and Joseph Blake as Comm. DOWER: 3/16/1793. Comm.: Tho. Bartlett, Sherbun Blake, Levi Mead, Samuel Johnson and John Crockett. Of Widow Elizabeth Piper. Oaths 3/16/1793 Comm. to Jona. Clark, JP. Allowed. CLAIMS: 3/25/1793. Comm.: Sherbun Blake, Benja. Kelley and Levi Mead. Total L130.9.8. Oaths 3/25/1793 Comm. to Jona. Blake, JP. ACCOUNT: 1/27/1794. Of Admr. Allowed 1/27/1794, heirs of age notified but did not appear. PETITION: 4/5/1793. Of Admr. For License. Granted. LICENSE (D30:407): 4/5/1793. To Admr. To sell real est. to amount of L440.0.0. INVY.: Appr. 8/20/1794. Comm.: Benja. Kelley and Levi Mead. Value L184.6.2. ADDL. ACCOUNT: 3/23/1795. Allowed 3/25/1795 with order to Admr. pay heirs bal, in equal proportions, the Widow having heretofore had her allowance. Account includes main. 2 children.

2106. PLUMMER, SAMUEL (1799) #6532
EST. Hawke yoeman decd. testate. WILL: Drawn 11/13/1797. Legatees; Wife-Mary; Sons-Samuel, Nathan, Caleb, Henry and Moses; Daus.-Nancy Quimby, Alis Collins and Hannah Plumer. Exec.- son Samuel. His sig. Witnesses; Jacob Eastman, Barnard Currier and Jabez Eaton. CERT. WILL (D33/31): 1/21/1799. Presented by Exec. and witnesses Currier and Eaton. INVY.: Comm.: William Marshall, Jacob Eastman and Barnard Currier. Value $1,079.59. Oaths 4/13/1799 Comm. and Exec. to Thos. Page, JP.

2107. PLUMMER, WILLIAM (1798) #6486
EST. Portsmouth merchant decd. intestate. RENUN.: 8/16/1798. Of Tristram Plummer, father of William. Of Admin. Requests appointment of William Welstead Prout, a principal creditor. ADMIN. (D32:570): 8/28/1798. Admr. William Welstead Prout, Newburyport, Essex Co., MA merchant. Sureties: Nathaniel Dean of Portsmouth and William Faris of Newburyport, Essex Co., MA, merchants. INVY.: 11/5/1798. Comm.: Jereh. Libbey, Nathl. White and Edward Jennings Long. Value $2,742.12. Oaths and affirm. 11/5/1798 Comm. to George Gains, JP. Oath 11/19/1798 Admr. to Nichs. Pike, JP. PETITION: 2/27/1799. Of Admr. For Comm. Insolvency. Gives claims of about $4,000.00. Granted. CLAIMS WARR.: 2/27/1799. Comm.: Abraham Wheelwright and Theophilus Bradley Jr., merchants and Samuel Cutler, gent., all of Newburyport, Essex Co., MA. Claims 1/24/1800. Total $4,314.37, which does not include money paid by Prout for Admin. Oaths 1/22/1800 Comm. to Benaniah Titcomb, JP. ACCOUNT: 5/14/1800. Of Admr. Allowed 5/14/1800. PROP. & SETTLM.: Claims $4,314.38. Amount to be proportioned $3,843.11. Allowed 5/22/1800 with order to Admr. to pay.

2108. POLLARD, JOHN (1775) #4182
EST. Kingston yoeman decd. intestate. ADMIN.: 10/26/1775. Admx. Sarah Pollard, Kingston widow. Bond L1000.0.0. Sureties: Isaac Webster, Kingston gent. and David Clifford, Brentwood yeoman. Witnesses: Sam. Hale and Saml. Hale Jr. INVY. WARR.: 10/26/1775. Comm.: Thomas Johnson of Plaistow and Timothy Pearley of Kingston, husbandmen. INVY.: Appr. 12/19/1774. Value not tallied. Esti. L100.0.0+. Oaths 12/21/1775 Comm. to Joseph Welch, JP. Oath 12/28/1775 Admr. to

2109. POOL, JOSHUA (1771) #3861
EST. Haverhill yoeman decd. intestate. RENUN.: 7/30/1771. Of Abigail Poole, widow of Joshua. Of Admin., being at a great distance from Portsmouth and attended with difficulty. Requests appointment of her bro.-in-law Timothy Bedell, esq. ADMIN.: 8/12/1771. Admr.: Timothy Bedell,

esq. Bond L500.0.0. Sureties: Jacob Tilton and James Dwyer, Portsmouth innholders. Witness Samuel Parker. INVY.: Appr. 11/28/1771.Comm.: Asa Porter and Andw. Savage Crocker. Value L134.4.0. Includes a right of land in Haverhill except 75acres. in the 100 acre lot sold at vendue for taxes. Oath: 11/28/1771 Crocker to Asa Porter, JP. Oath 12/6/1771 unidentified nor does it say to whom. LICENSE: 7/17/1772. To Admr. To sell sufficient real est. to pay debts. CLAIMS: 2/9/1773. Comm.: Asa Porter and Andrew S. Crocker. Total L192.9.9. Oaths 1/14/1773 Comm. to Samll. Hale, JP. ACCOUNT: 2/9/1773. Includes "time in looking for said intestate's body, he being drowned." Also includes main. one child. Allowed 2/9/1773. ADDL. ACCOUNT: Allowed 1/20/1774. It notes that Haverhill is now Grafton Co. DOWER WARR.: 7/17/1772. Comm.: Asa Porter, esq.; Andrew Savage Crocker, gent. and Timothy Barnes, yoeman, all of Haverhill. Of Widow Abigail Pool. DOWER: 2.9.1773. Oaths 1/14/1773 Porter and Crocker to Samll. Hale, JP. PROP. & SETTLM. (D22:385): Claims L108.11.5. Amount to be proportioned L86.7.0. Allowed 1/20/ 1774 with order to Admr. to pay.

2110. POOR: ANNA, JESSE, LYDIA, POLLY & SALA (1792) #5753 GDP. Of the children of Daniel Poor Jr., Atkinson yoeman decd. GDP.: 3/27/1792. Of: Sala, a minor over 14 and of Polly, Anna, Jesse and Lydia, minors under 14. Gdn. Peter Clement, Atkinson gent. Bond L1000.0.0. Sureties: James Thurston, gent. and James Thurston Jr., trader, both of Exeter. Witnesses: Trueworthy Gilman and Samuel Gliden. PETITION: 12/15/1800. Of Jesse Poor, being about 18 years of age. Requests appointment of Samuel Webster as his Gdn. GDP.: 12/17/1800. Of Jesse, a minor over 14. Gdn. Samuel Webster, Atkinson yoeman. Bond $2,000.00. Surety George Reed, Londonderry esq. Witness W. Parker. Note: This file includes a Petition for Gdp. of Merril Poor which belongs with #5754 Merril Poor (1792) and is recorded there.

2111. POOR, DANIEL JR. (1791) #5620
EST. Atkinson yoeman decd. intestate. ADMIN.: 2/7/1791. Admr. Humphrey Noyes, Atkinson yoeman. Bond L1000.0.0. Sureties: Moses Greenough and Abijah Eaton, Atkinson gentlemen. Witnesses: Wm. Parker Jr. and W. Parker. PETITION: 3/26/1792. Of Admr. For License. Granted. LICENSE (D30:216): 3/27/1792. To Admr. To sell real est. to amount of L50.0.0. APPR. WARR.: 3/27/1792. Comm.: Nathaniel Peabody, esq.; Eliphalet Knight and Jesse Sawyer, gentlemen; Caleb Noyes and Samuel Noyes Little, yoemen, all of Atkinson. To view 2/3 real est. to see if it can be div. Div. or appr. INVY.: Comm.: Moses Greenough, William Cogswell and Jesse Sawyer. Value L574.7.5 Oaths 4/18/1791 Comm. to Peter Clement, JP. Oath 4/20/1792 Admr. to judge.

APPR.: 5/5/1792. Value L223.5.2. DOWER WARR.: 3/27/1792. Comm.: Nathl. Peabody, Elipht. Knight, Caleb Noyes, Jesse Sawyer and Samuel N. Little. Of Widow Sarah Poor. Dower: Oaths 11/2/1792 Comm. to Peter Clement, JP. Allowed. ACCOUNT: 12/3/1792. Of Admr. Allowed 12/3/1792 there being no objection from Gdn. of the minors. Account includes main. one child. DECREE SETTLM.: 12/15/1792. There being no son of age to take settlm., judge settles 2/3 real est. on Abijah Eaton, Atkinson gent., who married one of the daus., in right of his wife. Abijah to pay each of his co-heirs L31.17.02 1/2 in 12 months, with interest. BOND: 12/15/1792. Of Abijah Eaton, Atkinson gent. Bond L500.0.0. To pay his co-heirs per Decree. Settlm. Sureties: Nathaniel Peabody, esq. and Eliphalet Knight, gent., both of Atkinson. Witnesses to sig. of Eaton, C. Moore and Jos. Wardwell. Witnesses to sigs. of Peabody and Knight, Lemuel Johnson and Joshua Cushing. DUPLIOCATE COPY OF BOND: Gives bond as L400.0.0. DISCHARGE: 5/20/1792. Of Peter Clement as Gdn. of Sally Poor, Polly Poor, Anna Poor, Jesse Poor and Lydia Poor, all minor children of Daniel. He has received from Abijah Eaton, L165.01.07 as the children's proportion of 2/3 of the real est. est. and thereby discharges Eaton. Witnesses: Samuel Webster and Nathl. Peabody. Oath 4/8/1794 Peter Clement, Esq. to Nathl. Peabody, JP. ADDL. ACCOUNT. 6/13/1796. Of Admr. Allowed 6/13/1796, the Gdn. of children consenting. RECEIPT: 7/25/1796. Of Admr. Acknowledges he received of Peter Clement and Abijah Eaton L40.3.0, in full of his demand against est. Oath 7/27/1796. Humphrey Noyes to Jona. Payson, JP.

2112. POOR, DANIEL (1792) #5742
EST. Atkinson gent. decd. testate. WILL: Drawn 7/8/1791. Legatees: Wife-Lydia; Sons-Jonathan, David, John and Jeremiah; Grandsons-Merrill Poor and Jesse Poor sons of his son Daniel decd. and Charles Poor son of his son John; His negro girl Philis. Execs.-sons Jonathan and David. His sig. Witnesses: John Dow, Caleb Richards and Stephen Peabody. CERT. WILL (D30:191): 2/14/1792. Presented by Execs. and witnesses Richardson and Rev. Peabody. ADMIN.: 2/14/1792. Execs.: Jonathan Poor and David Poor, Atkinson gentlemen. Bond L5000.0.0. Sureties: Stephen Peabody, clerk and Caleb Richards, yoeman, both of Atkinson. Witnesses: Nathniel Souther and Nat Parker. INVY.: Comm.: Jonathan Webster, John Dow and Eliphalet Knight. Value L3514.1.0. Oaths 2/3/1792 Comm. to Peter Clement, JP.

2113. POOR, BRIG. GEN. ENOCH (1781) #4684
EST. Exeter esq. decd. intestate. ADMIN.: 1/24/1781. Admx. Martha Poor, Exeter widow. Bond L100000.0.0. Sureties: Henry Dearborn, esq. and Eliphalet Ladd, merchant, both of Exeter. Witnesses: Timothy

Chamberlain and Jedidiah Jewett to sigs. of Poor and Ladd; Nathl. Parker and W. Parker to sig. of Dearborn. INVY. WARR.: 1/31/1781. Comm.: James Thirstin, blacksmith; Eliphalet Ladd, merchant and Gideon Lamson, taylor, all of Exeter. INVY.: Value L193.8.6 plus L1500.0.0+ in land and bldgs. not completely tallied. Oaths 1/29/1783 Ladd and Lamson to W. Parker, JP. PETITION: 1/29/1783. Of O. Peabody atty. to Admx. Requests Comm. Insolvency. Gives claims as amounting to L600.0.0. LICENSE (D27:152): 1/29/1783. To Admx. To sell sufficient real est. to pay debts. DOWER: 12/24/1787. Comm.: Nathaniel Gilman, Jona. Cass, Oliver Peabody and Wm. Parker Jr., esquires and Gideon Lamson, trader. Of Widow Martha Poor Oaths 12/24/1787 Comm. to W. Parker, JP. Allowed.

2114. POOR, MERRIL (1792) #5754
GDP. of the son of Daniel Poor Jr., Atkinson yoeman decd., n.c.m. The following Petition found in #5753 Poor: Anna, Jesse, Lydia, Polly & Sala (1792) belongs here. PETITION: 3/13/1792. Of Samuel N. Little and John Knight Jr., Atkinson Selectmen and Overseers of the Poor. Request appointment of a gdn. For Merril Poor of Atkinson who is n.c.m. PETITION: 3/22/1792. Of Sarah Poor, widow of Daniel Poor. Requests a Gdn. For her oldest son Merril, about 25 years old, incapable of caring for himself or est. Requests appointment of Abijah Eaton. Eaton, who, having married her oldest dau., will be more likely to take proper care of Merril than a stranger. Witness Jesse Sawyer. GDP.: 3/28/1792. Of Merril, an adult adjudged n.c.m. Gdn. Abijah Eaton, Atkinson gent. Bond L1000.0.0. Sureties: Nathaniel Peabody of Atkinson and Timothy Eaton of Haverill, Essex Co., MA, gentlemen. Witnesses: Joshua Sawyer and Peter Clement to sig. of Eaton and Jonah Minot and John Taylor to sig. of Peabody. PETITION: 3/16/1801. Of Sarah Webster. She thinks that because of Abijah Eaton's circumstances it would be prudent to have someone else as Merril's Gdn. Requests appointment of her husb. Samuel Webster. Witness Jonathan Stickney. GDP.: 4/15/1801. Of Merril, an adult n.c.m. Gdn. Samuel Webster, Atkinson yoeman. Bond $3,000.00. Sureties: James Webster, gent. and Rawlings Webster, yoeman, both of Salem. Witness Wm. Parker. INVY.: 12/17/1801. Comm.: Humphrey Noyes, Eliphalet Knight and James Webster. Value $286.37 1/2. Oaths Comm. to John Vose, JP. Oath 4/21/1802 Gdn. to N. Parker, JP. REPORT OF ARBITRATORS: 12/12/1818. Comm.: Henry Noyes, John Webster and Jedediah Pettengill. In the matter of the Account of Samuel Webster Gdn. of Merril and the objections to Account of Jesse Poor, Haverhill, Essex Co. cordwainer and others, bros. and sisters of Merril. The Arbitrators rule that Samuel Webster should be allowed $100.00 in full of his Gdp. Account up to the time of reference. LETTER: 1/13/1819. From Arbitration Comm. To judge. Having understood that there is a difference

of opinion as to their award, they feel it proper to inform the judge that it was their intention that Samuel Webster be allowed the $100.00 in the award in addition to what he had already received, i.e. Merril's property, exclusive of his real est., for which Webster gave credit in his Account. ACCOUNT: 1819. Of Gdn. The Account was referred to an Arbitration Comm. Decree: Samuel Webster is allowed the $100.00 awarded for his demands to date. The bal. of $102.03 in Webster's hands is to be paid to the person appointed Merril's Gdn.

2115. POOR, MOSES (1775) #4181
EST. Salem yoeman decd. intestate. PETITION: 10/4/1775. Of Hannah Poor, widow of Moses. Requests appointment of Jonathan Tenney of Salem as Co-Admin. Granted. ADMIN: 10/13/1775. Admrs.: Hannah Poor, widow and Jonathan Tenney, gent., both of Salem. Bond L1000.0.0.Sureties: John Kelly and Henry Little, Salem gentlemen. Witnesses: Abner Bayley and Mary White. INVY. WARR.: 12/13/1775. Comm.: Deacon John Hall and Abbot Petingill, both of Salem. INVY.: Appr. 12/26/1775. Value L98.14.6. Oath 12/27/1775 Hall to Timothy Ladd, JP. Oaths 12/28/1775 Admrs. to judge. PETITION: 6/26/1776. Of Jonathan Tenney, an Admr. For Comm. Insolvency. CLAIMS WARR.: 6/26/1776. Comm.: John Hall and John Kelly, Salem yoeman. LICENSE: 6/26/1776 To Admrs. To sell sufficient real est. to pay debts. DOWER; 11/18/1776. Comm.: John Hall, John Kelly and Thos. Hadley. Of Widow Hannah Poor. Oaths 12/10/1776 Comm. to Timothy Ladd, JP. Allowed 4/30/1777. CLAIMS: 12/25/1776. Total L74.9.11. Oaths 11/15/1777 Comm. to Timothy Ladd, JP. ACCOUNT: Of Admrs. Allowed 4/30/1777 on oath of Tenney. Account includes main. 2 children. PROP. & SETTLM: Claims L74.9.11. Amount to be proportioned L36.3.10. Allowed 6/25/1777 with order to Admrs. to pay.

2116. POOR, NOAH (1787) #5294
GDP. Of the son of Lydia Graves of Deerfield. GDP.: 9/19/1787. Of Noah Poor, a minor over 14. Gdn. Richard Bartlet, Pembroke esq. Bond L1000.0.0. Sureties: Daniel Bickford, Pembroke hatter and Reuben Dow of Hollis, Hillsborough Co. Witnesses: Jacob Sherburne and Nathl. Parker.

2117. POTTER: ABIGAIL, DANIEL & SARAH (1788) #5339
GDP. Of the children of Daniel Potter, Ipswich, Essex Co., MA mariner decd. GDP.: 3/18/1788. Of: Sarah, Daniel and Abigail, minors under 14. Gdn. Mager Gould, Ipswich, Essex Co., MA taylor. Bond L500.0.0. Sureties: Nathaniel Gould and James Folsom, Exeter saddlers. Witnesses: Nathl. Parker and W. Parker.

2118. POTTER, DANIEL (1791) #5649
EST. Of Ipswich, Essex Co. MA. ADMIN.: 4/20/1791. Admr. William McQuesten, Londonderry yeoman. Bond L1000.0.0. Sureties: Isaac Thom, physician and Jacob Martin, gent., both of Londonderry. Witnesses: George Russell and (John?) March. INVY.: Comm.: Amos Gould, William Danforth and Josiah Jones. Value L220.12.1. Oaths 6/25/1791 Comm. to William McQuesten, JP. Oath 4/18/1792 Admr. to judge. On back, Admr. paid Invy. Comm. L12.0.0. Note: The following Pet., Notification and Div. Warr. recorded as #6600 Samuel Stinson(1799) belong here. PETITION: 8/21/1799. Of Samuel Stinson, Londonderry yoeman in right of his wife. For div. of land and bldgs. in Londonderry, late the est. of Daniel Potter of Ipswich, Essex Co., MA, which he holds in common with William McQueston, Londonderry yoeman and of which he owns 1/4. Order: For hearing. NOTIFICATION: 8/23/1799. To William McQueston, Londonderry yoeman. He is notified of Petition and hearing. Cert.: 9/6/1799. Of John Morrison, Depy. Sheriff. He left the orig. of the Notification with McQueston. DIV. WARR.: 9/18/1799. Comm.: Names omitted. To make Div. as in Petition between William McQueston and Samuel Stinson in right of his wife, both of Londonderry. ACCOUNT (D33:147):

2119. POTTLE, SIMON (1791) #5681
EST. Stratham yoeman decd. intestate. ADMIN.: 8/8/1791. Admr. William Pottle, Stratham gent. Bond L1000.0.0. Sureties: Benjamin Baker, esq. and Josiah Thurston, both of Stratham. Witnesses: Simeon Ladd and Nathl. Parker. INVY.: Comm.: Jonathan Piper and Enos Hoag. Value L245.3.6. Oaths 6/10/1792 Piper and Admr., affirm. Hoag to W. Parker. PETITION: 7/10/1792. Of Admr. For Comm. Insolvency. Gives list claims of L255.0.0 plus more not ascertained. He proposes a Comm. of Capt. Jona. Wiggin, Enos Hoag and Joseph Merrill, Stratham gentlemen. CLAIMS WARR.: 7/10/1792. Comm. as proposed. Claims: 1/10/1793. Value not tallied. Esti. L85.0.0+.

2120. POTTLE, WILLIAM (1785) #5138
EST. Stratham blacksmith decd. testate. WILL: Drawn 12/20/1783. Legatees: Wife-unnamed, referred to as living but no bequest; Son-William; Daus.-Deborah Barker and Hannah Hill; Grandson-Simon Pottle son of his son William. Exec.-son William. His sig. Witnesses: Paine Wingate, Joshua Wingate and Eunice Wingate. CERT. WILL (D28:296): 9/21/1793. Presented by Exec. and witnesses Paine Wingate and Joshua Wingate.

2121. POWERS, CAPT. PETER (1757) A#2412
EST. Hollis gent. decd. intestate. LICENSE (D30:240): 4/18/1792. To Francis Powers, Admr. d.b.n., Hollis, now Hillsborough Co., cordwainer. To sell real est. to amount of L150.0.0. Orig. Archives file includes Admin., Invy., License (1758), Dower, Account, Prop. & Settlm. and Admin. D.B.N.

PRESCOTT. See also Prescut, Prescutt

2122. PRESCOTT, BENJAMIN (1799) #6533
EST. Portsmouth merchant decd. intestate. RENUN.: 1/25/1799. Of Hannah Prescott, widow of Benjamin. Of Admin. Requests appointment of Benjamin's bro. George W. Prescott. Granted. ADMIN. (D33:42): 1/25/1799. Admr. George Washington Prescott, New Castle gent. Sureties: Henry Prescott, New Castle esq. and Edmund H. Quincy of Portsmouth. INVY.: Comm.: William Vennard, Thomas Bell and Foxwell Curtis. Value $744.08. Oaths 3/18/1799 Comm. to Geo. Frost, JP. Invy. shows him as owner of the Schooner Betsy. PETITION: 4/8/1799. Of Admr. For Comm. Insolvency. Shows claims already in of $3,300.00. Granted. CLAIMS WARR.: 4/10/1799. Comm.: Isaac Rindge, esq.; Edward Sargent, mariner and Edmund H. Quincy, merchant, all of Portsmouth. On 10/10/1799 Comm. allowed 10 months longer. Claims: 10/13/1800. Total $3,675.88. Oaths 10/14/1800 Sargent and Quincy to Isaac Rindge, JP. Note: A note in file says Pet. License and Account missing and not found in Docket Book.

2123. PRESCOTT, JAMES (1751) A#1580
EST. Hampton Falls yoeman decd. Note: The following Citation found in #4757 Elisha Prescutt (1781) belongs here. CITATION: 2/11/1784. To Elisha Prescutt, Epping gent. Complaint has been made to the judge that Elisha refuses to act in the admin. of his father's est. Creditors are kept out of their due and his co-administrator is prevented from settling. Elisha is ordered to appear to answer the complaint and submit to the law enjoining him. Cert.: 2/11/1784. Of Samull. Dearborn, Dept. Sheriff. He has cited Prescutt by delivering to him a copy of Citation. Orig. Archives file includes Will naming sons Samuel and Elisha Execs., Invy. Warr. and Invy.

2124. PRESCOTT, JEREMIAH (1781) #4721
EST. Epping yoeman decd. intestate. RENUN.: 6/27/1781. Of Mary Prescott, widow of Jeremiah. Of Admin. Requests appointment of her sons Jeremiah and Elisha. Witnesses: Darbon (Bedy, Beck?-unreadable) and William Prescott. ADMIN.: 6/27/1781. Admr. Jeremiah Prescott, Epsom

gent. Bond L80000.0.0. Sureties: Elisha Prescutt, gent., Samuel Prescutt and Joel Judkins, husbandmen, all of Epping. Witnesses: Elizabeth Parker and Nathl. Parker. INVY.: Appr. 7/3/1791. Comm.: Jona. Swain, Raymond gent.; James Norris, esq. and James Norris 3rd, yoeman, both of Epping. Value L849.12.5. Oath 7/25/1781 Admr. to W. Parker, Reg. APPR. WARR.: 1/1/1783. Comm.: Jonathan Swain, Raymond gent., James Norris, esq. and James Norris, yoeman, last 2 of Epping. To appr. the income of the real est., exclusive of taxes and expenses, for the last 2 years. APPR.: 1/21/1783. Value 70 silver dollars per year or L42.0.0. ACCOUNT: 1/29/1783. Of Elisha Prescutt, Admr. Note: This Account seems to be his own expenses for boarding Jeremiah, his widow and his "dater" Phebe as well as for settling est. to date. PETITION: 5/29/1783. Of Jeremiah Prescott, for himself and for his co-Admr. For License. Gives list debts of L46.48.11. Allowed. LICENSE: 5/29/1783. To Admrs. To sell sufficient real est. to pay debts. ACCOUNT: Of Elisha Prescutt, an Admr.

2125. PRESCOTT, JOHN (1781) #4716
EST. Epping husbm. decd. testate. WILL: Drawn 4/23/1781. Legatees: Sons-Jonathan, Samuel, John and Dudley; Daus.-Ratchel Lawrence, Mary Lawrence, Lucey Perkins, Leah Prescutt and Hannah Prescutt. Exec.-son John. His sig. Witnesses: Joseph Prescott, Nathan Gove Prescut and Abraham Perkins. Codicil: He adds additional bequests of sawmills which he forgot, provides for Leah to live in house and makes specific bequests from his personal est. to several children. His sig. Same witnesses. Proved 5/30/1781 on oaths all witnesses. Note: The sig. on Will has been altered by someone and appears to have been changed from Prescutt to Prescott. INVY. WARR.: 8/30/1781. Comm.: Abraham Perkins, esq.; Seth Fogg and Simon Dearborn, gentlemen, all of Epping. Note adds appr. must be in silver money. INVY.: Value L1558.05.0. Oaths 10/30/1781 Fogg and Dearborn to Abraham Perkins, JP.

2126. PRESCOTT, JOSHUA (1785) #5139
EST. Chester yoeman decd. testate. WILL: Drawn 12/8/1769. Legatees: Wife-Mary; Sons-Stephen, Joshua, John, Demenikes, Daniel Moulton Prescutt, Asa and Joseph; Daus.-Sarah True and Abigail Currier; Any additional children his wife may have by him. Exec.-wife Mary. His mark. Witnesses: Dorithy Emerson, John Pain and Saml. Emerson. CERT. WILL (D28:301): Presented by Exex. and witnesses Samuel Emerson and Dorithy Emerson. INVY. Appr. 10/20/1785. Comm.: Jona. Swain of Raymond, John Knowles and John Lane, both of Chester. Value not tallied. Esti. L475.0.0+. Oaths 10/29/1785 Knowles, Swain and Exex. to Robt. Wilson, JP.

2127. PRESCOTT, JOSIAH (1776) #4256
EST. Deerfield yoeman decd.ADMIN.:7/31/1776. Admx. Ruth Prescott, widow. Bond L500.0.0. Sureties: Jeremiah Eastman, esq. and David Kindrick, both of Deerfield. Witnesses: Thos. Rand and Elijah Ring. INVY.: Appr. 10/14/1776. Comm.: Thos. Rand, Benjamin Page and Jonathan Hill. Value L351.10.7. Oath10/14/1776. Admx. and Comm. to Jeremiah Eastman, JP. ACCOUNT: 5/18/1791. Of Admx. Allowed5/18/1791.Account includes main. of one child.

2128. PRESCOTT, JOSIAH (1783) #4949
EST. Deerfield yoeman decd. testate. WILL: Drawn 9/2/1783. Legatees: Wife- Elisabeth. Daus.-Elisabeth Prescott, Mary Prescott and Hannah Prescott; Josiah Prescott son of his bro. John. Execs.-wife Elisabeth and John Tucke. His sig. Witnesses: John Prescutt, Samuel Batchelder and Saml. Mooers. CERT. WILL: 11/19/1783. Presented by John Tucke, an Exec., the other refusing, and witnesses Prescutt and Batchelder. PETITION: 11/19/1783. Of Widow Elisabeth Prescott. She is dissatisfied with the provision made for her in Will and requests her Dower. INVY.: Appr. 2/6/1784. Comm.: Thomas Jenness, Moses Barnard and Samuel Batchelder. Value L477.1.6. Oaths 2/6/1784 Comm. to Daniel Ladd, JP. Oath 2/18/1784 Exec. to W. Parker, Reg.

2129. PRESCOTT, MARSTON (1799) #6576
GDP. Kensington yoeman n.c.m. PETITION: 6/3/1799. Of Josiah Prescot. States that his father, Marston Prescot of Kensington, who has considerable real property and a family to support, is often n.c.m. Requests he be appointed Gdn. of Marston. Order: 6/25/1799.To Kensington Selectmen. To make inquisition into condition of Marston. Report: 6/28/1799. Of: John Blake and Joseph Weare, Kensington Selectmen. They judge Marston to be n.c.m. and recommend Simon Rowe to be his Gdn. GDP.: 6/29/1799. Of Marston, an adult adjudged n.c.m. Gdns.: Josiah Prescot and Simon Rowe, Kensington yoemen. Bond $3,000.00. Surety Elisha Blake, Kensington husbm. Witnesses: Mary S. Parker and W. Parker. LETTER OF GDP.: 6/29/1799. To Simon Rowe and Josiah Prescot. INVY.: Comm.: Moses Shaw, Elisha Blake and Samuel Dearbon. Value $1,001.86. Oaths 7/13/1799 Comm. to Jere. Fogg, JP.

2130. PRESCOTT, MARY (1766) #1172 (as Mary Frost) & (1771) #3839
EST. Mary Prescott, Danvers, MA gentlewoman, formerly wife of John Frost of New Castle, N.H., widow decd. Note: All of the following documents are in #3839. LICENSE: 3/27/1771. To William and George Frost, surviving Execs. To sell land and bldgs. in Portsmouth and New Castle and a pewin New Castle Meeting House. BOND: 3/10/1773. Of

Execs. Bond L15.0.0. To account for sale of land by License; to pay Mary's just debts; the debts of their father, John Frost, esq. decd.; and to div. the remainder among the legatees or legal reps.-Charles Frost and Joseph Frost, esquires.; Jane Watkins and Dorothy Clifford. Surey George Frost Jr., New Castle merchant. Witnesses: Hophom Barlow and Samuel Frost. DIV. WARR.: 11/2/1773. Comm.: William Weekes, John Parker, Walter Bryent and Thomas Pierce, esquires and Elisha Hill, blacksmith, all of Rockingham Co. To div. a lot of land in Portsmouth in 10 equal shares among the heirs. DIV.: 11/4/1773. Divisees: William Frost, Heirs of John Frost, Andrew Pepperell Frost, Heirs of Sarah Hills, Miriam Raitt, Heirs of Charles Frost, Heirs of Joseph Frost, Jane Watkins, Dorothy Clifford and George Frost. Allowed 11/4/1773. MAP OF DIV. Orig. Archives file includes Will, and Pet. for License. Note: The confusion over the two names for the est. arises from the several marriages of Mary. Her Will was written when she was still the Widow of John Frost. She later wrote a codicil to the Will when she was about to marry her 2d husb. Rev. Benjamin Colman of Danvers, Essex Co., MA. In the Codicil she gave her negro woman Hagar her freedom. At the time of her death she was the widow of her 3d husb. Rev. Benjamin Prescott, DD of Salem, Essex Co., MA.

2131. PRESCOTT, NATHANIEL (1771) #3867
EST. Kensington yoeman decd. testate. WILL: Drawn 5/1/1764. Legatee: Wife-Abigail. Exex.-wife Abigail. His sig. Witnesses: Jeremiah Fellows, John Lane and Wm. Parker Jr. Proved 9/4/1771 on oaths of Lane and Parker. ADMIN.:9/4/1771. Admrs.: Benjamin James, yoeman and Abigail his wife as she is Exex. of est. of Benjamin Prescott. Bond: L300.0.0. Surety Joseph Chase Stilyard, yoeman. Witnesses: John Lane and Wm. Parker Jr.

2132. PRESCOTT, NATHANIEL (1792) #5750
EST. Brentwood yoeman decd. testate. WILL: Drawn 5/6/1782. Legatees: Wife-Sarah; Sons-Jeremiah and Samuel; Dau.-Sarah Prescott. Execs.-wife Sarah and son Jeremiah. His sig. Witnesses: John Tucke, Coffin Sanborn and Thos. Stow Ranney. CERT. WILL (D30:212): 3/21/1792. Presented by Jeremiah Prescott, one of Execs., the other refusing trust, and all witnesses. ADMIN.: 3/21/1792. Exec. Jeremiah Prescott, Brentwood yoeman. Bond L1000.0.0. Sureties: John Tucke, gent. and Coffin Sanborn, joiner, both of Brentwood. Witness Nathl. Parker. INVY.: Appr. 3/23/1792. Comm.: Samuel Cram and Coffin Sanborn. Value L104.13.0. Oaths 4/11/1792 Exec. to Exekl. Godfrey, JP. Oaths 4/11/1792 Comm. to Ezekl. Godfrey, JP.

2133. PRESCOTT, SAMUEL (1790) #5545
EST. Deerfield yoeman decd. testate. WILL: Drawn 12/18/1789. Legatees: Wife-Anna; Son-Samuel; Daus.-Sarah Prescott (oldest dau.) and Betty Prescott. Execs.-wife Anna and friend and bro. Abraham Prescott. His sig. Witnesses: Benjamin Fellows, Jesse Prescott and Dudley Ladd. CERT. WILL (D29:380): 5/19/1790. Presented by Execs. and witnesses Ladd and Fellows. ADMIN.: 5/19/1790. Execs.: Anna Prescutt, widow and Abraham Prescutt, yoeman, both of Deerfield. Bond L500.0.0. Sureties: Dudley Ladd and Benjamin Fellows, Deerfield yoemen. Witnesses: Michl. McClary and Nathl. Parker. INVY.: Appr. 5/18/1790. Comm.: Jonathan Philbrick and Benjamin Sanborn. Value L354.4.6. Oaths 5/18/1790 Comm. to Jeremiah Eastman, JP. PETITION: 7/18/1790. Of Abraham Prescott, an Exec. For License. Gives list claims L88.8.11. Notes decd. disposed of all personal est. by Will and heirs are minors who cannot give bond. Allowed. LICENSE: (D30:16): 2/15/1791. To Execs. To sell real est. to amount of L100.0.0. DOWER: 3/28/1791. Comm.: Jeremiah Eastman, Moses Barnard, Jonathan Philbrick, Robert Morrill and Nathan Prescutt. Of Widow Anna Prescutt. Oaths 4/11/1791 Barnard, Philbrick, Morrill and Prescutt to Jeremiah Eastman, JP. Allowed 5/18/1791. ACCOUNT: 1791. Of Execs. Oath 8/12/1791 Anna Prescott, an Exec., to George Evens, JP. Allowed 8/15/1791. PETITION: 12/24/1792. Of Abraham Prescott, an Exec. For License. There are still legacies and costs of admin. to be paid. Requests permission to sell all the rest of the real est. as selling part would be injurious to heirs. Cert.: Of Stephen Prescott, Gdn. of only son and sole divisee. He agrees that selling rest of real est. would benefit the divisee, especially since another legacy in money is due in a few years. LICENSE: 12/24/1792. To Execs. To sell all the rest of real est. BOND: 12/24/1792.Of Abraham Prescott, Deerfield yoeman. Bond L1000.0.0. To account for proceeds of sale of real est. by License. Sureties: Stephen Prescott, Deerfield yoeman and Stephen Fogg, Exeter carpenter. Witnesses: Saml. Parker and W. Parker. ADDL. ACCOUNT: 1/14/1796. Of Abraham Prescott, an Exec. Allowed 1/14/1796. Account shows payment of legacies to Sally Kimball and Betty Farnum.

2134. PRESCOTT, SAMUEL (1792) #5835
GDP. Of the son of Samuel Prescott, Deerfield yoeman decd. GDP.: 12/24/1792. Of Samuel, a minor under 14. Gdn. Stephen Prescott, Deerfield yoeman. Bond L1000.0.0. Sureties: Abraham Prescott, Deerfield yoeman and Stephen Fogg, Exeter carpenter. Witnesses: Saml. Parker and W. Parker. GDP.: 12/12/1795. Of Samuel, a minor over 14. Gdn. David Farnum, Pembroke tanner. Bond L1000.0.0. Sureties: Richard Bartlett, esq. and Jonathan Eliot, cordwainer, both of Pembroke. Witnesses: Nathl. Doyen and Phebe (uncertain but pos. Bartlett). ACCOUNT: 11/16/1796.

Of Stephen Prescott. Of his Gdp. Allowed 11/16/1796 having been consented to by present Gdn.

2135. PRESCOTT, WILLIAM PARTRIDGE (1783) #4888
EST. Raymond yoeman decd. intestate. ADMIN.: 4/4/1783. Admr. Samuel Nay, Raymond gent. Bond L500.0.0. Sureties: John Dudley, esq. and John Prescott Loveren, yoeman, both of Raymond. Witnesses: Jona. Swain and Francis Hodgkins. INVY. WARR.: 4/4/1783. Comm.: Jonathan Swain, esq.; Thomas Gordon, gent. and Matthias Hains, yoeman, all of Raymond. INVY.: Appr. 4/14/1783. Value L35.18.6. Oaths 6/28/1783 Swain, Gordon and Admr. to John Dudley, JP. CLAIMS WARR.: 4/21/1784. Comm.: Jonathan Swain, Thomas Gordon and Matthias Haines, all of Raymond. DOWER WARR.: 4/21/1784. Comm.: Jonathan Swain, Thomas Gordon, Matthias Haines, Francis Hodgkins and Thomas Bean, all of Raymond. Of Widow Elizabeth Prescott. LICENSE (D27:443): 4/21/1784. To Admr. To sell 2/3 of the real est. DOWER: 5/4/1784. Oaths 5/26/1784 Swain, Gordon and Bean to John Dudley, JP. Allowed. CLAIMS: 12/16/1784. Total L11.11.10. Oaths 12/29/1784 Swain and Gordon to John Dudley, JP. ACCOUNT: 3/16/1785. Of Admr. Allowed 3/16/1785. Account includes main, 2 children.

PRESCUT. See also Prescott, Prescutt

2136. PRESCUT, ABRAHAM (1789) #5476
EST. Kensington yoeman decd. testate. WILL: Drawn 5/29/1789. Legatees: Sons-Samuel, Abraham, Simon, Stephen, Jesse, David, Chase, Joseph and Benjamin; Daus.-Anna Bachelder, Sarah Prescott and Abigail Prescott (n.c.m.). Exec.- son Simon. His sig. Witnesses: Robert Kimball, Benjamin Tilton and Jere. Bachelder. CERT. WILL (D29:293): 8/18/1789. Presented by Exec. and witnesses Kimball and Bachelder. ADMIN.: 8/18/1789. Exec. Simon Prescutt of Kensington. Bond L1000.0.0. Sureties: Jeremiah Bachelder of Kensington and Robert Kilmball of Exeter, gentlemen. Witnesses; Jere. Fogg Jr. and W. Parker. INVY.: Appr. 10/5/1789. Comm.: Robert Kimball, Benjamin Tilton and Jere. Bachelder. Value not tallied. Esti. L269.0.0+. Oaths 1/30/1790 Tilton, Bachelder and Exec. to W. Parker, JP.

PRESCUTT. See also Prescott, Prescut

2137. PRESCUTT, ELISHA (1781) #4757
EST. Hampton Falls yoeman decd. testate. WILL: Drawn 12/2/1772. Legatees: Wife-Phebe; Sons-James, Stephen and Ebenezer, last two of Raymond; Exec.-son James. His sig. Witnesses: Nathl. Healey, Benjamin

Sanborn and Jeremiah Lane. CERT. WILL: 12/26/1781. Presented by Exec. and witnesses Sanborn and Lane. INVY.: Appr. 1/10/1782. Comm.: Nathl. Healey, Benjamin Sanborn and Jeremiah Lane. Value L1294.7.6. Oaths 1/16/1782 Comm. to Saml. Weare, JP. Oath 2/27/1782 Exec. to W. Parker, Reg. This file also includes a Citation which belongs with A#1580 Samuel Prescott (1751) and is recorded there.

2138. PRESCUTT, JOSIAH (1783) #4949
EST. Deerfield yoeman decd. testate. WILL: Drawn 9/2/1783. Legatees: Wife-Elizabeth; Daus.-Mary Prescutt, Elisabeth Prescutt and Hannah Prescutt; Josiah Prescutt son of his bro. John. Execs. wife Elizabeth and John Tucke, Brentwood gent. His sig. Witnesses: John Prescutt, Samuel Batchelder and Saml. Mooers. CERT. WILL: 11/17/1783. Presented by John Tucke, one of Execs., the other refusing trust, and witnesses Prescutt and Batchelder. RENUN.: 11/19/1783. Of Elizabeth Prescott, widow of Josiah. She is dissatisfied with the provision made for her in Will so relinquishes the bequest and requests her dower right instead. INVY.: Comm.: Thomas Jenness, Moses Barnard and Samuel Batchelder. Value L477.1.6. Oaths 2/6/1784 Comm. to Daniel Ladd, JP. Oath 2/18/1784 Exec. to W. Parker, Reg.

2139. PRESCUTT, SAMUEL (1798) #6413
EST. Kensington gent. decd. testate. WILL: Drawn 2/4/1797. Legatees; Wife-Hopee. Son-Robert; Daus.-Sarah Pike wife of Elias Pike and Olive Rowe wife of Jonathan Rowe; Granddaus.-Mehetable Dole and Ruth Chase dau. of Stephen Chase. Exec.- son Robert. His sig. Witnesses: Nathan Weare, John Blake and Joseph Lane. CERT. WILL (D32:421): 1/15/1798. Presented by Exec. and witnesses Blake and Lane. CERT.: 1/15/1798. Of Hopee Prescutt, widow of Samuel. She accepts the provision made for her in Will and has compounded with Exec. to render an Invy. unnecessary. Requests it be disposed of. ADMIN.: 2/1/1798. Exec. Robert Prescott, Kensington yoeman. Bond $3,000.00. Sureties: Jonathan Stuart and Moses Rowe, Kensington yoemen. Witnesses: Mary S. Parker and W. Parker.

2140. PRESCUTT, STEPHEN (1799) #6595
EST. Deerfield gent. decd. testate. PETITION: 7/20/1799. Of Widow Rebecca Prescutt. She is dissatisfied with provision made for her in Will and claims her Dower and requests it be set off. WILL: Drawn 6/24/1799. Legatees: Wife-Rebeca; Sons-Samuel, Nathan and Stephen; Daus.-Deborah Rawlings and Rebeca Brown. Execs.-sons Samuel and Stephen. His sig. Witnesses: Jeremiah Eastman, Edmund Chadwick and William Page. CERT. WILL (D33:137): 7/22/1799. Presented by Execs. and

witnesses Eastman and Chadwick, esq. ADMIN.: 7/22/1799. Execs.: Samuel Prescott and Stephen Prescott, Deerfield yoemen. Bond $3,000.00. Sureties: Edmund Chadwick, physician and Andrew Freese, gent., both of Deerfield. Witnesses: Jeremiah Eastman and W. Parker. DOWER WARR.: 7/22/1799. Comm.: Joseph March, Jeremiah Eastman and James Prescott, esquires; Andrew Freese, gent. and Benjamin James, yoeman, all of Deerfield. Of Widow Rebecca Prescott. INVY.: Appr. 9/17/1799. Comm.: Joseph March, Benjamin James and Andw. Freese. Value $755.24. Oaths 9/18/1799 James, Freese and Execs. to judge. PETITION: 9/18/1799. Of Execs. For License. They note claims already $1,819.48 and real est. would sell most advantageously at this time of year. BOND: 9/18/1799. Of Execs. Bond $4,000.00. To account for proceeds of sale of real est. by License. Sureties: Benjamin James, husbm. and Andrew Freese, gent., both of Deerfield. Witnesses: Asa Foster Jr. and Nathl. Parker. LICENSE: 9/18/1799. To Execs. To sell real est. to amount of $2,000.00. PETITION: 9/18/1799. Of Execs. For Comm. Insolvency. Give list claims of $1,819.48. Granted. DOWER: 1/27/1800. Oaths 5/13/1800 Comm. to Nathl. Weare, JP. Allowed 5/21/1800. CLAIMS: 4/17/1800. Comm.: Benjamin James, Andw. Freese and Joseph March. Total $1,741.47. Oaths 5/13/1800 Comm. to Nathl. Weare, JP. An added list of $595.69 crossed out and noted by judge "to be paid without deduction." Most are doctor bills. ACCOUNT: 6/30/1800. Of Execs. Allowed 6/30/1800. Note: The following Prop. & Settlm. found in #6505 Stephen Peaslee (1798). belongs here. PROP. & SETTLM.: Claims $1,724.97. Amount to be proportioned $1,446.06. Allowed 8/8/1800 with order to Admrs. to pay. Note: This file includes a Petition which belongs with #6582 Samuel Smith (1799) and is recorded there.

2141. PRINCE, REV. JOSEPH (1791) #5621
EST. Candia clerk decd. testate. WILL: Drawn 1/7/1791 at Newburyport, MA. Legatees: Wife-Sarah. Has done what his ability can afford for all his children, but much more for some than others, so makes adjustment. Sons-Thomas, James, Joseph, Isaac, Ezekiel, Caleb and John. Execs.-Wife Sarah and sons Ezekiel and Caleb. His sig. Witnesses: David Hale, Eliphalet Pilsbury and Enoch C. Toppan. CERT. WILL (D30:17): 2/18/1791. Presented by Execs. and witnesses Enoch Coleman Toppan and Hale. ADMIN. 2/17/1791. Execs.: Sarah Prince, widow and Caleb Prince, yoeman, both of Candia and Ezekiel Prince, Newburyport, MA blockmaker. Bond L1000.0.0. Sureties: John Carr and Ephraim Eaton, Candia yoemen. Witnesses: John Clery and Patty Prince. INVY.: 2/24/1791. Comm.: John Clay, Ephraim Eaton and John Karr. Value L298.2.2. Oaths 2/24/1791 Execs. and Comm. to Saml. Mooers, JP.

2142. PROCTOR, JAMES (1777) #4306
EST. Kingston blacksmith decd. intestate. ADMIN.: 1/30/1777. Admx. Abigail Procter, Kingston widow. Bond L200.0.0. Sureties: Jonathan Procter, blacksmith and Jacob Hook, esq., both of Kingston. Witnesses: Amos Gale and Wm. Parker. INVY.: Appr. 1/22/1777. Comm.: Jacob Hook, Amos Gale and Daniel Colcord. Value L180.17.6. Oaths 1/30/1777Comm. and Admx. to judge. PETITION: 7/29/1777. Of Admx. For Comm. Insolvency. Gives list claims of L211.1.1. CLAIMS WARR.: 7/29/1777. Comm.: Amos Gale, physician and Simmons Seccombe, gent., both of Kingston. Report: 5/27/1778. The Comm. states they advertised the times and place of their meetings and attended accordingly, but no Claims were brought in to them. ACCOUNT: 10/27(sic.)/1779. Of Admx. Allowed 2/28(sic.)/1779. APPR. WARR.: 10/29/1779. Comm.: Jacob Hook, esq.; John Calef; Simmonds Seccombe, gent.; Amos Gale, physician and Daniel Colcord, yoeman, all of Kingston. To view 2/3 of the real est. and see if it can be div. among his 9 children. Appr. or div. giving 2 shares to oldest son. APPR.: 3/28/1780. Value L2100.0.0. Oaths 3/29/1780 Hook, Calef, Gale and Colcord to Josiah Bartlett, JP. DOWER: 3/28/1780. Same Comm. as Appr. Of Widow Abigail Procter. Oaths 3/29/1780 Hook, Calef, Gale and Colcord to Josiah Bartlett, JP.

2143. PULSIFER, WILLIAM FURNALD (1792) #5737
GDP. Of the son of Freeman Pulsifer of Boston, Suffolk Co., MA. GPD.: 2/1/1792. Of William Furnald Pulsifer, a minor under 14. Gdn. Freeman Pulsifer, his father, Boston, Suffolk Co., MA whalebone cutter. Bond L1000.0.0. Sureties: Titus Salter, esq. and Thomas Manning, mariner, both of Portsmouth. Witnesses: Nathl. Adams and John P. Hale. GDP.: 1/31/1801. Of William Furnald Pulsifer, a minor over 14. Gdn. William Stavers, Portsmouth yoeman. Bond $2,000.00. Sureties: Mark Rogers and James Shapley, Portsmouth merchants. Witnesses: Saml. Penhallow Jr. and Wm. Dame. ACCOUNT: Of William Stavers, Gdn. William Furnald Pulsifer has examined the Account and requests it be allowed. Allowed 2/19/1806.

2144. PURCELL, GREGORY (1776) #4287
EST. Portsmouth esq. decd. testate. WILL: Drawn 10/25/1776. Legatee: Wife-Sarah. He leaves entire est. to wife for her to dispose of among the children for their support. Exex.-Wife Sarah. His sig. Witnesses: Mary Clapham, Rebecca Butler and Richard Hall Wentworth. CERT. WILL (D23:418) 11/27/1776. Presented by Exex. and witnesses Clapham and Butler. INVY.: Appr. 2/20/1777. Comm.: Jno. Parker and Willm. Torrey. Value L2075.14.0. Oaths 2/24/1777 Admx, and Comm. to Saml. Penhallow, JP.

2145. PURCELL, SARAH (1789) #5457
EST. Portsmouth widow decd. ADMIN.: 6/16/1789. Admx.: Margaret Purcell, Portsmouth single woman. Bond L60.0.0. Sureties: Joseph Haven, merchant and Clement Storer, physician, both of Portsmouth. Witnesses: Nathl. Adams and Eunice Adams. INVY.: Comm.: Dan. R. Rogers and Clement Storer. Value L38.1.4. Oaths 9/1/1789 Comm. and Admx. to Nathl. Adams, JP.

PURINGTON. See Puritun

2146. PURITUN, JOSEPH (1785) #5130
EST. Pittsfield yoeman decd. testate. WILL: Drawn 5/28/1785. Legatees: Wife-Abigail; Sons-James, Joseph and Jorge; Daus.-Mary Purintum and Abigail Purintum. Exec.- son James. His sig. Witnesses: Jonathan Bunker, Caleb Shaw and John Cram. CERT. WILL(D28:258): 8/17/1785. Presented by Exec. and on oaths 7/28/1785 of witnesses Shaw and Cram, esq. to W. Parker, Reg. & JP. Allowed 8/17/1785. INVY.: Comm.: Job Haskell, David Knowlton and Edmund Sanborn. Value L625.17.2. Oaths 9/14/1785Comm. to John Cram, JP. Oath 12/22/1786 Exec. to W. Parker, Reg. & JP. ACCOUNT: 4/17/1788. Of Exec. PETITION: 2/3/1789. Of Exec. For License. He notes Will gave much of personal est. to wife and daus. LICENSE: 2/3/1789. To Exec. To sell real est. to amount of L80.0.0. DIV. & DOWER: Comm.: David Knowles, Edmund Sanborn, Jonathan Leavitt, Job Haskell and James Cram. To div. the real est. giving Widow her Dower and 2/3 to children. Divisees: Widow; Sons-James (oldest), George, Share of Joseph decd. Oaths 8/25/1789 Leavitt, Haskell and Cram to John Cram, JP. Allowed 10/11/1794.Includes map. Note: This file also contains the following: NOTIFICATION: To the Clerk of General Sessions of the Peace for Rockingham Co. From: Peter Clement, James Noyes and Enoch Knight, Atkinson Selectmen. They report that at a legal meeting held at the meeting house 12/15/1788 for the purpose of voting for a treasurer for the county, there were 38 votes cast for Oliver Peabody, esq. and none for any other person. Attested to by John Dow, Town Clerk. Note: The file card gives Joseph's res. as Chichester and the land in Div. was in Chichester, but the Will and all other papers say Pittsfield.

2147. PURMOTT, MARK (1778) #4419
EST. Kingston joiner decd. ADMIN.: 1/30/1778. Admr. Joseph Purmott, Exeter cordwainer. Bond L500.0.0. Sureties: Abner Dollof and David Dollof, Exeter yoemen. Witnesses: Walter Robie and W. Parker.

2148. PURVEAR, JOSEPH (1793) #5850
EST. Hampton Falls yoeman decd. ADMIN.: 1/22/1793. Admr. Caleb Haskell, Hampton Falls physician. Bond L500.0.0. Sureties: Theophilus Sanborn, gent. and Josiah Bachelder, yoeman, both of Hampton Falls. Witnesses: W. Parker and Wm. P. Adams. INVY.: Appr. 1/22/1793. Comm.: Abner Sanborn, Benja. Pike and George Fifield. Value L32.12.1. Oaths 3/15/1793 Comm. to Caleb Tilton, JP. Oath 3/28/ 1793 Admr. to W. Parker, Reg. PETITION: 3/28/1798. Of Admr. For License and Comm. Insolvency., Gives list claims of L68.19.11. Granted. LICENSE (D30:394): 3/28/1798. To Admr. To sell real est. to amount of L75.0.0. CLAIMS: Comm.: Abner Sanborn, Benja. Pike and George Fifield. Total L76.3.8. Cert. of W. Parker that Comm. gave oaths to a justice on another paper. ACCOUNT: 1/10/1794. Of Admr. Allowed 1/10/1794 Nathl. Healy, rep. Of creditors consenting. Receipt: 1/10/1794. From Nathl. Healey. To Admr. He has received L33.14.3, he having purchased all the claims as listed by Comm., thereby superceding the need for Prop.

2149. QUENTON, JAMES (1777) #4319
EST. Chester gent. decd. testate. WILL: Drawn 12/23/1773. Legatees: Wife-Agness; Sons-Hugh, Joshua, John and David; Dau.-Elizabeth McFarland; Granddau.-Susannah (Watson?). Execs.-wife Agness and son David. His sig. Witnesses: John Shirley, William Shirley and Saml. Emerson. CERT. WILL: 2/26/1777. Presented by Execs. and witnesses William Shirley and Emerson, esq. PETITION: 1/20/1777. Of Widow Agnes Quintin. She does not accept the provision made for her in Will and requests she be endowered in his est. according to law. Witness W. Parker. INVY.: Appr. 12/21/1776. Comm.: Saml. Emerson, John Tolford and Hugh Shirley. Value L444.4.0. Oaths 1/27/1777 Comm. to Robt. Wilson, JP. Oath 2/26/1777 David Quinton, an Exec. to judge.

QUIMBY. See also Quinby

2150. QUIMBY: ANNA, JOHN & SARAH (1788) #4584 1/2
GDP. Of the children of Jacob Quimby, Candia yoeman decd. PETITION: 10/14/1788. Of Anna, John and Sarah Quinby. They choose Walter Robie, esq. as their Gdn. Witnesses: James Varnum and John Karr. GDP.: 10/15/1788. Of: John, Sarah and Anne, minors over 14. Gdn. Walter Robie, esq. Bond L1000.0.0. Sureties: Samuel Buswell and John Sargent, Candia gentlemen. Witnesses: Samuel Flagg and Robert Wason.

2151. QUIMBY, COL. DAVID (1795) #6061
EST. Hawke esq. decd. RENUN.: 1/5/1795. Of: Mary Quimby, widow; Paul Quimby; Thomas Quimby; Joseph Busel and Lucy Busel, children of decd. Of Admin. They have agreed upon and request appointment of Thomas Page, esq. and the widow as Admrs. Allowed. ADMIN.: 1/9/1795. Admrs.: Mary Quimby, widow and Thomas Page, esq., both of Hawke. Bond L1000.0.0. Sureties: Joseph Williams and Josiah Tewksby, both of Hawke. Witnesses: Thomas Quimby, Barnard Collins and Polly Campbell. INVY.: Appr. 1/14/1795. Comm.: Nehemiah Sleeper, esq.; Simmons Seccombe, Matthias Bartlet and Benja. Pilsbey. Value L1320.2.7. Oaths 1/14/1795 Bartlet and Pilsbey to Simmons Secoombe, JP. Oath 4/13/1795 Mary Quimby, an Admr., to Thos. Page, JP.

2152. QUIMBY, JACOB (1776) #4196
EST. Hampstead gent. decd. intestate. ADMIN.: 1/31/1776. Admx. Miram Quimby, Hampstead widow. Bond L1000.0.0. Sureties: Aaron Quimby, housewright and Jabez Eaton, yoeman, both of Hawke. Witnesses: Ichabod Shaw and Jonathan Collins. INVY. WARR.:4/31/1776. Comm.: Ichabod Shaw, Sandown esq. and Edmund Moses, Hampstead gent. INVY.: Appr. 2/21/1776. Value L195.5.5. Oaths 4/24/1776 Admx. and Shaw, affirm. Moses to judge. CITATION: 8/25/1779. To Admx. To appear and exhibit account.ACCOUNT:9/29/1779. Of Admx. Allowed 9/29/1779. LICENSE D25:290): 9/29/1779. To Admx. To sell sufficient real est. to pay debts. ADDL. ACCOUNT: 11/24/1779. Of Admx. Allowed 11/24/1779. DOWER: 10/21/1779. Comm: Mark Emerson, Moses Welch, Jabez Eaton and Nehemiah Sleeper. Of Widow Mirriam Quimby. Includes Map. Oaths 10/25/1779 Comm. to Saml. Little, JP. Allowed 11/24/1779. DIV.: 3/24/1780. Comm.: Mark Emerson, Moses Welch and Jabez Eaton. To div, the real est. Divisees: Sons-Stephen (eldest, 2 shares), Jacob and William Dyer Quimby; Daus.-Mirriam (oldest dau.) and Sarah; the Widow, being the share that belonged to her son Pirkens, a minor decd. at age 4. Oaths 4/22/1780 Comm. to John Calfe, JP. Allowed. .

2153. QUIMBY: JACOB, SARAH & WILLIAM DYER (1779) #4584
GDP. Of the children of Jacob Quimby of Hampstead decd. GDP.: 11/24/1779. Of: Jacob and William Dyer Quimby, minors over 14 and of Sarah, a minor under 14. Gdn. Aaron Quimby of Hawke. Bond L1000.0.0. Sureties: Jabez Eaten of Hawke and Stephen Quimby of Hampstead, yoemen. Witnesses: Nathl. Adams and Nathl. Parker.

2154. QUINBY, ASHAEL (1776) #4204
EST. Candia joiner decd. ADMIN.: 2/28/1776. Admx. Elizabeth Quinby, Candia widow. Bond L1000.0.0. Sureties: John Dudley, Raymond esq. and Samuel Harper, Brentwood yoeman. Witnesses: Saml. Mooers and W. Parker Jr. INVY. WARR.: 2/28/1776. Comm.: Samuel Mooers and Nathaniel Emerson, esquires and Abraham Fitts, gent., all of Candia. INVY. Appr. 4/15/1776. Value L260.3.3. Oaths 4/15/1776 Admx. and Comm. to John Dudley, JP. DOWER WARR.: 4/25/1776. Comm.: Moses Baker and John Moors, gentlemen; Jeremiah Bean and John Clifford, all of Candia and Jonathan Swain, Raymond yoeman. Of Widow Elizabeth Quinby. DOWER: 5/6/1776. Oaths 5/6/1776 Swain, Baker and John Moors to John Dudley, JP. ACCOUNT: 2/1778. Of Admx. Allowed 2/26/1776. Account includes main. Harper. DIV. WARR.: 6/6/1781. Comm.: Nathaniel Emerson, esq.; Benj. Cass and Abraham Fitts, gentlemen; John Hills and John Lane, yoemen, all of Candia. To div. 2/3 of the real est., giving double share to oldest son and single share to each of the other children. DIV.: 4/20/1784. Divisees: Sons-Elisha (oldest), Bradbury and Harper; Daus.-Sarah Quinby and Mary Quinby. Oaths 4/25/1784 Fitts, Hill and Lane to Saml. Mooers, JP. Allowed. Note: The card file gives the name as Asahel Quimby, but all papers say Quinby.

2155. QUINBY: BRADBURY, ELISHA, MARY & SARAH (1776) #4206
GDP. Of the children of Asahel Quinby, Candia joiner decd. GDP.: 2/28/1776. Of: Elisha, Bradbury, Sarah and Mary, minors under 14. Gdn. Walter Robie, Candia esq. Bond L1000.0.0. Sureties: Samuel Mooers, esq. and Ezekiel Knowles, Candia yoeman. Witnesses: Samuel Jenness and W. Parker Jr. Note: The file card Index calls the children Quimby, but all papers say Quinby.

2156. QUINBY, JACOB (1776) #4205
EST. Candia yoeman decd. RENUN.: 2/26/1776. Of Ann Quinby, widow of Jacob. Of Admin. Requests appointment of Walter Robie, esq. Witness Samuel Mooers. ADMIN.: 2/28/1776. Admr. Walter Robie, Candia esq. Bond L1000.0.0. Sureties: Samuel Mooers, esq. and Ezekiel Knowles, yoeman, both of Candia. Witnesses: Saml. Jenness and Wm. Parker Jr. INVY.: Appr. 5/21/1776. Comm.: Saml. Mooers, Nathl. Emerson and Abrm. Fitts. Value L151.10.8. Oaths 6/5/1776 Admx. and Comm. to Saml. Emerson, JP. ACCOUNT: 1/30/1778 (sic). Of Admx. Allowed 1/29/1778(sic). Account includes main. 2 children. DOWER: 11/5/1788. Comm.: Moses Dustin, Simon French, Nathl. Emerson, John Lane and Thomas Wilson. Of Ann Varnum in est. Jacob Quinby. Oaths 11/28/1788 Emerson, Lane and Wilson to Saml. Mooers, JP. Allowed 8/18/1789.

DIV.:11/5/1788. Same Comm. as Dower. To div. 2/3 of real est. among the children, giving double share to oldest son. Divisees: Sons-Jonathan (oldest) and John; Daus.-Sarah Quinby and Anne Quinby. Oaths 11/28/1788 Emerson, Lane and Wilson to Saml. Mooers, JP. Allowed. Note: The Card Index calls him Quimby, but the papers all say Quinby.

2157. RAND, JOSHUA (1799) #6625
EST. Rye yoeman decd. intestate. ADMIN. 12/12/1799. Admx. Ruth Rand, Rye widow. Bond $2,000.00. Sureties: Joseph Parsons, esq. and Daniel Rand, yoeman, both of Rye. Witnesses: Samuel D. Parker and W. Parker. INVY.: Comm.: Joseph Parsons, esq.; Wm. Seavey and John Seavey. Value $812.90. Oaths 2/14/1800 Wm. Seavey and John Seavey to Joseph Parsons, JP. Oath 2/19/1800 Admx. to judge. ACCOUNT: 6/13/1801. Of Admx. Allowed 6/17/1801 the heir of age notified and Admx. also Gdn. of heirs. PETITION: 1/7/1802. Of George Rand, only surviving son. For Admin. D.B.N. ADMIN. D.B.N.: 1/7/1802. Admr. d.b.n. George Rand of Rye. Bond $3,000.00. Sureties: Thomas Rand and Jonathan Wedgwood, both of Rye. Witness W. Parker. INVY.: Comm.: William Mardin, Richd. Webster and Solomon Marden. Value $280.00. Oaths 2/11/1802 Comm. to Joseph Parsons, JP. Oath 2/17/1802 Admr. d.b.n. to judge. ADMIN. D.B.N.: 3/31/1803. Admr. d.b.n. John Rand, New Hampton, Strafford Co. yoeman, grandson, George Rand, Admr. d.b.n. now decd. Bond $2,000.00. Sureties: Joses Philbrick and Alexander Salter, Rye yoemen. PETITION: 6/15/1803. Of Admr. d.b.n. For Comm. Insolvency. Granted with Comm. of Daniel Humphreys and Isaac Rindge, esquires and Edward Sargent. ACCOUNT: 2/15/1804. Of John Rand, Admr. d.b.n. Allowed 2/15/1804. PETITION: 2/15/1804. Of Admr. d.b.n. For License so he may pay the bal. of $157.92 due him. Granted. LICENSE: 2/15/1804. To Admr. d.b.n. To sell real est. to amount of $180.00. PETITION: 3/21/1804. Of Admr. d.b.n. For License to sell all the real est. Order: 4/16/1804. For hearing, heirs to be notified. Granted 6/20/1804. CLAIMS WARR.: 6/15/1803. Comm. as noted. Claims 2/14/1804. Total $75.00. Oaths 2/15/1804 Comm. to George Gains, JP. ACCOUNT: Of George Rand, Admr. d.b.n. No date or allowance.

2158. RAND, THOMAS (1796) #6206
EST. Deerfield gent. decd. testate. WILL: Drawn 11/19/1794. Legatees: Wife-Elizabeth; Sons-Edmund and William; Daus.-Mary Hook wife of Frances Hook; Martha Griffin wife of John Griffin; Ruth Sanborn wife of John Sanborn and Isabella Sanborn wife of Edward Sanborn (4 oldest), Elizabeth Sanborn wife of Jetho Sanborn and Abigail Bickford wife of Eli Bickford (2 youngest). Execs.- son William and son-in-law John Sanborn His sig. Witnesses: Benjamin James, Joseph Mills and Nathl. Weare.

CERT. WILL (D32:129): 4/25/1796. Presented by Execs. and witnesses Weare, esq. and James. ADMIN.: 4/25/1796. Execs.: William Rand, Deerfield yoeman and John Sanborn, Loudon gent. Bond $2,000.00. Sureties: Benjamin James, yoeman and Nathaniel Weare, esq., both of Deerfield. Witnesses: Mary S. Parker and W. Parker. INVY.: Comm.: Job Chapman, Andw. Freese and James Prescott. Value $4,302.59. Oaths 5/18/1796 Comm. and Rand, an Exec., to judge.

2159. RAND, WILLIAM (1790) #5611
EST. Chester yoeman decd. ADMIN.: 12/15/1790. Admr. Abraham Libbee, Raymond yoeman. Bond L1000.0.0. Sureties: Benjamin Page, physician and Richard Brown, gent., both of Chester. Witnesses: James Betton and Nathl. Parker. INVY.: Comm.: Benja. Page and Richard Brown. Value L32.11.8. Oaths 2/4/1791 Comm. and Admr. to W. Parker, JP. PETITION: 2/4/1791. Of Admr. For Comm. Insolvency and License. Gives list claims of L23.5.5 and main. 2 children. Granted. LICENSE (D30:11): 2/4/1791. To Admr. To sell real est. to the amount of L30.0.0. CLAIMS WARR.: 2/4/1791. Comm.: Benjamin Page, physician and Richard Brown, gent., both of Chester and Samuel Nay, Raymond gent. On 12/21/1791 Comm. given 3 months longer. CLAIMS: 3/27/1792. Total not tallied. Esti. L14.0.0+. Note: There is in the file a fragment which is obviously part of an Account but there is not enough to abstract it.

RANDALL. See also Randel, Randell

2160. RANDALL, JACOB (1795) #6085
ACT OF LEG. for Jacob (of Newmarket?) ACT OF NH GENERAL COURT: Passed House 1/22/1794 and signed by Nathl. Peabody, Spkr. Passed Senate 1/23/1794 and approved 1/23/1794 by Josiah Bartlett. Cert. of Nathl. Parker, Depy. Shef. as a true copy. The Act grants Jacob Randall permission to sell house and land in Newmarket belonging to his 2 children, minors under 14, in right of their mother decd., which house is in disrepair and the rents insufficient to cover repair costs. BOND: The Bond is of Jacob to account for sale, but it is crumbling away and not possible to handle.

2161. RANDALL, JACOB (1798) #6512
EST. Exeter barber decd. ADMIN (D32:547): 11/29/1789. Admr. Josiah Adams, Newmarket esq. Sureties: Nathl. Lord and Daniel Hill, both of Newmarket. INVY.: (D33:56): Comm.: Nathl. Rogers, John Shute and Daniel Hill. Value $181.59. Oaths 3/20/1799 Comm. to Nathl. Kidder, JP. Oath 3/20/1799 Admr. to Wm. Parker, JP. ACCOUNT: Of Admr. Allowed 11/8/1804 having been consented by to heirs. Account includes payment to Gdn of "first children, they having been their mother's."

2162. RANDALL, WILLIAM (1780) #4675
GDP. Of the son of Benjamin Randall, Hampton mariner decd. GDP.: 12/22/1780. Of William, a minor over 14. Gdn. John Weeks, Greenland gent. Bond L30000.0.0. Sureties: Simeon Ladd, gent. and Stephen Leavitt Creighton, cordwainer, both of Exeter. Witnesses: Nat. Parker and W. Parker.

RANDEL. See also Randall, Randell

2163. RANDEL, BENJAMIN (1777) #4388
EST. Hampton mariner decd. intestate. ADMIN.: 9/24/1777. Admrs.: Thankful Randel, widow and John Weeks, gent., both of Greenland. Bond L500.0.0. Sureties: Samuel Haines of Greenland and Richard Haines of Canterbury, yoemen. Witnesses: Nathl. Parker and Wm. Parker. INVY.: Appr. 9/29/1777. Comm.: John Johnson, Samuel Haines and Joshua Brackett. Value L45.16.0. Oaths 9/30/1777 Comm. to Wm. Weeks, JP. Oaths 11/26/1777 Admrs. to W. Parker, Reg. & JP. ACCOUNT: 11/1778. Of Admrs. Allowed 11/26/1778. Account includes main. one child. Note: Found folded into the Invy. a list of claims which belongs with #4377 Aaron Smith (1777) and is recorded there.

2164. RANKIN, WILLIAM (1797) #6333
PET. GDP. Of Londonderry yoeman. PETITION: 4/19/1797. Of Robt. McMurphy Jr. States that his friend and neighbor, William Rankin, Londonderry yoeman, is very infirm and unable to care for himself or property. Requests that the Selectmen make inquisition into his need for a Gdn.

2165. RANSOM, THOMAS (1779) #4528
EST. Portsmouth yoeman decd. testate. WILL: Drawn 2/13/1779. Legatee: Mrs. Mary Tilton of Portsmouth. Exex.-Mary Tilton. His sig. Witnesses: Perkins Ayers, Phillip Pendexter and Daniel Cate. CERT. WILL: 3/31/1779. Presented by Exex. and all the witnesses, who were previously sworn before a justice. A note with Will says the claims against the est. on 2/13/1779 are two Notes, one to Eliph. Hanson, in the hands of Jno. Burnham Hanson, for L2.10.0 and another to Widow Hope for L0.30.0. "Is all I owe." Possibly written by Ransom when he wrote his Will, but unsigned. INVY. WARR.: 3/3/1779. Comm.: Perkins Ayers, cordwainer; Edward Hart, baker and Joseph Walker, caulker, all of Portsmouth. INVY.: Appr. 3/3/1779. Value L49.2.0. Oaths 3/3/1779 Ayers, Hart and Exex. to W. Parker, Reg.

RAWLINGS. See also Rollings, Rollins

2166. RAWLINGS, ALICE (1775) #4175
EST. Newington widow decd. intestate. ADMIN.: 8/11/1775. Admr.: Paul Rawlings, Newington husbm. Bond L1000.0.0. Sureties: Samuel Rawlings, Newington husbm. and Hunking Wentworth, Portsmouth esq. Witnesses: Saml. Hale Jr. and Benjamin Slade. INVY. WARR.: 10/11/1775. Comm.: Wintrop Pickering, husbm. and John Hodgdon, weaver, both of Newington. INVY.: Appr. 8/18/1775. Value L13.14.6. Oaths 8/21/1776 Admr. and Comm. to judge. DECLARATION: Of Sarah Rawlings, dau. of Alice. Claims that sundry articles in the Invy. were hers. She lists them. Also says that other articles in the Invy. belong to her, she having purchased her bro. Samuel's two shares and her own and that she let her mother have the improvement of them, excepting the cow and sheep. CLAIMS WARR.: 8/30/1775. Comm.: Benjamin Adams, esq. and Timothy Dam, yoeman, both of Newington. CLAIMS: Not tallied. Esti. L7.9.14. Oaths 10/30/1776 Comm. to judge. One item in Claims struck out as having been allowed in Account. ACCOUNT: 11/1776. Of Admr. Allowed 11/27/1776. PROP. & SETTLM.: Claims not tallied. Esti. L7.0.0+. Amount to be proportioned L2.4.6 1/4. Allowed 3/27/1777 with order to Admr. to pay. Note: Claims in (D23:523) give claims of L1.15.5 1/4 (sic.). Amount to be proportioned as L2.4.6 1/4 (sic).

READ. See also Reed, Reid

2167. READ, DOROTHY (1787) #5310
EST. Portsmouth widow decd. ADMIN.: 12/18/1787. Admr. Joseph Low, Portsmouth baker. Bond L500.0.0. Sureties: Jonathan Warner, esq. and James Haslett, leather dresser, both of Portsmouth. Witnesses: Timothy Ham and Daniel Warner. INVY. WARR: 12/18/1787. Comm.: Giles Seaward, mariner; Daniel Peirce and Daniel Symes, traders, all of Portsmouth. Invy.: Appr. 1/3/1788. Value not tallied. Esti. L114.0.0.+. Oaths 2/19/1788 Admr. and Comm. to George Gains, JP. PETITION: 2/20/1788. Of Admr. For License and Comm. Insolvency. Notes a claim of L337.13.4. LICENSE (D29:171): 2/20/1788. To Admr. To sell sufficience real est. to pay debts. CLAIMS WARR.: 2/20/1788. Comm.: John Evans, Daniel Peirce and Jacob Walden, Portsmouth traders. On 10/15/1788 Comm. granted 2 more months. CLAIMS: Total L205.13.1. Oaths 12/17/1788 Comm. to Geo. Gains, JP. ACCOUNT: Of Admr. Allowed 4/15/1789. PROP. & SETTLM.: Claims L205.13.1. Amount to be proportioned L37.7.10. Allowed 4/15/1789 with order to Admr. to pay.

2168. READ, PHILIP (1785) #5131
EST. Portsmouth mariner decd. ADMIN.: 8/17/1785. Admr. Joseph Low, Portsmouth baker. Bond L500.0.0. Sureties: James Haslett, leather dresser and John Davenport, goldsmith, both of Portsmouth. Witnesses: W. Parker and Nathl. Parker.

2169. REDMAN, HANNAH (1799) #6621
GDP.: Of the dau. of Joanna Casey, Portsmouth single woman and Tristram Redman of North Hampton. GDP.: Of Hannah, a minor under 14. Gdn. Joanna Casey, Portsmouth single woman, her mother. Bond $2,000.00. Sureties: Ebenr. Chadwick, gent. and George Nutter, merchant, both of Portsmouth. Witnesses: Jere. Mason and Ob. Lang. GDP.: 3/9/1802. Of Hannah, a minor under 21. Gdn. Joanna Casey, Portsmouth single woman. Bond $2,000.00. Sureties: Ebenr. Chadwick and George Nutter, Portsmouth traders. Witnesses: Nathl. Adams and John W. Adams.

2170. REDMAN, JOHN (1797) #6371
EST. Hampton yoeman decd. RENUN.: 9/11/1797. Of Sarah Redman, widow of John. Of Admin. Requests appointment of her son Joseph. Witnesses: John Lamprey and Abraham Marston. ADMIN.: 9/11/1797. Admr. Joseph Redman, Hampton yoeman. Bond $3,000.00. Sureties: John Green and Jacob Marston, Hampton yoemen. Witnesses: Christor. Toppan and Stephen Smith. INVY.: Appr. 11/23/1797. Comm.: Joseph Dow, John Lamprey and Jona. Garland. Value $1,898.00. Oaths 12/6/1797 Comm. to Christo. Toppan, JP. Oath 12/7/1797 Admr. to judge.

2171. REDMAN, TRISTRAM (1797) #6356
EST. North Hampton husbm. decd. testate. CAVEAT: 6/13/1797. Of Mary Howell, Hampton widow and sister of Tristram, by her atty. Geo. Sullivan. Claims that on or about 6/1/1797 Tristram made a Will, but he was n.c.m. and died on or about 6/2/1797. Requests Will not be allowed until the heirs may be heard. Order: For hearing. WILL: Drawn 5/31/1797. Legatees: Wife-Mary; Joanna Casey who now resides with him; Hannah the natural dau. of Joanna Casey. Execs.-John Fogg and Joanna Casey. His sig. Witnesses: Daniel Lamprey, Jonathan Godfree and Stephen Batchelder. On 6/28/1797 the witnesses appearing and confessing that they did not sign in the presence of, or in the same room with, the testator, Will not allowed. WILL: Drawn 5/27/1797. Legatees: Joanna Casey; Hannah Redman. Execs.-Joanna Casey and Dr. John Fogg. His sig. Witnesses: James Batchelder, Benjamin Brown and John Lamprey. CERT WILL (D32:322): 6/28/1797. Presented by Dr. Fogg, an Exec., the other renouncing, oath of witness Batchelder and affirm. Of witness Lamprey. RENUN.: 6/28/1797. Of Joanna Casey. Of Admin. Requests Admin. be

granted to other Exec. named in Will. ADMIN.: 6/28/1797. Exec. John Fogg, North Hampton esq. Bond $3,000.00. Sureties: Moses Leavitt and John Dearborn, both of North Hampton. Witnesses: Saml. Parker and W. Parker. INVY.: Comm.: Moses Leavitt, Joseph Brown and John Dearborn. Value $3,401.11. Oaths 7/7/1797 Leavitt and Dearborn to John Fogg, JP. Oath 7/19/1797 Exec. to W. Parker. DOWER: Comm.: Moses Leavitt, John Dearborn, James Batchelder, Joseph Brown and Simon Ward. Of Widow Mary Redman. Oaths 7/7/1797 Comm. to John Fogg, JP. Allowed 7/19/1797. PETITION: 2/24/1798. Of Exec. For Comm. Insolvency. Notes that decd. sold lands during lifetime which the Widow is now sueing against for her dower rights, has already recovered against two of them and will expect compensation from est., together with other costs. Also, he feels he cannot, in justice to heirs, pay some of the demands exhibited. He also informs the judge that the heirs have commenced an Act of Ejectment for the whole real est. against him. Comm. Insolvency granted. PETITION: 11/1/1798. Of Exec. For License. Notes that decd. made no provision in Will for payment of debts. Allowed. LICENSE (D32:536): 11/1/1798. To Exec. To sell real est. to amount of $1,250.00. BOND 11/1/1798. Of Exec. Bond $2,000.00. To account for proceeds of sale of real est. by License. Sureties: Moses Leavitt, esq. and Capt. Simon Ward, gent., both of North Hampton. Witnesses: Nathl. Parker and W. Parker. CLAIMS: 10/31/1798. Comm.: Moses Leavitt, Joseph Dearborn and Simon Ward. Total $1,083.77. Oaths 11/1/1798 Comm. to W. Parker, JP. PETITION: 11/16/1799. Of Exec. For License. States there is still a bal. of $320.00 unpaid. Granted. LICENSE ((D33:165): 11/16/1799. To Exec. To sell real est. to the amount of $350.00. PETITION: 11/29/1799. Of Joanna Casey Portsmouth single woman and Hannah Redman Portsmouth, a minor under 14 of whom Joanna is Gdn. To appeal Decree of 11/16/1799 granting License. Granted. BOND: 11/29/1799. Of Joanna Casey, Portsmouth single woman. Bond $200.00. To appeal Decree allowing License. Sureties: Ebenezer Chadwick and George Nutter, Portsmouth merchants. Witness Ob. Lang. ACCOUNT: 3/19/1800. Of Exec. Allowed 3/19/1800 the objections of Joanna Casey, Gdn. of sole heir, notwithstanding. PETITION: 3/29/1800.Of Joanna Casey, Portsmouth single woman and Hannah Redman, Portsmouth minor. To appeal Decree allowing Account. Granted 5/16/1800. BOND: 3/29/1800. Of Joanna Casey. Bond $200.00.ToappealDecree allowing Account. Sureties: Ebenezer Chadwick and George Nutter, Portsmouth traders. Witnesses: Daniel Brown and Thomas Cotton Jr. ADDL. ACCOUNT: 12/10/1800. Of Exec. Allowed 12/10/1800 having been consented to by atty. of Gdn. of principal heir. Note: Joanna did not prosecute her appeal against first Account. LICENSE: 12/10/1800. To Exec. To sell real est. to the amount of $460.00.

REED. See also Read, Reid

2172. REED: BETSY, HANNAH DAM, NABBY, POLLY, SAMUEL & SARAH ANN (1799) #6598
GDP. Of the children of John Reed, Portsmouth caulker decd. GDP.: 8/17/1799. Of: Hannah Dam Reed and Polly, minors over 14 and of Samuel, Betsy, Nabby and Sarah Ann, minors under 14. Gdn. Sarah Reed, Portsmouth widow. Bond $1,000.00. Sureties: Thomas Manning, merchant and Richard Cutts Shannon, esq., both of Portsmouth. Witnesses: Reuben Shapley and N. Newman.

2173. REEVE, WILLIAM (1786) #5218
EST. Bristol, Great Britain merchant decd. intestate. ADMIN.: 9/20/1786. Admr. Joshua Brackett, Portsmouth esq. Bond L2000.0.0. Sureties: Joseph Whipple and John Parker, Portsmouth esquires. Witnesses: Nathl. Parker and W. Parker. PETITION: 9/21/1787. Of Jonathan Warner, Portsmouth esq. States that decd. died leaving considerable est., real and personal, and no relations with right of admin. As the principal, if not the only, creditor to est., Warner feels the law gives him the right of Admin. rather than Joshua Brackett who is not a creditor and was appointed without notification to creditors. Requests appeal from Decree allowing Admin. Granted 10/17/1787. COPY OF PETITION. BOND: 10/28/1787. Of Jonathan Warner, Portsmouth esq. Bond L100.0.0. To appeal the Decree allowing Admin. Sureties: Oliver Peabody, Exeter esq. and William Plummer, Epping gent. Witnesses: Ebenezer Dearing and Richard Jackson. INVY. WARR.: 9/20/1786. Comm.: John Parker, Supply Clap and Jeremiah Libbey, Portsmouth esquires. Invy.: Appr. 11/14/1791. Value L530.0.0. Oaths 11/13/1791 Clap and Admr., affirm. Libbey to Nathl. Adams, JP. PETITION: 1/11/1792. Of Admr. For License. States he can find no est. In county for the company of Devonshire and Reeve of Bristol, G.B. and needs to sell the land to pay creditors. The firewards are threatening to pull the property down and the collectors to sell it for taxes. LICENSE (D30:179): 1/16/1792. To Admr. To sell real est. to the amount of L1000.0.0. PETITION: 2/15/1792. Of Admr. For Comm. Insolvency. Gives a claim against est. by est. of John Moffat esq. as L987.0.3. Granted. CLAIMS WARR.: 2/15/1792. Comm.: Supply Clap, William Gardner and George Wentworth, Portsmouth esquires. On 8/15/1792 Comm. extended 9 months longer. Claims: Total L922.3.5. Oaths 9/5/1793 Comm. to Geo. Gains, JP. Called "claims against the est. of William Reeve decd., surviving partner of the late company of Devonshire & Reeve, merchants of Bristol." ACCOUNT: 2/20/1794. Of Admr. Allowed 2/20/1794.

REID. See also Read, Reed

2174. REID, JOHN (1796) #6253
EST. Portsmouth caulker decd. ADMIN.: 9/8/1796. Admx. Sarah Reid, Portsmouth widow. Bond $1,000.00. Sureties: Thomas Manning and Richd. Cutts Shannon, Portsmouth esquires. Witness Joseph Simes. INVY.: Appr. 10/19/1796. Comm.: Edward Sargent, Saml. Drowne and Nathl. Marshall. Value: $31.26. Oaths 10/19/1796 Comm. to Jonathan Warner, JP. PETITION: 8/9/1799. Of Thomas Walton, Portsmouth mariner. For an appr. of land in Portsmouth which he holds in common with the heirs of John Reed, decd., which was set off to them to Walton and Reid as their share in the est. of Thomas Clark of Portsmouth decd. The land cannot be div. without prejudice. Requests that it be settled on one heir who will pay the others their share. APPR. WARR.: 9/4/1799. Comm.: Samuel Hutchings, gent.; Edward Sargent and Edward Coffin, mariners; Stacy Hall and William Stavers, yoemen, all of Portsmouth. To view the land held in common equally between the heirs of John Reed and the heirs of Sarah Walton and div. or appr. If. appraising, assign the whole to one party and award the sum of money to be paid to the other party. APPR.:9/12/1799. The Comm. set off the whole to the heirs of John Reed, who are to pay the heirs of Sarah Walton$125.00.Oaths 9/14/1799 Comm. to Saml. Penhallow, JP.

2175. RESIDE, JOHN (1779) #4523
EST. Londonderry yoeman decd. intestate. ADMIN. (D25:12): 1/7/1779. Admr. Matthew Thornton, Londonderry esq. Sureties: Joseph Gregg, gent. and William Cochran, yoeman, both of Londonderry. INVY.: Comm.: Robert McColom, Saml. Alls and Archibald McMurphy. Value L737.5.0. Oaths 2/19/1779 Comm. to John Bell, JP. Oath 3/8/1779 Admr. to W. Parker, Reg. & JP. LICENSE: 11/24/1779. To Admr. To sell sufficient real est. to pay debts.

2176. REYNOLDS, COL. DANIEL (1796) #6180.
EST. Londonderry esq. decd. ADMIN.: 2/20/1796. Admrs.: Hannah Reynolds, widow and Stephen Reynolds, joiner, both of Londonderry. Bond $3,000.00. Sureties: John Bell, esq. and David Patterson, gent., both of Londonderry. Witnesses: Benja. Carter and John Neal. INVY: Appr. 4/26/1796. Comm.: John Betton, John Neal and Robert McMurphy. Value $1,584.18. Oaths 12/28/1796 Comm. to Isaac Thom, JP. Oaths 4/19/1797 Admrs. (Runnels) to Saml. Tenney, JP.

2177. RICE, ANNA (1785) #5146
EST. Exeter widow decd. testate, formerly wife of John Rice, esq. decd. WILL: Drawn 3/28/1783. Legatees: Sister-Jude wife of Capt. Biley Lyford and Capt. Biley; Mary Odlin wife of Dr. John Odlin; Rev. Isaac

Mansfield; Elizabeth Taylor who now lives with her; Lydia Hall who formerly lived with her; Jude Odlin wife of William Odlin; The Assessors of 1st Parish in Exeter of which Rev. Isaac Mansfield is minister, income to go for support of the minister. But if the parish should neglect to support a regular minister, the income to support a grammar school in Exeter. Provides for gravestones for Sarah Blunt who formerly lived with her, her husband and herself. Ref. to her father Deacon Thomas Wilson decd. Exec.-bro.-in-law Biley Lyford. Her sig. Witnesses: Saml. Hobart, Samuel Sawyer and William Fogg. CERT. WILL (D28:332): 11/4/1785. Presented by Exec. and on 10/31/1785 oath of witness Hobart, esq. and on 11/4/1785 oath of witness Sawyer, both to Wm. Parker, JP & Reg. Allowed 11/4/1785. ADMIN.: 11/1/1785. Exec. Biley Lyford, Brentwood gent. Bond L1000.0.0. Sureties: Samuel Brooks, esq. and Benjamin Lamson, innholder, both of Exeter. Witnesses: W. Parker and Nathl. Parker.

2178. RICE, JOHN (1780) #4614
EST. Exeter esq. decd. testate. WILL: Drawn 2/20/1778. Legatees: Wife-Anna; The Parish in Exeter of which Rev. Mr. Isaac Mansfield is minister or a grammar school in Exeter should the church cease to exist. Exec.-wife Anna. His sig. Witnesses: Geo. King, Jonathan Lovewell and Saml. Cutts. Codicil: 10/14/1779. He adds John Giddinge, esq. as an Exec. with his wife. Witnesses: Josiah Gilman, Nicho. Gilman and Samuel Brooks. CERT. WILL: 3/29/1780. Presented by Anna Rice, one of the Execs., the other having refused the trust, and witnesses George Atkinson, formerly King, and Samuel Cutts, esquires, having sworn previously to a justice. Oaths 3/21/1780 Nicholas Gilman and Brooks, esquires, to the Codicil. ADMIN.: 3/29/1780. Exec. Anna Rice, Exeter widow. Bond L10000.0.0. Sureties: Noah Emery, esq. and John Odlin Jr., physician, both of Exeter. Witnesses: Simeon Ladd and Nathl. Parker.

2179. RICHARDS: ABIAH (1791) #5650
See Richards: Abraham, Lydia & Sarah (1791) #5650

2180. RICHARDS: ABRAHAM, LYDIA & SARAH (1791) #5650
GDP. Of the children of Daniel Richards of Atkinson decd. GDP.: 4/20/1791. Of: Abraham, Lydia and Sally, minors under 14. Gdn. Jonathan Poor, Atkinson gent. Bond L1000.0.0. Sureties: Peter Clement, esq. and William Page, yeoman, both of Atkinson. Witnesses: George Russell and Humphrey Noyes. Note: The card catalog incorrectly calls this file Abiah instead of Abraham.

2181. RICHARDS, BENJAMIN (1797) #6341
EST. Atkinson gent. decd. testate. RENUN.: 5/18/1797. Of Caleb Richards. Of Admin. RENUN.: 2/20/1797. Of Peter Clement. He presents the Will of Caleb Richards (sic.), Atkinson yeoman decd. and refuses to accept Executorship. WILL: Of Benjamin Richards. Drawn 2/26/1788. Legatees: Wife-Abigail; Sons-Samuel, Benjamin and Bradley; Daus.-Mary Page, Abigail Swett and Sarah Emerson; Dau.-in-law-Hannah Richards widow of his son Daniel decd.; Mary, Joseph, Elisabeth, Caleb, Joshua, Hannah, Abraham, Lydia and Sarah children of his son Daniel. Execs.-grandson Caleb and friend Peter Clement, esq. His sig. Witnesses: Nathl. Peabody, Benjamin Stone, William Cogswell and Stephen Peabody. No proving or Cert. of Will.

2182. RICHARDS, BENJAMIN (1793) #5878
See #5543 Capt. Daniel Richards (1790)

2183. RICHARDS, CAPT. DANIEL (1790) #5543
EST. Atkinson gent. decd. intestate. RENUN.: 5/17/1790. Of Hannah Richards, widow of Daniel Of. Admin. Requests appointment of her son Caleb Richards and Jonathan Poor. Caleb Richards declines Admin. ADMIN.: 5/17/1790. Admr. Jonathan Poor, Atkinson gent. Bond L500.0.0. Sureties: Peter Clement, esq. and William Page, husbm., both of Atkinson. Witnesses: Oliver Peabody and N. Parker. INVY.: Appr. 7/19/1790. Comm.: Jeremiah Poor, John Dow and William Page. Value L34.0.6. Oaths 11/9/1790 Comm. to Peter Clement, JP. Oath 11/17/1790 Admr. to judge. PETITION: 11/24/1790. Of Admr. He suspects some of the est. has been secreted. Requests the following persons from Atkinson be cited to appear and be examined under oath concerning embezzlement of the est.: Stephen Peabody, clerk; Peter Clement, esq.; Capt. Eliphalet Knight; John Dow, esq.; Benja. Richards, gent.; Hannah Richards, widow; Caleb Richards, yoeman and James Dow, gent. CITATION: 11/24/1790. To those listed in Petition. To appear and be examined concerning the concealing, embezzlement or conveyeing away of the est. Cert.: 12/3/1790. Of James Dow, Atkinson Constable. He summoned all those cited by reading the Citation to them or having them read it, except Caleb Richards at whose home he left a copy. W. Parker, Reg., notes that Rev. Steph. Peabody; Peter Clement, esq.; James Dow and John Dow, esq. were all examined under oath and their depositions filed. The others did not appear. DEPOSITION: 12/6/1790. Of Rev. Stephen Peabody. Asked what knew about a deed Benjamin Richards gave to his son Daniel decd. for one half of Benjamin's homeplace in Atkinson, Peabody replied that sometime the last of 1788 he was called to write a Will for Ensign Benjamin Richards. After conversing about the Will, he understood the one half of

the homeplace had been disposed of by deed some years before to the son Samuel. Benjamin wished to dispose of his est. equitably among his children and to the children of his son Daniel, but Joshua was the oldest son of Daniel and would get a double share of his father's est. Rev. Peabody tried to influence Joshua to give up his double share, but with no effect. Therefore, Benjamin, in making his Will, gave a single share to Joshua and two shares to each of Joshua's bros. Caleb and Joseph. In making provision for his dau.-in-law, Daniel's widow, he gave her full and free use and improvement of bldgs. and land as long a she remained Daniel's widow as an inducement to her to continue her dutiful attention to Benjamin and his wife. Benjamin also said the greater part of the stock belonged to Daniel's family. When the Will was written and signed, it was left in his hands by Benjamin. About the same time, Hannah Richards put into his hands a deed to one half of the homeplace formerly belonging to Benjamin and asked Peabody to keep it until she called for it. The deed remained with him until the spring of 1790 when Caleb Richards came as a messenger from his mother asking that the deed be returned to her. Peabody gave it to Caleb with a caution not to do wrong respecting it. DEPOSITION: 12/6/1790. Of Peter Clement, esq. Regarding the deed in question Clement replied that in his lifetime Daniel had told him that he had a deed to one half of his father's place. After Daniel's death, Daniel's widow told Clement there was such a deed and asked him if it was best to record it or what to do with it. Clement told her to record it and put it in some safe place. He was asked what he knew about the personal est. and replied by giving the Invy. submitted by Daniel to the Selectmen, including 10 creatures Daniel declared to be his own. In April 1786 Daniel's widow was taxed on an Invy. of 8 creatures. He replied that Daniel was rated for more than 1/2 of the homeplace in 1785 and a year or two before. Deposition: 12/6/1790. Of John Dow, esq. About Daniel's deed he replied that last spring, when talking to Caleb, Daniel's son, Caleb said his grandfather had sent him to Rev. Peabody for the deed. He took it home and put it in his grandfather's chest where his writings were and did not see it afterwards. As to the personal est., Dow said Daniel had a horse and a watch he supposed were Daniel's. Deposition: Of James Dow. He deposed that about last April at his house he heard a conversation between Genl. Peabody and Caleb Richards, son of Daniel decd. Peabody said he had been to see Caleb's mother about Follansbee's demand against them and asked her to give him power of atty. to manage the business, which she would consider. Caleb said he would give Peabody L30.0.0 to clear him of the demand. Then Gen. Peabody asked Caleb if the deed his grandfather gave to his father was safe and Caleb said he had or would take care of it. Dow did know that Daniel had a horse he bought from Ingalls and a watch he bought from Bradley Richards. He also said Daniel had told him he had a deed to half his father's homestead and half of the Watts place and soon expected a deed to all of the homeplace. After Daniel's death his widow asked Dow about the deeds, saying her husb. had 2 deeds to the homeplace and Watts place and she was afraid they would not be safe in the house, neither being on record. Dow advised her to administer on the est. and record them. He never heard of Daniel owing his father any money. The following Petition recorded as #5878 Benjamin Richards (1793) belongs here. PETITION: 4/12/1793. Of Benjamin Richards of Atkinson and Jona. Poor. They state that some time in 1782 Benjamin gave to Daniel Richards, who was then in full life, a deed to one full half of all his real est. in Atkinson. Daniel's est. is now under the Admin. of Jona. Poor. Request div. in order for settlm. DIV. WARR.: 4/17/1793. COMM.: John Dow, esq.; Moses Greenough and Eliphalet Knight, gentlemen; Humphrey Noyes and William Page, yoemen, all of Atkinson. To div. land in Atkinson held in common by Benjamin Richards, Atkinson gent. and the Heirs of Daniel Richards into 2 equal shares. DIV.: To div. est. of Benja. Richards. Divisees: Benjamin Richards and Heirs of Capt. Daniel Richards. Oaths 12/17/1793 Dow, Greenough and Noyes to Nathl. Peabody, JP. Allowed. APPR. WARR.: 4/17/1793. Comm.: John Dow, esq.; William Page and Humphrey Noyes, yoemen. To appr. the neat income of est. ADDL. INVY.: 12/14/1790. Value L243.18.0. Includesthe1/2 part of homestead, the Watts land, animals sold by the Widow and the watch. Oaths12/15/1790 Comm. to Peter Clement, JP. Note: The following Div. Warr. and Div. recorded as #6327 Emery & Richards (1790) belongs here. DIV. WARR.: 5/13/1793. Comm. same as previous Warr. To div. land in Atkinson held in common by Jona. Poor, Moses Emery, Caleb Richards and the Heirs of Capt. Daniel Richards decd. Poor, Emery and Caleb Richards own 1/2 and the Heirs 1/2. DIV.: Divisees: Heirs of Capt. Richards and Lt. Moses Emery. Oaths 12/7/1793 Greenough, Dow and Noyes to Nathl. Peabody, JP. Allowed. APPR.: Value of income L2.10.0 per year. Oaths 12/17/1793 Dow and Noyes to Nathl. Peabody, JP. ADDL. INVY.: 3/3/1797. Value L31.4.0. Oaths 3/3/1797 Dow and Poor and on 3/9/1797 Page to William Cogswell, JP. PETITION: 3/22/1797. Of Admr. For License. Granted. LICENSE (D32:279): 3/22/1797. To Admr. To sell real est. to amount of $600.00. BOND 3/22/1797. Of Admr. Bond $1,000.00. To account for sale of real est. by License. Sureties: James Noyes Jr. of Atkinson and Benja. Kimball of Kingston, gentlemen. Witness Saml. Parker. DOWER: Comm. same as for Div. Of Widow Hannah Richards. Oaths 12/17/1793 Greenough, Dow and Noyes to Nathl. Peabody, JP. Allowed 3/22/1797. DIV.: 12/26/1797. Same Comm. To div. 2/3 of the real est. Divisees: Sons-Joshua (oldest, double share), Joseph, Abraham and Caleb; Daus.-Polly Osgood, Hannah Richards, Sally Richards, Lydia Richards and Betsey Kelley. Oaths

1/1/1798 Comm. to William Cogswell, JP. Allowed 11/16/1803. ACCOUNT: Of Admr. Allowed 11/16/1803 the heirs having been notified but not present. LIST CLAIMS: Total L181.9.3. PETITION: 3/15/1824. Of: Caleb Richards for himself and for Mary Morrill and Betsey Kelley; Joseph Richards and Porter Clark for Abraham Richards, Lydia Clark and Sally Richards. For div. of the Dower, of which they each own 1/9. Request Comm. to Col. William Page, esq.; Capt. Edmund Wright, both of Atkinson and Benja. George, Plaistow esq. and two others if necessary. Granted 4/15/1824. DIV. WARR.: 4/15/1824. Comm. as requested. To div. the Dower among the heirs. Divisees: Caleb Richards, Mary Morrill wife of ____(sic.) Morrill, Betsey Kelley wife of Amasa Kelley, Sally Richards, Lydia Clark wife of Porter Clark, Abraham Richards, Joshua Richards, Hannah Emerson wife of Perley Emerson and Joseph Richards. Oaths 5/11/1824 Page and Wright to Benjamin George, JP. Allowed 6/10/1824.

2184. RICHARDSON, ABIJAH (1785) #5124
EST. Pelham yoeman decd. ADMIN.: 7/20/1785. Admx. Judith Richardson, Pelham widow. Bond L500.0.0. Sureties: Benjamin Coburn and Abial Barker, Pelham husbandmen. Witnesses: Jacob Marsh and John Wilson. INVY. WARR.: 6/20/1785. Comm.: John Ferguson, Ezra Marsh and Benjamin Coburn, all of Pelham. INVY. Appr. 10/29/1785. Value L228.2.6. Oath 11/8/1785 Admx. and Comm. to James Gibson, JP. ACCOUNT: 11/16/1787. Of Admx. Allowed 11/21/1787. Account includes main. one child born posthumously.

2185. RICHARDSON, AMOS (1797) #6338
EST. Pembroke cordwainer decd. intestate. ADMIN.: 5/17/1797. Admx. Polly Richardson, Pembroke widow. Bond $2,000.00. Sureties: Richard Bartlett and Anthony Somersbee Stickney, Pembroke esquires. Witnesses: Joseph Barker and Nathl. Parker. INVY.: Appr. 9/18/1797. Comm.: Joseph Emery, William Cochran and Thomas Robinson. Value L338.18.6. Oaths 9/20/1797 Comm. to Richard Bartlett, JP. PETITION: Of Admx. For Comm. Insolvency. Gives list claims of $627.62 and more not exhibited. Granted 9/20/1797. PETITION: 5/16/1798. Of Admx. For more time for Comm. Insolvency as all claims not yet in. CLAIMS WARR.: 5/16/1798. Comm.: Daniel Knox, esq.; Joseph Emery and Caleb Bartlett, gent. They are granted 3 months longer. CLAIMS: 8/29/1798. Total $854.59. Oaths 9/19/1798 Knox and Emery to judge. PETITION: 9/19/1798. Of Admx. For License. Gives claims as $854.59 with more not in. Granted. LICENSE (D32:527): To Admx. To sell real est. to amount of $700.00. BOND: 9/19/1798. Of Admx. of Reading, Middlesex Co., MA. Bond $2,000.00. To account for sale of real est. by License. Sureties: Daniel

Knox, esq. and Joseph Emery Jr., both of Pembroke. Witnesses: William Cochran and Nathl. Parker. DOWER WARR.: 9/19/1798. Comm.: Deacon William Cochran; Daniel Knox, Richard Bartlett and Samuel Daniels, esquires and Joseph Emery Jr., all of Pembroke. Of Widow Polly Richardson of Reading, Middlesex Co., MA. DOWER: 10/1/1798. Oaths 5/15/1799 Cochran, Knox and Emery to judge. Allowed 5/15/1799. ACCOUNT: 5/15/1799. Of Admx. Allowed 5/15/1799. PROP. & SETTLM.: Claims $854.59. Amount to be proportioned $625.78. Allowed 5/17/1799 with order to Admx. to pay. Note: In one Petition the Admx. says, "When the decd. moved to Pembroke." It appears the move may have been from Epsom.

2186. RICHARDSON, MOSES (1785) #5155
EST. South Hampton yoeman decd. testate. WILL: Drawn 1/30/1755. Legatees: Wife-Lydia; Dau.-Lydia wife of Humphry Pierce; Grandsons-Humphrey Pierce and Moses Pierce; Granddau.-Dau. of Humphrey and Lydia Pierce. Exex.-wife Lydia. His mark. Witnesses: Richard Fitts, Henry Currier and Abner Morrill. CERT. WILL (D28:383): 12/1/1785. Presented by Exec. and witness Fitts.

2187. RICHARDSON, RACHEL (1791) #5695
EST. Of Hampstead decd. ADMIN.: 9/28/1791. Admr. Eliphalet Richardson, Hampstead husbm. Bond L1000.0.0. Sureties: Hezekiah Hutchins and Ezekiel Gile, Plaistow esq. Witnesses: Nat. Parker and W. Parker. INVY.: 10/3/1791. Comm.: Amos Sawyer and Ezekiel Gile. Value L13.0.0. Oath 10/6/1791 Gile, affirm. Sawyer to John White, JP. Oath 10/10/1791 Admr. To judge. LICENSE (D30:135): 10/10/1791. To Admr. To sell real est. to amount of L15.0.0. Note: In #5696 Hannah Roberts (1791) there is a list of claims for that est. which also includes claims for this Rachel Richardson est. with notation "befour maragg." Total L7.3.2. The Admr. for both of these ests. was Eliphalet Richardson.

2188. RICHARDSON, RHODA (1798) #6520
GDP. Of the dau. of Abijah Richardson of Pelham decd. GDP.: 12/19/1798. Of Rhoda, a minor over 14. Gdn. Josiah Gage, Pelham esq. Sureties: Benjamin Hamblett of Pelham and Abel Webster of Salem.

2189. RICHARDSON, THOMAS (1776) #4250
EST. Pelham yoeman decd. ADMIN.: 7/15/1776. Admx. Lucy Richardson, Pelham widow. Bond L500.0.0. Sureties: Josiah Gage, esq. and Jesse Wilson, gent., both of Pelham. Witnesses: James Abbot and James Gibson. INVY.: Appr. 10/14/1776. Comm.: James Gibson, Miles Flint and Benjamin Colburn. Value L188.14.3. Oath 11/16/1776 Admx.

and on 11/18/1776 Comm. to Josiah Gage, JP. Added: Items omitted valued at L2.15.0. old tenor. ACCOUNT: 4/19/1786. Of Admx. Oath 4/17/1786 Admx. To Josiah Gage, JP. Allowed 4/19/1786.

2190. RICHARDSON, THOMAS (1795) #6167
EST. Chester yoeman and carpenter decd. ADMIN.: 12/16/1795. Admr. Capt. Pearson Richardson, Chester gent. Bond $3,000.00. Sureties; William Bell, innholder and John Bannister, cooper, both of Chester. Witnesses: James Doack and W. Parker. INVY.: Appr. 3/31/1796. Comm.: Josiah Flagg, esq.; Willm. White and Josiah Bradley. Value $94.06. Oaths 3/31/1796 White, Bradley and Admr. to Josiah Flagg, JP. PETITION: 5/5/1796. Of Admr. For Comm. Insolvency. Granted.

2191. RICHARDSON, CAPT. WILLIAM (1776) #4279
EST. Pelham gent. decd. testate. WILL: Drawn 4/1/1776. Legatees: Wife-Elizabeth; Sons-Asa and Daniel; Daus.-Elizabeth Butterfield wife of Capt. Jos. Butterfield; Mary Butterfield wife of Capt. Reuben Butterfield; Mary (sic.) Fletcher wife of Jacob Fletcher; Sarah Gage wife of Benjamin Gage and Hannah Richardson, single woman. Hannah is n.c.m. Her inheritance is to be paid to a proper Gdn. for her use, the Gdn. To be nominated by the minister of Pelham; Sons-in-law-Joseph Butterfield, Reuben Butterfield and Jacob Fletcher. Execs.-sons Asa and Daniel. His sig. Witnesses: Ebenezer Palmer, David Clement and Jno. Varnum. CERT. WILL (D23:207) 11/7/1776. Presented by Execs. and witnesses Varnum and Clement. ACCEPTANCE OF ADMIN.: 11/6/1776. OF Daniel Richardson, one of Execs. Requests Will be accepted and he accepts the trust of executorship. Witnesses: Jno. Varnum and David Clemons. INVY.: Appr. 9/25/1776. Comm.: James Sherburne, Joshua Hamblet and Ebenezer Palmer. Value not tallied. Esti. L1000.0.0+. Oaths 9/25/1776 Comm. to Jno. Varnum, JP. Oath 11/7/1776 Asa Richardson, an Exec., to judge.

2192. RICHEY, ALEXANDER (1783) #4939
EST. Windham weaver and yoeman decd. testate. WILL: Drawn 3/5/1783. Legatees: Wife-Sarah; Sons-James and Alexadr.; Daus.-Mary Donnechew, Elizabeth Thompson and Hannah Hamilton. Exec.-friend Gain Armour. His mark. Witnesses: Danl. Mcilvaine, Timothy Ladd and Eliphalet Ladd. CERT. WILL (D27:310): 9/24/1783. Presented by Exec. and witnesses Mcilvaine and Eliphalet Ladd. INVY. WARR.: 9/24/1783. Comm.: Daniel Mcilvaine, Benja. Thom and Alexander Morrow, all of Windham. INVY.: Value L239.9.9. Oaths 9/10/1784 Thom and Morrow to Timothy Ladd, JP. Oath 9/15/1784 Exec. to judge. DOWER WARR.: 9/15/1784. Comm.: James Betton, esq.; James Gilmore, gent.; Alexr.

Morrow, Benjamin Thom and John Morrison, all of Windham. Of Widow Sarah Richey. DOWER: 9/29/1784. Oaths 10/1/1784 Gilmore and Morrow to James Betton, JP. Allowed. ACCOUNT: 2/20/1788. Of Admr. Allowed 2/28/1788. ADDL. INVY.: 4/4/1792. Value L63.0.0. being an Addl. Invy. Of real est. Signed by Morrow and Thom.

2193. RINDGE, DANIEL (1799) #6535
EST. Portsmouth esq. decd. testate. WILL: Drawn 5/15/1798.Legatees: Jacob Sheafe, esq. for the benefit of such of his children by his present wife as he chooses; Bros.-Isaac Rindge, esq. and Jotham Rindge; Sister-Madam Mehetabel Rogers; Children of his sister Ann Peirce decd.; Mrs. Hannah Prescott and her sister Miss Olive Sheafe; Daniel Sheafe son of Jacob Sheafe; Friend-Col. William Gardner; Mrs. Mary Sheafe wife of Jacob Sheafe, esq.; His Exec.; Jacob Sheafe, esq.; Daniel Sheafe; Mr. E.H. Quincy; His former servant Romeo Freeman; Charles Mary Wentworth son of John Wentworth; Relation-Miss S.A. Fisher. Exec.-Friend and relation-Joseph Peirce, esq. His sig. Witnesses: Samuel Sherburne, Edward Hart and Samuel Larkin. Codicil: 9/3/1798. As his bro. Jotham is now dead gives that bequest to Jotham's sons John Rindge and Thomas Wentworth Rindge; Changes bequest to Jacob Sheafe, esq. for his children to a stated sum which Jacob is to div. between Hannah Prescott, Olive Sheafe and Daniel Sheafe and makes an addl. change; Discharges the accounts he holds against his late bro.-in-law Daniel Rogers, esq. and his bro. Isaac Rindge, esq. His sig. Witnesses: William Hart, Alexander Ewen and John P. Rindge. CERT. WILL (D33:37): Presented by Exec. and witnesses Sherburne and Larkin to Will and Hart and Rindge to Codicil. INVY.: Appr. 2/14/1799. Comm.: Joshua Brackett, William Gardner and Alexander Ewen. Value $40,190.31. Oaths 2/16/1799 Comm. to Saml. Penhallow, JP. Oath 2/20/1799 Exec. to judge. PETITION: Dated by clerk 2/20/1799. Of Exec. For License to sell personal est. Granted to amount of $6,000.00. ACCOUNT: 4/14/1801. Of Exec. Allowed 4/27/1801 the divisees and those interested being present and making no objections. ADMIN. D.B.N.: 10/10/1812. Admr. d.b.n. Mark Wentworth Peirce, Portsmouth merchant. Bond $10,000.00. Sureties: John Peirce and Samuel Sheafe, Portsmouth merchants. Witnesses: Samuel Marsh and Wm. Bennett Parker. LETTER OF ADMIN. D.B.N.: 10/10/1812. Joseph Peirce, esq., the Exec., having died without completing admin., Mark W. Peirce is appointed Admr. d.b.n. ACCOUNT: 2/12/1813. Of Execs. est. Joseph Peirce, esq. decd. Allowed 2/15/1813 there being no objections. ACCOUNT: 2/10/1815. Of Execs. of est. of Joseph Peirce, esq. decd. who was Exec. of Daniel Rindge. Signed by M.W. Peirce and John M. Peirce, Execs. est. of John Peirce, esq.

2194. RINDGE, JOHN (1787) #5235
EST. Portsmouth merchant decd. intestate. ADMIN.: 1/1/1787. Admr. Daniel Rindge, Portsmouth esq. Bond L1000.0.0. Sureties: Thomas Rindge Rogers and Daniel Rindge Rogers, Portsmouth merchants. Witnesses: Nathl. Parker and John Parr. Rindge. INVY. Appr. 1/1/1787. Comm.: Jno. Parker, Joshua Brackett and Wm. Gardner. Value L1893.19.0 1/2. Oaths 3/4/1787 Brackett and Gardner, esquires and on 3/23/1787 Admrs. to Oliver Whipple, JP. PETITION: 3/24/1787. Of Admr. For Comm. Insolvency. Gives list claims of L2740.0.0. CLAIMS WARR.: 3/29/1787. Comm.: Joshua Brackett, John Parker and William Gardner, Portsmouth esquires. LICENSE: 9/19/1787. To Admr. To sell sufficient real est. to pay debts. CLAIMS: 10/30/1787. Total L2944.15.10 3/4. Oaths 10/30/1787 Comm. to George Gains, JP. ACCOUNT: Of Admr. Allowed 4/16/1788. PROP. & SETTLM.: Claims L2944.15.10 3/4. Amount to be proportioned L1321.12.8. Allowed 4/16/1788 with order to Admr. to pay.

2195. RING, DAVID (1773) #4044
EST. Salisbury, Essex Co., Mass. Bay yoeman decd. intestate. ADMIN.: 9/29/1773. Admx. Mary Ring, Salisbury, Essex Co., Mass. Bay widow. Bond L500.0.0. Sureties: James Hadlock of South Hampton and Abraham Rowell of Hopkinton, Hillsborough Co. Witnesses: Benjamin Clough and Samuel Parker. Note: The file jacket says, "Incorrectly listed in Docket as David King. Should be David Ring. See Decree Recorded Vol. 22 Page 290."

2196. RING, PAGE (1797) #6302
PET. DIV. PETITION: 1/18/1797. Of Page Ring of Salisbury, Essex Co., MA. For div. of land in South Hampton which he owns in common with Ruth Morril, widow and Heirs of Richd. Morril of Amesbury, Essex Co., MA decd. He owns 6 of the 9 acres. Order: 1/18/1797. For hearing, Petitioner to serve others with copies of Petition and Order. COPY OF PETITION AND ORDER: Cert. 1/21/1797. Of Wm. (Tucker?), constable of Amesbury, Essex Co., MA. He read the Petition and Order to the widow and Heirs. DIV. WARR.: 2/6/1797. Comm.: Israel Sawyer and John Hale Pillsbury, yoemen and Joseph Jones, gent., all of South Hampton; Christopher Sargent, esq. and Ezekiel Worthen, gent., both of Amesbury, Essex Co., MA. Frank Brown of Salisbury is appointed agent for Widow and Heirs. Div.: 4/12/1797. Divisees: Page Ring, Ruth Morrill and Heirs of Richard Morrill decd. Oaths 4/12/1797 Sawyer, Jones, Sargent and Worthen to Jacob Brown, JP. Allowed.

2197. RING: REUBEN FRENCH & TIRZAH SAWYER (1787) #5242
GDP. Of the children of David Ring, Salisbury, Essex Co., MA yoeman decd. GDP.: 1/17/1787. Of Tirzah Sawyer Ring and Reuben French Ring, minors over 14. Gdn. James Hadlock, South Hampton yoeman. Bond L500.0.0. Sureties: John Currier, South Hampton gent. and Levi Hadlock, Deering, Hillsborough Co. yoeman. Witnesses: Nathan Currier and Ezekiel Currier.

2198. ROACH, THOMAS (1792) #5790
See #3868 Thomas Wallingford(1771) and #6040 John Noble et. als. (1794).

2199. ROBERTS, ALEXANDER (1777) #4376
EST. Brentwood yoeman decd. intestate. ADMIN.: 7/29/1777. Admrs.: Lydia Roberts, Brentwood widow and Samuel Johnson, Northwood gent. Bond L500.0.0. Sureties: Zadock Sanborn and Thomas Roberts, Brentwood yoemen. Witnesses: W. Parker and Nathl. Parker. INVY.: Appr. 8/26/1777. Comm.: Thomas Gordon, Thomas Roberts and Joseph Greely. Value L122.15.9. Oaths 8/27/1777 Comm. and Admrs. to judge. DOWER: 12/24/1777. Comm.: Levi Morrill, William Morrill, Joseph Greely, Thomas Gordon and James Robinson. Of Widow Lydia Roberts. Oaths 12/31/1777 Levi Morrill, William Morrill and Greely to judge. LIST CLAIMS: 7/21/1783. Total L118.2.0. Order: 7/21/1783. To William Parker, esq., Reg. To write up a Commission Insolvency, Comm. may be Deacon Williams and Dr. Parker. ACCOUNT: 5/19/1784. Of Admrs. Allowed 5/19/1784. LICENSE: 5/19/1784. To Admrs. To sell 2/3 of real est. CLAIMS: 5/19/1784. Comm.: Eliphalet Hale and W. Parker Jr. Total L58.6.9 1/4. ADDL. ACCOUNT: 9/3/1790. Of Samuel Johnson, surviving Admr. Allowed 10/19/1790. PROP. & SETTLM.: Claims L58.6.9 1/4. Amount to be proportioned L44.18.7. Allowed 10/19/1790 with order to Admr. to pay.

2200. ROBERTS, BENJAMIN (1795) #6114
EST. Brentwood yoeman decd. ADMIN.: 6/16/1795. Admr. Thomas Roberts of Brentwood. Bond $3,000.00. Sureties: Thomas Gordon, gent. and Thomas Leavitt, yoeman, both of Brentwood. Witnesses: Mary S. Parker and W. Parker. INVY.: Comm.: Jona. Sleeper, Thomas Gordon and Thomas Leavitt. Value L23.7.6. Oaths 11/24/1795 Gordon, Leavitt and Admr. to W. Parker, JP. PETITION: 4/27/1796. Of Admr. For Comm. Insolvency. Says claims amount to L21.1.7 and there will be an allowance to Widow. Granted. PETITION: 9/20/1796. Of Admr. For License. Gives list claims of L27.5.0. Granted. LICENSE (D32:188):9/20/1796. To Admr. To sell real est. to amount of $100.00. ACCOUNT: 1/1797. Of Admr.

Allowed 1/10/1797. Account includes payment to Widow for relinquishing Dower.

2201. ROBERTS, CAPT. EDMUND (1788) #5322
EST. Portsmouth mariner decd. intestate. ADMIN.: 1/16/1788. Admx.: Sarah Roberts, Portsmouth widow. Bond L1000.0.0. Sureties: John Furnald, Portsmouth brazier and Gideon Lamson, Exeter trader. Witnesses: Deborah Furnald and Mary Sherburne. INVY.: Comm.: Joshua Brackett, esq.; Nathl. Marshall and Martin Parry. Value L255.17.9 1/2. Oaths 5/20/1788 Comm. to Saml. Penhallow, JP. Oath 5/1788 Admx. to judge. PETITION: 9/3/1790. Of Moses Woodward. For Comm. Insolvency. Gives claims of L630.12.5. Witnesses: Jere. Libbey, John Furnald and Nathl. Marshall. Note: These men are probably the Claims Commissioners. DOWER WARR.: 10/20/1790. Comm.: Joshua Brackett and Jeremiah Libbey, esquires; John Furnald, brazier; Nathl. Marshall, mariner and Martin Parry, goldsmith, all of Portsmouth. Of Sarah Woodward, in est. of Edmund Roberts. Dower: 11/13/1790. Oaths 11/13/1790 Brackett, Furnald and Marshall, affirms. Libbey and Parry to Geo. Gerrish, JP. Allowed. PETITION: 2/16/1791. Of Nathl. Adams for Admx. For License. Gives claims of L645.4.7. LICENSE (D30:15): 2/16/1791. To Moses Woodward and Sarah Woodward, Admrs. To sell real est. to amount of L300.0.0. ACCOUNT: 2/20/1793. Of Admrs. Oaths 2/20/1793 Moses and Sarah Woodward to Nathl. Adams, JP. Allowed 4/29/1793. Account includes main. Edmund Roberts. ADMIN. D.B.N.: 12/16/1805. Admx. d.b.n: Sarah Roberts, Portsmouth single woman. Bond $4,000.00. Sureties: Gideon Lamson and George Sullivan, Exeter esquires. Witness W. Parker. PETITION: 12/24/1805. Of Admx. d.b.n, a dau., one of the heirs at law. Claims that Moses Woodward, Portsmouth esq., in right of his late wife Sarah Woodard decd., Admx., has in his hands a bal. of $900.00 due heirs. Requests settlm. of Account by Woodward. Order: 12/24/ 1806. Moses Woodward to be cited to appear and show cause why he should not settle Account. CITATION: 12/30/1805. To Moses Woodward. To appear and exhibit Addl. Account of Admin. as court has been informed he holds effects of est. not accounted for in his Account of 4/29/1793. Cert.: 1/8/1806. Of Richard Lane, D. Sherf. He served Citation. PETITION: 4/4/1806. Of Admx. b.d.n. Requests appeal against Decree on Woodward's Account. Granted 4/19/1806. BOND: 4/26/1896. Of Sarah Roberts. Bond $100.00. To appeal Decree on Account. Sureties: George Sullivan, esq. and Gideon Lamson, mariner, both of Exeter. PETITION: Of Moses Woodward, Portsmouth esq. He holds land in Portsmouth, part of a farm lately owned by Benjamin Lear of Portsmouth decd., with John Carroll, Hampstead merchant who owns the other part. Requests div. Signed by Moses Woodward and Philip Carrigan Jr., atty. Order:

5/27/1806. For hearing, Carroll to be served with notice. Cert.: 6/1806. Of F. B. Eastman, D. Sheriff. He served notice. REPLY: 6/18/1806. Of John Carroll by his atty. David Humphreys. Denies that Moses Woodward is seized in his demesne of the land in Portsmouth. Claims the land is his alone.

2202. ROBERTS, HANNAH (1791) #5696
EST. Plaistow single woman decd. ADMIN.: 9/28/1791. Admr. Eliphalet Richardson, Hampstead husbm. Bond L1000.0.0. Sureties: Hezekiah Hutchins of Hampstead and Ezekiel Gile of Plaistow, esquires. Witnesses: Nat. Parker and W. Parker. INVY.: Appr. 10/3/1791. Comm.: Amos Sawyer and Ezekiel Gile. Value L23.6.5. Oath 10/6/1791 Gile, affirm. Sawyer to John White, JP. PETITION: 10/10/1791. Of Admr. For Comm. Insolvency. Gives claims already in of L28.14.0. LICENSE (D30:135): 10/10/1791. To Admr. To sell real est. to the amount of L16.0.0. LIST OF CLAIMS: Total 28.14.0. Note: This list also includes claims for est. #5695 Rachel Richardson (1791) for L7.3.2. Note: Eliphalet Richardson was Admr. for both of these ests. CLAIMS: 4/2/1792. Comm.: John White, Ezekiel Gile and Amos Sawyer. Total L27.0.1. Oath Gile, affirm. Sawyer to John White, JP. PROP. & SETTLM.: Claims L20.12.9. Amount to be proportioned L4.17.10. Allowed 7/4/1792 with order to Admr. to pay. ACCOUNT: 4/18/1792. Of Admr. Allowed 10/18/1792.

2203. ROBERTS, JOHN (1773) #3994
EST. Somersworth yoeman decd. intestate. ORDER: 1/29/1773. To Mrs. Sussanah Roberts of Somersworth. To appear and take administration on or before 2/11/1773 or admin. will be granted to a creditor. Susanna appeared and renounced admin. in favor of Moses Varney. ADMIN.: 2/11/1773. Admr. Moses Varney, Dover yeoman. Bond L1000.0.0. Sureties: William Watson, Dover yeoman and Ephraim Folsom, Durham joiner. Witnesses: John Taylor and Samuel Parker.

2204. ROBERTS, JOSHUA (1772) #3901
EST. Somersworth husbm. decd. testate. WILL: Drawn 11/26/1771. Legatees: Wife- Sarah; Son-Joshua; Daus.-Hannah Foss, Betty Roberts and Lydia Knight; Grandsons-Jonathan Roberts son of his son Thomas decd. and Samuel Roberts son of his dau. Molly decd. Granddaus.-Olive Roberts dau. of his dau. Molly decd. and Molly dau. of his son Thomas decd. Exec.-son Joshua. His sig. Witnesses: William Stiles, Gershom Plumer and Samuel Roberts Jr. Proved 1/11/1772 on oaths of witnesses Plumer and Roberts.

2205. ROBIE, DANIEL (1793) #5895
EST. Raymond yoeman decd. ADMIN.: 5/13/1793. Admx. Nane Robie, Raymond widow. Bond L1000.0.0. Sureties: Stephen Prescott and John Osgood, Raymond yoemen. Witnesses: Jona. Swain and Ruth Robinson. INVY.: Appr. 5/22/1793. Comm.: Jona. Swain, Elisha Towle and Ebenezer Prescutt. Value L499.2.10. Oaths 6/71793 Towle, Prescutt and Admx. to Jona. Swain, JP.

2206. ROBIE, HENRY JR. (1788) #5383
EST. Hampton Falls yoeman decd. ADMIN.: 10/15/1788. Admx. Ruth Robie, Hampton Falls widow. Bond L500.0.0. Sureties: James Prescut Jr., gent. and Nathan Robie, yoeman, both of Hampton Falls, Witnesses: Samuel Parker and W. Parker. INVY.: Appr. 12/5/1788. Comm.: James Prescut Jr. and Benjamin Tilton. Value L100.14.8. Oaths 12/17/1788 Comm. and Admx. to W. Parker, JP. PETITION: 9/16/1792. Of Admx. For License. Gives list claims of L87.13.2 and main. 4 children. Granted. LICENSE (D30:302): 9/16/1792. To Admx. To sell real est. to amount of L50.0.0. PETITION: 2/11/1794. Of Isaac Marston and his wife, Admx. For License for housekeeping and continued main. one child. Granted. LICENSE (D31:172): 2/11/1794. To Admrs. To sell real est. to amount of L22.10.0.

2207. ROBIE, ICHABOD (1776) #4217
EST. Candia yoeman decd. intestate. ADMIN.: 3/27/1776. Admx. Anna Robie, Candia widow. Bond L1000.0.0. Sureties: Samuel Clough of Candia and Henry Robie of Hampton Falls. Witnesses: Benjamin Case and John Colby. INVY. Appr. 4/29/1776. Comm.: Saml. Mooers, Abrm. Fitts and Sherburne Reed. Value L236.14.2. Oaths 10/28/1776 Comm. and Admx. to John Dudley, JP. ACCOUNT: 11/15/1786. Of Eleazer Goodwin and Anna his wife, Admx. Allowed 11/15/1786. Account includes main. 2 children. DIV. WARR.: 4/18/1787. Comm.: Jonathan Hill, Benjamin Case, John Lane, Saml. Morril and Stephen Fifield, all of Candia. To div. 2/3 of real est., giving double share to oldest son and single to each of other children. Walter Robie, esq. is appointed agent for the children under age to see they are equally dealt with. DIV.: 6/16/1787. Divisees: Sons-Levi (oldest) and Loell; Daus.-Anna Robie and Sarah Robie. Oaths 6/16/1787 Case, Morril and Lane to Samuel Mooers, JP. Allowed 2/28/1793. DOWER: 6/16/1787. Comm.: Walter Robie, John Lane, Benjamin Case, Saml. Morril and Jonathan Hill. Of Anna Goodwin in est. Ichabod Robie. Oaths 6/16/1787 Robie, Case and Morril to Saml. Mooers, JP. Allowed 2/28/1793.

2208. ROBIE, ICHABOD (1799) #6585
GDP. Of the son of Henry Robie, Hampton Falls yoeman decd. GDP.: 6/18/1799. Of Ichabod, a minor over 14. Gdn. James Sanborn, Kensington yoeman. Bond $2,000.00. Sureties: Benjamin Rowe, physician and Jewett Sanborn, esq., both of Kensington. Witnesses: Christor. Toppan and Nathl. Parker.

2209. ROBIE: ICHABOD LEAVITT & PAIN ROW (1794) #5988
GDP. Of the sons of Henry Robie Jr., Hampton Falls yoeman decd. GDP.: 4/14/1794. Of Ichabod Leavitt Robie, a minor under 14. Gdn. Benjamin Leavitt, Hampton Falls yoeman. Bond L300.0.0. Sureties: James Thurston, gent. and James Rundlett, yoeman, both of Exeter., Witnesses: Joseph Hoit and Saml. Barker. GDP.: 10/2/1794. Of Pain Row Robie, a minor over 14. Gdn. Michael Tilton, Hampton Falls yoeman. Bond L1000.0.0. Surety Jonathan Burnham, Hampton Falls esq. Witnesses: W. Parker and Jno. Parker.

2210. ROBIE, JOHN (1794) #6052
EST. North Hampton yoeman decd. testate. WILL: Drawn 9/6/1794. Legatees: Wife- Elizabeth; Son-John; Daus.-Hannah, Patty and Sarah Cotton who is living separate from her husb. Joseph Cotton. His mark. Witnesses: John Fogg, Isaac Marston and Simeon Marston. CERT. WILL (D31:411): 12/15/1794. Presented by Exec. and witnesses Isaac Marston and Simeon Marston. ADMIN.: 12/15/1794. Exec. John Robie of North Hampton. Bond L1000.0.0. Sureties: Simeon Marston and Isaac Marston, both of North Hampton. Witnesses: Jere. Fogg and W. Parker.

2211. ROBINSON: CLERK & JONATHAN (1793) #5871
GDP. Of the sons of Daniel Robinson, Exeter yoeman decd. GDP.: 3/22/1793. Of: Jonathan and Clerk, minors over 14. Gdn. Josiah Rollins Jr., Exeter cooper. Bond L1000.0.0. Sureties: Daniel Robinson, yoeman and Francis Mason, miller, both of Exeter. Witnesses: Wm. Parker and N. Parker.

2212. ROBINSON, DANIEL A#2839 (1761)
EST. Daniel Robinson. ACCOUNT & DISCHARGE: 1/12/1803. Of Mary Driscall, lately Mary Robinson, only heir of Daniel. She has received from Jonathan Warner, esq., Admr., L3.9.1., the balance of the Admin. account and discharges him. Witness 1/15/1803 Isaac Rindge. Oath 1/15/1803 Driscall to Isaac Rindge, JP. Orig. Archives file includes Will, Claims Warr., License, Claims, Invy., Citation to Account, Account.

2213. ROBINSON, DANIEL (1783) #4932
EST. Exeter shipwright decd. RENUN.: 9/18/1783. Of Mary Robinson, widow of Daniel. Of Admin. As there is no relative of decd. near, requests appointment of Gideon Lamson of Exeter. ADMIN.: 9/18/1783. Admr. Gideon Lamson, Exeter taylor. Bond L500.0.0. Sureties: Joseph Smith Gilman, trader and Dudley Odlin, gent., both of Exeter. Witnesses: Nathl. Parker and W. Parker. INVY. WARR.: 9/18/1783. Comm.: Noah Emery Jr., esq.; Benja. Lamson, innholder and Joseph Swasey Jr., shipwright, all of Exeter. INVY.: Appr. 11/19/1783. Value L10.12.0. Oaths 11/19/1783 Lamson, Emery and Admr. to Wm. Parker, JP. CLAIMS WARR.: 8/18/1784. Comm.: Jedediah Jewett, Noah Emery Jr. and William Parker Jr., Exeter esquires. CLAIMS: Total L52.7.0. Oaths 3/16/1785 Comm. to W. Parker, JP. ACCOUNT: 4/1785. Of Admr. Allowed 4/21/1785. Account includes main. one child. PROP. & SETTLM.: Claims L52.7.0. Amount to be proportioned L36.12.8 1/2. Allowed 7/20/1785 with order to Admr. to pay.

2214. ROBINSON, DANIEL (1793) #5859
EST. Exeter husbm. decd. ADMIN.: 3/7/1793. Admr. Daniel Robinson, Exeter yoeman. Bond L1000.0.0. Sureties: Jeremiah Robinson and Francis Mason, Exeter yoemen. Witnesses: W. Parker and J. Huard Lanoiraix. INVY.: Appr. 3/1793. Comm.: Thomas Folsom, Joseph Robinson and Trueworthy Robinson. Value L32.17.0. Oaths 6/15/1793 Comm. and Admr. to Wm. Parker, JP. PETITION: 3/13/1794. Of Admr. For Comm. Insolvency. Gives list claims of L140.13.6. Requests Comm. of Capt. Thomas Folsom, Trueworthy Robinson and John Sanborn, all of Exeter. Granted.

2215. ROBINSON, DANIEL (1799) #6624
GDP.: Of the son of John Robinson, Sanbornton, Strafford Co. yoeman. GDP.: 11/22/1799. Of Daniel, a minor over 14. Gdn. Samuel Hoyt, Sanbornton, Strafford Co. yoeman. Bond $1,000.00. Surety Kinsley Hall, Exeter cordwainer. Witness W. Parker.

2216. ROBINSON, EDE (1790) #5529
GDP. Of the son of John Robinson of Stratham decd. GDP.: 3/31/1790. Of Ede, a minor over 14. Gdn. Samuel Goodhue, Deerfield yoeman. Bond L500.0.0. Sureties: Benjamin Green and Solomon Smith, Stratham yoemen. Witnesses: W. Parker and Eliza. Parker.

2217. ROBINSON, JEDEDIAH (1778) #4457
EST. Brentwood yoeman decd. testate. WILL: Drawn 4/6/1778. Legatees: Mother-Allice Robinson; Sister-Mary Robinson; Bros.-Jonathan and

Josiah; Congregational Church of Brentwood; Bros. And sisters, unnamed; Children of his sister Allice Bachelder decd.; Children of his sister Esther Perkins; "Cozen" Jonathan Robinson son of his bro. Jonathan. Exec.-bro. Jonathan. His sig. Witnesses: Thomas Stow Ranney, David Robinson and Nathl. Trask. CERT. WILL: 5/27/1778. Presented by Exec. and witnesses Ranney and Robinson. INVY.: Appr. 8/15/1778. Comm.: Thos. Stow Ranney, physician; David Robinson and Joseph Greely, yoemen. Value L767.16.0. Oaths 8/15/1778 Comm. and Exec. to W. Parker, JP.

2218. ROBINSON, CAPT. JOHN (1784) #5013
EST. Of Deerfield decd. intestate. INVY. WARR. 6/14/1784. Comm.: Richard Jenness and Ezekiel Gilman, gent., both of Deerfield and Zechariah Clifford of Candia. ADMIN.: 6/15/1784. Admr. Thomas Robinson, Deerfield yoeman. Bond L500.0.0. Sureties: John Dudley, Raymond esq. and John Underhill, Chester gent. Witnesses: Elizabeth Adams and Nathl. Parker. INVY.: Value not tallied. Esti. L62.0.0+. Oaths 7/20/1784 Comm. and Admr. to John Dudley, JP.

2219. ROBINSON, JOHN (1786) #5213
GDP. Of the son of John Robinson, Stratham yoeman decd. GDP.: 9/11/1786. Of John, a minor over 14. Gdn. Samuel Goodhue of Deerfield. Bond L500.0.0. Sureties: Samuel Goodhue, Stratham yoeman and Samuel Daniels, Pembroke esq. Witnesses: Elizabeth Adams and W. Parker.

2220. ROBINSON, JONATHAN (1782) #4817
EST. Brentwood gent. decd. testate. WILL: Drawn 3/12/1782. Legatees: Wife-unnamed, his sons to care for her as she is not capable of caring for herself; Sons-Jonathan and Samuel; Dau.-Elizabeth Robinson; Church in Brentwood as provided in Will of his bro. Jedediah. Exec.-son Jonathan. His sig. Witnesses: James Robinson, David Robinson and Nathanael Trask. CERT. WILL (D26:418): 6/26/1782. Presented by Exec. and witnesses James Robinson and David Robinson. INVY. WARR.: 6/26/1782. Comm.: James Robinson, gent.; Thos. Stow Ranney, physician and David Robinson, yoeman, all of Brentwood. INVY.: Appr. 9/17/1782. Value not tallied. Esti. L1000.0.0+. Oaths 9/25/1782 Comm. and Exec. to judge.

2221. ROBINSON, JONATHAN (1791) #5617
EST. Brentwood yoeman decd. testate. WILL: Drawn 11/11/1790. Legatees: Dau.-Molly Robinson; Bro.-Samuel, Samuel to provide for his mother Widow Elizabeth Robinson; His "intended companion"-Mary Perkins. He provides for Mary her right of dower and the right to live in his house as long as she remains unmarried and bequeaths her ½ of his

side saddle. Exec.-Bro. Samuel. His sig. Witnesses: David Robinson, Dudley Robinson and Thomas Stow Ranney. CERT. WILL (D30:13): 2/4/1791. Presented by Exec. and witnesses David Robinson and Dudley Robinson. ADMIN.: 2/4/1791. Exec. Samuel Robinson, Brentwood yoeman. Bond L1000.0.0. Sureties: David Robinson, gent. and Dudley Robinson, yoeman, both of Brentwood. Witnesses: Jno. Parker and Wm. Parker. INVY.: Comm.: David Robinson, James Robinson and Gilman Leavitt. Value L601.13.0. Oaths 5/16/1791 David Robinson and Leabitt to Tho. Stow Ranney, JP. Oath 5/7/1791 Exec. to W. Parker, Reg.

2222. ROBINSON, COL. JONATHAN (1798) #6509
EST. Stratham esq. decd. intestate. ADMIN. (D32:543): 11/9/1798. Admrs.: Abigail Robinson, his widow and Shadrach Robinson, son. Sureties: Andrew Wiggin, esq. and Walter Weeks. INVY.: Comm. Walter Weeks, John Adams and Josiah Brown. Value $5,324.56. Oaths 1/9/1799 Admrs., Weeks and Adams to W. Parker, JP. PETITION: 3/26/1799. 3/26/1799. Of: Shadrach Robinson, Ebenr. C. Robinson, Abednego Robinson, Bradbury Robinson, Noah Robinson and Meshach Robinson, heirs. By mutual consent they have agreed to and sold to Adednego Robinson all the real est. and reversion of the Dower for $230.17 each share. But they also agree that some of heirs are minors and some may oppose selling. Request an appr. and nominate a Comm. of Simon Wiggin and Andrew Wiggin, esquires and Capt. Joshua Avery, gent., all of Stratham. APPR. WARR.: 5/29/1799. Comm. as requested. To appr. the real est. as in Petition. Appr.: 6/19/1799. Value $2,800.00. Oaths 6/19/1799 Comm. to Josiah Bartlett, JP. DECREE SETTLM.: 4/12/1800. Abednego, a son, appearing and consenting, the real est. settled on him, Abednego to pay his co-heirs $233.33 each, his bros.-Shadrach, Meshech, Ebenezer, Jonathan, Bradbury and Noah; His sisters-Abigail, Jane Clark and Elizabeth Robinson with six months; The heirs of his sisters Mercy Boardman and Mary Clark decd. within 12 months, all with interest. BOND: 4/12/1800. Of Abednego Robinson, Stratham yoeman. Bond $5,000.00. To pay his co-heirs per Decree Settlm. Sureties: Thomas Bordman of Stratham and Shadrach Robinson of Greenland, yoemen. Witnesses: Enoch Clark and W. Parker. Receipt: Of Shadrach Robinson, Bradbury Robinson, Noah Robinson and Enoch Clark Gdn. of his child. They have each received $230.33. ACCOUNT: 4/1801. Of Admrs. Allowed 5/14/1801 some heirs present and making no objections.

2223. ROBINSON, JOSIAH (1782) #4807
EST. Poplin yoeman decd. ADMIN.: 5/29/1782. Admx. Judith Robinson, Poplin widow. Bond L1000.0.0. Sureties: Josiah Robinson, Poplin gent. and Samuel Shepard, Brentwood clerk. Witnesses: W. Parker and John

Beck. INVY.: Appr. 6/11/1782. Comm.: Coffin Sanborn, Josiah Robinson and Exekl. Godfrey. Value L153.4.5. Oaths 8/28/1782 Sanborn, Godfrey and Admx. to judge.

2224. ROBINSON, MARTHA (1777) #4368
EST. Stratham spinster decd. testate. WILL: Drawn 6/6/1770. Legatees: Sister-Hannah Coleby or her heirs; Kinswomen-Tirza Healey or her heirs and Elizabeth Bradley; John Dearborn of Stratham; Kinsman-Sergeant Heath or his heirs; James Dearborn son of John Dearborn and David Wiggin son of Nathaniel Wiggin of Stratham. Exec.-John Dearborn of Stratham. Her mark. Witnesses: Reuben Gove Dearborn, Joshua Lane and Nathaniel Wiggin Jr. CERT. WILL (24:40): 6/25/1777. Presented by Exec. and witnesses Dearborn and Wiggin. A note calls Martha "widow." INVY.: Comm.: Reuben Gove Dearborn, Joshua Lane and Nathaniel Wiggin Jr. Value L80.16.3. Oaths 7/8/1777 Comm. to W. Parker, JP.

2225. ROBINSON, MARY (1789) #5438
EST. Brentwood spinster decd. testate. WILL: Drawn 10/15/1788. Legatees: Cousins-Mary Perkins dau. of Joseph Perkins, Mary Robinson dau. of her cousin Jonathan; Nephew-Jonathan Robinson son of her bro. Jonathan Robinson decd. Who now lives in the house with her (she calls him cousin). Ref. to her father Jonathan Robinson decd. Exec.-cousin Jonathan Robinson. Her mark. Witnesses: Daniel Robinson, Dudley Robinson and Thomas Stow Ranney. CERT. WILL (D29:265): Presented by Exec. and all witnesses. ADMIN.: 4/15/1789. Exec. Jonathan Robinson, Brentwood yoeman. Bond L500.0.0. Sureties: David Robinson, gent. and Thomas Stow Ranney, esq. both of Brentwood. INVY.: Appr. 6/26/1789. Comm.: Thos. Stow Ranney, James Robinson and David Robinson. Value L139.10.6. Oaths 7/15/1789 James Robinson, David Robinson and Exec. to W. Parker, JP.

2226. ROBINSON, MOSES (1782) #4771
EST. Hampton Falls clothier decd. RENUN.: 1/17/1782. Of Mary Robinson, widow of Moses. Of Admin. Requests appointment of her bro. Jeremiah Bachelder of Kensington. She notes that the est. is small and there are a number of children to support. ADMIN.: 1/30/1782. Admr. Jeremiah Bachelder, Kensington gent. Bond L500.0.0. Sureties: Noah Emery, esq. and James Folsom, shopkeeper, both of Exeter. Witnesses: Seth Fogg and W. Parker. INVY.: Appr. 3/6/1782. Comm.: Joseph Wells, Abner Sanborn and George Fifield. Value L123.11.8. Oaths 4/22/1782 Comm. to Meshech Weare, JP. Oath 4/24/1782 Admr. to W. Parker, Reg. PETITION: 4/24/1782. Of Admr. For Comm. Insolvency. Gives claims of L127.18.8. ADDL. INVY.: Appr. 3/6/1782. Value L12.3.9. Returned

10/28/1782. LICENSE (D27:112): 11/27/1782. To Admr. To sell sufficient real est. to pay debts. CLAIMS: 3/5/1783. Comm.: Caleb Sanborn, Jonathan Burnham and Samll. Weare. Total L187.15.7. Oaths 12/8/1785 Comm. to Ebenr. Clifford, JP. ACCOUNT: 1/18/1785. Of Admr. Allowed 1/18/1785. Account includes main. Sarah, Jeremiah and Stephen.

2227. ROBINSON, THOMAS (1781) #4685
EST. Salem yoeman decd. testate. WILL: Drawn 12/13/1780. Legatees: Wife-Mehetebel; Sons-Thomas, Daniel and Stephen; Daus.-Mehetebel, Elizabeth, Louis(sic) and Mary. Exec.-wife Mehetebel. His sig. Witnesses: Adner Bayley, Nathl. Gorrell and Robert Cambell. CERT. WILL (D26:2): 1/31/1781. Presented by Exex. and witnesses Gorrell and Campbell. INVY. WARR.: 1/31/1781. Comm.: Thomas Douglass, Nathaniel Gorrell and Robert Cambell, Salem yoemen. INVY.: Appr. 4/11/1781. Value L21076.9.0. Oaths 4/23/1781 Comm. to Timothy Ladd, JP.

2228. ROGERS, REV. DANIEL (1785) #5162
EST. Exeter clerk decd. testate. WILL: Drawn 2/22/1785. Legatees: Sons-Daniel Denison Rogers, Thomas and William; Daus.-Anna, Elizabeth Gilman and Martha. Of Anna he makes particular note of "the extraordinary care she gave me and her mother." Exec. Thos. Odiorne, Exeter shopkeeper. His sig. Witnesses: John Dean, Thomas Dean and Simon Wiggin. CERT. WILL (D28:369): Presented by Exec. and witnesses Thomas Dean and Wiggin. INVY. WARR.: 12/21/1785. Comm.: John Phillips and Samuel Hobart, esquires and James Thurston, innholder, all of Exeter. INVY.: Appr. 1/10/1786. Value L500.17.0 plus a Note of Hand from son Daniel of L130.17.3, part of which has been paid. Oaths 5/17/1786 Comm. and Exec. to W. Parker, JP. ACCOUNT: 4/8/1788. Of Exec. Allowed 11/19/1788.

2229. ROGERS, DANIEL (1795) #6159
EST. Portsmouth esq. decd. testate. WILL: Drawn 9/29/1795. Legatees: Wife-Mehitable; His children-Thomas Rindge Rogers, Sarah Rogers, Daniel Rindge Rogers, Mark and William Rindge Rogers; Children of his dau. Widow Ann Treadwell, decd.-Ann Elliot, Mary Treadwell, Mehitabel Treadwell, George R. Treadwell, Jacob Treadwell, William Treadwell, Charles Treadwell and Daniel Treadwell. Exex.-wife Mehitabel. His sig. Witnesses: Joshua Brackett, Danl. Humphreys and Nat. Rogers. CERT. WILL (D32:64): 11/18/1795. Presented by Exex. and all witnesses. ADMIN.: 11/18/1795. Exex. Mehitable Rogers, Portsmouth widow. Bond $3,000.00. Sureties: Mark Rogers, Portsmouth trader and Thomas Rindge Rogers, Nottingham gent. Witnesses: Joshua Brackett and Danl. Humphreys.

2230. ROGERS, JOHN (1798) #6482
GDP. Of the son of Wm. Rogers, Newbury, Essex Co., MA esq. decd. GDP. (D32:510): 8/11/1787. Of John, a minor under 14. Gdn. William Rogers, Londonderry cordwainer. Sureties: Robert Rogers, gent. and Robert Ramsey, yoemen, both of Londonderry. Note: The jacket for this file is empty.

2231. ROGERS, NANNY (1797) #6378
EST. Of Salem decd. testate. WILL: Drawn 8/26/1797. Legatees: Son-Benjamin Rowllings Rogers; Daus.-Nancy Bowles and Martha Rogers; Sisters-Molly Emery, Mehitable Webster, Sarah Stewart and Patty Merrill. Exec.-Capt. James Webster. Her mark. Witnesses: Silas Wheeler, David Wheeler and Joseph Wardwell. CERT. WILL (D32:378): 9/22/1797. Presented by Exec. and witnesses Silas Wheeler and Wardwell. ADMIN.: 9/22/1797. Admr. James Webster, gent. Bond $2,000.00. Sureties: Joseph Wardwell, esq. and Silas Wheeler, yoeman. Witnesses: Mary S. Parker and W. Parker. INVY.: Appr. 9/26/1797. Comm.: Joshua Merrill, Stephen Webster and Joseph Wardwell. Value $29.15.8 (sic.) Oaths 9/26/1797 Merrill and Webster to Joshua Wardwell, JP. Oath 10/21/1797 Exec. to judge. ACCOUNT: 5/18/1800. Of Exec. Allowed 5/18/1800.

2232. ROGERS, NATHANIEL (1782) #4804
See #4320 Christopher Rymes (1777)

2233. ROGERS, STEPHEN (1786) #5179
EST. South Hampton yoeman decd. testate. WILL: Drawn 8/3/1779. Legatees; Wife-Mary; Son-Josiah; Dau.-Mary Morrill. Exec.-son Josiah. His sig. Witnesses: Jacob Collins, Timothy Flanders and John Pilsbury. CERT. WILL (D28:491): 3/20/1786. Presented by Exec. and witnesses Collins and Pilsbury. INVY.: Appr. 6/21/1786. Comm.: Benja. Clough and William Graves. Value L484.6.8. Oaths 6/21/1786 Comm. and Exec. to judge. DOWER: 12/25/1789. Comm.: Benja. Clough, Reuben Currier, William Graves, Barnard Currier and John H. Pillsbury. Of Widow Mary Rogers. Includes Map. Oath 1/5/1790 of Graves, affirms. Clough and Barnard Currier to judge. Allowed. ACCOUNT: 3/17/1790. Of Exec. Allowed 3/18/1790. CITATION: 11/1/1790. To Exec. To appear and exhibit an Addl. Account. Cert. 11/4/1790. Of John Morrill. He notified Josiah Rogers by giving him a copy of Citation.

2234. ROLFE, BENJAMIN (1772) #3909
EST. Concord esq.decd.intestate.ADMIN.: 2/5/1772. Admx. Sarah Rolfe, Concord widow. Bond L1000.0.0. Sureties: Timothy Walker Jr., gent. and Simon Trumbal, yoeman, both of Concord. Witnesses: Stephen Scales and

Peter Green. INVY.: Comm.: Capt. John Chandler, gent. and Joseph Hall Jr., yoeman, both of Concord. Appr. 4/1/1772. Value L4082.10.11. Oaths 9/11/1772 Comm. to Andr. McMillan, JP. Oath 9/25/1772 Admx. to judge. LETTER: 5/12/1773. To Andrew McMillan, Concord esq. From judge. It has been represented to the judge that Sarah Thompson, Admx., is not in a capacity to travel to Portsmouth. Requests that McMillan take her oath on the Account and enter his fee into it. ACCOUNT: Of Benjamin Thompson and Sarah his wife, formerly Sarah Rolfe, Admx. Oath 5/17/1773 Admx. to Andrew McMillan, JP. Oath 5/19/1773 Benjamin Thompson to judge. Account includes main. of Paul Rolfe. ACCOUNT: Of Benjamin Thompson and Sarah, Admx. Oath 11/11/1782 Admx. to Timo. Walker, JP. Oath 11/16/1782 Admx. to Joseph Gilman, JP, her husb. being out of state. Account includes an item re a negro man who died in the Army. ADMIN. D.B.N. 5/29/1793. Admr. d.b.n Timothy Walker, Concord esq. Bond L1000.0.0. Sureties: John Calfe of Hampstead and Thomas Bartlett of Nottingham, esquires. Witnesses: Ebenr. Chadwick and W. Parker.

2235. ROLFE, JANE (1788) #5325
GDP. Of the dau. of Joseph Rolfe, Londonderry yoeman decd. PETITION: 1/18/1788. Of Jenny (sig. Jean) Rolfe. Requests appointment of James Macgregore esq. as her Gdn. Witnesses: John Neal and David Blair. Allowed 2/20/1788. GDP.: 2/21/1788. Of Jenny, a minor over 14. Gdn. James Macgregore, Londonderry esq. Bond L500.0.0. Sureties: Archibald McMurphy of Londonderry and Nathl. Peabody of Atkinson, esquires. Witness W. Parker.

2236. ROLFE, JOSEPH (1784) #4981
EST. Londonderry yoeman decd. intestate. ADMIN.: 3/17/1784. Admx. Ann Rolfe, Londonderry widow. Bond L1000.0.0. Sureties: James Dinsmor, yoeman and Samuel Gerrish, both of Londonderry. Witnesses: Jonathan Adams, Timothy Harington and Archibald McMurphy. INVY. WARR.: 6/15/1784. Comm.: James Ramsey, Jonathan Adams and Acd. McMurphy, all of Londonderry. INVY.: Appr. 7/12/1784. Value L535.10.6. Oaths 10/19/1784 Comm. and Admx. to John Bell, JP. DIV. & DOWER: 3/29/1788. Comm.: James Macgregore, Archd. McMurphy and Jonathan Wallace. To div. real est. among Widow and children. Divisees: Mrs. Ann Rolf, her Dower; Moses Rolfe; Mrs. Esther wife of David Blair; Miss Jenny Rolf and Miss Judeth Rolf. Oaths 3/5/1792 Comm. to Isaac Thom, JP. Allowed 4/17/1793. MAP OF DIV.

2237. ROLFE, JUDITH (1788) #5326
GDP. Of the dau. of Joseph Rolfe, Londonderry yoeman decd. PETITION: 1/17/1788. Of Anna Rolfe. Requests appointment of Archibald McMurphy, Londonderry esq. as Gdn. of her minor dau. Judah Rolf, age 9. Witness J. Macgregore. GDP.: 2/21/1788. Of Judith, a minor under 14. Gdn. Archibald McMurphy, Londonderry esq. Bond L500.0.0. Sureties: James Macgregore of Londonderry and Nathl. Peabody of Atkinson, esquires. GDP.: 4/17/1793. Of Judith, a minor over 14. Gdn. Archibald McMurphy, Londonderry esq. Bond L1000.0.0. Sureties: Daniel Runnels, esq. and John McKeen, gent., both of Londonderry. Witnesses: John Morrison and Nathl. Parker.

2238. ROLFE, PAUL (1773) #4064 & (1785) #5105
GDP. Of the son of Benjamin Rolfe, Concord esq. decd. GDP. (#4064): 12/17/1773. Of Paul, a minor under 14. Gdn. Timothy Walker Jr., Concord merchant. Bond L1000.0.0. Sureties: Timothy Walker, clerk and Abiel Chandler, gent., both of Concord. Witnesses: Robie Morrill and Simon Trumbel. BOND (#5105): 6/11/1785. Of Gdn. Bond L1000.0.0. To account for sale of as much of real est. of the minor as will be necessary to defray the expense of supporting and educating him according to his rank and charges of Gdp., as allowed by an Act of the NH General Court 6/10/1784. Sureties: Peter Green of Concord and Nathaniel Folsom of Exeter, esquires. Witnesses: W. Parker and John Prentice. ACCOUNT (#5105): Of GdP. by Gdn. Allowed 2/6/1797, being consented to by Paul Rolfe. Receipt: Of Paul Rolfe. To Gdn. For L434.19.5 in full of bal. due on Account. Account includes a journey to Cambridge, MA to enter Paul in college.

ROLLINGS. See also Rollins, Rawlings, Rollins

2239. ROLLINGS, JOSEPH (1748/9) A#1473
EST. Of Newington decd. The following Div. recorded as #4962 Rollins & Nutter (1784) belongs here. DIV.: 12/16/1783. Comm.: John Fabyan, Benjamin Adams, Benjamin Miller and Wm. Thompson. To set off to heirs of Samuel Rollins of Newington 1/3 part of the land contained in 2 pieces in Newington, being part of the farm of Joseph Rollins of Newington decd. Divisees: Saloma Nutter, Susanna Rawlings; Heirs of Samuel Rollings decd.-Sarah, Aaron, George and Samuel Rollings. Includes ref. to a Plan of land set off to the heirs of Samuel Rollings which is not in file. This Plan includes an Anthony and a Joseph who not named in text and does not include Saloma. Orig. Archives file includes Will and Invy.

2240. ROLLINGS, REUBEN (1773) #4068
GDP. Of Sanbornton, Strafford Co. GDP. RELEASE: 11/24/1773. Reuben Rollins, Sanbornton, Strafford Co. yoeman, in consideration of L0.05.0 received from David Lawrence of Epping, releases Lawrence from all claims as Gdn. Witnesses: William Parker and David Brewster. Oath 11/24/1773 Rollings to William Parker, JP.

ROLLINS. See also Rawlings, Rawlins, Rollings

2241. ROLLINS, AARON (1790) #5588
EST. Deerfield yoeman decd. ADMIN.: 11/9/1790. Admx. Elizabeth Rollins, widow and Elijah Rollins, yoeman, both of Deerfield. Bond L1000.0.0. Sureties: Jesse Prescut and Jonathan Jenness, Deerfield yoemen. Witness Samuel Parker. INVY.: Appr. 1/15/1791. Comm.: Jesse Prescut, Moses Barnard and Jona. Jenness. Value not tallied. Esti. L301.0.0+. Oaths 1/15/1791 Comm. and Admrs. to Richard Jenness, JP. ACCOUNT: 2/26/1799. Of Admrs. Allowed 2/26/1799 on oath of Elijah Rollins, an Admr., the heirs having seen and approved it.

2242. ROLLINS, JOHN (1782) #4826
EST. Chichester yoeman decd. ADMIN.: 8/5/1782. Admr. David Greely, Loudon yoeman. Bond L1000.0.0. Sureties: David Thomson of Kingston and Samuel Jewett of Exeter, yoemen. Witnesses: Elizabeth Parker and W. Parker. INVY. WARR.: 8/5/1782. Comm.: Joseph Smith and William Tilton, yoemen and John Sanborn, gent., all of Loudon. INVY.: Appr. 10/28/1782. Value L20.10.6. Oaths 10/28/1782 Comm. to Nathan Bachelder, JP. Oath 10/29/1782 Admr. to W. Parker, JP.

2243. ROLLINS & NUTTER (1784) #4962
See A#1473 Joseph Rollings (1748/9)

2244. ROLLINS, THOMAS (1768) A#3506
EST. Lee yoeman decd. LICENSE (D32:117): 4/18/1796. To Jonathan Rollins, Nottingham yoeman, Admr. d.b.n. To sell real est. to amount of L133.00. Orig. Archives file includes Admin. D.B.N., Invy. and Account.

2245. ROWE, DR. BENJAMIN (1790) #5544
EST. Kensington physician decd. testate. WILL: Drawn 11/28/1777. Legatees: Wife-Susanah; Son-Benjamin; Daus.-Mary Rowe, Betty Leavit and Susannah Tilton. Exec.-son Benjamin. His sig. Witnesses: Samuel Prescutt, James Fogg and Elijah Tilton. Codicil: 6/5/1786. As his dau. Betty Leavit is now decd., he makes bequest to her children who live to 21. Gives addl. bequest to dau. Susanna Tilton. His sig. Witnesses: Samuel

Prescutt, Philemon Blake Jr. and Wm. Parker. CERT. WILL (D29:376): 5/17/1790. Presented by Exec. and witnesses Prescutt and Fogg to Will and Prescutt and Parker to Codicil. ADMIN.: 5/17/1790. Exec. Benjamin Rowe, Kensington physician. Bond L1000.0.0. Sureties: James Fogg, husbm. and Saml. Prescutt, gent., both of Kensington. INVY.: Appr. 7/12/1790. Comm.: Samuel Prescutt, Philemon Blake and Joshua Lane. Value L793.7.0. Oaths 9/11/1790 Comm. to Ebenr. Clifford, JP. Oath 9/13/1790 Exec. to W. Parker, JP.

2246. ROWE: JANE, JOSIAH, MOSES & MEHITABEL (1779) #4509
GDP. Of the children of Jonathan Rowe of Kensington decd. PETITION: 10/26/1778. Of Josiah and Jane. They choose Jeremiah Fellows, Kensington blacksmith, as their Gdn. Their sigs. Witnesses: Benja. Rowe and Benj. Rowe Jr. Oaths 10/26/1778 Josiah and Jane to Benja. Rowe, JP. GDP. (D25:48): 2/24/1779. Of: Moses and Mehetabel, minors under 14. Gdn. Winthrop Rowe. Sureties: Benjamin Rowe, esq. and Jeremiah Fellows, yoeman, all of Kensington. GDP. (D25:48): 2/24/1779. Of: Josiah and Jane, minors over 14. Gdn. Jeremiah Fellows. Sureties: Benja. Rowe and Winthrop Rowe.

2247. ROWE, JEREMIAH (1777). #3938
EST. Brentwood yoeman decd. intestate. ADMIN.: 5/28/1777. Admx. Judith Row, Brentwood widow. Bond L300.0.0. Sureties: Jeremiah Rowe, Brentwood yoeman and Daniel Tilton, Exeter esq. Witnesses: Eleazer Ferguson and Wm. Parker Jr. INVY.: Appr. 5/28/1772. Comm.: Jonathan Cram and Joseph Greely. Value not tallied. Esti. L593.0.0+. Oaths 6/8/1772 Comm. to Wm. Parker, JP. DIV. WARR. DIV. WARR.: 10/15/1773. Comm.: Jonathan Cram, Joseph Godfrey, Joseph Shaw, Jonathan Taylor and Joseph Greely, all of Brentwood. To div. the real est. among the Widow and children, giving the widow her Dower and a double share to oldest son. ACCOUNT: 2/1774. Of Admx. Allowed 2/23/1774 with order to Admx. to div. bal. of L103.13.9 3/4 among heirs according to law. DIV.: 10/27/1773. Divisees: The Widow; Sons-Jeremiah (oldest) and Aretas; Daus.-Judith Hanes and Charloty (youngest dau.). Oaths 10/27/1774 Cram, Godfey and Greely to Wm. Parker, JP.

2248. ROWE, JONATHAN (1778) #4479
EST. Kensington yoeman decd. testate. WILL: Drawn 6/8/1778. Legatees: Sons-Jonathan, Josiah and Moses; Daus.-Abigail Smith, Jane Rowe and Mehittable Rowe. Exec.-son Jonathan. His sig. Witnesses: Ebenezer Swasey, Nathaniel Weare and Benjamin Rowe. CERT. WILL: (24:340): 9/30/1778. Presented by Exec. and witnesses Swasey and Rowe, esquires. INVY.: Appr. 12/9/1778. Comm.: John Lane, esq.; Samll. Tucke, gent.

and Ebenr. Potter. Value L1874.0.0. Oaths 12/14/1778 Comm. to Benja. Rowe, JP. Oath 12/29/1778 Exec. to W. Parker, Reg. & JP.

2249. ROWE, JOSEPH (1773) #4038
EST. Kensington yeoman decd. testate. WILL: Drawn 6/1/1769. Legatees: Wife Ruth; Sons-Joseph and Sherburne; Daus.-Ruth Page, Hitty Manfield, Jane Rowe and Elizabeth Rowe. Exec.-son Joseph. His sig. Witnesses: Eliza Parker, Nicholas Dudley and William Parker Jr. CERT. WILL: 8/23/1773. Presented by Exec. and witnesses William Parker Jr. and Elizabeth Parker. INVY. WARR.: 8/23/1773. Comm.: Jeremiah Lane of Hampton Falls and Elisha Blake of Kensington, yeomen. INVY.: Appr. 8/26/1773. Value L484.7.5. Oaths 9/9/1773 Comm. and Exec. to Wm. Parker, JP.

2250. ROWE: JOSEPH & MOSES (1796) #6264
GDP. Of the sons of Sherburne Rowe, Candia yoeman decd. GDP.: 10/8/1796. Of: Moses and Joseph, minors over 14. Gdn. Stephen Fifield, Candia yoeman. Bond $2,000.00. Sureties: Chase Smith and Isaiah Rowe, Candia yoemen. Witnesses: Walter Robie and Benj. Batchelder.

2251. ROWE, PAINE (1795) #6126
GDP. Hampton Falls gent. adjudged n.c.m. PETITION: 7/27/1795. Of Benjamin Leavitt, Hampton Falls yoeman. States his friend and neighbor is debilitated with infirmities of old age and needs a Gdn. Order: 7/27/1795. To Hampton Falls Selectmen. To make inquisition into state of Paine. Return: 7/27/1795. Of: David Nason, Peter Tilton and George Fifield, Hampton Falls Selectmen. They judge Paine to be n.c.m. and in need of a Gdn. GDP.: 7/31/1795. Of Paine Rowe, Hampton Falls yoeman, an adult adjudged n.c.m. Gdns.: David Nason and Michael Tilton, Hampton Falls husbandmen. Bond $3,000.00. Surety Benjamin Leavitt, Hampton Falls husbm. Witnesses: Elizabeth Parker and W. Parker. INVY.: Appr. 8/20/1795. Comm.: James Prescott, Benjamin Leavitt and James Sandborn. Value L370.8.6. Oaths 9/23/1795 Comm. and David Nason, a Gdn., to W. Parker, JP. LIST OF CLAIMS: 9/21/1795. Of David Nason, a Gdn. Total L156.10.0.

ROWEL. See also Rowell

2252. ROWEL, ENOCH (1776) #4290
EST. Candia housewright decd. Admin.: 12/21/1776. Admx. Miriam Rowell, Candia widow. Bond L500.0.0. Sureties: Willm. Baker, yoeman and Saml. Mooers, esq., both of Candia. Witnesses: John Sargent and Jacob Bagley. INVY.: Appr. 3/21/1777. Comm.: Nathl. Eastman, esq.;

Abram. Fitts, gent. and Willm. Baker, esq. Value not tallied. Esti. L196.0.0+. Oaths 3/24/1777 Comm. and Admx. to Saml. Mooers, JP. DIV. WARR.: 5/30/.1781. Comm.: John Sargent, Benjamin Bachelder and Jonathan Bagley, gentlemen; John Lane and Aaron Brown, yoemen, all of Candia. To div. 2/3 of the real est. among the children, giving two shares to eldest son and one share to each of the others. DOWER WARR.: 5/30/1781. Same Comm. as Div. Of Widow Miriam Rowel. DIV.: 7/11/1781. Divisees: Widow Mirriam Rowel, her dower; Sons-Enoch (oldest), Daniel (2d) and Eliphalet (youngest); Daus.-Mirriam Cammet (oldest), Judith Rowel (2d) and Mary Rowel (3d). Oaths 7/11/1781 Comm. to Saml. Mooers, JP. Allowed 7/25/1781.

2253. ROWEL, JOHN (1791) #5713
EST. Epping yoeman decd. RENUN.: 11/16/1795. Of Hannah Rowell, widow of John. Of Admin. Requests appointment of her oldest son John. Witnesses: Saml. Plumer Jr. and Jonathan Rowell. ADMIN.: 11/16/1791. Admr. John Rowell, Epping yoeman. Bond L1000.0.0. Sureties: Samuel Plumer Jr. and Levi Tilton, Epping yoemen. Witnesses: Volintine Pickering and Nathl. Parker. INVY.: Appr. 1/18/1792. Comm.: Josiah Folsom, Thomas Norris and Saml. Plumer Jr. Value L214.17.3. Oaths 1/18/1792 Comm. to Wm. Parker, JP.

ROWELL. See also Rowell

2254. ROWELL, BENONI (1798) #6453
EST. Salem yoeman decd. intestate. PETITION: 4/18/1798. Of Mary Rowell, widow of Benoni of Salem. Requests admin. be granted to her and her son Israel. Granted. ADMIN.: 4/18/1798. Admrs. Mary Rowell, widow and Israel Rowell, yoeman, both of Windham (sic.). Bond $3,000.00. Sureties: James Betton of Windham and John Morrison of Londonderry, esquires. Witness Jona. Holmes. INVY.: Comm.: Nathl. Gorrell, Jesse Webster and Henry Little. Value L153.92. Oaths 4/27/1798 Comm. to Silas Betton, JP. Oaths 8/15/1798 Admrs. to judge. PETITION: 12/19/1798. Of Admrs. (both of Salem). For Comm. Insolvency. Give claims as about $200.00. Granted. LICENSE (D33:21): 12/19/1798. To Israel Rowell, an Admr. To sell all the real est. BOND: 12/19/1798. Of Israel Rowell, an Admr. Bond $500.00. To account for proceeds of sale of real est. by License. Sureties: Moody Morse, physician and John Morrison, gent., both of Londonderry. Witnesses: Robert Paige and Jeremiah H. Woodman. CLAIMS: Comm.: Jeremiah Dow, Nathl. Gorrell and Moody Morse. Total $203.96. Oaths 7/1/1799 Comm. to Silas Betton, JP. ACCOUNT: 12/18/1799. Of Admrs. Allowed 12/18/1799.

2255. ROWELL, DANIEL (1778) #4431
EST. East Kingston yoeman decd. RENUN.: 2/29/1778. Of Anne Rowell, widow of Daniel. Of Admin. Requests appointment of her son Jacob. Witnesses: Jeremiah Currier and John Blasdel. ADMIN.: 2/25/1778. Admr. Jacob Rowell. Bond L500.0.0. Sureties: Jeremiah Currier and Daniel Busel, Kingston yoemen. Witness James Betton. INVY.: Appr. 3/17/1778. Comm.: Nathl. Bachellor, Ezra Currier and Jeremiah Currier. Value L1119.19.6 with a note that a privilege in a sawmill omitted from Invy. Oaths 3/25/1778 Comm. and Admr. to judge. ACCOUNT: 9/29/1779. Of Admr. Allowed 9/29/1779. APPR. WARR.: 9/30/1779. Comm.: Ezra Currier, gent.; Phillip Morril, Henry Blasdel and Nathaniel Whitcher, yoemen, all of Kingston and Moses Flanders of South Hampton. To view 2/3 of the real est. Div., giving oldest son double share and single share to each of other children or their reps. or appr. APPR.: 11/19/1779. Value L4826.5.0. Oaths 11/19/1779 Comm. to judge. DOWER: 11/19/1779. Comm. same as for Appr. Of Widow Ann Rowell. Includes map. Oaths 11/19/1779 Comm. to judge. DOWER WARR.: 3/9/1780. Comm.: Richard Boynton and Nathl. Bacheldor, esquires; John Blasdell, Thomas Thompson and Jeremigh Currier, yoemen, all of Kingston. Of Widow Ann Rowell. To set off Dower and view 2/3 of realest. to see if it can be div. or appr. DOWER: 3/29/1780. Oaths Comm. to judge. Allowed 3/17/1780. Note: There is no explanation of why there were 2 Dowers, the second appearing to be the same except for a few minor word changes. ACCOUNT: 3/29/1780. Of Admr. Allowed 3/29/1780. DECREE SETTLM.: 3/19/1780. Jacob Rowell, oldest son, appearing and consenting, 2/3 of the real est. settled on him, Jacob to pay each of his co-heirs or their reps. L1128.18.4 within 6 months, with interest. BOND: 3/29/1780. Of Jacob Rowell, Kingston yoeman. Bond L30000.0.0. To pay his co-heirs per Decree Settlm. Sureties: Stephen Long of Sandown and Daniel Rowell of Barrington, Strafford Co., yoemen. Witnesses: Simeon Ladd and Nathl. Parker.

2256. ROWELL, ELIJAH (1774) #4130
EST. South Hampton yoeman decd. intestate. RENUN.: 10/25/1774. Of Jane Rowell, widow. Of Admin. Requests appointment of her son Nathl. Rowell. Oath 10/25/1774 Jane Rowell to Joseph Merrill, JP. ADMIN.: 10/26/1774. Admr. Nathaniel Rowell, South Hampton yoeman. Bond L1000.0.0. Sureties: Joseph Merrill, esq. and James Hadlock, yoeman, both of South Hampton. Witnesses: James Cram and Saml. Hale Jr. INVY.: Appr. 11/3/1774. Comm.: Eliphalet Merrill and Parker Flanders. Value L97.9.1. Oaths 1/24/1775 Comm. to Joseph Merrill, JP. Oath 1/25/1775 Admr. to judge. A note gives several items not inventoried. ACCOUNT: 4/29/1777. Of Admr. Allowed 4/30/1777. DOWER:

7/14/1777. Comm.: Moses Flanders, Benja. Brown, Abel Brown, Israel Sawyer and Joseph Merrill. Of Widow Jane Rowell. Oaths 9/13/1777 Benja. Brown, Flanders and Abel Brown to judge. Allowed. Includes Map.

2257. ROWELL, HANNAH (1783) #4912
EST. Of Hampton decd. testate, widow of Phillip Rowel of New Chaster decd. WILL: Drawn 5/3/1783. Legatees: Bros.-Moses Williams, Thomas Williams and John Williams; Sisters-Sarah Watson and Sister Wells wife of Reuben Wells; Sisters-in-law-Mehetabel Williams wife of her bro. Moses, Alice Williams wife of her bro. John and Sarah Williams wife of her bro. Thomas; Deliverance Gile dau. of her sister Gile decd.; Hannah Wells dau. of her sister Wells. Makes ref. to her "last" husb.'s joyner's tools. Exec.-bro. Moses Williams. Her mark. Witnesses: John Brown, Bethelemew Heath and Samuel Little. CERT. WILL (D27:249): 6/25/1783. Presented by Exec. and witnesses Little, esq. and Brown.

2258. ROWELL, JOHN (1771) #3862
EST. Salem yoeman decd. intestate. RENUN.: 8/7/1771. Of Mary Rowel, widow of John. Of Admin. Requests appointment of Timothy Beedel, esq. WitnessR. Young. ADMIN.: 8/13/1771. Admr. Timothy Beedle, Bath esq. Bond L500.0.0. Sureties: Jacob Tilton and James Dwyer, Portsmouth innholders. Witness Samuel Parker. INVY.: Appr. 8/20/1771. Comm.: Jonathan Wheeler and Robert Young. Value L69.2.7. Oaths 11/4/1771 Comm. to Timothy Ladd, JP. LICENSE: 7/17/1772. To Admr. To sell sufficient real est. to pay debts. ACCOUNT: 2/9/1773. Of Admr. Allowed 2/9/1773. Note: A Docket ref. calls Admr. "Knowell."

2259. ROWELL, MARY (1781) #4686
GDP. Of Sandown widow, an adult adjudged n.c.m. PETITION: 1/11/1781. Of: Sherburne Sanborn and Ezra French, Sandown Selectmen. Request that William Rowel be appointed Gdn. of his mother Widow Mary Rowel, who is n.c.m., for as long as she continues so. Allowed 1/17/1781.

2260. ROWELL, NEHEMIAH (1779) #4563
EST. Portsmouth saddler decd. ADMIN.: 9/27/1779. Admx. Elizabeth Rowell, Portsmouth widow. Bond L2000.0.0. Sureties: George Gains, esq. and Nathaniel Pitman, blacksmith, both of Portsmouth. Witnesses: Nathaniel Clark and John March Jr. INVY. WARR.: 9/27/1779. Comm.: Noah Parker, gent.; Jerh. Libbey, merchant and John Furnald, brazier, all of Portsmouth. INVY.: 10/1779. Value L3559.6.0. Oaths 2/7/1780 Comm. and Admx. to Geo. Gains, JP.

2261. ROWELL, WILLIAM (1785) #5090
EST. Newton esq. decd. testate. WILL: Drawn 8/28/1779. Legatees: Sons-Jacob, William and Christopher (oldest); Daus.-Anne Calfe, Hannah Rogers, Elizabeth Carleton and Sarah Sargent; Grandchildren-Joseph Rowell and Sarah Rowell children of his son William. Exec.-son William. His sig. Witnesses: Timothy Favour, Micah Hoit and Daniel Morse. Codicil: 6/17/1783. He bequeaths part of his est. not yet disposed of and clarifies the meaning of his real est. gifts to his sons. His sig. Witnesses: Timothy Favour, Daniel Morse and Micah Favour. He refers to land called Osgood's lot given to his wife by her mother, part of which his son Christopher and daus. Elizabeth, Hannah and Sarah are entitled to. They are to acquit the land to their bro. Jacob, or if they refuse, his Exec. is not to pay their legacies but give all the money to Jacob. CERT. WILL (D28:105): 3/29/1785. Presented by Hannah Rowell, the Exec. named being dead and witnesses Favour and Morse. ADMIN.: 3/29/1785. Admx. Hannah Rowell, Newton widow. Bond L1000.0.0. Sureties: Daniel Morse and Timothy Favour, Newton yoemen. Witnesses: Micah Favour and William Favour. INVY.: Comm.: Timothy Favour, Eliphalet Bartlet and Robert Stuart. Value L388.4.8. Oaths 6/11/1785 Comm. to Mathias Bartlet, JP and W. Parker certs. that Admx. was sworn at the same "as appears by his separate certificate."

2262. ROWELL, LT. WILLIAM JR. (1785) #5091
EST. Newton gent. decd. ADMIN.: 3/29/1785. Admx. Hannah Rowell, Newton widow. Bond L1000.0.0. Sureties: Daniel Morse and Timothy Favour, Newton yoemen. Witnesses: Thomas Favour and Micah Favour. INVY.: Comm.: Timothy Favour, Eliphalet Bartlet and Robert Stuart. Value L226.2.0. Oaths 6/11/1785 Comm. to Mathias Bartlet, JP and W. Parker attests that Admx. sworn at the same time as appears by separate certificate. PETITION: Dated by clerk 5/17/1786. Of Admx. For License. Gives list of claims of L125.8.0. and main. 2 children. LICENSE (D29:16): 5/17/1786. To Admx. To sell the real est.

RUNDLET. See also Rundlett

2263. RUNDLET, THEOPHILUS (1777) #4381
EST. Stratham yoeman decd. testate. WILL: Drawn 2/15/1774. Legatees: Wife-Leah; Sons-James, Jacob and Theophilus. Daus.-Prissilla Norris, Leah Allene, Esther Smith and Rachel Stockbridge. Exec.-son Jacob. His mark. Witnesses: Joseph Hoit, Daniel Clark and Jonathan Hoit. CERT. WILL: 7/30/1771. Presented by Exec. and witnesses Joseph Hoit, esq. and Clark. ADMIN.: 7/29/1777. Exec. Jacob Rundlet, Stratham yoeman. Bond L500.0.0. Sureties: Daniel Clark, yoeman and Joseph Hoit, esq., both of Stratham. Witnesses: Nathl. Parker and William Parker.

RUNDLETT. See also Rundlet

2264. RUNDLETT, JAMES (1794) #6038
EST. Exeter yoeman decd. ADMIN.: 10/17/1794. Admx. Olive Rundlett, Exeter widow. Bond L1000.0.0. Sureties: James Gordon, Exeter yoeman and Joshua Brown Jr., Epping husbm. Witnesses: W. Parker and N. Parker. INVY.: Appr. 10/1794. Comm.: Jabez Dodge and Joseph Osborne. Value L40.13.10. Oaths 6/1794 Comm. to judge.

2265. RUNDLETT, JOHN (1789) #5468
EST. Stratham saddler decd. testate. WILL: Drawn 3/31/1784. Legatees: Wife-Mary; Sons-William, Noah, Levi, Reuben, Phinehas and Simeon; Daus.-Patte, Mercy, Susanna, Molley and Olive. Exec.-son Simeon. His sig. Witnesses: Saml. Lane, John Stockbridge and Jeremiah Foss. CERT. WILL (D29:290): 7/15/1789. Presented by Exec. and witnesses Lane, esq. and Stockbridge. ADMIN.: 7/15/1789. Exec. Simeon Rundlett, Stratham yoeman. Bond L500.0.0. Sureties: John Stockbridge and Abraham Stockbridge, Stratham yoemen. Witnesses: W. Parker and Nathl. Parker. RECEIPT: 7/15/1789. Of Mary Rundlet, widow. She has received what her husb. gave her in his Will and is fully satisfied. Witness Saml. Lane.

2266. RUSSELL, ELEAZER (1798) #6514
EST. Portsmouth esq. decd. testate. WILL: Drawn 8/22/1798. Legatees: Sisters-Anna and Martha; Kinsman-Daniel Waldron of Dover. Exec.-kinsman Daniel Waldron. His sig. Witnesses: Thos. Marston, Thomas Chadbourn and Andrew Halliburton. CERT. WILL (D32:1): 12/5/1798. Presented by Exec. and witnesses Chadbourn, esq. and Halliburton. INVY. (D33:98): Comm.: Daniel Humphreys, Thomas Chadbourn and Thomas Sparhawk, esquires. Value $3,161.61. Oaths 4/6/1799 Exec. and Comm. to R. Cutts Shannon. LIST OF NOTES: Belonging to est. at Russell's death which have come to hands of Exec. Total $941.00. Note: This file also includes Admin. of est. Elizabeth Gould of Pembroke (1798) #6515 and is recorded there.

2267. RUSSELL: HANNAH, PAGE & RUTH (1798) #6464
GDP. Of the children of James Russell, Bow yoeman decd. PETITION: 5/16/1798. Of Jeremiah Russell, Bow yoemen. His bro. James Russell died leaving three children under 14. Their mother, due to sickness, is an invalid and her senses considerably impaired. As no other person has appeared to be Gdn., requests appointment. Cert. Of Jeremiah Page that Jeremiah Russell's statement is just and he would be a suitable Gdn. Granted. GDP.: 5/16/1798. Of: Page, Hannah and Ruth, minors under 14. Gdn. Jeremiah Russell, Bow yoeman. Bond $2,000.00. Sureties: Samuel

Gault, Bow gent. and Jeremiah Page, Dunbarton, Hillsborough Co. esq. Witnesses: Joseph Baker and Nathl. Parker. LETTER OF GDP.: 5/16/1798. To Jeremiah Russell. PETITION: 9/19/1898. Of: Jeremiah Russell, Gdn., and Ephraim Carter, Admr. est. of the children's father. For certain reasons, it is agreed that Russell relinquish Gdp. and some other person be appointed. They request that Russell be discharged and Capt. John Mills of Dunbarton, Hillsborough Co. be appointed Gdn. GDP.: 9/19/1798. Of Page, Hannah and Ruth, minors under 14. Gdn. John Mills, Dunbarton, Hillsborough Co. gent. Bond $2,000.00. Sureties: Ephraim Carter, Concord gent. and Jeremiah Russell, Bow yoeman. Witnesses: Daniel Knox and Nathl. Parker.

2268. RUSSELL, JAMES (1798) #6467
EST. Bow yoeman decd. RENUN.: 5/26/1798. Of Hannah Russell, widow of James. Of Admin. and all children are minors. Requests appointment of her father Ephraim Carter. Witnesses: Solomon Heath and Dorcas Carter. ADMIN.: 5/26/1798. Admr. Ephraim Carter, Concord gent. Bond $3,000.00. Sureties: David Carter, yoeman and David Stickney, gent., both of Concord. Witnesses: Timo. Walker and Timothy Abbott. INVY. (D33:27):Comm.: Solomon Heath and David Stickney. Value $798.67. Oaths 10/5/1798 Comm. and Admr. to Timo. Walker, JP. ACCOUNT: 9/18/1799. Of Admr. Allowed 9/18/1799 having been consented to by Gdn. of children. Ordered that $20.00 of the bal. be allowed to widow. Note: This file also includes a letter of 1890 (sic.) from Robert Collins to Judge regarding Will of Daniel E. Janvrin which does not belong with this book.

2269. RUSSELL, MARTHA (1799) #6584
EST. Portsmouth single woman decd. intestate. RENUN.: 5/30/1799. Of Anna Russell. Of Admin. of est. her sister. Requests appointment of her friend Daniel Waldron. ADMIN.: 6/19/1799. Admr. Daniel Waldron, Portsmouth merchant. Bond $3,000.00. Sureties: James Sheafe, esq. and Matthew Marsh, merchant, both of Portsmouth. Witnesses: Richd. Salter and Rob. Rice. INVY. WARR.: 6/19/1799. Comm.: Daniel Humphreys and Thomas Chadbourn, esquires and Capt. Thomas Sparhawk, gent., all of Portsmouth. Invy.: Value $615.21. Oaths 10/1799 Chadbourn and Sparhawk and on 10/8 Admr. to R. Cutts Shannon, JP. ACCOUNT: 2/17/1802. Of Admr. Allowed 2/17/1802. Anna Russell, heir, is satisfied with Account.

2270. RUST, DR. RICHARD (1786) #5174
EST. Stratham physician decd. testate. WILL: Drawn 3/3/1784. Legatees: Wife-Martha; Bro.-Henry Rust; Sister-Eleanor Folsom wife of Andrew

Folsom; Niece-Eleanor Folsom dau. of his sister Eleanor. Exex.-wife Martha. His sig. Witnesses: Joseph Merrill, Benjamin Barker Jr. and Levi Giles. CERT. WILL (D28:437): 2/15/1786. Presented by Exex. and witnesses Barker and Merrill. ADMIN.: 2/15/1785. Exex. Martha Rust, Stratham widow. Bond L1000.0.0. Sureties: Paine Wingate, gent. and Joseph Merrill, yoeman, both of Stratham. Witnesses: Josiah Thirston and Mary Wiggin. ACCOUNT: Dated by clerk 1/16/1792. "Danl. Clark's Account of the cost of partition of lands in Exeter." Allowed 1/16/1792. Billed to Saml. Rust, James Leavitt, Judith Odlin and Joseph Young.

2271. RYMES, CHRISTOPHER (1777) #4320
EST. Exeter merchant decd. testate. WILL: Drawn 2/4/1777. Legatees: Wife-Sarah; Dau.-Dorothy Sherburne Rymes; Bro.-Nathaniel Rogers; Sister-Widow Dorothy Coffin; Sister-in-law-Elizabeth Hale; Nephew-John Coffin; Nieces-Dorothy Coffin and Ann Barrel. Execs.-bro. Nathaniel Rogers and Thomas Odiorne. His sig. Witnesses: Beja. Safford, Saml. Folsom Gilman and Jonathan Young York. CERT. WILL (23:468): Presented by Nathaniel Rogers, one of Execs. and all witnesses. INVY.: Appr. 3/25/1777. Comm.: Josiah Barker, Josiah Gilman Jr. and Trueworthy Gilman. Value L1270.14.6. Oaths 7/4/1774 Comm. to Wm. Parker, JP. CITATION: 7/26/1779. To: David Gilman, esq. and Abigail his wife; and Nathaniel Gilman, physician and Ann his wife, all of Exeter. To appear and answer under oath the complaint of Nathaniel Rogers, an Exec., that he suspects some of the goods of decd. have been concealed, embezzled or conveyed away, to which some of the cited may be privy. PETITION: 9/12/1780. Of Widow Sarah Rymes. Requests div. of land to which she has one half for lifetime and Christopher's dau., a minor, has the other half. Order: Petition to be filed and Col. Daniel Gilman, Gdn. of the minor, be notified so he may appear. Consent of Daniel Gilman and they have agreed to a Comm. of Thomas Odiorne and Josiah Gilman, esquires; Josiah Barker, Joseph Lamson and Stephen Thing, yoemen, all of Exeter. DIV. WARR.: 9/12/1780. Comm. as requested. To div. the real est., one half to Widow and one half to dau. DIV.: 10/1/1780. Divisees: Dorothy, the dau. and Widow Sarah Rymes. Oaths 9/5/1781 Lamson, Barker and Gilman to W. Parker, JP. Allowed. The following 2 items are recorded as #4804 Nathaniel Rogers (1782) but belong here: PETITION: 5/3/1782. Of Nathl. Rogers. States that he, Dorothy wife of Anthony Willet, carpenter and Ann Barrel late of Portsmouth, dau. of Colburn Barrel, late of NY, are tenants in common of land partly in Exeter and partly in Brentwood, part of the real est. of Christopher Rymes, Exeter yoeman decd., each owning 1/3. As Ann is a minor and absent, requests div. Order: 5/3/1782. For hearing, Petitioner to advertise in newspaper. COPY OF PETITION. DIV. WARR.: 11/11/1834. Comm.: Benjamin

Ahern of Portsmouth; John Colcord and Daniel Smith of Brentwood. To div. the real est. setting off to Nathaniel Rogers 1/5 part. Note: See #4369 Dorothy Sherburne Rymes for Div. This file includes a copy of the newspaper ad. Judge notes there was no dispute about Petition. No explanation as to why Rogers received 1/5 instead of 1/3 or why the Warr. date of 1834. The file does contain a note that other papers are missing.

2272. RYMES, DOROTHY SHERBURNE (1777) #4369
GDP. & EST. Of Exeter single woman decd. GDP. Of the dau. of Christopher Rymes, Exeter merchant decd. GDP.: 6/26/1777. Of Dorothy Sherburne Rymes, a minor over 14. Gdn. Daniel Gilman, Exeter esq. Bond L500.0.0. Sureties: Nicholas Gilman and Samuel Brooks, Exeter esquires. Witnesses: Nathl. Parker and Wm. Parker. GDP.: 12/27/1780. Of Dorothy, a minor over 14. Gdn. John Taylor Gilman, Exeter merchant. Bond L50000.0.0. Sureties: Simeon Ladd, gent. and Moses Jewett, yoeman, both of Exeter. Witnesses: W. Parker and Nathl. Parker. ADMIN. 11/28/1782 (sic.), but an error as clerk dates '81. Of est. of Dorothy Sherburne Rymes. Admr. Nathaniel Rogers, Newmarket esq. Bond L1000.0.0. Sureties: Jona. Colcord Jr., Newmarket yoeman and Daniel Tilton, Exeter esq. Witnesses: Elizabeth Parker and W. Parker. INVY. WARR.: 11/28/1781. Comm.: Josiah Adams, esq; Samuel Baker, gent. and Jonathn. Colcord Jr., yoeman, all of Newmarket. Invy.: Appr. 5/6/1782. Value L606.4.7. Oaths 10/30/1782 Comm. to judge. DIV.: 11/4/1782. Comm.: Joseph Lamson, Paul Jewett and Capt. Josiah Gilman Jr. To div. the real est. Divisees: Nathaniel Rogers, esq.; Dorothy Carpenter and Ann Barrell. Oaths 11/4/1782 Comm. to Nichl. Gilman, JP. Allowed 11/27/1782. Note: See #4320 Christopher Rymes for Pet. Div.

2273. SALTER: HANNAH & SALLY (1791) #5619
GDP. Of the daus. of Titus Salter of Portsmouth decd. GDP.: 2/16/1791. Of Sally and Hannah, minors over 14. Gdn. Hannah Marshall, Portsmouth widow. Bond L200.0.0. Sureties: Henry Bickford, blockmaker and Elisha Plaisted, joiner, both of Portsmouth. Witnesses: George Hart and Mark Seavey.

2274, SALTER, CAPT. TITUS JR. (1776) #4191
Est. Portsmouth mariner decd. intestate. ADMIN. (D23:204): 9/5/1775. Admx. Hannah Salter. Sureties: Richard Mills and Mark Seavey, all of Portsmouth INVY.: Comm.: Nathl. Treadwell and Jona. Shillaber. Appr. 9/26/1775. Value L536.3.4 1/2. Oaths 1/1776 Admx. and Comm. to judge. ACCOUNT: 6/15/1785. Of William Marshall and Hannah Marshall, Admx. Allowed 6/15/1783. Account includes main. Sarah, Titus and Hannah. BOND: 7/28/1785. Of Mark Seavey, Portsmouth taylor. Bond

L100.0.0. To sue the Bond of Admin. of Hannah Salter, Admx, now Hannah Marshall. Witness W. Parker. PETITION: 2/16/1791. Of Mark Seavey, Portsmouth taylor. Requests div. of a lot of land in Portsmouth held in common with Widow Hannah Marshall and heirs of Titus Salter Jr. Note: The following Div. recorded as #6368 Mark Seavey et. al. (1797) belongs here. DIV.: 4/1/1791. Comm.: Josha. Wentworth, Supply Clap, George Hart, Geo. Gains and Benja. Dearborn. To div. land in Portsmouth as in Pet. Divisees: Mark Seavey (2 shares), Hannah Marshall and Heirs of Titus Salter Jr. Oaths Clap, Hart, Gains and Dearborn, esquires to Oliver Whipple, JP. Allowed 8/22/1797 there being no objections.

2275. SALTER, TITUS (1798) #6516
EST. Portsmouth esq. decd. ADMIN. (D33:7): 12/10/1798. Admrs. Titus Salter, mariner and Samuel Bowles, trader, both of Portsmouth. Sureties: George Wentworth and Richard Cutts Shannon, Portsmouth esquires. INVY. (D33:17): Comm.: Saml. Drowne and Nathl. Marshall. Value $227.11. Oaths 12/20/1798 Comm. and Admrs. to Saml. Penhallow, JP. Note: The entire file for this est. is missing from the original files. At some time the file number was given to 2 ests. but at this time there appears to be no duplication and the Brentwood card index assigns this number to Titus Salter.

SAMBORN. See also Sanborn, Sandborn

2276. SAMBORN, JOHN (1771) #3876 & (1773) #4013
EST. Lee cordwinder decd. testate. WILL (#3876): Drawn 4/30/1770. Legatees: His loving wife; Sons-John, Benjamin and Ebenezer; Daus.-Anne, Elizabeth and Susannah (3 oldest), Dorcas, and Abigail (youngest). Execs.-wife and Benjamin Peas. His sig. Witnesses: James Stacey, Moses Jewet and Jeremiah Bingham. Note says all the witnesses swore in court. INVY. WARR. (#4013): 10/30/1771. Comm.: Joseph Sias, esq. and Saml. James Stevens, yoeman, both of Lee. To be shown by Benjamin Pease and Anna Sandborn, Execs. INVY. (#4013): Appr. 2/24/1772. Value L135.15.9. Oath 2/24/1772 Stevens to Joseph Sias, JP. Oath 7/28/1773 Benjamin Pease, an Admr., to judge.

2277. SAMSON, ABRAHAM (1796) #6243
EST. Londonderry yoeman decd. testate. WILL: Drawn 7/24/1796. Legatees: Wife-Huldy; Sons-Branch and Asa; Daus.-Ruth Samson and Zenthigh Samson. Execs.-son Branch and Amos Phillips. His sig. Witnesses; William Anderson, Jonathan Holms and Elijah Chandler. CERT. WILL (D32:174): 8/17/1796. Presented by Execs. And witnesses Anderson and Holms. ADMIN.: 8/17/1796. Exec. Branch Samson and

Amos Phillips, both of Londonderry. Bond $2,000.00. Sureties: William Anderson and Jona. Holms, both of Londonderry. Witnesses: W. Parker and John Morrison.

SANBORN. See also Samborn, Sandborn

2278. SANBORN, ABNER (1780) #4599
EST. Hampton Falls yoeman decd. testate. WILL: Drawn 3/28/1761. Legatees: Sons-Caleb, Daniel, John, Abner, Timothy and Coffin; Daus.-Elizabeth Smith, Rachel Bennett and Mary Philbrick. Exec.-son Abner. His sig. Witnesses: Meshech Weare, Richard Nason and Francis Marshall. CERT. WILL: 10/25/1790. Presented by Exec. and witness Marshall. Oath 2/28/1780 witness Weare, esq. to Wm. Parker, Reg. & JP. ADMIN.: 2/23/1780. Exec. Abner Sanborn, Hampton Falls yoeman. Bond L10000.0.0. Sureties: Samuel Weare, esq. and Isaac Green, yoeman, both of Hampton Falls. Witnesses: W. Parker and Nathl. Parker.

2279. SANBORN, ABRAHAM (1798) #6485
Est. Exeter gent. decd. testate. CAVEAT: 8/2/1798. Of Moses Pike. Petitions judge not to allow Abraham's Will until there has been a hearing as he has proof that Abraham was not of sound mind when he made it. WILL: Drawn 6/10/1798. Legatees: Wife Mary; Daus.-Mary Shaw and Theodate Pike; Grandson Abraham Sanborn Pike; His grandchildren then alive if grandson Abraham Sanborn Pike dies without issue. Execs.: Wife Mary and son-in-law Benjamin Shaw. His mark. Witnesses: Wm. F. Rowland, Joseph Hoyt and Jeremiah Smith. CERT. WILL (D32:519): 8/23/1789. Presented by Execs. And all witnesses. INVY. (D32:528): Appr. 9/27/1798. Comm.: Gideon Lamson, Caleb Tilton and Jona. Cram. Value $6,548.24. Oaths 9/27/1798 Comm. and on 11/26/1798 Execs. to W. Parker, JP. PETITION: 3/17/1800. Of Execs. For License to sell real est. as most of the est. is out at interest. Granted. LICENSE (D31:224): 3/17/1800. To Admrs. To sell real est. to amount of $2,500.00. BOND: 3/17/1800. Of Execs. Bond $3,000.00. To account for proceeds from sale of real est. by License. Surety Jeremiah Smith, Exeter esq. Witnesses: Mary S. Parker and W. Parker. ACCOUNT: Of Execs. Allowed 3/9/1801 as there was no objection from heirs.

2280. SANBORN: ANDREW & JOSIAH (1772) #3973
GDP. Of the sons Josiah Sanborn decd. GDP.: 12/25/1772. Of: Josiah and Andrew, minors under 14. Gdn. Jeremiah Sanborn, Epping yoeman. Bond L500.0.0. Sureties: Abraham Sanborn, yoeman and Gideon Bartlet, both of Epping. Witnesses: Wm. Parker and Lydia Parker. Note: The file card says "Epping?"

2281. SANBORN: ANNA, MOSES & STEPHEN (1791) #5616
GDP. Of the children of Moses Sanborn, Raymond yoeman decd. GDP.: 1/18/1791. Of: Moses, a minor over 14 and of Stephen and Anna, minors under 14. Gdn. Joseph Dudley, Raymond yoeman. Bond L1000.0.0. Sureties: James Thurston, gent. and Benjamin Boardman, esq., both of Exeter. Witnesses: Peter Hanaford and Isaac Lord. GDP.: 2/7/1791. Of Moses. Gdn. Ebenezer Osgood, Raymond yoeman. Bond L500.0.0. Sureties: Jonathan Dearborn, Raymond gent. and Eliphalet Ladd, Exeter esq. Witnesses: W. Parker and N. Parker.

2282. SANBORN, BENJAMIN (1782) #4818
EST. Sandown yoeman decd. intestate. ADMIN.: 6/26/1782. Admx. Hannah Sanborn, Sandown widow. Bond L1000.0.0. Sureties: James Thom and Jacob Thom, both of Kingston. Witness Nathl. Parker. INVY. WARR.: 6/26/1782. Comm.: Robert Collins, gent; David Moulton, yoeman and Daniel Kelley, joiner, all of Sandown. INVY.: Value not tallied. Esti. L117.0.0+. Oaths 9/2/1782 Comm. to Reuben Clough, JP. Oath 9/25/1782 Admx. to judge.

2283. SANBORN, BENJAMIN (1796) #6216
GDP. Of the son of Daniel Sanborn, Chichester yoeman decd. GDP.: 5/18/1796. Of Benjamin, a minor over 14. Gdn. Jeremiah Sanborn, Chichester yoeman. Bond $3,000.00. Sureties: Joseph Sanborn, Chichester gent. and Josiah Knowles, Epsom yoeman. Witness Allen Gilman.

2284. SANBORN: BETTY, HANNAH, HENRY & RHODA (1785) #5085
GDP. Of the children of Henry Dearborn Sanborn of Exeter decd. GDP.: 3/16/1785. Of: Henry, a minor over 14 and of Rhoda, Betty and Hannah, minors under 14. Gdn. Jacob Blasdel, Epping gent. Bond L1000.0.0. Sureties: Josiah Robinson and Abraham Sanborn, Exeter gentlemen. Witness Nat. Parker.

2285. SANBORN, CALEB (1794) #6013
EST. Hampton Falls esq. and gent. decd. testate. WILL: Drawn 12/16/1777. Legatees: Wife-Mehetable; Son-Meshech; Daus.-Judith Sanborn, Rachel Lamson and Molley Stivers. Exec.-son Meshech. His sig. Witnesses: Abner Sanborn Jr., Joseph Wells and Zebulon Hilyard. CERT. WILL (D31:325): 7/16/1794. Presented by Exec. and witness Sanborn, Wells being dead and Hilyard at a distance though in county. Oath 8/13/1794 Hilyard to judge. ADMIN.: 7/16/1794. Exec. Meshech Sanborn, Hampton Falls husbm. Bond L3000.0.0. Sureties: Abner Sanborn, Hampton Falls hubam. and Dudley Sanborn, Chichester gent. Witnesses:

Nathl. Parker and Wm. Parker. INVY.: Comm.: Abner Sanborn, Benja. Pike and George Fifield. Value L1206.5.0. Oaths 8/28/1794 Comm. to Caleb Tilton, JP.

2286. SANBORN, DANIEL (1782) #4848
EST. Brentwood husbm. decd. testate. WILL: Drawn 6/29/1772. Legatees: Wife-Abigail; Sons-Josiah, Abraham, Daniel and John Prescut Sanborn; Daus.-Elizabeth Sanborn, Huldah Sanborn, Lydia Sanborn and Rebeckah Judkins wife of Joseph Judkins. Exec.-son Daniel. His sig. Witnesses: Jeremiah Bean, Abraham Morril and Joseph Greeley. CERT. WILL (D27:70): 10/30/1782. Presented by Exec. and witnesses Morril and Greeley. INVY.: Appr. 11/28/1782. Comm.: Levi Morrill and Abraham Morril. Value L265.0.9. Oaths 1/25/1783 Comm. to William Morrill, JP. Oath 1/25/1783 Exec. to W. Parker, JP. ADDL. INVY.: Dated by clerk 11/1783. Value L30.6.6. ACCOUNT: 12/17/1783. Of Exec. Allowed 12/17/1783.

2287. SANBORN, DANIEL (1787) #5277
EST. North Hampton esq. decd. testate. WILL: Drawn 8/22/1764. Legatees: Wife-Kathrine; Sons-Daniel, Thomas, Moses of Raymond, Aaron and Abijah; Daus.-Ann Thomas, Kathrine Foss, Rachel Piper, Sarah Jewell and Phebe Dearborn. Exec.-son Thomas. His sig. Witnesses: Stephen Page, Christopher Smith and Josiah Sanborn. CERT. WILL (D29:129): 6/20/1787. Presented by Exec. and all witnesses.

2288. SANBORN, EBENEZER (1794) #5995
EST. North Hampton gent. decd. testate. WILL: Drawn 2/20/1779. Legatees: Sons-John, Josiah, Benjamin, Ebenezer and William; Daus.-Ruth Leavitt and Elisabeth Leavitt; Heirs of dau. Anne decd. Exec.-son William. His sig. Witnesses: Josiah Hobbs, Jacob Low and Christopher Smith. CERT. WILL (D31:265): 5/7/1794. Presented by Exec. and witnesses Low and Smith. ADMIN.: 5/7/1794. Exec. William Sanborn, North Hampton yoeman. Bond too water damaged to read. Sureties: Jacob Low, Stratham cooper and Christopher Smith, North Hampton gent. Witnesses: W. Parker and Jno. Parker.

2289. SANBORN, ELIPHALET (1794) #6025
EST. Epsom gent. decd. testate. WILL: Drawn 8/3/1790. Legatees: Wife-Margaret; Sons-William, Andrew, Simon, Caleb, Eliphalet Jr. and Josiah; Daus.-Lydia McGaffey, Rachel Sanborn, Margaret Sanborn and Jane Sanborn. Exec.-son Josiah. His mark. Witnesses: Reuben Sanborn, David McC. Hendricks and Michl. McClary. CERT. WILL (D31:353): 9/17/1794. Presented by Exec. and witnesses Sanborn and McClary.

CERT.: 9/17/1794. Of Margaret Sanborn, widow of Eliphalet. She accepts provision made for her in Will in lieu of her Dower and is content no Invy. be taken as she has already received from Exec. the households goods given to her. Witnesses: Nathl. Allen and Anna Sanborn. ADMIN.: 9/17/1794. Exec. Josiah Sanborn, Epsom husbm. Bond L1000.0.0. Sureties: Reuben Sanborn, yoeman and Michael McClary, esq., both of Epsom. Witnesses: Philip Sargent and W. Parker.

2290. SANBORN, ELISHA (1787) #5243
EST. Brentwood esq. decd. testate. WILL: Drawn 10/17/1786. Legatees: Wife-Lydia; Sons-Elisha, John and Edward; Dau.-Lydia Sanborn. Makes ref. to his "bro." Stephen Leavitt decd. Exec.-son Edward. His sig. Witnesses: Nathaniel Trask, Nathaniel Graves and Hawley Marshall Jr. Proved 1/17/1787 on oaths of witnesses Graves and Marshall. INVY.: Appr. 2/22/1787. Comm.: Thos. Stow Ranney and Nathaniel Graves. Value L530.19.2. Oaths 2/27/1787 Comm. and Exec. to W. Parker, JP.

2291. SANBORN, ELIZABETH (1773) #4029
EST. Hampton spinster decd. testate. WILL: Drawn 5/8/1773. Legatee Dudley Lamprey, a minor, son of her cousin Daniel Lamprey. Exec.-cousin Daniel Lamprey. Her mark. Witnesses: Joseph Dow, Nathan Brown and James Hobbs. Proved 6/30/1773 on oaths of Dow and Brown.

2292. SANBORN, ENOCH (1794) #6026
EST. Poplin yoeman decd. intestate. ADMIN.: 9/18/1794. Admr. Willoughba Taylor, Sidney, Lincoln Co., MA/ME yoeman. Bond L1000.0.0. Sureties: Stephen Hobbs of Poplin and Levi Hoit of Chester, yoemen. Witnesses: John Wason and Nathl. Parker. INVY.: Appr. 9/23/1794. Comm.: Enoch Brown, Enoch Smith and Stephen Hobbs. Value L65.2.4. Oaths 9/24/1794 Comm. and Admr. to John Scribner, JP. ACCOUNT: 10/1797. Of Admr. Allowed 10/2/1797. Account includes main. a son. PETITION: 10/2/1797. Of Admr. To sell all the real est. as selling less would be injurious to the child, of whom Admr. Is Gdn. Granted. LICENSE (D32:386): 10/2/1797. to Admr. To sell all the real est. BOND: 10/2/1797. Of Admr. Bond L1000.0.0. To account for proceeds of sale of real est. by License. Surety Levi Hoit, Chester yoeman. Witnesses: Nicholas Emery and W. Parker.

2293. SANBORN, HANNAH (1793) #5899
EST. Kingston widow decd. ADMIN.: 5/25/1793. Admr. Samuel Stevens, Kingston yoeman. Bond L1000.0.0. Sureties: Joseph Fifield, Kingston gent. and Jonathan Swain, Raymond esq. Witnesses: N. Parker and W. Parker. INVY.: Appr. 5/28/1793. Comm.: Saml. French, Amos Gale and

Eliphalet Webster. Value L57.10.9. Oaths 5/29/1793 Gale and Webster to Simmons Seccombe, JP. Oath 6/3/1793 Admr. to W. Parker, JP. ACCOUNT: 4/14/1794. Of Admr. Allowed 4/14/1794 there being no objections from heirs.

2294. SANBORN, HENRY (1798) #6470
EST. Epping cordwainer decd. ADMIN.: 6/18/1798. Admx. Anna Sanborn, Epping widow. Bond $3,000.00. Sureties: Henry Sanborn, cordwainer and Winthrop Dow, yoeman, both of Epping. Witnesses: Mary S. Parler and W. Parker. INVY.: Appr. 6/20/1798. Comm.: Samuel Morrill, Winthrop Dow and Joseph Shepard. Value $1,163.00. Oaths 6/20/1798 Comm. and Admx. to Jona. Swain, JP. APPR. WARR.: 1/28/1800. Comm.: Joseph Shepard, Theophilus Blake, Winthrop Dow, Benjamin Folsom and Joseph Peaslee, Epping husbandmen. To appr. 2/3 of the real est. so it may be settled on one or more of his sons. APPR.: 1/30/1800. Value $590.00. Affirm. 1/30/1800 Peaslee, oaths Blake, Dow and Shepard to Ezekl. Godfrey, JP. BILL: 1797. From Henry Dearborn Jr. To Henry Dearborn. Cert.: 3/4/1800. Of: Ebne. Sanborn and Moses Sanborn, heirs. They consent to the Bill and agree that it should be taken out of the appr. of 2/3 of the real est. DOWER: 1/30/1800. Comm. same as for Appr. Of Anna Fifield in est. Henry Sanborn. Oaths 1/30/1800 Shepard, Blake, Dow and Folsom, affirm. Pealsee to Exekl. Godrrey, JP. Allowed. BOND: 3/5/1800. Of: Henry Sanborn and Moses Sanborn, Epping yoemen. Bond $1,100.00. The 2/3 of the real est. having been settled on them, they bond themselves to pay their co-heirs per Decree Settlm. Sureties: David Fifield and Ebenezer Sanborn, Brentwood yoemen. Witnesses: Samuel Smith and Wm. Parker. ACCOUNT: 4/1801. Of David Fifled and Anna his wife, Admx. Allowed 4/27/1801 objections of heirs having been considered. Admx. ordered to distribute bal. to heirs.

2295. SANBORN, HENRY DEARBORN (1785) #5084
EST. Exeter yoeman decd. intestate. ADMIN.: 3/16/1785. Admr. Jacob Blasdel Epping gent. Bond L1000.0.0. Sureties: Josiah Robinson and Abraham Sanborn, Exeter gentlemen. Witnesses: Nathl. Weare and Dudley Hobart. This file includes a Petition for Div. which belongs with #4928 William Sanborn (1783) and is recorded there. The heirs of Henry Dearborn Sanborn are Divisees.

2296. SANBORN: ISRAEL & JONATHAN (1782) #4801
GDP. Of the sons of Jonathan Sanborn, Kingston yoeman decd. GDP.: 4/24/1782. Of: Jonathan and Israel, minors over 14. Gdn. Samuel Sanborn, Sandown gent. Bond L1000.0.0. Sureties: Ebenezer Long and Henry Judkins, both of Kingston. Witness Nathl. Parker.

2297. SANBORN, JAMES (1784) #5055
EST. Kingston husbm. decd. testate. WILL: Drawn 5/12/1772. Legatees: Son-Henry; Dau.-Elizabeth Sanborn. Exec.-son Henry. His sig. Witnesses: Samuel Hobbs, Benjamin James Jr. and Joseph Tilton. CERT. WILL (D27:530): 11/17/1784. Presented by Exec. and witnesses Hobbs and James. INVY.: Appr. 1/12/1785. Comm.: Benjamin Tilton, Benjamin James and Theophilus Sanborn. Value not tallied. Esti. L514.0.0+. Oaths 2/11/1785 Tilton and James to W. Parker, Reg.

2298. SANBORN, JANE (1783) #4872
EST. Of Nottingham decd. ADMIN.: 1/29/1783. Admr. Matthew Nealey Sanborn, her son. Bond L400.0.0. Sureties: Joseph Nealey and Joseph Hodgdon, both of Nottingham. Witnesses: Paul Jewett and Nathl. Parker. APPR. WARR.: 1/29/1783. Comm.: Thomas Bartlet, esq.; Jonathan Gove, gent.; Rice Rowell and John Harvey yoemen and John Ford, blacksmith, all of Nottingham. To view the real est. and see if it can be div. among all the children. Div. or appr. APPR.: Value of 2/3 of real est. L44.0.0. Oaths 3/29/1783 Comm. to Thomas Bartlet, JP. INVY.: Comm.: Thomas Bartlet, esq. and Rice Rowell. Value L44.0.0. Oaths 3/29/1783 Comm. to Benjamin Butler, JP. Oath 4/12/1783 Admr. to W. Parker, Reg. Note: The Invy. and Appr. were the same because there was no personal est. DECREE SETTLM.: 4/12/1783. Matthew Nealey Sanborn, oldest son, appearing and consenting, the real est. settled on him, Matthew to pay oldest bro. and sister L6.4.7 each within 3 months and his youngest bro. and sister the same amount within 12 months, with interest. ACCOUNT: 4/12/1783. Of Admr. Allowed 4/12/1783.

2299. SANBORN, JEREMIAH (1772) #3946
EST. Kensington husbm. decd. testate. WILL: Drawn 12/14/1771. Legatees: Wife-Abigail; Sons-Theophiless, Jeremiah, David and Jonathan; Daus.-Hannah Sandborn, Abigail Sandborn and Rebekah Sandborn. Execs.-wife Abigail and son Theophiless. His sig. Witnesses: Joseph Tilton, Thomas Sanborn and Samuel Hobbs. CERT. WILL (D21:390): 6/24/1772. Presented by Execs. and witnesses Tilton and Hobbs. INVY. WARR.: 6/25/1772. Comm.: Joseph Tilton, esq. and Samuel Hobbs, yoeman, both of Kensington. Invy.: Appr. 6/16/1772. Value not tallied. Esti. L367.0.0+. Oaths 7/30/1772 Comm. and Theophilus Sanborn, an Exec., to judge.

2300. SANBORN, CAPT. JEREMIAH (1784) #4998
EST. Hampton gent. decd. testate. WILL: Drawn 2/24/1783. Legatees: Wife-Lydia; Sons-Jeremiah and John; Daus.-Anna Calley, Mary Perkins, Abigail Leavitt, Lydia Leavitt and Ruth Batchelder. Exec.-son John. His

sig. Witnesses: John Fogg, Henry D. Taylor and William Batchelder. CERT. WILL (D27:441): 4/21/1784. Presented by Exec. and witnesses Taylor and Batchelder. INVY. WARR.: 4/21/1784. Comm.: Dearborn Taylor and John Fogg, both of Hampton and David Fogg of Exeter. INVY.: Appr. 7/20/1784. Value not tallied. Esti. L92.0.0+. Oaths 7/22/1784 Exec. and Comm. to judge.

2301. SANBORN, JETHRO (1781) #4729
EST. Sandown esq. decd. ADMIN.: 7/25/1781. Admx. Elizabeth Sanborn, Sandown widow. Bond L50000.0.0. Sureties: John Sanborn, Sandown yoeman and William Sanborn, Kingston gent. Witnesses: Nathl. Parker and W. Parker. INVY. WARR.: 7/25/1781. Comm.: Timothy Tilton and Benjamin Taylor, gentlemen and John Sleeper, yoeman, all of Sandown. INVY.: Appr. 9/13/1781. Value L198.06.0. as money was in 1775 or L1329.18.0. Oaths 9/19/1781 Tilton, Sleeper and Admx. to Robt. Wilson, JP. Note: It is difficult to tell if of the Invy. L173.8.0 is land in Hopkinton, Hillsborough Co. and L198.8.0 is land in Unity, Cheshire Co. in addition to the total given or are a part of the total.

2302. SANBORN, JOHN (1783) #4880
GDP. Of the son of Benjamin Sanborn, Epping yoeman decd. GDP.: 2/26/1783. Of John, a minor over 14. Gdn. William Lowney, Epping schoolmaster. Bond L1000.0.0. Sureties: Benjamin Dearborn of Epping and Andrew Freese of Deerfield, gentlemen. Witnesses: Benj. Brown and Nathl. Parker.

2303. SANBORN, JOHN (1785) #5127
EST. Newmarket tanner decd. testate. WILL: Drawn 1/21/1785. Legatees: Wife-Sarah; Sons-Israel, John (2 oldest), Jeremiah, Joseph and Daniel; Dau.-Anna. Exec.-Samuel Gilman, esq. His sig. Witnesses: John Gilman, Benjn. Peas and Edward Wells. CERT. WILL: 7/20/1794. Presented by Exec. and witness Wells. Oaths 6/24/1785 Gilman and Peas to Nathl. Folsom, JP. INVY. WARR.: Comm.: Thomas Hanaford and Levi Chapman. Value L104.11.0. Oaths 12/19/1787 Comm. to Enoch Coffin, JP. Oath 12/3/1788 Exec. to W. Parker, JP. ACCOUNT: 2/6/1792. of Exec., who was also atty. to John Sanborn during his lifetime. Allowed 2/6/1792. Note: Exec. gives the Invy. as being only the personal est. He lists many Notes due, "part of which were indorsed to him in John's lifetime, in trust, the business beginning in John's lifetime and completed since by Samuel as atty. and Exec. His final bal. for the income, including personal est., is L1022.16.0. ADDL. ACCOUNT: 1/27/1794. Of Exec. Allowed 1/27/1794.

2304. SANBORN, JOHN JR. (1793) #5900
EST. East Kingston husbm. decd. testate. WILL: Drawn 10/24/1792. Legatees: Wife-Elizabeth; Sons-John, Peter, Stevens, Jacob Hook Sanborn, Phinehas and Moses; Daus.-Molly Sanborn and Hannah Sanborn. Ref. to his late father Tristram Sanborn. Exex.-wife Elizabeth. His sig. Witnesses: Jacob Ordway, Abraham Sanborn and Nathl. Parker. CERT. WILL (D30:439): 5/27/1793. Presented by Exex. and all witnesses. ADMIN.: 5/27/1793. Exec. Elizabeth Sanborn, East Kingston widow. Bond L1000.0.0. Sureties: Jacob Ordway, East Kingston gent. and Jacob Hook, Kingston esq. Witnesses: Abraham Sanborn and W. Parker. INVY.: Appr. 6/13/1793. Comm.: Abraham Sanborn, David Tilton and Jacob Ordway. Value L337.11.7. Oaths 8/7/1793 Tilton, Ordway and Exex. to Nathl. Bachellor, JP.

2305. SANBORN: JOHN, JONATHAN & MOLLY (1794) #5998
GDP. Of the children of Worster Sanborn, Newton yoeman decd. GDP.: 5/19/1794. Of: Jonathan, a minor over 14 and of Molly and John, minors under 14. Gdn. Hannah Sanborn, Newton widow. Bond L1000.0.0. Sureties: John Chase, Plaistow yoeman and Nathan Currier of Amesbury, Essex Co., MA. Witness Mary S. Parker.

2306. SANBORN, JOHN (1795) #6145
EST. Kingston yoeman decd. testate. WILL: Drawn 2/18/1791. Legatees: Wife-Elizabeth; Son-Enoch (or this may be the following. Wording unclear); Son-in-law Enoch Sanborn and dau. Elizabeth. Exec.-son-in-law Enoch Sanborn. His mark. Witnesses: Richard Smith, Edward Greeley and Reuben Greely. CERT. WILL (D32:54):10/6/1795. Presented by Exec. and witnesses Smith and Edward Greeley. ADMIN.: 10/7/1795. Exec. Enoch Sanborn, East Kingston joiner. Bond $2,000.00. Sureties: Richard Smith, gent. and Edward Greeley, both of East Kingston. Witnesses: Wm. Parker and Wm. Duguerny. INVY.: Appr. 11/27/1795. Comm.: David Tilton, Richard Smith and Eliphalet Webster. Value $2,357.99. Oaths 12/1/1795 Comm. and Exec. to Edward Greeley, JP.

2307. SANBORN, JONATHAN (1782) #4800
EST. Kingston yoeman decd. intestate. ADMIN.: 4/24/1782. Admrs.: Samuel Sanborn, Sandown gent. and Mary Sanborn, Kingston widow. Bond L1000.0.0. Sureties: Ebenezer Long and Henry Judkins, Kingston yoemen. Witness Nathl. Parker. INVY. WARR.: 4/24/1782. Comm.: Josiah Bartlett and Jacob Hook, esquires and Ebenezer Long, yoeman, all of Kingston. INVY.: Appr. 5/1/1782. Value not tallied. Esti. L300.0.0+. Oaths 5/28/1782 Hook and Long and on 7/8/1782 Admrs. To Josiah Bartlett, JP. ACCOUNT: Of Admrs. Allowed 9/24/1783. GDP. Of the son

of Jonathan Sanborn, Kingston yoeman decd. GDP.: 9/24/1783. Of Joseph, a minor under 14. Gdn. Mary Sanborn, Kingston widow. Bond 500.0.0. Sureties: Samuel Sanborn of Sandown and Elisha Bachelder of Hawke, husbandmen. Witness Nathl. Parker. DOWER WARR.: 9/24/1783. Comm.: Jonathan Swain of Raymond and Jacob Hook of Kingston, esquires; Simmonds Seccombe and John Eastman, gentlemen and Ebenr. Long, yoeman, all of Kingston. Of Widow Mary Sanborn. DIV. WARR.: 9/24/1783. Comm. same as for Dower. To div. the real est. giving 2 shares to oldest son and single share to each of the other children. DIV.: Divisees: The Widow, her Dower; Sons-Jonathan (oldest), Joseph and Israel. Oaths 1/26/1784 Swain, Hook, Long and Seccombe to Josiah Bartlett, JP. ADDL. ACCOUNT: 4/21/1784. Of Admrs. Allowed 4/21/1784 on oath of Mary Sanborn, an Admr.

2308. SANBORN, JONATHAN (1786) #5231
EST. Newmarket yoeman decd. ADMIN.: 12/20/1786. Admx. Anna Sanborn, Newmarket widow. Bond L1000.0.0. Sureties: John Wedgewood and Jacob Burleigh, Newmarket yoemen. Witness Nathl. Parker. INVY.: Comm.: Enoch Coffin, Jacob Burleigh and Josiah Burleigh. Value not tallied. Esti. L562.0.0+. Oaths 6/18/1787 Admx., Josiah Burleigh and Jacob Burleigh to Enoch Coffin, JP.

2309. SANBORN, JONATHAN (1790) #5550
EST. Hawke gent. decd. testate. WILL: Drawn 9/30/1786. Legatees: Wife-Mary; Sons-John, Jethro and Jonathan; Dau.-Mary wife of Jedediah Philbrick; Heirs of son John; Grandson-Samuel Adams Sanborn. Execs.-sons Jethro and Jonathan. His sig. Witnesses: Abraham Hook., Peter Emerson and Elisha Hook. CERT. WILL (D29:373): 5/27/1790. Presented by Execs. and witnesses Abraham Hook and Elisha Hook. ADMIN.: 5/27/1790. Execs.: Jethro Sanborn and Jonathan Sanborn, Hawke yoemen. Bond L1000.0.0. Sureties: Elisha Hook of Poplin and Abraham Hook of Sandown, gentlemen. Witnesses: Nathl. Parker and W. Parker. INVY.: Comm.: Thos. Page, Abraham Hook and Reuben Hill. Value L870.19.6. Oaths 7/20/1790 Execs., Hook and Hill to Thos. Page, JP.

2310. SANBORN, JONATHAN (1796) #6251
EST. Epping cordwainer decd. testate. WILL: Drawn 5/25/1796. Legatees: Wife-Sarah; Son-James; Daus.-Diedamia Sanborn and Sally Sanborn. Exex.-wife Sarah. His sig. Witnesses: Peter Holt, John Shaw and Eliphalet Cilley. CERT. WILL (D32:182): 9/5/1796. Presented by Exex. and witnesses Shaw and Cilley. ADMIN.: 9/5/1796. Exex. Sarah Sanborn, Epping widow. Bond $3,000.00. Sureties: John Shaw and Eliphalet Cilley, Epping yoemen. Witnesses: Mary S. Parker and W. Parker. INVY.: Appr.

9/27/1796. Comm.: Francis Harvey and Cutting Cilley, both of Nottingham and David Lawrence of Epping. Value $1,285.98. Oaths 9/27/1796 Cilley, Lawrence and Exex. to Benjamin Butler, JP.

2311. SANBORN. LT. JOSEPH (1773) #3988
EST. Hampton Falls gent. decd. intestate. RENUN. 2/1/1773. Of Dorothy Sanborn, widow of Joseph. Requests appointment of Joseph Sanborn and Jeremiah Lane. Witnesses: Thomas Moore and (Rhoda?) Perkins. ADMIN.: 2/1/1773. Admrs.: Joseph Sanborn of Brentwood and Jeremiah Lane of Hampton Falls, yeomen. Bond L500.0.0. Sureties: Ebenezer Neal of North Hampton and Simeon Morgan of Brentwood, yoemen. Witnesses: Joseph Champney, John Parker and Samuel Parker. INVY. WARR.: 2/1/1773. Comm.: Benjamin Moulton and Henry Blake, both of Hampton Falls. INVY. Appraised 2/4/1773. Value L256.2.0. Oaths 2/22/1773 Comm. to Nathn. Healey, JP. Oath 2/24/1773 Admrs. to judge. LICENSE; 10/27/1773. To Admrs. To sell sufficient real est. to pay debts. ACCOUNT: 10/21/1774. Of Admrs. This appears to be only a 2d page with a "Bal. Forward" at top. DOWER WARR.: 3/2/1773. Comm.: Jeremiah Blake, gent.; Samuel Prescutt and David Batchelder, yoemen, all of Hampton Falls. Of Widow Dorothy Sanborn. DOWER: 3/11/1773. Oaths 5/24/1773 Comm. to Nathn. Healey, JP. Allowed 5/26/1773. PETITION: 4/22/1773. Of Widow Dorothy Sanborn. Requests judge to allow her a cow to replace one she received by the death of a dau. she had by another husb., which the Invy. Comm. judged to be of Joseph's est. though Joseph never intended that she should be deprived of it. Also, requests something for some household goods. ACCOUNT: 10/21/1774. Of Admrs. Allowed 10/21/1774.

2312. SANBORN, JOSIAH (1770) A#214
EST. Epping yoeman decd. testate. DOWER (D23:102): 3/2/1773. Comm.: Jacob Burley, Gideon Bartlett and Abraham Perkins. Of Widow Jemima Sanborn. Oaths 3/8/1773 Bartlett and Perkins to David Lawrence, JP. Orig. Archives file includes Will and Invy.

2313. SANBORN, JOSIAH (1789) #5405
EST. Exeter tanner decd. testate. WILL: Drawn 10/5/1784. Legatees: Wife-Deborah; Sons-Josiah and John; Niece-Deborah Rowell; Josiah Chandler son of Thomas Chandler. Exex.-wife Deborah. His sig. Witnesses: Saml. Brooks, Elisabeth Brooks, Mary Brooks and Saml. Hobart. CERT. WILL (D29:238): 1/21/1789. Presented by Exex. and witnesses Samuel Brooks, esq. and Mary Brooks. INVY.: Appr. 3/3/1789. Comm.: John Fogg, Joseph Cram and Seth Fogg. Value L974.10.2. Oaths 4/18/1789 Cram, Seth Fogg and Exex. to W. Parker, Reg.

2314. SANBORN, MESHECH (1797) #6319
EST. Hampton Falls innholder decd. ADMIN.: 3/6/1797. Admx. Hannah Sanborn, Hampton Falls widow. Bond $3,000.00. Sureties: Abner Sanborn and Nathaniel Hubbard Dodge, Hampton Falls yoemen. Witness W. Parker. INVY.: Comm.: Abner Sanborn, Nath. H. Dodge and George Fifield. Value L971.18.0. Oaths 4/14/1797 Comm. to Elisha Brown, JP. Oath 4/15/1797 Admx. to judge. PETITION: 4/15/1797. Of Admx. For License. Gives claims already known as $1,328.17. Granted. LICENSE (D32:288): 4/15/1797. To Admx. To sell real est. to amount of $1,020.00. BILL: 12/1/1797. From Davis Nason. To est. Total $136.50. For various services. Cert.: Dudley Dodge, Gdn. of 2 of the children and Nathl. Chase, husb. of the other. They approve of the Bill. ACCOUNT: Of David Nason and Hannah his wife, Admx. Allowed 3/22/1803. Account includes main. 1 child. ADMIN. D.B.N.: 3/22/1803. Admr. d.b.n. David Nason, Hampton Falls yoeman. Bond $2,000.00. Sureties: Joseph Dow of Hampton Falls and Nathaniel Weare of Deerfield, esquires. Witness W. Parker. PETITION: 3/22/1803. Of Admr. d.b.n. For License to settle the bal. due from last Account. Granted. LICENSE (D34:303): 3/22/1803. To Admr. d.b.n. To sell real est. to amount of $350.00. PETITION: 11/28/1804. Of Admr. d.b.n. For License as another claim of $119.75 has been presented. LICENSE: 11/28.1804. To Admr. d.b.n. To sell real est. to amount of $130.00. DOWER WARR.: 11/28/1804. Comm.: Theophilus Sanborn and Aaron Merrill, gentlemen.; Moses Wells, innholder; Joseph Dow, esq. and Thomas Leavitt, yoeman, all of Hampton Falls. Of Hannah Nason wife of David Nason in est. Meshech Sanborn. DOWER: Oaths 12/6/1804. Comm. to Peter Tilton, JP. Allowed. DIV.: Comm.: Same as for Dower. To div. 2/3 of the real est. Divisees: Daus.-Sophia Chase wife of Nathaniel Chase (oldest), Hariot (2d) and Charlotte (3d). Oaths 12/6/1804 Comm. to Peter Tilton, JP. Allowed. ACCOUNT: 12/11/1804. Of Admr. d.b.n. Allowed 12/11/1804 having been consented to by the husb. of the heir of age and the Gdn. of the minor heir.

2315. SANBORN, MOSES (1779) #4583
EST. Raymond yoeman decd. ADMIN. (D25:200): 6/17/1779. Admx. Judith Sanborn, Raymond widow. Sureties: Joseph Dudley and Reuben Tilton, Raymond yoemen. INVY.: 9/29/1779. Comm.: Jona. Swain, Joseph Dudley and Reuben Tilton. Value L1863.18.0. Oaths 11/20/1779 Swain, Tilton and Admx. to John Dudley, JP. APPR. WARR.: 6/21/1786. Comm.: Jonathan Swain, esq.; John Fullerton, gent. and Benja. Cram, yoeman, all of Raymond. To appr. the neat income of 2/3 of the real est. for the last 8 years, including the current year. APPR.: 11/11/1786. Value L6.0.0 per year. ACCOUNT: 11/18/1789. Of Judith Meloon, Admx. Examined 11/18/1789 and Admx. ordered to notify heirs to attend next

court and make any objections they may have to its being allowed. Account includes main. 1 child. ACT OF NH GENERAL COURT: Passed Senate 12/11/1791 and House 12/13/1792. Granting the Petition of Judith Meloon wife of Josiah Meloon of Raymond to complete the Admin. of est. her former husb. Moses Sanborn decd. Admin. was granted to her about 12 years ago, but Josiah Mellon "refuses to intermeddle with settlement and has absconded." ADMIN.: 1/14/1793. Admx. Judith Meloon wife of Josiah Meloon of Raymond. To admin. the est. of Moses Sanborn as if she were a femsole. Bond L500.0.0. Sureties: Jeremiah Holman, gent. and Moses Sanborn, yoeman, both of Raymond. Witnesses: Jno. Parker and John Prescut (Louren?). PETITION: 1/22/1793. Of Moses Sanborn on behalf of Admx. For License. Includes list claims of L41.7.10 1/2 and will be others. Granted. LICENSE (D30:352): 1/22/1793. To Admx. To sell real est. to amount of L50.0.0. ADDL. ACCOUNT: 1/13/1794. Of Admx. (sig. Mellon). Allowed 1/13/1794.

2316. SANBORN, NATHAN (1784) #4999
EST. Epping yoeman decd. testate. WILL: Drawn: 7/6/1775. Legatees: Wife-Cattarine; Sons-Nathaniel and Nathan; Daus.-Hannah Cass and Mary Dow. Exec.-son Nathan. His mark. Witnesses: Edward Lawrans, Paul Brown and Abraham Perkins. CERT. WILL (D27:433): 4/21/1784. Presented by Exec. and witnesses Brown and Perkins.

2317. SANBORN, PETER (1797) #6383
GDP. Of the son of Enoch Sanborn, Poplin taylor decd. GDP.: 10/2/1797. Of Peter, a minor under 14. Gdn. Willowba Taylor, Sidney, Lincoln Co., MA/ME yoeman. Bond $1,000.00. Surety Levi Hoit, Chester yoeman. Witnesses: Wm. P. Adams and W. Parker.

2318. SANBORN, PHINEAS (1773) #4014
EST. Hawke husbm. decd. testate. WILL: Drawn 7/7/1773. Legatees: Wife- Mary; Son and only child Samuel Adams Sanborn; Bros.-John, Jethro and Jonathan if his son dies. Execs.: Wife Mary and bro. Jethro. His sig. Witnesses: John Page, Thos. St. Ranney and Zaccheus Cholby. CERT. WILL.: 7/28/1773. Presented by Execs. and witnesses Rev. Page and Dr. Ranney. ADMIN.: 7/28/1773. Execs.: Jethro Sanborn, yeoman and Mary Sanborn, widow, both of Hawke. Bond L500.0.0. Sureties: John Page, Hawke clerk and Joseph Wright, Salem esq. Witnesses: Joseph Dudley and Samuel Parker.

2319. SANBORN: PHINEHAS & TRISTRAM (1773) #4030
GDP. Of the sons of Joshua Sanborn, Epping yeoman decd. GDP.: 6/30/1773. Of Phinehas, a minor over 14. Gdn. Jacob Burleigh of

Newmarket. Bond L100.0.0. Surety Daniel Sanborn of Epping. Witnesses David Bacheler and Samuel Parker. GDP.: 5/30/1781. Of Tristram, minor over 14. Gdn. Moses Dolton, Epping blacksmith. Bond: L30000.0.0. Sureties: Simon Dearborn, gent. and John Towle, yoeman, both of Epping. Witnesses: Wm. Parker Jr. and W. Parker.

2320. SANBORN, RICHARD (1773) #4047
EST. Kensington husbm. decd. testate. WILL: Drawn 4/28/1772. Legatees: Wife-Judith; Sons-Jonathan, Richard and Moses; Heirs of his son David; Heirs of his dau. Mary Cough; Children of his son Jeremiah-Theophilus, David, Jonathan, Hannah Sanborn, Abigail Sanborn and Rebekah Sanborn; Great granddau.-Betty Page dau of Daniel Page. Exec.-grandson Theophilus. His sig. Witnesses: Joseph Tilton, Samuel Hobbs and William Brown. CERT. WILL: 9/29/1773. Presented by Exec. and witnesses Hobbs and Brown. INVY. WARR.: 9/29/1773. Comm.: Samuel Hobbs and Jeremiah Bachelder, both of Kensington. INVY.: Appr. 10/19/1773. Value not tallied. Esti. L442.0.0+. Oaths 11/1/1773 Comm. and Exec. to Wm. Parker Jr., JP. CITATION: 1/30/1777. To Exec. To appear and answer a Petition of John Prescott on behalf of Judith Sanborn, relict of Richard, for her Dower. Exec. appeared, had no objection, so a Dower Warr. ordered.

2321. SANBORN, TRISTRAM (1789) #5495
EST. Kingston yoeman decd. testate. WILL: Drawn 10/13/1789. Legatees: Wife- unnamed; Son-John; Daus.-Elizabeth wife of Joseph Fifield and Mary wife of Samuel Stevens; Grandson-Stevens Sanborn son of his son John; Granddau.-Hannah Fifield dau. of his dau. Hannah Fifield decd. Exec.-son John. His sig. Witnesses: Richard Jenness, Thomas Mathis and Simon Norton. CERT. WILL (D29:314): 11/18/1789. Presented by Exec. and all witnesses. ADMIN.: 11/18/1789. Exec. John Sanborn, Kingston husbm. Bond L500.0.0. Sureties: Richard Jenness, esq. and Simon Norton, yoeman, both of Deerfield. Witnesses: Richard Jenness and Nathl. A. Haven. INVY.: Appr. 12/15/1789. Comm.: Richard Jenness, esq. ; David Tilton and Jacob Ordway. Value L316.16.9. Oaths 1/7/1790 Tilton, Ordway and Exec. to judge. ACCOUNT: 11/17/1790. Of Admr. Allowed 11/17/1790.

2322. SANBORN, WILLIAM (1772) #3929
EST. Of Deerfield, decd. testate. WILL: Drawn 11/14/1771. Legatees: Wife-Eunice; Dau.-Mary Moulton Sanborn. Exex.-wife Eunice. His mark. Witnesses: William Sanborn, Simon Marston and Enoch Robie. Note: Gives his daughter "all his first wife's household goods and clothes." CERT. WILL: 4/29/1772. Presented by Admx. and witnesses Sanborn and

Marston. ADMIN.: 4/29/1772. Exex. Eunice Sanborn, Deerfield widow. Bond L500.0.0. Sureties: Simon Marston, Deerfield gent. and William Sanborn, Exeter gentleman. Witnesses: Saml. Hale Jr. and Samuel Parker.

2323. SANBORN, WILLIAM (1783) #4928
EST. Exeter yoeman decd. testate. WILL: Drawn 6/20/1783. Legatees: Wife-Elisabeth; Sons-Simon and Josiah; Daus.-Elisabeth Sanborn wife of Daniel Sanborn of Brentwood, Hannah Chase, Mary Chase, Anne Sanborn wife of John Sanborn of Exeter; Elisabeth Sanborn widow of his son Henry Dearborn Sanborn; Children of his son Henry Dearborn Sanborn; Grandson-Jonathan Sanborn Cram. Exec.-son Simon; His mark. Witnesses: Patton Simpson, Moses Chase and Dudley Ladd. CERT. WILL (D27:290): 8/26/1783. Presented by Exec. and witnesses Chase and Ladd. DIV. WARR.: 10/29/1783. Josiah Robinson, gent. and Daniel Jones, blacksmith, both of Exeter; Jeremiah Lane, Stephen Tilton and Nehemiah Cram, all of Hampton Falls. To div. the real est. in 3 equal parts according to Will. INVY.: Appr. 11/18/1783. Comm.: Josiah Robinson, Jeremiah Lane and Stephen Tilton. Value L1567.16.0. Oaths 2/18/1784 Robinson, Tilton and Exec. to W. Parker, Reg. DIV.: 12/26/1783. Divisees: Widow Elisabeth Sanborn; Simon Sanborn, son; Elisabeth Sanborn widow of Henry Dearborn Sanborn. Oaths 11/17/1784 Comm. to judge. Allowed. Includes Map. The following Petition found in #5084 Henry Dearborn Sanborn (1785) belongs here. PETITION: 9/19/1791. Of Simon Sanborn. Requests div. of that part of the est. of William Sanborn, Hampton Falls yoeman which was the Dower. He and the Heirs of Henry Dearborn Sanborn are tenants in common. The Gdn. of heirs being present consented to Petition. Parties agreed upon a Comm. of Jeremiah Bachdelder, gent.; Ebenezer Clifford, esq., both of Kensington; Caleb Tilton, esq., James Prescutt Jr. and George Fifield, gentlemen, all of Hampton Falls. Signed by W. Parker, Reg. DIV.: Comm. as in Petition. Divisees: Heirs of Henry Dearborn Sanborn late of Exeter decd. and Simon Sanborn. Oaths 9/25/1791 Prescutt, Bachelder, Tilton and Fifield to Ebenr. Clifford, JP. Oath 9/28/1791 Ebenezer Clifford to Caleb Tilton, JP. Allowed. ACCOUNT: 11/19/1791. Of Exec. Allowed 6/18/1792.

2324. SANBORN, WINTHROP (1796) #6291
EST. Hampton husbm. decd. testate. WILL: Drawn 1/2/1795. Legatees: Wife-Abigail; Son-Abner; Dau.-Molly Blake; Grandson-Josiah Sanborn; Granddau.-Abigail Hale. Execs.-Major Josiah Dearborn and wife Abigail. His sig. Witnesses: Simon Marston, Saml. Page and Isaiah Dow. CERT. WILL (D32:232): 12/26/1796. Presented by Execs. and witnesses Marston and Dow. ADMIN.: 12/26/1796. Execs.: Josiah Dearborn, esq. and Abigail Sanborn, widow, both of Hampton. Bond $2,000.00. Sureties: Simon

Marston and Isaiah Dow, Hampton yoemen. Witnesses: Joseph Dow and Morris Hobbs. INVY.: Appr. 3/15/1797. Comm.: Jonathan Marston, Philip Towle and John Drake. Value $1,657.00. Oaths 3/15/1797 Towle and Drake and on 3/17/1797 Execs. to Christo. Toppan, JP.

2325. SANBORN, WOSTER (1794) #5999
EST. Newton yoeman decd. testate. WILL: Drawn 4/11/1794. Legatees: Wife-unnamed; Sons-Josiah, Jonathan, William, Ebenezer and John; Daus.-Dotey, Elizabeth and Mary. Makes ref. to his daus. "1st mother." Execs.-wife and John Chase of Plaistow. His sig. Witnesses: Nathan Currier, Sarah Andrews and John Chase. CERT. WILL (D31:274): 5/19/1794. Presented by Hannah Sanborn, an Exec. named, the other refusing, and witnesses Currier and Chase. RENUN.: 5/19/1794. Of John Chase, Plaistow joiner. Of Admin. Witness W. Parker. ADMIN.: 5/19/1794. Exex. Hannah Sanborn, Newton widow. Bond L1000.0.0. Sureties: John Chase, Plaistow joiner and Nathan Currier, Amesbury, Essex Co., MA yoeman. Witnesses: Joseph Akerman and W. Parker. INVY.: Appr. 6/2/1794. Comm.: Francis Chase Jr., Mark Whittier and John Chase. Value L286.7.6. Oaths 7/3/1794 Comm. to John White, JP. Oath 7/11/1794 Exex. to Matthias Bartlet, JP.

SANDBORN. See also Sanborn

2326. SANDBORN, JOSIAH (1772) #3972
EST. Epping yoeman decd. intestate. ADMIN.: 12/24/1772. Admr.: Jeremiah Sandborn, Epping yoeman, "in the room of Abra. Sanborn who resigns that trust." Bond L500.0.0. Sureties: Abra. Sanborn and Gideon Bartlet, Epping yoemen. Witnesses: William Parker and Catharine Parker. DOWER WARR.: 12/24/1772. Comm.: Abraham Perkins, innholder; Gideon Bartlet, Jacob Burley, Job Perkins and Timo. Jones, yoemen, all of Epping. Of Jemima Sandborn. DOWER: 3/2/1773. Oaths 3/8/1773 Burley, Bartlet and Perkins to David Lawrence, JP.

SANDER. See also Sanders, Saunders

2327. SANDER, CAPT. WILLIAM (1782) #4862
EST. Salem gent. decd. testate. WILL: Drawn 8/29/1782. Legatees: Wife-Elizabeth; Son-James; Daus.-Mary wife of Caleb Balch and Easther wife of Jonathan Gordon; Grandson-William Sanders son of his son James; Execs.-son James and son-in-law Caleb Balch. His sig. Witnesses: Jeremiah Dow, Saml. Sweetra and Timothy Ladd. CERT. WILL (D27:115): 11/27/1782. Presented by Execs. and witnesses Dow and Ladd. Widow Elizabeth approves and accepts the provision made for her in Will.

Same witnesses as Will. INVY. WARR.: 11/27/1782. Comm.: Timothy Ladd, esq.; Jerh. Dow, gent. and Wm. Duty, yoeman, all of Salem. INVY.: Appr. 12/26/1782. Value L679.2.9. Oaths 2/26/1782 Dow, Duty and Execs. to Timothy Ladd, JP. LETTER: From: James Saunders, Caleb Balch and Jonathan Gordon. To judge. They notify judge that they have appointed Deacon Samuel Morison, Windham yoeman, for one of the Comm. to settle the est. of Capt. Wm. Saunders of Salem instead of Mr. David Nevens. They note men formerly appointed were Capt. John Emery, Derry gent.; Wm. Stevens, Salem cordwainer and David Nevens. REFEREES WARR.: 4/21/1790. James Sanders of Salem, one of the Execs., has demands against the est. which are objected to by Caleb Balch, the other Exec. The judge appoints as Referees Samuel Morison, Windham yoeman; William Stevens, yoeman and John Emery, gent., both of Londonderry, as agreed to by the parties. The referees to settle all demands on the est. in dispute. Report of Referees: 6/10/1790. After hearing the parties and examining the evidence, the Referees award and determine that Balch recover from Sanders L36.13.7, to be paid L32.0.6 out of the standing debt. and Balch and Jonathan Gordon, one of the heirs, are each to receive from Sanders L2.6.6. The L3.14.0 cost of the Referees to be div. equally among Sanders, Balch and Gordon. Decree: 1/14/1791. It having been suggested that there is a mistake in the written report, the parties agree that Mr. Morison and Mr. Stevens shall consider alterations as they think just. Report: 3/15/1791. Stevens and Morison determine there was a mistake. Sanders is to pay L24.10.6 of the outstanding debt and to pay L2.15.9 to each of Balch and Gordon.

SANDERS. See also Sander, Saunders

2328. SANDERS, SARAH (1796) #6221
EST. Bow spinster (sic. Will) decd. testate. WILL: Drawn 5/6/1796. Legatees: Sons-Joseph and Jesse; Dau.-Widow Molly Dow; Grandson-James Sanders; Granddau.-Sally Dow dau. of her dau. Mary. Exex.-dau. Widow Molly Dow. Her mark. Witnesses: Jacob Green and Benja. Sargent. CERT. WILL (D32:144): 6/8/1796. Presented by Exex. and both witnesses. INVY.: Appr. 7/5/1796. Comm.: Jacob Green and Willeby Colby. Value L49.16.4. Oaths 9/1/1796 Comm. to Jno. Bryent, JP. Oath of Exex. given without date or JP. Sarah called widow in Invy. Note: Only about 1/3 of the 2 documents in this file exist, both being badly water damaged. They have been sealed by the Archivist but can be photocopied from the Docket book.

2329. SARGENT, ABRAHAM (1795) #6129
See #5396 Sargent, Winthrop (1788)

2330. SARGENT, CHRISTOPHER (1799) #6556
GDP. of the son of Elijah Sargent of Windham decd. GDP.: 4/18/1799. Of Christopher, a minor over 14. Gdn. William Thom, Salem esq. Bond $2,000.00. Surety Isaac Thom, Londonderry esq. Witnesses: Isaac Sargent and Nathl. Parker.

2331. SARGENT, DAVID (1796) #6256
EST. Of Pittsfield. Missing. Research

2332. SARGENT, EDWARD (1794) #6017
EST. Pittsfield yoeman decd. ADMIN.: 8/13/1794. Admr. John Sargent, Pittsfield yoeman. Bond L1000.0.0. Sureties: Robert Tibbets, husbm. and James Drake, gent., both of Pittsfield. Witnesses: John Harper and N. Parker.

2333. SARGENT, ELIJAH (1798) #6483
EST. Windham yoeman decd. ADMIN. (D32:510): 8/11/1798. Admr. Isaac Thom, Londonderry esq. Sureties: Daniel Miltimore and James Doak, both of Londonderry. INVY. (D32:515): Comm.: Saml. Senter, John Davison Jr. and Joseph Cottle. Value $492.31. Oaths 8/23/1798 Comm. to Isaac Thom, JP. Oath Admr. to John Nesmith Jr., JP. PETITION: 12/20/1798. Of Exec. For Comm. Insolvency. Notes the high expense of Elijah's last sickness, main. of a child, claims of about $350.00 and uncertainty of some Notes in Invy. Granted. CLAIMS: 4/16/1800. Comm.: Robert McNeill, James Doak and John Betton. Partial total $505.73. Oaths 4/16/1800 Comm. to judge. ACCOUNT: 4/16/1800. Of Admr. Allowed 1/19/1801 no creditors appearing to object. Admr. notes real est. inventoried did not belong to decd. Account includes main. Susannah. ADDL. ACCOUNT: 4/1801. Of Admr. Allowed 4/15/1801. PROP. & SETTLM.: Claims $367.10. Amount to be proportioned $234.71. Allowed 4/15/1801 with order to Admr. to pay.

2334. SARGENT, ELIZABETH (1772) #3903
EST. Newton widow decd. testate. WILL: Drawn 11/17/1760. Legatees: "Son"-Reuben Hoyt; Dau.-Hannah Hoyt wife of Reuben; Exec.-son Reuben Hoyt. Her mark. Witnesses: Josiah Fowler, David Elliot and Gideon Bartlet. CERT. WILL: 1/23/1772. Presented by Exec. and witnesses Elliot and Bartlet. INVY. WARR. 1/24/1772. Comm.: Jacob Rowell and David Bagley, Newton yeomen. INVY.: Appr. 1/28/1772. Value L22.4.5. Oaths 4/13/1772 Comm. to Nicalos White, JP.

2335. SARGENT, JACOB (1787) #5279
EST. Candia yoeman decd. ADMIN.: 6/28/1787. Admx. Alice Sargent, Candia widow. Bond L500.0.0. Sureties: John Clifford, gent. and Jacob Clifford, husbm., both of Candia. Witnesses: Elisabeth Dudley and John Dudley. INVY.: Appr. 8/22/1787. Comm.: John Clifford and Saml. Scribner. Value L207.10.11. Oaths 8/22/1787 Comm. and Admx. to Saml. Mooers, JP. PETITION: 5/21/1788. of Joseph Dudley atty. to Admx. For License and Comm. Insolvency. Gives list claims of L163.6.6. LICENSE (D29:193): 5/21/1788. To Admx. To sell sufficient real est. to pay debts. DOWER WARR.: 5/21/1788. Comm.: Jonathan Swain, esq.; Joseph Dudley, yoeman; Thomas Gordon, gent., all of Raymond; John Clifford, gent. and Thomas Wason, yoeman, both of Candia. Of Widow Alice Sargent. DOWER: 6/2/1788. Oaths 7/14/1788 Swain, Gordon and Clifford to Samll. Mooers, JP. CLAIMS: 12/25/1788. Comm.: Jonathan Swain and Thomas Gordon. Total L126.10.0 1/2. Oaths 2/2/1789 Comm. to John Scribner, JP.

2336. SARGENT, JESSE (1795) #6063
EST. Newton yoeman decd. ADMIN.: 1/31/1795. Admr. Philip Sargent, Weare, Hillsborough Co. yoeman. Bond L1000.0.0. Sureties: Robert Stuart, gent. and David Sargent, yoeman, both of Newton. Witnesses: Jno. Parker and W. Parker. INVY.: Appr. 2/2/1795. Comm.: Capt. Robert Stuart, Josiah Sargent and James Peaslee. Value L224.0.2. Affirms. 2/25/1795 Comm. to Matthias Bartlet, JP. Oath 2/26/1795 Admr. to W. Parker, JP. PETITION: 3/2/1795. Of: Philip Sargent, Margaret Sargent, Dorothy Sargent, Nathl. Sargent, Abel Sargent and Noah Sargent, the heirs. As land must be sold to pay claims, they have agreed all the land should be sold at public vendue and the money div. by all lawful charges. PETITION: 4/6/1795. Of Admr. For License. Granted heirs having consented. LICENSE (D31:501): 4/6/1795. To Admr. To sell all the real est. BOND: 4/6/1795. Of Admr. Bond L400.0.0. To account for proceeds of sale of real est. by License. Sureties: Robert Stuart, gent. and Obediah Peaslee, yoeman, both of Newton. Witness Saml. Parker.

2337. SARGENT, JOHN (1797) #6403
EST. Candia gent. decd. testate. WILL: Drawn 4/10/1794. Legatees: Wife-Susannah; Sons-John, Jacob and James; Daus.-Dorithy Emery, Hannah Sargent and Sarah Sargent. Execs.-sons Jacob and James. His sig. Witnesses: Jonathan Rowe, Samll. Mooers and Nathl. Emerson. Oaths 1212/1797 witnesses Emerson and Rowe. Proved 12/22/197. ADMIN.: 4/16/1798. Execs. Jacob Sargent and James Sargent, Candia yoemen. Bond $3,000.00. Surety John Sargent, Candia gent. Witnesses: Jere. Mason and W. Parker. INVY.: Appr. 7/11/1798. Comm.: Walter Robie,

Nathl. Emerson and Jonathan Pilsbury. Value $2,193.50. Oaths 7/11/1798 Emerson, Pilsbury and Execs. to Walter Robie, JP.

2338. SARGENT: OLLY & SIMEON (1796) #6259
GDP. Of the children of Daniel Sargent, Pittsfield yoeman decd. PETITION: 8/10/1796. Of: Simeon Sargent and Oley Sargent of Pittsfield. They choose Nathaniel Chase to be their Gdn. Witnesses: John Cram, George Curtis, Robert Johnson and Obediah Johnson. GDP.; 9/21/1796. Of: Simeon and Olly, minors over 14. Gdn. Nathaniel Chase, Pittsfield yoeman. Bond $1,000.00. Sureties: James Drake of Pittsfield and James Harvey McClary of Epsom, gentlemen. Witnesses: Michl. McClary and W. Parker.

2339. SARGENT, SAMUEL (1796) #6275
EST. Hawke labeer decd. testate. WILL: Drawn 4/14/1792. Legatees: Wife-Elisebeth; Samuel Sargent son of Chalice Sargent "who we took in and brought up." Exex.-wife Elisebeth. His sig. Witnesses: Joseph Williams, Josiah Tuxbury and Anne Tuxbury. CERT. WILL (D32:210): 11/9/1796. Presented by Exex. and witnesses Williams and Josiah Tuxbury. ADMIN.: 11/10/1796. Admx. Elizabeth Sargent, Hawke widow. Bond $2,000.00. Sureties: Joseph Williams, gent. and Josiah Tuxbury, husbm., both of Hawke. Witnesses: W. Parker and Nathl. Parker. INVY.: Appr. 12/5/1796. Comm.: Joseph Williams and Josiah Tuxbury. Value $781.06. Note: It is difficult to tell if some Notes are included in total. Oaths 12/5/1796 Comm. and Admx. to Solomon Wheeler, JP.

2340. SARGENT, SAMUEL (1798) #6494
EST. Canterbury yoeman decd. CONSENT: 9/18/1798. Of: Marriam Sargent, widow of Samuel and Ezra and Aaron, sons. To appointment of Samuel Sargent as Admr. His father's est. Petition: Of Samuel Sargent. For Admin. ADMIN. (D32:525): 9/19/1798. Admr. Samuel Sargent, Canterbury yeoman. Sureties: Elijah Sargent and Simon Stevens, both of Canterbury. INVY. (D33:143): Comm.: David McCrillis, Obediah Clough and Simon Stevens. Value $1,840.02 of est. of Samuel Sargent of Canterbury. Oaths 12/14/1799 Comm. and on 9/18/1799 Jereh. Clough, Admr. (sic.) to judge. Note: There is no other Samuel est. to which this Invy. can belong and no explanation for Clough as Admr. DOWER: 9/9/1800. Comm.: David McCrillis, Jesse Stevens, Leavitt Clough, William Hazeltine and Saml. Haines. Of Widow Marriam Sargent. Oaths 9/13/1800 Clough, Hazeltine and Haines to Jereh. Clough, JP. Allowed 9/17/1800.

2341. SARGENT, SARAH (1771) #3879
EST. Portsmouth widow decd. intestate. PETITION: 10/12/1771. Of D. Peirce. Requests that Admin. of est. of his sister Sarah Sargent be granted to her son John Winslow. Allowed 10/12/1771. ADMIN.: 10/14/1771. Admr.: John Winslow, Boston, Suffolk Co., MA gent. Bond L500.0.0. Sureties: Daniel Peirce and George King, esquires, both of Portsmouth. Witnesses: Wm. Parker and Richd. Cutts Shannon. INVY.: Comm.: Saml. Penhallow and Peter Pearse. Appr. 10/14/1771. Value L200.9.10. Oaths 10/14/1771 Comm. and Admr. to judge. ADMIN. D.B.N.: 11/15/1773. Admr. d.b.n. Joseph Peirce, Portsmouth merchant. Bond L1000.0.0. Sureties: Daniel Peirce, esq. and John Peirce, merchant, both of Portsmouth. Witnesses: Tobias Warner and Richd. Leader Nelson.

2342. SARGENT, STARLING (1794) #6003
EST. Allenstown gent. decd. testate. WILL: Drawn 6/26/1792. Legatees: Wife-Mary; Sons-Simeon, Jonathan and Philip; Daus.-Lydia Webster wife of Samuel Webster, Molle Sargent and Jemima Clough wife of Daniel Clough. Ref. to his father Jonathan Sargent. Exec.-son Philip. His mark. Witnesses; John Leonard, John Leonard Jr. and Molley Leonard. CERT. WILL (D31:285): 5/21/1794. Presented by Exec. and witnesses John Leonard and John Leonard Jr. ADMIN.: 5/21/1794. Exec. Philip Sargent, Allenstown gent. Bond L1000.0.0. Sureties: John Leonard, Allenstown yoeman and Richard Bartlett, Pembroke esq. Witnesses: Thomas Baker and W. Parker. INVY.: Appr. 6/20/1794. Comm.: Benja. Noyes, James Cochran and Joshua Clement. Value L196.14.10. Oaths 9/16/1794 Cochran and Clement to Thomas Adams, JP. Oath 9/17/1794 Exec. to judge.

2343. SARGENT, WINTHROP (1788) #5396
EST. Chester yoeman decd. RENUN.: 12/15/1788. Of Phebey Sargent, widow of Winthrop. Of Admin. Requests appointment of her son Moses Sargent. ADMIN.: 12/17/1788. Admr. Moses Sargent, Candia yoeman. Bond L1000.0.0. Sureties: John Sanborn, Candia yoeman and Jeremy Towle, Hawke gent. Witnesses: Simeon Ladd and Nathl. Parker. INVY.: Appr. 2/23/1789. Comm.: Willm. White, Jethro Colby and James Dunlap. Value L282.4.8. Oaths 2/23/1789 Comm. to Josiah Flagg, JP. Oath 4/15/1789 Amdr. to judge. NOTIFICATION: 12/12/1792. To Heirs. They are notified that the Admr. will exhibit his Account and they may attend if they see fit. Cert.: Of: David Hall, Jonathan Smith, Samuel Darbon, John Sanborn and John Sargent. They have been notified by Abraham Sargent. ACCOUNT: 1/14/1793. Of Admr. Allowed 1/14/1793. Judge notes the Admr. has not charged himself with the income of the real est. for 4 years and unless he settles with the heirs, he must be accountable for it. ADDL

ACCOUNT: 9/19/1794. Of Admr. Allowed 9/19/1794. PETITION: 2/13/1795. Of: John Sanborn and Elizabeth his wife, Jeremy Towle and Mary his wife, Jonathan Smith and Phebe his wife, Samuel Darborn and Sarah his wife and David Hall and Judith his wife, heirs. They suspect the Admr. and Abraham Sargent, an heir, have embezzled certain papers and other matters belonging to est., conveyed them away and refuse to discover them. Request the two be cited to appear and be examined. Signed by Jonathan Smith on behalf of Petitioners. CITATION: 2/13/1795. To: Moses Sargent of Candia and Abraham Sargent of Chester, husbandmen. To appear and be examined under oath regarding the complaint that they may be involved in the embezzlement of money, goods, chattels and papers of est. Cert.: 2/17/1795. Of John Buswell, Constable. He has notified Moses Sargent of Citation. Cert.: 2/21/1795. Of David Mills, Constable. He notified Abraham Sargent by reading Citation to him and gave William White, esq. a summons. EXAMINATION: Dated by clerk 3/9/1795. Of Abraham Sargent. Asked if he has ever had in his hands, or knowledge of since his father's death, any deed, bond or other papers given to his father or belonging in any way to his est., Abraham answered no. DEPOSITION: 3/9/1795. Of Phebe Sargent, of full age. Deposes that Abraham Sargent claims, by deed, out of his father's est. 15 acres. There "was" 2 other pieces given to Abraham in lieu of them, the one contains 10 acres and the other 6 acres. The following Petition recorded as #6129 Abraham Sargent (1795) belongs here. PETITION: 8/17/1795. Of Abraham Sargent, Chester yoeman. For div. of land in Chester late the est. of Winthrop Sargent, Chester yoeman decd. which he holds in common with Jeremiah Towle, Hawke gent.; John Sanborn of Sandown; David Hall of Chester; and Jonathan Smith and Samuel Darborn of Candia, yoemen, all except Winthrop Sargent in right of their wives. Order: 8/17/1795. For hearing, Petitioner to serve the other parties with copies of the Petition and Order.

2344. SATERLY, JACOB (1776) #4260
EST. Hampton Falls saddler decd. ADMIN.: 8/29/1776. Adms.: Sarah Sately, widow and Abner Sanborn Jr., yoeman, both of Hampton Falls. Bond L500.0.0. Sureties: Caleb Sanborn, gent. and Meshech Weare, esq., both of Hampton Falls. Witnesses: Nathaniel Weare and Lowell Long. INVY.: Comm.: Caleb Sanborn, Joseph Wells and Obediah Worth. Value L176.7.1. Oaths 10/1776 Comm. to Saml. Weare, JP. Oath 4/30/1777 Abner Sanborn, an Admr., to judge.

2345. SATERLY, JACOB (1791) #5714
GDP.: Of the son of Jacob Saterly, Hampton Falls gent. decd. GDP.: 11/19/1791. Of Jacob, a minor over 14. Gdn. Joseph Saterly, Epsom cordwainer. Bond L500.0.0. Sureties: James Gray, esq. and David How, husbm., both of Epsom. Witnesses: Joseph Sherburne and Samuel Lock.

SAUNDERS. See also Sander, Sanders

2346. SAUNDERS: ABIGAIL, ELIZABETH & THOMAS (1772) #3900
GDP. No father or res. given. GDP.: 1/9/1772. Of Abigail, a minor over 14 and under 21. Gdn. John Gage, Dover esq. Bond L1000.0.0. Sureties: Otis Baker, Dover esq. and James Knowles, Rochester gent. Witnesses: Thomas Ransom and Saml. Hale Jr. GDP.: 1/9/1772. Of Elizabeth, a minor over 14 but under 21. Gdn. John Gage, Dover esq. Bond L1000.0.0. Sureties: Otis Baker, Dover esq. and James Knowles, Rochester gent. Witnesses: Thomas Ransom and Saml. Hale Jr. GDP.: 1/9/1772. Of Thomas, a minor over 14 but under 21. Gdn.: John Gage, Dover esq. Bond L1000.0.0. Sureties: Otis Baker, Dover esq. and James Knowles, Rochester gent. Witnesses: Thomas Ransom and Saml. Hale Jr. Note: These may be children of Edward Saunders who married Abigail [Wallingford] dau of Hon. Thomas Wallingford of Somersworth, Strafford Co. See Evans, Helen F. ABSTRACTS OF THE PROBATE RECORDS OF STRAFFORD CO., NH.

2347. SAUNDERS, JOHN (1771) #3881
EST. Rye Mariner decd. intestate. ADMIN.: 10/18/1771. Admrs.: Tryphena Saunders and Robert Saunders Jr., both of Rye. Bond L500.0.0. Sureties: Robert Saunders of Rye and Thomas Berry of Greenland. Witnesses: William Parker and Lydia Parker. INVY.: Comm.: Saml. Wallis and Jonathan Brown. Appr. 11/27/1771. Value L193.1.0. "All sworn in court." LICENSE: 4/28/1773. To Admrs. To sell as much real est. as will raise L25.0.0. ACCOUNT: 4/28/1773. Allowed on oath of Admr. Robert Saunders Jr. Note The card index gives John's name as Sanders, but all documents are spelled Saunders.

2348. SAVAGE, JOHN (1778) #4463
EST. Portsmouth yoeman decd. ADMIN.: 7/25/1778. Admr. John Savage, Portsmouth yoeman. Bond L5000.0.0. Sureties: Samuel Jones and Mark Broughton, Portsmouth yoemen. Witnesses: Wm. Parker and Jno. Parker. INVY.: Appr. 9/15/1778. Comm.: George Ayers, Sam. Langdon and John Jones. Value not tallied. Est. L159.0.0+. Oaths 9/15/1778 Comm. to Saml. Penhallow, JP. Oath 9/30/1778 Admr. to judge.

2349. SAVAGE, JOHN (1796) #6190
GDP. Of the son of Hannah Crosby, Newmarket single woman and spinster. GDP.: 3/21/1796. Of John Savage, a minor under 14. Gdn. Jonathan Clark, Northwood esq. Bond $500.00. Surety Levi Mead, Northwood yoeman. Witnesses: Jno. Parker and W. Parker.

2350. SAWYER, JOSIAH (1792) #5803
EST. South Hampton yoeman decd. testate. CERT.: 9/6/1792. Of: Josiah Sawyer, Matthias Sawyer, John Sawyer, Moss Sawyer and Terzah Shawyer. They have received from their bros. Israel and Richard, Execs. of Will of their father, what was left them in the Will and accept it as their full part in the est. Cert.: 9/6/1792. Of Mary Sawyer, widow of Josiah. She has received from her sons Israel and Richard, Execs. of Josiah's est., all that was given her in Will and accepts the provision for sons to provide for her. Witnesses to both Certs. Er Colby and Ichabod Colby WILL: Drawn 4/14/1783. Legatees: Wife-Mary; Sons-Josiah, Israel, Matthias, John, Moses and Richard; Dau.-Tirzah Sawyer. Execs.-sons Israel and Richard. His sig. Witnesses: William Cooper, Nathaniel Flanders and Ebenezer French. CERT. WILL (D30:293): 9/17/1792. Presented by Execs. and witnesses Cooper and Flanders. ADMIN.: 9/18/1792. Execs.: Israel Sawyer and Richard Sawyer, yoemen. Bond L1000.0.0. Sureties: Nathaniel Flanders, yoeman and William Cooper, Kingston gent. Witnesses: Nat. Parker and W. Parker.

2351. SAWYER, MOLLY (1782) #4836
EST. South Hampton spinster decd. ADMIN. 8/28/1782. Admr. Josiah Sawyer, South Hampton yoeman. Bond L500.0.0. Sureties: Israel Sawyer and Richard Sawyer, South Hampton yoemen. Witnesses: Josiah Sawyer Jr. and Parker Merrill. INVY. WARR.: 8/28/1782. Comm.: Abel French, gent.; Er Colby and Ebenr. French. INVY.: Appr. 9/3/1782. Value L9.3.0. Oaths 10/3/1782 Abel French, Ebenezer French and Admr. to judge.

2352. SAWYER, MOSES (1784) #5022 & (1786) #5177
EST. Newbury, Essex Co., MA husbm. decd. intestate. ADMIN. (#5022): 7/22/1784. Admr. Moses Sawyer, Newbury, Essex Co., MA physician. Bond L2000.0.0. Sureties: Israel Sawyer and Richard Sawyer, South Hampton husbandmen. Witnesses: Jemima Sawyer and Molly Sawyer. INVY. WARR.: (#5022) 7/22/1784. Comm.: Peter Emerson, physician; Elisha Bachelder, yoeman, both of Hawke and Daniel Davis of Sandown. INVY. (#5022): Appr. 7/24/1784. Value L315.0.0. Oaths 7/24/1784 Comm. to David Tilton, JP. Oath 10/20/1784 Admr. to W. Parker, JP. DIV. WARR. (#5177): 10/20/1784. Comm.: Enoch Smith of Poplin; Daniel Davis of Sandown; Thomas Page, Elisha Bachelder and Peter

Emerson of Hawke. To div. the real est. among the children, giving double share to oldest son. DIV. (#5177): 11/9/1784. Divisees: Sons-Thomas, Joseph and Moses; Heirs of Matthias Plant Sawyer (oldest son) decd.; Dau.-Hannah Sawyer. Oaths 11/9/1784 Comm. to David Tilton, JP. Allowed.

2353. SAYLER, JOHN (1760) No#
EST. Dunstable, Hillsborough Co. taylor decd. ACCOUNT (D21:376): ACCOUNT: Of David Frick, Admr. d.b.n. by his atty. James Lovell. Allowed 5/29/1772. PROP. & SETTLM. (D21:372): Claims L151.4.3 1/2. Amount to be proportioned L2.0.0. Allowed 5/29/1772 with order to atty. to pay. Orig. Archives file includes Admin. with Wm. Greenleaf Admr., Lic. Invy. and Admin. D.B.N. with David Frick Admr. d.b.n.

2354. SCALES, ABRAHAM (1797) #6380
EST. Nottingham yoeman decd. testate. WILL: Drawn 11/14/1795. Legatees: Wife-Sarah; Son-Ebenezer; Daus.-Abigail, Hannah and Lois; Grandson-Samuel Scales. Exex.-wife Sarah. His sig. Witnesses: Samuel Tasker, Philip Hoitt and Thos. Bartlett. CERT. WILL (D32:382): 9/27/1797. Presented by Exex. and all witnesses. ADMIN.: 9/27/1797. Exex. Sarah Scales, Nottingham widow. Bond $2,000.00. Sureties: Thomas Bartlett, Nottingham esq. and Philip Hoitt, Northwood yoeman. Witnesses: Samuel Tasker and Wm. Parker. INVY.: Appr. 12/1/1797. Comm.: John Kelsey, Thos. Glass and Joseph Leavitt. Value $2,931.05. Oaths 12/18/1797 Comm. to Thos. Bartlett, JP.

2355. SCRIBNER: MARGARET & SARAH (1794) #6027
GDP. Of the daus. of Benjamin Scribner of Salisbury, Hillsborough Co. decd. Note: His est. says he was Raymond yoeman. GDP.: 9/18/1794. Of: Sarah and Margaret, minors over 14. Gdn. John Clifford, Candia gent. Bond L1000.0.0. Sureties: John Wason, Candia gent. and Saml. Scribner of Raymond. Witnesses: Willoughba Taylor and Nathl. Parker.

2356. SEAVEY, MARK ET. AL. (1797) #6368
See #4191 Capt. Titus Salter Jr. (1776)

2357. SEAVEY, MOSES (1795) #6102
EST. Deerfield yoeman decd. testate. WILL: Drawn 4/15/1794. Legatees: Wife-Huldah; Sons-Samuel, Moses, Elijah, Jonathan and Levi; Dau. Abigail Sevey; Granddau.-Nabby Sevey. Exec.-son Levi. His mark. Witnesses: William Mudget, Moses Barnard and Samuel Bachelder. CERT. WILL (D31:533): 5/20/1795. Presented by Exec. and witnesses Barnard and Bachelder. ADMIN.: 5/20/1795. Exec. Levi Seva, Deerfield yoeman. Bond L1000.0.0. Sureties: Simon Norton, yoeman and Samuel

Bachelder, gent., both of Deerfield. Witnesses: Thos. Adams and W. Parker. INVY.: Appr. 6/24/1795. Comm.:: Moses Barnard, Thomas Jenness and William Mudget. Value L715.10.4. Oaths 8/18/1795 Comm. to Nathl. Weare, JP. Oath 8/19/1795 Exec. to judge.

2358. SEAVEY, THOMAS (1794) #5972
EST. Portsmouth yoeman decd. intestate. ADMIN.: 2/19/1794. Admx. Sarah Sevey, Portsmouth widow. Bond L1000.0.0. Sureties: Joseph Akerman and John Ayers, Portsmouth yoemen. Witnesses: E. Livermore and W. Parker. INVY.: Appr. 4/9/1794. Comm.: Nathl. Gookin, Walter Akerman and Samuel Whidden. Value L2045.9.2. Oaths Admx. and Comm. to Geo. Gains, JP. DOWER WARR.: 2/18/1795. Comm.: Isaac Rindge, esq. and Israel Marden, yoeman, both of Portsmouth; Stephen March of Greenland and Benjamin Garland of Rye, esquires; and Richard Dame, Newington gent. Of Widow Sarah Seavey. DOWER: 6/9/1795. Oaths 6/10/1795 Comm. to R. Cutts Shannon, JP. Allowed 6/11/1795. DIV.: 6/9/1795. Comm. same as for Dower. To set off in equal shares 2/3 of the real est. among his children. Divisees: Jno. Seavey, Mary Whidden widow of Joseph Whidden decd., Michael Seavey and Betsy Seavey. Oaths 6/10/1795 Comm. to R. Cutts Shannon, JP. Allowed 6/9 (sic.)/1795. PETITION: 2/19/1805. Of John Seavey, son of decd. The Admx., has lately died. He relinquishes his right to Admin. as only surviving son in favor of Joseph Akerman, a creditor. Witness: Nahum Ward. A.P.S. adds that the Petitioner has 2 sisters, children of decd. One is incapable of business and the other is a widow who declines admin. and also wishes that Akerman take Admin. ADMIN. D.B.N: 2/20/1805. Admr. d.b.n: Joseph Akerman, Portsmouth cordwainer. Bond $2000.00. Sureties: Joseph Clark Jr., goldsmith and Benjamin Akerman, cordwainer, both of Portsmouth. Witnesses: Danl. Humphreys and Nathl. Parker. INVY. WARR.: 5/20/1805. Comm.: Jeremiah Libbey, Robert Ham and William Walker, all of Portsmouth. INVY.: Appr. 6/17/1805. Value $126.00. Oaths 6/17/1806 Admr. d.b.n and Comm. to George Gains, JP.

SEAWARD. See also Seawer, Seward

2359. SEAWARD, CAPT. GILES (1798) #6423
EST. Portsmouth mariner decd. testate. WILL: Drawn 8/22/1789. Legatees: Sons-Joseph, John, George and William; Dau.- Deborah Shackford; Grandsons-Giles Seaward son of his son Giles, John Place and James Place sons of his late dau. Christian Place. Execs.-friend Isaac Rindge and son William. His sig. Witnesses: Wm. McHard, Saml. Griffen and John Gooch. Proved 2/12/1798, being presented by Isaac Rindge and Wm. Seawards, the named Execs., who refused trust, and John Seaward, a

son, named instead. RENUN.: 12/7/1797 Of Isaac Rindge. Of Co-admin. as provided Will. Requests appointment of some other person. RENUN.: 1/10/1798. Of William Seaward. Of Co-admin. as provided in his father's Will. Witness: Jos. Seaward. ORDER: 3/14/1798. To John Seaward, Portsmouth mariner. John ordered to appear and assume admin. which has been refused by the 2 Execs. named in Will. ADMIN.: 3/14/1798. Exec.: John Seaward, Portsmouth mariner. Bond $3,000.00. Sureties: Isaac Rindge, esq. and William Stavers, yoeman, both of Portsmouth. Witnesses: Mary Trafton, Samuel Appleton and Geo. Andrews. LETTER OF ADMIN.: 3/14/1798. To John Seaward. INVY. WARR.: 3/14/1798. Comm. Isaac Rindge, esq.; Nathaniel Gookin, gent. and Jacob Waldron, innholder, all of Portsmouth. Invy.: Appr. 3/15/1798. Value $71.24. Oaths 3/17/1798 Waldron, Gookin and Exec. to Isaac Rindge, JP. PETITION: 3/21/1798. Of Exec. For Comm. Insolvency. Allowed. CLAIMS WARR.: 4/3/1798. Comm.: Isaac Rindge, esq.; Jacob Waldron, innholder and Mark Rogers, trader, all of Portsmouth. Claims: Total $176.73. Oaths Comm. to R. Cutts Shannon, JP. ACCOUNT: 10/17/1798. Of Exec. Allowed 10/17/1798.

2360. SEAWARD, JOHN DREW (1773) #4016
EST. Portsmouth caulker decd. intestate. ADMIN.: 5/10/1773. Admx. Sarah Seaward, Portsmouth widow. Bond L500.0.0. Sureties: Eliphalet Daniels and Samuel Hale Jr., Portsmouth gentlemen. Witnesses: Sally Drew and Samuel Parker. INVY. WARR.: 5/10/1773. Comm.: William Knight, esq. and Thomas Martin, merchant, both of Portsmouth. INVY.: Appr. 5/27/1773. Value L28.2.9. Oath 7/10/1773 Knight and on 7/30/1773 Admx. to judge. PETITION: 10/10/1773. By Samuel Hall of Portsmouth, Collector of Parish Taxes. Requests judge to order the Exex. to pay the sum due him as Collector. Oath 10/10/1773 Hall to judge. CLAIMS WARR.: 5/19/1773. Comm.: Samuel Hale Jr., gent. and Gillam Butler, merchant, both of Portsmouth. Oaths 12/7/1773 Comm. with no judge or JP. CLAIMS: 4/29/1774. Total L55.18.8 1/2. Oath 4/30/1774 Butler to judge. Included in this packet are the following items: 1. Bill dated 1764 To John Sherburne, Esq. From Seaward. For caulking. L43.8.11.0. 2. Receipt for payment by est. to John Sherburn of L23.6.0., leaving a bal. due on 8/28/1773 of L8.15.4. 3. Bill too Seaward. From Daniel and Saml. Sherburne dated 3/1771-12/1772. Due L44.7.10 1/2. This appears to be a store account. 4. Bill. To Admx. est. Dennis Drew. From Gillam Butler. Dated 4/29/1774 Due L2.14. 5. Promisory Note 4/10/1777. Of Daniel and Saml. Sherburne. To John Drew Seaward for 150 gallons of West India Rum in one month. 6. Bill 4/29/1774. To est. From Gillam Butler for L1.16 for expenses of Claims Commission. Signed by Butler as paid by Admx. 7. Bill? Of Capt. Wolden Kinston of Kittery. Due L6.3.0. 8. Bill.

7/1770. From Gillam Butler. To Sarah Drew. Due L1.12.2. For what purpose unreadable.

2361. SEAWARD, WILLIAM (1793) #5930
EST. Portsmouth caulker decd. testate. WILL: Drawn 9/19/1793. Legatees: Wife-Sarah; Sons-John who is blind, James and Abraham; Daus.-Elizabeth widow of William Chandler decd., Sarah wife of Richard Elliot and Catharine wife of John How. Exex.-wife Sarah. His sig. Witnesses: A. R. Cutter, Sam. Sherburne and Samuel Hutchings. CERT. WILL (D31:89): 10/16/1793. Presented by Richard Elliot, the Exex. named being dead, and all witnesses. ADMIN.: 10/16/1793. Admr. Richard Elliot, Portsmouth yoeman. Bond L1000.0.0. Sureties: Samuel Sherburne, esq. and Samuel Hutchings, trader, both of Portsmouth. Witnesses: George Hart and W. Parker. INVY.: Appr. 10/30/1793. Comm.: Nathl. Marshall, Saml. Hutchings and Saml. Drowne. Value L168.2.5. Oaths 6/16/1794 Comm. and Admr. to Nathl. Adams, JP. ACCOUNT: Of Admr. Of ests. Of William and Widow Sarah. Consent to Account of: Nathl. Hilton and Edward Sargent atty to James Seaward and Catharine How, heirs. Allowed 2/15/1804. Account includes funeral expenses for bro. John.

2362. SEAWER, PHILLIP (1773) #4057
EST. Portsmouth mariner decd. intestate. ADMIN.: 11/22/1773. Admr.: Samuel Hutchings, Portsmouth yoeman. Bond L1000.0.0. Sureties: William Cotton Jr. and Nathanael Babb, Portsmouth yoemen. Witnesses: Samuel Hale Jr. and John Parker. Note: The sig. on Admin. was Nathanael Ball but changed by clerk to Babb.

2363. SENTER, JANE (1777) #4363
EST. Londonderry single woman decd. ADMIN.: 5/29/1777. Admr. Reuben Senter, Londonderry yoeman. Bond L500.0.0. Sureties: John Dickey of Francistown, Hillsborough Co. and Alexander Parker of Society Land, Hillsborough Co. yoemen. Witnesses: Nicholas Gilman and Wm. Parker. INVY.: Appr. 6/12/1777. Comm.: Josiah Jones, Thomas Petterson and Joseph Curtice. Value L55.6.0. Oaths 8/9/1777 Comm. to James Betton, JP. LICENSE: 5/23/1778. To Admr. To sell sufficient real est. to pay debts. ACCOUNT: 7/1/1779. Of Admr. Allowed on oaths of Admr. to W. Parker, Reg. 7/1/1779.

2364. SERVICE, ELIZABETH (1784) #5000
EST. Portsmouth widow decd. testate. WILL: Drawn 1/23/1784. Legatees: Rev. Samuel Haven; Dr. Ammi Ruhamah Cutter; Good friend John Davenport. Exec.-John Davenport. Her sig. Witnesses: Peter Man, Joseph

Haven and Elizabeth Man. CERT. WILL (D27:442): 4/21/1784. Presented by Exec. and witnesses Peter Man and Elizabeth Man. ADMIN.: 4/21/1784. Exec. John Davenport, Portsmouth goldsmith. Bond L1000.0.0. Sureties: Peter Man, barber and Benjamin Miller, both of Portsmouth. Witnesses: Ebenezer Fogg and Nathl. Parker.

2365. SEVERANCE, JACOB (1774) #4095
EST. Kingston yoeman decd. RENUN.: 3/29/1774. Of Catherine Severance, widow of Jacob. Of Admin. Requests appointment of Samuel Severance of Kingston. Witnesses: Ebenr. Stevens and Josiah Bartlett. ADMIN.: 3/30/1774. Admr. Samuel Severance, Kingston yoeman. Bond L1000.0.0. Sureties: Josiah Bartlett and Ebenezer Stevens, Kingston esquires. Witnesses: John Wadleigh and Samll. Philbrick. INVY. WARR.: 6/30/1774. Comm.: Joseph Fellows and John Wadleigh, Kingston yoemen. INVY.: Appr. 6/27/1774. Value L166.16.7. Oaths 6/27/1774 Comm. to Josiah Bartlett, JP. Oath 6/29/1774 Admr. to judge. PETITION: 9/26/1774. Of Catharine Severance. States that Jacob died about 4 months after they married, leaving no Will. She is entitled to l/3 of his personal est. after debts and expenses are paid and use of 1/3 of the real est. during her life, but she will renounce those rights if the judge will permit the Admr. to make her a competent allowance for same. DECLARATION: Of Admr. He consents that the Pet. be granted, the amount to be determined by the judge. Allowed 10/3/1774. The widow to receive L20.0.0. upon her giving a release of her right to dower and also releasing her part of the personal est. to Admr. for the use of the creditors and heirs. PETITION: 10/30/1776. Of Admr. For License. There is need for main. of 2 children and the decd.'s aged mother to whom decd. gave his bond for her main. LICENSE: 10/30/1776. To Admr. To sell sufficient real est. to pay debts. REPORT: Of the public vendue held 11/13/1776 of 21+/- acres of land, part of est. Struck off to Benjamin Webster Sillaway for L1.18.0. Consented to and signed by Sillaway. ACCOUNT: 3/25/1778. Of Admr. Allowed 3/25/1778. The Account lists an item for advice about the children, but no main.

SEWARD. See also Seaward, Seawer

2366. SEWARD, MARY (1787) #5291
EST. Portsmouth single woman decd. intestate. ADMIN.: 9/18/1787. Admr. Giles Seaward, Portsmouth mariner. Bond L1000.0.0. Sureties: Shackford Seaward, laborer and Jos. Seaward, mariner, both of Portsmouth. Witnesses: Deborah Shackford and Debby Shackford.

2367. SEWARD, SARAH (1793) #5929
EST. Portsmouth widow decd. testate, widow of William Seaward decd. WILL: Drawn 10/1/1793. Legatees: Son-John, to be cared for lifelong by Richard Elliot; Her other children or their heirs; Son-in-law-Richard Elliot. Exec.-son-in-law-Richard Elliot. Her mark, Witnesses: A. R. Cutter, Rebecca Marden and Samuel Hutchings. CERT. WILL (D31:91): 10/16/1793. Presented by Exec. and witnesses Cutter, esq. and Hutchings. ADMIN.: 10/16/1793. Exec. Richard Elliot, Portsmouth yoeman. Bond L1000.0.0. Sureties: Samuel Sherburne, esq. and Samuel Hutchings, trader, both of Portsmouth. Witnesses: George Hart and W. Parker. INVY.: Appr. 10/30/1793. Comm.: Nathl. Marshall, Samuel Hutchings and Saml. Drowne. Value L168.2.5. Oaths 6/10/1794 Comm. and Exec. to Nathl. Adams, JP.

2368. SHACKFORD, JOHN (1765) A#3207
EST. Portsmouth mariner decd. DIV. (D21:96): 4/9/1771. Comm.: John Wendell, Jno. Parker and Woodbury Langdon. Divisees: Widow Katharine Shackford, her Dower; Daus.-Katharine Tilton, Dorothy Moulton, Elizabeth Shackford and Mary Shackford. Oaths 4/11/1771 Comm. to judge. Orig. Archives file includes Admin., Invy. Warr. and Invy.

2369. SHACKFORD, JOHN JR. (1779) #4547
EST. Chester miller decd. testate. WILL: Drawn 3/15/1779. Legatees: Wife-Sarah; Sons-Samuel, Jonathan and Richard; Daus.-Betty Shackford and Sarah Shackford; Provides for the support of his father. Exex.-wife Sarah. His sig. Witnesses: James Stickna, Ephraim Fitts and Saml. Emerson. CERT. WILL (D25:157): 6/30/1779. Presented by Exex., witnesses Emerson, esq. and Fitts having given oaths to W. Parker, JP & Reg. on 6/10/1779. INVY.: Comm.: John Webster and Benja. Hill. Value not tallied. Esti. L4500.0.0+. Oaths 12/10/1779 Exex. And Comm. to Saml. Emerson, JP. Note: This file also contains a Renun. which belongs to #6631 Jonathan Shackford (1799) and is recorded there.

2370. SHACKFORD, JONATHAN (1799) #6631
EST. Chester yoeman decd. Note: The following Renun. found in #4547 John Shackford Jr. (1779) belongs here. RENUN.: 12/17/1799. Of Sarah Shakford. Of Admin. of est. her son Jonathan of Chester decd. Requests appointment of her son Samuel Shakford. Witnesses: Willm. White and Richard Shackford. ADMIN: 12/18/1799. Admr. Samuel Shackford, Chester yoeman. Bond $2000.00. Sureties: William White and Jonathan Dearborn, Chester esquires. Witnesses: Robert Moor and W. Parker. INVY.: Appr. 12/28/1799. Comm.: Isaac Hill and Josiah Forsith. Value $237.80. Oaths 12/20/1799 Comm. to William White, JP. Note by W.

Parker, Reg. that Admr. sworn 12/17/1800. PETITION: 9/25/1806. Of Daniel French on behalf of Bradbury Quimby who married one of heirs. For Admr. to appear and settle account. CITATION: 10/18/1806. To Admr. To appear to settle his account for distribution of est. Cert.: 10/27/1806. Of John Morrison, D. Sheriff. He gave Admr. the orig. copy of the Citation. DEPOSITION: Of Richard Shackford of Salem, Essex Co., MA, of lawful age. Says he has known his bro. Jonathan from the time he was 21 to his death. He spent a great deal of time with his bro. Samuel and boarded in his family. He knows no reason why his bro. Samuel received any consideration or pay for board from Jonathan. Oath 4/2/1807. Richard to Ezekiel Savage, JP. DEPOSITION: Of Josiah Lane, of lawful age. States he was in and out of Samuel Shackford's house during Jonathan's last sickness, about 2 1/2 yrs. Jonathan was able to do little or no work and he, Josiah, understood from his wife that Jonathan never paid any board. Oath 4/13/1807 Josiah to Willm. White, JP. DEPOSITION: Of Sarah Shackford, of lawful age, mother of Jonathan. States that her son Jonathan spent several winters at Samuel's home, where she also lived, and also the period of his last sickness. Jonathan never set aside enough to board himself and was unable to do much to assist Samuel. Oath 4/13/1807 Sarah to William White, JP. ACCOUNT: 12/17/1806. Of Admr. Allowed 4/15/1807.

2371. SHACKFORD, WILLIAM (1773) #3981
EST. Portsmouth esq. decd. testate. WILL: Drawn 12/26/1772. Legatees: Wife-Eleanor dau. of Nathaniel Mendum; Son-Josiah; Ref. to his negro girl Bess. Exex.-wife Eleanor. His sig. Witnesses: John Marshall, Danl. Grant, Abner Blazdel and Saml. Hutchings. Codicil: 1/11/1773. Provides for his children Samuel, Josiah and Abigail(also called "dau Cooper."). Ref. to his negro woman Venus. His sig. Witnesses: Deborah Marshall, Nanny Partridge and Saml. Hale Jr. CERT. WILL: 7/24/1773. Presented by Exex. and all witnesses to both Will and Codicil. INVY. WARR.: 2/24/1773. Comm.: William Knight, esq. and John Marshall, boatbuilder, both of Portsmouth. INVY.: Appr. 5/27/1773. Value L435.17.0. Oaths 5/29/1773 Exex. and on 7/31/1773 Comm. to judge.

2372. SHANNON, JOHN (1778) #4480
See John McShannon (1777) #4359

2373. SHANNON, NATHANIEL (1792) #5812
EST. Portsmouth yeoman decd. ADMIN.: 10/17/1792. Admrs.: Elizabeth Shannon, widow and Nathaniel Shannon, yoeman, both of Portsmouth Bond L1000.0.0. Sureties: Isaac Rindge and George Wentworth, Portsmouth esquires. Witnesses: Nathl. Folsom and W. Parker. INVY.:

Appr. 11/21/1792. Comm.: Is. Rindge, esq.; Capt. Geo. Wentworth and James Ayers. Value L566.18.3. Oaths 12/1/1792 Comm. to Oliver Whipple, JP. Oath 3/15/1793 Nathaniel Shannon, an Admr., to judge. PETITION: 3/15/1793. Of Admrs. by Nathaniel Shannon. For License so they may redeem mortgage on part of the land which will soon expire. Also request Comm. Insolvency. Give list claims in as L641.19.11. License and Comm. granted. LICENSE (D30:371): 3/15/1793. to Admrs. To sell real est. to amount of L300.0.0. ACCOUNT: 3/20/1799. Of Admrs. Signed by Nath. Shannon and Nathl. Adams atty. to Elizabeth Shannon, an Admr. Allowed 3/20/1799 having been consented to by the heirs of age. Account includes main. Of Eliza, John D. and George. DIV.: 4/6/1799. Comm.: Seth Walker, esq.; Nathaniel Jackson and Samll. Nutter, yoemen, all of Portsmouth; Benja. Miller, yoeman and Richd. Dame., esq., both of Newington. To div. the real est., except Dower, among his children. Divisees: Sons-Nathaniel, Samuel, John and George; Daus.-Margaret Nelson wife of John Nelson and Elizabeth Shannon. Includes Map. Oaths 4/8/1799 Walker, Nutter, Miller and Dame to Nathl. Adams, JP. Allowed.

2374. SHAW, ALICE & JOSIAH (1773) #4021
GDP. Of the children of Josiah Shaw, Hampton yoeman decd. testate. GDP.: 5/26/1773. Of Alice and Josiah, minors under 14. Gdn. John Taylor Jr., Hampton yoeman. Bond L1000.0.0. Sureties: Robert Moulton of Hampton and Samuel Stevens of Brentwood, yoemen. Witnesses: Jeremiah Lane and Samuel Parker. Note: Alice called "Elline" in father's Will.

2375. SHAW, CALEB (1792) #5739
EST. Kensington gent. decd. testate. WILL: Drawn 12/11/1787. Legatees: Wife-Abigail; Sons-John, Caleb, Elijah and Nathaniel; Dau.-Hannah Ladd; Heirs of his dau. Sarah Sibley. Exec.-son Elijah. His sig. Witnesses: Jeremiah Lane, Jeremiah Lane Jr. and Joshua Lane. CERT. WILL (D30:185): 2/4/1792. Presented by Exec. and witnesses Jeremiah Lane and Jeremiah Lane Jr. ADMIN.: 2/4/1792. Exec. Elijah Shaw, Kensington wheelwright. Bond L1000.0.0. Sureties: John Shaw, Pittsfield wheelwright and Jeremiah Lane, Hampton Falls taylor. Witnesses: W. Parker and Nathl. Parker.

2376. SHAW, EDWARD (1777) #4382
EST. North Hampton yoeman decd. testate. WILL: Drawn 10/23/1770. Legatees: Wife-Love; Sons-Josiah and John; Benjamin Mason son of Francis and Mary Mason; Mary Jewell dau. of David Jewell. Exex.-wife Love. His mark. Witnesses: Ebenezer Sanborn, John Tilton and Levi Dearborn. CERT. WILL: 7/30/1777. Presented by Exex. and witnesses

Sanborn and Dearborn. INVY.: Appr. 11/24/1777. Comm.: Ebenr. Sanborn, Christopher Smith and Thomas Sanborn. Value not tallied. Esti. L893.0.0+. Oaths Comm. and Exec. to W. Parker, JP.

2377. SHAW, EDWARD (1788) #5323
EST. Hampton husbm. decd. testate. WILL: Drawn 2/1/1783. Legatees: Wife-Ruth; Sons-Jeremiah, Samuel Ichabod (if he be living), Simeon, John and Levi; Dau.-May Shaw. Execs.-sons Simeon and John. His sig. Witnesses: Simon Ward, Cotton Ward and Joseph Dow. CERT. WILL (D29:166): 1/16/1788. Presented by Execs. And witnesses Cotton Ward and Dow, esq.

2378. SHAW, ELIHU (1784) #5023
EST. Kensington husbm. decd. testate. WILL: Drawn 8/25/1775. Legatees: Wife-Mary; Sons-Nathan, Joseph and Abraham; Daus.-Hannah Dow, Ann Ward, Mary Gilman and Betty Shaw. Exec.-son Nathan. His sig. Witnesses: Jeremiah Dearbon, David Shaw and Joseph Tilton. CERT. WILL (D27:484): 7/21/1784. Presented by Exec. And witnesses Dearbon and Shaw.

2379. SHAW, GIDEON (1789) #5449
EST. Hampton husbmn. decd. testate. WILL: Drawn 2/25/1779. Legatees: Wife-Rachel; Sons-Joshua and Benjamin Brown Shaw; Daus.-Rachel James, Elizabeth Blake and Mary Towle. Exec.-son Benjamin Brown Shaw. His mark. Witnesses: Jona. Garland, Jacob Palmer and Joseph Dow. CERT. WILL (D29:278): Presented by Exec. and witnesses Garland and Dow. ADMIN.: 5/20/1789. Exec. Benjamin Brown Shaw, Hampton yeoman. Bond L500.0.0. Sureties: Jonathan Garland, gent. and Joseph Dow, esq., both of Hampton. Witness W. Parker.

2380. SHAW, ICHABOD (1789) #5450
EST. Sandown esq. decd. RENUN.: 5/19/1789. Of Hanah Shaw, widow of Ichabod. Of Admin. Requests appointment of her son-in-law Thomas Cotton. ADMIN.: 5/20/1789. Admr. Thomas Cotton, Sandown gent. Bond L1000.0.0. Sureties: Israel Dimond and Jacob Eastman, both of Hawke. Witnesses: John Calfe and W. Parker. INVY.: Appr. 6/2/1789. Comm.: Israel Dimond, Benja. Pilsbury and Jacob Eastman. Value L328.1.0. Oaths 8/19/1789 Admr. And Comm. to Thos. Page, JP. PETITION: 10/21/1789. Of Admr. For Comm. Insolvency. Gives claims as L165.5.0. Signs "in right of his wife the only heir." CLAIMS WARR.: 10/21/1789. Comm.: Jacob Eastman and Jabez Eaton, both of Hawke and Benja. Pilsbury, Sandown gent. CLAIMS: 4/9/1790. Total L170.13.0. Oaths 4/14/1790 Comm. to Edmund Mooers, JP. ACCOUNT: 4/22/1790. Of Admr. Allowed 4/22/1790.

2381. SHAW, ICHABOD (1783) #4875
EST. Hampton mariner decd. ADMIN.: 2/8/1783. Admr. Edward Shaw, Hampton yoeman. Bond L500.0.0. Sureties: Jonathan Moulton and John Moulton, Hampton esquires. Witnesses: Jerh. Shaw and Jonathan Moulton. ADMIN. D.B.N.: 10/25/1788. Admr. d.b.n. Jeremiah Shaw, Moultonborough, Strafford Co. clerk. Bond L500.0.0. Sureties: Josiah Moulton, Hampton gent. and Isaac Mansfield, Exeter clerk. Witness W. Parker.

2382. SHAW, JOHN (1785) #5115
EST. Nottingham yoeman decd. RENUN.: 6/15/1785. Of Susanna Shaw, widow of John. Of Admin. Requests appointment of her son-in-law John Chesley. Witnesses: Sarah Chesley and Joseph Sias. ADMIN.: 6/15/1785. Admr. John Chesley, Nottingham yoeman. Bond L1000.0.0. Sureties: Asa Forster, Canterbury yoeman and Joseph Sias, Lee, Strafford Co. esq. Witnesses: Robt. Young and Nathl. Parker. INVY.: Appr. 7/8/1785. Comm.: Joseph Sias, Nathl. Goodhue and Benja. Watson. Value L359.12.0. Oaths 8/30/1785 Watson and Goodhue to Joseph Sias, JP. Oath 12/26/1789 Admr. to W. Parker, Reg.

2383. SHAW, JONATHAN (1780) #4637
EST. Hampton yoeman decd. testate. WILL: Drawn 5/28/1780. Legatees: Sons-Jonathan, Benjamin and Josiah; Daus.-Elizabeth Peabody, Mary Clark, Susanah Shaw and Bathshaba Shaw. Exec.-son Benjamin. His sig. Witnesses: Nathl. Trask, Jonathan Robinson and Thomas Stow Ranney. CERT. WILL (D25:349): 6/28/1780. Presented by Exec. and witnesses Robinson and Ranney. INVY.: Appr. 8/30/1780. Comm.: Simon Sanborn, Philip Marston and John Fogg. Value not tallied. Esti. L1100.0.0+, rated at Indian corn at 4 shil. bu. Oaths 8/30/1780 Comm. and Exec. to judge.

2384. SHAW, JONATHAN (1785) #5145
EST. Brentwood yoeman decd. testate. WILL: Drawn 1/24/1785. Legatees: Wife-Elisabeth; "Bro."-Mayhew Clark; Nephews-Thomas Peabody Clark and Jonathan Shaw son of his bro. Benjamin; Niece-Elizabeth Peabody; Mary Mills; Cousins-Elizabeth Peabody and Thomas Peabody Clark; Michael Parks. Execs.-wife Elizabeth and bro. Mayhew Clark. His sig. Witnesses: Porter Kimball, Hawley Marshall Jr. and Nathl. Trask. CERT. WILL (D28:317): 10/5/1785. Presented by Execs. and Capt. Marshall and Porter. INVY. Appr. 10/6/1785. Comm.: Samuel Cram, Porter Kimball and Jonathan Taylor. Value L721.0.0. Oaths 11/16/1785 Comm. to judge. LETTER OF ADMIN. D.B.N.: 3/15/1786. To Samuel Cram, Brentwood yoeman. Widow Elizabeth Shaw refused Admin. and Admin. was granted to Mayhew Clark, who died before executing est. Widow Elizabeth still refuses to Admin. By his legal right, the judge

appoints Samuel Cram. BOND OF ADMIN.: 3/15/1786. Admr. d.b.n. Samuel Cram, Brentwood yoeman. Bond L500.0.0. Sureties: James Thurston, innholder and Simeon Ladd, gent., both of Exeter. Witnesses: Jere. Fogg and Nathl. Parker. INVY. WARR.: 5/17/1786. Comm.: Jonathan Taylor, John Shaw and Aretas Rowe, all of Brentwood. INVY.: Appr. 5/2/1786. Value L425.1.6. Oaths 6/28/1786 Comm. and Admr. d.b.n. to W. Parker, JP. PETITION: 5/22/1786. Of Admr. d.b.n. For Comm. Insolvency. States claims appear to be L350.0.7. CLAIMS WARR.: 11/15/1786. Comm.: Ezekiel Godfrey, Poplin gent., Jabez Smith and Jonathan Taylor, Brentwood yoemen. On 5/16/1787 Comm. allowed 6 months longer. LICENSE (D29:164): 12/19/1787. To Admr. d.b.n. To sell sufficient real est. to pay debts. CLAIMS: 12/19/1787. Total L277.2.8. Oaths 12/19/1787 Comm. to W. Parker, Reg. DOWER: 11/21/1786. Comm.: Samuel Harper Jr., Jona. Veasey Jr., Ezekl. Godfrey, Jabez Smith and Jonathan Taylor. Of Widow Elizabeth Shaw. Oaths 11/25/1786 Comm. to William Morrill, JP. Allowed 12/20/1786. ACCOUNT: 1/14/1799. Of Admr. d.b.n. Allowed 1/14/1799 heirs consenting. ADDL. ACCOUNT: Dated by clerk 1/14/1799. Pos. part of previous.

2385. SHAW, MOSES (1791) #5683
EST. Kensington yoeman decd. testate. WILL: Drawn 4/28/1789. Legatees: Wife-Mary; Sons-Moses and David; Dau.-Sarah Smith. Exec.-son Moses. His sig. Witnesses: Jere Fogg Jr., Abraham Shaw and Edward Lock. CERT. WILL (D30:104): 8/15/1791. Presented by Exec. and witnesses Fogg, esq. and Lock. ADMIN.: 8/15/1791. Exec. Moses Shaw, Kensington esq. Bond L1000.0.0. Sureties: Jeremiah Fogg, esq. and Edward Lock, yoeman, both of Kensington. Witnesses: Nathl. Parker and W. Parker. INVY.: Appr. 8/15/1791. Comm.: Jere. Fogg, Jeremiah Dearborn and Elisha Blake Jr. Value L283.5.6. Oaths 8/22/1791 Dearborn and Blake to Jere Fogg, JP.

2386. SHAW, SAMUEL (1784) #4975
EST. Epping yoeman decd. testate. WILL: Drawn 11/17/1783. Legatees: Wife-Margaret; Sons-John and Samuel; Daus.-Sarah Sanborn, Elizabeth Shaw, Rachel Shaw, Nabby Shaw and Dolley Shaw; Grandson-John Shaw; Granddau.-Ruanne Shaw. Exex.-wife Margaret. His mark. Witnesses: Joseph Sias, esq.; John Page and Samuel French. CERT. WILL (D27:388): 2/18/1784. Presented by Exex. and all witnesses ADMIN.: 2/18/1784. Exex. Margaret Shaw, Epping widow. Bond L1000.0.0. Sureties: John Page and Samuel French, Epping yoemen. Witnesses: Nathl. Parker and W. Parker.

2387. SHAW, STEPHEN (1783) #4892
EST. North Hampton yoeman decd. testate. WILL: Drawn 2/18/1783. Legatees: Wife-Elizabeth; Son-Benjamin; Daus.-Sarah Shaw and Abigail Shaw. Exex.-wife Elizabeth. Hs mark. Witnesses: Thomas Sanborn, William Sanborn and William Palmer. CERT. WILL (D27:206): 4/30/1783. Presented by Exex. and witnesses Thomas Sanborn and Palmer.

2388. SHEAFE, JACOB (1791) #5675
EST. Portsmouth esq. decd. testate. WILL: Drawn 1/11/1786. Legatees: Wife-Abigail; Sons-Jacob Jr., Thomas, James, William and John; Daus.-Abigail Pickering, Sarah Marsh, Hannah Henderson, Mary Willard and Mehitabel Sheafe. Execs.-sons Jacob, Thomas and James. His sig. Witnesses: John Noble, Jos. Haven, John Hale and Willm. King Jr. CERT. WILL (D30:95): 7/11/1791. Presented by Execs. and witnesses Noble and Haven. ADMIN.: 7/8/1791. Execs.: Jacob Sheafe, Thomas Sheafe and James Sheafe, Portsmouth merchants. Bond L20000.0.0. Sureties: John Pickering, esq. and William Sheafe, merchant, both of Portsmouth. Witnesses: Charles Walker and Charles (Cutter?-very faded). INVY. (D20:180): Comm.: John Peirce, Danl. R. Rogers and Jerh. Libbey. Value L5118.8.1. Oaths 2/14/1792 Comm. to N. Adams, esq. Oaths 2/15/1792 Execs. to judge. NOTE: The Invy. is so fragile it cannot be handled so abstract taken from Docket book. ACCOUNT: 8/31/1809. Of Execs. Jacob S. Pickering Admr. est. of Jno. Pickering, esq. decd.; Sarah Marsh; John Sheafe, W. Hart, Wm. Sheafe, Hannah Hart, Mary Willard, Ebenr. Smith and Mehitable Smith approve the Account and acknowledge receipt of the sums set by their names. Allowed 8/14/1810 heirs consenting.

2389. SHEAFE, SAMPSON (1772) #3964 & (1791) #5702
EST. New Castle esq. decd. testate. WILL (#3964): Drawn 5/18/1763. ("Portsmouth esq."). Legatees: Wife-Sarah; Sons-Sampson, Jacob, Samuel and Henry; Daus.- Mary Bell, Sarah Simpson, Mehetabel Burleigh and Elizabeth Branscomb; His grandchildren. Execs.: wife Sarah, sons Sampson and Jacob, John Burleigh and John Simpson. His sig. Witnesses: Joseph Abbet, John Randel, Levi Connor, Allcock Stevens and Nathaniel (Remick or Kennick?). CERT. WILL (#3964): 11/5/1772. Presented by Jacob Sheafe, an Exec., and witnesses Randel and Abbet. INVY. (#5702): Appr. 9/22/1791. Comm.: Henry Prescutt, William Vennard and Joseph Frost. Value L115.18.8. Oaths 9/22/1791 Comm. and John Simpson, an Exec., to Geo. Frost, JP.

2390. SHEAFE, SAMPSON (1791) #5702
See #3964 Sampson Sheafe (1772)

SHEPARD. See also Shepherd

2391. SHEPARD, JAMES (1795) #6138
EST. Hampstead blacksmith decd. testate. WILL: Drawn 1/19/1788. Legatees: Wife-Mary; Bro.-Jonathan; Sister-Hannah Dow; Jonathan Shepherd son of his bro. Thomas; James Shepherd Kimball son of Ebenezer Kimball of Enfield, Grafton Co. Exec.-wife Mary. His sig. Witnesses: Thomas Muzzey, Henry Johnson and John Calfe. CERT. WILL (D32:39): 8/20/1795. Presented by Exec. and witnesses Muzzey and Calfe, esquires. ADMIN.: 8/20/1795. Exex. Mary Shephard, Hampstead widow. Bond $3,000.00. Sureties: John Calfe and Thomas Muzzey, Hampstead esquires. Witnesses: Joseph Blanchard and Wm. Parker.

2392. SHEPARD, THOMAS (1773) #4059
EST. Of Barrington, decd. testate. WILL: Drawn 6/4/1771. Legatees: Wife-Dorothy; Sons-Samuel, Thomas, Jacob and John; Dau.-Susanna Shepard. Exec.-Son Jacob. His sig. Witnesses: Hercules Mooney, Abraham Ellison and Thos. Fisher. Proved 11/29/1771. With the Will in the Docket Book is the notation, "I find indorsed in Major John Wentworth's handwriting 'sworn y 29th Nov. 1771' the usual mark of his Probate of Wills. Saml. Hale Junr. L. F. Reg." Marked on back by clerk "Returned 11/29/1771. Recd. in the Probate Office 12/1773." Note: Major John Wentworth was a Judge of Probate.

SHEPHERD. See also Shepard

2393. SHEPHERD, ABNER (1791) #5677
EST. Est Kingston yoeman decd. ADMIN.: 7/20/1791. Admr. Moses Shepard, East Kingston yoeman. Bond L1000.0.0. Sureties: Jacob Ordway, East Kingston gent. and John Sheppard, South Hampton yoeman. Witnesses: Jonath Collins and W. Parker. INVY.: 9/7/1791. Comm.: Ezra Currier and Jacob Ordway. Value L319.6.0. Oaths 9/15/1791 Comm. and Admr. to Nathl. Bacheller, JP. AGREEMENT: 3/19/1793. Of: Mary Shepard, widow and Moses Sheppard. Mary and her sons have agreed upon the following Dower Comm.: Capt. Ezra Currier and Jacob Ordway, gentlemen; Edward Greeley and Joseph Fifield, yoemen, all of East Kingston and Capt. Jeremiah Bacheller, Kensington gent. DIV. WARR.: 3/20/1793. Comm. same as for Dower. To set off to Moses Shepherd his 1/3 proportion of the real est. ACCOUNT: 3/1793. Of Admr. Allowed 3/20/1793. As the whole family has lived on the real est. and have had equal share of income, Admr. does not account for it. DOWER: 3/39/1793. Comm. as requested. Of Widow Mary Sheppard. Oaths 3/29/1793 Comm. to Nathl. Bacheller, JP. Allowed. DIV.: 3/29/1793. Divisee Moses

Sheppard. Oaths 3/29/1793 Comm. to Nathl. Bacheller, JP. ADDL. ACCOUNT: 1/19/1795. Of Admr. Allowed 1/19/1795.

2394. SHEPHERD, DANIEL (1788) #5348
EST. Northfield yoeman decd. ADMIN.: 4/24/1788. Admx. Elizabeth Shepherd, Northfield widow. Bond L500.0.0. Sureties: Henry Gerrish, Boscawen, Hillsborough Co. esq. and Thomas Clough of Northfield. Witnesses: Edward Blanchard and Thomas Cross. INVY.: Appr. 5/7/1788. Comm.: Edward Blanchard, Thomas Clough and Thomas Cross. Value L36.16.1. Oaths 5/7/1788 Admx. and Comm. to Henry Gerrish, JP.

2395. SHEPHERD, JESSE (1789) #5477
EST. Hampstead yoeman decd. RENUN.: 8/17/1789. Of Mehitabel Bodge. Of Admin. of est. her son Jesse Shepherd. Requests appointment of James Shepard. Witness John Morss. ADMIN.: 8/18/1789. Admr. James Shepard, Hampstead blacksmith. Bond L500.0.0. Sureties: Nehemiah Sleeper, Hawke gent. and Jacob Paslee, Kingston esq. Witnesses: Nathl. Parker and Jere. Fogg Jr.

2396. SHEPHERD, JONATHAN (1785) #5116
GDP. Of the son of Thomas Shepherd of Haverhill decd. GDP.: 6/15/1785. Of Jonathan, a minor over 14. Gdn. James Shepherd, Hampstead blacksmith. Bond L1000.0.0. Sureties: Jonathan Eastman, gent. and John Kimball, yoeman, both of Hampstead. Witnesses: Samll. Shepard and Nathl. Parker. Note: There is no indication as to whether the res. of Jonathan's father was Haverhill, Grafton Co., NH, to which many families of the area moved as pioneer settlers, or Haverhill, Essex Co., MA, which is close to Hampstead.

SHERBURN. See also Shurburne

2397. SHERBURN JOHN (1777) #4278 1/2
EST. Portsmouth chaisemaker and yoeman decd. intestate. ADMIN.: 3/26/1777. Admr. Samuel Sherburne, Portsmouth husbm. and yoeman. Bond L100.0.0. Sureties: Thomas Odiorne, trader and Theophilus Smith, esq., both of Exeter. Witness Nathl. Parker. ACCOUNT (D24:328): 8/21/1778. By Admr. Allowed 8/26/1778.

SHERBURNE. See also Sherburn

2398. SHERBURNE, DANIEL (1779) #4529
EST. Portsmouth merchant decd. testate. WILL: Drawn 11/1778. Legatees: His mother; Bros.-Samuel, esq. and Nathaniel; Sister-Dorothy Sherburne; Daniel Lang grandson of Richard White of Portsmouth who now lives with Capt. Jotham Blanchard; His negro man Casar, his freedom but to live with family if he wishes; Free negro boy Phillip who lives with him. Exec.-bro. Nathaniel. His sig. Witnesses: John Wendell, William Martin and Elizabeth Chivers. CERT. WILL (D25:52):3/31/1779. Presented by Exec., witnesses Wendell, esq. and Chivers having given oaths to W. Parker, JP. & Reg. on 3/4/1779. INVY.: Appr. 5/21/1779. Comm.: Dean Fowle, John Wendell and Josh. Seaward. Value L2391.9.0. Oaths 5/21/1779 Comm. to H. Wentworth, JP. Oath 5/27/1779 Exec. to judge. LICENSE (D26:443):6/19/1781. To Exec. To sell sufficient real est. to pay debts. PETITION: 3/8/1783. of Exec. For Comm. Insolvency. ADMIN. D.B.N.: 3/20/1799. Exec. d.b.n. Samuel Sherburne, Portsmouth esq. Bond $2,000.00. Sureties: Jonathan Warner, esq. and George Wentworth, both of Portsmouth. Witnesses: Richd. Champney and Mark Rogers. LETTER ADMIN. D.B.N.: 3/1779. To Samuel Sherburne, Portsmouth esq. A copy. LETTER : 9/11/1799. From Lt.? Joseph Peirce. To judge or Reg. Col. Saml. Sherburne has applied to Peirce for papers respecting the late D. Sherburne's est. in keeping of Mr. Rindge. What Peirce found, he is enclosing, thinking it not proper to give them to Col. Sherburne and that they should be deposited in the Registrar's office. PAPERS: The following loose papers, mostly receipts, seem to be what Peirce sent and appear to be papers that were in hands of the Comm. Insolvency. 1. To Daniel Sherburne. His account with Samuel Sherburne. For L4583.18 (1/4?). Signed by Saml. Sherburne and dated 9/12/1786. 2. Account of the late company of Danl. And Saml. Sherburne in account with Saml. Sherburne L11707.17.2 1/2 and an account of Est. Daniel Sherburne with Saml. Sherburne undated, including what is apparently payment by Est., leaving a bal. of L4628.12.7 1/4. On back dated 4/10/1797 "Col. Sherburne desired to have this acct. with me to accompany an acct. he formerly left before I (recinded?) my appointment as Comm." 3. Bill to Est. Daniel Sherburne from A. R. Cutter L35.18.6. Dated 9/18/1786. Oath 9/18/1786 Dr. A. R. Cutter to Geo. Gains, JP. 4. Bill to est. From: John Penhallow, Thomas Martin, Joshua Wentworth, Ammi R. Cutter, Samuel Sherburne, George Turner, Nathaniel Folsom, Richard Champney, Moses Woodard, Nich. McIntyre, Robert Furniss, Keith Spence, Thomas Dalling and Jacob Treadwell. L50.18.0. For expense of defending the cause of Mr. Doane vs. the Props. of the McClarey. Signed by Jacob Treadwell as agent for the Props. of the McClarey. 3/30/1786. 5. Bill to Daniel Sherburne decd. From Joshua Brackett. L15.1.0 plus L5.14.4. 6. Bill from Israel Marsden for work on

barn. L0.4.0/day, 1 1/2 days for him and 2 days for son in 9/1778. Dated 1/1779. 7. Bill to Est. from Stephen Hardy. L8.3.8 plus 3.10.4 1/2. For making uniform for Col. Wingate. Total L11.14.0 1/2. 8. Bill to Est. From Joseph Tarlton @ 114 dollars (Spanish milled) /mo. And credit for one pair shoes 9 (Spanish milled) dollars. 9. Bill to Est. from James Tarlton. L3.17.9 1/2. Oath 9/5/1785 Tarlton to Geo. Gains, JP. 10. D. Sherburne. Rcd. Sarah Basher L66.13.4 plus 9 items to several persons amounting to L4600.0.0+. 11. Rcpt. Witness Saml. Abbot. From Mrs. Sarah Barker 7/6/1776 for L50 sterling, it being a legacy left Mary Gibson by her uncle Joseph Gibson, equal to L66.13.4 lawful money which is in full for said legacy per D. Sherburne. 12. Bill from Dr. Hall Jackson for medicine and services L9.12.9. 7/1785. Oath 7/1785 Jackson to Clemt. March, JP.

2399. SHERBURNE, DEBORAH (1786) #5167
EST. Kensington widow decd. testate. WILL: Drawn 3/31/785. Legatees: Sons-Nathaniel, Daniel, Nathan and Joseph; Dau.-Betty Fowler; Grandson-John Huse; Granddau.-Elizabeth Fogg (unm.). Exec.-son Nathaniel. Her sig. witnesses; Samuel Tucke, Ebenr. Potter and Elijah Shaw. CERT. WILL (D28:390): 1/18/1786. Presented by Exec. and witnesses Potter and Tucke. INVY.: Comm.: Samuel Tucke and Ebenezer Potter. Value not tallied. Esti. L61.11.0. Oaths 3/21/1788 Comm. and Exec. to Jere. Fogg, JP.

2400. SHERBURNE, EDWARD (1777) #4522
EST. Of Portsmouth decd. testate. WILL: Drawn 4/4/1777. Legatee: Mother-Sarah Sherburne. Exec.-Sarah Sherburne. His sig. Witnesses: John Wendell, D. Sherburn and Saml. Sherburne. CERT. WILL: 3/31/1779. Presented by Exex., witnesses Wendell and Saml. Sherburne, esq. having given oaths on 3/4/1779 to W. Parker, JP. & Reg. Witness Daniel Sherburn decd.

2401. SHERBURNE, GEORGE JR. (1778) #4471
EST. Loudon yoeman decd. ADMIN.: 9/23/1778. Admx. Elizabeth Sherburne, Loudon widow. Bond L500.0.0. Sureties: Joseph Leavit, cooper and Jonathan Norris, gent., both of Exeter. Witnesses: Nathl. Parker and W. Parker. INVY. WARR.: 9/23/1778. Comm.: William Davis and William Boynton, both of Loudon and Joseph Sanborn of Canterbury. Oaths 11/3/1778 Davis and Boynton to Nathan Bachelder, JP. INVY.: Value not tallied. Esti. L593.0.0+. Oath 11/3/1778 Sanborn and Admx. to Archelaus Moore, JP. DIV.: Comm.: Benjamin Sias, William Davis and Leavitt Clough, of a 5 man Comm. appointed by an Act of the NH General Court. To set off to Jacob Sherburne of Loudon 1/2 of a 100 acre lot in Loudon, it being the est. of George Sherburne Jr. where he lived until his

death. Divisees: Jacob Sherburne and Heirs of George Sherburne Jr. Oaths 8/3/1779 Comm. to Archelous Moore, JP.

2402. SHERBURNE, GEORGE (1782) #4827
EST. Loudon yoeman decd. RENUN.: 7/2/1782. Of Abigail Sherburne. Of Admin. Requests appointment of Jacob Sherburne as it is agreeable to the whole family. Witnesses: William Boynton and Nathanael Moore. ADMIN.: 8/6/1782. Admr. Jacob Sherburne, Loudon yoeman. Bond L15000.0.0. Sureties: Richard Whitcher, Brentwood yoeman and Ebenezer Smith, Meredith, Strafford Co. esq. Witness Nathl. Parker. INVY.: Appr. 8/26/1782. Comm.: Archelaus Moore, Benja. Sias and William Davis. Value L207.15.0. Oaths 8/26/1782 Comm. to Nathan Bachelder, JP. Oath 8/26/1782 Admr. to W. Parker, JP. & Reg. ACCOUNT: 9/19/1787. Of Admr. Allowed 9/19/1787 with note of Comm. that the reversion of about 1/4 acre of land near Plains in Portsmouth omitted from Invy. Judge notes that income from the real est. to be accounted for in a future Account.

2403. SHERBURNE, HENRY (1767) A#3399
EST. Portsmouth esq. decd. LICENSE (D27:50): 9/25/1782. To Widow Sarah Sherburne, Admx. To sell real est. Orig. Archives file includes Admin., Invy., Petition, Account and License 1771.

2404. SHERBURNE, JAMES (1799) #6538
EST. Pelham yoeman decd. testate. WILL: Drawn 6/11/1789. Legatees; Wife-Anna; Sons-Benjamin and William; Daus.-Margaret Wright, Dorothy Barker and Sarah Hebbard. Exec.-son William. His sig. Witnesses: Abial Coburn, Caleb Coburn and Nathan Coburn. CERT. WILL (D33:40):2/19/1799. Presented by Exec. and witnesses Abiel Coburn and Nathan Coburn. CERT.: 2/11/1799. Of: Benjamin Sherburne, Abiel Wright, John Hebberd and Ebenezer Barker, heirs or husbands or heirs. They are satisfied with Will. Witnesses: Mark Gould, Sarah Sherburne and John Barker. Cert.: Of Anna Sherburn, widow of James. She is satisfied with Will. Witnesses: Nathan Coburn and James Sherburn. INVY. (D33:66): Comm.: Asa Richardson, Benja. Hamblett and Abiel Coburn. Value $2,522.58. Oaths 4/15/1799 Comm. to Josiah Gage, JP. Oath 4/17/1799 Exec. to judge.

2405. SHERBURNE, JOHN (1767) A#3384
EST. Kensington joyner decd. Note: The following License and Account found in #4121 1/2 John Sherburne (1774) belong here. LICENSE: 12/31/1777. To Deborah Sherburne, Admx., his widow. To sell as much real est. as needed to pay debts. ACCOUNT: 12/31/1777. Of Admx. Allowed 12/31/1777. Account includes main. 3 children. Orig. Archives file includes Admin. and Invy.

2406. SHERBURNE, JOHN (1774) #4121 1/2
EST. Kensington yoeman decd. testate. WILL: Drawn 4/2/1774. Legatees: Mother-Deborah Sherburne; Bros.-Nathaneal, Daniel, Nathan and Joseph; Sisters-Betty Perkins, Zervia, Mary and Hannah; Heirs of his father John Sherburne given freedom to move the barn and shop on land he bequeaths to bro. Nathaniel to the other part of the est. which was his father's, if they wish. Execs.-mother Deborah and bro. Nathaneal. His sig. Witnesses: Nathl. Healy, John Lane and Samuel Tucke. CERT. WILL (D24:168): 12/31/1777. Presented by Execs. and witnesses Lane, esq. and Tucke. Note: An earlier oath of 9/24/1774 has been crossed out. Judge also notes the Exex. Unable to travel to Portsmouth. INVY.: Appr. 10/3/1774. Comm.: Joseph Tilton and Samuel Tucke. Value not tallied. Esti. L110.0.0+. Oath 11/20/1774 of Tucke only, Tilton being dead, to Wm. Parker, JP. Note: This file includes a License and an Account which belong with A#3384 John Sherburne (1767) and are recorded there.

2407. SHERBURNE, CAPT. JOHN (1794) #6042
EST. Portsmouth mariner decd. ADMIN.: 11/6/1794. Admr. Clement Storer, Portsmouth esq. Bond L1000.0.0. Sureties: Edward Gove, gent. and Edward Hart, baker, both of Portsmouth. Witnesses: R. Cutts Shannon and W. Parker. INVY. WARR.: 11/6/1794. Comm.: Isaac Rindge, George Wentworth and Jeremiah Libbey, Portsmouth esquires. INVY. (D31:397): 11/10/1794. Value L232.0.7 plus 1/3 of the cargo of his Schooner Adventure, amount not yet known. Oaths 11/10/1794 Rindge, Wentworth and Admr., affirm. Libbey to Nathl. Adams, JP. PETITION: 11/25/1794. Of Admr. For Comm. Insolvency. Gives claims already exhibited as L352.13.2. Requests Comm. of Isaac Rindge, Geo. Wentworth and Jeremiah Libbey, esquires. Granted. CLAIMS WARR.: 11/25/1794. Comm. as requested. CLAIMS: 6/8/1795. Total $1,203.25. Oaths 6/8/1795 Rindge and Wentworth to R. Cutts Shannon, JP. ACCOUNT: 6/17/1795. Of Admr. Gives income from voyage of Schooner Adventure by report of Referees as L239.19.9 plus two accounts which appear to be due from West Indies. Allowed 6/17/1795. POWER OF ATTY. (D33:100): 3/17/1798. Of Henry Sherburne, Conway, Strafford Co. blacksmith. To Robert McClintock, Conway, Strafford Co. mariner. To demand, prosecute and receive from Clement Storer, Portsmouth physician, Admr. of est. of John Sherburne, Portsmouth mariner decd., all things relative to est. Witnesses: Obed. Hall and Catty Sherburne. Oath 8/11/1798 Henry Sherburne to Obed. Hall, JP. PROOF OF POWER OF ATTY. (D33:101): 6/18/1799. Daniel Humphreys, Notary Public, certs. this is a true copy of the Power of Atty. and he witnessed the receipt and discharge made and executed by McClintock to Dr. Clement Storer. Receipt: 3/5/1799. Of Henry Sherburne by his atty. Robert McClintock. To Dr. Clement Storer,

Admr. est. Capt. John Sherburne of Portsmouth decd. For $300.00 in full of all monies due him from est. as heir of John decd. Witness Daniel Humphreys.

2408. SHERBURNE, HON. JOHN (1797) #6326
APPOINTMENT & EST. Portsmouth esq. decd. APPOINTMENT (D22:335): 11/26/1773. Of John Sherburne, esq. He is appointed Judge of Probate for the County of Rockingham. Signed by John Wentworth, esq., Governor and Commander in Chief of the Province of NH and Theodore Atkinson, secy. Recorded in the Book of Commissions 11/30/1773 by Geo. King, secy. Oath of Office 11/30/1773 by John Sherburne. Signed by Theodore Atkinson and Jonathan Warner, Comm. ADMIN.: 3/20/1797. Admr. John Samuel Sherburne, Portsmouth esq. Bond $10,000.00. Sureties: Joshua Brackett and Supply Clap, Portsmouth esquires. Witnesses: George Wentworth and Nathan Goss. INVY.: Comm.: Joshua Brackett, George Wentworth and R. Cutts Shannon. Value $9,809.92. Oaths 8/2/1797 Comm. to Saml. Penhallow, JP. Affirm. 8/101797 Admr. to W. Parker. RELEASE (D33:288): 7/1/1801. Of: John Langdon, Portsmouth esq. and Elisabeth his wife in her right as an heir to her late father John Sherburne, Portsmouth esq. decd. To John Samuel Sherburne, Portsmouth esq., Admr. For $4,000.00 received they release and discharge him of all demands of one moiety of est. Witnesses: R. Cutts Shannon and Charles Prilay. Oaths 8/5/1800 John Langdon and Elizabeth Langdon to R. Cutts Shannon, JP.

2409. SHERBURNE: MOLLY & NATHANIEL (1797) #6382
GDP. Of the children of Nathl. Sherburne, Kensington yoeman decd. GDP.: 9/30/1797. Of: Molly and Nathaniel, minors under 14. Gdn. Sarah Sherburne, Kensington widow. Bond $1,000.00. Sureties: John Bacheller and Elijah Shaw, Kensington yoemen. Witnesses: Samuel Bachelder and Nathl. Parker. GDP.: 3/25/1800. Of: Molly and Nathaniel, minors over 14. Gdn. Josiah White, Pittsfield yoeman. Bond $3,000.00. Sureties: John Hilyard, gent. and Jeremiah Lane, yoeman, both of Chichester. Witness W. Parker.

2410. SHERBURNE, NATHANIEL (1757) A#2289
EST. Portsmouth shopkeeper decd. Note: The following items found in #6036 Nathaniel Sherburne (1794) belong here. PETITION: 10/3/1774. Of Mehetabel Sherburne, Admx. For Comm. Insolvency. Allowed 10/3/1774 with Comm. of John Parker and John Sparhawk, esquires. PETITION: 2/2/1775. Of Admx. For License. Granted. LICENSE: 2/2/1775. To Admx. To sell sufficient real est. to pay debts. Orig. Archives file includes Admin., Invy. Warr. and Invy.

2411. SHERBURNE, NATHANIEL (1788) #5389
EST. Kensington yoeman decd. intestate. ADMIN.: 11/19/1788. Admx. Sarah Sherburne, Kensington widow. Bond L1000.0.0. Sureties: John Bacheller, esq. and Samuel Tucke, gent., both of Kensington. Witnesses: Nathl. Parker and W. Parker. INVY.: Comm.: John Lane and Ebenr. Potter. Value L181.17.3. Oaths 2/17/1789 Comm. and Admx. to Jere. Fogg, JP. PETITION: 2/3/1797. Of Admx. For License to sell all the real est., as selling part would be injurious to children and Admx., and 1/2 a pew. LICENSE: 2/5/1797. To Admx. To sell all the real est. and half a pew in Kensington Meeting House. BOND: 2/5/1797. Of Admx. Bond $2,000.00. To account for sale of real est. and pew by License. Sureties: Elijah Shaw and John Shaw, Raymond yoemen. Witness W. Parker. APPR.: 9/27/1797. Comm.: John Lane, Benjamin Tilton and Jere. Fellows Jr. They appr. the neat income of 2/3 of the real est. since Nathaniel's death at $15.50 per year. Oaths 9/27/1797 Comm. to Jere. Fogg, JP. ACCOUNT: Of Admx. Allowed 9/30/1797 being sworn to by Accountant who is also Gdn. of heirs. Account includes main. Molly, Nathaniel and a babe who died at 6 months.

2412. SHERBURNE, CAPT. NATHANIEL (1794) #6036
EST. Portsmouth mariner decd. ADMIN.: 10/15/1794. Admx. Elizabeth Sherburne, Portsmouth widow. Bond L1000.0.0. Sureties: Jonathan Warner, esq. and Daniel Warner, merchant, both of Portsmouth. Witnesses: Jos. Seaward to Mrs. Sherburne's sig.; John Haven to Warner's sig. and Geo. Seaward to all sigs. INVY.: Appr. 2/12/1795. Comm.: Capt. George Wentworth, Isaac Rindge and Saml. Drowne. Value L167.14.3. Oaths 2/12/1795 Wentworth and Drowne and on 2/14/1795 Admx. to R. Cutts Shannon, JP. ACCOUNT: 2/16/1803. Of Admx. Oath 2/17/1803 Admx. to Isaac Rindge, JP. Allowed 2/17/1803. Account includes main. Jno. This file also contains A Pet. for Comm. Insolvency, Petition for License, License and Account which belong with A#2289 Nathaniel Sherburne (1757) and are recorded there.

2413. SHERBURNE, NATHANIEL (1799) #6581
EST. Portsmouth merchant decd. testate. PETITION: 7/9/1799. Of Samuel Sherburne, Portsmouth esq. He states that the Exec. named in Will has refused to administer, the only children are minor girls and the mother of decd. is aged. As largest creditor, requests Admin. WILL: Drawn 12/20/1788. Legatees: Daus.-Polly Cutter Sherburne, Sally Warner Sherburne and Betsy Sherburne. Exec.-father-in-law Dr. Ammi Ruhamah Cutter. His sig. Witnesses: Jona. M. Sewall, Danl. R. Rogers and Danl. Cutter. CERT. WILL: 7/12/1799. Presented by Exec. named and witnesses Rogers and Danl. Cutter. Exec. Having refused Admin., judge appoints

Samuel Sherburne Admr. RENUN.: 6/19/1799. Of A. R. Cutter, esq. Of Admin. ADMIN.: 7/12/1799. Admr. Samuel Sherburne, Portsmouth esq. Bond $3,000.00. Sureties: Jonathan Warner, Portsmouth esq. and Joseph Tilton, Exeter physician. LIST OF CLAIMS: 8/6/1801. Signed by Admr. Total $931.48.8 (sic.) plus an unspecified claim of est. of Danl. Sherburne. ACCOUNT: 10/21/1801. Of Admr. Allowed 10/21/1801 the heirs and creditors having been notified.

2414. SHERBURNE, NOAH (1782) #4854
EST. New Castle yoeman decd. testate. WILL: Drawn 1/25/1782. Legatees; Wife-Elizabeth; Son-John. Execs.-wife and son John. His mark. Witnesses: William Seavey, Nadab Moses and George F. Blunt. No probing of Will. ADMIN.: 5/29/1782. Execs.: Elizabeth Sherburne, widow and John Sherburne, yoeman, both of New Castle. Bond L1000.0.0. Sureties: Richard Jenness, Rye esq. and John Beck, Portsmouth gent. Witnesses: Nathl. Parker and W. Parker. INVY.: Appr. 10/28/1782. Comm.: Joseph Edmonds and William Seavey. Value L265.15.0. Oaths 10/28/1782 Comm. to Amos Seavey, JP. Oaths 10/30/1782 Admrs. to judge. DOWER WARR.: 10/30/1782. Comm.: Samuel Wallace of Rye; Samuel Sherburne and Joseph Banfill of Portsmouth; and James Seavey and Joseph Edmonds. Of Widow Elizabeth Sherburne. PETITION: 1/29/1783. Of John Sherburne, an Admr. For License. Gives list claims of L110.3.4. LICENSE (D27:149): 1/29/1783. To Admrs. To sell sufficient real est. to pay debts. CLAIMS: Comm.: Joshua Brackett, Nathl. Treadwell and Moses Woodward. Total L134.10.2. Oaths 2/12/1784 Comm. to George Gains, JP. DOWER: Oaths 2/28/1783 Comm. to Amos Seavey, JP. Allowed. MAP OF DOWER. ACCOUNT: 7/22/1784. Of Admrs. Allowed 7/22/1784. PROP. & SETTLM.: Claims L134.10.2. Amount to be proportioned L96.14.0. Allowed 7/22/1784 with order to Admrs. to pay.

2415. SHESLEY, SAMUEL (1775) #4159
See #4159 Daniel Shirley (1775)

SHIELDS. See also Sheills

2416. SHIELDS, RICHARD (1779) #4558
EST. Portsmouth mariner decd. ADMIN.: 7/28/1779. Admr. John Bason, Portsmouth mariner. Bond L1000.0.0. Sureties: Joseph Baker and Joe Hutchings, Portsmouth mariners. Witnesses: John Weeks and W. Parker.

SHIELLS. See also Shields

2417. SHIELLS, JAMES (1773) #4065
EST. Canterbury peddler and traveling merchant decd. intestate. ADMIN.: 12/17/1773. Admr. Timothy Walker Jr., Concord merchant Bond L1000.0.0. Sureties: Timothy Walker, clerk and Abiel Chandler, gent., both of Concord. Witnesses: Daniel Parker and Ephraim Eddy. INVY.: Appr. 12/27/1773. Comm.: Capt. Stephen Gerrish, and Jeremiah Clough, esq., both of Canterbury. Value L75.17.2 1/2. Oaths 7/6/1774 Comm. to George Jackman, JP. Oath 9/29/1774 Admr. to judge. PETITION: 9/27/1774. Of Admr. For Comm. of Insolvency. Allowed 9/27/1774. Comm.: Stephen Gerrish of Canterbury and Abiel Chandler of Concord. CAVEAT: 7/20/1787. Dated at Concord. Of William Wallace of Newbury, Cohas, VT. He states that Mr. Shields, a traveling man, who died at the house of Capt. Gerrish, now decd., in Canterbury with Col. Timothy Walker of Concord, Admr. his est., was late of Great Britain. Shields left property here, now impounded as insolvent and there are large sums due in Scotland by Shields. Wallace has written Shields' friends in Scotland and requests that in order for justice to be done further action on the est. be delayed until claims can be received from Scotland.

2418. SHILLABER, JONATHAN (1791) #5666
EST. Portsmouth potter decd. intestate. ADMIN.: 6/8/1791. Admr. Joseph Stacy, Portsmouth mariner. Bond L1000.0.0. Sureties: Stacy Hall and John Melcher, Portsmouth gentlemen. Witnesses: Nathl. Adams and Joseph Md. Fitzgerald. INVY.: Comm.: John Evans and Is. Rindge. Shown by Jacob Walden atty. to Admr. Value L276.18.6. Oaths 6/20/1791 Comm. to Jonathan Warner, JP. Oath 9/21/1791 Admr. to judge. PETITION: 7/2/1791. Of Jacob Walden atty. to Admr. For Comm. Insolvency. Gives list claims of L375.13.4 1/2. DOWER: 9/14/1791. Comm.: Is. Rindge, Saml. Hutchings and Stacy Hall. Of Widow Elizabeth Shillaber. PETITION: 9/21/1791. Of Admr. For License. States claims already in are more than Invy. Granted. LICENSE (D30:126): 9/21/1791. To Admr. To sell real est. to amount of L260.0.0. CLAIMS WARR.: 7/2/1791. Comm.: Isaac Rindge and Jeremiah Libbey, esquires and John Evans, merchant, all of Portsmouth. Claims: 5/29/1792. Total L363.10.9 3/4. Oaths 5/29/1792 Rindge and Libbey to Geo. Gains, JP. ACCOUNT: 5/30/1792. Of Admr. Allowed 5/30/1792. PROP. & SETTLM.: Claims L363.10.9.3/4. Amount to be proportioned L165.8.9. Allowed 5/30/1792 with order to Admr. To pay.

SHIRLA. See also Shirley

2419. SHIRLA, JAMES (1796) #6242
EST. Chester gent. decd. testate. WILL: Drawn 5/13/1783. Legatees: Sons-Hugh, William and John; Daus.-Margret Shirla and Agnes MacNear. Exec.-son John. His sig. Witnesses: Robert MacMurphy, Margrit Moore and Daniel Hunter. CERT. WILL (D32:171): 8/17/1796. Presented by Exec. and witnesses MacMurphy and Moore. ADMIN.: 8/17/1796. Exec. John Shirley, Chester yoeman. Bond $1,000.00. Sureties: Robert MacMurphy, yoeman and John Morrison, esq., both of Londonderry. Witnesses: Jonathan Holms and W. Parker.

SHIRLEY. See also Shirla

2420. SHIRLEY, DANIEL (1775) #4159 & (1775) #4160
GDP. of the son of John Shirley, Chester yoeman decd. PETITION (#4159): 3/15/1775. Of Daniel Shoulley. Sates that he has an est. which has fallen to him and no Gdn. With the advice of friends, he has chosen Joseph Lynn of Chester to be his Gdn. Witness Samuel Emerson. Oath 3/15/1775. Of Daniel Shirley to Saml. Emerson, JP. Allowed 3/22/1775 and judge orders a Letter of Gdp. for Daniel "Sharley." GDP.(#4160). 3/22/1775. Of Daniel Shirley, a minor over 15. Gdn. Joseph Lynn, Chester yoeman. Bond L1000.0.0. Sureties: John Webster and Samuel Emerson, Chester esquires. Witnesses: Saml. Robie and Robt. Wilson. Note: The #4159 file is mistakenly called Samuel Shesley but all papers say Daniel. Because of the multiple spellings of Daniel's last name, the entry has been put under the spelling of Shirley, as with his father.

2421. SHORES, PETER (1790) #5509
EST. Portsmouth mariner decd. testate. WILL: Drawn 1/12/1789. Legatees: Son-John; Ref. to son Peter "where he lately lived;" Grandchildren-6 children of his dau. Mary Nason; Grandchildren-Susannah Gardner and Mary Shores, sisters; Grandson-James Shores; Children of his grandson Peter Shores. He gives son John the house and land in Portsmouth which Peter Ball gave his wife during her lifetime. Execs.-friends Geo. Jerry Osborn Sr. and Joseph Walton. His mark. Witnesses: Saml. Drowne, Benjamin Drowne and Arthur Blunt. CERT. WILL (D29:334): Presented by Execs. and oaths of all witnesses on 1/15/1790 to Nathl. Adams, JP. Allowed. ADMIN.: 1/15/1790. Execs.: George Jerry Osborn, gent. and Joseph Walton, clerk, both of Portsmouth. Bond L1000.0.0. Sureties: George Wentworth, mariner and Edward Dimpsey, yoeman, both of Portsmouth. Witnesses: Nathl. Adams and Joseph W. Woodward. INVY.: Appr. 1/23/1790. Comm.: John Evans and Nathl. Marshall. Value L397.4.0. Oaths 1/24/1790 Comm. and George Jerry Osborn, an Exec., to Nathl. Adams, JP.

2422. SHORTRIDGE, RICHARD (1777) #4326
EST. Portsmouth esq. decd. intestate. ADMIN.: 3/20/1777. Admx. Mary Shortridge, Portsmouth widow. Bond L500.0.0. Sureties: John Furnald, brazier and Nahum Ward, trader, both of Portsmouth. Witnesses: Humphrey Fernald and Hannah Dame. INVY.: Appr. 6/20/1777. Comm.: Thos. Hart, Richard Hart and Thomas Sheafe. Value L839.11.6. Oaths 6/20/1777 Comm. and on 6/23/1777 Admx. to Saml. Penhallow, JP. PETITION: Of Admx. by her atty. Oliver Whipple. For License. Gives claims as L379.10.7. Allowed 9/30/1778. LICENSE: 9/30/1778. To Admx. To Admx. To sell sufficient real est. to pay debts. ACCOUNT: 6/1779. Of Admx. Allowed 6/30/1779. Account includes main. 2 children. LICENSE (D27:188): 3/26/1783. To Admx. To sell sufficient real est. to pay debts. ADDL. ACCOUNT: 9/24/1783. Of John Donaldson and Mary his wife, Admx. Allowed.

2423. SHUTE: ANNA, HIRAM, LYDIA, MICHAEL & WILLIAM (1791) #5641
GDP. Of the children of Michael Shute, Newmarket boatbuilder decd. GDP.: 4/18/1791. Of Michael, Hiram, William and Lydia, minors under 14. Gdn. Henry Wiggin, Newmarket joiner. Bond L500.0.0. Sureties: Henry Wiggin Jr., joiner and William Shute, boatbuilder, both of Newmarket. Witnesses: W. Parker and Jacob Randel. The following GDP. was together with the Gdp. of the children of Henry Wiggin #5245 Wiggin: Henry & Wealthan &Anna Shute (1787). The Gdp. of Anna is placed here and the Wiggin children left with #5245. GDP: 1/17/1787. Of Anna, a minor over 14, dau. of Michael Shute of Newmarket decd. Gdn. Henry Wiggin, Newmarket housewright. Bond L500.0.0. Surety John Shute, Newmarket innholder Witnesses: Nathl. Parker and W. Parker. See also #6404 for an addl. 1797 Gdp. for William.

2424. SHUTE, ELIZABETH (1793) #5873
EST. Exeter widow decd. ADMIN.: 3/25/1793. Admr. John Shute, Newmarket innholder. Bond L500.0.0. Sureties: Nathaniel Rogers, esq. and Daniel Hill, gent., both of Newmarket. Witnesses: Nancy Adams and Josiah Adams. INVY.: Appr. 3/30/1793. Comm.: Josiah Adams, Ichabod Hilton and John Colcord. Value L11.10.6. Oaths 4/1/1793 Comm. to Nat. Rogers, JP. PETITION: 4/2/1793. Of Admr. For Comm. Insolvency. Gives one claim of L20.0.0. and another not yet ascertained but large. PETITION: 3/10/1794. Of Admr. He suspects Jacob Pearson, trader and Jacob Randall, barber, both of Exeter, of concealing, embezzling or conveying away goods of est. Requests they be cited to appear and be examined under oath. CITATION: 3/10/1794. To: Jacob Pearson, gent. and Jacob Randell, barber, both of Exeter. To appear and be examined

under oath regarding the suspicion of Admr. that they have concealed, embezzled or conveyed away goods or chattels of est. Cert.: 3/17/1794. Of James Rundlett, Dpy. Sheriff. He has read the Citation to Pearson and Randell. EXAMINATION: Of Mr. Pearson: States the only article of est. he has had was one silk gown which Mrs. Randell (sic.) sent him before her death in a bundle with other articles with a request that he keep them for her children. Examination of Mr. Randel: States the Invy. does contain all the est. of Mrs. Shute at the time of her death which Mrs. Shute had not previously given to Mrs. Randel, except a gold necklace and a gold sleeve button. Mrs. Shute left only one silk gown not given to Mrs. Randel in Shute's lifetime, which Mrs. Randel afterwards had altered and wore as mourning, 2 chintz gowns and part of the feathers of one bed, the tick and remaining feathers being spoiled during Mrs. Shute's last sickness. ADDL. INVY.: Appr. 3/24/1794. Value L3.15/9. Includes the clothing, necklace and gold button. Oaths 3/31/1794 Adams and Hilton to James Smith, JP. CLAIMS WARR.: 4/2/1793. Comm.: Josiah Adams and Daniel Hill, Exeter esquires. Claims: 10/22/1793. Total L24.14.3. Oaths 3/31/1794 Comm. to James Smith, JP. ACCOUNT: Of Admr. Allowed 4/14/1794. PROP. & SETTLM.: Claims L24.14.3. Amount to be proportioned L9.14.10. Allowed 5/10/1794 with order to Admr. to pay. DUPL. COPY OF PROP. & SETTLM.

2425. SHUTE, JAMES (1791) #5640
GDP. Of the son of William Shute, Newmarket boatbuilder decd. GDP.: 4/18/1791. Of James, a minor over 14. Gdn. William Shute, Newmarket boatbuilder. Bond L500.0.0. Sureties: Henry Wiggin and Henry Wiggin Jr., Newmarket joiners. Witnesses: W. Parker and Jacob Randel.

2426. SHUTE, JOSEPH (1791) #5635
See Michael Shute (1784) #5056

2427. SHUTE, MICHAEL (1784) #5065
EST. Newmarket trader decd. testate. WILL: Drawn 9/1/1778. Legatees: Wife-Elizabeth; Sons-Michael, Thomas, Joseph, Benjamin, Walter, John and William; Daus.-Sarah Shute, Mary Shute, Lydia Wiggins and Elizabeth Shute. Exec.-son John. His sig. Witnesses: Moses Egerby, Josiah Adams and William Coffin. CERT. WILL: 12/15/1784. Presented by Exec. and witnesses Edgerly and Adams, esq. INVY.: Appr. 3/15/1785. Comm.: Saml. Baker, gent.; Nat. Rogers, esq. and Wm. Badger, shipwright, all of Newmarket. Value L918.17.8 3/4. Oaths 12/15/1785 Comm. to Josiah Adams, JP. Oath 3/16/1786 Exec. to W. Parker, JP. PETITION: 12/19/1786. Of: Michael Shute and Joseph Shute. For div. of land in Stratham and Sanbornton, Strafford Co. which they hold as tenants

in common with Anna Shute and the children of Lydia Wiggin decd. Anna and the children are minors. Signed by: Michael Wiggin (sic.), John Shute, William Shute, Walter Shute, John Marstes, Benjamin Shute, Nancy Shute and Joseph Shute. Order: 12/20/1786. For hearing, Petitioners to notify Gdns. of minors. DIV. WARR.: 1/17/1787. Comm.: Nathaniel Rogers, esq.; Hubartus Neal, Walter Neal, John Colcord and Benjamin Folsom, all of Newmarket. To div. the land as follows: to Michael Shute 2/11 of 3/11, to the children of Lydia Wiggin 1/11 of 3/11 and to each of the others 1/11 plus 1/11 of 3/11. DIV.: 4/13/1787. Divisees: Heirs of Lydia Wiggin decd., Walter Shute, John Marstes, Michael Shute, William Shute, Thomas Shute, Joseph Shute, Benjamin Shute, John Shute and Anna Shute. Oaths 11/17/1787 Hubartus Neal, Walter Neal, Colcord and Rogers to Josiah Adams, JP. Allowed 12/19/1787. The following Addl. Invy. found in #5662 Michael Shute (1791) belongs here. ADDL. INVY.: 2/17/1789. Of John Shute, Admr. Total L102.11.0. Contains land in Sanbornton. The following PETITION recorded as #5635 Joseph Shute (1791) belongs here. PETITION: 4/9/1791. Of Joseph Shute, John Marstes, Walter Shute, Jacob Randell and Benjamin Shute. Request division of a mansion house and land in Newmarket which they hold in common with 1. Some of the children of Michael Shute, Newmarket boatbuilder decd.; 2. The children of William Shute, Newmarket boatbuilder decd. and; 3. Other heirs of Michael Shute, Newmarket shipwright decd. Order: 4/11/1791. Petitioners to serve their co-heirs with a copy of Petition and an Order for a hearing thereon. TRUE COPY OF PETITION. The following Div. Warr., Div., Bill, Accounts and Petition found in #5662 Michael Shute (1791) belong here. DIV. WARR.: 4/18/1791. Comm.: Hubartus Neal, gent.; Gideon Colcord and Nathl. Lord, yoemen, all of Newmarket. To divide land held in common by the heirs of Michael Shute, Newmarket shipwright decd., 30 acres with buildings, in Newmarket, which Michael by Will devised to his widow until married or death. Divisees: John Shute; Heirs of William Shute; Walter Shute; Thomas Shute; Joseph Shute; Benja. Shute; John Marstes in the right of his wife; Jacob Randell in the right of his wife; and the heirs of Lydia Wiggin decd., each 1/11th part. The remaining: 2/11ths to John Shute 3 parts; to the heirs of William Shute, Walter, Thomas, Joseph, Benjamin Marstes and Randell 2 parts each and to the heirs of Michael Shute Jr., boatbuilder decd., 5 parts. Returned 5/14/1791. Oaths Comm. to Josiah Adams, JP. Allowed. BILL: 5/14/1791. By Div. Comm. To heirs of the est. of Michael Shute. For L3.18.6, their charge for doing the Division. Signed by Nathaniel Rogers for the Comm. ACCOUNT NO. 1: 7/25/1792. By John Shute, Exec. ACCOUNT NO. 2: Continuation of previous Account. ACCOUNT NO. 3: Further continuation. All Accounts allowed 7/25/1792, heirs having been heard. PETITION: 7/25/1792. Of John Shute, Exec. For License in amount of L145.0.0 to pay the claims and other demands not ascertained. Gives list of Claims of $138.7.0. tained. ACCOUNT: 5/13/1793. Of John Shute, Exec. Allowed there being no objections from heirs.

2428. SHUTE, MICHAEL (1791) #5662
EST. Newmarket boatbuilder decd. ADMIN.: 5/21/1791. Admr. John Marstes, Newmarket physician. Bond L500.0.0. Sureties: Dudley Watson, trader and Daniel Hill, esq., both of Newmarket. Witnesses: W. Parker and Benj. Abbott. INVY.: Comm.: Daniel Hill and Dudley Watson. Value L44.13.6. Oaths 3/14/1792 Comm. to Josiah Adams, JP. Oath 3/17/1792 Admr. to W. Parker, JP. ADMIN. D.B.N: 9/9/1799. Admr. d.b.n Dudley Watson, Newmarket trader. Bond $1000.00. Sureties: Josiah Adams, esq. and John Shute, innholder, all of Newmarket. Witnesses: John Shute Jr. and Mary Branscombe. The following Document found in this file has not been further identified. DOCUMENT: This document has been torn and half is missing. The clerk wrote on back "Partition of land held in common by heirs of Michael Shute of Newmarket decd. May 16, 1791." What is left of the document is an order to the constable of Exeter, Rock. Co. to apprehend one Tristram Taylor and bring him before the judge to answer the charges against him in the lost half. There is also a note to summon Joseph Smith Gilman and Nicholas Nicholls and to notify the complaintant. Dated 3/14/1789. The judge notes the respondent pled guilty and was ordered to pay a fine of 10 shillings and costs and stand committed until sentence performed. (It may be that this paper was used as a wrapper for a Div.)Note: The Probate card file indicates that this file also contains the est. of Michael Shute Jr., the numerous items of which have been placed with #2427 Michael Shute (1874).

2429. SHUTE, WILLIAM (1791) #5670
EST. Newmarket boatbuilder decd. RENUN.: 6/13/1791. Of Margry Shute, widow of William. Of Admin. Requests appointment of William Shute. Witness Danl. Hill. ADMIN.: 6/13/1791. Admr. William Shute, Newmarket yoeman. Bond L1000.0.0. Sureties: David Colcord, gent. and Walter Shute, yoeman, both of Newmarket. Witnesses: Nathl. Parker and W. Parker. NOTE: The following Invy. Mistakenly filed as #5712 William Nute (1791) belongs here. INVY.: Comm.: Nat. Rogers, Josiah Adams and Nathl. Lord. Value L55.14.8 plus list Notes not tallied with indorsements added. Oaths 10/6/1791 Adams and Lord to Nat. Rogers, JP. Oath 11/16/1791 Admr. to judge. PETITION: 11/16/1791. Of Admr. For Comm. Insolvency. Gives list claims of L54.10.0. DOWER WARR.: 1/5/1792. Comm.: Nathaniel Rogers, Josiah Adams and Daniel Tilton, esquires; Nathaniel Lord, innholder and Dudley Watson, trader, all of Newmarket. Of Widow Margery Shute. Dower: 4/25/1792. Oaths

3/18/1793 Comm. to James Smith, JP. Allowed. CLAIMS WARR.: 11/16/1791. Comm.: Nathl. Rogers and Josiah Adams, Newmarket esquires. Claims: 3/19/1793. Total L136.19.4 1/2. Oaths 3/20/1793 Comm. to judge. PETITION: 2/17/1794. Of Admr. For License. Granted. LICENSE (D31:181): 2/17/1794. To Admr. To sell real est. to amount of L120.0.0.

2430. SHUTE, WILLIAM (1797) #6404
GDP. Of the son of Michael Shute, Newmarket yoeman decd. GDP.: 12/23/1797. Of William, a minor over 14. Gdn. Samuel Chapman, Newmarket yoeman. Bond $2,000.00. Sureties: John Folsom Jr., yoeman and Andrew McClary Chapman, schoolmaster, both of Newmarket. Witnesses: Jona. Sherbune and W. Parker. See also #5641 Shute: Anna, Hiram, Lydia, Michael and William (1791) for an earlier Gdp. for William.

2431. SIBLEY, JONATHAN (1780) #4601
EST. Poplin yoeman decd. intestate. ADMIN.: 3/13/1780. Admx. Patience Sibley, Poplin widow. Bond L2000.0.0. Sureties: Daniel Brown, gent. and Nathan Merrill, innholder, both of Poplin. Witnesses: James Merrill and Thomas Clark. INVY.: Appr. 4/27/1780. Comm.: John Scribner, James Merrill and Nathan Brown. Value L347.2.0.6. Oaths 4/29/1780 Merrill, Brown and Admx. to Enoch Brown, JP. ACCOUNT.: 11/1781. Of Admx. Allowed 11/28/1781.

2432. SIBSON, MARY (1776) #4405 1/2
EST. Portsmouth single woman decd. ADMIN.: 9/17/1776. Admr. William Elliot, Dracut, Middlesex Co., Mass Bay yoeman. Bond L500. Sureties: Abraham Elliot, yoeman and Nathl. Sheaff Griffeth, both of Portsmouth. Witnesses: Deborah Adams and William Parker. INVY.: Appr. 6/17/1777. Comm.: Daniel Sherburn, John Marshall and Ephraim Ham. Value L16.12.5. Oaths 6/17/1777 Comm. to Saml. Penhallow, JP. Oath 12/17/1777 Admr. to judge.

2433. SILK, HUMPHREY (1783) #4873
EST. Of Londonderry decd. testate. WILL: Drawn 3/20/1780. Legatee-friend John Thompson of Londonderry. Exec.-John Thompson. His sig. Witnesses; Samuel Thompson, Elizabeth Prout and Margaret Thompson. CERT. WILL (D27:145): 1/29/1783. Presented by Exec. and witnesses Samuel Thompson and Prout.

2434. SILK, WILLIAM (1784) #5041
GDP. Of the son of Richard Silk of Boston, Suffolk Co., MA decd. GDP.: 10/19/1784. Of William Sisk, a minor over 14. Gdn. William Gregg Jr., Windham yoeman. Bond L1000.0.0. Sureties: James Betton, esq. and John Knox, yoeman, both of Windham. Witnesses: Ruth Betton and John Betton. Note: The clerk has used the name Sisk in the text, but Silk is given on card Index and file jacket.

2435. SILVER, DANIEL (1777) #4350
EST. Salem yoeman decd. RENUN.: 4/10/1777. Of Susannah Silver, widow of Daniel. Of Admin. Requests appointment of Robert Young. Also requests an Invy. Comm. of Benjamin Hall and Asa Colles or William Smith and William Thom. Witnesses: John Pettengill and Judith Pettengill. ADMIN.: 4/30/1777. Admr. Robert Young, Salem gent. Bond L500.0.0. Sureties: Richard Dow Jr., gent. and Moody Morse, physician, both of Salem. Witnesses: Nathl. Parker and W. Parker. INVY.: Appr. 5/8/1777. Comm.: Benja. Hall, William Smith and Asa Colles. Value L22.15.10. Oaths 9/16/1777 Comm. to Timothy Ladd, JP. Oath 2/26/1778 Admr. to judge. ACCOUNT: 2/26/1778. Of Admr. Allowed 2/26/1778. Account includes main. 3 children. Note: The Renun. gives the name of Asa as Corlis as does also the JP in the Invy. oaths.

2436. SILVER, ISAAC (1786) #5182
EST. Of Salem decd. intestate. RENUN.: 4/18/1786. Of Judith Silver. Of Admin. of est. her son Isaac. Requests appointment of Moody Morse, esq. Witnesses: George Cochran and Moses Cochran. States that Isaac had wages due him from "the other state," which cannot be come at without Admin.

2437. SILVER, JAMES (1797) #6335
EST. Chester gent. decd. ADMIN.: 4/17/1797. Admrs.: Mary Silver, widow and Joseph Silver, yoeman, both of Chester. Bond L500.0.0. Sureties: Thomas Fowler, yoeman and Benja. Hall, gent., both of Chester. Witnesses: Pheba Fowler and Charles McDuffee. INVY.: Appr. 5/11/1797. Comm.: Joseph Blanchard, Benja. Hall and Josiah Underhill. Value L39.6.0. Oaths 5/11/1797 Hall, Underhill and Admrs. to Joseph Blanchard, JP. DOWER: 5/11/1797. Comm.: Joseph Blanchard, Stephen Chase, Benja. Hall, Saml. Underhill and Josiah Underhill. Of Widow Mary Silver. Oaths 5/11/1797 Chase, Hall, Saml. Underhill and Josiah Underhill to Joseph Blanchard, JP. Note: It is odd that the Dower includes land, part of a house and barn and refers to "part of land he died seized of," yet there is no real est. included in Invy. ACCOUNT: 4/17/1799. Of Admrs. Allowed 4/17/1799 on oath of Joseph Silver, an Admr.. Oath 4/6/1798 Mary Silver, an Admr., to Thomas Cogswell, JP.

2438. SIMES: ANN, GEORGE, HANNAH, MARK, MARY & WILLIAM (1782) #4858
GDP. Of the children of Joseph Simes, Portsmouth painter decd. GDP.: 11/1/1792. Of: Ann and Hannah, minors over 14 and of Joseph, George, William, Mark and Mary, minors under 14. Gdn. Ann Simes, Portsmouth widow. Bond L1000.0.0. Sureties John Simes, painter and Thomas Simes, chaisemaker, both of Portsmouth. Witnesses: Martin Parry and Elliott Dearing. Note: The card file records the name as Simmes, but all documents say Simes.

2439. SIMES, JOHN (1789) #5465
EST. Portsmouth painter decd. ADMIN.: 6/16/1789. Admx. Alice Simes, Portsmouth widow. Bond L600.0.0. Sureties: Jonathan Ayers, cordwainer and John Salter Jr., mariner, both of Portsmouth. Witnesses: Nathl. Adams and Thomas Simes. INVY.: Appr. 7/30/1789. Comm.: Joshua Brackett, John Goddard and Danl. R. Rogers. Value L319.13.0 1/4. Oaths 8/5/1787 Comm. and Admx. to Nathl. Adams, JP. ACCOUNT: Of Admx. Allowed 10/19/1796. Account includes main. one child. ADMIN. D.B.N.: 7/18/1804. Admr. d.b.n George Richards, Portsmouth clerk. Bond $3,000.00. Sureties: Thomas Manning, merchant and John Wendell, esq., both of Portsmouth. Witness W. Parker. INVY.: 8/1/1804. Of Admr. d.b.n. Of sums receive since last Account, giving a bal. of $2,443.10. ACCOUNT: Of Admr. d.b.n. Allowed 10/17/1804 there being no objections. Admr. ordered to distribute the bal. of $1,608.09 1/2 (sic.) aggreably to law. Note: The only ref. to heirs is an item in Account of a sum due to Joseph, a son and a donation for Joseph "from Comm. for Relief of Sufferers by fire."

2440. SIMES, JOSEPH (1780) #4596
EST. Portsmouth painter decd. intestate. ADMIN.: 1/27/1780. Admrs.: Ann Simes, widow and John Simes, painter, both of Portsmouth. Bond L4000.0.0. Sureties: John Furnald, brazier and Jeremy Libbey, merchant, both of Portsmouth. Witnesses: Edmund Roberts and (Reuben Daniels?- too faint to read.) INVY. WARR.: 1/27/1780. Comm.: Joshua Brackett, Geoge Gains and Noah Parker, Portsmouth esquires. INVY.: Appr. 5/29/1781. Value L1850.14.10. Oaths 5/29/1781 Admrs., Brackett and Parker to Saml. Penhallow, JP. ACCOUNT: 10/30/1782. Of Admrs. Oaths 10/30/1782 Admrs. to Geo. Gains, JP. Allowed 10/31/1782. Account includes boarding and schooling of 2 children. DOWER WARR.: 10/30/1782. Comm.: Thomas Martin, Joshua Brackett, John Parker and George Gains, esquires and Noah Parker, gent., all of Portsmouth. Of Widow Ann Simes. DIV. WARR.: 10/30/1782. Comm. same as for Dower. To div. the real est. among the children. DIV.: 12/21/1782.

Divisees: Widow Ann Simes, her Dower; Sons-John (oldest, double share); Thomas, Joseph, George, Mark, and William Cadogan Simes; Daus.-Elizabeth, Anna, Hannah and Polly. Oaths 12/21/1782 Comm. to Saml. Penhallow, JP. Allowed 7/30/1783. ADDL. ACCOUNT: 12/24/1796. Of Ann Simes, an Admr. Allowed 12/24/1796. ADMIN. D.B.N.: 2/16/1803. Admr. d.b.n. George Simes, Portsmouth chaisemaker. Bond $2,000.00. Sureties: Jeremiah Libbey, esq. and Mark Simes, merchant, both of Portsmouth. PETITION: 2/16/1803. Of Admr. d.b.n. and signed by Geo. Richards rep. of Joseph Simes a minor and son of John Simes oldest son decd.; Betsey Simes, Hannah Simes, Ann Parry, Thomas Lunt in behalf of Mary his wife, Mark Simes and Jeremiah Libbey as Exec. est. of Thos. Simes. The Admr. d.b.n. states that the only part of the est. still unadministered is the Widow's Dower, being land and bldgs. on Market St., the bldgs. having been destroyed. Requests a Comm. to appr. the whole as it cannot be div. without prejudice. INVY. WARR.: 2/16/1803. Comm.: John Goddard and Jeremiah Libbey, esquires and Samuel Fernald, merchant, all of Portsmouth. APPR. WARR.: 2/17/1803. Comm.: James Sheafe and John Goddard, esquires; Nathaniel A. Haven, Peter Coffin and Samuel Fernald, merchants, all of Portsmouth. To appr. the Dower. Appr.: 3/3/1803. Value $1,400.00, whether part is taken off by Selectmen to widen the road or not. Oaths 3/3/1803 Comm. to Isaac Rindge, JP. PETITION: 3/4/1803. Of: Ann Parry, Hannah Simes, Wm. Simes, Mark Simes and Thomas Lunt in behalf of Mary his wife. They are satisfied with appr. And request that the land be set off to George Simes, oldest surviving son. DECREE SETTLM.: 3/14/1803. George Simes, a son, appearing and consenting, the Dower is settled on him, George to pay to the est. of John Simes, oldest son decd. $247.80 and to each of the other heirs $123.90, within 6 months. Other heirs: Mary Lunt, Betsy Simes, Ann Parry, Hannah Simes, William Simes and Mark Simes. BOND: 3/14/1803. Of George Simes, chaisemaker. Bond $3,000.00. To pay co-heirs per Decree Settlm. Sureties: William Simes, goldsmith and Thomas Lunt, mariner, both of Portsmouth. Witnesses: Oliver P. Kennard and John H. Shortridge. ACCOUNT: 3/1803. Of Admr. d.b.n. Allowed 3/14/1803. The heirs give their consent to Account and request it be accepted so they may receive their proportions. Signed by Jeremiah Libbey, Exec. est. Thomas Simes decd.; Geo. Perkins, rep. of Joseph Simes son of John Simes decd.; Betsy Simes; Hannah Simes; Ann Parry, William Simes, Mark Simes and Thomas Lunt for Mary his wife. Mary Lunt and Heirs of Thomas Simes purchased the right of Joseph Simes decd., a son.

2441. SIMES, JOSEPH (1796) #6271
GDP. Of the son of John Simes, Portsmouth painter decd. GDP.: 10/19/1796. Of Joseph, a minor under 14. Gdn. Alice Simes, Portsmouth widow. Bond $5,000.00. Sureties: Thomas Manning, merchant and Jonathan Ayers, cordwainer, both of Portsmouth. Witnesses: Geo. Long and W. Parker.

2442. SIMES, MARK (1792) #5818
GDP. Of the son of Joseph Simes of Portsmouth decd. GDP.: 11/20/1792. Of Mark, a minor. Gdn. Jeremiah Libbey, Portsmouth esq. Bond L300.0.0. Sureties: Thomas Simes, chaisemaker and Martin Parry, goldsmith, both of Portsmouth. Witnesses: Jno. Marsh and Mark Simes. ACT. OF NH GENERAL COURT: Passed House 12/5/1792. Passed Senate 12/7/1792. To allow the Petition of Jeremiah Libbey, Gdn. of Mark Simes, and Eliphalet Ladd to sell land of Libbey's ward held in common with Eliphalet Ladd. BOND: 12/24/1792. Of Jeremiah Libbey, Portsmouth esq. Bond L180.0.0. To account for proceeds of sale of land of his ward. Witnesses: Danl. Humphreys and Mark Simes. The following items are in this file although they actually belong with Mark's est. which is too late to be included in this volume. PETITION: 11/23/1886. Of Eleanor A. Scott of New York, NY, only surviving dau. of Mark Simes of Portsmouth decd.; Henry O. Simes and Mary Elizabeth Walker, children of Mark's decd. son. She states that Mark died leaving no widow. Admin. on his est. was granted to _____(sic.) who died before completing Admin. Requests appointment of Thomas Scott of New York, NY as Admr. Admin.: 11/26/1886. Admr. Thomas Scott of New York, NY. Bond $1,000.00. Sureties: John Sise and Joseph Sise, both of Portsmouth. Witnesses: W. G. Scott, New York, NY to sig. of Thomas Scott and William H. Rollins to sigs. of John Sise and Joseph Sise. Allowed 11/26/1886. PETITION: 12/19/1902. Of Francis M. Scott of New York, NY. States that Mark Simes of Portsmouth died 10/7/1834 intestate, leaving no widow. On 11/26/1886 Admin. D.B.N. was granted to Thomas Scott who has since died without having fully administered est. The only known next of kin are grandchildren Francis M. Scott and William G. Scott, both of New York, NY and Mary Elizabeth Walker and Henry O. Simes, both of Riverside, CT. Requests appointment of William E. Marvin of Portsmouth as Admr. d.b.n. He estimates the value of the est. at $2,020.00, a French Spoliation Award. Oath 12/19/1902. Francis M. Scott to Jas. L. McNeirry, JP. Cert.: 12/19/1902.. Of Thos. L. Hamilton, clerk Supreme Court of New York Co. That the JP. is authorized by the State of NY. Order: 12/22/1902. For hearing on Petition. Cert.: Hearing was advertised in Portsmouth Herald. Decree: 1/27/1903. After a hearing on Petition William E. Marvin appointed Admr. d.b.n. ADMIN. D.B.N.: 2/4/1903. Admr. d.b.n. William

E. Marvin of Portsmouth. Bond $3,000.00. Sureties: Charles H. Batchelder of Portsmouth and J. S. Frink of Greenland. Witness John G. Tobey, Jr. PROOF OF ADEQUATE SECURITY: 3/3/1903. Of Admr. d.b.n. States that he was appointed d.b.n for the purpose of prosecuting a French Spoliation Claim of est. An award of $2,020.00 was granted under the Act of Congress of 5/27/1902 and he herewith files a Bond of $3,000.00 for the legal distribution of the award. Allowed.

2443. SIMPSON, ALEXANDER (1789) #5406
EST. Windham yoeman decd. testate. WILL: Drawn 6/6/1788. Legatees: Sons-William, John, Alexander and Samuel; Sons-in-law and daus.-Thomas Atchison and Agnes his wife, George Wilson and Jennet his wife; William Smith and Sarah his wife; Grandchildren-John Simpson Bammer and Mary Darling. Execs.-James Betton, esq. And son John. His sig. Witnesses: Joseph Corliss, Robert McAdams and Gawin McAdams. CERT. WILL (D29:238): 1/21/1789. Presented by Execs. and witnesses Corliss and Gawin McAdams. INVY.: Comm.: Gain Armour, Benja. Thom and Joseph Corliss. Value L467.10.1 1/2. Oaths 3/24/1789 Comm. and Execs. to Josiah Page, JP. CERT.: 10/30/1789. Of: Wm. Smith, George Wilson and William Simpson, legatees. They have no objections to the Account of Execs. ACCOUNT: Of Execs. Allowed 11/18/1789 the heirs apparently having seen it and having no objections. ADDL. ACCOUNT: 4/10/1794. Of John Simpson, an Exec. Allowed 4/10/1794 the heirs having been notified.

2444. SIMPSON, ANDREW (1775) #4169
EST. Nottingham yoeman decd. testate. WILL: Drawn 3/9/1775. Legatees: Wife-Abigail; Sons-Thomas, Andrew, Patten and William; Dau.-Abigail Simpson. Exec. Friend John Banfill, physician. His mark. Witnesses: John Banfill, Samuel Gove and Joseph Nealey. CERT. WILL: (D23:178): 5/30/1775. Presented by Exec. and witnesses Gove and Nealey. INVY.: Comm.: Benjamin Butler and Josiah Clark. Value L103.1.1. Oaths 8/30/1775 Exec. and Butler, esq. to judge. Oath 9/11/1775 Clark to Benjamin Butler, JP.

2445. SIMPSON: ANN FROST AND RACHEL (1788) #5390
GDP. Of the daus. of Thomas Simpson, Portsmouth esq. decd. GDP.: 11/19/1788. Of: Ann Frost Simpson and Rachel, minors over 14. Gdn. Joseph Norris, Stratham gent. Bond L500.0.0. Sureties: Nathl. Folsom and Samuel Brooks, Exeter esquires. Witness W. Parker.

2446. SIMPSON: BENJAMIN, GEORGE, JOSEPH, PEGGY, SAMUEL & WILLIAM (1788) #5350

GDP. Of the children of William Simpson, Greenland husbm. decd. GDP.: Of: Benjamin, George and Joseph minors over 14 and of Peggy, Samuel and William minors under 14. GDP: 5/19/1788. Gdn.: Sarah Simpson, Greenland widow. Bond L1000.0.0. Sureties: Thomas Johnson and Nathan Johnson Jr., Greenland gentlemen. Witnesses: Thomas Nudd and Nathan Johnson.

2447. SIMPSON, THOMAS (1784) #4982

EST. Portsmouth mariner decd. testate. WILL: Drawn 4/10/1783. Legatees: Wife-Martha; His children that survive his wife; Mother-Sarah Simpson; Sisters-Sarah Simpson and Jane Simpson. He is intending a voyage to sea and gives his wife everything, being convinced she will provide for his children. Exex.-wife Martha. His sig. Witnesses: Nathl. Treadwell, Sarah Treadwell and Nathl. Treadwell Jr. CERT. WILL (D27:411): 3/17/1784. Presented by Exex. and witnesses Nathaniel Treadwell and Nathaniel Treadwell Jr. ADMIN.: 3/17/1784. Exex. Martha Simpson, Portsmouth widow with Woodbury Langdon as Principal for her. Bond L4000.0.0. Sureties: Pierse Long and Nathaniel Treadwell, Portsmouth merchants. Witnesses: Benjamin Barker Jr. and Nathl. Parker. PETITION: 11/19/1788. Of Joseph Norris, Stratham gent., Gdn. of Ann Frost Simpson and Rachel Simpson, children of decd. For the benefit of his wards requests div. of est. of their father now held in common with their bro. Thomas, Portsmouth mariner. Order: 11/19/1788. For hearing, Petitioner to serve Thomas with a copy of Petition so he may appear. MEMORIAL: 12/13/1788. Of Thomas Simpson. To judge. He has received the Citation and while he has no opposition to the div. as such, he feels that for the safety of his sisters and himself, the Petition should not be granted, at least for a time, for the following reasons: 1. The Will of their father made their mother tenant for life in est. By their benevolent dispositions the Hon. James Sullivan, esq. and Martha, his wife, who was the widow and Exex. of decd., did by deed of 6/17/1788 release the whole of the real est. of their father to Thomas and his sisters in common, though it may be subject to reversion to the Sullivans for the express purpose of paying the debts of est. of decd. The Memorialist has petitioned the NH General Court for an Act of Limitation for his father's creditors to bring in their claims so he and his sisters may have an unencumbered title. The Bill passed the House but was suspended by the Senate until the next session; 2. Although their mother has given her conditional release to the children, there is still another encumbrance against the est. He questions whether his sisters' Gdn. has seen or referred to his father's Will. The Will provides that if all the children die before their mother, which Thomas knows could happen, the est. passes to his father's sisters, Sarah and Jane Simpson, in acknowledgement of the tenderness they show their aged and infirm mother, but not until the death of the Widow Martha. Sarah and Jane might have the right to claim the reversion undivided. The Memorialist feels no court would thwart the intentions of his father's Will by overthrowing the provisions of it. If the judge does not dismiss the Petition, he requests suspension until Thomas can obtain the advice of his uncle The Hon. William Simpson, esq., who will be at the General Court session in Exeter on the 14th, as he wishes the advice of someone learned in the law. The following Petition recorded as William Simpson (1794) #6000 belongs here. PETITION: 5/5/1794. Of William Simpson, Portsmouth esq. For div. of land in Stratam and 2 lots of land in Portsmouth with bldgs. which he with Caleb Wiggin and David Barker in right of their wives hold in common, the property being the est. of Thomas Simpson, Portsmouth mariner decd. Order: 5/5/1794. For hearing, Petitioner to notify Wiggin and Barker of Petition and Order.

2448. SIMPSON, WILLIAM (1754) A#1922
EST. Portsmouth innholder decd. intestate. ACCOUNT (D27:287): 7/30/1783. Of Sarah Simpson, Admx. Allowed. Orig. Archives file includes Admin., Invy. and Relinquishment.

2449. SIMPSON, WILLIAM (1782) #4829
EST. Greenland yoeman decd. intestate. ADMIN.: 6/26/1782. Admx. Sarah Simpson, Greenland widow. Bond L1000.0.0. Sureties: David Simpson, Greenland yoeman and Daniel Jewell, Stratham gent. INVY.: Appr. 8/26/1782. Comm.: Wm. Weeks, esq.; Nathan Johnson and John Poor, gentlemen. Value L1107.7.0. Oaths 8/28/1782 Comm. to judge. ACCOUNT: 7/30/1783. Of Admx. Allowed 7/30/1783. Account includes main. 2 children. DOWER: 6/17/1788. Comm.: Nathan Johnson, Pelatiah Ayers, John Haines Jr. and Samuel Lane Jr. Of Widow Sarah Simpson. Oaths 6/17/1788 Comm. to Joshua Weeks, JP. Allowed 6/17/1788. DIV.: 6/17/1788. Comm. same as for Dower. To div. the real est. among his children. Divisees: Sons-John Simpson (oldest son), Samuel, George, David, William, Benjamin and Joseph; Daus,-Peggy Simpson, Susanna Nud wife of Thomas Nud, Mary Lang, wife of Thomas Lang, Sarah Simpson, Martha French wife of Andrew French and Jane Dam wife of Benjamin Dam. Oaths 6/17/1788 Comm. to Joshua Weeks, JP., Allowed 6/17/1788. Includes Map. APPR.: 7/15/1788. Comm.: Nathan Johnson and John Haines Jr. They appr. the neat yearly income of all of the real est. at L77.0.0. per year. ADDL. ACCOUNT: 7/16/1788. Of Admx. Allowed 7/19/1788. Account includes main. "another" child since settlement of the other Account. Pos. posthumous? The following 2 Petitions recorded as

#6000 William Simpson (1794) belong here. PETITION: 6/14/1802. Of William Simpson, Greenland yoeman, an heir of William Simpson, Greenland yoeman decd. For div. of the Dower among the heirs or that it be settled on one or more of them. Order: For hearing, Petitioner to notify heirs of Petition and Order. APPR. WARR.: 5/24/1802. Comm. Clement Weeks and Enoch Clark, esquires; Amos Davis, Ebenezer Johnson Jr. and Brackett Weeks, yoeman, all of Greenland. To view the Widow's Dower to see if it can be div. without prejudice. Div. giving double share to eldest son or appr. APPR.: 7/23/1804. Of Dower. Value $1420.00. DECREE SETTLM.: 7/23/1804. William Simpson, appearing and consenting, the real est. settled on him, William to pay $109.12 each of his co-heirs. To John, Jane Dame, Martha French, Sarah Simpson, Susanna Nudd, Margaret Simpson, David, George, Joseph, Samuel and Mary Lane in 6 months and to the heir of Benjamin decd. in 5 years, with interest.

2450. SIMPSON, WILLIAM (1794) #6000
See William Simpson #4829 (1782)

2451. SLADE, CATHERINE (1795) #6151
GDP. Of Portsmouth widow adjudged n.c.m. PETITION: 10/21/1795. Of Thomas Slade, Portsmouth tanner. For appointment of a Gdn. for his mother Catharine Slade, who is n.c.m. Order: 10/21/1795. To Portsmouth Selectmen. To make inquisition into Catherine's condition. Report: 10/21/1795. Of: Geo. Gains, Nathl. A. Haven and Supply Clap, Portsmouth Selectmen. They are of opinion Mrs. Slade is n.c.m. and needs a Gdn. GDP.: 10/21/1795. Of Catherine, an adult adjudged n.c.m. Gdn. Thomas Slade, Portsmouth tanner. Bond $1,000.00. Sureties: John Drew Seaward and Adam Simpson, Portsmouth cordwainers. Witness Hall Jackson. INVY. WARR.: 10/21/1795. Comm.: Jeremiah Libbey and George Wentworth, esquires and Jacob Walden, innholder, all of Portsmouth. Invy.: Appr. 1/19/1796. Value $238.31. Affirms. 2/6/1796 Libbey and Walden to Isaac Rindge, JP.

2452. SLEEPER, DAVID (1781) #4696
EST. Sandown gent. decd. ADMIN.: 2/28/1781. Admx. Ruth Sleeper, Sandown widow. Bond L40000.0.0. Sureties: Jethro Sanborn, esq. and John Sanborn, yoeman, both of Sandown. Witnesses: Henry Robie and W. Parker. INVY.: Appr. 3/24/1781. Comm.: Jethro Sanborn, esq.; John Sanborn, yoeman and Timothy Tilton, tanner. Value L64691.19.0. Oaths 5/30/1781 Tilton, John Sanborn and Admx. to judge. DOWER: 1/16/1787. Comm.: John Sleeper, William Rowel, Benjamin Taylor, John Sanborn and Timy. Tilton. Of Widow Ruth Sleeper. Oaths 1/16/177 Rowel, Taylor, Sanborn and Tilton to Moses Hook, JP. Allowed 1/17/1787. DIV.:

1/16/1787. Same Comm. as Dower. To div. 2/3 of real est. Divisees: Gidion (double share), Peter, John, David, Daniel, Jethro, Benjamin, Josiah, Nathan, Edmund, Samuel, Jonathan, Ruth and Mary. Oaths 1/16/1787 Comm. to Moses Hook, JP. Allowed 1/17/1787. ACCOUNT: 1/17/1787. Of Admx. Allowed 1/17/1787. Account includes main. Ruth, Nathan and Jonathan.

2453. SLEEPER, WILLIAM (1792) #5741
EST. Kingston yoeman decd. testate. WILL: Drawn 6/20/1787. Legatees: Wife-Ruth; Son-John Blasdel Sleeper; Daus.-Sarah Flanders, Dorothy Challis wife of John Challis, Anne Webster wife of Jeremy Webster and Elisabeth Cammet wife of Samuel Cammet. Exec.-son John. His sig. Witnesses: Josiah Bartlett, Josiah Bartlett Jr. and Ezra Bartlett. CERT. WILL (D30:188): 2/13/1792. Presented by Exec. and witnesses His Excelly. Josiah Bartlett, esq. and Ezra Bartlett. ADMIN.: 2/13/1792. Exec. John B. Sleeper, Kingston husbm. Bond L1000.0.0. Sureties: Ezra Bartlett, physician and Jacob Peaslee, esq., both of Kingston. Witnesses: Stephen Dearborn and W. Parker. INVY.: Appr. 3/6/1792. Comm.: Simmons Seccombe, Jacob Peaslee and Daniel Wadleigh. Value not tallied. Esti. L234.0.0+. Oaths 3/6/1792 Peaslee and Wadleigh to Simmons Seccombe, JP. Oath 4/6/1794 Exec. to judge.

2454. SLOPER, AMBROSE (1772) #3937
EST. Portsmouth housewright decd. testate. WILL: Drawn 5/10/1759. Legatees: Wife-Sarah; Sons-Ambrose, Richard, Benning, John, William, Joshua and Daniel. Daus.-Mary Lucy, Sarah Tucker, Susanna, Olive and Elizabeth. Appoints wife Gdn. of Benning and John while minors;. Execs.-wife Sarah and Wyseman Clagett. His sig. Witnesses: Hon. Jonathan Warner, Samuel Aris and Ebenezer Odiorne. CERT. WILL.: 5/27/1772. Presented by Sarah Sloper, one of the Execs. and witnesses Warner and Aris 3d. Wyseman Clagett, co-executor, renounced office. INVY. WARR.: 5/27/1772. Comm.: Richard Jenness, esq. and Amos Seavy, gent., both of Rye. INVY.: Appr. 9/30/1772. Value L338.1.3. Oaths 9/30/1772 Admx. and Comm. to judge. LICENSE: 1/7/1773. To Admx. To sell 11 acres of land to pay debts. DIV. WARR.: 1/7/1773. Comm.: Hunking Wentworth, esq.; Thomas Pierce, gent.; Benjamin Akerman, tanner; Woodbury Langdon, merchant and Joshua Brackett, physician, all of Portsmouth. To divide the real est. among the widow and children according to the Will. DIV.: 4/12/1773. Divisees: Heirs or legal reps. of Ambrose Sloper of Boston; Heirs or legal reps. of Richard Sloper of Boston; Benning Sloper and John Sloper; Widow Sarah Sloper, her Dower. Oaths 4/12/1773 Pierce, Akerman, Langdon and Brackett to judge. Allowed. PLAN OF DIV.: Of Sloper's Farm at North Hampton by Benja.

Hobbs, surveyor. PETITION: 1/24/1774. Of Benning Sloper, Portsmouth yoeman. For div. of land held in common with his bro. John, a minor. Granted 1/24/1774, Sarah Sloper, Gdn., and John, the minor, appearing and consenting. DIV. WARR.: D22:384): 1/25/1774. Comm.: John Gardner, taylor; Samuel Cate and Samuel Langdon, gentlemen.; Geo. Ayers, cordwainer and Moses Brewster, yoeman, all of Portsmouth. To div. land held in common by Benning Sloper and John Sloper, sons. DIV. (D22:383): 1/25/1774. Divisees as named. Oaths 1/24/1774 Comm. to judge. ACCOUNT: 12/19/1774. Of Admx. Allowed 12/19/1774. PETITION: 12/19/1774. Admx. For License so she can pay daus. their legacies according to Will. Granted. LICENSE: 12/19/1774. To Admx. To sell 4 acres of land.

2455. SLOPER, BENNING W. (1780) #4671
EST. Portsmouth mariner and yoeman decd. testate. WILL: Drawn 1/16/1778 "being bound to sea." Legatees: Wife-Henrietta heretofore called Henrietta Mitchell. Exex.-wife Henrietta. His sig. Benning W. Sloper. Witnesses: John Neal, Robert Drout and Lasarus Holmes. CERT. WILL: 11/29/1780. Presented by Exex. And John Neal, one of the witnesses who gave oath to Wm. Parker, Reg. & JP, the other witnesses being absent, if alive. INVY. WARR.: 1/8/1781. Comm.: Samuel Hall, gent.; Nathl. Melcher, boatbuilder and Mark Seavey, taylor, all of Portsmouth. INVY.: Appr. 4/23/1781. Value L36.1.3. Oaths 4/24/1781 Exex., Melcher and Seavey to Saml. Penhallow, JP.

2456. SLOPER, JOHN (1784) #5024
EST. Portsmouth mariner decd. intestate. ADMIN.: 7/22/1784. Admx. Sarah Sloper, Portsmouth widow. Bond L500.0.0. Sureties: John Langdon, esq. and Peter Pearse, merchant, both of Portsmouth. Witnesses: Robert O. Treadwell and Nat Barrett Jr. INVY.: Appr. 9/15/1784. Comm.: Samuel Hall and Saml. Drowne. Value L81.13.6. Oaths 9/22/1784 Comm. to Saml Pemhallow, JP. Oath 9/21/1784 Admx. to W. Parker, Reg. PETITION: Of Admx. For license. Shows claims of L30.9.11 plus main. of one child. Granted 10/20/1784. LICENSE (D27:517): 10/20/1784. To Admx. To sell sufficient real est. to pay debts.

2457. SMART, HILTON (1796) #6272
EST. Exeter mariner decd. ADMIN.: 10/14/1796. Admx. Batty Smart, Exeter widow. Bond $2,000.00. Sureties: John Smart of Exeter and Hezekiah Smith of Brentwood, yoemen. Witnesses: Mary S. Parker and W. Parker. INVY.: 12/28/1796. Comm.: Daniel Smith, Wm. Parker Jr. and Jonathan Connor. Value L387.5.7. Oaths 12/28/1796 Admx., Smith and Parker to judge.

2458. SMART, JOHN (1774) #4139
EST. Newmarket yoeman decd. intestate. ADMIN.: 12/28/1774. Admx. Betty Smart, Newmarket widow. Bond L1000.0.0. Sureties: Josiah Hilton and Nathanael Ames, Newmarket yeomen. Witnesses: John Taylor and Saml. Hale Jr. INVY.: Appr. 2/22/1775. Comm.: David Folsom and Benja. Mead. Value L135.1.11. Oaths 3/17/1775 Comm. to judge. Oath 11/27/1776 Admx. to Wm. Parker, JP.

2459. SMITH, AARON (1777) #4377
EST. Hampton Falls yoeman decd. intestate. ADMIN.: 7/29/1777. Admx. Dolly Smith, Hampton Falls widow. Bond L500.0.0. Sureties: Hilyard Shaw, Hampton Falls joiner and Peter Coffin, Gloucester, Essex Co., MA esq. Witnesses: Nathaniel Weare and Wm. Parker. INVY.: Appr. 7/29/1777. Comm.: Caleb Sanborn, Hilyard Shaw and Samll. Weare. Value L789.13.4. The Comm. notes that the widow showed them the whole of the income and produce for 1777 without any deduction for Dower. Oaths 9/24/1777 Comm. to Winthrop Gove, JP. Oath 9/24/1777 Admx. to Wm. Parker, JP. Note: The following List of Claims found in #4388 Benjamin Randel (1777) belongs here. LIST OF CLAIMS: 9/24/1777. For est. of Aaron Smith of Hampton. Signed by Dolly Smith. Total L313.19.1. PETITION: 9/24/1777. Of Admx. For License. She notes four children to be maintained. LICENSE: 9/24/1777. To Admx. To sell sufficient real est. to pay debts. ACCOUNT: Of Dolly Leighton, Admx. Allowed 8/17/1785. In this account she lists children Hannah, John, Peter, Lois and Abigail with their birth dates.

2460. SMITH, ABIGAIL (1773) #3996
GDP. Of the dau. of Paul Smith of Chester decd. GDP: 2/17/1773. Of Abigail, a minor over 14. Gdn.: William Gross, Chester yoeman. Bond L500.0.0. Surety Samuel Chapman, North Hampton gent. Witnesses: Samuel Parker and David Swett. DIV. WARR.: 3/5/1772. Comm.: Samuel Emerson, esq.; Samuel Robie and John Underhill, gentlemen; and John Robie and Stephen Morse, husbandmen, all of Chester. To div. the real est. of Abigail, a minor decd. and Huldah Smith, dau. of Sylvanus Smith, Chester gent. decd., also a minor, which est. Abigail and Huldah hold in common, each own in gone half. DIV.: 7/20/1772. Divisees: Abigail Smith and Huldah Smith. Oaths 7/24/1772 Comm. to judge.

2461. SMITH, ABRAHAM (1798) #6457
EST. Poplin yoeman decd. testate. WILL: Drawn 9/13/1797. Legatees: Wife-Mary; Sons-Samuel, Jonathan, Benjamin and Abraham; Daus.-Elisabeth Healy, Margaret wife of Jeremiah Quimby, Molley wife of Daniel Sanborn, Abigail wife of Josiah Sandborn, Meriam wife of Peter

Abot and Deborah Smith. Exec.-son Abraham. His sig. Witnesses: Elisha Hook, Enock Smith and Thomas Page. CERT. WILL (D32:478): Presented by Exec. and witnesses Hook and Smith. ADMIN.: 5/14/1799 (sic., a clerk's error). Exec. Abraham Smith, Poplin yoeman. Bond $3,000.00. Sureties: Enoch Smith and Elisha Hook, Poplin yoemen. Witnesses: Mary S. Parker and W. Parker. INVY.: Appr. 6/9/1798. Comm.: Elisha Hook, Jonathan Brown and Enoch Smith. Value $1,728.96. Oaths 6/12/1798 Brown and Smith to Thos. Page, JP. Oath 8/28/1798 Exec. to Thomas Page, JP.

2462. SMITH: ANNA, DOROTHY, ELIZABETH, JACOB, JOHN, LYDIA, MEHETABEL & SARAH (1779) #4530)
GDP. Of the children of Nathaniel Smith, Epping yoeman decd. GDP: 3/31/1779. Of: Anna, Sarah and Dorothy, minors under 14. Gdn. Seth Fogg, Epping gent. Bond L1000.0.0. Sureties: Benjamin Smith, blacksmith and Nathl. Gordon, Exeter yoeman. Witnesses: Micajah Morrill and Wm. Parker. GDP.: 3/31/1779. Of Jacob, a minor under 14. Gdn. Benjamin Smith, Epping blacksmith. Bond L1000.0.0. Sureties: Seth Fogg, Epping gent. and Nathaniel Gordon, Exeter yoeman. Witness Nathl. Parker. GDP.: 4/7/1779. Of: Mehetabel, Elizabeth and Lydia, minors over 14. Gdn., Obadiah Williams, Epping physician. Bond L2000.0.0. Sureties: Jacob Blasdel, gent. and Josiah Moody, yoeman, both of Epping. Witnesses: Nathl. Parker and W. Parker. GDP. (D25:78): GDP. Of John, a minor under 14. Gdn. Nathaniel Gordon. Sureties: Seth Fogg, gent. And Benja. Smith, blacksmith. ACCOUNT: 2/26/1783. Of Nathaniel Gordon, Gdn. of John Smith, a minor under 14, son of Nathaniel Smith, Epping yoeman decd. Allowed 2/26/1783. GDP.: 3/15/1786. Of Jacob, a minor over 14. Gdn. Seth Fogg, Epping gent. Bond L1000.0.0. Sureties: Danl. Tilton, Exeter esq. and Abraham Sanborn, Brentwood husbm. Witness W. Parker. ADDL. ACCOUNT: 3/17/1790. Of Nathaniel Gordon of Exeter decd. Of Gdp. of John. Exhibited by Nathaniel Gordon and John Gordon, Execs. est. Nathaniel Gordon decd. Account was objected to and parties agreed to refer Account to Eliphalet Hale, gent., Ephraim Robinson, merchant, both of Exeter and Enoch Coffin, Epping esq. as referees and to accept their decision as final settlm. Report: 5/31/1790. The referees rule that John Smith should receive from the Execs. of est. Nathaniel Gordon L37.12.8 in full of Gdp. Account, cost of reference being paid. Receipt: 5/31/1790. Of John Smith. To Execs. For their note for L37.12.8. which, when paid, will be final accounting of his Gdp. Includes a copy of Account. COPY OF ACCOUNT & RULING. PETITION: 3/20/1793. Of Wm. Plummer, atty. to Jacob Smith. Jacob requests permission to sue Bond Gdp. of Benjamin Smith, who was his Gdn. and refuses and neglects to settle his Gdp. Account though requested. CITATION: 3/20/1793. To

Benjamin Smith, late Epping blacksmith now of Newbury, Essex Co., MA. To appear and exhibit his Gdp. Account in order for settlm. Cert.: 4/8/1793. Of William Ingalls, Dept. Sheriff. He cited Benjamin Smith by reading Citation to him. DECREE: 4/17/1793. Benjamin Smith, though cited, did not appear so Jacob is allowed to sue Benjamin's Bond Gdp. On back is a notation re an Account of John Shute. As only part is here, appears the Account was torn apart to supply paper for Decree. Also on back is confirmation of Wm. Plummer, atty. to Jacob, that he has received from Wm. Parker the Bond of the Decree. BOND: 6/3/1793. Of Jacob Smith. Bond L100.0.0. For his suit against Bond Gdp. of Benjamin Smith and his sureties Seth Fogg and Nathaniel Gordon decd., which suit has been commenced and is now pending at Rockingham Co. Court of Common Pleas. Surety Daniel Watson. Witnesses: Nancy Smith, Wm. Plumer and Saml. Carpenter. ACCOUNT: 7/1793. Of Benjamin Smith. Of Gdp. of Jacob.

2463. SMITH, BRIDGET (1771) #3070 & ALSO AS BRIDGET CLIFFORD (1771) #3882
EST. Brentwood widow decd. intestate. ADMIN.: (#3870), Est. Bridget Clifford. 9/17/1771. Admr. Caleb Smith, Candia yoeman. Bond L500.0.0. Sureties: Daniel Clark, gent. and Joseph Wadleigh Jr., yoeman, both of Brentwood. Witnesses: Sam. Blodget and Samuel Parker. INVY. WARR.: (#3882) 9/17/1771. Comm.: Daniel Clark, gent. and Chase Smith, yoeman, both of Brentwood. INVY. (#3882): Appr. 9/18/1771. Value L32.19.7. Oaths 10/23/1771 Comm. to Noah Emery, JP. Note: On outside of file #3870 the clerk calls her Bridget Smith and the Index card for #3870 also calls her Smith, but the Admin. and Invy. in #3882 call her Clifford.

2464. SMITH, CALEB (1786) #5180
ATTACHMENT WARR. to Raymond gent. BILL: 12/17/1784. Of Theo. Gilman and Elipht. Gilman. To Caleb Smith of Raymond. For ox shoes, nails and two hoes for a total of L1.11.0. ATTACHMENT WARR.: 3/25/1786. To the Sheriff of Rockingham Co. or his Under-sheriff, or either of the constables of Raymond. To attach the goods or est. of Caleb Smith, Raymond gent. to the value of L3.0.0. or, for want of that, to take his body into safe keeping so that he may appear before William Parker, esq., JP. to answer Theophilus Gilman and Eliphalet Gilman, Exeter blacksmiths and partners in a plea against Smith, Smith owing the plaintiffs L1.11.0 for blacksmith work which he promised to pay them on demand but has not paid. Cert.: Of James Prince, Depy. Sheriff. He has attached a hat of Smith and gave him a summons. Note: From W. Parker. To Mr. Gilman. Parker tells Gilman that from what Gilman wrote he cannot determine the remaining cost. Smith says Gilman reckons only 45

shillings for all his boards, giving in the interest, which is true, only 12 shillings remains. Will Gilman please explain. Gilman replies that he did not mean to have any interest. "You know all the rest." Signed T. Gilman.

2465. SMITH, COMFORT (1789) #5455
GDP. Of the dau. of Hubartus Smith, Chichester husbm. decd. GDP.: 6/4/1789. Of Comfort, a minor over 14. Gdn. Francis Winkley, Canterbury blacksmith. Bond L500.0.0. Sureties: Benjamin Witcher, Canterbury yoeman and Abraham Brown Jr., Epping gent. Witnesses: W. Parker and Nathl. Parker.

2466. SMITH, EDWARD (1778) #4438
EST. Kensington yeoman decd. ADMIN.: 3/25/1778. Admr. Nathaniel Bacheller, Kingston esq. Bond L500.0.0. Sureties: Joseph Bean, gent. and Jonathan Collins, yoeman, both of Kingston. Witnesses: W. Parker and Saml. Gilman Jr. INVY.: Appr. 4/6/1778. Comm.: Jonathan Collins, David Tilton and Jonathan Greeley Jr., all of Kingston. Value L26.8.6. Oaths 4/9/1778 Comm. and Admr. to judge.

2467. SMITH, ELIZABETH (1776) #13080
EST. Of Brentwood decd. ADMIN. (D23:260): 2/28/1776. Admr. Alexander Gordon Smith of Brentwood. Sureties: Thomas Peabody and Hawley Marshall, both of Brentwood. Note: The est. was never entered into the clerk's Master Index until 1835 and was given a number current that year.

2468. SMITH, EZEKIEL (1780) #4672
EST. Raymond yoeman decd. intestate. ADMIN.: 11/29/1780. Admr. Alexander Smith, Raymond yoeman. Bond L20000.00. Sureties: Ithiel Gordon, yoeman and Thomas Gordon, gent., both of Raymond. Witnesses: O. Peabody and W. Parker. INVY.: Appr. 12/4/1780. Comm.: Ithiel Gordon, Jona. Swain and Francis Hodgkins. Value L3625.4.0. Oaths 3/5/1781 Comm. and Admr. to John Dudley, JP. PETITION: 11/21/1781. Of Admr. For license. Lists claims of L30.2.8. LICENSE: 11/28/1781. To Admr. To sell sufficient real est. to pay debts. CLAIMS: 10/18/1782. Comm.: Jona. Swain and Francis Hodgkins. Total L704.12.7. Oaths 12/16/1782 Comm. to John Dudley, JP. ACCOUNT: 10/1786. Of Admr. Allowed 10/18/1786. PROP.& SETTLM: Claims L704.12.7. Amount to be proportioned L22.13.7. Allowed 11/15/1786 with order to Admr. to pay.

2469. SMITH, HUBARTUS (1781) #4754
EST. Chichester yoeman decd. ADMIN.: 12/6/1781. Admr. Winthrop Smith, Chichester yoeman. Bond L40000.0.0. Sureties: Levi Morrill and Jabez Smith, tanner, both of Brentwood. Witnesses: Noah Greeley and Reuben Sanborn. INVY. WARR.: 12/8/1781. Comm.: John Sanborn, gent. and Nathan Bachelder, esq., both of Loudon and Thomas Johnson of Chichester. INVY.: Appr. 1/7/1782. Value not tallied. Real est. esti. L270.0.0. Oaths 1/7/1782 Comm. to John Cram, JP. Oath 1/30/1782 Admr. to W. Parker, Reg. DOWER WARR.: 1/30/1782. Comm.: John Sanborn, gent. and Nathan Bachelder, esq., both of Loudon; Thomas Johnson, Moses Rollings and Josiah Edgerly, all of Chichester. Of Widow Joanna Smith. PETITION: 5/30/1782. Of Admr. For License and Comm. Insolvency. He gives total Invy. as L315.0.0. Lists partial claims of L271.0.0. Judges notes Comm. of Nathan Bachelder, esq. and John Sanborn, gent., both of Loudon and Thos. Johnson, Pittsfield yoeman. LICENSE: 5/27/1782. To Admr. To sell sufficient real est. to pay debts. DOWER: 5/20/1784. Oaths Bachelder, Johnson, Sanborn and Rollings to John Cram, JP. Allowed. PETITION: Dated by clerk 3/1787. Of Admr. For Div. as the Claims Comm. found claims were no more than personal est. Requests Div. Comm. of John Sanborn, Loudon gent.; Stephen Blake, Thomas Johnson, Robert Tibbets, yoemen and Benja. Sias, esq., all of Pittsfield. Note: He calls Hubartus "late of Chichester now Pittsfield decd." This results from a town div. DIV. WARR.: 3/20/1787. Comm.: As requested. To div. 2/3 of real est., giving double share to oldest son and single share to other children. Oaths 4/5/1787 Sanborn, Johnson, Blake and Tibbets to Benja. Sias, JP. They will faithfully and impartially make the Div. DIV.: 4/3/1787. Divisees: Sons-Winthrop (oldest) and Richard; Daus.-Comfort (youngest dau.), Moley Hall wife of Silvenus Hall (oldest dau.), Dolley (3d dau.), Anna Green wife of Jabeth Green (4th dau.) and Joanna Louge wife of Gilman Louge (2d dau.). Oaths 4/6/1787 Johnson, Blake and Tibbets to Benja. Sias, JP. PETITION: 4/18/1787. Of Dolley Smith, a dau. States that her bro. Winthrop, Admr., has neglected to settle the est., whereby she and her co-heirs are injured. Requests permission to sue Bond of Admin.

2470. SMITH, HULDAH (1773) #3990
GDP. Of the dau. of Sylvanus Smith, Chester gent. decd. GDP.: 2/3/1773. Of Huldah, a minor under 14. Gdn. Stephen Morse, Chester yoeman. Bond L400.0.0. Surety Samuel Emerson, Chester esq. Witnesses: Jonathan Carleton and Samuel Parker. GDP.: 12/31/1777. Of Huldah, a minor over 14. Gdn. William Brown, Chester cordwainer. Bond L500.0.0. Sureties: John Webster and Robert Wilson, Chester esquires. Witnesses: W. Parker and Stephen Moore. ACCOUNT: Of Stephen Morse. Of Gdp. Allowed

12/31/1777. See also #3996 Abigail Smith (1773) for div. of land held in common by Abigail Smith and Huldah Smith. Note: This file also contains a Gdp. Release by Samuel Smith which belongs with A#3231 Samuel Smith (1767) and is recorded there.

2471. SMITH, JACOB (1776) #4197
EST. Seabrook yoeman decd. testate. WILL: Drawn 10/12/1775. Legatees: Sons-Daniel, John and Jacob; Daus.-Mary Briant, Sarah Mead, Anna Eaton and Rhoda Smith. Exec.-son Daniel. His sig. Witnesses: Samuel Smith, Richard Smith and Aaron Clough Jr. CERT. WILL (D23:236): 1/31/1776. Presented by Exec. and witnesses Samuel Smith and Clough.

2472. SMITH, JAMES JR. (1772) #3942
EST. Durham yoeman decd. intestate. ADMIN.: 6/24/1772. Admx. Tamison Smith, Durham widow. Bond L500.0.0. Sureties: Jeremiah Burnham Jr., yoeman and John Smith, gent., both of Durham. INVY. WARR.: 6/25/1772. Comm.: John Smith, gent. and Winborn Adams, yoeman, both of Durham. Value L76.4.3. Oath 11/25/1772 Adams to Jno. Sullivan, JP. Oaths Admx. and Smith to judge. INVY: Appr. 9/26/1772. Value L76.4.3. Oath 11/25/1772 Adams to Jno. Sullivan, JP.

2473. SMITH, JAMES (1773) #3998)
EST. Durham yoeman decd. testate. ADMIN.: 2/24/1773. Exec.: John Smith, Durham gent. Bond L1000.0.0. Surety: John Sullivan, Durham esq. Witnesses: Samuel Parker and John Marshall. WILL: Drawn 5/16/1765. Legatees: Wife-Unnamed; Son-John; Dau.-Abigail Smith. Exec. Son John. His sig. Witnesses: John Sullivan, Eben. Hill and James Sullivan. CERT. WILL: 2/24/1773. Presented by Exec. and witnesses James Sullivan and Hill.

2474. SMITH, JAMES (1789) #5451
EST. Atkinson yeoman decd. ADMIN.: 5/20/1789. Admx. Hannah Smith, Atkinson widow. Bond L1000.0.0. Sureties: John Merrill and William Page, Atkinson yoemen. Witnesses: John Calfe and W. Parker. INVY.: Comnm.: Peter Clement, Moses Greenough and William Bradly. Value L78.17.1. Oaths 4/16/1792 Greenough and Bradly to Peter Clement, JP. Oath 4/18/1792 Admx. to judge. ACCOUNT: 4/18/1792. Of Admx. Allowed 4/18/1792. Account includes item for nursing child 119 weeks and charges for two funerals, pos. the child and husband? And paid her father for boarding husband and her during husband's last sickness then moving "them" from Canaan. LICENSE (D30:239): 4/18/1792. To Admx. To sell real est. to the amount of L40.0.0.

2475. SMITH, JEDIDAH (1779) #4545
EST. North Hampton single woman decd. testate. WILL: Drawn 1/5/1773. Legatees: Children of Paul Smith Marston-Abigail and John; David Smith Marston. Execs.-John Leavitt, esq. and Paul Smith Marston, both of North Hampton. Her mark. Witnesses: Benjamin Leavitt, Mayhew Clark and Levi Dearborn. CERT. WILL (D25:128): 5/26/1779. Presented by Execs. and witnesses Leavitt and Dearborn.

2476. SMITH, HON. JEREMIAH (1800) No#
APPOINTMENT: 11 /8/1800. Jeremith Smith appointed Judge of Probate for Rockingham Co. Sworn 12/8/1800.

2477. SMITH, JOHN (1784) #5025
GDP. Of the son of Richard Smith, Exeter tanner decd. GDP.: 7/26/1784. Of John, a minor over 14. Gdn. Eliphalet Hale, Exeter gent. Bond L500.0.0. Sureties: John Taylor Gilman, esq. and Kinsley Hall, cordwainer, both of Exeter. Witnesses: Nathl. Parker and W. Parker.

2478. SMITH, JONATHAN JR. (1782) #4802
EST. Salem yoeman decd. PETITION: 4/16/1782. Of Jonathan Smith. States that his son Jonathan died about age 28, intestate, leaving no heirs. He conceives right of admin. falls to him but as there appear to be many difficulties in settlm. est. requests appointment of Nathl. Peabody, esq., who has consented to be Admr. ADMIN.: 4/24/1782. Admr. Nathaniel Peabody, Atkinson esq. Bond L1000.0.0. Sureties: James Noyes and Caleb Noyes, Atkinson husbandmen.

2479. SMITH, COL. JOSEPH (1782) #4855
EST. Newmarket esq. decd. intestate. ADMIN.: 9/25/1782. Admr. Winthrop Smith, Newmarket husbm. Bond L5000.0.0. Sureties: Hubartus Neal Jr., yoeman and Ichabod Hilton, gent., both of Newmarket, Witness Walter Bryent. INVY. WARR.: 9/25/1782. Comm.: Walter Bryent and Nathl. Rogers, esquires and Gideon Colcord, gent., all of Newmarket. INVY.: Appr. 12/24/1782. Value L579.13.0. Oaths 12/25/1782 Comm. to Joseph Adams, JP. Oath 1/29/1783 Admr. to W. Parker, Reg. & JP. PETITION: 2/14/1803. Of Ichabod Hilton and Hubartus Neal Jr., Sureties of Admr. They state the Admr. has not settled his Account and request he be cited to appear and do so in order that they may be released from their Bond. CITATION: 2/14/1803. To Admr. To appear and exhibit Account. PETITION: 4/18/1803. Of Ichabod Hilton and Hubartus Neal jr., 2 of heirs. For permission to sue Bond of Admin. as Admr. has neglected to settle his Account although cited to do so. BOND: 4/18/1803. Of Ichabod Hilton and Hubartus Neal Jr. Bond $200.00. To sue Bond of Admin.

DISCHARGE: 7/26/1803. Of: Hannah Gilman, Sarah Gilman, Ichabod Hilton in right of his late wife Susannah, John Folsom and his wife Elizabeth, Hubartus Neal Jr. and Mary his wife and Joseph Smith, heirs. They have received from Admr. $30.00 for their several and respective shares in the personal est. and request the judge to discharge the Admr. accordingly.

2480. SMITH, JOSIAH (1748) A#1385
EST. Of Stratham. The following Petition recorded as #4553 Josiah Smith & David Burleigh (1779) belongs here. PETITION: 7/15/1779. Of Josiah Smith, Stratham yoeman. States that he and some of the children of David Burleigh of Stratham are tenants in common of land in Stratham which was the Dower of Charity Smith in the est. of Josiah Smith decd. Some of the children are minors. Requests div. Orig. Archives file includes Will, Cert. Will, Invy., Account, Div. Warr. (1766) and Div. & Dower (1766). Note: A dau. of Josiah decd. was Anna Burleigh.

2481. SMITH, JOSIAH & DAVID BURLEIGH (1779) #4553
See #1385 Josiah Smith (1748)

2482. SMITH, NATHANIEL (1774) #4886
EST. Epping husbm. decd. testate. WILL: Drawn 12/10/1773. Legatees: Wife-Mehitabel; Sons-Nathaniel, John and Jacob; Daus.-Mary, Mehitabel, Elizabeth and Lydia (4 oldest), Anna, Sarah and Dorithy (3 youngest). Exex.: Wife-Mehitabel. His mark. Witnesses: Josiah Stearns, Seth Fogg and Abraham Perkins. CERT. WILL (D22:429). 2/23/1774. Presented by Exex. and witnesses Fogg and Perkins. INVY.: Appr. 2/28/1774. Comm.: Seth Fogg and Abraham Perkins. Value L1491.19.6. Oath "all sworn" 5/25/1774. DIV. WARR.: 4/7/1779. Comm.: Abraham Perkins and Jacob Blasdell, gentlemen; Jeremiah Sanborn, yoeman; and Abraham Tilton, blacksmith, all of Epping; and Thomas Bartlett, Nottingham esq. To div. the land in Epping and Raymond between the wife and children. DIV.: 5/25/1779. Divisees: Wife of Nathaniel now wife of Capt. Seth Fogg of Epping; Sons-Nathaniel (oldest), John and Jacob; Daus.-Mary Foulsom wife of James Foulsom; Mehitabel Smith, Elizebeth Smith and Lydia Smith. Oaths Comm. and approved 6/30/1770. NOTE: This Div. does not include the 3 youngest daus., who were bequeathed land in Sanbornton. ACCOUNT: 4/12/1787. Of Seth Fogg and Mehitabel his wife, Admx. Allowed 4/18/1787. The Account includes an item for "taking care of children under 7."

2483. SMITH, NEHEMIAH (1782) #4790
See Nicholas Smith (1780) #4651 & (1782) #4790

2484. SMITH, NICHOLAS (1780) #4651 & (1782) #4790
EST. Candia yoeman decd. ADMIN.: 9/11/1780. Admx. Abiel Smith, Candia widow. Bond L20000.0.0. Sureties: Saml. Mooers, esq. and Jonathan Brown, yoeman, both of Candia. Witnesses: Aaron Brown and Levi Brown. INVY.: Appr. 11/2/1780. Comm.: Benjm. Cass, Benjm. Hubbard and Aaron Brown. Value L9674.10.0. Oaths 1/1/1781 Comm. and Admx. to Saml. Mooers, JP. The following License recorded as #4790 Nehemiah Smith (1782) belongs here. LICENSE: 3/27/1782. To Abiel Smith, Admx. To sell sufficient real est. to pay debts. DOWER WARR.: 4/4/1782. Comm.: Walter Robie, Nathaniel Emerson and Saml. Mooers, esquires; Abraham Fitz and Benjamin Bachelder, gentlemen, all of Candia. Of Widow Abiel Smith. DOWER: 4/11/1782. Oaths 4/29/1782 Robie, Emerson and Bachelder to Saml. Mooers, JP. Allowed 10/20/1784. ACCOUNT: Of William Evens and Abiel his wife, Admx. Allowed 10/20/1784.

2485. SMITH, RICHARD (1778) #4439
EST. Exeter yoeman decd. testate. WILL: Drawn 1/15/1778. Legatees: Wife-Mary; Sons-Samuel, Zebulon and John; Daus-Mary Gilman, Sarah Mudget, Lydia Hopkinson, Abigail and Dorithy; His mother agreeable to his father's Will. Exex.-wife Mary. His sig. Witnesses: Caleb Robinson, Nehemiah Dane and Samuel Gilman Jr. CERT. WILL: 3/25/1778. Presented by Exex. and witnesses Dane (Deane in D) and Gilman, esq.

2486. SMITH, SAMUEL (1767) A#3231
GDP. of the son of Joseph Smith of Durham. RELEASE: 11/14/1773. Of Samuel Smith. To Daniel Meserve, his Gdn. Smith acknowledges receiving "from the beginning of the world to this day" L100.0.0 in full of all demands of all of his real and personal est. which Meserve had in his possession as Samuel's Gdn. Witnesses: Robert Hill and Jno. Sullivan. Oath 4/6/1776 Smith to John Sullivan, JP. Orig. Archives file of est. of Samuel's father A#3231 Joseph Smith (1767) contains the Gdp. for Samuel 1767.

2487. SMITH, SAMUEL (1773) #3992
EST. Londonderry yoeman decd. intestate. ADMIN.: 2/4/1773. Admr. John Smith, Londonderry husbm. Bond L500.0.0. Sureties: Joseph Butler of Pelham and John Hazeltine of Nottingham West, Hillsborough Co., gentlemen. Witnesses: Hough Smith and Jona. Lowell. INVY. WARR.: 2/4/1773. Comm.: Joseph Butler of Pelham and David Gregg of Windham, gentlemen. INVY.: Appr. 2/27/1773. Value L27.19.10. Oaths 3/18/1773 Comm. to James Betton, JP. Oath 3/31/1773 Admr. to judge. LICENSE: 3/31/1773. To Admr. To sell all the real est. LICENSE: Dupl. of previous.

CLAIMS WARR.: 3/31/1773. Comm.: James Betton, Windham esq. and Samuel Anderson, Londonderry yeoman. CLAIMS: 4/27/1773. Total L44.16.1. Oath 12/14/1773 Anderson to J. Holland, JP. Oath 3/30/1774 Betton to judge. PROP. & SETTLM.: Claims L44.16.0. Amount to be proportioned L37.9.0. Allowed 3/14/1775 with order to Admr. to pay. ACCOUNT: 3/22/1774. Of Admr. Allowed 3/30/1774.

2488. SMITH, SAMUEL (1776) No#
EST. Of Brentwood. decd. ADMIN.: (D23:259): 2/28/1776. Admr. Alexander Gordon Smith. Sureties: Thos. Peabody and Hawley Marshall, all of Brentwood.

2489. SMITH, SAMUEL (1778) #4441
EST. Epping yoeman decd. ADMIN.: 3/26/1778. Admr. Theophilus Stevens, Epping gent. Bond L500.0.0. Sureties: Ezekiel Worthen, Epping gent. and Josiah Fogg, Raymond esq. Witnesses: Nathl. Parker and W. Parker. INVY.: Appr. 6/22/1778. Comm. Josiah Fogg and Joseph Blake. Value L86.04.0. Oaths 10/28/1778 Comm. and Admr. to Wm. Parker, Reg. LICENSE: 6/30/1779. To Admr. To sell sufficient real est. to pay debts. ACCOUNT: 6/31/1779. Of Admr. Allowed 6/30/1779 (sic.)

2490. SMITH, SAMUEL (1799) #6582
EST. Newmarket blacksmith decd. intestate. RENUN.: 6/20/1799. Of Azubah Smith widow of Samuel. Of Admin. Requests appointment of John Shute of Newmarket, father-in-law of decd. ADMIN.: 6/20/1799. Admr. John Shute, Newmarket innholder. Bond $2,000.00. Sureties: Nathaniel Rogers, esq. and Dudley Watson, trader, both of Newmarket. Witnesses: Moses Dalton and John Shute Jr. INVY.: Appr. 7/19/1799. Comm.: Nathl. Rogers, Ichabod Hilton and Daniel Hill. Value $243.56. Oaths 7/19/1799 Rogers and Hill to Josiah Adams, JP. Oath 7/20/1799 Admr. to W. Parker, JP. DOWER WARR.: 7/23/1799. Comm.: Nathaniel Rogers, Josiah Adams and Daniel Hill, esquires; Dudley Watson, trader and Ichabod Hilton, yoeman, all of Newmarket. Of Widow Azubah Smith. DOWER: 10/7/1799. Oaths 10/11/1799 Rogers, Adams, and Watson to James Smith, JP. The following Petition found in #6595 Stephen Prescutt (1799) belongs here. PETITION: 4/2/1800. Of John Shute, Admr. est. Samuel Smith, Newmarket blacksmith. For Comm. Insolvency. Gives claims of $139.66. Granted. LICENSE (D33:293): 8/5/1800. To Admr. To sell all the real est. and reversion of Dower. CLAIMS: Comm.: Nat. Rogers, Josiah Adams and Dudley Watson. Total $220.74. Oaths 5/9/1801 Comm. to Enoch Coffin, JP. ACCOUNT: Of Admr. Allowed 5/12/1801. Account includes main. "the" children. PROP. & SETTLM.: Claims $220.74. Amount to be proportioned $39.57. Allowed 5/14/1801 with order to Admr. to pay.

2491. SMITH, SYLVANUS (1771) #3893
EST. Chester gent. decd. intestate. ADMIN.: 11/27/1771. Admr. William White, Chester yoeman. Bond L500.0.0. Sureties: John L. Derben, yoeman and Henry Moore, gent., both of Chester. Witnesses: Saml. Hale Jr. and Danl. Fowle. INVY.: Comm.: Saml. Emerson and John Webster, esquires. Value L278.1.1. Oaths 1/28/1772 Comm. to Walter Robie, JP. Oath 1/29/1772 Admr. to judge. LICENSE: 1/29/1772. To Admr. To sell sufficient real est. to pay debts. ACCOUNT: 1/19/1774. Of Admr. Oath 1/20/1774 Admr. to judge. ADDL. ACCOUNT: 8/25/1779. "Which also corrects mistake in former account." Allowed.

2492. SMITH, THEOPHILUS (1772) #3913
EST. Exeter esq. decd. testate. WILL: Drawn 7/3/1765. Legatees: Wife-Mary; Son-Theophilus; Daus.-Abigail Folsom, Doley Smith and Lydeah Smith; Grandsons-Theophilus Folsom son of his dau. Abigail and Theophilus Smith son of his son Theophilus; Second Church in Exeter. Exec.- son Theophilus. His sig. Witnesses: James Leavitt, James Thurstin and Benj. Boardman. CERT. WILL (D21:314): 3/19/1772 Presented by Exec. and witnesses Thurstin and Boardman. ADMIN.: 3/19/1772. Exec. Theophilus Smith, Exeter esq. Bond L500.0.0. Sureties: James Thurstin, blacksmith and Benjamin Boardman, saddler, both of Exeter. Witnesses: Wm. Parker Jr. and Samuel Parker.

2493. SMITH, WILLIAM (1773) #4040
EST. Portsmouth chocolate grinder decd. intestate. ADMIN.: 9/13/1773. Admr. Samuel Smith, Portsmouth chocolate grinder. Bond L200.0.0. Sureties: George Marshall Jr., sailmaker and William Yeaton, blockmaker, both of Portsmouth. Witnesses: Samuel Parker and John Williams. INVY. WARR.: 9/13/1773. Comm.: John Beck, hatter and Albert Denny, mariner, both of Portsmouth. INVY.: Dated by clerk 12/21/1773. Value L469.18.0 or L23.9.10 lawful money. Oaths 12/17/1773 Comm. and Admr. to judge.

2494. SMITH, WILLIAM (1785) #5098
EST. Kingston husbm. decd. testate. WILL: Drawn 2/11/1771. Legatees: Wife-Elisabeth; Sons-William, practioner in physick and Richard; Dau.-Sarah wife of Abraham French. Exec.-son Richard. His sig. Witnesses: Jeremy Webster, Israel Clifford, Jeremiah Webster, Nathl. Bachellor, Eliphalet Webster and Ebenazer Fifield. CERT. WILL (D28:124): 4/20/1785. Presented by Exec. and witnesses Bachellor, esq. and Fifield. ADMIN.: 4/20/1785. Exec. Richard Smith, Kingston yoeman. Bond L1000.0.0. Sureties: Nathaniel Bachellor, esq. and Ebenezer Fifield, yoeman, both of Kingston. Witnesses: John White and W. Parker.

2495. SMITH, WILLIAM (1794) #6023
EST. Salem yoeman decd. testate. WILL: Drawn 8/21/1794. Legatees: Wife-Pheebe; "Son"-Elisha Woodbury; Grandson-William Woodbury; Granddau.-Agnes Woodbury. Exec.-son Elisha Woodbury. His mark. Witnesses: Solomon Smith, John Clark and Wm. Thom. Proved 9/15/1794 on oaths of Clark and Thom. There being no seal on Will, it is allowed for personal est. only. ADMIN.: 9/15/1794. Admr. Elisha Woodbury, Salem yoeman. Bond L1000.0.0. Sureties: John Clark, yoeman and William Thom, gent., both of Salem. Witnesses: W. Parker and Jno. Parker. INVY.: Appr. 12/2/1794. Comm.: Wm. Thom, Asa Corlles and Francis Smith. Value L290.17.11. Oaths 12/2/1794 Comm. to Josiah Gage, JP. Oath 12/17/1794 Admr. To judge. DOWER: 12/2/1794. Comm. Wm. Thom, Asa Corlles, Francis Smith, John Clark and Samuel Cross. Of Widow Phebe Smith. Oaths 12/2/1795 Comm. to Josiah Gage, JP. Allowed 12/17/1794.

2496. SMITH, ZEBULON (1782) #4777
GDP. Of the son of Richard Smith, Exeter tanner decd. PETITION: 2/27/1782. Of Zebulon Smith, a minor over 14. He chooses Eliphalet Hale, Exeter gent., as his Gdn. His mark. Witness W. Parker and signed by judge.

2497. SNELL, JOHN (1781) #4758
GDP. Of the son of John Snell of Portsmouth decd. GDP.: 12/26/1781. Of John, a minor over 14. Gdn. Nathaniel Rogers, Newmarket esq. Bond L500.0.0. Surety Samuel Baker, Newmarket gent. Witnesses: Nathl. Parker and W. Parker.

2498. SNELL, REUBEN (1794) #6037
EST. Portsmouth boatbuilder decd. ADMIN.: 10/15/1794. Admx. Lucy Snell, Portsmouth widow. Bond L1000.0.0. Sureties: Elisha Hill, blacksmith and John Marshall, boatbuilder, both of Portsmouth. Witnesses: Isaac Rindge and W. Parker. INVY.: Appr. 10/27/1794. Comm.: Isaac Rindge and George Wentworth. Value L227.14.9. Oath 10/27/1794 Capt. Wentworth to R. Cutts Shannon, JP. Oath 2/18/1795 Admx. to judge. PETITION: 2/18/1794. Of Admx. For License as she has three infirm children almost blind to maintain and cannot afford to sell personal est. Allowed. LICENSE (31:464): 2/18/1795. To Admx. To sell real est. to amount of L120.0.0. PETITION: 11/19/1799. Of Admx. For Dower. Allowed 11/11/1799 with Comm. of Isaac Rindge, George Wentworth, George W. Wendell, Saml. Hutchings, merchants and Edw. Sargent, mariner. Of Widow Lucy Snell. DOWER: 12/10/1799. Oaths 12/12/1799 Rindge, Wentworth and Sargent to R. Cutts Shannon, JP.

Allowed. ACCOUNT: 2/19/1800. Of Admx. Oath 2/19/1800 Admx. to judge. Account shows expenses for 2 funerals and what may be a 3d.

2499. SOLLEY, SAMUEL (1785) #5163
EST. Portsmouth esq. decd. intestate. ADMIN.: 12/21/1785. Admr. George Jaffrey, Portsmouth esq. Bond L1000.0.0. Sureties: George Atkinson and John Parker, Portsmouth esquires. Witnesses: Thos. Odiorne and Teney Gilman.

2500. SPARHAWK, GEORGE KING (1788) #5342
GDP. Of the son of John Sparhawk, Portsmouth esq. decd. GDP.: 3/19/1788. Of George King Sparhawk, a minor over 14. Gdn. Daniel Humphreys, esq. Bond L2000.0.0. Sureties: William King, esq. And Abigail Sparhawk, widow. Witnesses: Alfred Butler and Abigail Humphreys. BOND: 7/4/1788. Of Daniel Humphreys, Gdn. By an Act of the NH General Court, the Gdn. is empowered to sell and convey any lands belonging to his ward, to compromise or refer any dispute concerning the title of such lands and to charge the minor's est. for such purposes. Bond L2000.0.0. To account for the proceeds of any lands sold as required by law. Sureties: Abigail Sparhawk, Portsmouth widow and William Atkinson, Dover esq. Witnesses: John Sparhawk and Abigail Humphreys.

2501. SPARHAWK, JOHN (1787) #5312
EST. Portsmouth esq. decd. intestate. ADMIN.: 12/19/1787. Admx. Abigail Sparhawke, Portsmouth widow. Bond L1000.0.0. Sureties: George Atkinson and Daniel Humphreys, Portsmouth esqures. Witnesses: George K. Sparhawk and Elizabeth Warner. INVY. WARR.: 12/19/1787. Comm.: John Parker and Jeremiah Libbey, esquires and John Evans, merchant, all of Portsmouth. Invy.: Appr. 3/6/1788. Value L891.10.0. Oaths 3/6/1788 Admx. and Comm. to Geo. Gains, JP. PETITION: 3/19/1788. Of Daniel Humphreys on behalf of Admx. For License and Comm. Insolvency. Gives list of claims of L2152.13.4. LICENSE (D29:188): 4/16/1788. To Admx. To sell sufficient real est. to pay debts. ADDL. INVY.: 9/15/1789. Value L89.19.10. CLAIMS: 10/10/1789. Comm.: Jno. Parker, Thomas Marden and Jeremiah Libbey, esquires. Total L2316.11.5. Oaths 10/13/1789 Comm. to Saml. Penhallow, JP. ACCOUNT: 10/21/1789. Of Admx. Allowed 10/21/1789. PROP. & SETTLM.: Claims L2316.11.5. Amount to be proportioned L989.17.8 1/2. Allowed 11/18/1789 with order to Admx. to pay. ACCOUNT: 6/1/1793. Of Admx. by her atty. Daniel Humphreys. Allowed 6/1/1793 with note by judge that taking into consideration the integrity of the Admx. in accounting for the appreciation of the State Notes charged in Account, he has made her an allowance of L65.0.0., which under the circumstances

might appear too large an allowance. ADDL. PROP. & SETTLM.: Claims L2316.11.5. Amount to be proportioned L603.10.7. Allowed 6/3/1793 with order to Admx. To pay. ADDL. ACCOUNT: 2/20/1799. Of Admx. by her atty. Daniel Humphreys. Allowed 2/20/1799. ADDL. PROP. & SETTLM. (D33:83): Claims L2316.11.5. Amount to be proportioned L173.13.8. or $568.95. Allowed 5/1/1799 with order to Admx. to pay.

2502. SPARHAWK, JOHN (1798) #6456
EST. Portsmouth merchant decd. intestate. RENUN.: 5/12/1798. Of Eliza Sparhawk, widow of John. Of Admin. Requests appointment of her bro.-in-law Thomas Sparhawk. ADMIN.: 5/12/1798. Admr. Thomas Sparhawk, Portsmouth merchant. Bond $4,000.00. Sureties: George King Sparhawk and Daniel Humphreys Jr., Portsmouth merchants. Witnesses: John P. Rindge and Edward Ordway. INVY. WARR.: 5/12/1798. Comm.: Jeremiah Libbey, Supply Clap and George Wentworth, Portsmouth esquires. Value $4,560.25. Oath 6/25/1798 Admr., affirms. Comm. to George Gains, JP.

2503. SPARHAWK, SAMUEL HIRST (1791) #5705
EST. Kittery, York Co., MA/ME gent. decd. intestate. PETITION: 11/2/1791. Of Danl. Humphreys, Portsmouth esq. States he is atty. to Sir William Pepperrell of London, the largest creditor to est., Sparhawk has no bro. or sister in NH and his mother consents to Humphrey being appointed Admr. ADMIN.: 11/3/1791. Admr. Daniel Humphreys, Portsmouth esq. Bond L2000.0.0. Sureties: John Sparhawk, Portsmouth gent. and William King Atkin-son, Dover, Strafford Co. esq. Witnesses: Wm. Dame and Geo. K. Sparhawk. INVY.: Appr. 11/15/1791. Comm.: Jeremiah Libbey, James Sheafe and Danl. Rogers, esquires. Value L680.0.0. Oaths 11/15/1791 Comm. to Nathl. Adams, JP. Oath 11/24/1791 Admr. to W. Parker, JP. PETITION: 11/24/1794. Of Admr. For License and Comm. Insolvency. Gives claims as L2310.0.0 with no personal est. in his hands. LICENSE (D30:150): 11/24/1791. To Admr. To sell real est. to the amount of L2300.0.0. CLAIMS WARR.: 11/23/1791. Comm.: Jeremiah Libbey, esq.; James Sheafe and Daniel Rindge Rogers, merchants, all of Portsmouth. Claims: 8/13/1792. Total L1627.15.3. Oaths 8/13/1792 Sheafe and Rogers, affirm. Libbey to Nathl. Adams, JP. ACCOUNT: Of Admr. Allowed 8/17/1792. ACCOUNT: Partially destroyed. Of Admr. Oath 3/17/1794 Admr. to Joseph Simpson, Judge Probate, York Co., MA/ME and Admr. to be accountable for bal. of L124.10.7 1/4. Cert. as a true copy by Daniel Sewall, Reg. ADDL. ACCOUNT: Of Admr. Allowed 6/18/1794. PROP. & SETTLM.: Claims L1627.15.3. Amount to be proportioned L738.3.1 1/2. Allowed 7/1/1794 with order to Admr. to pay. DUPL. COPY PROP.

2504. SPAULDING, MARY (1787) #5236
EST. Windham widow decd. ADMIN.: 1/5/1787. Admr. Alexander McCay, Windham yoeman. Bond L1000.0.0. Sureties: James Betton, esq. and William Gregg Jr., yoeman, both of Windham. Witnesses: Henry Campbell Jr. and Willm. Reed. INVY.: 1/29/1787. Comm.: James Betton, William Gregg and Henry Campbell Jr. Value L90.17.11 1/2. Oaths 1/29/1787 Gregg, Admr. and Campbell to James Betton, JP.

2505. STACEY, JOSEPH (1777) #4408
EST. Exeter cordwainer decd. testate. WILL: Drawn 9/12/1777. Legatees: Wife-Mercy; Dau.-Betty Thurstin; Grandchildren-Joseph Stacey Thurstin and Peggy Thurstin. Exec.-wife Mercy. His sig. Witnesses: Timothy Chamberlain, Jedediah Jewett and Noah Emery. CERT. WILL (D24:171): 12/31/1777. Presented by Exex. and witnesses Chamberlain and Emery, esq. INVY.: Appr. 1/22/1778. Comm.: Charles Rundlet, Trueworthy Gilman and Benja. Lamson. Value L493.6.9. Oaths Comm. and on 2/6/1778 Admx. to W. Parker, JP.

2506. STANYAN, LT. JONATHAN (1778) #4434
EST. Chichester gent. decd. ADMIN.: 2/26/1778. Admx. Molly Stanyan, Chichester widow. Bond L500.0.0. Sureties: John Cram, Chichester esq. and Jeremiah Prescott, Epsom gent. Witnesses: Samuel Daves and Caleb Daves. INVY.: Comm.: Benjamin Goodwin, Epsom blacksmith; Edmund Rand Leavitt, gent. and Jeremiah Sanborn, yoemen, both of Chichester. Value not tallied. Esti. L294.0.0+. Oaths 8/18/1778 Comm. and on 8/31/1778 Admx. to John Cram, JP.

2507. STAVERS, JOHN (1797) #6384
EST. Portsmouth innholder decd. testate. WILL: Drawn 12/30/1793. Legates: Sons-John Jr. and William; Daus.-Margaret Davis wife of Theodore Davis, Mary Frazier widow of John Frazer, Sukey Appleton widow of Jotham Appleton and Elizabeth Seaward wife of John Seaward. Execs.-son William and Jeremiah Libbey. His sig. Witnesses: Hall Jackson, Saml. Drowne and George Ham. CERT. WILL (D32:387): 10/5/1797. Presented by Execs. And witnesses Drowne and Ham. ADMIN.: 10/5/1797. Execs.: William Stavers, yoeman and Jeremiah Libbey, esq., both of Portsmouth. Bond $3,000.00. Sureties: John Seaward, mariner and Samuel Drowne, goldsmith, both of Portsmouth. Witnesses: George Ham and W. Parker. INVY.: Appr. 10/18/1797. Comm.: Saml. Drowne, Nathl. Marshall and Edmund H. Quincy. Value $7,729.9(mills). Oaths 10/18/1797 of Mary Frazer and Susannah Appleton, daus. who lived in the house and had the care of the property. They had informed the Execs. of all property. Affirms. of Execs. and oaths Comm. to R. Cutts Shannon, JP. The following Petition recorded as

#6387 William Stavers et. al. (1797) belongs here. PETITION: 1-/18/1797. Of William Stavers, Portsmouth yoeman. For div. of real est. owned in common with his 3 sister-Mary Frazer, Sukey Appleton and Elizabeth Seaward. Consent: 10/18/1797. Of the sisters to Petition. They all request Comm. of Dr. John Goddard, George Gains, Samuel Drowne, Edward Sargent and Nathl. Marshall. Witness Jere. Libbey. DIV. WARR.: 10/18/1797. Comm. as requested. To div. the real est. among the 4 children. DIV.: 11/25/1797. Divisees: William, Mary Frazer, Susannah Appleton and Elizabeth Seaward. Oaths 11/27/1797 Comm. to Saml. Penhallow, JP. Cert.: Of Mary Frazer, William Stavers, Elizabeth Seaward and Susannah Appleton. They accept the Div. and request acceptance by judge. Allowed 12/6/1797. Note: The Will states that John Jr. and Margaret had received their shares and were given in Will grants for love and affection so are not included in Div. MAP OF DIV.. ACCOUNT: Of Execs., the property having passed wholly through the hands of Exec. William Stavers. Consent: 11/7/1790. Of Mary Frazer, Susanna Appleton and Jno. Seaward. Allowed 11/8/1798. Note: This file also includes a Petition which belongs with #6147 Josiah Akerman (1795) and is recorded there.

2508. STAVERS, MARTHA (1792) #5757
EST. Of Portsmouth, widow of Bartholomew Stavers, decd. testate. WILL: Drawn 2/18/1792. Legatees: Son-William; Daus. Catherine Slade and Sally Hutchings. Exec.: Dr. John Jackson. Her mark. Witnesses: James Rand, Robert Yeaton and Tho. Bickford. CERT. WILL (D30:219): 4/16/1792. Presented by Exec. and witnesses Yeaton and Bickford. ADMIN.: 4/16/1792. Exec. John Jackson, Portsmouth physician. Bond L1000.0.0. Sureties: John Hale, esq. and Thomas Bickford, merchant, both of Portsmouth. INVY.: Appr. 5/2/1792. Comm.: Thos. Bickford, Peter Coues and Saml. Drowne. Value L151.5.7. Oaths 6/20/1792 Coues, Drowne and Exec. to W. Parker, Reg. PETITION: Dated by clerk 7/15/1793. Of Exec. For License to sell the personal est. to bal. the Account. Jeremiah Libbey as Gdn. to Wm. Stavers, to whom the above legacy was given, consents to sale. ACCOUNT: 6/18/1794. Of Exec. Examined 6/17/1794 by Jeremiah Libbey, Gdn. of Wm. Stavers Jr. and has no objections to it. Account also examined by Thomas Slade on behalf of his mother Katherine Slade, an heir, and has no objections. Allowed.

2509. STAVERS, WILLIAM (1792) #5774
GDP. Of the son of Bartholomew Stavers, of Castle Camps, Great Britain, formerly Portsmouth yoeman, decd. GDP.: 5/23/1792. Of William, a minor over 14. Gdn. Jeremiah Libbey, Portsmouth esq. Bond L1000.0.0. Sureties: John Stavers and William Stavers, Portsmouth yoemen. Witnesses: Mary Frazer and Elizabeth Stavers.

2510. STAVERS, WILLIAM (1797) #6387
See #6384 John Stavers (1797).

2511. STEARNS: CATHARINE, CHARLES, JOHN, JOSEPH, MARTHA, MARY & THOMAS (1782) #4863
GDP. Of the children of John Stearns and his late wife Martha decd. of Watertown, Middlesex Co., MA. GDP.: 11/27/1782. Of: Catharine, John, Thomas and Joseph, minors over 14 and of Martha, Charles and Mary, minors under 14. Gdn. John Stearns, Watertown, Middlesex Co., MA tanner, their father. Bond L1000.0.0. Sureties: Phinehas Stearns, gent. And Daniel Barnard, yoeman, both of Watertown, Middlesex Co., MA. Witnesses: Thomas Drowne and Sarah Drowne.

2512. STEARNS, REV. JOSIAH (1788) #5365
EST. Epping clerk decd. testate. WILL: Drawn 4/21/1788. Legatees: Wife-Sarah; Sons-Dudley (oldest), John, Josiah, Samuel, Timothy and William; Daus.-Sarah (oldest), Esther, Molley and Elizabeth. Exec.-son Samuel. His sig. Witnesses: Enoch Coffin, Jonathan Fogg and Enoch Coffin Jr. CERT WILL (D29:206): Presented by Exec. and all witnesses. Note: This file contains an Inferior Court of Common Pleas return dated 5/1/1783 wherein Jonathan Greeley 3d, Kingston esq., was plaintiff against George March, Stratham husbm., defendent wherein March has not paid a note he signed. March failed to appear so Plaintiff granted L4.13.0. damages. After which March appealed to the Superior Court. On Back: Greeley complains that the appeal has not been prosecuted and requests affirmation of his judgment, plus interest an costs.

STEEL. See also Steele

2513. STEEL, JOSEPH (1794) #6014
GDP.: Exeter yoeman, an adult adjudged n.c.m. PETITION: 7/5/1794. Of Jeremiah Leavitt, Exeter hatter. States that Joseph is n.c.m. and needs a Gdn. Order: 7/5/1794. To Exeter Selectmen. To hold an inquisition into condition of Joseph. Report: 7/5/1794. Of: Eliphalet Giddings, Gideon Lamson and Geo. Odiorne, Exeter Selectment. They are of opinion Joseph is n.c.m. and needs a Gdn. GDP. 7/24/1794. Of Joseph, an adult n.c.m. Gdn. Benjamin Moulton, Kensington husbm. Bond L1000.0.0. Sureties: Stephen Fogg, carpenter and Benjamin Clark Gilman, goldsmith, both of Exeter. Witnesses: Nathl. Parker and Wm. Parker. INVY.: 8/29/1794. Comm.: Jere. Bachelder, Stephen Fogg and Benjamin Leavitt. Value L55.10.0. Oaths 10/8/1794 Comm. and Gdn. to judge. Note: The following Petition recorded as #6084 Benjamin Moulton (1795) belongs here. PETITION: 4/4/1795. Of Benjamin Moulton, Gdn. of Joseph Steel of

Exeter, an adult n.c.m. For div. of land and house which his ward and 2 sisters own as tenants in common. Requests Comm. of Jeremiah Bachelder, esq.; Weare Nudd and Simon Prescott, yoemen, all of Kensington; Robert Kimball, gent. and John Gordon, yoeman, both of Exeter. Consent of: Ephraim Moulton, Nathaniel Davis, Jeremiah Moulton, Jacob Carter, Abigail Carter and Nancy Steel. DIV. WARR.: 4/7/1795. Comm.: As requested. To div. land and house owned in common by Joseph and his sisters Abigail Carter and Nanny Steel, setting of 1/2 to Joseph. DIV.: 4/10/1795. Comm. divided only Joseph's share. Oaths 7/4/1795 Bachelder, Nudd and Gordon to W. Parker, JP. Allowed. ACCOUNT: 1/23/1796. Of Gdn. Allowed 1/23/1797. ACCOUNT: 9/6/1798. Of Gdn. Allowed 9/6/1798. ADDL. ACCOUNT: 5/4/1799. Of Gdn. Allowed 5/4/1799.

STEELE. See also Steel

2514. STEELE, HENRY (1780) #4654
EST. Exeter yeoman decd. testate. WILL: Drawn 7/8/1780. Legatees: Wife-Marcy; Son-Joseph; Daus.-Abigail Carty wife of Jacob Carty and Anna Steel; Grandchild-Nathaniel Davis son of Jonathan Davis. Exec.-son Joseph. His mark. Witnesses: Benja, Kimball, Moses Kimball and Jere. Bachelder. CERT. WILL (D25:369): 9/27/1780. Presented by Exec. and all witnesses. INVY. WARR.: 9/27/1780. Comm.: Benja. Kimball, yoeman and Robert Kimball, gent., both of Exeter and Jeremiah Bachelder, Kensington gent. INVY.: Appr. 1/5/1780. Value not tallied. Esti. L5959.0.0+. Oaths 1/6/1781 Comm. and Exec. to W. Parker, Reg.

2515. STEELE, REBECCA (1786) #4889
GDP. Of the dau. of John Steel of Londonderry decd. PETITION: 4/7/1786. Of Rebecca Steel, a minor over 14. She chooses as her Gdn. Hugh Montgomery, Londonderry yoeman. Witness James Betton.

2516. STEVENS, ANNA (1788) #5345
EST. Hampstead widow decd. RECOMMENDATION: 4/3/1788. Of: Francis Stevens, Moses Stevens, William Lacy and Molley Lacy, heirs. They recommend appointment of Parker Stevens as Admr. ADMIN.: 4/12/1788. Admr. Parker Stevens, Piermont, Grafton Co. yoeman. Bond L1000.0.0. Sureties: Jabez Hoit, Chester esq. and Ela Dow, Sandown gent. Witnesses: Charles Pressey and Abigail Dow. INVY.: Appr. 4/15/1788. Comm.: Ela Dow, Thomas Muzzey and Jabez Hoit. Value L20.5.2. Oaths 4/15/1788 Muzzey and Dow to Jabez Hoit, JP. Oath 4/16/1788 Admr. to W. Parker, Reg. PETITION: 4/16/1788. Of Admr. For Comm. Insolvency. Gives list claims of L55.0.0. CLAIMS WARR.: 4/16/1788. Comm.: Jabez

Hoit, Chester esq.; Ela Dow, Sandown gent. and Thomas Muzzey, Hampstead blacksmith. LICENSE: 9/17/1788. To Admr. To sell sufficient real est. to pay debts. CLAIMS: 10/15/1788. Total not tallied. Esti. L55.0.0+. Oaths 10/14/1788 Comm. to John Calfe, JP. ACCOUNT: 12/16/1789. Of Admr. Allowed 12/16/1789 after considering objections made on behalf of John Hogg, esq., one of creditors.

2517. STEVENS, BENJAMIN (1776) #4227
EST. Kingston yoeman decd. testate. WILL: Drawn 3/22/1776. Legatees: Wife-Elizabeth; Sons-Benjamin and Ebenezer. Execs.-sons Benjamin and Ebenezer. His sig. Witnesses: Samuel Stevens, Ebenezer Colcord and Ebenr. Stevens. CERT. WILL: 4/24/1776. Presented by Execs. and all witnesses. PETITION: Dated by clerk 4/24/1776. Of Widow Elizabeth Stevens. She thinks that her husband, in his Will, did not make provision for her equal to what the law allows. She rejects the provision of the Will and requests her Dower. INVY.: Appr. 4/30/1776. Value L1729.9.3. Oaths 7/31/1776 Comm. and Execs. to judge.

2518. STEVENS: BENJAMIN WOODS, GRACE, JOHN, MABEL JENNER, STEPHEN GREENLEAF & THOMAS JENNER (1793) #5858
GDP. Of the children of John Stevens, Concord esq. decd. GDP.: 3/1/1793. Of: Mabel Jenner Stevens and Grace, minors over 14 and of John, Stephen Greenleaf Stevens, Thomas Jenner Stevens and Benjamin Wood Stevens, minors under 14. Gdn. Sally Stevens, Concord Widow. Bond L1000.0.0. Sureties: Thomas Wilson, saddler and William Partridge, merchant, both of Concord. Witnesses: Peter Green Jr. and Robert Eastman.

2519. STEVENS: CHACE, ELISABETH, HANNAH, LYDIA, MARY, PRUDENCE & RUTH (1773) #4022
GDP. Of the children of Moses Stevens, Plaistow yoeman decd. GDP.: 5/24/1773. Of: Hannah and Ruth, minors over 14 and of Chace, Lydia, Mary, Elisabeth and Prudence. Gdn. David Stevens of Plaistow. Bond L500.0.0. Sureties: Dustin Chaney and Moses Stevens, both of Plaistow. Witnesses: James Cheney and Daniel Stevens.

2520. STEVENS, DAVID (1773) #4006
EST. Strathem husbm. decd. testate. WILL.: Drawn 1/16/1773. Legatees: Wife-Sarah; Sons-Nathaniel and Joseph. Daus.- Hannah Caule, Sarah Wiggin and Elisabeth Stevens. Exec.-son Nathaniel. His sig. Witnesses: Thomas Moore Jr., Samuel Pottle and Saml. Shepard. CERT. WILL.: 4/28/1773. Presented by Exec., and witnesses Moore and Pottle. DECLARATION: 4/22/1773. Of Sarah Stevens, widow. She states that

during his lifetime David bequeathed to her 1/4 part of the income of his farm. She promises to remain satisfied with the provisions of the Will. Witness William Calley. ADMIN.: 4/28/1773. Exec. Nathanael Stevens. Bond L500.0.0. Sureties: Samuel Pottle, yoeman and Thomas Moore Jr., gent., both of Strathem. Witnesses: Nathaniel Rogers and Saml. Parker.
2521. STEVENS, DAVID (1799) #6542
EST. Plaistow husbm. decd. testate. WILL: Drawn 12/25/1798. Legatees: Wife-Anna; Son-David; Dau.-Molly wife of Zebediah Sargeant; Grandson-John Stevens. Execs.-son David and dau. Molly Sargeant. His sig. Witnesses: Joseph Smith, Humphrey Noyes, Moses Harriman, Joshua Dow, Nathaniel Cheney and John White. CERT. WILL (D33:55): Presented by David Stevens, one of Execs., and witnesses Smith and Dow. CERT.: 3/1/1799. Of Widow Anna Stevens. She accepts Will. Witnesses: Joshua Dow and Jos. Smith. INVY. (D33:142): Comm.: Joseph Smith, Joshua Dow and Ezekial Gile. Value $98.70. Oaths 9/16/1799 Comm. to Josh. Welch, JP.

2522. STEVENS, EBENEZER 3RD (1799) #6545
EST. Kingston yoeman decd. ADMIN. (D33:60): 3/7/1799. Admx. Eleanor Stevens, Kingston widow. Sureties: Ebenezer Eastman Jr. of Kingston and Benjamin Hills of Chester. INVY. (D33:117): Comm.: Jacob Hook, Jacob Webster and Simmons Seccombe. Value $553.41. Oaths 3/19/1799 Hook, Webster and Admx. To Simmons Seccombe, JP. ACCOUNT: 11/20/1800. Of Admx. Allowed 11/20/1800. Account includes main. of 3 children.

2523. STEVENS, EDWARD (1787) #5244
EST. Brentwood yoeman decd. testate. WILL: Drawn 6/28/1785. Legatees: Wife-Hannah; Sons-Samuel, Edward, Hale and James; Daus.-Sarah wife of Samuel Thing, Mehetabel Hill wife of Isaac Hill, Abigail Thing wife of Eliphalet Thing, Anna Hill wife of Stephen Hill and Betty Stevens. Grandchildren-John Stevens Dudley and Sarah Dudley children of his dau. Hannah Dudley decd. late wife of Winthrop Dudley. Execs.-sons Samuel and Edward. His sig. Witnesses: Benjamin Dearborn, Saml. Hobart, Sarah Dearbon and Dudley Hobart. CERT. WILL (D29:96): Presented by Execs. and witnesses Saml. Hobart, esq., Dudley Hobart and Sarah Dearbon. ACCEPTANCE: 1/16/1787. Of Hannah Stevens, widow of Edward. She accepts provision made for her in Will. Witnesses: Joseph Wadleigh Jr. and Saml. Hobart. INVY.: Appr. 4/10/1787. Comm.: Saml. Hobart and Joseph Wadleigh Jr. Value L1219.7.6. Oaths 4/18/1787 Comm. and Execs. to W. Parker, JP.

2524. STEVENS, HUBBARD (1771) #3842
EST. Durham tanner decd. testate. WILL: Drawn 7/12/1770. Legatees: Sons-Joseph and Hubbard or his heirs; Granddau.-Abigail Clough; Niece-Hannah Stevens dau. of his bro. Moses. Exec.-son Joseph. His sig. Witnesses: John Griffen, Joseph Parsons and John Smith. Proved 4/11/1771. Does not say on oaths of whom. ADMIN.: 4/11/1771. Admr.: Joseph Stevens, Durham tanner. Bond L1000.0.0. Surety: Ebenezer Thompson, Durham physician. Witnesses: Otis Baker and Richd. Jenness.

2525. STEVENS, JOHN (1793) #5857
EST. Concord esq. decd. ADMIN.: 3/1/1793. Admx. Sally Stevens, Concord widow. Bond L1000.0.0. Sureties: Thomas Wilson, saddler and William Partridge, merchant, both of Concord. Witnesses: Peter Green Jr. and Robt. Eastman. INVY.: 3/20/1793. Comm.: Wm. Manly, merchant; Peter Green Jr., physician and Robert Eastman, yoeman, all of Concord. Value not tallied. Esti. L1599.0.0+ and probably does not include interest on a long list of Notes. Oaths 6/20/1793 Green, Manley and Admx. to Peter Green, JP. LETTER: 9/11/1796. From: Peter Green Jr. and Wm. Manley, appraisers. They report a material error they made in estimating the weight of the silver plate. They reported it was 316 oz. and find it was only 185 oz. DOWER WARR.: 12/6/1796. Comm.: Timothy Walker and John Bradley, esquires; Peter Green, physician; Reuben Kimball and Jonathan Eastman, gentlemen, all of Concord. Of Widow Sarah Stevens. PETITION: 12/3/1796. Of Admx. For a certificate from judge stating it is necessary for her to sell the wild land in Mass. (ME). Notes great expense of Admin., main. children, cost of taxes on the wild land and limited income from lands rented. Gives list claims of L556.17.9. ACCOUNT: 9/22/1797. Of Admx. Allowed 9/22/1797, reps. of a majority of the heirs present and consenting. DOWER: 12/5/1797. Oaths 12/11/1797 Bradley, Eastman and Kimball to Timo. Walker, JP. Allowed. DIV. WARR.: 5/17/1799. Comm. same as for Dower. To div. 2/3 of the real est. equally among his children. DIV.: 6/23/1800. Divisees: Sons-John, Greenleaf, Thomas Jenners Stevens and Benjamin Wood Stevens; Daus.-Mable Jenners Stevens and Grace Stevens. Oaths 8/4/1800 Kimball and Jonathan Eastman to Timo. Walker, JP. Allowed 8/15/1800. Includes Map. BOND: 1/18/1803. Of Admx. Bond $10,000.00. To account for sale of 8,000 acres of land in Pennicook, Dist. of Maine, MA by License from Leg. of MA. Sureties: Peter Green, physician and David Wait, trader. Witnesses: Timo. Walker and Wm. Manly.

2526. STEVENS, JOSEPH (1772) #3918
GDP. Of the son of Thomas Stevens of Portsmouth decd. GDP.: 4/5/1772. Of Joseph, a minor over 14. Gdn.: Joseph Walton, Portsmouth yoeman. Bond L100.0.0. Surety Joseph Day, Portsmouth yoeman. Witnesses: Samuel Hale Jr. and Joseph Ward.

2527. STEVENS, MOSES (1799) #6543
EST. Plaistow yoeman decd. testate. WILL: Drawn 7/7/1778. Legatees: Wife-Mary; Sons-David, Nicholas and Daniel who has had his share; Daus.-Hannah wife of Job Eaton and Lydia wife of John Colbey; Children of his son Moses decd. Execs.-sons David and Nicholas. His sig. Witnesses; Jos. Smith, Moses Bradley and John Knight. CERT. WILL (D33:54): 3/4/1799. Presented by David Stevens, an Exec., the other being dead, and witness Smith, the other two being dead. ADMIN. (D33:60): 3/4/1799. Exec. David Stevens of Plaistow. Sureties: Joseph Smith and Joshua Dow, both of Plaistow. INVY. (D33:142): Comm.: Joseph Smith, Joshua Dow and Ezekiel Gile. Value $1,037.39 1/2. Oaths 9/16/1799 Comm. to Josh. Welch, JP.

2528. STEVENS, NATHANIEL (1773) #4023
EST. Brentwood yoeman decd. testate. WILL.: Drawn 4/3/1773. Legatees: Wife-Sarah; Sons-Nathanael and John. Dau.-Sarah Stevens. Execs.-son Nathanael and Deacon Joseph Wadleigh. His mark. Witnesses: Jeremy Webster, David Clifford and Samuel Stevens. Codicil: 4/9/1773. Gives his wife the remaining 2/3 of all the moveable goods and effects indoors. His mark. Witnesses: Jeremy Webster, David Clifford and Samuel Stevens. CERT. WILL: 5/26/1773. Presented by Execs. and witnesses David Clifford, who affirmed, and Samuel Stevens who gave oath. INVY. WARR.: 5/26/1773. Comm.: Benjamin Stevens, Kingston yoeman and Ebenezer Colcott, Brentwood gent. INVY.: Appr. 7/20/1773. Value L402.9.0. Oaths 7/23/1773 Comm. and Execs. to Noah Emery, JP. Oaths 7/28/1773 Execs. to judge. ACCOUNT: 1/5/1775. Of Nathaniel Stevens, an Admr. Consent: 12/27/1774. Joseph Wadleigh, an Exec., consents to paying the charge of Nathaniel Stevens, the other Exec., as in the Account, as Stevens transacted and settled the business without Wadleigh. Allowed 1/5/1775.

2529. STEVENS, NATHANIEL (1798) #6484
EST. Stratham gent. decd. testate. WILL: Drawn 7/19/1798. Legatees: Wife-Anna; Sons-Simeon, Nathaniel and John; Daus.-Anna French, Sarah Sanborn, Rachel Smith, Elizabeth, Abigail and Polley (last 3 unmarr.). Exec.-son Simeon. His sig. Witnesses: Christopher Smith, Thomas Moore and Nich. Rollins. CERT. WILL (D32:518): 8/22/1798. Presented by

Exec. and all witnesses. CERT.: 8/22/1798. Of Widow Anna. She accepts what her husb. gave her in Will. Witnesses: Thomas Moore and Nich. Rollins. INVY. (D32:530): Comm.: Christopher Smith, Abra. Tilton and Nichs. Rollings. Value $1,902.95. Oaths 10/13/1798 Comm. and Exec. to W. Parker, JP. PETITION: 1/9/1800. Of Daniel Mason in right of his wife, a legatee. States that the Admr. d.b.n. has never paid the legacies or settled his Account. Requests he be cited. ADMIN. D.B.N.: 4/25/1803. Admr. d.b.n. Nicholas Rollins, Stratham esq. Bond $3,000.00. Sureties: Jacob Low Jr., yoeman and Abraham Tilton, gent., both of Stratham. Witness W. Parker. PETITION: 3/21/1804. Of Daniel Mason for Widow Anna Stevens. She states that the Admr. d.b.n. refuses to provide for her as in Will. Requests permission to sue Bond of Admin. Order: 3/21/1804. For hearing, Admr. d.b.n. to be cited to appear. PETITION: 12/28/1804. Of Admr. d.b.n. For License. No personal est. has come to his hands, there are legacies of over $360.00 unpaid and an annuity due Widow. Granted. LICENSE (D36:31): 12/28/1804. To Admr. d.b.n. To sell real est. to the amount of $500.00. CITATION: 1/9/1809. To Admr. d.b.n. To appear and settle his Account for distribution of est. Cert.: 1/10/1809. Of Walter Weeks, Stratham Constable. He left a copy of Citation at Rollins' house. DECREE: 1/16/1809. In answer to the Petition of Daniel Mason, a legatee in right of his wife, the Admr. d.b.n. was cited, appeared and declared his resolution not to pay the legacies. Mason granted leave to sure Bond of Admin. PETITION: 9/27/1809. Of Admr. d.b.n. For License. Gives list of legacies and claims of $362.00. Granted. LICENSE (D39:158): 9/22/1809. To Admr. d.b.n. To sell real est. to amount of $370.00. ACCOUNT: Of Admr. d.b.n. Allowed 3/20/1810 no objections being made. Account shows legacy payments to Wm. Wiggin's wife, John and Daniel Mason's wife.

2530. STEVENS, NATHANIEL (1799) #6548
GDP. Of the son of Nathaniel Stevens, Stratham gent. decd. GDP.: 3/30/1799. Of Nathaniel, a minor over 14. Gdn. Simeon Stevens, Stratham yoeman. Bond $3,000.00. Surety Nicholas Rollins, Stratham esq. Witnesses: W. Parker and (Mrs. P. Adams?). File is a photocopy of orig.

2531. STEVENS, SAMUEL (1771) #3845
EST. Newmarket husbm. decd. ADMIN. 5/7/1771. Admr. Walter Bryent, Newmarket esq. Bond L500.0.0. Sureties: Sarah Hicks, Madbury, Strafford Co. widow and Andrew McMellen, Concord esq.

2532. STEVENS, SAMUEL (1789) #5466
EST. East Kingston yoeman decd. testate. WILL: Drawn 1/22/1789. Legatees: Sons-Samuel, Ebenezer, Benjamin, Moses, Daniel, Peter, Edward and Jacob; Daus.-Shuah Morrison, Sarah Stevens (married), and Hannah Stevens. Ref. to his bros. John and Benjamin. Execs.-sons Edward and Peter. His sig. Witnesses: Moses Greeley, John Tappan and Jonathan Greeley Jr. CERT. WILL (D29:289): 6/15/1789. Presented by Execs. and witnesses Moses Greeley and Jonathan Greeley Jr. ADMIN.: 6/17/1789. Execs.: Edward Stevens and Peter Stevens, East Kingston yoemen. Bond L1000.0.0. Sureties: Jona. Greeley Jr., esq. and John Morill, gent., both of East Kingston. Witnesses: W. Parker and Nathl. Parker. INVY.: appr. 7/6/1789. Comm.: Ebenr. Loveren, Jacob Ordway and Ezra Currier. Value not tallied. Esti. L1302.0.0+. Oaths 10/29/1789 Comm. and Execs. to judge.

STEWARD. See also Stewart, Stuart

2533. STEWARD, DAVID (1788) #5366
EST. Kensington blacksmith decd. intestate. ADMIN.: 8/20/1788. Admx. Abigail Steward, Kensington widow. Bond L1000.0.0. Sureties: Jeremiah Fogg, esq. And Jeremiah Fellows Jr., clockmarker, both of Kensington. Witnesses: David Prescott and Jeremiah Blake. INVY.: Comm.: Jere. Fellows Jr., Philemon Blake and Jeremiah Fogg Jr. Value L372.17.6. Oaths 10/13/1788 Blake, Fellows and Admx. to Jere. Fogg, JP. DOWER: Comm.: Stephen Page, Philemon Blake, Jere. Bachelder, Joseph Brown and Moses Shaw Jr. Of Widow Abigail Steward. Oaths 10/28/1789 Comm. to Jere. Fogg, JP. Allowed 4/16/1792. DIV.: Same Comm. as Dower. To div. the real est. Divisees: Nabba Johnston, David and Jonathan (oldest sons, twins, 3 shares) and Josiah Steward. Oaths 10/28/1789 Comm. to Jere. Fogg, JP. Allowed. ACCOUNT: Of Admx. Allowed 4/16/1792.

STEWART. See also Steward, Stuart

2534. STICKNEY, CAPT. ANTHONY (1774). #4131
EST. Chester gent. & yoeman decd. intestate. ADMIN.: 11/9/1774. Admr. Anthony Somersby Stickney, Newburyport, Mass. Bay cooper. Bond L1000.0.0. Sureties: David Griffith and Samuel Bowles, Portsmouth merchants. Witnesses: Anna Rogers and Saml Hale Jr. INVY.: Appr. 11/11/1774. Comm.: Isaac Towl and David Wetherspoon. Value L42.4.6. Oaths 12/6/1774 Comm. to Saml. Emerson, JP. Oath 1/25/1775 Admr. to judge. A note says that 2 shirts and 1 pr. plated buckles not appraised. LIST OF CLAIMS: Top half missing. Total L55.4.10. 3/22/1775 judge allows petition for Comm. Insolvency and orders a Warr. CLAIMS

WARR.: 3/23/1775. Comm.: Samuel Emerson and Samuel Robie, Chester esquires. CLAIMS: 9/23/1775. Total L55.3.3.3. Oaths 4/30/1776 Comm. to Robt. Wilson, JP. ACCOUNT. 9/24/1776. Of Admr. Allowed 9/24/1776. PROP. & SETTLM.: 9/30/1776. Claims L55.3.3.3. Amount to be proportioned L23.15.10. Allowed with order to Admr. to pay.

2535. STICKNEY, JOHN (1776) #4240
EST. Raymond yoeman decd. ADMIN.: 5/29/1776. Admrs.: Mary Stickney, Epping (sic.) widow and Josiah Fogg, Raymond esq. Bond L1000.0.0. Sureties: Jonathan Swain and Ithiel Gordon, Raymond yoemen. Witnesses: Joseph Pearson and W. Parker. INVY. WARR.: 5/29/1776. Comm.: Jonathan Swain and Ithiel Gordon of Raymond and Jeremiah Prescut of Epping. INVY.: Appr. 6/5/1776. Value L277.2.9. Oaths 6/12/1776 Swain, Prescut and Admrs. to Wm. Parker, JP. DOWER: 11/26/1776. Comm.: Jona. Swain, Jeremiah Prescut and Benjamin Morgan. Of Widow Mary Stickney. Oaths 11/26/1776 Comm. to John Dudley, JP. Allowed 11/27/1776. LICENSE: 11/27/1776. To Admrs. To sell sufficient real est. to pay debts. PETITION: 11/27/1776. Of Josiah Fogg, an Admr. For Comm. In-solvency. Gives list claims of L114.9.8 and expects more. CLAIMS WARR.: 11/27/1776. Comm.: John Dudley and Jonathan Swain of Raymond. CLAIMS: Total L90.2.9. Oaths 1/28/1778 Comm. to W. Parker, JP. ACCOUNT: 2/25/1778. Of Admrs. Allowed 2/25/1778. Account includes main. children under 7, number and names not given. PROP. & SETTLM.: Claims L90.2.9. Amount to be proportioned L83.9.9. Allowed 7/28/1779 with order to Admrs. to pay. COPY OF PROP. & SETTLM.

2536. STICKNEY, JONATHAN (1793) #5839
EST. Concord gent. decd. of smallpox. RENUN.: 12/21/1792. Of Anna Stickney, widow of Jonathan. Of Admin. Requests appointment of her son David. Witness Timo. Walker. ADMIN.: 1/3/1793. Admr. David Stickney, Concord gent. Bond L1000.0.0. Sureties: Thomas Stickney, gent. and William Stickney, yoeman, both of Concord. Witnesses: Timo. Walker and Caleb Chase. INVY.: Appr. 1/29/1793. Comm.: Joshua Abbot and Caleb Chase, gentlemen and Abel Hutchins, yoeman. Value L906.2.8. Oaths 1/29/1793 Comm. to Timo. Walker, JP. GDP. of the children of Jonathan. GDP.: 11/30/1793. Of: Jonathan, Samuel and Hannah, minors under 14. Gdn. Anna Stickney, Concord widow. Bond L1000.0.0. Sureties: Ezekiel Knowlton, yoeman and Moses Trussell, schoolmaster, both of Hopkinton, Hillsborough Co. Witnesses: Joseph Story and Betsay Knowlton. PETITION: 4/2/1794. Of Admr. For License. Gives claims already exhibited as L422.18.11 and 3 children to main. Granted. LICENSE (D31:230): 4/2/1794. To Admr. To sell real est. to amount of

L255.0.0. DOWER: 4/12/1794. Comm.: Timo. Walker, Asa Herrick, Ephraim Carter, Thomas Wilson and Danl. Stickney. Of Widow Anna Stickney. Oaths 4/12/1794 Herrick, Carter, Wilson and Stickney to Timo. Walker, JP. Allowed. ACCOUNT: Of Admr. Allowed 5/15/1799 the heirs having been notified. APPR. WARR.: 5/15/1799. Comm.: Asa Herrick and Ephraim Carter, both of Concord and Samuel Farington of Hopkinton, Hillsborough Co., gentlemen. To appr. the neat income of 2/3 of the real est. for past 6 years. APPR.: 5/25/1799. Value $50.00 per annum or $300.00 for 6 years. Oaths 5/25/1799 Comm. to Timo. Walker, JP. ADDL. ACCOUNT: Of Admr. Allowed 3/20/1806 the heirs having no objections. Note: This file also contains a Petition which belongs with #5538 Robert Collins Jr. (1791) and the Gdp. of Jeremiah Burns (1793) No#. Both have been recorded in their proper places.

2537. STINSON, SAMUEL (1799) #6600
See #5649 Daniel Potter (1791)

2538. STOCKBRIDGE, JOHN (1782) #4778
EST. Stratham yoeman decd. intestate. ADMIN.: 2/27/1782. Admr. John Stockbridge, Stratham gent. Bond L1000.0.0. Sureties: Paine Wingate, gent. and Thomas Veasey, yoeman, both of Stratham. Witnesses: Nathl. Parker and W. Parker. INVY. WARR.: 2/27/1782. Comm.: Samuel Lane, esq.; Paine Wingate and Jonathan Wiggin, gentlemen, all of Stratham. Invy.: Appr. 3/27/1782. Value L755.18.0. Oaths 3/27/1782 Comm. and Admr. to judge. DOWER WARR.: 2/18/1784. Comm.: Paine Wingate and Jonathan Wiggin, gentlemen; Samuel Lane and Theophilus Smith, esquires and Daniel Clark, yoeman, all of Stratham. Of Widow Sarah Stockbridge. Dower: 4/20/1784. Oaths 4/21/1784 Wingate and Smith to judge. Allowed. Note: On back clerk incorrectly called widow Mary, but text says Sarah. DIV. WARR.: 2/18/1784. Comm.: Same as for dower. To div. 2/3 of the real est. with double share to oldest son and one share to each of the other children. Div.: 4/21/1784. Divisees: Sons-John (oldest), Abraham in his own right and the right of his sister Hannah Piper which he purchased from her, Reuben in his own right and the right of his sister Sarah Rundlet which he purchased from her, Israel and Jacob; Daus.-Elizabeth and Abigail (youngest dau.). Oaths 4/21/1784 Lane, Wingate and Smith to judge. Allowed. ACCOUNT: Of Admr. Allowed 1/18/1785. DIV. WARR.: 2/16/1785. Comm.: Paine Wingate and Jona. Wiggin, gentlemen; Samuel Lane and Thos. Smith, esquires and Daniel Clark, yoeman. To div. the real est. which was the Dower, giving double share to oldest son and one share to other children. Div.: 5/18/1785. Divisees: Sons-John (oldest), Jacob in his own right and in the rights of his bro. Israel and his sister Elizabeth Allen which he purchased, Reuben in his own right and the right of his sister Sarah Rundlet which he purchased,

Abraham in his own right and the right of his sister Hannah Piper which he purchased; Dau.-Abigail. Oaths 5/17/1786 Wingate, Lane and Wiggin to W. Parker, JP. Allowed.

2539. STOCKBRIDGE, REUBEN (1785) #5144
EST. Stratham yoeman decd. intestate. ADMIN.: 10/19/1785. Admx. Anna Stockbridge, Stratham widow. Bond L1000.0.0. Sureties: Abraham Stockbridge, mason and Josiah Allen jr., yoeman, both of Stratham. Witnesses: Nat. Parker and W. Parker. INVY. WARR.: 10/19/1785. Comm.: Paine Wingate and Thomas Moore, gentlemen and Enos Hoag, yoeman, all of Strathem. Invy.: Appr. 2/10/1786. Value not tallied. Esti. L155.0.0+. Oath Admx., Wingate and Moore to W. Parker, Reg.

2540. STOKELL, ROBERT (1764) A#3362
Of Portsmouth decd. ACCOUNT (D22:448): 4/29/1774. Of William Furnald and Mary his wife, formerly Mary Stokell. Account includes main. dau. Mary. Note: The original Archives file is missing. The card file lists an Admin. and Invy. for the est., Admx. Widow Mary. It is assumed the Account was not with orig. papers.

2541. STOODLEY: ELIZABETH & NATHANIEL (1796) #6183
GDP.: Of the children of William Stoodley, Portsmouth merchant decd. GDP.: 2/26/1796. Of Elizabeth and Nathaniel, minors under 14. Gdn. Elijah Hall, Portsmouth merchant. Bond $2,000.00. Sureties: Samuel Storer, merchant and Isaac Rindge, both of Portsmouth. Witnesses: Jno. Manning and John P. Rindge.

2542. STOODLEY, JAMES (1779) #4586
EST. Portsmouth esq. decd. testate. WILL: Drawn 4/26/1779. Legatees: Wife- Elizabeth; Son-William; Daus.-Mary Folsom, Sarah Lewis and Elizabeth Stoodley. Execs.-wife Elizabeth and son William. His sig. Witnesses: George King, A. R. Cutter and Wm. Hart. CERT. WILL: 12/8/1779. Presented by Execs. and witnesses Hart; George Atkinson, formerly King; and Cutter, esquires who gave oath to Wm. Parker, Reg. & JP.. INVY.: Comm.: Wm. Knight, A. R. Cutter and John Furnald. Value L95130.0.3 3/4. Oaths 3/24/1780 Comm. and on 4/25/1789 Admx. to Geo. Gains, JP. PETITION: 10/16/1793. Of Elijah Hall, Portsmouth mariner. For div. of land in Durham, Strafford Co. in right of his wife. "NB. The said Hall is atty. to Sarah Lewis, the other of them." Nathl. Folsom, standing by courtesy in the right of one of them, consents to div.. DIV. WARR.: 10/16/1793. Comm.: Ammi Ruhamah Cutter, Isaac Rindge, George Gains and Supply Clap, esquires and Wm. Hart, gent., all of Portsmouth. To div. land devised to his 3 daus. by William and which they

took possession of immediately after his death. If it cannot be div. equally, Comm. to settle with daus. on money to make equal. ACCOUNT. 10/17/1793. A note by clerk says "this is no more than a list of demands against said est. in order to get License to sell, of which a notification was made by Execs. to heirs for a hearing." Total claims L421.8.0. PETITION: 10/17/1793. Of William Stoodley, Portsmouth yeoman, surviving Exec. For License to sell enough real est. to pay the share of the debts to be paid by James' daughters from their inheritance, he having paid his share. Order: For hearing. Nathl. Folsom, tenant by courtesy in right of his late wife Mary Folsom decd. and Gdn. of her children, minor heirs, consents. Elijah Hall as owner in right of his wife of part of the dwelling house and as atty. to Sarah Lewis, an heir, consents. LICENSE (D31:272): 5/19/1794. To Exec. To sell all of the dwelling house set off to the Widow. BOND: 5/19/1794. Of Exec. Bond L1500.0.0. To account for sale of real est. by License. Sureties: Nathl. Folsom, esq. and Elijah Hall, mariner, both of Portsmouth. Witness W. Parker. DIV.: Divisees: Mrs. Sarah Lewis; Capt. Elijah Hall and Elizabeth his wife in her right; Heirs of Mrs. Mary Folsom decd. and to make shares equal they are to pay Mrs. Lewis L80.0.0 and the Halls L40.0.0. Oaths 5/14/1794 Cutter, Rindge and Hart to Geo. Gains, JP. RECEIPT: 5/14/1794. Of Nathaniel Folsom as Gdn. of his children, heirs. To Exec. For L40.0.0 and certs. that L80.0.0 was paid to Capt. Lewis on behalf of his wife and another heir. Oath 5/14/1794. Of Nathl. Folsom, as tenant by courtesy in right of his late wife and Gdn. to her children. He is content with Div. Witnesses: Isaac Rindge and Wm. Hart. Allowed 5/19/1794. ACCOUNT 2/17/1796. Of William Stoodley, surviving Exec. Statement: 2/10/1796. The Account was made out by William Stoodley but left at his death without his sig. It has been examined and approved by heirs. They agree the bal. is to be divided between Sarah Lewis, the heirs of Mary Folsom and Elizabeth Hall, their prop. of the debts having been paid. Signed by the judge. Statement: 2/10/1796. Of Nathaniel Folsom, E. Hall and Elijah Hall for Sarah Lewis. That Account was made out by William Stoodley as a final settlm. of est. and they believe it to be just and are willing it should be confirmed.

2543. STOODLEY, WILLIAM (1795) #6134
EST. Portsmouth merchant decd. ADMIN.: 8/24/1795. Admx. Mary Stoodly, Portsmouth widow. Bond $3,000.00. Sureties: Elijah Hall, merchant and Isaac Rindge, esq., both of Portsmouth.. Witnesses: Saml. Sparhawk and Daniel French. INVY.: Comm.: Isaac Rindge, esq.; Capt. Geo. Wentworth, and Wm. Hart. Value: $519.86. Oaths 11/3/1795 Admx. and Comm. to Geo. Gains, JP. ACCOUNT: Of Elijah Hall atty. to Admx. Allowed 2/16/1804.

2544. STORY, NEHEMIAH (1785) #5108
EST. Manchester, Essex Co., MA mariner decd. ADMIN.: 6/14/1785. Admr. Elnathon Whitney, Manchester, Essex Co., MA baker. Bond L1000.0.0. Sureties: Jacob Allen, housewright and Eleazer Crafts, esq., both of Manchester, Essex Co., MA. Witnesses: Saml. Adams and W. Parker. INVY.: Appr. 6/15/1785. Comm.: John Bell, esq.; James Aiken, gent. and John Morse, yoeman. Value L316.10.6. Oaths 6/15/1785 Aiken, Morse and Admr. To John Bell, JP. Invy. is all land in Londonderry. DOWER WARR.: 7/15/1789. Comm.: John Bell and John Pinkerton, esquires; James Aiken, gent.; David Patterson and James Nesmith, yoemen, all of Londonderry. Of Widow Lucy Whitney in est. Nehemiah Story. Dower: 7/16/1789. Oaths 7/16/1789 Pinkerton, Aiken, Nesmith and Patterson to John Bell, JP. Oath 7/16/1789 Bell, esq. to Archd. McMurphy, JP. Allowed. ACCOUNT: 8/18/1789. Of Admr,. who is also Gdn. of heirs. Allowed 8/18/1789 heirs not being notified.

2545. STRAW, DAVID (1782) #4849
EST. Sandown yoeman decd. ADMIN.: 10/30/1783(sic.). Admx. Mary Straw, Sandown widow. Bond L1000.0.0. Sureties: Alexander Campbell and Benjamin Fuller, Chester husbandmen. Witnesses: Jabez Hoit and Jonathan Straw. INVY. WARR.: 10/30/1782. Comm.: Jabez Hoit of Chester, Nathl. Ingalls and David Moulton of Sandown. INVY.: Appr. 1/21/1783. Value not tallied. Esti. L300.0.0+. Oaths 1/21/1783 Comm. and Admx. to Reuben Clough, JP.

2546. STRAW, SAMUEL (1773) #4053
EST. South Hampton husbm. decd. testate. WILL: Drawn 10/10/1764. Legatees: Wife-Elizabeth; Sons-Jonathan, Exekiel, Jacob, Samuel and Israel; Daus.-Hannah Straw; Elizabeth Goarden wife of Abner Goarden and Abiah Osgood wife of John Osgood. Exec.-son Israel. His sig. Witnesses: James Merrill, Ezekiel Flanders and Joseph Merril Jr. CERT. WILL: 10/27/1773. Presented by Exec. and witnesses Flanders and Joseph Merril; Jr. ADMIN.: 10/27/1773. Exec. Israel Straw of Weare, Hillsborough Co. Bond L500.0.0. Sureties: Ezekiel Flanders and Joseph Merril, both of South Hampton. Witnesses: Samuel Parker and John Parker.

2547. STRAW, WILLIAM (1785) #5141
EST. Epping yoeman decd. ADMIN.: 8/29/1785. Admr. Ebenezer Straw, Epping yoeman. Bond L1000.0.0. Sureties: Josiah Robinson, gent. and Richard Emery, mariner, both of Exeter. Witness W. Parker. INVY. WARR.: 8/29/1785. Comm.: Jeremiah Sanborn, Josiah Tilton and Dudley Ladd, Epping yoemen. INVY.: Appr. 10/21/1785. Value L1168.09.10. Oaths 2/20/1786 Comm. and Admr. to W. Parker, Reg.

STUART. See also Steward, Stewart

2548. STUART: DAVID, JONATHAN & JOSIAH (1789) #5489
GDP. Of the sons of David Stuart, Kensington blacksmith decd. GDP.: 10/19/1789. Of: David, Jonathan and Josiah, minors over 14. Gdn. Abigail Stuart, Kensington widow. Bond L500.0.0. Sureties: Jeremiah Fogg Jr. and Moses Shaw Jr., Kensington esquires. Witnesses: Philimon Blake and Jere. Fellows Jr.

2549. STUART, JOHN (1786) #5232
EST. Londonderry yoeman decd. testate. WILL: Drawn 6/7/1786. Legatees: Sons-Robert, Samuel, John and Thomas; Daus.-Elisabeth Gibson and Margrat Humphrey; Granddau.-Jean Gibson. Execs.-Samuel Gibson and John Morrison. His mark. Witnesses: John Moor, Robert Barnet and Ezra Waldon. CERT. WILL(D29:88):12/20/1786. Presented by Execs. and witnesses Moor and Barnet. A TRUE COPY OF WILL. INVY.: Appr. 1/19/1787. Comm.: Robert Barnet and John Adams. Value not tallied. Esti. L49.12.1. Oaths 2/20/1787 Comm. to Geo. Reid, JP. Oath 2/21/1787 Execs. to judge. PETITION: 2/21/1787. Of Execs. For Comm. Insolvency. Give list of claims of L39.15.7. CLAIMS WARR.: 2/21/1787. Comm.: James Underwood, Litchfield, esq. and Jacob McGraw of Merrimack, both of Hillsborough Co. CLAIMS: Total L37.0.0. Oaths 10/26/1787 Comm. to William McQuesten, JP. ACCOUNT: 4/1788. Of John Morrison, an Exec. Allowed 4/16/1788. ACCOUNT: Of Samuel Gibson, an Exec. Allowed 4/16/1788. PROP. & SETTLM.: Claims L37.0.0. Amount to be proportioned L18.4.11. Allowed 4/16/1788 with order to Execs. to pay. 2550. STUART, ROBERT (1782) #4810 EST. Newton yoeman decd. testate. WILL: Drawn 8/31/1781. Legatees: Wife-Anne; Sons-Robert and Stephen; Daus.-Sarah Chase widow of Samuel Chase decd., Anne Hoyte wife of Barnard Hoyte, Mary Chase wife of Samuel Chase and Elizabeth Currier wife of Reuben Currier; Grandson-Samuel Stuart son of his son Samuel decd.; Granddau.-Abigail Brown wife of Enoch Brown and dau. of his son Samuel decd. Exec.-son Robert. He appoints his son Stephen to be Gdn. of his grandson Samuel Stuart. His sig. Witnesses: Enoch Brown, James Brown and Thos. Clarke. CERT. WILL: 5/27/1782. Presented 4/24/1782 by Exec. and on oaths of witnesses James Brown and Thomas Clarke and the affirm. On 5/27/1782 of Enoch Brown. INVY. WARR.: 5/30/1782. Comm.: David Bagley, Abraham Kimball and Samuel Hoit, Newton gentlemen. INVY.: Value not tallied. Esti. L1900.0.0+. Oaths 8/20/1782 Comm. to William Rowell, JP. Oath 8/28/1782 Exec. to judge.

2551. SWAIN, CALEB (1773) #4071
EST. Hampton Falls yoeman decd testate. WILL: Drawn 10/15/1773. Legatees: Wife-Anna; Sons-Dudley and Jeremiah; Daus.-Bettey Swain and Olly Swain. Execs.-wife Anna and son Jeremiah. His sig. Witnesses: Jeremiah Blake, Jeremiah Lane and Henry Blake. Cert Will: 12/29/1773. Presented by Anna Swain, one of the Execs., and witnesses Jeremiah Blake and Lane. INVY. WARR.: 12/29/1773. Comm.: Jeremiah Blake, gent. and Jeremiah Lane, husbm., both of Hampton Falls. INVY.: Appr. 1/4/1774. Value L262.7.0. Oaths 2/17/1774 Comm. and on 2/22/1774 Anna Swain, an Exec., to Meshech Weare, JP. ACCOUNT: 1/25/1775. Of Anna Swain, Exex. Allowed 1/25/1775.

2552. SWAIN, ELIZABETH (1799) #6494 1/2
EST. Of Raymond, wife of Jonathan Swain of Raymond, decd. testate. WILL: Drawn 1/14/1799. Legatees: Son-Isaac Towle; Grandaus.-Elizabeth Derburn, Elizabeth dau. of her son Simon Towle and Betsy dau. of her son Isaac Towle. Exec.-son Isaac Towle. Her mark. Witnesses: Levi Swain, Francis Hopkins and John Prescot. Consented to by Jonathan Swain. No proving or cert.

2553. SWAIN, MOLLY (1796) #6175
EST. Raymond widow decd. intestate, late wife of Jonathan Swain, Raymond esq. ADMIN.: 1/18/1796. Admr. Isaac Blasdel, New Salisbury, Hillsborough Co. gent. Bond L1000.0.0. Sureties: Stephen Chase, esq. and Josiah Chase, yoemen, both of Chester. Witnesses: Rhoda Chase and Dolly Blake. INVY.: Appr. 2/2/1796. Comm.: Jacob Chase, Willm. White and Benja. Brown. Value $1,482.60. Oaths 2/4/1796 Comm. to Walter Robie, JP. Oath 2/4/1796 Admr. to Willm. White, JP. DIV.: 2/4/1796. Comm.: Jacob Chase, Ebenezer Dearborn, Willm. White, Jacob Elliot and Benja. Brown. To div. all the real est. in Chester. Divisees: Isaac Blasdel, David Blasdel, Abigail Blasdel, Heirs of Hannah Morss decd., Ebenezer Blasdel, Molley Wadleigh, Abner Blasdel, Anna Chase and Lydia Chase. Oaths 2/4/1796 White, Elliot and Brown to Walter Robie, JP. Allowed. CERT.: 1/12/1797. Of Stephen Chase. At the request of Admr. he has notified 5 of the heirs and sent a letter to 2 who were at a great distance that the Admr. will exhibit his Account. ACCOUNT: 1/6/1797. Of Admr. Allowed 1/16/1797.

2554. SWAIN, REUBEN (1780) #4643
EST. Northwood yoeman decd. intestate. ADMIN.: 8/25/1780. Admr. Samuel Tucke, Kensington cordwainer. Bond L5000.0.0. Sureties: James Fogg, husbm. and William Fogg, gent., both of Kensington. Witnesses: Nathl. Parker and W. Parker. INVY.: Appr. 9/2/1780. Comm.: Sherbun

Blake, Phineas Blake and Levi Dearborn. Value L5288.12.0. Appraised at fifty to one. Oaths 10/18/1780 Comm. to Jeremiah Eastman, JP. Oath 11/29/1780 Admr. to judge. ACCOUNT: Of Admr. The account notes a journey to Northwood to get inquisition on body, he being drowned.

2555. SWAIN, STEPHEN (1799) #6546
GDP. Hampton Falls yoeman n.c.m. PETITION: 3/6/1799. Of Stephen Swain Jr. of Hampton Falls. States that his uncle Stephen Swain of Hampton Falls is n.c.m. and needs a Gdn. Order: 3/6/1799. To Hampton Falls Selectmen. To conduct inquisition into the condition of Stephen. Report: 3/8/1799. Of: Samuel Lane, Caleb Tilton and Theo. Sanborn, Hampton Falls Selectmen. They are of the opinion that Stephen is n.c.m. and needs a Gdn. GDP. (D33:60): 3/9/1799. Of Stephen, an adult adjudged n.c.m. Gdns.: James Sanborn and Theophilus Sanborn, Hampton Falls yoemen. Sureties: Caleb Tilton, esq. and James Prescutt Jr., both of Hampton Falls. INVY. (D33:95): Comm.: Newell Healey, Michael Tilton and James Prescott. Value $1,047.11. Oaths 6/6/1799 Comm. and Gdns. to W. Parker, JP. ACCOUNT: 1/27/1800. Of Gdns. Allowed 1/27/1800. ACCOUNT: 3/1801. Of Gdns., Stephen now decd. Allowed 3/18/1801 the Admr. of est. present and having no objections.

SWEAT. See also Swett

2556. SWEAT, DEACON ELISAH (1788) #5391
EST. Kingston gent. decd. testate. WILL: Drawn 6/10/1778. Legatees: Wife-Abigail; Sons-Joseph of Hawke, Stephen and Elisah; Daus.-Esther wife of Capt. John Judkins, Abigail wife of Capt. John Moody, Hannah wife of Thomas Sweat and Sarah Sweat. Exec.-son Stephen. His sig. Witnesses: Jonathan Collins, Jacob Graves and Nathl. Bacheller. Proved 11/19/1788 on oaths of Graves and Bacheller, esq. ADMIN.: 11/19/1788. Exec. Stephen Sweat of Kingston. Bond L2000.0.0. Sureties: John Currier and Moses Sheppard, both of Kingston. Witness W. Parker.

SWETT. See also Sweat

2557. SWETT, BENJAMIN (1787) #5308
EST. Kingston yoeman decd. ADMIN.: 11/21/1787. Admr. John Darling Swett, Kingston yoeman. Bond L500.0.0. Sureties: John Eastman, esq. and Jacob Webster, gent., both of Kingston. Witnesses: Nathl. Parker and W. Parker. INVY.: Appr. 12/15/1787. Comm.: John Eastman and Jacob Webster. Value L134.10.1. Oaths 12/18/1787 Comm. to Josiah Bartlett, JP. Oath 12/19/1787 Admr. to W. Parker, Reg. PETITION: 12/19/1787. Of Admr. For License. Gives list claims of L32.16.4. LICENSE

(D29:159): 12/19/1787. To Admr. To sell sufficient real est. to pay debts. PETITION: 9/28/1787. Of Abigail Sweat, widow of Benjamin. To have her Dower set off. DOWER WARR.: 10/30/1788. Comm.: Jacob Hook, Simmons Seccombe and John Eastman, esquires and Henry French, yoeman, all of Kingston and Nehemiah Sleeper, Hawke gent. Of Widow Abigail Swett. DOWER: 10/31/1788. Oaths 11/3/1788 Eastman, Sleeper and French to Solomon Wheeler, JP. Allowed 11/19/1788. REPORT: On 1/16/1792 Admr. exhibited his Account, to many articles of which John Calfe, esq. objected. The parties agreed to submit the Account to a Comm. of Simmonds Seccombe, esq.; Amos Gale and Daniel Colcord, all of Kingston. Report: 3/22/1792. The Comm. considered the disputes and evidence and decided that the Admr.'s Account of L76.14.4 should be reduced to L72.4.4. and no more. Signed by Gale and Colcord. Allowed. ACCOUNT: 6/1791. Of Admr.

2558. SWETT, JOHN (1776) #4278
EST. Raymond yoeman decd. intestate. ADMIN.: 10/31/1776. Admx. Lydia Swett, Raymond widow. Bond L500.0.0. Sureties: Joseph Dudley and Joseph Dudley Jr., Raymond yoemen. Witnesses: Mary Dudley and John Dudley. INVY.: Appr. 12/4/1776. Comm.: Jona. Swain and Joseph Dudley. Value L58.0.8. Oaths 11/3/1777 Comm. and Admx. to John Dudley, JP. DOWER WARR.: 3/11/1779. Comm.: Francis Hodgkins, physician; Jona. Swain, Ithiel Gordon, Alexander Smith and Daniel Moody, yoemen, all of Raymond. Of Widow Lydia Swett. DOWER: 4/5/1779. Oaths 4/26/1779 Swain, Hodgkins and Gordon to judge. LICENSE: 5/26/1779. To Admx. To sell sufficient real est. to pay debts.

2559. SWETT, WILLIAM (1790) #5563
EST. Kingston blacksmith decd. ADMIN.: 7/21/1790. Admx. Elizabeth Swett, Kingston widow. Bond L1000.0.0. Sureties: Charles Chase, hatter and Joseph Calef, cordwainer, both of Kingston. Witnesses: W. Parker and N. Parker. INVY.: Appr. 9/7/1790. Comm.: Jacob Hook, esq. and Amos Gale. Value L355.9.1. Oaths 10/18/1790 Comm. to Solomon Wheeler, JP. Oath 11/18/1790 Admx. to W. Parker, JP.

2560. SYLVESTER, PHILIP (1785) #5154
EST. Portsmouth mariner decd. intestate. ADMIN.: 11/16/1785. Admr. William Symmonds, Portsmouth mariner. Bond L500.0.0. Sureties: George Akerman and William Gates, Portsmouth mariners. Witnesses: Wm. Parker and Nathl. Parker. INVY. WARR.: 11/16/1785. Comm.: William Meserve, mariner and Benja. Chandler, shopkeeper, both of Portsmouth. INVY.: Value L8.2.1. Oaths 1/20/1786 Comm. to Oliver Whipple, JP.

2561. TABOR, EBENEZER (1771) #3844
EST. Greenland cordwainer decd. intestate. ADMIN.: 4/24/1771. Admr.: James Berry, Greenland yoeman. Bond L1000.0.0. Sureties: Francis Berry and Samuel Chapman, Greenland yoemen. Witnesses: Joseph Boyd and Wm. Parker. INVY.: Appr. 5/15/1771. Comm.: Enoch Clark and Samuel Chapman. Value L99.19.6. Oaths 8/26/1771 Comm. and Admr. to judge. ACCOUNT: 8/30/1780. Of Admr. Allowed. 8/30/1780. Account includes main. 3 children.

2562. TALLANT, HUGH (1796) #6176
EST. Pelham husbm. decd. testate. WILL: Drawn 7/17/1795. Legatees: Wife-Mary; Sons-John, Hugh, William, George and Andrew; Daus.- Abiah Cutter and Sarah Tallant. Exec.-son Andrew. His sig. Witnesses: Samuel Senter, John Davidson Jr. and John Davidson 3d. CERT. WILL (D32:82): 1/19/1796. Presented by Exec. And witnesses Senter and John Davidson Jr. ADMIN.: 1/19/1796. Exec. Andrew Tallant, Pelham yoeman. Bond $3,000.00. Sureties: Samuel Senter and John Davidson Jr., Windham yoemen. Witnesses: Joseph Blanchard and W. Parker. INVY.: Appr. 3/8/1796. Comm.: Jesse Smith, John Ferguson and Samuel Gains. Value $115.36. Oaths 4/16/1796 Comm. to Josiah Gage, JP. Oath 4/20/1796 Exec. to judge. PETITION: 4/20/1796. Of Exec. For Comm. Insolvency. Gives list claims of $150.00. Allowed. CLAIMS WARR.: 4/20/1796. Comm.: John Ferguson of Pelham and Samuel Armour of Windham, gentlemen and Samuel Senter, Windham yoeman. CLAIMS: 11/21/1796. Total L121.17.5.2. Oaths 11/21/1796 Senter and Armour to Josiah Gage, JP. ACCOUNT: 3/28/1800. Of Exec. Allowed 3/28/1800.

2563. TALLANT, JAMES (1790) #5576
EST. Canterbury yeoman decd. intestate. ADMIN.: 9/15/1790. Admx. Margaret Tallant, Centerbury widow. Bond L1000.0.0. Sureties: David McCrillis and Thomas Curry, Canterbury gentlemen. Witnesses: Michl. McClary and Wm. Parker.

2564. TATE, ROBERT (1777) #4390
EST. Portsmouth mariner decd. ADMIN.: 9/27/1777. Admr. Nicholas Spinney, Kittery, York Co., Mass. Bay/ME yoeman. Bond L500.0.0. Sureties: Nathaniel Jackson, cordwainer and Henry Sherburne, blacksmith, both of Portsmouth. Witnesses: Samuel Briard and Nahum Ward. INVY.: Appr. 11/8/1777. Comm.: Joseph Cotton, Nahum Ward and Jeremiah Libbey. Value L708.17.10 1/4. Oaths 11/8/1777 Comm. to Saml. Penhallow, JP. Oath 11/26/1777 Admr. to W. Parker, Reg. ACCOUNT: 9/30/1778. Of Admr. Allowed 9/30/1778. Account includes 2 counterfeit shillints. MEMO: No date. "A being possessed of a considerable personal

est. died intestate, leaving a wife ensient, who afterwards hath a child. Then the mother dies and soon after the child dies also, leaving grandparents both on the paternal and maternal side. How shall the est. be distributed, to whom, and in what proportion? Note: This last seems to be the judge's notation with no further action or comment.

2565. TAYLOR, JOHN (1779) #4537
EST. Poplin yoeman decd. testate. WILL: Drawn 1/12/1779. Legatees: Wife-Elizabeth; Sons-Phinehas and Willeba; Daus.-Bette Batchelder, Doley Kimball, Hille Taylor and Anna Taylor. Exex-wife Elizabeth. His sig. Witnesses: Daniel Sanbun, John Scribner and Jona. Swain. CERT. WILL: 4/23/1779. Presented by Exex. and witnesses Sanbun and Scribner. INVY. WARR.: 7/28/1779. Comm.: John Scribner, Daniel Sanbun and Enoch Smith, all of Poplin. INVY.: Appr. 6/4/1779. Value L2715.4.0. Oaths 6/19/1779 Comm. and Exex. to John Dudley, JP.

2566. TAYLOR, JOHN (1787) #5264
EST. Of Londonderry, decd. testate. WILL: Drawn 1/29/1784. Legatees: Wife-Margaret; Sons-Matthew, James and John; Daus.-Jennet McKeen and Agnes McKeen. Execs.-son John and son-in-law John McKeen. His sig. Witnesses: William Taylor, David Paul and Samuel Pilsbury. CERT. WILL (D29:110): 3/21/1787. Presented by the Execs. and witnesses Taylor and Paul. INVY. WARR.: 3/21/1787. Comm.: Moody Morse, Salem esq.; David Paul and John Emery, Londonderry gentlemen. INVY.: Appr. 3/30/1787. Value L142.18.6. Oaths 3/30/1787 Paul and Emery to Moody Morse, JP. Oath 2/20/1788 John McKeen, an Exec., to W. Parker, Reg. ANNEXED INVY.: "of the particulars." Otherwise same as previous.

2567. TAYLOR, JOHN (1795) #6075
EST. North Hampton yoeman decd. testate. WILL: Drawn 10/28/1782. Legatees: Wife-Mary; Sons-Joseph, Richard, John and Abraham; Daus.-Abigail wife of John Cotton, Anna wife of Increase Batchelder, Elizabeth wife of Nathaniel Batchelder, Sarah Taylor, Hannah Taylor and Mary Taylor. Exec.-son Abraham. His sig. Witnesses: Levi Dearborn, Morris Hobbs and Thomas Hobbs. CERT. WILL (D31:470): 2/18/1795. Presented by Exec. and witnesses Morris Hobbs and Thomas Hobbs. ADMIN.: 2/18/1795. Exec. Abraham Taylor, North Hampton husbm. Bond L1000.0.0. Sureties: Morris Hobbs and Thomas Hobbs, North Hampton husbandmen. Witnesses: Jonathan Warner and W. Parker. INVY.: Comm.: John Fogg, Simon Brown and Nathaniel Drake. Value $1,313.18. Oaths 6/29/1795 Comm. to Moses Leavitt, JP. Oath 7/28/1795 Exec. to W. Parker, JP.

2568. TAYLOR, JOHN (1796) #6192
EST. Hampton joiner decd. testate. WILL: Drawn 7/2/1778. Legatees: Sons-John and Henery Dearborn Taylor; Daus.-Sarah Blake, Elisabeth Batchelder and Abigail Shaw; Grandsons-Henry Batchelder and Simon Batchelder sons of his dau. Mary Batchelder decd. Exec.-son Henery. His sig. Witnesses: John Fogg, Deaniel Leampary and Joseph Dow. CERT. WILL (D32:108): 3/29/1796. Presented by Exec. And witnesses Fogg and Leampary. ADMIN.: 3/29/1796. Exec. Henry Dearborn Taylor of Hampton. Bond L1000.0.0. Sureties: John Fogg and Daeniel Leampary.

2569. TAYLOR, JONATHAN (1785) #5071
EST. Canterbury yoeman decd. ADMIN.: 1/26/1785. Admx. Ruth Taylor, Canterbury widow. Bond L1000.0.0. Surety Asa Foster, Canterbury yoeman. Witnesses: W. Parker and Nathl. Parker. INVY.: Appr. 2/3/1785. Comm.: Laben Morrill, gent.; David Forster and John Lyford, yoemen. Value not tallied. Esti. L388.17.5. Oaths 3/7/1785 Comm. and Admx. to Archelaus Moore, JP. PETITION: 6/1785. Of Asa Forster for Admx. For License. Gives list claims of L110.8.8. plus main. 3 children, one born posthumously. LICENSE (D28:522): 6/15/1785. To Admx. to sell real est. DOWER: 6/18/1785. Comm.: David Forster, Obediah Hall, Jonathan Bradey, Laban Morrill and John Lyford, all of Canterbury. Of Widow Ruth Taylor. Oaths Forster, Hall and Bradey to Archelaus Moore, JP. Allowed 6/15/1785. PETITION: 3/27/1786. Of Admx. For Comm. Insolvency. Witness Asa Forster Jr. CLAIMS: 5/3/1788. Comm. Jere. Clough Jr. and Obediah Hall. Total L211.16.0. Oaths 5/3/1788 Comm. to Abiel Foster, JP. ACCOUNT: 7/16/1788. Of Gideon Leavitt and Ruth his wife, Admx. Allowed 7/16/1788. PROP. & SETTLM.: Claims L211.16.0. Amount to be proportioned L192.15.11. Allowed 8/20/1788 with order to Admx. to pay.

2570. TENNEY, SAMUEL (1793) No#
APPOINTMENT (D31:1): 6/20/1793. Of Samuel Tenney, esq. as Judge of Probate. Signed by Josiah Bartlett, esq., Gov. Oath 6/28/1793 Tenney to Joseph Pearson and Oliver Peabody, JPs.

TEWKESBURY. See also Tewksbury, Tuxbury

2571. TEWKESBURY: ELIZABETH, MOSES, PETER & SARAH (1792) #5817
GDP. Of the children of Thomas Tewksbury, South Hampton gent. decd. GDP.: 11/21/1792. Of: Peter and Sarah, minors over 14 and of Elizabeth and Moses, minors under 14. Gdn. Sarah Tewksbury, South Hampton widow. Bond L1000.0.0. Sureties: Joseph Tewkesbury of South Hampton

and Jacob Tuxbury of Newton, yoemen. Witnesses: W. Parker and Josiah Tewkesbury.

TEWKSBURY. See also Tewkesbury, Tuxbury

2572. TEWKSBURY, THOMAS (1791) #5628
EST. South Hampton gent. decd. intestate. ADMIN.: 3/16/1791. Admx. Sarah Tuxsbury, South Hampton widow. Bond L1000.0.0. Sureties: James Hadlock, yoeman and Benjamin Clough, esq., both of South Hampton. Witnesses: Josiah Tewksbury, Wm. White and Thomas Currier. INVY.: Appr. 3/25/1791. Comm.: Nathan Currier, Benja. Clough and Joseph Merrill. Value not tallied. Esti. L643.0.0+. Oaths 3/25/1791 Comm. and Admx. To Nathl. Bacheller, JP. DOWER: 4/12/1791. Comm.: Benja. Clough, Joseph Merrill, Thomas Currier, Nathan Currier and Christopher Sargeant. Of Widow Sarah Tuxbury. Allowed 1/16(sic.)/1791. Includes Map. PETITION: 3/31/1791. Of Josiah Tewksbury. For License and Comm. Insolvency. Gives list claims of L361.11.7. CLAIMS WARR.: 3/31/1791. Comm.: Joseph Merrill and Benja. Clough of South Hampton and Christopher Sargeant of Amesbury, Essex Co., MA, esquires. Claims: 10/31/1791. Total L222.13.8. Oaths 10/31/1791 Comm. to Matthias Bartlet, JP. LICENSE (D30:179): 1/16/1792. To Admx. To sell real est. to amount of L90.0.0. OATH: 3/6/1792. Of Admx. In disposing of the est. for which she has a License, she will use her best judgment in setting the time and sell to best advantage of heirs. To Joseph Merrill, JP. APPR.: 4/16/1792. Comm.: Benja. Clough, Nathan Currier and Thomas Currier. They appr. the income of 2/3 of the real est. for 1791 at L15.0.0 and for 1792 at L12.10.0. Oaths 4/16/1792 Comm. to Joseph Merrill, JP. ACCOUNT: 6/18/1792. Of Admx. Allowed 6/18/1792. Account includes main. one child. LICENSE (30:266): 6/18/1792. To Admx. To sell real est. to the amount of L26.0.0. PETITION: 7/2/1792. Of Daniel Collins of Bradford, Orange Co., VT. and Jedediah Flanders of Salisbury, Essex Co., MA in right of their wives. Request div. of 2/3 of the real est., of which they are each entitled to 1/12. Order: 7/2/1792. For hearing, the co-heirs to be served with copies of Petition and Order. COPY OF PETITION. DIV.: 11/22/1792. Comm.: Joseph Merrill, Christopher Sargeant, Abraham Kimball, Thomas Currier and Benjamin Clough. To div. 2/3 of the real est. into 12 equal shares. Divises: Judith Flanders wife of Jedediah Flanders; Anne Tewksbury wife of Josiah Tewksbury; Mary Collins wife of Daniel Collins; Thomas Tewksbury; Philip Tewksbury; Jacob Tewksbury; Dorothy Rowe wife of Elijah Rowe; Joseph Tewksbury; Sarah Tewksbury; Peter Tewksbury; Elizabeth Tewksbury and Moses Tewksbury. There is due to the Admx. from each share L2.3.4 for debts and costs that have been allowed plus a proportion of cost of Div. Oaths 1/23/1793 Kimball,

Currier and Clough to Joseph Merrill, JP. Allowed. BOND: 1/23/1793. Of Sarah Tuxbury Gdn. of heirs Sarah, Peter, Elisabeth and Moses. Bond L300.0.0. To pay her wards' proportion of debts and costs. Sureties: Philip Tewksbury and Elijah Rowe, Bradford, Orange Co., VT. husbm. Witnesses: Josiah Tuxbury and Joseph Rowe. BOND: 1/23/1793. Of: Thomas Tuxbury of Nottingham, Jacob Tuxbury of Newton, Joseph Tuxbury of South Hampton and Josiah Tuxbury of Hawke, yoemen; Philip Tuxbury and Elijah Rowe, Bradford, Orange Co., VT husbandmen. Bond L300.0.0. To pay their proportion of debts and costs of est. Sureties: Micah Hoit, gent. and Timothy Goodwin, yoeman, both of Newton. Witnesses: Caleb Atwood and Joseph Rowe. BOND: 7/2/1792. Of: Jedediah Flanders, Salisbury, Essex Co., MA and Daniel Collins, Bradford, Orange Co., VT, yoemen. Bond L60.0.0. To pay their proportion of debts and costs of est. on behalf of their wives. Sureties: James Hadlock, yoeman and Joseph Merrill, esq., both of South Hampton. Witnesses: Ezekiel Merrill and Benjamin Merrill. ADDL. ACCOUNT: 9/8/1796. Of Admx. Oath 9/8/1796 Admx. to Joseph Merrill, JP. Allowed 9/22/1796. Account includes main. Moses. PETITION: 7/27/1812. Of Peter Tuxbury. Requests Admin. D.B.N. as the Dower has not been administered. ADMIN. D.B.N.: 7/27/1812. Admr. d.b.n. Peter Tuxbury, South Hampton husbm. Bond $2,000.00. Sureties: John H. Pillsbury, South Hampton esq. and Williba Colby, Newton gent. Witness John J. Parker. INVY. WARR.: 7/27/1812. Comm.: John H. Pillsbury, South Hampton esq.; Benjamin Farmer and Jonathan Kimball, Newton yoemen. INVY.: Appr. 9/30/1812. Value $1,200.00. Oaths 11/5/1812 Farmer and Kimball to John H. Pillsbury, JP. Oath 11/9/1812 Admr. d.b.n. to Wm. Parker, JP. PETITION: 11/9/1812. Of Admr. d.b.n. For comm. to view Dower to see if it can be div. Granted with Comm. of John H. Pillsbury, esq.; Isaiah Palmer and Thomas Currier, yoemen, all of South Hampton and Benjamin Farmer and Jonathan Kimball of Newton, yoemen.

2573. THAYER, REV. EBENEZER (1792) #5816
EST. Hampton clerk decd. ADMIN.: 11/6/1792. Admx. Martha Thayer, Hampton widow. Bond L1000.0.0. Sureties: Ward Clark Dean, merchant and Stephen Lamson, yoeman, both of Exeter. Witnesses: James Rundlett and Nathl. Thayer. INVY.: Comm. Christo. Toppan, Jos. Knight and Jona. Garland. Value 232.17.5 1/4. The Comm. did not appr. for present some bldgs. built by decd. which would have value to someone living in house but little if torn down. Oaths 4/2/1793 Comm. to Moses Leavitt, JP. SHORT LIST OF NOTES: Prob. part of Invy. Value without interest $1,281.78 plus two at L163.0.0+ uncertain.

2574. THING, BENJAMIN (1774) #4077
EST. Exeter gent. decd. testate. WILL: Drawn 9/8/1773. Legatees: Wife-Deborah; Sons-Coffin, Winthrop and Samuel; Daus.-Pernal Trask wife of Rev. Nathl. Trask of Brentwood, Mary Clough wife of Capt. Zaccheus Clough of Poplin and Anna Folsom wife of Samuel Folsom, esq. Exec.-son Winthrop. His sig. Witnesses: John Odlin Jr., Mary Odlin and Saml. Brooks. CERT. WILL (D22:382): 1/26/1774. Presented by Exec. and witnesses John Odlin Jr. and Brooks.

2575. THING, STEPHEN (1791) #5701
EST. Exeter yeoman decd. testate. WILL: Drawn 6/10/1776. Legatees: Wife-Mehitable; Dau.-Betty Thing; Sisters-Martha Thing and Eunice; Uncle-Henry Clerk of Candia; Trustees of Church in new parish in Exeter where Rev. Mr. Daniel Rogers is Pastor. Exec.-Joseph Gilman. His sig. Witnesses: Nichl. Gilman, Jno. Taylor Gilman and Nichl. Gilman Jr. Oaths 10/1/1791 Nicholas Gilman, esq. and on 10/17/1791 John Taylor Gilman to judge. Allowed. ADMIN.: 10/17/1791. Admr. Jeremiah Bachelder, Kingston gent. Bond L1000.0.0. Sureties Benjamin Conner Jr. and James Rundlett, Exeter yoemen. Witness John Parker. Note: There is no explanation why Joseph Gilman was not Exec. INVY.: Comm.: Simeon Ladd, esq.; Benjamin Conner and James Rundlett. Value L362.9.9. Oaths 12/19/1791 Ladd, Rundlett and Admr. to judge. DOWER: 4/6/1792. Comm.: Zebulon Gilman, Theophilus Smith, Jabez Dodge, Jeremiah Leavitt and Samuel Colcord. Of Widow Mehitable Thing. Oaths 4/8/1792 Comm. to Wm. Parker, JP. Allowed. CONSENT: 11/23/1792. Of: Martha Thing and Eunice Thing. They consent to sale at public auction of their bro. Stephen' est. of meadow and pasture land on Little River. PETITION: 12/12/1792. Of Admr. For License. Gives claims of L160.0.6. Granted. LICENSE (D30:333): 12/12/1792. To Admr. To sell real est. to amount of L68.0.0. DISCHARGE: 4/11/1795. Of: Martha Thing and Eunice Thing. They have received from Exec. L46.19.0 in full bal. of the est. due them on settlm. Witnesses: Jona. Connor and Danl. Connor. Oaths 6/20/1796 Martha Thing and Eunice Thing to Jere. Fogg, JP. ACCOUNT: 9/16/1793. Of Admr. Allowed 9/16/1793.

THIRSTON. See also Thurston

2576. THIRSTON, JOHN (1774) #4078
EST. Stratham husbm. decd. testate. WILL: Drawn 6/21/1773. Legatees: Wife-Phebe; Son-John; Daus.-Hannah Stockbridge and Phebe Thirston; His wife's dau. Hannah Wiggin. Exec.-friend Stephen Piper. His sig. Witnesses: Moses Clark, Edmund Chapman and Saml. Shephard. CERT. WILL (D22:376): 1/26/1774. Presented by Exec. and witnesses Clark and

Shephard. INVY.: Appr. 4/27/1774. Comm.: Benjamin Barker and Moses Clark. Value L558.5.3. Oaths 4/27/1774 Exec. and Comm. to judge. ACCOUNT: Of Exec. Allowed 6/31/1776. ADDL. ACCOUNT: 2/28/1781. Of Exec. Allowed 2/28/1781. The Addl. Account notes a payment to the heirs of dau. Phebe decd.

2577. THIRSTON, JOHN (1774) #4098
GDP. Of the son of John Thirston of Stratham decd. GDP.: 4/27/1774. Of John, a minor over 14. Gdn. Moses Clark, Stratham clothier. Bond L1000.0.0. Sureties: Benjamin Barker, clothier and Stephen Piper, yoeman, both of Stratham. Witnesses: Benja. Mead and Saml. Hale Jr. RELEASE: 2/28/1781. Upon receipt of two shillings, John releases Moses Clark of all Gdp. responsibilities. Witnesses: O. Peabody and Nathl. Parker. Oath 2/28/1781 John Thirston to W. Parker, JP.

2578. THOM, WILLIAM (1795) #6093
EST. Windham husbm. decd. testate. WILL: Drawn 4/14/1788. Legatees: Sons-John, William, Samuel, Isaac and Benjamin; Dau.-Jennet; Granddau.-Elisabeth Woodbury. Execs.-sons Isaac and Benjamin. His sig. Witnesses: John Morison, Alexander Morison and Saml. Morison. CERT. WILL (D31:511): 4/15/1795. Presented by Execs. and witnesses John Morison and Alexander Morison. ADMIN.: 4/15/1795. Execs.: Isaac Thom, Londonderry esq. and Benjamin Thom, Windham gent. Bond L1000.0.0. Sureties: John Hopkins, Londonderry yoeman and John Morison, Windham gent. Witnesses: James Doak and W. Parker.

2579. THOM, WILLIAM (1798) #6447
See #6451 John Moreland (1798)

2580. THOMAS, JOSEPH MERRILL (1778) #4418
EST. Deerfield gent. decd. intestate. ADMIN.: 1/29/1778. Admx. Anna Thomas, Deerfield widow. Bond L500.0.0. Sureties: Joseph Mills, Deerfield yoeman and Benjamin Norris, Pembroke gent. Witnesses: John (Turner?) and W. Parker. INVY.: Appr. 4/27/1778. Comm.: Simon Marston, John McCrilles and Zebulon Ring, all of Deerfield. Value not tallied. Esti. L158.0.0+. Oaths 4/27/1777 McCrelles, Ring and Admx. to Jeremiah Eastman, JP.

2581. THOMLINSON, JOHN THE ELDER (1797) #6406
EST. London, Great Britain esq. decd. ADMIN.: 12/26/1797. Admr. Jonathan Warner, Portsmouth esquire. Bond $3,000.00. Sureties: Samuel Sherburne and Joshua Wentworth, Portsmouth esquires. Witnesses: Charles Wentworth and Joshua Wentworth Jr. PETITION: 1/5/1798. Of

John Peirce, atty. to Edward Baston Long, Bath, Great Britain esq., who is married to Mary Thomlinson dau. of John Jr., London merchant decd. and granddau. And sole heir of John the elder decd. They are dissatisfied with Decree allowing Admin. to Warner and request appeal against it. Granted 1/5/1798. BOND: 1/5/1798. Of John Peirce. To appeal Decree granting Admin. to Warner. Bond $100.00. Sureties: Jonathan Clark and Daniel Rindge Rogers, Portsmouth esquires. Witnesses: Nathl. A. Haven and Stacy Hall.

2582. THOMPSON, JANE (1792) #5765
EST. Londonderry spinster decd., dau. Of Benja. Thompson of Londonderry decd. ADMIN.: 4/18/1792. Admx. Jenet Clindenine, Londonderry widow. Bond L1000.0.0. Sureties: John McKeen Jr. and Robert Barnet, gent., both of Londonderry. Witnesses: David Webster and W. Parker. INVY.: Appr. 4/21/1792. Comm.: Robt. Barnet and John McKeen Jr. Value L54.0.0. Oaths 8/15/1792 Admx. and Barnet to W. Parker, JP. Oath 11/3/1792 McKeen to Isaac Thom, JP. PETITION: 8/16/1792. Of Admx. For License. Notes that Jane died after age 7 and lists her charges for nursing and medicines for past 8 years as L66.0.0. Allowed. LICENSE (D30:284): 8/15/1792. To Admx. To sell real est. to amount of L66.0.0. ACCOUNT: 8/1796. Of Admx. Allowed 8/17/1790. Account includes sale of Admx.'s thirds in Jane's real est.

2583. THOMPSON, JOHN (1789) #5504
EST. Exeter mariner decd. ADMIN.: 12/16/1798. Admr. Benjamin Boardman, Exeter esq. Bond L500.0.0. Sureties: James Thurston and Simeon Ladd, Exeter gentlemen. Witnesses: Trueworthy Gilman and Eliza Thurston. INVY.: Comm.: James Thurston and Eliphalet Hale. Value L71.16.3. Oaths 1/20/1790 Comm. and Admr. To W. Parker, JP. PETITION: 3/17/1791. Of Admr. For License. Allowed. LICENSE (D30:19): 3/17/1791. To Admr. To sell real est. to amount of L35.0.0. ACCOUNT: 10/23/1790. Of Admr. Allowed 10/23/1790. Account includes main. 2 children.

2584. THOMPSON, NANCY (1796) #6260
GDP. Of the dau. of Samuel Thompson, Concord cordwainer decd. GDP.: 9/21/1796. Of Nancy, a minor over 14. Gdn. Joshua Thompson, Concord gent. Bond $1,000.00. Sureties: Anthony Potter and Joseph Potter, Concord husbandmen. Witnesses: Edmund Leavitt and Joseph Hall.

2585. THOMPSON, ROBERT JR. (1793) #5951
EST. Londonderry yoeman decd. ADMIN.: 12/18/1793. Admr. Robert Thomson of Londonderry. Bond L1000.0.0. Sureties: Robert Moore and Thomas Thomson, both of Londonderry. Witnesses: John Morrison and N. Parker.

2586. THOMPSON, SAMUEL (1795) #6103
EST. Concord cordwainer decd. ADMIN.: 5/20/1795. Admx. Miriam Thompson, Concord widow. Bond L1000.0.0. Sureties: Edmund Leavitt, Chichester gent. and Benjamin Kimball, Concord yoeman. Witnesses: Michl. McClary and W. Parker. INVY.: Appr. 5/26/1795. Comm.: Thos. Stickney, Joshua Abbott and David Hall., Value L47.12.0. Oaths 7/7/1795 Comm. to Timo. Walker, JP. Oath 9/16/1795 Admx. to judge. LIST OF NOTES DUE EST.: Dated by clerk 9/1795. Value L540.10.0. GDP. Of the children of Samuel Thompson decd. GDP.: 4/22/1797. Of: Sally, Reuben and John, minors under 14. Gdn. Miriam Thompson, Concord widow. Bond $1000.00. Sureties: Reuben Kimball of Concord and Edmund Leavitt of Chichester, gentlemen. Witnesses: William Hook and Thomas Leavitt. ACCOUNT: 5/17/1797. Of Admx. by her atty. Edmund Leavitt. Allowed 5/17/1797. Account includes main. one child.

2587. THOMPSON, WILLIAM (1791) #5656
EST. Portsmouth husbm. decd. intestate. RENUN.: 2/15/1791. Of Susannah Thompson. Of Admin. est. her husb. William. Requests appointment of her sons John and Samuel. Witness: Nabby Thomson. ADMIN.: 4/29/1791. Admrs.: John Thompson, goldsmith and Samuel Thomson, taylor, both of Portsmouth. Bond L1000.0.0. Sureties: Aaron Hodgdon, Portsmouth joiner and Joseph Adams, Newington husbm. Witnesses: Nathl. Adams and Nathl. Parker. INVY.: Comm.: James Ayers, Aaron Hodgdon and Joseph Adams. Appr. 6/14/1791. Value L139.9.0. Oaths 6/14/1791 Comm. and Admrs. to Nathl. Adams, JP.

THOMSON. See also Thompson

2588. THOMSON, WILLIAM (1783) #4926
EST. Londonderry weaver decd. testate. WILL: Drawn 2/14/1783. Legatees: Wife-Naomi; Sons-John and William. Execs.-Archebald McMurphy and Robert McColam. His sig. Witnesses: John Pinkerton, John Cochran and John Bell. CERT. WILL (D27:289): 8/26/1783. Presented by Execs. And witnesses Pinkerton and Bell. INVY. WARR.: 8/26/1783. Comm.: John Pinkerton, esq.; James Aiken and William Adams, gentlemen, all of Londonderry. INVY.: Value L187.18.9. Oaths 3/15/1784 Comm. and Execs to John Bell, JP.

2589. THORN, JAMES (1796) #6226
EST. Hawke yoeman decd. testate. WILL: Drawn 6/22/1790. Legatees; Wife-Hannah; Sons-James and Nathan; Daus.-Sarah Thorn, Betty Thorn, Abegail Thorn, Hannah Clemmons wife of Rebuen Clemmons and Molley Tandy wife of Parker Tandy. Exec.-son James. His sig. Witnesses: Thos. Page, Joseph Williams and Nathaniel Brown. CERT. WILL (D32:146): 6/13/1796. Presented by Exec. and witnesses Williams and Brown. ADMIN.: 6/13/1796. Exec. James Thorn, Hawke yoeman. Bond $3,000.00. Sureties: Joseph Williams, gent. and Nathaniel Brown, yoeman. Witnesses: Jos. Smith and W. Parker. INVY.: Comm.: John Eastman, Thomas Page and Jonathan Sanborn. Value $718.75. Oaths 6/22/1796 Eastman and Sanborn and on 7/13/1796 Exec. to Thomas Page, JP.

2590. THORN, JOHN (1790) #5589
EST. Hawke yoeman decd. testate. WILL: Drawn 9/18/1771. Legatees: Wife-Elisabeth; Sons-Jacob and John; Dau.-Elisabeth; Grandchildren-Daus. of his dau. Jemimah Lovering. Exec.-son Jacob. His sig. Witnesses: Samuel Sweat, John Darling Sweat and Moses Sweat. CERT. WILL (D29:440): 11/12/1790. Presented by Exec. and witnesses John Darling Sweat and Moses Sweat.

2591. THRESHER, HENRY (1792) #5735
EST. Raymond yoeman decd. testate. WILL: Drawn 10/21/1785. Legatees: Wife-Mary; Sons-Jacob, Joseph and David; Daus.-Hannar, Mary, Sarah and Rhoda (all marr.). Exec.-son David. His sig. Witnesses: Jos. Swain, Levi Swain and Hannah Swain. CERT. WILL (D30:177): 1/16/1792. Presented by Exec. and witnesses Levi Swain and Jonathan Swain. ADMIN.: 1/16/1792. Exec. David Thresher, Raymond yoeman. Bond L1000.0.0. Sureties: Levi Swain, yoeman and Jonathan Swain, esq., both of Raymond. Witnesses: Thomas Shute and W. Parker. INVY.: Comm.: John Dudley, esq., Jona. Swain and Joseph Dudley. Value L309.15.0. Affirms. 1/31/1792 John Dudley, Joseph Dudley and Exec. to Jona. Swain, JP.

THURSTIN. See also Thirston, Thurston

2592. THURSTIN, SAMUEL (1783) #4882
EST. Epping gent. decd. intestate. ADMIN.: 2/28/1783. Admx. Elizabeth Thurstin, Epping widow. Bond L1000.0.0. Sureties: Daniel Gordon of Epping and Edward Robie of Candia, gentlemen. Witnesses: Jonathan McCostain and W. Parker. INVY.: Comm.: James Norris 3d, esq. Daniel Gordon and Saml. Morrill. Value L527.03.0. Oaths 5/20/1783 Comm. to Enoch Coffin, JP. Oath 7/20/1783 Admx. To David Lawrence, JP.

PETITION: 10/20/1784. Of Admx. For License. Gives total claims of L86.14.9.2. LICENSE (D27:517): 10/20/1784. To Admx. To sell sufficient real est. to pay debts. DOWER WARR.: 9/17/1785. Comm.: Enoch Coffin, esq.; William Plummer, Gordon Lawrence and Jonathan Clarke Jr., yoemen, all of Epping, and Nicholas Smith of Brentwood. Of Widow Elizabeth Thurstin. ACCOUNT: 10/18/1786. Of Admx. Allowed 10/18/1784. Account includes main. one child. DIV.: Comm.: Enoch Coffin, esq.; Seth Fogg, Jona. Clarke Jr., Gordon Lawrence and Daniel Barber. To div. 2/3 of real est. among the children. Divisees: Sons-Jonathan (oldest, double share), Nathaniel, Gilman, Samuel and Ezekiel; Daus.-Elizabeth, Shuer Freese wife of Andrew Freese, Dolly Pike wife of Henry Pike, Anna Pike wife of John Pike and Sarah Bartlett wife of John Bartlett who received her share in money during father's lifetime. Oaths 3/31/1793 Lawrence and Barber to Enoch Coffin, JP. Allowed. DOWER: 12/20/1785. Oaths 2/8/1786 Coffin, Clarke and Lawrence to Thos. Bartlet, JP. Allowed 2/27/1795.

THURSTON. See also Thirston, Thurstin

2593. THURSTON: ANNA, ELIZABETH, GILMAN, NATHANIEL & SAMUEL (1784) #5064
GDP. Of the children of Samuel Thurston, Epping gent. decd. GDP.: 12/15/1784. Of: Samuel and Anna, minors over 14 and of Elizabeth, Gilman and Nathaniel, minors under 14. Gdn. Samuel Morrill, Epping gent. Bond L1000.0.0. Sureties: Seth Fogg, Epping gent. and Benjamin Lamson, Exeter innholder. Witnesses: Jona. Rawson and N. Parker. GDP.: 4/18/1787. Of: Gilman, Samuel and Elizabeth, minors over 14 and of Nathaniel, a minor under 14. Gdn. Andrew Freese, Deerfield gent. Bond L500.0.0. Sureties: John Pike, Epping yoeman and John Magner, Nottingham schoolmaster. Witnesses: Nathl. Parker and W. Parker.

2594. THURSTON, JOHN PHILLIPS (1796) #6172
GDP. Of the son of Rev. Benjamin Thurston of North Hampton. GDP.: 1/8/1796. Of John Phillips Thurston, a minor over 14. Gdn. Benjamin Thurston, North Hampton clerk, his father. Bond $1,000.00. Surety James Rundlett, Exeter yoeman. Witnesses: Mary S. Parker and W. Parker.

2595. THURSTON, ROBERT (1788) #5337
EST. Stratham mariner decd. RENUN.: 3/11/1788. Of Elizabeth Thurston, Stephen Thurston Jr. and Moses Thurston, mother and bros. of Robert. Of Admin. Request appointment of Capt. John Marble. Witness Stephen Thurston. ADMIN.: 3/12/1788. Admr. John Marble, Stratham mariner. Bond L1000.0.0. Sureties: Ephraim Tebbets, physician, and Ward Mason,

yoeman, both of Stratham. Witness W. Parker. INVY.: Appr. 3/14/1788. Comm.: Stephen Batson and Jno. Tuckerman. Value L34.10.0. Oaths 3/14/1788 Comm. to Saml. Penhallow, JP. Oath 3/19/1788 Admr. to W. Parker, Reg. Invy. shows Robert owns 1/2 of the Schooner Sally. PETITION: 3/19/1788. Of Admr. For Comm. Insolvency. Gives list claims of L152.6.0. LICENSE (D29:177): 3/19/1788. To Admr. To sell sufficient real est. to pay debts. CLAIMS WARR.: 3/19/1788. Comm.: Simon Wiggin, esq. and Jonathan Wiggin, gent., both of Stratham. CLAIMS: 9/25/1788. Total L178.17.3 1/2. Oaths 8/1790 Comm. to W. Parker, JP. ACCOUNT: 1/14/1791. Of Admr. Allowed 1/14/1791. PROP. & SETTLM.: Claims L178.17.3 1/2. Amount to be proportioned L23.10.6. Allowed 1/27/1791 with order to Admr. to pay.

2596. THURSTON, SALLY (1788) #5397
GDP. Of the dau. of Jonathan Thurston, Canterbury yoeman decd. GDP.: 12/17/1788. Of Sally, a minor under 14. Gdn. John Pingrey Williams, Nottingham trader. Bond L500.0.0. Sureties: Thomas Bartlet and Henry Butler, Nottingham esquires. Witnesses: Nathl. A. Haven and Nathl. Parker.

TIBBETS. See also Tibbetts

2597. TIBBETS, EPHRAIM (1781) #4711
GDP. Of the son of Gideon Tibbets, Rochester, Strafford Co. yoeman decd. GDP.: 4/25/1781. Of Ephraim of Stratham. Gdn. Enos Hoag, Stratham yoeman. Bond L30000.0.0. Sureties: Enoch Barker, Stratham yeoman and John Weeks, Greenland esq. Witnesses W. Parker and Nathl. Parker.

TIBBETTS. See also Tibbets

2598. TILTON, ABRAHAM (1792) #5758
EST. Stratham blacksmith decd. testate. WILL: Drawn 3/24/1789. Legatees: Wife-Abigail; Son-Abraham; Daus.-Aigail Rowlings, Anna Avery, Hannah Lane and Molloy Knowles; Grandson-Abraham Tilton son of John Tilton of Stratham decd.; Granddau.-Comfort Tilton. Execs.-Wife Abigail and grandson Abraham Tilton. His sig. Witnesses: John Shaw, Jacob Low Jr. and Nich. Rollins. CERT. WILL (D30:220):4/16/1792. Presented by Execs. and witnesses Low and Rollins, esq. RENUN.: 4/16/1792. Of Abigail Tilton, widow of Abraham. Of Co-admin. due to age. She is content that her grandson named in Will be sole Exec. Witnesses: Jacob Low Jr. and Nich. Rollings. ADMIN.: 4/16/1792. Exec. Abraham Tilton, Stratham yoeman. Bond L1000.0.0. Sureties: Nicholas

Rollins, esq. and Jacob Low Jr., yoeman, both of Stratham. Witnesses: Nat. Parker and W. Parker. INVY.: Appr. 6/25/1792. Comm.: Jacob Low Jr., Christopher Smith and Nich. Rollins. Value L242.8.1. Oaths 6/25/1792 Comm. and Exec. to W. Parker, JP.

2599. TILTON: ABRAHAM, JOHN, NANCY & POLLY (1797) #6385
GDP. Of the children of Abraham Tilton, Stratham gent. GDP.: 10/16/1797. Of: Polly, Nancy, John and Abraham, minors under 14. Gdn. Abraham Tilton, Stratham gent., their father. Bond $2,000.00. Sureties: Nicholas Rollins, esq. and Daniel Jewell, gent., both of Stratham. Witnesses: Joshua Lane and W. Parker.

2600. TILTON: BENJAMIN & NATHANIEL (1794) #6039 & BENJAMIN (1794) #6029
GDP. Hampton Falls adults adjudged n.c.m. PETITION (#6039): 8/25/1794. Of Stephen Tilton, Hampton Falls gent. Requests appointment of a Gdn. for his bros. Nathaniel and Benjamin, adults n.c.m. Order: 8/25/1794. To Hampton Falls Selectmen. To make inquisition into condition of Nathaniel and Benjamin. Report: 8/27/1794. Of: David Nason, Peter Tilton and Aaron Merrill, Hampton Falls Selectmen. They are of opinion Nathaniel and Benjamin do not have strength of mind to care for themselves or ests. and need Gdns. GDP. (#6039): 10/24/1794. Of Benjamin, an adult adjudged n.c.m. Gdn. Stephen Tilton, Hampton Falls gent. Bond L1000.0.0. Sureties: Peter Tilton, esq. and David Bacheldor, yoeman, both of Hampton Falls. Witnesses: Phineas Tilton and W. Parker. GDP. (#6039): 10/24/1794. Of Nathaniel, an adult adjudged n.c.m. Gdn. Phineas Tilton, Deerfield yoeman. Bond L1000.0.0. Sureties: David Bacheldor, yoeman and Peter Tilton, esq., both of Hampton Falls. Witnesses: Stephen Tilton and W. Parker. INVY. (#6039): Appr. 1/2/1795. Of est. Nathaniel. Comm.: David Bacheldor and Peter Tilton. Value not tallied. Esti. L101.0.0+. Oaths 1/6/1795 Comm. to Caleb Tilton, JP. INVY. (#6029): 1/2/1795. Of est. Benjamin. Comm.: David Bachelder and Peter Tilton. Value not tallied. Esti. L143.0.0+. Oaths 1/6/1795 Comm. to Caleb Tilton, JP. Oath 1/17/1795 Gdn. to judge.

2601. TILTON, BENJAMIN (1798) #6508
EST. Pittsfield yoeman decd. testate. WILL: Drawn 9/26/1798. Legatees: Wife-Hannah; Sons-John and Abraham; Daus.-Marcy Tilton and Unice Tilton. Exex.- wife Hannah. His mark. Witnesses: Samuel Brown, John Tilton, John Shaw and Abraham Brown. CERT. WILL (D32:536): 11/2/1798. Presented by Exex. and witnesses Tilton and Shaw. RENUN.: 11/2/1798. Of Hannah, widow of Benjamin. Of all legacies given her in Will and claims her Dower and Admin. INVY. (D33:38): Comm.: John

Shaw, Jacob Bachelder and Saml. Brown. Value $722.84. Oaths 1/16/1799 Comm. to John Cram, JP. Oath 2/1/1799 Exex. to W. Parker, JP. CAVEAT: 7/24/1799. Of Enoch Butler of Pittsfield, a large creditor of est. Requests a Comm. of Insolvency not be allowed before he has been heard. States that some of the Invy. has not been disclosed, especially a Note of Hand for $800.00. If the Exex. does not waste the est., there is sufficient to pay claims. Also requests a hearing on Dower before it is allowed, the Comm. having given her more than 1/3 share and div. it in such a way as to injure the remaining 2/3. ADDL. INVY.: 9/16/1799. Value $50.00. For hay which was left out when copying Invy. DOWER: 8/20/1799. Comm.: Robert Tibbets, Samuel Brown, Enoch Blake, Edmund Sanborn and Jacob Bacheldor. Of Widow Hannah Tilton. Oaths 8/20/1799 Comm. to John Cram, JP. Allowed 9/18/1799 provided the widow holds 20 acres and no more. Includes Map. PETITION: 9/18/1799. Of Admx. For Comm. Insolvency and License. Gives list claims of $2,167.66 plus expense of Dower and Admin. Granted for both. LICENSE: 9/18/1799. To Admx. To sell real est. to amount of $2,000.00. BOND: 9/18/1799. Of Admx. Bond $5,000.00. To account for proceeds from sale of real est. by License. Sureties: Robert Tibbets and John Shaw, Pittsfield esquires. Witnesses: Enoch Butler and N. Parker. CLAIMS: 7/25/1797 and 3/14/1800. Comm.: John Shaw, Robert Tibbets and Samuel Brown. Total $2,019.61. Also includes list payments of Admx. on note of Enoch Butler. Oaths 5/31/1800 Comm. to John Cram, JP. LICENSE: 2/21/1800. To Admx. To sell reversion of Dower. APPR. WARR.: 2/21/1800. Comm.: John Shaw and Robert Tibbets, esquires and Samuel Brown. To appr. neat income of 2/3 of real est. for one year, exclusive of taxes and expenses of carrying on the place. Appr.: 5/14/1800. Value $20.00. Oaths 5/14/1800 Brown and Shaw to Robert Tibbets, JP. ACCOUNT: 2/21/1800. Of Admx. Allowed 5/25/1800. Account includes main. 2 children. PROP. & SETTLM.: Claims $2,019.61. Amount to be proportioned $1,171.00. Allowed 8/11/1800 with order to Admx. to pay. MAP. Unidentified but is not Dower. Note: This file also includes a Citation which belongs in #6663 Abraham Trefethen (1800) est. which is not included in this book.

2602. TILTON, BETSEY (1783) #4878
GDP. Of the dau. of Jacob Tilton, Portsmouth esq. decd. GDP.: 2/24/1784. Of Betsy, a minor over 14. Gdn. Daniel Tilton, Exeter gent. Bond L1000.0.0. Sureties: Eliphalet Hale, gent. and James McClure, esq. both of Exeter.

2603. TILTON, DAVID (1783) #4913

EST. Sandown miller decd. testate. WILL: Drawn 5/3/1783. Legatees: Wife-Miriam; Sons-John and Joseph; Daus.-Moly Tilton and Margaret Tilton. Exex.-wife Miriam. His sig. Witnesses: Joseph Tilton, John Tilton and Jeremiah Tilton. CERT. WILL (D27:245): 6/25/1783. Presented by Exex. and witnesses Joseph Tilton and Jeremiah Tilton. INVY.: Appr. 9/19/1783. Comm.: Wm. Rowel, Moses Hook and Timy. Tilton. Value L223.17.0. Oaths 9/19/1783 Comm. and Exex. to Reuben Clough, JP. PETITION: 8/18/1784. Of Exex. For License and Comm. Insolvency. Lists partial claims of L90.0.0., expects more and believes real est. when sold will not be as much as the appr. LICENSE (D27:495): 8/18/1784. To Admx. To sell sufficient real est. to pay debts. DOWER WARR.: 8/18/1784. Comm.: John Calfe of Hampstead and Reuben Clough, esquires; David Fuller, Sherburne Sanborn and William Rowel, yoemen, all of Sandown. Of Widow Miriam Tilton. DOWER: Oaths 9/6/1784 Clough, Rowel and Sanborn to John Calfe, JP. Oath 9/15/1784 Calfe to W. Parker, Reg. CLAIMS: 2/7/1785. Comm.: Reuben Clough, William Rowel and John Calfe. Total L79.9.1. Oaths 2/7/1785 Clough and Rowel to John Calfe, JP. CITATION: 6/13/1791. To Parker Stevens and Miriam his wife, Exex. In reply to a complaint of some of heirs, they are cited to appear and exhibit their Account. ACCOUNT: 9/1791. Of Exex. Allowed 9/17/1791.

2604. TILTON, CAPT. JACOB (1782-sic) #4840

EST. Portsmouth esq. decd. intestate. ADMIN.: 11/5/1777. Admx.: Mary Tilton, Portsmouth widow. Bond L500.0.0. Sureties: Perkins Ayers, cordwainer and Samuel Ham Jr., yoeman, both of Portsmouth. Witnesses: Thomas Ransom and Philip Brewster. ADMIN. D.B.N: 10/19/782. Admrs. d.b.n.: Jonathan Tilton, Hampton Falls gent. and Daniel Tilton, Exeter esq. Bond L1000.0.0. Sureties: Joseph Tilton, physician and Benjamin Lamson, innholder, all of Exeter. Witnesses: Elizabeth Parker and W. Parker. INVY.: Appr. 12/5/1782. Comm.: John Parker, George Gains and Jacob Treadwell. Value L637.4.4. Oaths 12/5/1782 Comm. to Saml. Penhallow, JP. Note: This Invy. Includes land in Warner and Cockermouth and ½ house and land in Portsmouth occupied by Capt. George King. PETITION: 2/7/1783. Of Daniel Tilton, an Admr. d.b.n. For Comm. Insolvency. Allowed. INVY.: Appr. 2/24/1783. Comm.: Joseph Lamson, Eliphalet Hale and James McClure. Value L105.6.0. Note: this Invy. includes a house, barn and land in Exeter and land in Westmoreland. LICENSE (D27:182): 2/26/1783. To Execs. d.b.n. To sell sufficient real est. to pay debts. CLAIMS WARR.: 12/17/1783. Comm.: Samuel Hobart and Samuel Brooks, esquires and Jedediah Jewett, merchant, all of Exeter. On 6/22/1784 Comm. allowed 6 more months. CLAIMS: 3/31/1785. Total

L713.13.5. Oaths 4/5/1785 Brooks and Jewett to W. Parker, JP. ACCOUNT: 3/15/1786. Of Execs. d.b.n. Oath 3/15/1786 of Daniel Tilton, an Admr. d.b.n. "who did all the business." Allowed. PROP. & SETTLM. Claims L713.13.5. Amount to be proportioned L475.8.0. Allowed 4/19/1786 with order to Execs. d.b.n. to pay.

2605. TILTON, JOHN (1769) A#3601
EST. Hampton Falls gent. decd. intestate. Note: The following Petition, Div. Warr. and Div. found in #5086 John Tilton (1785) belong here. PETITION: 4/1/1785. Of: Jeremiah Sanborn of Gilmanton, Strafford Co. and Philip Greeley of Hopkinton, Hillsborough Co., gentlemen. For div. of land in Kensington and Hampton Falls of which they, in right of their wives, heirs of John Tilton, Hampton Falls gent. decd., are tenants in common, which was the Dower of Sarah Tilton, widow of John decd. Abraham Sanborn owns 2/10 and to each of the Petitioners 1/10. One of the heirs is a minor. Order: For hearing, Petitioners to notify Abraham Sanborn, the heirs and Gdn. of the minor. Consent: Of: Isaac Hills on behalf of the minor, Paul Eaton, Sarah Tilton, Jere. Sanborn on behalf of Jonathan Leavitt, Abraham Sanborn, Asa Tilton, Jere. Sanborn, Philip Greeley and Daniel Tilton, who are the rest of the heirs. They consent to div. and request a Comm. of Capt. Jonathan Tilton and Lt. Zebulon Hilyard, gentlemen; Col. Jonathan Cram, esq. and Deacon Jeremiah Lane, yoemen, all of Hampton Falls and Lt. Samuel Prescott, Kensington gent. DIV. WARR.: 4/5/1785. Comm. as requested. To div. the Dower of Sarah Wilson decd., widow of John. DIV.: 4/7/1785. Divisees: Abraham Sanborn who purchased the right of one of heirs; Asa Tilton a son; Sarah Tilton a dau.; Daniel Tilton; Lucretia Hill, Dorothy Greeley; Lydia Sanborn; Mary Eaton; Anna Leavitt. Oaths 4/7/1785 Tilton, Prescott and Lane to Saml. Weare, JP. Allowed. Orig. Archives file includes Admin., Invy. Warr., Invy., Div. Warr. 1772 and Div. 1773.

2606. TILTON, JOHN (1785) #5086
EST. Kensington gent. decd. testate. WILL: Drawn 6/21/1782. Legatees: Wife-Hannah; Sons-Joseph, John, David and Jeremiah; Daus.-Mary Cramb wife of Benja. Cramb, Abigail Rowe wife of Robert Rowe and Hannah Gilman wife of Samuel Gilman decd.; Jonathan Hobbs husb. of his dau. Margaret decd.; Grandchildren-Edmund James and Elisabeth James. Exec.-son Jeremiah. His sig. Witnesses: Benjamin Tilton, Theophilus Sanborn and Jeremiah Bachelder. CERT. WILL (D28:82): 3/16/1785. Presented by Exec. and witnesses Sanborn and Bachelder. INVY.: Appr. 6/30/1785. Comm.: Jeremiah Bachelder, Benjamin Moulton and Theophilus Sanborn, all of Kensington. Value not tallied. Esti. L320.0.0+. Oaths 7/4/1785 Bachelder, Sanborn and Exec. to Jere. Fogg,

JP. Note: File also includes a Pet. for Div., Div. Warr. and Div., all of which belong to #A3601 John Tilton (1769) and an Account which belongs to #6348 Jonathan Tilton (1797). All are recorded in their proper places.

2607. TILTON, JOHN SULLIVAN (1782) #4864
GDP. Of the son of Jacob Tilton, Portsmouth esq. decd. GDP.: 12/2/1782. Of John Sullivan Tilton, a minor under 14. Gdn. Daniel Tilton, Exeter esq. Bond L1000.0.0. Surety Jonathan Tilton, Hampton Falls gent. Witnesses: Nathl. Parker and N. Terry Parker.

2608. TILTON, JONATHAN (1797) #6348
EST. Kensington yoeman decd. ADMIN.: 6/19/1797. Admx.: Fanny Tilton Kensington widow. Bond $3,000.00. Sureties: Winthrop Rowe, Kensington gent. and Ephraim Robinson, Exeter merchant. Witnesses: Enoch Rowe and W. Parker. INVY.: Comm.: Jere. Fogg, Philemon Blake and Benjamin Melcher. Value $6,286.38. Oaths 7/28/1797 Blake and Melcher to Jere. Fogg, JP. Oath 8/14/1797 Admx. to judge. LICENSE (D32:498): 6/27/1798. To Admx. To sell real est. to amount of $2,000.00. ACCOUNTS: 1797, 1799 & 1799. Of Admx. Allowed 1/31/1801 after various hearings and considering objections of Dr. Joseph Tilton, sole heir. Note: All of the following items found in #6415 Jonathan Tilton of Hampton Falls (1798) belong here: PETITION: 3/28/1798. Of: Daniel Tilton, Caleb Tilton, Joseph Tilton, Fanny Tilton and Peter Tilton. They request a comm. to adjust and settle accounts existing unsettled between Dr. Joseph Tilton and Jonathan decd. They have agreed upon a Comm. of Eph. Robinson of Exeter, chair. and Dr. Thomas Stow Ranney of Brentwood, esquires and Nathaniel Hubbard Dodge, Hampton Falls yoeman. REFERENCE WARR.: 5/14/1798. Comm. as requested. Report: 5/31/1798. The Referees decide the Admx. of est. of Jonathan Tilton of Kensington decd. should pay Dr. Joseph Tilton $495.00 in full of his demands. Allowed 8/31/1798. PETITION: 6/27/1798. Of Joseph Tilton and Enoch Rowe for Admx. For License. Give claims of L500.16.5 1/4 and others not yet in. Granted. BOND: 6/28/1798. Of Admx. Fanny Tilton. Bond $3,000.00. To account for sale of real est. by License. Sureties: Joseph Tilton and Enoch Rowe, Exeter yoemen. Witnesses: Benja. Morse and Benja. Melcher. DOWER WARR.: 6/28/1798. Comm.: Jeremiah Fogg, Jeremiah Bachelder, Philemon Blake, Newell Healey, esquires and Robert Prescott, yoeman, all of Kensington. Of Widow Fanny Tilton. DOWER: 7/6/1798. Oaths 7/6/1798 Bachelder, Blake, Healey and Prescott to Jere. Fogg, JP. Allowed. APPR. WARR.: 12/1/1798. Comm.: Enoch Coffin, Epping esq.; Aaron Wells, innholder and Nathaniel Hubbard Dodge, yoeman. To appr. the neat income of the real est. of Jonathan

Tilton of Kensington since death. Appr.: Value $240.00. Oaths 12/24/1798 Wells and Dodge to Enoch Coffin, JP. ADDL. ACCOUNT(D33:407): Of Fanny Tilton, Admx. Allowed 1/31/1801 after objections of Dr. Joseph Tilton, sole heir by purchase, heard and hearing there one.

2609. TILTON, JONATHAN (1798) #6415
EST. Hampton Falls gent. decd. testate. WILL: Drawn 5/22/1793. Legatees: Sons-Peter, Daniel, Jonathan, Caleb, Joseph and Josiah; Heirs of his son Jacob decd. Exec.-son Peter. His sig. Witnesses: Stephen Tilton, Jonathan Cram Jr. and Phinehas Felch. CERT. WILL (D32:425): 1/19/1798. Presented by Exec. and witnesses Tilton and Cram. ADMIN.: 1/19/1798. Exec. Peter Tilton, Hampton Falls esq. Bond $3,000.00. Sureties: Stephen Tilton and Jona. Cram Jr., Hampton Falls gentlemen. Witnesses: W. Parker and Elizabeth Parker. INVY.: Comm.: Jonathan Cram, Stephen Tilton and Levi Healey. Value $6,136.50. Oaths 4/2/1798 Comm. to Caleb Tilton, JP. Oath 4/9/1798 Exec. To W. Parker, JP. The accounts included in Invy. include an appr. of the est. of his son Jona. Tilton (#6348) "which fell to him." This file also includes the following which belong with #6348 Jonathan Tilton of Kensington (1797): Petition for referees, Referees warr. And report, Petition for License, Bond, Dower Warr., Dower and Appr. Warr.

2610. TILTON, JOSEPH (1778) #4432
EST. Kensington husbm. decd. testate. WILL: Drawn 6/4/1773. Legatees: Wife-Elisabeth; Son-Elijah; Daus.-Susanna Coffin and Mary Coffin. Exec.-son Elijah. His sig. Witnesses: Samuel Prescutt, Phelemon Blake Jr. and Josiah White. CERT. WILL (D24:227): 2/25/1778. Presented by Exec. and witnesses Blake and Prescutt. ADMIN.: 2/25/1778. Exec. Elijah Tilton, Kensington yoeman. Bond L500.0.0. Sureties: Samuel Prescutt and Philemon Blake Jr., Kensington gentlemen. Witnesses: Josiah Fogg and W. Parker. PETITION: Dated by clerk 1/17/1784. Of Eliza. Tilton, widow of Joseph by her atty. Enoch Coffin. Requests permission to sue Bond of Admin. as Exec. has not paid her the annual half of the income of est. or cows or moveables as given her in Will. Allowed, "giving caution according to law."

2611. TILTON, JOSIAH (1796) #6273
EST. East Kingston gent. decd. testate. WILL: Drawn 8/24/1784. Legatees: Wife-Sarah; Sons-David, Philip, Josiah and Ebenezer, latter 2 both of Deerfield; Daus.-Meribah wife of Benja. Smith and Sarah wife of Elisha Blake; Grandsons-Samuel Smith son of Benjamin Smith and Dearborn Blake son of Elisha Blake or his next youngest sibling if he dies before 21; Next child of Benjamin Smith. Exec.-son David. His sig.

Witnesses: Nathl. Bachellor, Jonathan Lad Webster and Elipht. Webster. CERT. WILL (D32:206): 10/31/1796. Presented by Exec. and witnesses Jonathan Lad Webster and Eliphalet Webster. ADMIN.: 10//31/1796. Exec. David Tilton, East Kingston yoeman. Bond $3,000.00. Sureties: Timothy Batchelder and Eliphalet Webster, East Kingston yoemen. Witnesses: Jonathan Webster and W. Parker. INVY.: Appr. 11/18/1796. Comm.: John Tappan, Eliphalet Webster and Richard French. Value $5,812.00. Oaths 11/18/1796 Comm. and Exec. to Edward Greeley, JP.

2612. TILTON, MARY (1782) #4838
EST. Portsmouth widow decd. intestate, widow of Capt. Jacob Tilton. ADMIN.: 10/19/1782. Admrs.: Jonathan Tilton, Hampton Falls gent. and Daniel Tilton, Exeter esq. Bond L1000.0.0. Sureties: Joseph Tilton, physician and Benjamin Lamson, innholder, both of Exeter. Witnesses: Elizabeth Parker and W. Parker. INVY.: Appr. 12/5/1782. Comm.: John Parker, Geo. Gains and Jacob Treadwell. Value L115.16.6. Oaths 12/6/1782 Comm. and Admrs. to Saml. Penhallow, JP. PETITION: 2/26/1783. Of Daniel Tilton, an Admr. For Comm. Insolvency. Gives list claims of L355.0.0. CLAIMS WARR.: 2/26/1783. Comm.: Samuel Hobart and Samuel Brooks, esquires and Jedediah Jewett, merchant, all of Exeter. On 9/24/1783 Comm. allowed 6 more months. On back a note that Comm. met 12 times at the Recorder's office and also a note dated 6/25/1784 that it is agreed to set on the Comm. to sit the first Wed. of July, Col. Moulton agreeing to be present. CLAIMS: 3/31/1785. Total L335.4.6. Oaths 4/5/1785 Brooks and Jewett to W. Parker, JP. ACCOUNT: 3/15/1786. Of Admrs. Allowed 3/15/1786 on oath of Daniel Tilton, an Admr. PROP. & SETTLM.: Claims L335.4.6. Amount to be proportioned L32.9.0. Allowed 4/19/1786 with order to Admrs. to pay.

2613. TILTON, NATHAN (1793) #5941
EST. Hampton Falls yoeman decd. testate. WILL: Drawn 1/6/1775. Legatees: Wife-Hannah; Sons-Nathan, Benjamin, Nathaniel, David, Phinehas, Ebenezer and Stephen. Exec.-son Stephen. His sig. Wit- nesses: David Bachelder, Jeremiah Lane and Peter Tilton. CERT. WILL (D31:121): 11/25/1793. Presented by Exec. and witnesses Lane and Tilton. ADMIN.: 11/25/1793. Exec. Stephen Tilton, Hampton Falls gent. Bond L1000.0.0. Sureties: dA:RO13 Jeremiah Lane, yoeman and Peter Tilton, esq., both of Hampton Falls. Witness W. Parker. INVY.: Appr. 1/21/1794. Comm.: Jeremiah Lane, David Bachelder and Peter Tilton. Value L1100.12.9. Oaths 1/21/1794 Comm. and Exec. to W. Parker, Reg. & JP.

2614. TILTON, SAMUEL (1777) #4409
EST. Deerfield husbm. decd. testate. WILL: Drawn 4/29/1775. Legatees: Wife-Rebeckah. Exex.-wife Rebeckah. His sig. Witnesses: Josiah Sawyer, James Brown and Benjamin Butler. He notes in Will he has no issue by his wife and particularly specifies that she is not to have any lands he may or ought to have of his father's est., those to be disposed of as the law directs. CERT. WILL (D24:179): 1/1/1778. Presented by Exex., and witnesses Sawyer and Brown. INVY.: Appr. 1/16/1778. Comm.: John McCrilles, Patton Simpson and Samuel Hobbs. Value not tallied. Esti. L147.0.0+. Oaths 1/16/1778 Comm. to Jeremiah Eastman, JP. Oath 2/26/1778 Exex. to judge. The Invy. Comm. noted that the Widow had disposed of oxen and a cow valued at L24.12.0.

2615. TILTON, SAMUEL (1796) #6292 & (1796) #6293
EST. Hampton Falls yoeman decd. ADMIN. (#6292): 12/31/1796. Admx. Joanna Tilton, Hampton Falls widow. Bond $2,000.00. Sureties: Caleb Tilton, esq. and James Prescutt Jr., gent., both of Hampton Falls. Witnesses: W. Parker and Wm. P. Adams. INVY. (#6293): Appr. 1/11/1797. Comm.: James Prescutt Jr., Peter Tilton and Levi Healey. Value $1,240.77. Oaths 3/3/1797 Comm. to Caleb Tilton, JP. PETITION: 3/8/1798. Of Ebenezer Tilton for Admx. For License. Shows claims as needed repairs to bldgs. of $559.39. Granted. LICENSE (D32:447): 3/8/1798. To Admx. To sell real est. to amount of $350.00. DOWER (#6293): 3/22/1798. Comm. Jeremiah Lane, James Prescutt Jr., Peter Tilton, Levi Healey and Jonathan Cram Jr. Of Widow Joanna Tilton. Oaths 3/26/1798 Comm. to Caleb Tilton, JP. Allowed. ACCOUNT: 4/8/1801. Of Admx. Allowed 4/20/1801 objections of heirs notwithstanding.

2616. TILTON, SHERBURN (1785) #5125
EST. Kensington husbm. decd. testate. WILL: Drawn 3/13/1767. Legatees: Wife-Anna; Sons-Sherburne, Timothy and Benjamin; Daus.-Elizabeth wife of Richard Sanborn and Sarah wife of Nathaniel Emerson; Heirs of dau. Anna former wife of Daniel Sanborn. Exec.-son Benjamin. His sig. Witnesses: Samuel Tucke, James Fogg and Timothy Hilyard. CERT. WILL (D28:234): 7/20/1785. Presented by Exec. And witnesses Tucke and Fogg. INVY.: Appr. 3/17/1786. Comm.: James Fogg and Benjamin James. Value L460.17.6. Oaths 12/4/1786 Comm. and Exec. to W. Parker, JP & Reg.

2617. TILTON, TIMOTHY (1785) #5087
EST. Loudon yoeman decd. testate. WILL: Drawn 3/13/1780. Legatees: Wife-Martha; Sons-Joseph, Nathan, William and David; Daus.-Joanna Row and Elizabeth Tilton. Exec.-son William. His sig. Witnesses: Thomas Taylor, Peaslee Badger and Joseph Badger. CERT. WILL (D28:73): 3/16/1785. Presented by Exec. and witnesses Peaslee Badger and Joseph Badger, esq. who gave oaths to Wm. Parker, JP. INVY.: Appr. 5/27/1783. Comm.: Joseph Smith, Timothy French and Abel French. Value L806.01.1. Oaths 5/27/1785 Comm. to Nathan Bachelder, JP. Oath 6/6/1785 Exec. to W. Parker, the Exec. saying that a yoke of oxen and a cow claimed by his bro. David not appr.

2618. TINSDELL, RICHARD (1782) #4867
See Trusdel.

2619. TIRRELL: DOROTHY & WOODBURY (1798) #6465
GDP. Of the children of Seth Tirrell of Canterbury decd. intestate. PETITION: 5/15/1798. Of Leavitt Clough of Canterbury. States that Seth Tirrell died leaving 2 minor children. Their mother, the widow, declines Gdp. and has asked him to be their Gdn. Requests appointment. Granted. GDP.: 5/16/1798. Of: Dorothy and Woodbury, minors under 14. Gdn. Leavitt Clough, Canterbury yoeman. Bond $2,000.00. Sureties: William Tirrell and Joseph Kinnison, Canterbury yoemen. Witnesses: Joseph Baker and Nat Parker.

2620. TIRRELL, WILLIAM (1794) #6004
GDP. Canterbury yoeman adjudged n.c.m. PETITION: 5/21/1794. Of Seth Tirrill, Canterbury yoeman. States his father William is n.c.m. Requests judge to take action thereon. Order: 5/21/1794. To Canterbury Selectmen To hold an inquisition into the state of William Tirrell. Report: Of: Abiel Foster and Leavitt Clough, Canterbury Selectmen. They adjudge William to be insane and in need of a Gdn. GDP.: 5/21/1794. Of William an adult adjudged n.c.m. Gdns. Abiel Foster, esq. and Leavitt Clough, yoeman, both of Canterbury. Bond L1000.0.0. Sureties: Seth Tirrill and William Tirrill Jr., Canterbury yoemen. Witnesses: Jonathan Clough and W. Parker. INVY.: Comm.: Nehe. Clough, Masten Morrill and Obadiah Clough. Value L743.19.10. Oaths 9/16/1794 Morrill and Clough to Asa Forster, JP. Oath 9/17/1794 Abiel Foster, a Gdn., to judge. ACCOUNT #1: Of Gdns. No sigs., no allowance. ACCOUNT #2: 1795. Of Gdns. Allowed 5/20/1795. ADDL. ACCOUNT: Of Gdns. Exhibited by Leavitt Clough on behalf of Abiel Foster, a Gdn. Allowed 9/26/1797. Note: See also #6339 William Terrell (1797) for est.

2621. TIRRELL, WILLIAM (1797) #6330
EST. Canterbury yoeman decd. intestate. RENUN.: Of: Joseph Young on behalf of the Widow and sons John Tirrell and William Tirrell. Of Admin. Request appointment of Leavitt Clough. ADMIN.: 5/17/1797. Admr. Leavitt Clough, Canterbury yoeman. Bond $3,000.00. Sureties: Joseph Young, gent. and John Shepard, esq., both of Gilmanton, Strafford Co. Witnesses: James H. McClary and Nathl. Parker to sigs. of Young and Shepard; Jonathan Davis and Leavitt Clough Jr. to sig. of Leavitt Clough. INVY.: Appr. 6/17/1797. Comm.: Masten Morrill, Obadiah Clough and Jedediah Clough. Value $2,063.08/58. Oath 9/20/1797 Admr. to judge. ACCOUNT: 5/16/1798. Of Admr. Allowed 5/16/1798 having been consented to by heirs attending. ADDL. ACCOUNT: 5/15/1799. Of Admr. Allowed 5/15/1799.

2622. TITCOMB, CAPT. MOSES (1797) #6359
EST. Pelham mariner decd. ADMIN: 7/7/1797. Admx. Sarah Titcomb, Pelham widow. Bond $3,000.00. Sureties: Gershom Bartlett and Jonathan Bartlett, Newton yoemen. Witnesses: Saml. Parker and W. Parker. INVY.: Appr. 8/15/1797. Comm.: Joseph Kittridge, Timothy Clark and Wm. Thom. Value $298.28 plus 3 Notes valued at $215.00. Oaths 8/15/1797 Comm. and on 9/12/1797 Admx. to Josiah Gage, JP. ACCOUNT: 10/1804. Of Admx. Allowed 10/15/1804 the children being minors not notified.

2623. TOBIE, WILLIAM (1782) #4808
EST. Deerfield joiner decd. testate. WILL: Drawn 5/11/1782. Legatees: Sons-William and Nathan; Daus.-Hulday Tobie, Abigail Tobie and Elizabeth Tobie. Exec.-bro. Richard Tobie. His sig. Witnesses: Andrew Freese, Moses Clark and Hannah Severence. CERT. WILL: 5/29/1782. Presented by Exec. and witnesses Freese and Clark. INVY. WARR.: 5/29/1782. Comm.: Andrew Freese; Joseph Hilton, gent. and John Bartlett, yoeman, all of Deerfield. INVY.: Appr. 7/30/1782. Value not tallied. Esti. L300.0.0+. Oaths 8/17/1782 Comm. to Jeremiah Eastman, JP. Oath 8/28/1782 Admr. to judge. The Admr. notes that several small items were omitted from Invy.

2624. TODD, ANDREW (1777) #4398
EST, Londonderry esq. decd. testate. WILL: Drawn 7/27/1775. Legatees: Sons-Alexander and Andrew; Sons-in-law and their wives-Moses Morrison and Rachel, William Millar and Jean, Robert Duncan and Sarah, Jonathan Murrey and Margaret; Dau.-in-law-Martha Grier; Son-in-law-Thomas Morison; Grandsons-John Todd, Andrew Todd, Andrew Todd Morison, Andrew Todd Millar, Andrew Todd Murrey; Granddaus.-

Rachell Morison, Mary Morison, Elisabeth Todd and Genet Morison. Execs.-Andrew Todd and John Bell. His sig. Witnesses: John Pinkerton, James Aiken and John Bell. CERT. WILL: 10/30/1777. Presented by Andrew Todd, one of the execs., the other declining to serve, and witnesses Pinkerton and Aiken. INVY.: Comm.: John Pinkerton, James Aiken and John Aiken. Value L1076.19.6. Oaths 3/25/1778 Comm. to John Bell, JP. Oath 3/25/1778 to an Addl. Invy. of L40.8.0 Comm. to John Bell, JP. Oath 10/28/1778 Exec. to judge.

2625. TOLFORD, JANE (1793) #5847
EST. Chester widow decd. testate. WILL: Drawn 7/5/1792. Legatees: Son-Joshua; All her other children-unnamed; Granddau.-Jane McMurphy. Execs.-Robert Forsaith and Hugh Tolford. Her sig. Witnesses: Ichabod S. Davis, Elizabeth McFarland and Arch. McMurphy. CERT. WILL (D30:349): 1/14/1793. Presented by Execs. and witnesses Davis and McMurphy, esq. ADMIN.: 1/14/1793. Execs.: Robert Forsaith, gent. and Hugh Tolford, yoeman, both of Chester. Bond L1000.0.0. Sureties: Ichabod S. Davis, Chester goldsmith and Archibald McMurphy, Londonderry esq. Witnesses: Josiah Adams and N. Parker. INVY.: Appr. 2/9/1793. Comm.: John Stevens and Benja. Haseltine. A long list of notes not tallied. Appr. 2/12/1793 of personal est. Value L67.6.3. Oaths 4/17/1793 Comm. and Execs. to Joseph Blanchard, JP.

2626. TOLFORD, JOHN JR. (1781) #4687
GDP. Chester yoeman, an adult adjudged n.c.m. PETITION: 1/4/1781. Of: Isaac Hills, Josiah Forsith and Josiah Flagg, Chester Selectmen. State that John, son of Deacon William Tolford of Chester, has for the past 7 years been n.c.m. During this time, John's father has cared for him and his est. The Selectmen feel it is reasonable that Deacon Tolford be paid for his care and expense. They recommend as Gdns. his father William, Hugh Tolford of old Chester and Robert Forsith of New Chester, Grafton Co., husbandmen. GDP.: 1/31/1781. Of John, son of William Tolford n.c.m.. Gdns.: Robert Forsith, New Chester, Grafton Co. gent.; William Tolford, gent. and Hugh Tolford, yoeman, both of Chester. Bond L40000.0.0. Sureties: Robert Smith, Londonderry gent. and Matthew Forsith, Chester yoeman. Witnesses: William Forsith, David Blair, Joshua Tolford and John Tolford. INVY. WARR.: 1/10/1782. Comm.: Joshua Tolford, Alexandria, Grafton Co. esq.; Carr Huse, esq. and John Smith Millar, both of New Chester, Grafton Co.; Matthew Forsith, Chester yoeman and Robert Smith, Londonderry gent. Invy.: Appr. at New Chester, Grafton Co. 1/30/1782. Value 1475 in silver dollars = L442.10.0. lawful money. Oaths at New Chester 1/30/1782 Joshua Tolford and John Smith Millar to Carr Huse, JP. Note: It is almost impossible to read some of this Invy. It

appears to be all land. INVY.: Appr. 6/5/1782 at Chester. Value L243.1.0. Oaths 4/29/1783 Mattw. Forsith and Robert Smith to John Webster, JP. INVY. WARR.: A dupl. copy. See also #4989 John Crafford (1790) for a petition for div. of land held in common by John Tolford n.c.m. and John Crafford decd.

2627. TOLFORD, JOHN (1790) #5569
EST. Chester esq. decd. testate. WILL: Drawn 3/7/1781. Legatees: Wife-Jean; Sons-Hugh, Joshua and John; Sons-in-law- William Ranken, William Ayers and William Murry and Jean his wife; Granddau.-Jean and her husb. Robert McMurphy Jr., gent. Execs.-wife Jean and son Hugh. His sig. Witnesses: Robert Forsith, Thomas Sever and Alexander Campbell. CERT. WILL (D29:410): 8/18/1790. Presented by Execs. and witnesses Forsith and Campbell. ADMIN.: 8/18/1790. Execs.: Hugh Tolford, husbm. and Jane Tolford, widow, both of Chester. Bond L1000.0.0. Sureties: Robert Forsith, gent. and Alexander Campbell, husbm., both of Chester. Witnesses: John W. Cox, Silas Barker and Robert McMurphy Jr. INVY.: Comm.: Robt. Forsith, Alexdr. Campbell and Thomas Sever. Value not tallied. Esti. L126.0.0+. Oaths 12/15/1790 Comm. to Oliver Peabody, JP.

2628. TOLFORD, WILLIAM (1792) #5810
EST. Chester yoeman decd. testate. WILL: Drawn 5/31/1787. Legatees; Son-John; Daus.-Elisabeth wife of William Powell or her heirs and Mary wife of Daniel McMurphy or her heirs; Son-in-law Robert Forsith. Exec.-son-in-law Robert Forsith. His sig. Witnesses: Hugh Tolford, Thomas Sever and John Calfe. CERT. WILL (D30:304): 10/10/1792. Presented by Exec. and witnesses Tolford and Sever. ADMIN.: 10/6/1792. Exec. Robert Forsith, Chester gent. Bond L1000.0.0. Sureties: Hugh Tolford and Thomas Sever, Chester yoemen. Witnesses: David Copp Jr. and Nat Parker. INVY.: 12/9/1792. Comm.: Hugh Tolford and Ichabod S. Davis. Value not tallied. Esti. L76.0.0+. Oaths 4/17/1793 Comm. and Exec. to Joseph Blanchard, JP.

2629. TOWLE, ABIGAIL 1775) #4173
GDP of the dau. of Caleb Towle Jr., Hawke yoeman decd. GDP.: 6/17/1775. Of Abigail, a minor over 14. Gdn. Ruth Towle, Sandown widow. Bond L1000.0.0. Sureties: Henry Page of Sandown and Thomas Page of Hawke, yoemen. Witnesses: Joseph Tilton and Richard Grefin. ACCOUNT: Of Caleb Towle of his Gdp. of Abigail Towle, a minor. Consent: 5/27/1778 of Ruth Towle, her present Gdn. and mother of Abigail. She consents to Account and acknowledges that she has received from Caleb, Abigail's late Gdn., the sum of L24.19.0 in full of the bal., having been the interest of Abigail's real est. for 6 years 1769-1774. There

is also in the Account an item for a hearing "on the other account." Allowed 5/27/1778. Note: The orig. Gdp. for Abigail is in A#3246 Caleb Towle Jr., Abigail's father. That file gives Widow Ruth Towle as Admx.

2630. TOWLE, CALEB (1795) #6068
EST. Hawke innholder decd. testate. WILL: Drawn 12/3/1782. Legatees; Wife-Rebecca; Sons-Elisha, Jeremy and James; Daus.-Annah now wife of Ebenezer Long and Mary now wife of Aaron Quinby; Grandchild-Abigail now wife of Joseph Brown dau. of his son Caleb decd. Execs.-wife Rebecca and son Jeremy. His sig. Witnesses: Josiah Bartlett, John Eastman and Reuben True Jr. CERT. WILL (D31:458): 2/13/1795. Presented by Jeremy Towle, surviving Exec. and witnesses Bartlett and Eastman, esquires. ADMIN.: 2/13/1795. Exec. Jeremiah Towle, Hawke gent. Bond L1000.0.0. Sureties: James Towle of Hawke and John Eastman of Kingston, esquires. Witnesses: Jno. Parker and W. Parker. INVY.: Appr. 2/24/1795. Comm.: Amos Gale, Jonathan French and Nehh. Sleeper. Value $8,237.20. Oaths 2/24/1795 Gale, French and Exec. to Nehh. Sleeper, JP. with notation that one iron bar omitted. ACCOUNT: 7/24/1799. Of Exec. Allowed 7/24/1799 objections of Ebenezer Long notwithstanding.

2631. TOWLE, ISAAC (1791) #5694
EST. Chester yoeman decd. ADMIN.: 9/23/1791. Admrs.: Elizabeth Towle, widow and Abraham Towle, yoeman, both of Chester. Bond L1000.0.0. Sureties: Wm. White, esq. and Benja. Hall, gent., both of Chester. Witnesses: Dearborn Richardson, Henry Moore, Joseph Hill and Joseph Spiller. INVY.: Appr. 11/28/1791. Comm.: Willm. White, Stephen Chase and Benja. Hall. Value not tallied. L803.0.0+. Oaths 11/28/1791 Comm. to Josiah Flagg, JP. Oaths 12/21/1791 Admrs. to judge. DOWER: 11/28/1791. Comm.: Joseph Blanchard, Willm. White, Stephen Dearborn, Stephen Chase and Benja. Hall. Of Widow Elizabeth Towle. Oaths 11/28/1791 White, Dearborn, Chase and Hall to Josiah Flagg, JP. Allowed 12/21/1791. ACCOUNT: Of Admrs. Allowed 9/15/1794 on oath of Abraham Towle, an Admr., the other having been sworn by a justice, and heir present. Oath 9/13/1794 Elizabeth Towle, an Admr., to Joseph Blanchard, JP. The following Petition recorded as #6127 Sherburne Dearborn (1795) belongs here. PETITION: 8/12/1795. Of Sherborn Dearborn, Chester esq. in right of his wife. For div. of land and bldgs. in Chester from est. of Isaac Towle, 2/3 of which he holds in common with Abraham Towle and others. In his wife's right he owns 1/4 part. Order: 8/12/1795. For hearing. Petitioner to notify Abraham Towle and Simon Towle, esq. NOTIFICATION: 8/12/1795. To: Simon Towle, esq. and Abraham Towle, gent., both of Chester. Of a hearing on a Petition of Sherborn Dearborn, Chester, esq. for div. in right of his wife, tenant in

common with them of 2/3 of the buildings and 1/3 of the orchard in Chester of which their late father died seized, Dearborn owning 1/4 right. Cert.: 8/17/1795. Of D. Dichardson, Dept. Sheriff. He summoned Simon Towle and Abraham Towle by reading the Notification to them. PETITION: 5/11/1820. Of Abraham Towle, an heir. For a Comm. to div. the Dower among the heirs, his mother having died. Order: For hearing, Petition to be advertised in Concord Patriot. Hearing was held and no objections made, a comm. ordered. DIV. WARR.: 9/5/1820. Comm.: John Folsom, esq.; William Graham, gent.; John Coffin, Jesse J. Underhill and William H. Underhill, all of Chester. To div. the Dower among the heirs according to their rights in est. DIV.: 10/5/1820. Divisees: Sons-Abraham Towle of Chester; Simon Towle late of Haverhill, Grafton Co. decd. having left several children and Isaac Towle of Chester who has conveyed his share to his bro. Abraham; Dau.-Elizabeth Dearborn decd. wife of Sherburne Dearborn of Chester, leaving her husb. and several children living. Consent: Of Edward Towle of Haverhill, Grafton Co., Exec. of est. of Simon. Oaths 10/5/1820 Graham, Coffin, Jesse Underhill and William Underhill to John Folsom, JP. Allowed 1/1/1821.

2632. TOWLE, JAMES (1783) #4927
EST. Hampton yoeman decd. testate. WILL: Drawn 3/11/1783. Legatees: Wife-Ann; Sons-James, Jonathan, David, Simon and Perkins. Exec.-wife Ann. His sig. Witnesses: William Godfree, Abraham Perkins Towle and Moses Elkins. CERT. WILL (D27:292): 8/26/1783. Presented by Exec. And witnesses Godfree and Towle, the judge crossing out the name Abraham Perkins Towle and changing it to Jonathan Perkins Towle, even though the sig. on Will is plainly Abraham. INVY. WARR.: 8/27/1783. Comm.: Moses Leavitt, North Hampton esq.; Joseph Towle Jr. and Moses Elkins of Hampton. INVY.: Appr. 11/18/1783. Value L538.18.0. Oaths 11/18/1783 Comm. and Exex. to Joseph Dow, JP.

2633. TOWLE: JOANNA & POLLY (1797) #6318
GDP. Of the daus. of Samuel Towle, Hampton yoeman decd. GDP.: 2/24/1797. Of Joanna, a minor over 14. Gdn. Levi Batchelder, Hampton yoeman. Bond $2,000.00. Sureties: Benjamin Shaw, gent. and Jeremiah Towle, yoeman, both of Hampton. Witnesses: Caleb Towle and W. Parker. GDP.: 2/24/1797. Of Polly, a minor over 14. Gdn. Jonathan Lane, Hampton Falls gent. Bond $2,000.00. Sureties: Jona. Marston, gent. and John Dearborn, yoeman, both of Hampton. Witnesses: Caleb Towle and W. Parker. RELEASE OF GDP. (D35:3): 11/12/1803. Of Joanna Towle, Hampton spinster. To Levi Batchelder, her Gdn. She has received from him $76.53 the bal. of his Gdp. Account and discharges him. Oath 11/12/1803 Joanna to Wm. Parker, JP & Reg.

2634. TOWLE, JOHN (1787) #5254
EST. Hampton gent. decd. testate. CAVEAT: 1/17/1787. Of Josiah Towle on behalf of John Towle, Epping yoeman. John suspects his father was not of sound mind when making his Will and requests the opportunity to present evidence before the Will is proved. CITATION: 1/5/1787. To Zachariah Towle, Samuel Smith and William Godfrey of North Hampton and Jethro Blake, Small Moulton, Moses Elkins, John Lamprey, Samuel Blake and Ward Lane of Hampton. To appear and give evidence of what they know about the soundness of mind of John Towle at the time of, before and after he executed his Will. Cert.: 2/1/1787. Of David Page, Depety. Sher. That on 2/1/1787 he summoned Zachariah Towle, Samuel Smith, William Godfree, Jethro Blake, Small Moulton, Moses Elkins and Samuel Blake and on 2/10/1787 he summoned John Lampson (sic.) and Ward Lane. WILL: Drawn 12/2/1786. Legatees: Son-John; Daus.-Abigail Robie and Mehetibel Towle; Grandaus.-Lydia Hobbs and Mary Towle daus. of his son Lemuel decd.; Grandsons-Lemuel Towle son of his son Lemuel decd. and Dearbon Fogg. Execs.-grandson Dearbon Fogg and dau. Mehetibale. His mark. Witnesses: Benj. Mason, Samuel Blake and Joseph Garland. CERT. WILL (D29:105): 2/21/1787. Presented by Execs. and witnesses Mason and Garland. Blake refused to declare that Towle was of sound mind when he made his Will, but the others testified that he was. Will approved.

2635. TOWLE, JONATHAN (1776) #4228
EST. Of Candia, decd. ADMIN.: 4/24/1776. Admr. Walter Robie, Candia esq. Bond L1000.0.0. Sureties: Moses Baker, gent and William Baker, yoemen, both of Candia. Witnesses: Benjamin Boardman and W. Parker. INVY.: Appr. 5/21/1776. Comm.: Nathll. Emerson and Abram. Fitts. Value not tallied. Esti. L103.15.3. Oaths 7/12/1776 Comm. and Admr. to Samll. Mooers, JP. ACCOUNT: 5/1777. Of Admr. Allowed 5/29/1777. Account includes main. one child. Receipt: 6/2/1773. From Ann Quinby. To Admr. For L1.5.5 in money in full of her thirds in est. after debts and costs paid. Witnesses: Moses Duston and Mary Duston. Cert. to as a true copy by Wm. Parker, Reg. DOWER: 4/16/1777 Comm.: Natha. Emerson, Moses Baker and Simon French. Of Ann Quinby in est. her former husb. Jonathan Towle. Oaths 4/15/1777 Comm. to Saml. Mooers, JP. Allowed 5/28/1777.

2636. TOWLE, LEMUEL (1778) #4464
EST. Hampton yoeman decd. ADMIN.: 7/29/1778. Admx. Mary Towle, Hampton widow. Bond L500.0.0. Sureties: Gideon Shaw, yoeman and John Taylor Jr., gent., both of Hampton. Witnesses: W. Parker and Nathl. Peabody. INVY.: Appr. 9/28/1778. Comm.: Henery Batchilder, John

Taylor, Jr. and Joseph Towle Jr. Value L415.15.0. Oaths 10/16/1778 Comm. to Joseph Drew, JP. Oath 10/28/1778 Admx. to Wm. Parker, Reg. ADMIN. D.B.N.: 8/29/1781. Admr. d.b.n. Samuel Hobbs, Hampton yoeman. Bond L10000.0.0. Sureties: Moses Leavitt, gent. and Benjamin Brown Shaw, yoeman, both of Hampton. Witnesses: W. Parker and Elizabeth Parker. INVY.: Appr. 11/26/1781. Value L129.18.11. Oaths 11/26/1781 Comm. to Joseph Dow, JP. INVY. WARR: 11/29/1781. Comm.: William Lane, James Towle, yoemen; and Philip Towle Jr., gent., all of Hampton. Shown by Admr. d.b.n. ACCOUNT: 6/15/1785. Of Admr. d.b.n. Allowed 6/16/1786. ADDL. ACCOUNT: 7/1/1785. Of Admr. d.b.n. Allowed 7/1/1785. DIV.: 6/22/1785. Comm.: Stephen Page and Simeon Marston, gentlemen; Isaac Marston and Benja. Hobbs, yoemen, all of North Hampton and Philip Towle, Hampton gent. To div. the est. into 3 equal shares. Divisees: son-Samuel Hobbs, double share? and dau.-unnamed, both minors. Oaths 6/25/1783 Hobbs, Isaac Marston, Simeon Marston and Page to Moses Leavitt, JP. Allowed 7/20/1785.

2637. TOWLE, LEMUEL & MARY (1785) #5088
GDP. Of the children of Lemuel Towle, Hampstead yoeman decd. GDP.: 3/21/1785. Of Lemuel, a minor over 14. Gdn. Dearborn Fogg, North Hampton yeoman. Bond L1000.0.0. Sureties: Levi Marston of North Hampton and Daniel Jones of Exeter, yoemen. Witnesses: Nat Parker and Jere. Fogg. GDP.: 6/20/1785. Of Mary, a minor under 14. Gdn. Samuel Hobbs, Parsonstown, York Co., MA/ME yoeman. Bond L1000.0.0. Sureties: Dearborn Fogg and Josiah Hobbs, North Hampton yoemen. Witnesses: Nathl. Parker and W. Parker.

2638. TOWLE, MARY ET. AL (1794) #6028
See #5940 Samuel Towle (1793)

2639. TOWLE, NATHANIEL ET. AL. (1796) #6179
See #5973 Charles Treadwell (1794).

2640. TOWLE, PERKINS (1798) #6416
EST. Concord clothier decd. testate. WILL: Drawn 1/19/1798. Legatees: Wife-Abigail; Mother-Ann Towle. Exec.-Robert Tibbets. His sig. Witnesses: Asahel Green, James Hight and John Hill. CERT. WILL (D32:428): 2/1/1798. Presented by Exec. and witnesses Green and Hill. ADMIN.: 2/1/1798. Exec. Robert Tibbets, Pittsfield esq. Bond $4,000.00. Sureties: Asahel Green and John Hill, Pittsfield husbandmen. Witnesses: Samuel Huston and Wm. Parker. INVY.: Appr. 2/7/1798. Comm.: Thomas R. Swett, Asahel Green and John Shepard. Value $455.13. Oaths 2/7/1798 Comm. to Robert Tibbets, JP. Oath 5/23/1798 Exec. to Wm. Parker. A

note that his real est. was held in partnership with his bro. Jonathan Towle. ACCOUNT: Of Exec. Allowed 2/20/1801 Asahel Green, Gdn. of the only child, consenting.

2641. TOWLE, PHILIP (1785) #5104
EST. Hampton carpenter decd. testate. WILL: Drawn 7/6/1771. Legatees: Son-Philip; Daus.-Easter Leavitt and Patience Towle; Grandsons-Jonathan Leavitt and Jabez Towle; Presbyterian Church of Seabrook. Exec.-son Philip. His sig. Witnesses: Thomas Rand, Cotton Ward and John Moulton. CERT. WILL (D28:155): Presented by Exec. and witnesses Ward and Moulton.

2642. TOWLE, PHILIP (1798) #6443
EST. Hampton carpenter decd. testate. WILL: Drawn 3/16/1798. Legatees: Sons-Jabez and Philip; Daus.-Anna Towle and Lydda Towle. Exec.-son Philip. His sig. Witnesses: Jona. Marston, Ephraim Fellows and James Sanborn. Codicil: 3/18/1798. Makes addl. bequests to sons. Witnesses: John Fogg, Ephraim Fellows and Hannah Drake. CERT. WILL (D32:483): 3/17/1798. Presented by Exec. and witnesses Marston and Fellows and Fellows to Codicil. ADMIN.: 3/17/1798. Exec. Philip Towle, Hampton yoeman. Bond $3,000.00. Sureties: Ephraim Fellows, blacksmith and Jonathan Marston, gent., both of Hampton. Witness W. Parker.

2643. TOWLE, REUBEN (1777) #4336
GDP. Of the son of Jonathan Towle of Candia decd. GDP.: 3/26/1777. Of Reuben, a minor over 14. Gdn. Walter Robie, Candia esq. Bond L500.0.0. Surety Samuel Mooers, Candia esq. Witnesses: Eliz. Parker Jr. and Wm. Parker.

2644. TOWLE, SAMUEL (1793) #5940
EST. Candia gent. decd. ADMIN.: 11/20/1793. Admx. Mary Towle, Candia widow. Bond L1000.0.0. Sureties: Thomas Towle, yoeman and Walter Robie, esq., both of Candia. Witnesses: Nathl. Emerson and Simon French. INVY.: Appr. 1/10/1794. Comm.: Nath. Emerson and Walter Robie, esquires and Simon French. Value L52.5.0. Oaths 1/10/1794 Robie, French and Admx. to Nathl. Emerson, JP. PETITION: 1/13/1794. Of Admx. For Comm. Insolvency. Gives list claims of L62.12.0. Granted 1/13/1794. CLAIMS: Comm.: Walter Robie, Nathl. Emerson and Abram. Fitts. Total L43.3.2.2. The following Petition, Div. Warr. and Div. recorded as #6028 Mary Towle et. al belong here. PETITION: 8/19/1794. Of Mary Towle, Admx. est. Samuel Towle; Joshua Moore, Jesse Eaton, Jon. Baglay and John Sargent. For div. of land held in common by est. of

Samuel Towle and Petitioners. Request a Comm. of Nathl. Emerson and Walter Robie, esquires; Simon French, yoeman and Thomas Wilson Jr., gent., all of Candia and Joseph Blanchard, Chester esq. PETITION: 9/19/1794. Of Walter Robie atty. to Admx. For License. Granted. LICENSE (D31:358): 9/19/1794. To Admx. To sell real est. to amount of L60.0.0. DIV. WARR.: 9/19/1794. Comm. as requested. To div. land in Candia, giving Sargent 1/4, Eaton 1/4, Bagley 1/4, Moore 11 acres and remaining to est. Samuel Towle. DIV.: 10/8/1794. Divisees as in Warr. Oaths 10/20/1794 Emerson and Wilson to Walter Robie, JP. Oath 10/20/1794 Robie to Nathl. Emerson, JP. Allowed. ACCOUNT: 12/17/1794. Of Admx. Allowed 12/17/1794. PROP. & SETTLM.: Claims L43.3.2 1/2. Amount to be proportioned L11.12.0. Allowed 1/1/1795 with order to Admx. to pay.

2645. TOWLE, SAMUEL (1796) #6224
EST. Hampton yoeman decd. intestate. ADMIN.: 6/13/1796. Admr. Caleb Towle, New Hampton, Strafford Co. yoeman. Bond $3,000.00. Sureties: Jeremiah Towle and Stephen Coffin, Hampton yoemen. Witnesses: Jos. Smith and W. Parker. INVY.: Comm.: Cotton Ward, Jona. Marston Jr. and Stephen Coffin. Value $3,005.75. Oaths 6/18/1796 Comm. to Oliver Whipple, JP. Oath 6/18/1796 Admr. to W. Parker. APPR. WARR.: 11/1/1796. Comm.: Benjamin Shaw and Jonathan Marston, gentlemen and Levi Bachelder, yoeman, all of Hampton. To appr. the real est. at its true value. APPR.: 11/5/1796. Comm. appr. At $2,625.00. Oaths 1/24/1797 Comm. to W. Parker. DECREE SETTLM.: 2/24/1797. Caleb Towle and Jeremiah Towle, the two sons, appearing and consenting, the real est. is settled on them, they to pay their co-heirs $300.00 each, Anna Page and Zipporah Towle within 6 months; Rachel Towle and Polly Towle within 9 months; Joanna Towle in 2 years and Betty Towle in 3, with interest. BOND: 2/24/1797. Of Caleb Towle of New Hampton, Strafford Co. and Jeremiah Towle of Hampton, yoemen. Bond $4,000.00. To pay their co-heirs per Decree Settlm. Sureties: Benjamin Shaw, gent. and Levi Batchelder, yoeman, both of Hampton. Witnesses: Jona. Marston and W. Parker.

2646. TOWLE, ZACHARIAH (1787) #5309
EST. North Hampton yoeman decd. intestate. ADMIN.: 11/21/1787. Admrs.: Susanna Towle, widow and Zachariah Towle, yoeman, both of North Hampton. Bond L1000.0.0. Sureties: Moses Leavitt and John Dearborn, North Hampton esquires. Witnesses: Jos. Moulton and W. Parker. INVY.: Appr. 11/17/1787. Comm.: Isaac Marston, William Godfree and Thomas Leavitt. Value L197.18.6. Oaths 12/18/1787 Comm. to Moses Leavitt, JP. Oath 12/19/1787 Admrs. to W. Parker, JP.

ACCOUNT: Of Susanna Norton late wife of Zachariah and Zachariah Towle, Admrs. Allowed 10/17/1791 heirs having been notified. PROMISORY NOTE (D27:551): 4/21/1787. Of Zachariah Towle, North Hampton yoeman. To John Dearborn, North Hampton gent. For L200.0.0.

2647. TOWNER, ASA (1788) #5356
EST. Portsmouth mariner decd. intestate. ADMIN.: 6/11/1788. Admx. Sarah Towner, Portsmouth widow. Bond L500.0.0. Sureties: William Gerrish, mariner and Samuel Drowne, goldsmith, both of Portsmouth. Witnesses: N. Emery and W. Parker. INVY.: Appr. 8/21/1788. Comm.: Saml. Drowne, Joseph Clark and William Vaughan. Value L14.8.0. Oaths 9/16/1788 Admx. and Comm. to Geo. Gains, JP.

2648. TOWNSEND, TIMOTHY (1782) #4794
GDP. Father and res. not given. GDP.: 4/10/1782. Of Timothy of Hampstead, a minor over 14. Gdn. John Darling, Hampstead yoeman. Bond L1000.0.0. Surtey John Calfe, Hampstead esq. Witnesses: John Shackford Tilton and Nathl. Parker.

2649. TRASK, REV. NATHANIEL (1790) #5516
EST. Brentwood clerk decd. testate. WILL: Drawn 5/6/1785. Legatees: Wife-Pernal; Sons-Samuel and Jonathan; Daus.-Betty (& Elisabeth) Trask and Mary Perkins; Grandson-Nathaniel Trask Perkins. Execs.-sons Samuel and Jonathan. His sig. Witnesses; David Robinson, Samuel Robinson and Thomas Stow Ranney. CERT. WILL (D29:335): 1/20/1790. Presented by Execs. and witnesses Samuel Robinson and Ranney. ADMIN.: 1/20/1790. Execs.: Samuel Trask and Nathaniel Trask, Brentwood yoemen. Bond L1000.0.0. Sureties: Samuel Robinson, yoeman and Thos. Stow Ranney, physician, both of Brentwood. Witness William Plumer. INVY.: Appr. 3/25/1790. Comm.: William Morrill, James Robinson and Thos. Stow Ranney. Value L571.4.0. Oaths 3/30/1790 Comm. and Execs. to W. Parker, JP.

TREADWELL. See also Tredwell

2650. TREADWELL, CHARLES (1794) #5973
EST. Portsmouth merchant and shopkeeper decd. testate. WILL: Drawn 9/1/1783. Legatees: Sons-Nathaniel and Jacob; Dau.-Hannah Cutter. Execs.-sons Nathaniel and Jacob. His sig. Witnesses: Joseph Haven, John Adams, Willm. King Jr. and John Pickering. CERT. WILL (D31:186): Presented by Nathaniel Treadwell, surviving Exec., and witnesses Haven and Adams. ADMIN.: 2/19/1795 (sic.-error). Exec. Nathaniel Treadwell, Portsmouth merchant. Bond L1000.0.0. Sureties: George Wentworth,

merchant and Joseph Akerman, yoeman, both of Portsmouth. Witnesses: Saml. Thompson and W. Parker. INVY.: Appr. 2/18/1794. Comm.: Jeremiah Libbey and Capt. George Wentworth. Value L1393.3.11. Affirm. Libbey, Oaths Wentworth and Exec. 2/18/1794 to Nathl. Adams., JP. LIST NOTES OF HAND BELONGING TO EST.: 2/17/1794. Total L163.2.3 1/2. REFERENCE WARR.: Referees: William Gardner, James Sheafe and Nathaniel Adams. To examine and determine the personal account of Nathaniel Treadwell, Portsmouth merchant, amounting to $1,419.05, which he submitted on 6/17/1795 with his Account of Admin. and to which Jeremiah Libbey, esq. made objections on behalf of the other heirs. The parties agree to binding decision of Referees and the judge's decision thereon. Return: 7/9/1795. Referees decide that Nathaniel Treadwell should receive from the est. $250.00 in full payment of his Account. ACCOUNT: 7/15/1795. Of Exec. Allowed 7/15/1795, having been consented to by atty. to other heirs. ADDL. ACCOUNT: 6/15/1796. Of Exec. Allowed 6/15/1796. The following 2 items are recorded as #6179 Nathaniel Treadwell, et. al. (1796) belong here: PETITION 2/17/1796. Of Nathaniel Treadwell, Portsmouth merchant. For div. of land and bldgs. in Portsmouth and lands in Epsom, Rochester, Barrington and elsewhere bequeathed by his father to Nathaniel and his bro. Jacob. Jacob now decd. and his children minors. Cert.: Of Jeremiah Libbey, Gdn. to minors and atty. of the heirs of Jacob of age. Consents to Petition. Requests a Comm. of: Nathl. Rogers of Newmarket, John Hale and John Pierce of Portsmouth, all esquires; Samuel Wallace, Epsom gent. and Joseph March of Deerfield. DIV.: 6/14/1796. Comm. as requested. Divisees: Heirs of Jacob Treadwell and Nathaniel Treadwell. Oaths 6/14/1796 Hale, March and Wallace to Sam. Penhallow, JP. Allowed 6/15/1796, having been consented to by parties.

2651. TREADWELL, JACOB (1787) #5289
EST. Portsmouth merchant decd. intestate. RENUN.: 8/30/1787. Of Ann Treadwell, widow of Jacob. States that there are a number of children, none of age, and she is incapable of Admin. Requests appointment of her bro. Daniel Rindge Rogers. ADMIN.: 8/30/1787. Admr. Daniel Rindge Rogers, Portsmouth merchant. Bond L2000.0.0. Sureties: Ammi Ruhamah Cutter and Clement Storer, Portsmouth physicians. Witnesses: Willm. Cutter and Jacob Cutter. INVY. Appr. 10/30/1787. Comm.: Thomas Parker, Jno. Parker and John Pierce. Value L1663.19.4. Oaths 10/30/1787 Comm. and Admr. to Geo. Gains, JP., the Comm. reporting they did not see the appr. lands and goods in Northumberland, Grafton Co. PETITION: 11/21/1787. Of Admr. For License and Comm. Insolvency. Gives list claims of L1385.0.0. LICENSE (D29:156): 11/21/1787. To Admr. To sell sufficient real est. to pay debts. CLAIMS: 5/26/1787. Comm.: Jno. Parker

and Jeremiah Libbey. Total L1398.15.2. Oath 5/26/1787 Parker, affirm. Libbey to W. Parker, JP. DOWER WARR.: 11/21/1787. Comm.: John Parker, Pearse Long and Jeremiah Libbey, esquires; Alexander Ewin, merchant and Peter Coues, mariner, all of Portsmouth. Of Widow Ann Treadwell. Dower: Oaths 1/2/1788 Parker, Long and Ewen, affirm. Libbey to Geo. Gains, JP. Allowed 1/16/1788. ACCOUNT: Of Admr. Allowed 7/21/1790. Account includes cost of boarding, clothing and schooling for Daniel. PROP. & SETTLM.: Claims L1398.15.2. Amount to be proportioned L707.2.2. Allowed 9/10/1790 with order to Admr. to pay. GDP. Of the children of Jacob Treadwell, Portsmouth merchant decd. GDP.: 6/10/1794. Of: William Kelly Treadwell and Charles Cutter Treadwell, minors over 14. Gdn. John Elliot, Boston, Sussex Co., MA clerk. Bond L1000.0.0. Sureties: Nath. Goodwin, Boston, Suffolk Co. merchant and Jeremiah Libbey, Portsmouth esq. Witnesses: Ebenr. Lane to signing of Elliot and Goodwin; Sarah Stone, Benja. Penhallow and Mark Simes to signing of Libbey.

2652. TREADWELL, MEHETABLE (1782) #4796
GDP. Of Mehetable the wife of William Earl Treadwell of Portsmouth an adult adjudged n.c.m. GDP.: 4/16/1782. Gdns.: Samuel Penhallow and Ammi Ruhamah Cutter, Portsmouth esquires. Bond L2000.0.0. Sureties: Peter Pearse, merchant and William Appleton, stationer. Gdp. granted pursuant to an Act of the Legislature passed last season. Witnesses: John Penhallow and Michael Frost. PETITION: 5/18/1789. Of Peter Pearse, merchant and Mary his wife in her right; Samuel Penhallow and Ammi Ruhamah Cutter as Gdns. of Mehitable. Request div. of shares in the mansion house of Mehitable Odiorne of Portsmouth decd. and land and buildings of est. of Jotham Odiorne, esq. decd. held in common with interest of Widow Sarah Appleton. They agree on a Comm. of Isaac Rindge, Joseph Whipple, George Gains and Jeremiah Libby, esquires and William Hart. Note: For Div. See #1578 1/2 Jotham Odiorne (1751). ACT OF NH GEN. COURT: Passed House 1/6/1790. Passed Senate 1/12/1790. To authorize Judge of Probate to appoint Gdn. for Mehitable Treadwell, wife of William Earl Treadwell of Portsmouth, she being n.c.m. Enables guardians to sell real est. for her support and payment of taxes. Includes request of Gdns. that they be allowed to resign Gdp. Request appointment of Robert Odiorne Treadwell only son of Mehitable. Request made with consent of Robert and his father. Act of 3/26/1782 is refuted. GDP.: 8/19/1790. Gdn. Robert Odiorne Treadwell Bond L2000.0.0. Sureties: William Earl Treadwell and Peter Pearse Jr., both of Portsmouth. Witnesses: Peter Pearse and Mary Pearse.

2653. TREADWELL, NATHANIEL, ET. AL. (1796) #6179
See #5973 Charles Treadwell (1794)

2654. TREADWELL, WILLIAM EARL (1793) #5919
EST. Portsmouth merchant decd. intestate. ADMIN.: 8/19/1793. Admr. Robert Odiorne Treadwell, Portsmouth merchant. Bond L500.0.0. Sureties: Peter Pearse and Peter Pearse Jr., both of Portsmouth. Witnesses: Mary Pearse and Stephen Pearse. INVY.: Appr. 8/22/1793. Comm.: Isaac Rindge, William Hart and Peter Pearse Jr. Value L16.5.0. Oaths 8/22/1793 Comm. to Saml. Penhallow, JP. Oath 1/17/1794 Admr. to W. Parker, JP. ACCOUNT: 2/19/1794. Of Admr. Allowed 2/19/1794.

TREDWELL. See also Treadwell

2655. TRECOTHICK, BARLOW (1797) #6405
(Called Trewthic in Probate Index)
EST. London, Great Britain esq. decd. ADMIN.: 12/25/1797. Admr. Jonathan Warner, Portsmouth esq. Bond $3,000.00. Sureties: Samuel Sherburne and Joshua Wentworth, Portsmouth esquires. Witnesses: Charles Wentworth and Joshua Wentworth Jr. PETITION: 2/21/1798. Of James Ivers, Boston, Suffolk Co., MA merchant and Hannah, his wife, Hannah being heir at law of and next of kin to Barlow Trecothick. For an appeal against the Decree granting Admin. to Jonathan Warner. BOND: 2/1798. Of James Ivers, Boston, Suffolk Co., MA merchant. Bond $200.00. Sureties: John Pierce and Jeremiah Mason, Portsmouth esquires. To make an appeal by James Ivers and Hannah, his wife to Superior Court of Judicature of Rockingham County. Signed by John (Bisor?) atty. for James Ivers and sureties. Witnesses: Jona. Hamilton and Danl. R. Rogers. DEPOSITION: 4/12/1790. Signed at Boston, Suffolk Co., MA. Of: Caleb Blanchard, Shrimpton Hutchinson and Thomas Bulfinch, all of Boston, Suffolk Co., MA. They depose that they have been well acquainted with the family of Barlow Trecothick and that Hannah Ivers, present wife of James Ivers, is the sister of Barlow, decd. and that there is no other kindred as close now living or that was living at his death. The present James Trecothick of London is a nephew of Barlow decd. and assumed that name in compliance with Barlow's Will. He is the only son of James and Hannah Ivers. Oaths of Blanchard, Hutchinson and Bulfinch to (Theaj?ashush) Bourne, JP. They make this deposition in support of the appeal against Decree allowing Admin. DEPOSITION: 4/12/1798 at Boston, Suffolk Co., MA. Of: James Ivers and Jona. L. Austin. They depose that the Will of Barlow Trecothick under the seal of the Perogative Court of Canterbury is a copy of the Will received from Dr. Commons and that the persons interested in the est. of Barlow have always acknowledged the Will to be good and authentic; that the est. has been held by the Will and mostly settled pursuant to it; that they and others have acted under and by authority of the Exec. named therein. Oaths 4/12/1790 of Ivers and Austin

to Theajashu (?) Bourne, JP. that the Deposition was taken at the request of James Ivers and Hannah his wife in support of their appeal from the Decee of Admin. PETITION: 2/21/1798. Of James Ivers, Boston, Suffolk Co., MA merchant and Hannah his wife. They declare that Hannah is the sister of Barlow Trecothic of London and sole heir and next of kin. There being no widow living, James in the right of Hannah is entitled to claim and have admin. of the est. of Barlow if he died intestate; that the judge granted Admin. to Jonathan Warner without summoning James and Hannah to take upon themselves, or either of them, Admin.; nor have either of them ever refused to accept Admin. Admin. was given to Warner without their knowledge or consent and he is neither kin nor creditor to the est. The Admin. was granted on a false suggestion of Warner. They request revocation of the Decree of Admin. and that Warner be cited for a hearing. Signed by John Peirce, atty. for James Ivers and Hannah his wife. ORDER: 2/20/1798. For a hearing, the Petitioners to notify Warner to appear. CERT.: 2/26/1798. Of Edward Hart, Sheriff. He summoned Jonathan Warner by reading to him the Order. DECREE: 4/16/1798. At the hearing it appeared that admin. was granted to Jonathan Warner, esq. on the supposition that the Execs. of the last Will were all dead. That being a mistake, Warner's admin. is revoked and he is ordered to give it up. PETITION: 4/19/1798. Of Jonathan Warner, esq. He requests an appeal from the Decree revoking his admin. Granted. PETITION: A copy of previous. BOND: 4/19/1798. Of Jonathan Warner, Portsmouth esq. Bond $200.00. To prosecute his appeal. Witnesses: William Ham and Joseph Moulton. Sureties: Daniel Rindge and Samuel Sherburne, Portsmouth esquires. Witnesses: William Ham and Joseph Moulton.

2656. TREDICK, CAPT. EDWARD (1793) #5926
EST. New Castle mariner decd. RENUN.: 9/16/1793. Of Margret Tredick, widow of Edward. Of Admin. Requests appointment of Edward's bro. William. ADMIN.: 9/16/1793. Admr. William Tredick, New Castle mariner. Bond L1000.0.0. Sureties: Henry Tredick Jr., New Castle mariner and Martin Parry, Portsmouth goldsmith. Witness Nathl. Parker. INVY .: 11/14/1793. Comm. Geo. Frost, William Vennard and Thomas Bell. Value L153.13.0. Oaths 11/15/1793 Venard and Bell and on 11/16/1793 Admr. to Geo. Frost, JP. PETITION: 9/15/1794. Of Nathl. Adams atty. to Admr. For Comm. Insolvency. Gives list claims of L102.9.6 1/2 and the Dower. CLAIMS WARR.: 2/179(5? torn). Comm.: George Frost, esq.; William Vennard, mariner and Thomas Bell, innholder, all of New Castle. Claims: 8/13/1795. Oaths 8/13/1795 Vennard and Bell to Geo. Frost, JP. Note: This document is badly damaged and the total missing. A note in file says no record in Docket books. ACCOUNT: Of Admr. Oath 8/11/1796 of Admr. Allowed 2/15/1797 Margret Tredick consenting on behalf of her

children. PETITION: 11/24/1812. Of Thomas Stapels for Margaret Tredick. For Admin. D.B.N. as Admr. has died without completing Admin. Granted. ADMIN. D.B.N.: 1/2/1812. Admx. d.b.n. Margraet Tredick, New Castle widow. Bond $3,000.00. Sureties: Thomas Stapels, housewright and Hall J. Locke, gent., both of New Castle. Witnesses: Samuel Staples and Aaron Wilson. INVY. WARR.: 1/2/1812. Comm.: George Vennard, mariner; Nathan Priest, trader and Hall J. Locke, gent., all of New Castle. INVY.: Appr. 2/7/1813. Value $200.00. Oaths 1/7/1813 Comm. to Nat. Rogers, JP. Oath 2/17/1813 Admx. d.b.n. to Henry Prescott Jr., JP. ACCOUNT & PETITION: 1/17/1813. Of N. Priest for Admx. d.b.n. For License to defray expenses in Account. Granted. Account shows expenses of lying-in at birth of dau. Margaret E. Tredick, her main. and main. of Joseph W. LICENSE: 2/17/1813. To Admx. d.b.n. To sell real est. to amount of $400.00. ACCOUNT: Of Admx. d.b.n. Allowed 10/20/1813.

2657. TREDICK, HENRY (1785) #5156
EST. New Castle mariner decd. intestate. PETITION: 12/5/1785. Of: Elizabeth Tredick, Mary Amazeen, Elizabeth Clark, Christopher Amazeen, William Clark and Noah Emery Jr., heirs. They have agreed on Edward Tredick to be Admr. CITATION: 12/8/1785. To: William Tredick and Henry Tredick, New Castle mariners. They are notified that their bro. Edward has applied for admin. as recommended by his mother, sisters and their husbands. They are cited to appear and show any cause why Edward should not be appointed. Cert.: Of Thomas Bell, a Selectman. He cited William and Henry by reading and explaining the Citation to them. ADMIN.: 12/8/1785. Admr. Edward Tredick, New Castle mariner. Bond L500.0.0. Sureties: Geo. Heart Jr., merchant and Stephen Batson, shipwright, both of New Castle. Witnesses: Nathl. Batson and Sarah Batson. INVY. WARR.: 2/17/1786. Comm.: Thomas Bell, George Frost, merchants and Stephen Batson, shipwright, all of New Castle. INVY.: Appr. 4/12/1786. Value L156.10.6. Oaths 4/13/1786 Admr. and Comm. to George Gains, JP.

2658. TREDWELL, NEHEMIAH (1782) #4767
File jacket says, "Papers missing." Listed in Docket Index as a Gdp. Not found.

TREWTHIC. See Trecothick

2659. TRICKEY: EPHRAIM & JAMES (1783) #4881
GDP. Of the sons of Joshua Trickey of Newington decd. GDP.: 2/26/1783. Of Ephraim, a minor over 14, and of James, a minor under 14. Gdn. Benjamin Adams, Newington esq. Bond L1000.0.0. Surety John Colman, Newington yoeman. Witnesses: Andrw. Freese and Nathl. Parker.

2660. TRICKEY, JOSEPH (1774) #4108
EST. Newington yoeman decd. intestate. ADMIN.: 6/22/1774. Adms. Elizabeth Trickey, widow and Thomas Trickey, yoeman, both of Newington. Bond: L1000.0.0. Sureties: Samuel Shackford, husbm. and Jonathan Trickey, yoeman, both of Newington. Witnesses: Benjamin Slade and Saml. Hale Jr. INVY. WARR.: 6/22/1774. Comm.: Timothy Dame and James Colman, Newington husbandmen. INVY.: Appr. 7/19/1774. Value L117.15.0. Oaths 7/27/1774 Comm. and Admrs. to judge.

2661. TRUE, CAPT. HENRY (REV.) (1782) #4822
EST. Hampstead clerk decd. ADMIN.: 7/20/1782. Admx. Ruth True (sig. "Mary"), Hampstead widow. Bond L1000.0.0. Sureties: John Darling, gent. and John Calfe, esq., both of Hampstead. Witnesses: Moses Kimball and Elipht. Poor. INVY.: Appr. 10/23/1782. Comm.: John Darling, Jonathan Carleton and Elipht. Poor. Value L804.19.8 plus a long list of Notes due est. not tallied. Oaths 10/23/1782 Comm. and Admx. to John Calfe, JP.

2662. TRUE: HENRY, JAMES, MARY, RUTH & SARAH (1783) #4940
GDP. Of Hampstead gent. adjudged n.c.m. and of the children of Henry True, Hampstead clerk decd. GDP.: 10/1/1783. Of James True, Hampstead gent. an adult adjudged n.c.m. Gdn. John Calfe, Hampstead esq. Bond L5000.0.0. Sureties: John True, Hampstead yoeman and James Thurston, Exeter innholder. Witnesses: Nat Parker and Wm. Parker. GDP. Of the children of Henry True, Hampstead clerk decd. GDP.: 10/1/1783. Of: Ruth and Sarah, minors over 14 and of Henry and Mary, minors under 14. Gdn. John Calfe, Hampstead esq. Bond L1000.0.0. Sureties: John True, Hampstead yoeman and James Thurston, Exeter blacksmith.

2663. TRUE, ISRAEL (1794) #5974
EST. Portsmouth joiner decd. ADMIN.: 1/24/1794. Admr.: Jeremiah Hill, Portsmouth esq. Bond L1000.0.0. Sureties: James Hill, blacksmith and George Wendell, merchant, both of Portsmouth. Witnesses: Robt. O. Treadwell and W. Parker. INVY.: Appr. 3/26/1794. Comm.: Edward Sargent, George Wentworth and Solomon Cotton. Value L325.12.7. Oaths 4/2/1794 Comm. and Admr. to Nathl. Adams, JP. DIV. WARR.: 2/18/1795. Comm.: Edward Sargent, mariner; George Wentworth, esq.;

Nathl. Treadwell, merchant; John Noble, yoeman and Solomon Cotton, joiner, all of Portsmouth. To div. est. in four equal parts. Div.: 6/9/1795. Divisees: Abigail Lewis, Mrs. Jemima Peirce wife of Daniel Peirce. Mary Hill wife of Jeremiah Hill and Comfort Hill wife of Elisha Hill. Oaths 6/9/1795 Capt. Sargent, Wentworth, Treadwell and Cotton to R. Cutts Shannon, JP. Allowed 6/17/1795. ACCOUNT: 6/15/1797. Of Admr. Allowed 6/21/1797. Oaths 6/16/1797. Of: Abigail Hill, Elisha Hill and Jemima Peirce. As heirs they have examined the Account and approve it. NOTE: This file also contains Cert. Will of John Jackson which belongs with #4874 John Jackson (1783) and is recorded there.

2664. TRUE, JOHN (1795) #6141
EST. Pembroke yoeman decd. testate. WILL: Drawn 7/15/1795. Legatees: Wife-Anne; Bros.-Benjamin and Daniel. Exex.-wife Anne. His sig. Witnesses: Richard Bartlett, Nathan Holt and Benjamin Lovejoy. CERT. WILL (D32:53): Presented by Exex. and witnesses Holt and Lovejoy. ADMIN.: 10/3/1795. Exex. Anne True, Pembroke widow. Bond L500.0.0. Sureties: Richard Bartlett, Pembroke esq. and Theodore Shackford of Allenstown. Witnesses: Nathan Holt and Phebe Bartlett. INVY.: Appr. 11/13/1795. Comm.: Stephen Bartlett, Isaac Morrison and Caleb Bartlett. Value L139.3.7. Oaths 1/18/1796. Comm. and on 5/13/1796 Exex. to Richard Bartlett, JP.

2665. TRUSDEL, RICHARD (1782) #4867
EST. Portsmouth butcher decd. ADMIN.: 10/11/1782. Admx. Lydia Trusdel, Portsdel widow. Bond L1000.0.0. Sureties: Nathaniel Thwing, merchant and Samuel Trusdel, chaisemaker, both of Portsmouth. Witnesses: Aaron Hastings and Hannah Dame. to mark of Lydia Trusdel; Willm. Pearn and Supply Clap to sigs. of Thwing and Trusdel. INVY. WARR.: 12/2/1782. Comm.: Supply Clap, esq.; George Wentworth and Thomas Bickford, merchants, all of Portsmouth. INVY.: Appr. 12/12/1782. Value L80.3.6. Oaths 1/2/1783 Comm. and on 1/3/1783 Admx. to Geo. Gains, JP. PETITION: 1/3/1783. Of Artemas Ward Trusdel on behalf of Admr. For Comm. Insolvency. Gives list claims of L108.0.0 and more not ascertained.

TUCK. See also Tucke

2666. TUCK, EDWARD (1772) #3943
EST. Kensington yeoman decd. testate. WILL: Drawn 4/15/1763. Legatees: Sons-John, Samuel and Jesse. Daus.-Sarah Prescott, Bethiah Veasey, Mary Tuck and Hannah Tuck. Exec. Son Jesse. His sig. Witnesses: Philemon Blake, Joseph Tilton and Isaac Fellows Jr. CERT.

WILL: 6/24/1772. Presented by Exec. and witnesses Blake and Tilton, esq. ADMIN.: 6/24/1772. Exec. Jesse Tuck, Kensington yeoman. Bond L500.0.0. Sureties: Philemon Blake, yoeman and Joseph Tilton, esq., both of Kensington. Witnesses: Saml. Hale Jr. and Samuel Parker.

TUCKE. See also Tuck

2667. TUCKE, BENJAMIN (1789) #5440
EST. Hampton yoeman decd. testate. WILL: Drawn 10/8/1787. Legatees: Wife-Sarah; Daus.-Rachel, Tabitha, Hannah French and Anna Tucke. Exex.-dau. Anna. His sig. Witnesses: Saml. Tucke, Joshua James and Stephen Coffin. CERT. WILL (D29:267): 4/15/1789. Presented by Exex. and witnesses James and Coffin. ADMIN.: 4/15/1789. Exex. Anna Tucke, Hampton spinster. Bond L500.0.0. Sureties: Joshua James and Stephen Coffin, Hampton yoemen. Witnesses: Peter Pearse and W. Parker.

2668. TUCKE, REV. JOHN (1773) #4039
EST. Gosport clerk decd. intestate. ADMIN.: 9/10/1773. Admr.: John Tuck, Epsom clerk. Bond: L500.0.0. Sureties: John Sherburne, Esq. and Daniel Peirce, shopkeeper, both of Portsmouth. Witnesses: Samuel Parker and John Parker. INVY. WARR.: 12/10/1773. Comm.: Henry Carter, esq., John Varrell and William Muchamore, Gosport shoremen. INVY.: Value L168.16.3 "excepting a quantity of fish came to hand since Invy." Oaths 2/9/1775 Admr., Carter and Muchamore to judge.

2669. TUCKE, REV. JOHN (1777) #4342
EST. Epsom clerk decd. intestate. ADMIN.: 4/18/1777. Admx. Mary Tucke, Epsom widow. Bond L500.0.0. Sureties: John McClary, esq. and George Wallace, yoeman, both of Epsom. Witnesses: Michl. McClary and John Casey. INVY.: Appr. 5/15/1777. Comm.: Timothy Upham, Jeremiah Eastman and Daniel Page. Value L464.4.11. Oaths 7/25/1777 Comm. and Admx. to John McClery, JP. PETITION: 11/16/1785. Of Admx. For License. Gives list of claims in as L190.6.0. OPINION: 9/21/1791. Of John McCleary and Michl. McClary "being desired to give our opinion in regard to income of the real est. since death. "Their opinion is that it has produced no income and has, instead, cost the Admx. Samuel (F.?) Tucke, oldest son, agrees with opinion. ACCOUNT: 9/21/1791. Of Admx. Allowed 9/21/1791. Account includes main. of Joseph, Richard and Abigail.

2670. TUCKE, JOHN (1792) #5821
EST. Hampton yeoman decd. ADMIN.: 11/21/1792. Admrs. John Tucke and Thomas Leavitt, both of Hampton. Bond L1000.0.0. Sureties: Moses

Elkins of Hampton and Francis B. Eastman, Exeter taylor. Witnesses: John Shute and W. Parker. INVY.: Appr. 1/23/1793. Comm.: Philip Towle, John Dearborn and Elisha S. Marston. Value L219.6.6. Oaths 1/23/1793 Comm. and Admrs. to Christo. Toppan, JP. PETITION: 12/19/1793. Of John Tucke, Hampton joiner. For div. of the homestead owned in common with heirs and of which 1/2 belongs to him. Order: 12/19/1793. For hearing, Petitioner to serve heirs with copies of Petition and Order. Consent: Of heirs Thomas Leavitt Jr. for himself and wife, Jeames Tucke and Nathaniel Haaden to Petition and to setting off Dower. DIV.: WARR.: 12/23/1793. Comm.: Philip Towle, gent.; John Dearborn, esq.; Elisha Smith Marston, Jabez Towle and Jonathan Philbrick, yoemen, all of Hampton. To set off 1/2 of est. in Hampton to son John Tucke, Hampton joiner, according to the deed given when decd. sold to his son during his lifetime and to set off to Widow Sarah Tucke her Dower, including 1/3 of the half sold to son John, the heirs having signified to judge that they have agreed that her thirds in John's half be set off to her out of the remaining half after John's is div., so she is entitled to 2/3 of the remaining half. They are also to appr. the neat income of the remaining 1/3 of the 1/2 for past year. PETITION: 12/23/1793. Of Thomas Leavitt, an Admr. For License. Gives list claims of L75.5.10 1/2. Granted. LICENSE (D31:141): 12/23/1793. To Admrs. To sell real est. to amount of L60.0.0. APPR.: 4/1/1794. Value of neat income for 2 years past L4.19.0. DIV.: 10/25/1796. Divisee John Tucke. Oaths 10/28/1796 Philip Towle, Marston and Jabez Towle to Oliver Whipple, JP. Allowed. DOWER: 10/25/1796. Oaths 10/25/1796 Philip Towle, Marston and Jabez Towle to Oliver Whipple, JP. Allowed. ACCOUNT: 12/1796. Of Admrs. Allowed 12/23/1796.

2671. TUCKE, JONATHAN JR. (1780) #4673
EST. Hampton yoeman decd. intestate. ADMIN.: 11/29/1780. Admx. Huldah Tucke, Hampton widow. Bond L20000.0.0. Sureties: Josiah Moulton, Hampton esq. and James Batchelder, North Hampton yoeman. Witnesses: O. Peabody and W. Parker. GDP.: Of the children of Jonathan Tucke, Hampton yeoman decd. GDP.: 1/31/1781. Of: Betty, Josiah, Jonathan, Samuel and John, minors under 14. Gdns. James Batchelder, North Hampton gent. and Huldah Tucke, Hampton widow. Bond L20000.0.0. Sureties: Henry Elkins, gent. and Jeremiah Moulton, yoeman, both of Hampton. Witnesses: Nathl. Parker and Wm. Parker. INVY.: Appr. 7/23/1781. Comm.: Joseph Dow, Morris Hobbs and John Dearbon. Value L553.12.0 at rate of corn at 4 shil./bu. Oaths 7/23/1781 Dow, esq. And Dearbon to Levi Dearborn, JP. Oath 7/25/1781 Admx. to W. Parker, Reg. PETITION: 7/25/1781. Of John Tucke, Hampton yeoman. States that he is tennant in common with the children of his bro. Jonathan Jr. of

Hampton decd, he owning half and children, who are minors, owning half. Requests div. Signed by John Tucke Jr. in behalf of the Petition of his father. Consent: Of Gdns. They have agreed with John Tucke Jr. on a Comm. of Joseph Dow, esq.; Philip Towle Jr. and Josiah Dearbon, gentlemen; Elisha Smith Marston and Abner Page, yoemen. Witness W. Parker. Order: 7/25/1781. For Div. Warr. DIV. WARR.: 7/25/1781. Comm. as requested. To div. the lands and marsh according to the deeds of Jonathan Tucke to his sons Jonathan Tucke Jr. and John Tucke. DIV.: 9/25/1791. Divisees: Heirs of Jonathan Tucke Jr. and John Tucke. Oaths 9/26/1791 Dearbon and Marston to Joseph Dow, JP. PETITION: 10/30/1782. Of Admx. Evid. for License. Lists claims and main. of children of L114.15.11 1/4. LICENSE: 10/30/1782. To Admx. To sell sufficient real est. to pay debts. APPR.: 12/15/1794. Comm.: Isaac Moulton, Simeon Marston and John Robie. To appr. neat income of 2/3 of the real est. for the 14 years past. Value L70.0.0., exclusive of the marsh sold which was esti. at L4.0.0. Oaths 12/21/1794 Comm. to W. Parker only son of age being present and Admx. bein Gdn. to rest of children. ACCOUNT: 12/15/1794. Of Admx. Allowed 12/15/1794. Account includes main. of Jonathan, Samuel and John.

2672. TUCKE, JONATHAN (1781) #4720 1/2
EST. Hampton yoeman decd. intestate. RENUN.: 5/23/1781. Of John Tuck, oldest son. Of Admin. Requests appointment of his bro. Samuel Tucke. Benjamin Tucke consents. Witnesses: Thomas Leavitt and Joseph Frese Darbon. ADMIN.: 6/27/1780. Admr. Samuel Tucke, Kensington cordwainer. Bond L20000.0.0. Sureties: Benjamin Tucke, Hampton husbm. and Noah Emery, Exeter esq. Witnesses: Jedediah Jewett and Nathl. Parker. INVY. WARR.: 6/27/1781. Comm.: Josiah Moulton Jr., Philip Towle and Josiah Dearbon, Hampton gentlemen. INVY.: 10/30/1781. Value L15.17.8. Oaths 1/29/1782 Moulton and Dearbon to Joseph Dow, JP. PETITION: 4/20/1782. Of Admr. He has reason to believe that Joseph Dow, Hampton esq., has in his possession papers belonging to est., the detention of which is injurious to est. Requests Dow be cited to appear. Allowed. CITATION: 4/20/1782. To Joseph Dow, Hampton esq. To appear and be examined on the concealing and embezzling of money, goods or chattels belonging to est. Cert.: 4/22/1782. Of Nathl. Shannon, Constable. At request of John Tucke Jr., he has read the Citation to Joseph Dow, esq. APPR. WARR.: 12/15/1794. Comm.: Joseph Dow and Josiah Dearbon, esquires; Morris Hobbs and Philip Towle, gentlemen and Daniel Philbrook, yoeman. To view 2/3 of real est. to see if it can be div. among all the children. Div., giving double share to oldest son, or appr. APPR.: 12/21/1794. Value of 2/3 of the real est. L298.16.0. The appr. Is also signed by James Batchelder, Gdn. Oaths

12/24/1794 Philbrook, Hobbs and Towle to Oliver Whipple, JP. DECREE SETTLM.: 12/26/1794. Decree includes reversion of Dower as well as 2/3 real est. Josiah Tuck, oldest son, appearing and consenting, real est. is settled on him, including incumbrance of Dower, Josiah to pay his co-heirs L49.10.0 each, with interest, Betty Leavitt in 2 months, Jonathan Tucke and Samuel Tucke in one year and John Tucke in 2 years. BOND: 12/26/1794. Of Josiah Tuck, Hampton yoeman. Bond L600.0.0. To pay his co-heirs per Decree Settlm. Sureties: James Moulton of Hampton and Edward Tucke of Brentwood, yoemen. Witnesses: John Parker and W. Parker.

2673. TUCKE, JOSEPH (1778) No#
GDP. Of the son of Samuel Tucke of Kingston. GDP.(D24:242). 3/26/1778. Of Joseph, a minor over 14. Gdn. Samuel Philbrick, esq. Sureties: Timothy Chamberlain, baker and Samuel Robinson, yoeman, both of Exeter.

2674. TUCKE, SAMUEL (1777) #4410
EST. Brentwood yoeman decd. intestate. ADMIN.: 12/31/1777. Admx. Anna Tucke, Brentwood widow. Bond L500.0.0. Sureties: John Tucke of Brentwood and Jesse Tucke of Kensington, gentlemen. Witnesses: Daniel Smith and W. Parker. INVY.: Appr. 1/26/1778. Comm.: Joseph Smith, Joseph Johnson and Joseph Greely. Value L1334.12.4. Oaths 1/26/1778 Comm. and Admx. to Wm. Morrill, JP. ACCOUNT: 2/20/1792. Of Admx. Allowed 2/20/1792. Account includes main. 4 children.

2675. TUCKE, SAMUEL (1789) #5407
EST. Kensington gent. decd. testate. WILL: Drawn 12/9/1788. Legatees: Wife-Martha; Son-Jonathan; Daus.-Abigail, Betty, Lydia, Love (all married), Martha Tucke, Mary Tucke and Tabitha Tucke. Exex.-wife Martha. His sig. Witnesses: Jere. Fogg, Benjamin Tilton and Benja. Rowe Jr. CERT. WILL (D29:237): 1/21/1789. Presented by Exex. and witnesses Fogg, esq. and Tilton. INVY.: Comm.: John Lane, Ebenr. Potter and Benja. Tilton. Value not tallied. Esti. L197.0.0+. Oaths 5/11/1789 Lane, Potter and Admx. to Jere. Fogg, JP.

2676. TUCKER, EBENEZER (1776) #4241
EST. Hawke husbm. decd. testate. WILL: Drawn 5/4/1776. Legatees: Wife-Deborah; Sons-Joseph, Ebenezer and Jacob; Dau.-Hannah wife of William Rowe; Grandsons-Jonathan Tucker son of his son Ebenezer and Henry. Exec. son Joseph. His mark. Witnesses Jonathan French Jr., John Page and Timothy Worth. CERT. WILL (D23:301): 5/29/1776. Presented by Exec. and witnesses Page and Worth. INVY. WARR.: 5/28/1776.

Comm.: Edward Eastman and David Quinby, gentlemen and Annes Campbell, all of Hawke. INVY.: Appr. 6/22/1776. Value L87.0.1. Oaths 6/26/1776 Comm. to W. Parker, JP.

2677. TUCKER, EBENEZER (1789) #5430
EST. Hawke yoeman decd. testate. Note: Ebenezer's Will is missing and has not been found by Probate Office or during research for this book. DECREE: 3/18/1789. In his Will Ebenezer appointed his son Joseph Exec. of his est. Joseph has died without settling est. By his power under the law, judge appoints Ebenezer Tucker as Admr. ADMIN.: 3/18/1789. Admr. Ebenezer Tucker, Andover, Hillsborough Co. yoeman. Bond L500.0.0. Sureties: Thomas Page, esq. and Humphry Hook, husbm., both of Hawke. Witnesses: Jedediah Philbrick and Daniel Page. INVY.: Appr. 3/21/1789. Comm.: Thomas Page, Humphry Hook and David Quimby. Of land and bldgs. Value L54.9.9. Oaths 3/21/1789 Hook, Admr. and Quimby to Thos. Page, JP. INVY.: Appr. 4/23/1789. Comm.: Samuel Blake and Josiah Batchelder. Of personal est., being the est. in Hillsborough Co. Value L8.1.9. Oaths 4/23/1789 Comm. to Jonathan Weare, JP. PETITION: Dated by clerk 11/1789. Of Admr. For Comm. Insolvency. Gives claims already in as L26.0.0 and many more expected. He doubts the real est. will sell for as much as appr. CLAIMS WARR.: 11/18/1789. Comm.: Thomas Page and David Quimby, esquires and Israel Hook, yoeman, all of Hawke. CLAIMS: Total L24.1.8. Oaths 1/26/1791 Quimby and Hook to Thos. Page, JP. LICENSE (D30:14): 2/4/1791. To Admr. to sell real est. to the amount of L35.0.0.

2678. TUCKER, JAMES (1795) #6100
EST. Poplin gent. decd. testate. WILL: Drawn 3/30/1795. Legatees: Wife-Miriam; Sons-John, True, James, Daniel and Benjamin; Daus.-Miriam Robinson, Hannah Badcock, Mary Tucker and Eleanor Lock. Execs.-Enoch Smith and son Benjamin. His sig. Witnesses: Benja. Clough, Betsey Smith and Reuben Smith. CERT. WILL (D31:524): 5/18/1795. Presented by Execs. and witnesses Clough and Betsey Smith. ADMIN.: 5/18/1795. Execs.-Enoch Smith and Benjamin Tucker, Poplin yoemen. Bond L1000.0.0. Sureties: Benjamin Clough and William Morrill, Poplin yoemen. Witnesses: Betsey Smith and W. Parker. INVY.: Appr. 8/13/1795. Comm.: Enoch Smith, Jonathan Brown and William Morrill. Value not tallied. Esti. L448.0.0+. Oaths 8/13/1795 Brown, Morrill and Execs. to John Scribner, JP.

2679. TUCKER, JOSEPH (1782) #4860
GDP. Of the son of Joseph Tucker, Hawke yoeman decd. GDP.: 11/20/1782. Of Joseph, a minor over 14. Gdn. John Eastman, Kingston gent. Bond L500.0.0. Sureties: John Calfe of Hampstead and Ebenr. Webster, Salisbury, Hillsborough Co. gent. Witnesses: Tabby Gilman and W. Parker.

2680. TUCKER, LEMUEL (1791) #5632
EST. Concord yoeman decd. INVY.: 4/18/1791 (sic.) Comm.: Timo. Walker, Phinehas Virgin and Chandler Lovejoy. Value L233.11.0. Oaths 4/18/1791 Virgin and Lovejoy to Timo. Walker, JP. ADMIN: 3/29/1792. Admr. Eliphalet Tucker, Concord yoeman. Bond L1000.0.0. Sureties; Ebenezer Eastman and Stephen Gage, Concord yoemen. Witnesses: Samuel Parker and W. Parker. This file also includes a Caveat of Samuel Tucker Jr. of Portsmouth against the awarding of Admin. of his mother's est. An est. after 1800 not needed for this book.

2681. TURNER, WILLIAM (1797) #6297
EST. Candia yoeman decd. testate. WILL: Drawn 10/28/1796. Legatees: Wife-Sarah; Son-Moses; Daus.-Sarah Turner, Molly Sargent, Susanah Brown and Abial Patton. Exec.-son Moses. His sig. Witnesses: John Lane, Peter Mooers and Nathl. Emerson. CERT. WILL (D32:239): 1/16/1797. Presented by Exec. and witnesses Lane and Emerson, esq. ADMIN.: 1/16/1797. Exec. Moses Turner, Candia yoeman. Bond $2,000.00. Sureties: Nathaniel Emerson, esq. and John Lane, yoeman, both of Candia. Witnesses: Wentworth Cheswill and W. Parker. INVY.: Appr. 1/26/1797. Comm.: Abraham Fitts, gent.; Nathl. Emerson and Walter Robie, esquires. Value $679.47. Oaths 1/26/1797 Fitts, Emerson and Exec. to Walter Robie, JP.

2682. UNDERHILL, BETSEY & REUBEN (1797) #6402
GDP. Of the children of Jeremiah Underhill, Chester yoeman decd. GDP.: 12/20/1797. Of Betsey, a minor over 14. Gdn. Richard Dearborn, Chester gent. Bond $1,000.00. Sureties: Jabez Hoit, Chester esq. and Taylor Hoit, Deerfield husbm. Witnesses: Nicholas Emery and John Morrison. GDP.: 11/20/1799. Of Reuben, a minor over 14. Gdn. Richard Dearborn, Chester gent. Bond $1,000.00. Sureties: Jabez Hoit of Chester and Moses Greenough, Atkinson, gent. Witnesses: Joseph Knight Jr. and W. Parker. Note: For earlier Gdp. of Betsey and Reuben see #6046 est. Jeremiah Underhill, their father (1794).

2683. UNDERHILL, JEREMIAH (1794) #6046
EST. Chester yoeman decd. intestate. ADMIN.: 11/20/1794. Admx. Anna Underhill, Chester widow. Bond L1000.0.0. Sureties: Thomas Merrill, yoeman and Josiah Underhill, gent., both of Chester. Witnesses: Stephen Chase and Reuben Clark. GDP. Of the children of Jeremiah Underhill, Chester yoeman decd. GDP.: 11/20/1794. Of: David, Elijah and Benjamin, minors over 14. Gdn. Reuben Clark, Chester yoeman. Bond L1000.0.0. Sureties: Samuel Underhill, yoeman and Stephen Chase, esq., both of Chester. Witnesses: Josiah Underhill and Josiah Chase. GDP. Of the children of Jeremiah. GDP.: 11/20/1794 Of: Betsy, Reuben, Joanna, James, Samuel and John, minors under 14. Gdn. Anna Underhill, Chester widow. Bond L1000.0.0. Sureties: Joseph Hills, gent. and Samuel White, yoeman, both of Chester. Witnesses: Stephen Chase and Dolly Blake. PETITION: 11/21/1794. Of: Stephen Underhill; Samuel Underhill; John Underhill; Anna Underhill as Admx. and Gdn. of 6 of the children of decd.; Reuben Clark, Gdn. of the rest of children of decd. For div. of a lot in Chester of which decd. owned 1/4. Request a Comm. of: Stephen Chase, esq.; Josiah Underhill, Richard Dearborn and Benja. Hall, gentlemen and B. Pike Chase, yoeman. Witness Reuben Clark. DIV. WARR.: 11/20/1794. Comm. as requested. To set off to heirs of decd., his children, 1/4 part of a lot of land. DIV.: 1/2/1795. Divisees: Stephen Underhill, Samuel Underhill, John Underhill, Heirs of Jeremiah Underhill. Oaths 1/31/1795 Stephen Chase, B. Pike Chase, Dearborn and Underhill to Willm. White, JP. Allowed. INVY.: Comm.: Benjamin Hall, Stephen Chase and B. Pike Chase. Value L215.7.1. Oaths 1/31/1795 Stephen Chase, B. Pike Chase and Admx. To Willm. White, JP. ACCOUNT: 4/19/1797. Of Admx. by her atty. Oath 4/18/1797 Admx. to Josiah Flagg, JP. Witnesses: Stephen Chase and Betsy V. M. Flagg. Allowed 4/19/1797 having been vouched for by Admx. as Gdn. of some of minor children and atty. of Gdn. of rest of minor children. Account includes main. of James, Samuel and John. DOWER & DIV.: 5/8/1797. Comm.: Stephen Chase, B. Pike Chase, Richard Dearborn "and others." To. set off her Dower to the Widow and div. 2/3 among the children in single shares. Divisees: Widow Anna Underhill, her Dower; Sons-David Jr., Elijah, Benjamin, Reuben, James, Samuel 3d and John Jr.; Daus.-Betsee Underhill and Anna Underhill. Oaths 5/8/1797 Comm. to Willm. White, JP. Allowed 11/20/1799. ADDL. ACCOUNT: Of Admx. Oath 2/13/1801 Admx. to Stephen Chase, JP. Allowed 3/6/1801. Note: For addl. Gdps. of Betsey and Reuben see #6402 Underhill: Betsey & Reuben (1797).

2684. UNDERHILL, JOHN (1793) #5922
EST. Chester gent. decd. testate. WILL: Drawn 9/15/1785. Legatees: Sons-Moses, John, Jeremiah, David and Samuel; Daus.-Betty Bussell,

Molly Pearce, Sarah Underhill and Joanna Presson; Grandson-Stephen Underhill. Execs.-sons David and Samuel. His sig. Witnesses: Thos. Sargeant, John Manning and Josiah Flagg. CERT. WILL (D31:60): 8/21/1793. Presented by Execs. and witnesses Sargeant and Flagg, esq. ADMIN.: 9/21/1793. Execs.: David Underhill and Samuel Underhill, Chester yoemen. Bond L1000.0.0. Sureties: Josiah Flagg, esq. and Thomas Sargeant, physician, both of Chester. Witnesses: Moody Morse and Benja. Gordon.

2685. UNDERWOOD, CAPT. BENJAMIN (1773) #4056
EST. Of Portsmouth decd. intestate. ADMIN.: 11/12/1773. Admr. John Underwood, Marblehead, Essex Co., MA ropemaker. Bond L1000.0.0. Sureties: Benjamin Hart, ropemaker and Samuel Hart, yoeman, both of Portsmouth. Witnesses: Benja. Mackay and Saml. Hale Jr. CLAIMS WARR.: 11/17/1773. Comm.: Joseph Whipple and John Sparhawk, Portsmouth merchants. ACCOUNT: 4/10/1774. Of Capt. Abraham Trefethen Jr. For going to Falmouth (state?) to get Gift, a negro man. Oath 5/11/1774 Trefethen to judge. INVY.: Appr. 5/5/1774. Comm.: Henry Prescott and Benja. Hart. Value L145.5.6. Oaths 7/8/1774 Comm. and Admr. to judge. Invy. Includes negro man Gift. Note: The Invy. calls Capt. Benjamin of New Castle and all his est. was in New Castle. BILL: From John Underwood. To Est. of his father. Total L14.12.0. PETITION: 11/29/1774. Of Admr. For License. LICENSE: 11/29/1774. To Admr. To sell sufficient real est. to pay debts. Includes a statement from John Sparhawk of Claims Comm. that claims will be more than L100.0.0. ACCOUNT OF VENDUE: 11/29/1774. Of sale of house, a negro and household goods. Total L91.2.9. Signed by Henry Langmaid. PETITION: 11/29/1774. Of Admr. For License. BILL: 7/30/1774. From Abra. Trefethen Jr. To est. Total L4.2.3. For settling affair of negro man Gift belonging to est. Receipt: 12/1/1774. From Trefethen. To est. For payment of L4.2.3. in full. BILL: 12/1/1774. Of Admr. For expenses with additions made by judge. CLAIMS: Comm.: John Sparhawk and J. Whipple. Claims L113.18.5 1/2. Oaths 1/20/1783 Comm. to Saml. Penhallow, ACCOUNT: 2/1783. Of John Sparhawk atty. to Admr. Of money left in his hands by Admr. who is out of state. Includes a note that Claims to be sent to Sparhawk, who will pay the proportion though it is only a partial settlm. ACCOUNT: Dated by clerk 2/1783. Of John Sparhawk atty. to Admr. Allowed 2/26/1783 with order to atty. that bal. to be proportioned among creditors. PROP. & SETTLM.: Claims L113.18.5 1/2. Amount to be proportioned L39.19.11 1/2. Allowed 3/26/1783 with order to John Sparhawk, atty. to pay. There are also in the file 6 small bills to the est. with oaths and receipts.

2686. UNDERWOOD, JOHN (1799) #6617
EST. Portsmouth ropemaker testate. WILL: Drawn 8/7/1799. Legatees: Wife-Lydia; His children-John, Lydia Underwood and Mary wife of Joseph Carter ropemaker. Exec.-bro-in-law-Samuel Drowne. His sig. Witnesses: James Hickey, Andw. Newman and Timy Gerrish. CERT. WILL (D33:158): 10/16/1799. Presented by Exec. and all witnesses. INVY. ADMIN.: 10/16/1799. Exec. Samuel Drowne, Portsmouth goldsmith. Bond $3,000.00. Sureties: Saml. Hutchings, trader and John Underwood, ropemaker, both of Portsmouth. Witnesses: Richard Long and W. Parker. INVY.: Comm.: Edward Sargent, Nathl. Marshall and Saml. Hutchings. Value $1,950.42. Oaths 2/20/1800 Marshall, Hutchings and Exec. to W. Parker, JP.

2687. UNDERWOOD, PHINEHAS (1757) A#2305 & (1774) #4134
EST. Merrimack Underwood, Hillsborough Co. decd. Note: All of the following documents are in (#4134.) PETITION: 10/12/1774. Of Phinehas Underwood of Merrimack, oldest son of decd. States that his father left a considerable est. His mother was appointed Admx. She has married twice since his father's death and the present Admrs. have on hand considerable personal est. plus real est. undivided, unless they have wasted it. Request that Nathanael Garfield, the present husb. of his mother, be cited to account. PETITION: 11/30/1774. Of Phinehas Underwood for himself and his sisters. He notes that after the death of his father his mother married, first, Robert Mordough. He claims that there appears to be due the est. a bal. of L669.14.10 = L33.9.9 lawful money, which neither the Admx. nor her husbands Mordough or Garfield have paid to the Petitioners or accounted for. The Admrs. have wasted the est. and refused to appear to account though they have been legally cited. Requests that Bond of Admx. Mary be decreed forfeit and ordered to be put in suit for the benefit of the heirs. Decree: 11/30/1774. It appearing by sundry depositions that the Admrs. have wasted and misapplied the est., and because the Admrs. failed to appear this day as cited, the judge decrees the Bond of Admin. be freed and Petitioner to give security to sue. Oaths 11/30/1774. Of Phinehas Underwood and Timothy Taylor. They will hold the Judge of Probate harmless in any action they commence on the Bond. DEPOSITION: Of: Joseph Barns and Charity Lund, of lawful age. They depose that they were near neighbors of Phinehas decd. a number of years before and at his death. Underwood raised 200 or 300 bushels of grain yearly on his farm. He left the bldgs. and fences in good repaid when he died. He left 2 yoke of oxen, a good horse, 3 or 4 cows, several young creatures and a good stock of farming utensils. They depose that the farm is now very much out of repair, the bldgs. very much gone to ruin and fences in general very bad. In reply to questions they stated: 1. The grain

and everything else now raised on the farm for a year or two would not pay to repair fencing; 2. They think that Robert Murdough did leave the farm in good repair when he died; 3. As to whether Murdough deserved any pay for repairs of bldgs. or breaking up land, they think the profits he received from the est. fully paid him for everything he paid out; 4. Yes, they think Underwood cut yearly sufficient hay to keep the cattle. They further say that they believe the personal est. and the debts due the est. would have been sufficient to pay all the est. debts. and to have brought up the children under age. Their sigs. DEPOSITION: Of Joseph Dix. Deposes that since Nathaniel Garfield has come to the est., he has cut a number of board logs on the est. of decd. by Garfield's order. He helped Garfield draw the logs to Merrimack River, helped raft and take them down river and delivered them to James Tyng. In reply to questions: 1. He thinks he helped cut and draw about 30 logs. 2. He thinks that Garfield did not keep honest accounts with him. His sig. DEPOSITION: Of John Stearns. He deposes: 1. He helped Gearfield cut and draw a considerable quantity of pine board logs of the est. of Underwood, some of which he helped to draw to the river, which were sent down river by Gearfield and some hauled to house of decd.; 2. He helped Col. Lytwyche draw a parcel of fencing stuff from est., which Gearfield told him he had sold to Lytwyche; 3. Daniel Bixbe, Nathaniel Parker and others cut the same; 4. He lived by Gearfield from the time Gearfield first came to est. until spring 1773 and he never saw Gearfield repair any bldgs., but, rather, let them go to ruin. When he, Stearns, first come to live by est., the fences were in good repair. Now they are out of repair In reply to questions: 1. He thinks near 30 logs were cut and hauled; 2. He thinks Col. Lytwyche drew away 70 or 80 lengths of fencing; 3. He does not remember that Gearfield ever hired a school master or mistress in house to teach decd.'s children; 4. He believes in times past Gearfield has not kept honest and just records. His general character has been that he does not. His sig. DEPOSITION: Of Thomas Lancy. He deposes that since Garfield has come to est. he helped draw a parcel of fencing stuff from the est. for Col. Lytwyche. Nathaniel Parker cut the same. He understood from Lytwyche he bought the fencing from Garfield. He also says there has been a great deal of timber cut and conveyed from the farm since Underwood's death. In reply to questions: 1. He thinks the personal est. would have paid all debts and brought up the children who were under age. The questioner noted that Lancy had lived with Underwood before and at the time of Underwood's death and with the Widow after the death of Underwood; 2. He thinks Garfield has not honest and just accounts. His sig. STATEMENT SENT WITH DEPOSITIONS: Dated Dunstable 11/17/1771. Of Robt. Fletcher, JP. He gave oath to all the deposings per notes and states that Nathl. Garfield and wife were notified but notpresent. Orig. Archives file (#2305) includes Admin. with Widow

Mary Underwood Admx., Invy. Warr., Invy. and Account Of Robert Murdoe and Mary his wife 1759, which includes main. 2 children.

2688. VANCE, JOHN (1777) #4370
EST. Londonderry yoeman decd. intestate. RENUN.: 6/7/1777. Of Sarah Vance, widow of John. Of Admin. through age and infirmity. States that two of the sons are considerably indebted to est. so she deems it inappropriate for them to administer. The third son refuses. Requests appointment of Moses Barnett, esq. Witness: (JA.?) Vance. ADMIN.: 6/25/1777. Admrs.: Moses Barnett, Londonderry esq. Bond L500.0.0. Sureties: Samuel Allison, Londonderry gent. and James Betton, Windham esq. Witnesses: Stephen March and Jabez Hoit. INVY.: Comm.: Andrew Clendinin and David Anderson. Value L222.8.3. Oaths 9/10/1777 Comm. to Matthew Thornton, JP. Oath 9/18/1777 Admr. to Wm. Parker, JP.

2689. VAUGHAN, ELLIOT (1758) A#2443
Portsmouth esq. decd. DIV. & APPR. WARR. (D21:381): 3/23/1772. Comm.: Samuel Livermore, esq.; Woodbury Langdon, Peter Pearse and John Wentworth, merchants and Joshua Brackett, physician, all of Portsmouth. To div. the real est. in 6 equal shares, with a double share to the oldest son, or appr. APPR. (D21:381): 6/9/1772. Value L1400.0.0. Oaths Comm. to William Parker, JP. DECREE SETTLEM. (D21:382). 6/24/1772. William Vaughan, oldest son, appearing and consenting, the real est. is settled on him, William to pay each of his co-heirs 1/6 part within a year, except those under 21, who are to be paid when they come of age. BOND (D21:382): 6/24/1772. Of William Vaughan. To pay co-heirs per Decree Settlem.. Orig. Archives file includes Admin., Invy., 2 licenses and Appr. Warr. 1758.

2690. VEACH, ELIZABETH (1783) #4945
EST. Portsmouth widow decd. testate. WILL: Drawn 9/26/1783. Legatees: Her children-Sarah Veach and Elizabeth Veach. Exex.-sister Sarah Cotton. Her mark. Witnesses: William White, Peirse Long and Mary Long. CERT. WILL (D27:322): 10/29/1783. Presented by Exex. And witnesses Peirse Long, esq. and Mary Long.

VEASEY. See also Veazey

2691. VEASEY, JONATHAN (1792) #5751
EST. Brentwood gent. decd. testate. WILL: Drawn 3/22/1790. Legatees: Wife-Bethiah; Sons-Jonathan and Jeremiah; Daus.-Mary Sanborn and Sarah Sanborn. Execs.-sons Jonathan and Jeremiah. His mark. Witnesses: Porter Kimball, Susa. Morgain and Coffin Sanborn. CERT. WILL

(D30:216): 3/21/1792. Presented by Execs. and witnesses Kimball and Sanborn. ADMIN.: 3/21/1792. Exec. Jonathan Veazey and Jeremiah Veazey, Brentwood yoemen. Bond L1000.0.0. Sureties: Coffin Sanborn, yoeman and Porter Kimball, esq., both of Brentwood. Witness Nathl. Parker. INVY.: Appr. 3/27/1792. Comm.: Porter Kimball, Jabez Smith and Ezekl. Godfrey. Value L247.16.5. Oaths 3/27/1792 Execs., Kimball and Smith to Ezekl. Godfrey, JP.

2692. VEASEY, THOMAS, ET. AL. (1791) #5657
PET. DIV. Of Brentwood yoeman. PETITION: 3/29/1791. Of Thomas Veazey, Brentwood yoeman. Requests div. of land and bldgs. in Stratham, part of the est. of Thomas Veasey decd., which he holds in equal shares with Nathaniel Wiggin, Stratham joiner. Order: 3/29/1791. For hearing, Wiggin to be notified. CAVEAT: 4/6/1791. Of Nathaniel Wiggin, Stratham joiner. Requests that the Div. made by the Comm. not be accepted until he has an opportunity to show why it should not be. DIV.: 4/5/1791. Comm.: Joseph Norris, Danl. Clark, Nich. Rowlings, Thomas Moore and Phinehas Merrill. To div. the land and bldgs. in Stratham in equal shares. Divisees: Thomas Veasey of Brentwood and Nathaniel Wiggin, Stratham joiner. Oaths 5/3/1791 Comm. to W. Parker, JP. Allowed 5/3/1791. Note: The est. of the Thomas Veasey referred to in Petition not identified.

2693. VEASEY, THOMAS (1797) #6367
EST. Of Stratham decd. testate. WILL: Drawn 7/13/1797. Legatees: Wife-Anne; Sons-Joshua, Simon and Thomas; Daus.-Anna Wedgewood and Olive Davis. Exex.- wife Anne. His sig. Witnesses: Josiah Bartlett, Joshua Wingate and Dudley L. Chase. CERT. WILL (D32:349): 8/19/1797. Presented by Exex. and witnesses Bartlett and Wingate. ADMIN.: 8/19/1797. Exex. Anne Veasey, Stratham widow. Bond $2,000.00. Sureties: Thomas Veasey, yoeman and Josiah Bartlett, physician, both of Stratham. Witnesses: Wm. P. Adams and Wm. Parker.

VEAZEY. See also Veasey

2694. VEAZEY, HENRY (1774) #4135
EST. Stratham yoeman decd. intestate. RENUN.: 11/29/1774. Of Hannah Vesey, mother of Henry. Of Admin. Requests appointment of her son Nathaniel Wiggin, Jr. ADMIN.: 11/30/1774. Admr. Nathaniel Wiggin Jr. Bond L1000.0.0. Sureties: Samuel Smith, yoeman and Joseph Fifield, gent., both of Stratham. Witnesses: John Pickering Jr. and Saml. Hale Jr. INVY. WARR.: 11/30/1774. Comm.: Samuel Lane, esq. and John Clark, yoeman, both of Stratham. INVY.: Appr. 2/22/1775. Value L36.6.2 1/2. Oaths 2/22/1775 Comm. and Admr. to judge.

2695. VEAZEY, JOHN (1772) #3961
EST. Stratham yoeman decd. testate. WILL: Of John of Stratham. Drawn 3/20/1772. Legatees: Wife-Hannah; Son-Samuel; Daus.-Mary, Anna, Hannah, Elisabeth and Lydia, all unmarried. Exex.-wife Hannah. His sig. Witnesses: Benjamin Leavitt, Thomas Veasey and Samuel Lane. CERT. WILL: 9/30/1772. Presented by Exex. and witnesses Leavitt and Lane, esq. INVY. WARR.: 9/30/1772. Comm.: Samuel Lane, Stratham esq. and Isaac Diman, Epping husbm. To be shown by Exex. Hannah Veazey of Epping, est. of John late of Epping. INVY.: Appr. 10/26/1772. Value L257.10.0. Oath 10/27/1772 Dimond to Joseph Sias, JP. Oath 12/30/1772 Lane to judge. Of est. of Joseph of Epping. Note: There is no explanation of why the both Stratham and Epping given as residences for John and no other John of Epping found.

2696. VIRGIN, EBENEZER (1789) #5499
EST: Of Concord decd. PETITION: 6/20/1787. Of Phinehas Virgin, Concord gent. For div. of land in Concord which was the est. of his father Ebenezer Virgin of Concord decd., held in common with his bros. Ebenezer and William and the children of his bro. John decd. Ebenezer Virgin, William Virgin and Chandler Lovejoy consent to the granting of the Petition. DIV. WARR.: 12/12/1787. Comm.: Timothy Walker, esq.; Reuben Kimball, John Bradley and John Chandler, gentlemen and Joseph Eastman Jr., all of Concord. To div. about 400 acres of land in Concord from est. of Ebenezer Virgin of Concord decd. among his heirs, giving 2 shares to Phinehas 2/6 and 1/4 of 1/6; to Ebenezer 1/6 and 1/4 of 1/6; to William 1/6 and 1/4 of 1/6 and to Heirs of John decd. 1/6 or 1/4 of 1/6. Chandler Lovejoy is appointed agent for the Heirs of John. DIV.: 12/1/1788. Divisees as in Warr. Oaths 2/3/1789 Kimball, Chandler, Eastman and Bradley to Timo. Walker, JP. Allowed. This file also contains a Petition and Div. which belong with #A3028 Ephraim Worthen (1763) and are placed there.

2697. VIRGIN: JOEL, JOHN, SALLY & SUSANNA (1792) #5807
GDP. Of the children of John Virgin, Concord yoeman decd. intestate. PETITION: 9/18/1792. Of Susanna, a minor over 14. She chooses Chandler Lovejoy, Concord yoeman, as her Gdn. PETITION: 9/18/1792. Of Betsy Virgin, widow of John. Requests appointment of Chandler Lovejoy, Concord yoeman, as Gdn. of her children Sally, John and Joel, minors under 14. On back: "Betsy Virgin recd. of Chandler Lovejoy L45.0.0. in full of what allowed for main. of her children under age. N.B. He had License 16 March last to sell real est. to that amount." GDP.: 9/19/1792. Of: Susanna, a minor over 14, and of Sally, John and Joel, minors under 14. Gdn. Chandler Lovejoy, Concord yoeman. Bond

L1000.0.0. Sureties: Abiel Foster, esq. and Obadiah Hall, gent., both of Canterbury. Witnesses: Huard Lanoiraix and W. Parker. PETITION: 8/5/1800. Of: John Virgin and Joel Virgin, minors over 14. They choose John Bradley, Concord esq. as their Gdn. Witnesses: John Lovejoy and Eben. Lovejoy.

2698. VIRGIN, JOHN (1787) #5278
EST. Concord yoeman decd. intestate. POWER ATTY.: 5/11/1787. Of Bettee Virgin, Concord widow. She grants Power of Atty. in all her affairs to Chandler Lovejoy, Concord yoeman. Witnesses: William Wheeler and Sarah Graham. ADMIN.: 6/20/1787. Admr. Chandler Lovejoy, Concord yoeman. Bond L1000.0.0. Sureties: Phinehas Virgin, Concord gent. and John Clough, Poplin yoeman. Witnesses: Mark Wiggin and W. Parker. INVY.: Appr. 12/1/1788. Comm.: John Chandler, Timo. Walker and John Bradley. Value L283.2.0. Oaths 2/4/1789 Walker and Bradley to Abiel Foster, JP. Oath 2/18/1789 Admr. to W. Parker, JP. DOWER WARR.: 2/18/1789. Comm.: Robert Ambross, Timothy Bradley, Nathaniel Eastman, John Chandler and Joseph Eastman Jr., all of Concord. Of Widow Bettee Virgin. DOWER: Oaths 1/13/1790 Ambrose, Chandler and Joseph Eastman to Jno. Stevens, JP. Allowed. ACCOUNT: 5/16/1792. Of Admr. Account includes main. 3 children. LICENSE (D30:244): 5/16/1792. To Admr. To sell real est. to amount of L45.0.0. PETITION: 5/9/1803. Of: John Bradley as Gdn. of John and Joel Virgin; Ebenezer Lovejoy and Sally Virgin, heirs. For div. of real est. Request Comm. of Jonathan Eastman, Jacob Eastman, John Eastman and Edmund Leavitt, gentlemen and Nathaniel Ambrose, husbm., all of Concord. Cert.: 1/16/1804. Of Chase, Lovejoy and Admr. That John Virgin decd. "made his exit" in 5/1786. PETITION: 5/9/1804. Of: John Bradley as Gdn. of Joel Virgin; Ebenezer Lovejoy and Sally Virgin, heirs. Also signed by John Virgin who is entitled to double share as oldest son. P.S. John Virgin decd. died 5/19/1786. Request same Comm. DIV.: Divisees: John Virgin (oldest son, double share); Joel Virgin, Sally Virgin and Ebenezer Lovejoy husb. of Susy decd. a dau. Oaths 1/13/1806 Jonathan Eastman, John Eastman, Jacob Eastman and Leavitt to Stephen Ambrose, JP. Allowed.

WADDLE. See also Wadleigh, Wadley, Wendell

2699. WADDLE, JAMES (1798) #6497 & (1798) #6497
EST. Londonderry yeoman decd. intestate. Note: All items from #6498 are recorded as John Waddel et. al. (1798) but belong here. RENUN. (#6498): 9/17/1798. Of Jean Waddel, widow of James. Of Admin. Requests appointment of James Wason Jr. of Chester. Witness M. Morse. PETITION (#6498): 9/20/1798. Of John Waddell, father of James of

Londonderry decd. Requests div. of land in Londonderry on which John now lives, of which James owned 1/2. Consent of James Wason Jr., Admr. est. James and Gdn. of his children. ADMIN. (D32:525): 9/25/1798. Admr. James Wason Jr. of Chester. Sureties: Joseph Blanchard and Isaac Hills, Chester esquires. DIV. WARR. (#6497): 9/25/1798. Comm.: Stephen Chase, esq.; and Stephen Morse, yoeman, both of Chester; Nathaniel Brown and Nathaniel Jewett, yoemen and Moody Morse, esq., all of Londonderry. To div. land partly in Londonderry and partly in Chester held in common and in equal shares by John Waddel of Londonderry and heirs of James Waddell of Londonderry decd. PETITION (#6498): 10/9/1798. Of Admr. and Nathaniel Brown. For div. of land in Londonderry held in common by heirs of James Waddel and Nathaniel Brown. Witnesses: John Grimes and M. Morse. DIV. WARR. (#6497): 10/16/1798. Comm.: William White and Stephen Chase, esquires and Stephen Morse, gent., all of Chester; Moody Morse, esq. and Nathaniel Jewett, yoeman, both of Londonderry. To div. land in Londonderry held in common and in equal shares, by Nathaniel Brown of Londonderry and heirs of James Waddel decd. INVY. (D32:534): Comm.: William White, Jona. Adams and Thos. Jewett. Value $1,431.29. Oaths 10/24/1798 Comm. to Josiah Flagg, JP. DIV.(#6498): 10/18/1798. Same Comm. Divisees: John Waddell and Heirs of James Waddell. Of land that lately belonged to the est. of Capt. James Blair of Londonderry decd. Oaths 10/19/1798 Stephen Morse, Chase, Moody Morse and Brown to Willm. White, JP. Allowed 4/16/1800. ACCOUNT (#6497): 4/16/1800. Of Admr. Allowed 4/16/1803. Account includes main. one child. PETITION (#6497): 4/20/1808. Of Admr. For Comm. to view real est. as it cannot be div. Granted with Comm.: Wm. White, David Clark and Robert Clark. Note: This file also includes the Dower of Ruth Colby which belongs with #6500 Thomas Colby (1798) which is recorded there. File #6497 includes a Petition and 2 Depositions and #6498 2 Depositions, all of which belong with a Gdp. of a James Waddle of 1826 and are not part of this book.

WADDELL. See also Waddel, Waddle, Wadleigh

2700. WADDELL, JOHN ET. AL. (1798) #6498
See #6497 James Waddel (1798)

2701. WADDLE, SUSANNA (1786) #5205
EST. Windham widow decd. RENUN.: 6/27/1786. Of John McCay. Of Admin. of est. his mother. Requests appointment of James Betton, esq. ADMIN.: 6/27/1786. Admr. James Betton, Windham esq. Bond L1000.0.0. Sureties: Alexander McCay, cordwainer and George Clark, yoeman, both of Windham. Witnesses: John Betton and Elizabeth Betton.

INVY.: Comm.: David Gregg. William Gregg Jr. and James Davidson. Value L54.8.6. Oaths 7/4/1786 William Gregg Jr. and Davidson to James Betton, JP. Oath 2/21/1787 Admr. to W. Parker.

WADLEIGH. See also Waddle

2702. WADLEIGH, EDWARD (1785) #5097
EST. Exeter cordwainer decd. ADMIN.: 4/21/1785. Admr. John Wadleigh, Exeter yoeman. Bond L1000.0.0. Sureties: Benjamin Lamson, innholder and Simeon Ladd, gent., both of Exeter. Witnesses: Theophilus Smith and Nathl. Parker. INVY.: Comm.: Jeremiah Leavitt, Joseph Osborne and Jabez Dodge. Value L19.1.5. Oaths 7/19/1785 Leavitt and Dodge to W. Parker, Reg. LIST CLAIMS: Total L9.19.8. CLAIMS WARR.: 11/3/1785. Comm.: Jeremiah Leavitt, hatter and Stephen Fogg, joiner, both of Exeter. CLAIMS: Total L48.14.6. Oaths 4/19/1786 Comm. to W. Parker, JP. LICENSE (D28:520): 4/19/1786. To Admr. To sell sufficient real est. to pay debts. ACCOUNT: Of Admr. Allowed 1/17/1788. PROP. & SETTLM.: Claims L48.14.6. Amount to be proportioned L1.14.10. Allowed 2/20/1788 with order to Admr. To pay.

2703. WADLEIGH: EPHRAIM, HENRY & SUSANNA (1788) #5334
GDP. Of the children of Thomas Wadleigh of Hampstead decd. GDP.: 2/20/1788. Of Susanna, a minor over 14 and of Henry, a minor under 14. Gdn. Moses Atwood, Hampstead husbm. Bond L500.0.0. Sureties: Aaron Wadley of Hampstead and Thomas Wadley of Sutton, Hillsborough Co., husbandmen. Witness W. Parker. GDP.: 2/20/1788. Of Ephraim, a minor over 14. Gdn. Thomas Wadley, Sutton, Hillsborough Co. husbm. Bond L500.0.0. Sureties: Moses Atwood and Aaron Wadley, Hampstead husbandmen. Witnesses: W. Parker and Nathl. Parker. BOND: 2/14/1794. Of Moses Atwood, Hampstead yoeman, Gdn. of Henry Wadley of Hampstead. Bond L1000.0.0. By an Act of the NH General Court, Atwood is permitted to sell at public auction his ward's real est., the proceeds of the sale to be at interest for the benefit of the minor until he becomes of age, when Gdn. to account to him. Sureties: John Calfe and John Hogg Jr., Hampstead esquires.

2704. WADLEIGH, JOHN (1776) #4257
EST. Kingston blacksmith and yoeman decd. intestate. ADMIN.: 7/31/1776. Admx. Mary Wadleigh, Kingston widow. Bond L1000.0.0. Sureties: Thomas Wadleigh, yoeman and Benjamin Little Jr., esq., both of Hampstead. Witnesses: Nathl. Parker and W. Parker. INVY.: Appr. 10/281776. Comm.: Benjm. Little Jr., Edward Sleeper and William Sleeper. Value L447.19.1. Oaths 10/28/1776 Comm. to Samuel Little, JP.

Oath 10/30/1776 Admx. to judge. CLAIMS WARR.: 10/30/1776. Comm.: Samuel Philbrick and Simmonds Seccombe, Kingston esquires. DOWER: 11/7/1776. Comm.: Benja. Little Jr., John Mills, Richard Hubbard Jr., Edward Sleeper and William Sleeper. Of Widow Mary Wadleigh. Oaths 11/7/1776 Comm. to Ebenr. Stevens, JP. Allowed 4/30/1777. CLAIMS: 8/28/1777. Total 1598.9.9.3. Oaths 8/28/1777 Comm. to W. Parker, JP. LICENSE: 9/24/1777. To Admx. To sell 2/3 of the real est. to pay debts. ACCOUNT: 12/31/1777. Of Admx. Allowed 12/31/1777. PROP. & SETTLM.: Claims L598.9.9.3. Amount to be proportioned L447.14.0. Allowed 3/25/1778 with order to Admx. to pay. PETITION: 3/11/1811. Of Daniel Wadleigh, Kingston esq., son of decd. States that Mary Wadleigh, Admx., settled est. as insolvent as provided by law, but she had been granted her Dower, which at the time of settlm. could not be sold. Admx. has since died and there is no one to admin. the Dower. Requests Admin. D.B.N. Granted. ADMIN. D.B.N.: 3/11/1811. Admr. d.b.n. Daniel Wadleigh, Kingston esq. Bond $3,000.00. Sureties: Benjamin Kimball, gent. and Benjamin Badger, husbm., both of Kingston. Witness John J. Parker. INVY. WARR.: 3/11/1811. Comm.: Matthias Bartlett, Newton esq.; John Webster and Daniel Peaslee, Kingston gentlemen. INVY.: 3/15/1811. Value $858.00. Oaths 3/15/1811 Webster and Peaslee to Matthias Bartlett, JP. Oath 3/18/1811 Admr. d.b.n. to Wm. Parker, JP. PETITION: 3/18/1811. Of Admr. d.b.n. For License. LICENSE: 3/18/1811. To Admr. d.b.n. To sell all the real est. ACCOUNT: Of Admr. d.b.n. Allowed 11/16/1814, there being no objections. PROP. & SETTLM.: Claims $1,996.35. Amount to be proportioned $1,082.83. Allowed 12/19/1814 with order to Admr. d.b.n. to pay. Note: This file also contains an 1848 Petition for Div. by Dorothy A.H. Rowe of Haverhill, MA and Daniel Wadleigh of Kingston, Gdns. of Daniel Wadleigh 3d. For div. of the homestead farm of which they are only heirs. And Div. This must be the est. of a later John Wadleigh as the Licenses of 1811 permitted all land of this est. to be sold to settle claims and no other John of Kingston has been found.

2705. WADLEIGH, JOHN (1795) #6120
EST. Hampton Falls yoeman decd. testate. WILL: Drawn 4/29/1795. Legatees: Wife-Hannah; Daus.-Leah Wadleigh and Hannah Wadleigh. Exex.-wife Hannah. His sig. Witnesses: James Sanborn, Benjamin Sanborn Jr. and Joseph Lawrence. CERT. WILL (D32:17): 7/13/1795. Presented by Exec. and witnesses James Sanborn and Benjamin Sanborn Jr. ADMIN.: 7/13/1795. Exex. Hannah Wadleigh, Hampton Fall widow. Bond $3,000.00. Sureties: Benjamin Sanborn Jr. of Hampton Falls and Joseph Wadleigh Jr. of Kensington, yoemen. Witnesses: John Prentice Jr. and W. Parker. INVY.: Comm.: Nathan Brown, Jeremiah Lane and Peter

Tilton. Value $761.1.3. Oaths 10/16/1795 Lane and Tilton to Caleb Tilton, JP. OATH TO INVY.: 10/16/1795 Admx. to Caleb Tilton, JP.

2706. WADLEIGH, JOSEPH (1779) #4538
EST. Kensington millwright decd. testate. WILL: Drawn 3/13/1765. Legatees: Sons-Theophilus, Benjamin, James and Joseph; Dau.-Lydia Robinson; Granddaus.-Mary Coffin and Sarah Coffin (sisters, their mother apparently dead). Exec.-son Joseph. His sig. Witnesses: Meshech Weare, Adner Sanborn Jr. and Timothy Sanborn. CERT. WILL (D25:93): 4/28/1779. Presented by Exec. and witnesses Weare and Abner Sanborn. Note: He bequeaths to his granddau. Mary all his wife's clothing at her decease but does not otherwise mention his wife in Will. INVY. (D25:204): Comm.: John Lane, esq.; Samuel Prescott and Abraham Sanborn. Value L1740.8.0. Oaths 7/20/1779 Lane and Sanborn to Benjamin Rowe, JP. Oath 7/28/1779 Exec. to judge.

2707. WADLEIGH, JOSEPH (1792) #5752
EST. Brentwood yoeman decd. testate. WILL: Drawn 1/6/1787. Legatees: Son-Joseph; Daus.-Hannah wife of Caleb Smith of Raymond, Anna wife of Joseph Woodman of Kingston and Rachel Wadleigh; His sister Abagail Wadleigh. Exec.-son Joseph. Witnesses; Daniel Clark, Edward Stevens and Saml. Hobart. CERT. WILL (D30:214): 3/21/1792. Presented by Exec. and witnesses Clark and Stevens. ADMIN.: 3/21/1792. Exec. Joseph Wadleigh, Brentwood yoeman. Bond L1000.0.0. Sureties: Daniel Clark, gent. and Edward Stevens, yoeman, both of Brentwood. Witness Nat Parker. INVY.: Appr. 5/28/1792. Comm.: Nathaniel Stevens and Samuel Stevens. Value L460.18.3. Oaths 6/19/1792 Comm. and Exec. to judge.

2708. WADLEIGH, THOMAS (1787) #5237
EST. Hampstead yeoman decd. testate. WILL: Drawn 9/8/1787. Legatees: Wife-Miriam; Sons-Aaron, Henry, Benjamin, Jonathan, Joseph, Thomas, John, Moses and Ephraim; Daus.-Judith Attwood, Betty Wodley and Susanna Wodley. Execs.-son Aaron and Amos Whitmore. His mark. Witnesses: Amos Whitmore, Moses Brown and James Brown. CERT. WILL (D29:153): 11/21/1787. Presented by Execs. (Sig. Wodley) and all witnesses. INVY.: Appr. 3/18/1788. Comm.: Jonathan Eastman, Moses Brown and Robert Emerson. Value L487.4.6. Oaths 3/20/1787 Eastman and Brown to John Calfe, JP. Oath 4/16/1788 One of Execs. to W. Parker. CITATION: 10/15/1790. To Execs. To appear and exhibit Account so est. may be settled according to Will. ACCOUNT: Of Execs. Allowed 7/21/1790. DIV. WARR.: 7/21/1790. Comm.: John Calfe and Jonathan Eastman, esquires; Job Kent and Robert Emerson, gentlemen; and Moses

Brown, yoeman, all of Hampstead. To divide the real est. according to Will. DIV.: 7/27/1790. Divisees: Widow Miriam Wodley, Aaron Wodley and Henry Wodley. Oaths 8/3/1790 Kent, Brown, Emerson and Eastman to John Calfe, JP. Allowed.

2709. WAIT, SAMUEL (1783) #4883
GDP. Of the son of Samuel Wait of Newburyport, Essex Co., MA. GDP.: 3/8/1783. Of Samuel, a minor over 14, now residing in Hawke. Gdn. Thomas Page, Hawke husbm. Bond L500.0.0. Surety Elisha Hook, Poplin yoeman. Witnesses: Jethro Sanborn and Israel Hook. Note: The card catalog incorrectly lists this Gdp. as Thomas Wait, probably a clerk's error using the name of the Gdn.

2710. WAIT, THOMAS (1783) #4883
See #4883 Samuel Wait (1783)

2711. WALDRON: JAMES, MARY AND SAMUEL (1772) #3907
GDP. Of the children of Richard Waldron of Dover decd. GDP: 1/29/1772. Of Mary, a minor under 14. Gdn. John Waldron, Dover husbm. Bond L500.0.0. Sureties: Joseph Waldron and John Conner, Dover husbandmen. Witnesses: Jno. Hayes and Saml. Hale Jr. GDP: 1/29/1772. Of Samuel and James, minors over 14. Gdn. John Waldron, Dover husbm. Bond L500.0.0. Sureties: John Conner and Joseph Waldron, Dover husbandmen. Witnesses: Mark Wiggin and Jno. Hayes.

2712. WALDRON, CAPT. RICHARD (1772) #3925
EST. Dover gent decd. testate. WILL: Drawn 8/26/1771. Legatees: Wife Elizabeth; Sons-John, Richard, Samuel, Joseph and James; Daus.-Hannah Hayes, Elizabeth Shapleigh and Mary Waldron. He wills his negro girl Peggy to his wife. Execs.: sons John and Joseph. His sig. Witnesses: Samuel Ambrose, John Conner and Thomas Wb. Waldron. CERT. WILL (D21:285): 1/29/1772. Presented by Execs. And witnesses Ambrose and Conner. INVY.: Comm.: Thos. Wb. Waldron, esq. and Nehemiah Kimbal. Value L3018.4.8 1/2. Oaths 4/25/1772 Comm. to Otis Baker, JP. DIV.: 1/2/1773. Comm.: Ebr. Thompson, John Plummer and Job Clements. To div. the real est. according to Will. Divisees: Mrs. Elizabeth Atkinson, wife of Joseph Atkinson, esq., late widow of Richard Waldron; Joseph Waldron; Richard Waldron, Samuel Waldron and James Waldron. Oaths 1/14/1773 Plummer and Thompson, esquires and Clemens to judge. Allowed no objections being made.

2713. WALDRON, RICHARD (1787) #5238
EST. Portsmouth yoeman decd. testate. WILL: Drawn 10/9/1777. Legatees: Wife-Sarah; Bro:-Daniel Waldron and his heirs, or, his bros. and sisters or their heirs who survive Daniel. Execs.-Wife Sarah and Dr. Hall Jackson. Specifically revokes the Will he made when he went to sea and was unmarr., which his uncle George Waldron has put on record. His sig. Witnesses: Moses Brewster, John Melcher and John Dennet. Proved 11/27/1787 on oaths of witnesses Brewster and Dennet and presented by Execs. CERT. WILL (D29:152): 11/1/1787. INVY.: Appr. 12/3/1787. Comm.: Sam. Sherburne; John Wendell, esq. and Robert Ham. Value L1204.9.6. Oaths 12/4/1787 Comm. to Saml. Penhallow, JP. Oath 2/20/1788 Sarah Waldron, an Exec., to W. Parker, JP. LIST OF CLAIMS; 9/17/1788. Of Hall Jackson, an Exec. Total L842.8.11. He notes that many claims have not been submitted and he has reason to believe several large accounts are unjust. PETITION: 9/17/1788. Of Execs. For Comm. of Insolvency. PETITION: 4/20/1793. Of Hall Jackson, surviving Exec. Requests that Thomas Shannon, Dover, esq. and Gdn. of the heir or divisee of the Will, be cited to show cause why a License should not be granted. CLAIMS WARR.: 9/17/1788. Comm.: Elisha Hill and Jeremiah Libbey, esquires and Samuel Sherburne, yoeman, all of Portsmouth. Claims: 5/18/1789. Total L257.1.5 1/4. Oaths 5/18/1789 Sherburne and Hill, affirm. Libbey to Geo. Gains, JP. On back says: "Claims on Waldron est. as adjusted by Commissioners. ACCOUNT: 5/20/1793. Of Hall Jackson, Exec. Notes a receipt for money from the Gdn. of heir. Danl. Waldron accepts the Account and thanks Exec. 5/28/1793. Allowed 5/29/1793, the heir having expressed his approbation.

2714. WALKER, ELIZABETH (1771) No#
EST. Boston, Suffolk Co., MA gentlewoman decd. testate. WILL (D23:558): Drawn 4/24/1770. Legatees: John Walker who her bro. John decd. supposed and took to be his natural son and who sometime lived with bro. and is now abroad; If John dies or does not live soberly and viruously, his bequest goes to-Abigail Royal, Rebecca Byles, Sarah Taylor and William Taylor, children of her late friend Hon. William Taylor, esq. decd and to Abigail Taylor and Gillam Taylor, children of Dr. Gillam Taylor, Boston physician decd. who was son of William Taylor, esq. decd. Exec.-friend Joshua Green, Boston, Suffolk Co., MA merchant. Her mark. Witnesses: Saml. Quincy, Edward Green and Elizabeth Cromartie. Proved 3/19/1771 before Hon. Foster Hutchingson, esq., Judge Probate, Suffolk Co., MA, having been presented by Exec. and witnesses Quincy and Cromartie. Cert. as a true copy by Jno. Cotton, Reg. Copy examined by W. Parker, Reg., Rockingham Co. Probate.

2715. WALKER, GIDEON (1793) #5931
EST. Newington husbm. decd. testate. WILL: Drawn 4/27/1793. Legatees: Wife-Eleana; Sons-Samuel, Mark and Seth; Children of his dau. Elizabeth Thompson decd.; Children of his dau. Nancy Williams decd.; Grandson-John Walker son of John Walker decd.; Elizabeth Slate his servant maid. Exex.-wife Eleana. His mark. Witnesses: Noah Rawlings, Edward Park and John Shackford. CERT. WILL (D31:87): 10/16/1793. Presented by Exex. and all witnesses. ADMIN.: 10/16/1793. Exex. Eleanor Walker, Newington widow. Bond L1000.0.0. Sureties: Noah Rawlings, Newington yoeman and Seth Walker, Portsmouth miller. Witnesses: Saml. Sherburne and W. Parker. INVY.: 1/8/1794. Comm.: Richdd. Pickering, John Shackford and Saml. Rawlings. Value L360.12.0. Oaths 1/20/1794 Comm. and Exec. to Ephraim Pickering, JP.

2716. WALKER, SAMUEL (1789) #5420
GDP. Of the son of Nathaniel Walker, Portland, Cumberland Co. MA/ME tanner decd. GDP.: 2/18/1789. Of Samuel. Gdn. Theophilus Smith, Exeter esq. Bond L1000.0.0. Sureties: Ebenezer Chadwick, cordwainer and David Boardman, blacksmith, both of Exeter. Witness Nathl. Parker.

2717. WALKER, REV. TIMOTHY (1782) #4856
EST. Concord clerk decd. testate. WILL: Drawn 8/10/1782. Legatees: Son-Timothy Jr., esq.; Daus.-Sarah Thompson and Mary Goss; Granddau.-Judith Rolfe. Exec.-son Timothy. His sig. Witnesses: Abiel Foster, James Walker and Philip Abbot. CERT. WILL (D27:28): 9/13/1782. Presented by Exec. and witnesses Foster and Abbot.

WALLACE. See also Wallis, Walls

2718. WALLACE, GEORGE (1776) #4218
EST. Londonderry yoeman decd. PETITION: 2/25/1776. Of Mary Wallace, widow of George. To allow admin. to her and Col. Robert Moore. ADMIN.: 3/27/1776. Admrs.: Mary Wallace, widow and Robert Moore, yoeman, both of Londonderry. Bond L1000.0.0. Sureties: Stephen Holland, esq. And George Moore, yoeman, both of Londonderry. Witnesses: Richard Holland and John Moore. INVY. WARR.: 3/27/1776. Comm.: John Crombie, gent. and James Ramsey, yoeman, both of Londonderry. INVY.: Appr. 3/4/1776 (sic.). Value not tallied. Esti. L578.0.0+. Oaths 6/24/1776 1771 Comm. to Matthew Thornton, JP. Oath 6/26/1776 Admx. to judge. ACCOUNT: Of Admrs. Allowed 4/30/1777.

2719. WALLACE, GEORGE (1795) #6102.
See George Walls #6104 (1795)

2720. WALLACE, JAMES (1792) #5766
EST. Londonderry gent. decd. testate. WILL: Drawn 3/28/1791. Legatees: Wife-Mary; Sons-Robert, William and James; Grandson-James Wallace son of Thomas Wallace decd.. Ref. to his bro. Robert decd.; Son-in-law-Thomas Patterson. Execs.-sons Robert and William. His sig. Witnesses: Samuel Fisher, Joshua Sawyer and James Betton. CERT. WILL (D30:234): 4/19/1792. Presented by Execs. and witnesses Fisher and Betton, esq. ADMIN.: 4/19/1792. Execs.: Robert Wallace and William Wallace, Henniker, Hillsborough Co. esquires. Bond L1000.0.0. Sureties: James Betton of Windham and Thomas Patterson of Londonderry, gentlemen. Witnesses: Samuel Fisher and W. Parker. INVY.: Appr. 4/20/1792. Comm.: John Bell, John Dwinell and Wm. Anderson. Value not tallied. Esti. L311.0.0+. Oaths 4/20/1792 Dwinell, Anderson and Execs. to John Bell, JP.

2721. WALLACE, CAPT. JAMES (1793) #5885
EST. Londonderry gent. decd. intestate. ADMIN.: 4/17/1793. Admx. Mary Wallace, Londonderry widow. Bond L1000.0.0. Sureties: John Anderson, Londonderry husbm. and James Betton, Windham esq. Witnesses: Jona. Poor and N. Parker. PETITION: 10/22/1794. Of John Anderson, one of Admx.'s bondsmen and husb. of only child of decd., who has issue of her own. States that the Admx. has neglected to return an Invy. and to carry on Admin., whereby est. is decreasing in value and Petitioner is unable to settle his own Account with est. Requests Admx. be cited to return an Invy. and Account so Bond Admin. may be released. Order: 10/22/1794. That Admx. be cited to appear and exhibit Account and Invy. INVY.: Appr. 5/3/1793 (sic.). Comm.: John Barker, James Alexander and James Betton. Value L487.14.11. Oaths 5/4/1793 Barker, Alexander and Admx. to James Betton, JP. ADDL. INVY.: Value L17.8.0. Oaths 4/15/1795 Alexander and Barker to James Betton, JP. DOWER: 11/9/1795. Comm.: John Bell, Joseph Gregg, Thomas Patterson, Andrew Mack and David McKeen. Of Widow Mary Wallace. Oaths 11/9/1795 Gregg, Patterson, Mack and McKeen to John Bell, JP.

2722. WALLACE, JOHN (1778) #4490
EST. Londonderry yoeman decd. testate. PETITION: 9/28/1778. Of: Rebecca Wallace, William Clark, John Wallace, Anna Wallace, Matw. Wallace, Janet Dickey, Willm. Wallace, William Vance, Sarah Vance, Ann Clark and Jene Wallace, heirs of John Wallace decd. Samuel Wallace, son of decd. named Exec. in Will, has died. They request appointment of oldest son James Wallace. WILL: Drawn 5/4/1765. Legatees: Sons-James, Samuel, William and John; Daus.-Rebecca Wallace, Jennet Dickey wife of Matthew Dickey, Ann Clark wife of William Clark, esq. and Sarah

Vance wife of William Vance; Granddaus.-Jenny Wallace dau. of James Wallace and Annas Wallace dau. of John Wallace; Grandson-John Wallace son of William Wallace. Exec.-son Samuel. His sig. Witnesses: Richard Humphrey, Andrew Todd and Asa Liveston. CERT. WILL: 10/28/1778. Presented by James Wallace, Londonderry gent., the Exec. named being dead, and witness Andrew Todd. Robert Humphrey is now living in the state of New York and Asa Liveston is now dead. ADMIN.: 10/28/1778. Exec. Capt. James Wallace, Londonderry gent. Bond L500.0.0. Sureties: John Bell and John Pinkerton, Londonderry esquires. Witnesses: Wm. Parker Jr. and Wm. Parker. INVY.: Comm.: John Aiken, yoeman; Thomas Wallace Jr. and James Aiken, gentlemen. Value L737.10.0. Oaths 11/19/1778 Comm. and on 12/12/1778 Exec. to John Bell, JP. ACCOUNT: 4/16/1788. Of Exec., wholly consolidated by the scale of depreciation. Allowed 4/16/1788.

2723. WALLACE, JOHN (1790) #5535
EST. Londonderry cordwainer decd. RENUN.: Of Jenet Wallace, widow of John. Of Admin. She has agreed to Samuel Cherry as Admin. ADMIN.: 4/22/1790. Admr. Samuel Cherry, Londonderry esq. Bond L500.0.0. Sureties: John Morrison and James Choate, Londonderry yoemen. Witnesses: Thomas Cotton and N. Parker. INVY.: Appr. 7/17/1790. Comm.: John Morrison and James Choate. Value L29.13.6. Oaths 8/18/1790 Comm. and Admr. to W. Parker, JP. PETITION: 8/18/1790. Of Admr. For Comm. Insolvency. Gives list claims of L35.7.0. CLAIMS: Dated by clerk 12/15/1790. Comm.: Moses L. Neal and John W. Corr?). Total L27.5.4 3/4. DOWER: Dated by clerk 4/1791. Comm.: John Morrison, Robt. Barnet and James Choate. Of Widow Jenet Wallace. Noted as not sworn to but recorded. ADMIN. D.B.N.: 8/17/1796. Admr. d.b.n. John Morrison, Londonderry esq. Bond L1000.0.0. Sureties: Robert Clindenin and Jonathan Holms, Londonderry yoemen. Witnesses: W. Parker and T. C. Blodget. INVY.: Appr. 4/17/1797. Comm.: James Choate, John Warner and James Moor. Value $32.66, being the Dower. Oaths 4/19/1797 Admr. d.b.n. and Comm. to Saml. Tenney, JP. LICENSE: 4/19/1797. To Admr. d.b.n. To sell reversion of the Dower.

2724. WALLACE, CAPT. ROBERT (1782) #4868
EST. Londonderry gent. decd. intestate. PETITION: 12/24/1782. Of Thomas Wallace. States that his bro. Robert Wallace of Londonderry recently died intestate. Assuming that he has an equal right to Admin., requests that it be granted to him or in conjunction with any other legal heir as judge sees fit. As his own health prohibits him from attending court, requests that Admin. be granted to John Prentice, Londonderry esq. Witness James Macgregore. ADMIN.: 12/25/1782. Admrs.: James Betton,

Windham esq. and Thomas Wallace Jr. of Londonderry. Bond L2000.0.0. Sureties: John Bell, esq. and Deacon Saml. Fisher, both of Londonderry. Witnesses: Henry Campbell and Jos. Mark. INVY.: Comm.: John Bell, Saml. Fisher and Henry Campbell. Value L565.7.4. Oaths 3/3/1783 Comm. to James Betton, JP. Oaths 3/3/1783 Admrs. to John Bell, JP. PETITION: Dated by clerk 1/1783. Of James Wallace. States that Margaret Wallace, Widow of Capt. Robert Wallace, is advanced in years and desires that James Betton, esq. May take admin. in her stead. She is also asks that the oldest son Thomas Wallace be co-Admr. with Betton. He supposes that he has the right next to the Widow and asks that his oldest son Thomas Wallace take admin. with Betton. Statement: 12/31/1782. Of James Wallace Jr. States he is an heir to est. and joins with his bro. James Wallace in requesting Admin. be granted to James Betton and Thomas Wallace Jr. ACCOUNT: Of Admrs. Allowed 4/16/1788. Note: The following Pet. And Div. Warr. recorded as #5897 Samuel Dodge (1793) belong here. PETITION: 4/16/1793. Of Samuel Dodge of Londonderry. For div. of the farm formerly owned by Capt. Robert Wallace decd. of which he owns 14/15 shares and James Wallace, a minor, owns 1/15 share. Samuel Dodge and Wm. Wallace on behalf of the child request a Comm. of John Bell, esq.; James Nesmith; Elder Saml. Fisher, Wm. Anderson and John Dwinel. DIV. WARR.: 5/17/1793. Comm. as requested. Of the est. of Capt. Robert Wallace of Londonderry decd. Divisees: Samuel Dodge of Londonderry and James Wallace, a minor, son of Thomas Wallace of Londonderry decd. DIV.: Comm. has set off the share belonging to James and all the rest belongs to Dodge as defined in Dodge's deed from the heirs of est. Wallace. Oaths 8/6/1793 Fisher, Nesmith, Anderson and Dwinell to John Bell, JP. Allowed 4/7/1799.

2725. WALLACE, SAMUEL (1778) #4491
EST. Of Londonderry decd. intestate. RENUN.: 9/28/1778. Of Lettitia Wallace, widow of Samuel. Of Admin. Requests appointment of Capt. James Wallace. Witnesses: Andrew Todd and James Nesmith. ADMIN.: 10/28/1778. Admr. James Wallace, Londonderry gent. Bond L500.0.0. Sureties: John Bell and John Pinkerton, Londonderry esquires. Witness Wm. Parker Jr. INVY.: Comm.: John Aiken, yoeman, James Aiken, gent. and Thomas Wallace Jr. Value L1470.11.0. Oaths 11/19/1778 Comm. and on 12/12/1778 Admr. to John Bell, JP. ACCOUNT: Of Admr. who notes that he has on hand 198 paper dollars old emission and Account is on depreciated scale. Allowed 4/16/1788. SETTLM.: 8/21/1793. Of: Robert Clark, an heir, and on behalf of the other heirs and Mary Wallace, Admx. of est. of Capt. James Wallace of Londonderry decd., who was the Admr. of est. Samuel Wallace. They have agreed that during his lifetime Capt. James Wallace did in some measure settle the est. of Samuel decd., of

which he was Admr.. Acknowledged in court 8/21/1793 and attested to by W. Parker, Reg.

2726. WALLACE, SPENCER (1793) #5903
EST. Exeter shipwright decd. ADMIN.: 6/1/1793. Admx. Sarah Wallace, Exeter widow. Bond L1000.0.0. Sureties: Benjamin Conner, trader and Josiah Nelson, blacksmith, both of Exeter. Witness Nathl. Parker. INVY.: Appr. 6/29/1793. Comm.: Simeon Ladd, Benja. Conner and Edmd. Pearson. Value L90.9.5. Oaths 6/29/1793 Comm. and on 4/3/1794 Admx. to W. Parker, Reg. PETITION: 4/3/1794. Of Admx. For License. Gives list claims of L11.9.1. Granted and main. one child. LICENSE (D31:231): 4/3/1794. To Admx. To sell real est. to amount of L12.0.0.

2727. WALLACE, THOMAS (1789) #5452
EST. Londonderry gent. decd. testate. WILL: Drawn 4/30/1789. Legatees: Bro.-James; Sister-Mary Wallace; Widow Lydia Sergent; Betsey dau. of Widow Lydia Sergent; Children of his bro. James-Maj. Robert Wallace, William Wallace and Elizabeth Patterson; Lt. John Smith of Henniker, Hillsborough Co. and James Thomas Smith his son; Thomas Wallace son of Robert Wallace; Thomas Patterson son of Elisabeth Patterson. Execs.- Deacon Samuel Fisher, Deacon Thomas Patterson and Lt. John Smith. His sig. Witnesses: Ebenezer Fisher, John Fisher and Matthew Taylor. CERT. WILL (D29:273): 5/20/1789. Presented by Execs. Patterson, Smith and Robert Wallace (sic.) and witnesses Ebenr. Fisher and John Fisher. ADMIN.: 5/20/1789. Execs.: Samuel Fisher, Londonderry yoeman and John Smith of Henniker, Hillsborough Co., two of Execs. named in Will. Bond L1000.0.0. Sureties: Ebenezer Fisher and John Fisher, Londonderry yoemen. Witnesses: Nathl. Parker and W. Parker. INVY.: Appr. 5/25/1789. Comm.: Wm. Anderson and Robert Dickey. Value L433.11.7. Oaths 12/15/1789 Comm. and on 12/17/1789 Dea. Samuel Fisher and Dea. Thomas Patterson, esquires, Execs. to James Betton, JP. ACCOUNT (D33:69): 4/17/1799. Of Execs. Allowed 4/17/1799. The following Bond found in #5553 Thomas Wallace (1790) belongs here. BOND: 11/24/1797. Of: Robert Wallace, Henniker, Hillsborugh Co. esq., Gdn. of his son Thomas; John Smith of Henniker, Gdn. of his son Thomas; Thomas Patterson of Londonderry, Gdn. of his son Thomas Jr., gentlemen. Bond $3.000.00. To account for proceeds from sale of land in Londonderry lately the property of Thomas Wallace and of Capt. Robert Wallace decd. now held in common by their wards, all minors under 21, by License granted by the Superior Court. Witnesses: William Choate and Nathl. Parker to sig. of Wallace, John Morrison and Nicholas Emery to sigs. of Smith and Patterson.

2728. WALLACE, THOMAS (1790) #5533
EST. Londonderry yoeman decd. testate. WILL: Drawn 2/21/1790. Legatees: His father and mother; Son-James, who he puts under care of his bro. Wm. until 21; His 3 bros. and sister. Execs.-Bros. Robert and William. His sig. Witnesses: William Anderson, Jean Willson and James Betton. CERT. WILL (D29:359): 4/21/1790. Presented by Execs. and witnesses Betton, esq. and Anderson. ADMIN.: 4/21/1790. Execs.: William Wallace and Robert Wallace, Henniker, Hillsborough Co. gentlemen. Bond L1000.0.0. Sureties: William Anderson, Londonderry yoeman and James Betton, Windham esq. Witness N. Parker. INVY.: Appr. 5/25/1790. Comm.: James Betton, Wm. Anderson and Samuel Fisher. Value L363.16.4. Oaths 5/26/1790 Fisher, Anderson and Admrs. (Maj. Robt.) to James Betton, JP. ACCOUNT: Of Admrs. Allowed 4/17/1799. Note: this file also includes a Bond which belongs with #5452 Thomas Wallace (1789) and is recorded there.

2729. WALLINGFORD: OLIVE AND SAMUEL (1771) #3888
GDP. Of the children of Thomas Wallingford of Somersworth decd. GDP: 11/11/1771. Of: Olive and Samuel minors over 14. Gdn. Elizabeth Wallingford, Somersworth widow. Bond L5000.0.0. Sureties: James Stoodly, Portsmouth esq. and Samuel Lord. Witnesses: Thomas Wallingford and Sarah Stoodly. Note: Both the Probate file card and the file envelope call this file "Oliver" Wallingford, but the papers indicate that it was Olive.

2730. WALLINGFORD, OLIVER. See Olive Wallingford.

2731. WALLINGFORD, PETER (1772) #4035
Est. Rochester yoeman decd. testate. WILL: Drawn 4/18/1771. Legatees: Wife-Abigail; Sons-Jonathan, Jacob and David; Daus.-Sarah, Lydia and Mary Wallingford. Refers to his obligation under his father's Will to his mother who is still living. Exex.-wife Abigail. Witnesses: John McDuffie, Ebenezer Tebbets and Jona. Dame. CERT. WILL: 10/28/1772. Presented by Exex. and witnesses Tibbets and Dame. ADMIN.: 10/28/1772. Exex. Abigail Wallingford, Rochester widow. Bond L500.0.0. Sureties: Ebenezer Tebbets, esq. and Jonathan Dame, yoemen, both of Rochester. Witnesses: Samuel Parker to all sigs.; Archd. Achincloss to sig. Of the Widow; John Parker to sigs. of Tebbets and Dame. Clerk notes that the Bond of Admin. was not signed by bondsmen until 8/23/1773 at which time Tebbets gave oath and Dame affirmed.

2732. WALLINGFORD, THOMAS (1771) #3868

EST. Somersworth esq. decd. intestate. ADMIN.: 9/4/1771. Admx. Elizabeth Wallingford, Somersworth widow. Bond: L2000.0.0. Sureties: James Stoodley, esq. and Woodbury Langdon, merchant, both of Portsmouth. Witnesses: Joshua Hubbard and Samuel Parker. BOND: 9/4/1771. Of Thomas Wallingford, Somersworth gent. Bond L30.0.0. To appeal Decree denying him co-admin. with Elizabeth Wallingford. Surety John Wentworth, Somersworth esq. DIV. WARR.: 4/7/1772. Comm.: Hon. Thomas Westbrook Waldron and Otis Baker, both of Dover and Ebenezer Thompson of Durham, esquires; William Knight and Samuel Penhallow, both of Portsmouth. To div. the real est., giving one part to Widow and rest to children with double share to oldest son. DIV.: 9/10/1772. Divisees: Widow Elizabeth Waldron; Sons-Thomas (oldest), Ebenezer, Mark and Samuel; Daus.-Hannah wife of John Brown, Margaret wife of James Goodwin, Mary wife of Capt. Wm. Pearne, Elizabeth wife of Col. John Wentworth, Rachel wife of Silas Noel, Lydia wife of Samuel Lord and Olive Wallingford; Heirs of dau. Abigail decd. late wife of Edward Sanders. Oaths 9/10/1772 Comm. to judge. Allowed. PETITION: 12/1/1772. Of John Sullivan of Durham, Strafford Co. on behalf of Admx. as Gdn. of Samuel and Olive, minor children of decd. For appeal against Decree allowing Div. as she is dissatisfied with div. of land given to the children. Bond L100.0.0. Sureties: John Langdon and Nathaniel Folsom Jr., Portsmouth merchants. Also signed by John Sullivan. Witnesses: Joseph Prime and Samuel Parker. PETITION: 4/16/1773. Of William Pearne, Portsmouth merchant, and Mary his wife. To sue Bond of Admin. as Admx. has not paid them their distribution of personal est. Allowed 4/16/1773. ACCOUNT: 7/14/1773. Of Admx. Allowed after considering and altering objections of heirs. Order: Admx. to charge herself with interest on Notes to date. The bal. of L17550.4.6.3 is to be distributed by Admx, giving herself L5850.1.6.1; Thomas, oldest son, L1800.0.5.2 and L900.0.2.3 to each of the other children. PETITION: 12/4/1773. Of: Jno. Wentworth, Thomas Wallingford and Ebenezer Wallingford. They state Admx. is about to present an Account which contains many errors. They and some of heirs wish to be notified of date of exhibition of Account so they may be present and present their objections. OBJECTIONS TO ACCOUNT: 8/12/1774. By John Pickering Jr. by desire of many of heirs. Order: Admx. to be served with copy immediately. DEPOSITION: 9/27/1774. Of Abiel Hovey of Somersworth, Strafford Co. Deposes that some time the winter before last she heard Mrs. Elizabeth Wallingford offer a negro woman named Phillis to Capt. Pearne. Does not recall Pearne's answer, but Phillis appeared to Abiel to be in a perfect state of health. Oath 9/27/1774 Hovey to M. E. Wentworth, JP. REPLY TO OBJECTIONS: Of Exex. To objections against her Account. Includes information about the negros and that Phillis now dead. Marked by clerk as recd. and filed 11/15/1774 and a 2d copy on 12/3/1774. ADDL. ACCOUNT: 12/16/1774. Objections: Heirs Capt. Wallingford, Col. Wentworth and Capt. Pearne objected to several charges in Account. Their objections were filed and they were ordered to give Admx. a copy. She asked for time to answer. On 12/3 she filed her Account and it was expected council would be heard on the objections for Decree has been suspended for some time. Objections considered were: l. To the charge for entertaining Mr. Sullivan as it was charged in a former Account. Ruled it had not been allowed in former Account. 2. To the charge for the two negroes, they were the property of Admx. and when heirs asked for Div., Admx. said she would keep them, refusing to let heirs have either of them. Admx. denied and produced Deposition of Abiel Hovey as proof she did offer to let heirs have one of negroes named Phillis, who has since died. The other negro was put up for sale and struck off to one of heirs who afterward recanted and paid Admx. L5.0.0 to take her back. Ruled Admx., as widow of est., should not bear whole loss of negros. Heirs provided no proof so charge stands as in Account. 3. The silver plate said to be Olive's was bought and used by decd. and inventoried with his est. and accounted for by Admx. Admx. answered that it was well known that many of Col. Wallingford's daus. were given plate by their father during his lifetime. Since he bought this silver plate for Olive's use and her name ordered by him to be put on it, it should be hers. Ruled that the plate having been marked with Olive's name is a strong circumstance that it was given to her. It should be given to her and charge stands. 4. The item for the burying yard should not be allowed because the heirs were never notified and the property has always been claimed by the town. Admx. replied she did it to fulfill the intention of decd., for his reputation and on the advice of appraisers. Ruled item to stand as one heir has since removed objection, some others consenting and assisting in making the yard, and the decd. often talked of doing it during his lifetime. 5. The charge for repairing the sawmill. Ruled the article to be deducted from this Account and be considered when Admx. accounts for the net profits of the mill. Also ruled that 35,363 feet of boards credited for rent of mill be deducted from this Account and accounted for as in previous item. 6. Mr. Prime's bal. should not be allowed because it does not appear that the decd. ever owed him anything. As for Mr. Quint's demand, heirs suppose he owed est. considerable and it should not be allowed until examined and vouched. Ruled the Admx. would not have paid the balances unless she thought them due as 1/3 comes out of her own pocket. She did produce vouchers and made oath, while heirs have submitted no evidence to support objection. Ruled Account charge stands. 7. Admx. should not be allowed a commission because in a former Account she charged a large sum for Mr.

Sullivan's time and trouble settling est. The cost of Comm., expense of entertaining Mr. Sullivan and heirs, together with her own time, comes to nearly L200.0.0 and settling of personal est. was done with little expense to Admx. Ruled the article objected to is L546.12.0. A commission of 3% was charged on L18220.7.101/2, the amount of the personal est., for settling. In a former Account the sum heirs objected to was only L14.13.5., a sum the judge feels no person would think any way equal to settlm. of so large an est. The costs for Mr. Sullivan and the Comm. are considered incidental charges and are no way connected to any allowance to the Admx. As the charge is high, the judge has studied other practices and accounts in the Probate Office. Some use only the personal Invy. as a basis and some the whole est. He feels the present Account charge is too much and it should be changed to L300.0.0, a sum equal to the business and risk. Est. to be credited with an over-charge of L246.12.0. 8. A Note of Hand of Sarah Simpson for L21.4.0. was charged as bad when Account was exhibited. Ruled that it be credited for and the Admx. to endeavor to recover the money from Mrs. Simpson. If it cannot be recovered, it will be reconsidered. Decree: The Account to be allowed as it now stands with the corrections. The heirs are to pay the bal. of L1078.17.2.1 to the Admx. according to their just proportions, viz. L359.12.4. 3/4 to be paid by the Widow; L110.3.0.13 by Thomas Wallingford, oldest son and L55.6.6.4/13 by each of the other children or their legal reps. Account names negro girl Dinal who is disordered in mind and body. PETITION: 3/28/1775. Of John Wentworth, esq. and Thomas Wallingford, gent., both of Somersworth, Strafford Co., two of heirs and attys. for Ebenezer Wallingford and other heirs. For permission to sue Bond Admin. because Admx. has not exhibited Account. Allowed 4/4/1775 with order to cite Admx. to appear and show cause why Petition should not be granted. Cert.: Of S. Hale. He has received and filed the Petition and cited Admx. REPLY TO PETITION: 4/10/1775. Of Admx. States she has presented 2 Accounts, the bal. being held as instructed by judge. INVY.: Of the est. in Portsmouth. Appr. 9/18-28/1771. Comm.: Thomas W. Waldron, Moses Carr and James Stoodley. Value L23107.8.5 3/4. Oaths 10/17/1777 Comm. and Admx. to judge, Admx. to bring in an Addl. Invy. CERT.: 1/20/1789. Of Daniel Wood, Depy. Sheriff, Berwick, York Co., MA/ME. On 12/10/1788 he served Admx. with Citation to appear 1/21/1789 and settle her Account. ADDL. ACCOUNT: 7/21/1787. Of Admx. Oath 5/19/1789 Admx. to Dominicus Goodwin, JP. Notes by judge: At request of John Costeloe in right of his wife, an heir, Admx. was cited to exhibit Addl. Account. On 3d Wed. March 1789 John Cushing, son-in-law and atty. to Admx., and Costeloe appeared and agreed to an accounting 3d Wed. May. Allowed 6/17/1789, judge having heard objections of Amos Wallingford, an heir, and finding no evidence to support them. PETITION:

6/18/1789. Of Amos Wallingford. For appeal against Decree allowing Addl. Account. Granted. BOND: 8/16/1789. Of Amos Wallingford, Somersworth, Strafford Co. yoeman. Bond L60.0.0. To appeal Decree allowing Addl. Account of 1789. Sureties: Thomas Wallingford, Somersworth gent. and Amos Cogswell, Dover esq., both of Strafford Co. Witnesses: Henry Mellen and Saml. Roberts. Note: The following Petition recorded as #5790 Thomas Roach (1792) belongs here. PETITION: 8/16/1792. Of Thomas Roach, Portsmouth mariner. For div. of Wallingford Island in Piscatraqua River of which he owns 1 acre and the heirs of Thomas Wallingford of Somersworth, Strafford Co. decd. the remainder. Order: For hearing. There is also a notation with names of George Gains, Supply Clap, George Wentworth, Isaac Rindge and Wm. Hart (as Comm.?) See also #6040 John Noble et. als. (1794) for addl. information about this same Div. in which land is called "Wallingford's Island or Jackson's Island."

WALLIS. See also Wallace, Walls

2733. WALLIS, FURNAL (1772) #3905
GDP. Of the son Nathaniel Wallis, Epsom yeoman decd. GDP: 1/27/1772. Of Furnal Wallis, a minor over 14. Gdn. Samuel Allen Jr., Stratham yoeman. Bond L500.0.0. Sureties: William Blazo, Greenland yoeman and Thomas Manning of Portsmouth. Witnesses: Sarah Wentworth and Mary Hall. Note: Both the card file and the file envelope call this the file of "Nathaniel Wallis." There is a note on jacket that it is an error, the correct name being Furnal.

2734. WALLIS, NATHANIEL (1772) #3905
See #3905 Furnal Wallis (1772)

2735. WALLIS, SAMUEL (1794) #5975
EST. Rye husbm. decd. testate. WILL: Drawn 10/16/1793. Legatees: Son-Samuel; Daus.-Sarah, Hannah, Mary (apparently these 3 married), Martha, Abigail and Elizabeth (these 3 unmarried). Gives negro Philless to son. Exec.-son Samuel. His sig. Witnesses: Joseph Parsons, Billy Rand and Eben. Odiorne. CERT. WILL (D31:188): 2/19/1794. Presented by Exec. and witnesses Rand and Odiorne. INVY.: Comm.: David Lock, Richard Webster and John Garland. Value L1151.10.0. Oaths 3/13/1794 Comm. to Joseph Parsons, JP. Oath 3/19/1794 Exec. to judge.

2736. WALLIS, WALLIS (c1771) No#
EST. Of Peterborough decd. INVY. (D21:229): Appr. 11/20/1771. Comm.: John Swan Jr. and James Robie. Value L133.6.6. Oaths 11/25/1771 Comm. to Reuben Kidder, JP.

2737. WALLIS, WILLIAM (1772) #3944
EST. Greenland yoeman decd. testate. WILL: Drawn 6/16/1772. Legatees: Sons- Samll. and William; Daus.-Jean Moses, Martha Scaggel and Abagel Blazdal; Grandsons-Joseph Wallis, Waymouth Wallis, Nathaniel Wallis and Fernal Wallis; Son-in-law-Wm. Blazdell husb. of dau. Abagel. Execs.-son-in-law William Blazdell and grandson Joseph Wallis. His mark. Witnesses: Josiah Foss, Josiah Foss Jr. and Richd. Jenness. CERT. WILL: 6/24/1772. Presented by Execs. and all witnesses. ADMIN.: 6/24/1772. Execs.: William Blazdell and Joseph Wallis, both of Greenland. Bond L100.0.0. Sureties: Richard Jenness, Rye esq. and Josiah Foss of Greenland. Witnesses: Oliver Whipple and Samuel Parker.

WALLS. See also Wallace, Wallis

2738. WALLS, GEORGE (1795) #6104
EST. Epsom husbm. decd. testate. WILL: Drawn 1/10/1781. Legatees: Wife-Sarah; Sons-Ebenezer and George; Daus.-Patty Ham, Margaret Sanborn, Hannah McGaffey, Elizabeth and her husb. Thomas Babb and the heirs of Elizabeth's body; Grandson-John Gray. Execs.-"son" Thomas Babb and dau. Elizabeth. His sig. Witnesses: John McClery, Michael McClary, Sarah McClary and Jonathan Randell. CERT. WILL (D31:529): 5/20/1795. Presented by Execs. and witnesses John McClery and Michael McClary, esquires. ADMIN.: 5/20/1795. Exec. Thomas Babb, Epsom gent. Bond L1000.0.0. Sureties: John McClery and Michael McClary, Epsom esquires. Witnesses: F. G. Dearborn and W. Parker. INVY.: Appr. 9/12/1795. Comm.: Michl. McClary, Moses Osgood and James H. McClary. Value L1023.25.0. Oaths 9/12/1795 Osgood and James H. McClary to Michl. McClary, JP. Oath 9/16/1795 Exec. to judge. Note: This file is recorded as George Wallis but his sig. on Will is Walls.

2739. WALTON, JOHN (1774) #4137
EST. Newington yoeman decd. intestate. ADMIN.: 12/13/1774. Admrs.: George Walton, Portsmouth tanner and Shadrack Walton, Barnstead, Strafford Co. yoeman. Bond L1000.0.0. Sureties: John Pickering, Newington yoeman and Nathaniel Furbur, Portsmouth boatbuilder. Witnesses: James Picken and Saml. Hale Jr. INVY. WARR.: 12/13/1774. Comm.: Richard Downing, esq. and Jonathan Swett, gent., both of Newington. INVY.: Appr. 12/20/1774. Value L272.4.0. Oaths 12/22/1774 Shadrach Walton, an Admr., the other being sick, and Comm. to judge. CITATION: 3/29/1777. To Admrs. To appear and exhibit Account so est. may be distributed. Cert.: 10/11/1777. Of Ebenezr. Lord. He has summoned Admrs.

2740. WALTON, JONATHAN (1799) #6528
EST. Seabrook miller decd. testate. WILL: Drawn 11/21/1795. Legatees: Wife-Rebekah; Son-Samuel; Daus.-Hannah Eaton, Rachel Greele and Rebekah Dodge. Exec.-son Samuel. His sig. Witnesses; Elisha Brown, Daniel Smith and John Smith. CERT. WILL (D33:28): 1/18/1797. Presented by Exec. and witnesses Brown, esq. and John Smith. ADMIN.: 1/18/1799. Exec. Samuel Walton, Seabrook yoeman. Bond $2,000.00. Sureties: Elisha Brown, esq. and John Smith, gent., both of Seabrook. Witnesses: Mary Parker and W. Parker. INVY.: Appr. 4/1/1799. Comm.: Elisha Brown, Daniel Smith and Winthrop Eaton. Value $2,020.00. Oaths 4/1/1799 Smith and Eaton to Elisha Brown, JP. Oath 4/12/1799 Exec. to W. Parker, JP. Note: Both the Admin. and Invy. are photocopies.

2741. WALTON, TEMPERANCE (1782) #4828
GDP. Of the dau. of George Walton, Portsmouth tanner decd. GDP.: 8/17/1782. Of Temperance, a minor under 14. Gdn. Stacy Hall, Portsmouth truckman. Bond L1000.0.0. Sureties: Samuel Hall, truckman and Benjamin Drowne, goldsmith, both of Portsmouth. Witnesses: D. Hart and Jeremiah Libbey.

2742. WARD, DANIEL (1787) #5254 1/2
EST. Brentwood taylor decd. testate. WILL: Drawn 2/15/1786. Legatees: Wife-Sarah; Sons-Nathaniel, Jeremiah, Daniel, Benjamin and Andrew; Dau.-Sarah Mead. Exex.-wife Sarah. His mark. Witnesses: Nicholas Smith, George Fuller, Samuel Judkins and Saml. Shepard. CERT. WILL (D29:103): 2/21/1787. Presented by Exex. and witnesses Smith and Fuller. INVY.: Appr. 11/20/1787. Comm.: Thos. Stow Ranney and George Fuller. Value L106.18.3. Oaths 11/21/1787 Comm. to judge. PETITION: 11/21/1787. Of Exex. For License. Gives list of claims of L18.0.0. LICENSE (D29:156): 11/21/1787. To Admx. To sell sufficient real est. to pay debts.

2743. WARD, HANNAH (1782) #4837
EST. Kensington single woman decd. testate. WILL: Drawn 8/1/1782. Legatee: Sister-Elizabeth Ward. Exex.-sister Elizabeth. Her mark. Witnesses: Isaac Fellows and Jonathan Flanders. CERT. WILL: 8/28/1782. Presented by Exex. and Flanders (oath) and Fellows (affirm.), the two witnesses. ADMIN.: 8/28/1782. Admx. Elizabeth Ward, Kensington widow. Bond L40000.0.0. Sureties: Jonathan Flanders, blacksmith and Isaac Fellows, tanner, both of Kensington. Witnesses: Paul Jewett and Nathl. Parker.

2744. WARD, JOHN (1787) #5255
EST. Kensington yoeman decd. testate. NUNCUPATIVE WILL: 2/21/1787. Philimon Blake Jr., Jere. Fellows Jr. and Jonathan Flanders state that on or about 1/15/1787 they were at the dwelling house of John Lamprey of Kensington, where John Ward decd. then lived and was sick of his last illness. Ward asked them to bear witness that it was his will that after his debts were paid he gave all his est. to his bro. Melcher Ward. Oaths 2/21/1787 Blake, Fellows and Flanders to W. Parker, JP. & R. Prob. The heirs having been notified and being present in court and declaring they had no objections to the foregoing being allowed as a nuncupative will, it was proved and allowed. ADMIN.: 2/27/1787. Admr. Jeremiah Fellows Jr., Kensington blacksmith. Bond L300.0.0. Surety Philemon Blake Jr., Kensington gent. Witnesses: John Dean Jr. and Nathl. Parker. INVY.: Comm.: Philemon Blake Jr. and Enoch Worthen. Value L7.18.10. Oaths 10/16/1787 Comm. to Jere. Fogg Jr. JP. ACCOUNT: 2/20/1788. Of Admr. Allowed 2/20/1788.

2745. WARD, JONATHAN (1787) #5258
EST. Kensington yoeman decd. ADMIN.: 2/21/1787., Admx. Mercy Ward, Kensington widow. Bond L1000.0.0. Sureties: Jonathan Purinton, yoeman and Joseph Brown, gent., both of Kensington. Witnesses: Jere. Fellows Jr. and Nathl. Parker. INVY.: Comm.: Joseph Brown, Jonathan Purinton and Enoch Worthen. Value L639.5.8. Oaths 5/10/1787 Admx., Purinton and Worthen to Jere. Fogg, JP. ACCOUNT: Of Admx. Oath 12/22/1804 Admx. to Jacob B. Moore, JP. Allowed 5/15/1805.

2746. WARD, NATHANIEL (1787) #5313
GDP. Of Brentwood, an adult adjudged n.c.m. PETITION: 12/19.1689. Of William Morrill and Josiah Hook, Brentwood Selectmen and Overseers of the Poor. They adjudge Nathaniel Ward n.c.m. and in danger of squandering his est. as principle heir of the est. of his father Daniel Ward. Request appointment of a gdn. and recommend Dr. Thomas Stow Ranney. GDP. APPOINTMENT: 12/19/1787. Thomas Stow Ranney, Brentwood physician, is appointed Gdn. of Nathaniel Ward, an adult n.c.m. GDP. 12/19/1787. Of Nathaniel, an adult adjuded n.c.m. Gdn. Thomas Stow Ranney, Brentwood physician. Bond L1000.0.0. Sureties: William Morrill, esq. and Josiah Hook, yoeman, both of Brentwood. Witnesses: David Norris and Nathl. Parker. INVY. WARR.: 12/19/1787. Comm.: Samuel Dudley, esq.; Winthrop Dudley, gent. and David Robinson, yoeman, all of Brentwood. INVY.: Appr. 12/21/1787. Value L75.0.0. RECEIPT: 9/26/1820. Of: Josiah Dudley and Andrew Dudley, Brentwood Selectmen. They have received from the Gdn., for safe keeping, all of Nathaniel's property until another Gdn. is appointed. They find the value of the est. to

be $448.22, which they promise to account for to the Probate Office, and are satisfied with the accounting. GDP. (D46:439): 2/15/1821. Gdn. Jesse Robinson. Sureties: William Morrill and Andrew Dudley, all of Brentwood. INVY. (D46:517): Josiah Dudley and Jonathan Rowe. Value $471.61. Oaths 4/19/1821 Comm. to John S. Dudley, JP. ACCOUNT: 1821. Of Gdn. Cert.: 8/30/1822. Of: William Morrill, Jonathan Rowe and Michael Fellows, Brentwood Selectmen. They have examined the Account and are satisfied that it is true and reasonable. A bal. of $426.50 is in the hands of the Gdn. The Account includes an item for digging the grave. Note: Admin. of Nathaniel's est. is 1823.

2747. WARD, NATHANIEL (1798) #3773
PET. Kensington yoeman. PETITION: For div. of land in Deerfield, Twp. of Nottingham, which he owns as tenant in common with others unknown. He owns 1/4. Order: 6/26/1798. For hearing, Petitioner to notify interested parties by advertising Petition and Order in newspaper. REPLY: 7/30/1798. Of Dudley Ladd, Deerfield husbm. States that he and others are the lawful owners of the whole lot referenced in Petition, are now and have been for more than 20 years in peaceable and quiet possession thereof. Therefore, Ward is not an owner of any part of the lot and has never been in possession of it. Requests judge to decide the question of title and possession and to dismiss Petition. Decree: 7/30/1798. The plea having been considered, Petition is dismissed.

2748. WARNER: ABIGAIL, DANIEL & ELIZABETH (1779) #4511
GDP. Of the children of Samuel Warner, Portsmouth mariner decd. intestate. PETITION: 2/22/1779. Of Eliza Warner. Requests her bro.-in-law Jonathan Warner, esq. be appointed Gdn. of her daus. Elizabeth and Abigail. GDP. (D25:48): 2/24/1779. Of Elizabeth and Abigail, minors under 14. Gdn. Jonathan Warner, Portsmouth esq. Sureties: Nathl. Folsom and Daniel Tilton, Exeter esquires. GDP.: 4/27/1780. Of Daniel, a minor over 14. Gdn. Jonathan Warner, Portsmouth esq. Bond L10000.0.0. Sureties: John Parker of Portsmouth and John Giddinge of Exeter, esquires. Witnesses: Jeremiah Holman and Wm. Parker.

2749. WARNER, COL. DANIEL (1778) #4496
EST. Portsmouth esq. decd. intestate. RENUN.: 11/2/1778. Of Sarah Warner, widow of Daniel. Of Admin. because of advanced age. Requests appointment of her son Jonathan. Witness Hannah Sherburne. ADMIN. (D24:427): 11/4/1778. Admr. Jonathan Warner, esq. Sureties: Oliver Whipple of Portsmouth and Nathaniel Folsom of Exeter, esquires. INVY. WARR.: 11/4/1778. Comm.: Samuel Penhallow and William Knight, esquires and Giles Seaward, mariner, all of Portsmouth. INVY.: Appr.

12/15/1778. Value L17587.6.1. Oaths 2/4/1779 Comm. to H. Wentworth, JP. Oath 2/6/1779 Admr. to Saml. Penhallow, JP. PETITION: 2/24/1779. Of Admr. For license. LICENSE: 2/24/17789. To Admr. To sell sufficient real est. to pay debts. PETITION : 8/26/1783. Of Admr. For Comm. Insolvency. Granted. CLAIMS: 10/1/1784. Comm.: Wm. Knight, Geo. Atkinson and Isaac Rindge. Total L9326.0.8. Oaths 10/6/1784 Comm. to Saml. Penhallow, JP. ACCOUNT: 8/23/1781. Of Admr. Allowed 3/16/1785. PROP. & SETTLM.: Claims L9326.0.8. Amount to be proportioned L3495.16.5 1/2. Allowed 3/17/1785 with order to Admr. to pay. CITATION: 6/15/1796. To Admr. It has been represented to judge that since his last Account, the Admr. has received large sums of money due the est. for which he has not accounted. He is cited to appear and exhibit an Addl. Account so est. may be settled. Cert.: Of Edward Hart, Depy. Sherrif. He has delivered the orig. of Citation to Warner. ADDL. ACCOUNT: 7/8/1796. Of Admr. Shows addl. income of L1087.17.7. Allowed 9/27/1797. PETITION: 12/14/1799. Of George Jaffrey by his atty. Jere. Mason. States that Admr. has never paid him the L89.10.11 1/2 ordered by judge as his part of prop. of Addl. Account of 1797. Requests permission to sue Bond Admin. Cert.: Of W. Parker, Reg. The proportion was ordered paid to Jaffrey as stated. Petition granted 12/14/1799. PROMISE: 12/14/1799. Of Jere. Mason on behalf of George Jaffrey, esq. To indemnify judge in his suit against the Bond Admin.

2750. WARNER, JONATHAN (1789) #5485
Pet. for Div. See #4437 Moses Millar (1778)

2751. WARNER, SAMUEL (1773) #3997
EST. Portsmouth merchant decd. intestate. ADMIN.: 2/17/1773. Admr. Daniel Warner, Portsmouth esq. Bond L1000.0.0. Sureties: Jonathan Warner, esq. and Elias Warner, merchant, both of Portsmouth. Witnesses: John Phillips and John Wentworth to sig. of Jonathan Warner. INVY. WARR.: 10/20/1771(sic.) Comm.: John Marshall, boatbuilder, Pierse Long, mariner and Elias E. Warner, merchant, all of Portsmouth. INVY.: 10/1771. Value L216.11.7 1/4. Oaths 2/18/1773 Comm. to judge. ADMIN. D.B.N. (D25:48): 2/4/1779. Admr. d.b.n. Jonathan Warner, Portsmouth esq. Sureties: Nathl. Folsom and Daniel Tilton, Exeter esquires. ACCOUNT: 7/16/1786. Of Admr. d.b.n. Allowed 7/19/1786. Account includes main. Abigail.

2752. WARREN, DR. PELETIAH (1787) #5256
EST. Portsmouth physician decd. ADMIN.: 2/21/1787. Admx. Peggy Warren of Exeter, his widow. Bond L1000.0.0. Sureties: Daniel Tilton, esq. and Joseph Tilton, physician, both of Exeter. Witnesses: W. Parker to

sigs. of Daniel and Joseph and Nathl Parker to all sigs. INVY.: No Comm. given. Value L13.8.4 1/2. Oath 3/21/1787 Admx. to W. Parker, Reg. CLAIMS: Dated by clerk 11/1787. Comm.: Dudley Odlin and Oliver Peabody. Total L127.7.7. ACCOUNT: 9/1787. Of Admx. Oath Admx. to W. Parker, JP. Allowed 9/15/1787. Account includes main. one child. PROP. & SETTLM.: Claims L127.7.7. Amount to be proportioned L3.8.9 1/2. Allowed 11/21/1787 with order to Admx. to pay.

2753. WASON, THOMAS (1792) #5785
EST. Candia yoeman decd. ADMIN.: 6/18/1792. Admx. Mercy Wason, Candia widow. Bond L1000.0.0. Sureties: Walter Robie, Candia esq. and James Wason of Chester. Witnesses: Saml. Mooers and Joshua Moore. INVY.: Appr. 7/2/1792. Comm.: Walter Robie and Joshua Moore. Value L269.9.8. Oaths 7/2/1792 Comm. and Admx. to Saml. Mooers, JP. GDP. Of the children of Thomas Wason, Candia yoeman decd. GDP.: 8/20/1794. Of: Elizabeth, a minor over 14 and of Sarah, Jane and Thomas, minors under 14. Gdn Walter Robie, Candia esq. Bond L1000.0.0. Sureties: Joseph Blanchard and Stephen Dearborn, Chester esquires. Witnesses: John Dinsmoor and W. Parker. ACCOUNT: 12/17/1794. Of Samuel Nay and Mary his wife, Admx. Allowed. Account includes main. of Jenna and Thomas. DOWER: 10/7/1794. "Part of" the Comm.: Nathl. Emerson, Joseph Blanchard and John Wilson. Of Mary Nay in est. of Thomas Wason. Oaths 10/7/1794 Emerson, Blanchard and Wilson to Walter Robie, JP. DIV.: 10/7/1794. Comm. "maj. part": Nathl. Emerson, Jas. Blanchard and John Wilson. To div. part of a lot held in common and in equal shares by heirs of Thomas Wason and James Wason, Chester yeoman. Divisees: Heirs of Thomas Wason and James Wason. Walter Robie, Gdn. of heirs, is satisfied with Div. Oaths 10/7/1794 Emerson, Blanchard and Wilson to Walter Robie, JP. Allowed 10/31/1794. DIV.: 10/7/1794. Comm.: Nathl. Emerson, Joseph Blanchard, John Wilson, Joshua Moore and John Clifford. To div. the real est. among all his children. Divisees: Son-Thomas; Daus.-Anne wife of Jona. Sargent, Elizabeth Wason, Sarah Wason and Jenny Wason. Oaths 10/7/1794 Emerson, Blanchard and Wilson to Walter Robie, JP. Allowed 12/17/1794.

2754. WATSON, WINTHROP (1777) #4385
EST. Exeter yoeman decd. testate. WILL: Drawn 3/25/1777. Legatees: Wife-Abigail; Sons-Daniel, Stephen, David and Dudley; Daus.-Mary, Sarah, Elizabeth and Rebecca. Exec.-son Dudley. His sig. Witnesses: Ebenezer Smith, Daniel Smith, David Hason and Joseph Connor. CERT. WILL (D24:106): 8/27/1777. Presented by Exec. and witnesses Daniel Smith and Connor. Oath: 8/27/1777. Of Abigail Watson. She accepts the provisions made for her in Will and desires proving of Will. Witnesses:

Wm. Parker and Daniel Smith. INVY.: Appr. 1/29/1778. Comm.: John Connor, Daniel Smith and Zebulon Gilman. Value L1857.3.0. Oaths 1/29/1778 Exec., Smith and Gilman to judge.

2755. WAUGH, JOSEPH (1771) #3847
EST. Windham yoeman decd. testate. WILL: Drawn 11/29/1770. Legatees: Dau.-Margaret Carswell wife of Richard; Son-in-law-Richard Carswell; Grandchildren-Joseph Carswell, Rachel Carswell, Samuel Carswell, Mary Waugh, James Waugh, John Waugh, William Waugh, Janet Waugh, Ann Waugh, Robert Waugh and Agness Waugh. Exec.-Matthew Thornton, Londonderry esq. His mark. Witnesses: Simon Williams, Capt. Joseph Clyd and Joseph Smith. Proved 5/27/1771 on oaths of witnesses Rev. Williams and Smith to Matthew Thornton, JP by order of the court.

2756. WEARE, DEBORAH (1783) #4933
EST. Seabrook widow decd. intestate. RENUN.: 9/20/1783. Of Jonathan Weare of Seabrook, only surviving child of decd. States that Deborah left an est. that needs to be administered and requests appointment of Nathl. Weare of Kensington, only child of Deborah's oldest son, decd. ADMIN.: 9/20/1783. Admr. Nathaniel Weare, Kensington yoeman. Bond L500.0.0. Sureties: Jonathan Weare, Seabrook yoeman and Jonathan Weare, Andover, Hillsborough Co. esq. Witnesses: Moses Hook and W. Parker. INVY. WARR.: 9/24/1783. Comm.: Benjamin Eastman, Isaac Fellows and Moses French. INVY.: Value not tallied. Esti. L39.0.0+. Oaths 6/16/1784 Eastman and Fellows to Benjamin Rowe, JP. Oath 6/16/1784 Admr. to Wm. Parker. CITATION: 3/9/1784. To: Richard Smith, gent.; Elizabeth Smith, spinster and Stephen Smith, yoeman, all of Seabrook. To appear and be examined under oath concerning the concealing, embezzlement or conveying away of the money, goods or chattels of Widow Deborah Weare decd. Cert.: Of Jonathan Leavitt, Constable of Seabrook. That he has notified those cited of the time and place.

2757. WEARE, JOHN (1773) #4072
EST. Kensington yoeman decd. testate. WILL: Drawn 10/5/1773. Legatees: Wife-Lucy; Son-Joseph; Dau.-Lydia Weare. Execs.-wife Lucy and Nathanael Weare son of his bro. Joseph late of Kensington decd. His sig. Witnesses Stephen Brown, Onesiphorus Page and Jonathan Palmer. CERT. WILL: (D22:358). 12/30/1773. Presented by Nathaniel Weare, one of the Execs., and witnesses Brown and Palmer. DECLARATION: 12/24/1773. Of Lucy Weare, widow and co-exec. She notes that circumstances make it difficult for her to attend court with her co-Exec. for proving the Will, but she is willing to accept co-Admin. INVY.: Appr.

2/1774. Comm.: Meshech Weare and Moses French. Value L694.10.2 1/2. Oaths 2/9/1774 Comm. to Jona. Fifield, JP. Oath 2/25/1774 Lucy Weare, an Exec., to Meshech Weare, JP. Noted on back as returned 2/25/1774. ACCOUNT: Of Execs. Allowed 7/29/1777. Includes a Receipt 7/29/1777 of Lucy Weare, to her co-Exec. for the full bal. of the Account and discharges him from all demands against the same. Oath Lucy Weare to Wm. Parker, JP.

2758. WEARE, JONATHAN (1772) #3976
See Joseph Weare #3976 (1772)2758 Incorrectly filed as Jonathan.

2759. WEARE, JONATHAN (1790) #5598
EST. Seabrook yoeman decd. testate. WILL: Drawn 9/3/1787. Legatees: Wife-Mary; Sons-Peter, Jonathan and John; Dau.-Abigail Toppan wife of John Toppan; Grandchildren-Children of his dau. Hannah Page decd. Exec.-son John. His sig. Witnesses: Elisha Brown, Edward True and Moses Rowe. CERT. WILL (D29:437): Presented by Exec. and witnesses Brown, esq. and True. ADMIN.: 11/17/1790. Exec. John Weare, Seabrook yoeman. Bond L1000.0.0. Sureties: Elisha Brown, esq. And Edward True, yoeman, both of Seabrook. Witness W. Parker. INVY.: Appr. 12/7/1790. Comm.: Joseph Brown, Stephen Gove and Elisha Brown. Value L420.9.4. Oaths 3/15/1791 Joseph Brown and Gove to Elisha Brown, JP.

2760. WEARE, JOSEPH (1772) #3976
EST. Of Kensington decd. intestate. ADMIN.: 12/30/1772. Admr. Nathaniel Weare, Kensington yoeman. Bond L500.0.0. Sureties: Meshech Weare, Hampton Falls esq. and Samuel Collins, Seabrook yoeman. Witnesses: John Taylor and Samuel Parker. INVY. WARR. 12/30/1772. Comm.: Jonathan Purrington and Samuel Clifford, Kensington yoemen. INVY.: Value L1184.17.0. Oaths 2/4/1773 of Clifford, affirm. Purington, a Quaker, to Meshech Weare, JP. Oath 3/8/1773 Admr. to judge. Note: This est. was incorrectly filed under Jonathan Weare in the card file. Has been changed to Joseph as the papers read.

2761. WEARE, HON. MESHECH (1786) #5175
EST. Hampton Falls esq. decd. testate. WILL: Drawn 12/26/1785. Legatees: Sons-Samuel, Nathan, Thomas, Wibert, Nathaniel and Redford. Ref. to his son Capt. Richard decd; Daus.-Mary, Hannah and 2 unnamed; Granddau.-Elizabeth Lang; All the children of his late wife Mehitable by him. Execs.-sons Thomas, Wibert and Redford. His sig. Witnesses: Abner Sanborn, Barnard Tucker and Oliver Peabody. CERT. WILL (D28:423): 2/15/1786. Presented by Execs. and witnesses Tucker and Peabody, esq. INVY.: Comm.: Christo. Toppan and Abner Sanborn. Value L953.11.7. Oaths 9/20/1786 Comm. and Execs. to W. Parker, JP.

2762. WEARE, NATHAN (1799) #6634
EST. Hampton Falls gent. decd. ADMIN.: 12/27/1799. Admx. Hannah Weare, Hampton Falls spinster. Bond $2,000.00. Sureties: Peter Tilton of Hampton Falls and Nathl. Weare of Deerfield, esquires. Witnesses; W. Parker and Jno. Parker. INVY.: Appr. 3/15/1800. Comm.: Aaron Merrill, David Nason and Theophilus Sanborn. Value $474.60. Oaths 3/17/1800 Nason, Sanborn and Admx. to Caleb Tilton, JP.

2763. WEARE: SAMUEL & HANNAH HIS WIFE (1795) #6125
GDP. Hampton Falls esq. and his wife, adults adjudge n.c.m. PETITION: 7/24/1795. Of Peter Russel, Bradford, Essex Co., MA esq. Requests inquisition into condition of Samuel, his brother-in-law, and Samuel's wife. Order: 7/24/1795. To Selectmen of Hampton Falls. To make inquisition into condition of Samuel and his wife. Report: Of: David Nason, George Fifield and Peter Tilton, Hampton Falls Selectmen. They judge both Samuel and his wife Hannah to be n.c.m. GDP.: 7/30/1795. Of: Samuel Weare, Hampton Falls esq. and Hannah his wife, both adults adjudged n.c.m. Gdn. Peter Russel, of Bradford, Essex Co., MA. Bond $3,000.00. Sureties: Nathaniel Hubbard Dodge, Hampton Falls yoeman and Joseph Dow, Kensington esq. Witnesses: Mary S. Parker and Wm. Parker. INVY.: Comm.: Nathl. H. Dodge, David Nason and George Fifield. Value L2003.0.3. Also a Note for L18.0.0 and L8.0.0. due when Hannah relinquishes her dower right in marsh land sold. Oaths 9/17/1795 Dodge, Fifield and Gdn. to Nathl. Adams, JP. LIST CLAIMS: Dated by clerk 9/18/1795. Total $1,485.66. No sig. ACCOUNT: 8/1795. Of Gdn. Allowed 8/4/1795. ADDL. ACCOUNT: 2/2/1798. Of Gdn. Allowed 2/2/1798. ADDL. ACCOUNT: 9/17/1804. Of Gdn. Allowed 9/17/1804.

2764. WEATHERSPOON, ROBERT (1796) #6244
EST. Chester yoeman decd. testate. WILL: Drawn 7/9/1795. Legatees: Wife-Sarah; Son-John. Exec.-friend Joseph Blanchard, esq. His mark. Witnesses: Samuel Sharley, James Orr and Agness Weatherspoon. There is no proving of will. RENUN.: 8/17/1796. Of Joseph Blanchard, who presents Will but renounces Executorship.

2765. WEBSTER: ABIGAIL, BAILEY, BENAIAH, HANNAH, JONATHAN, MARTHA & SARAH (1793) #5886
GDP. Of the children of Nathan Webster, Salem yoeman decd. GDP.: 4/17/1793. Of: Bailey, Jonathan, Martha and Abigail, minors over 14 and of Hannah, Benaiah and Sarah, minors under 14. Gdn. Elijah Hall, Salem yoeman. Bond L1000.0.0. Sureties: Phinehas Gordon, yoeman and Joseph Wardwell, gent., both of Salem. Witnesses: Jona. Poor and Nat Parker.

2766. WEBSTER, BENJAMIN (1781) #4705
EST. Kingston gent. decd. testate. WILL: Drawn 10/20/1777. Legatees: Wife-Mary; Son-Jacob; Daus.-Elisabeth Hubbard, Mary Kelly, Anna Page, Dorithy Badger and Sarah Pollard; Benjamin Quimby son of Saml. Quimby; Benjamin Badger; Benjamin and Thomas Quimby sons of David Quimby; Benjamin Hubbard; Benjamin Webster son of Jacob Webster; Benjamin Kelley; Benjamin Page son of Anna Page. Exec.-son Jacob. His mark. Witnesses: Sarah George, Elisabeth Davis and Benjamin Sweat. CERT. WILL (D26:54): 3/28/1781. Presented by Exec. and witnesses Davis and Sweat. INVY.: Appr. 6/23/1781. Comm.: Samuel Severance and Benjamin Sweat. Value not tallied. Esti. L332.0.0+. Oaths 6/23/1781 Comm. to Josiah Bartlett, JP. Oath 7/25/1781 Exec. (Capt.) to W. Parker, Reg.

2767. WEBSTER, DANIEL (1780) #4618
EST. Chester husbm. decd. testate. WILL: Drawn 2/19/1780. Legatees: Wife-Martha; Granddau.-Martha Sargent. Exex.-wife Martha. His sig. Witnesses: John Haseltine, Moses Haseltine and Thomas Hoit. CERT. WILL (D25:363): 8/30/1780. Thomas Hoit, a witness, certified that he lived with Daniel at the time of his death. Three or four weeks before his death, Daniel asked Hoit to call some witnesses to witness his Will and he called the witnesses John Haseltine and Moses Haseltime, saw Daniel sign and seal his Will, which was previously drawn, and he judged Daniel to have been of sound mind. He also deposed that he saw John and Moses sign as witnesses at the same time, but he did not hear Daniel declare it his last Will. Proved, the last declaration not withstanding, the Will being designed as such. Oaths 8/30/1780 John Hazeltine and Moses Haseltine to Wm. Parker, JP. & Reg. and on the same date Thomas Hoit to judge. INVY.: Appr. 6/14/1780. Comm.: Saml. Hesseltine, Peter Hesseltine and Moses Haseltine. Value L256.14.0, equal to corn at 3 shillings a bushel plus L0.6.0. addl. Oaths 7/26/1780 Comm. to Saml. Emerson, JP. Oath 7/26/1780 Exex. to W. Parker, JP.

2768. WEBSTER, JEREMY (1773) #4031
EST. Kingston esquire decd. testate. WILL: Drawn 4/11/1769. Legatees: Wife-Elizabeth; Sons: Jeremiah, Jonathan, Nathaniel and Eliphalet; Dau.-Elizabeth wife of Joseph Bartlet. Execs.: wife Elizabeth and son Jonathan. His sig. Witnesses: Benjamin Lord, Benjamin French Jr. and Philip Tilton. CERT. WILL.: 6/30/1773. Presented by Execs. and witnesses French and Tilton. RENUN.: 8/26/1773. Of Elizabeth Webster, widow. Of co-admin. Requests that her co-Exec. be made sole Exec. Also says since she and Jonathan inherit all of the personal est., the Invy. can be dispensed with. Witnesses: W. Parker and Elijah Clough. ADMIN.: 6/30/1773. Exec.

Jonathan Ladd Webster, Kingston yoeman. Bond L200.0.0. Sureties: Eliphalet Webster and Benjamin French, Kingston yoemen. Witnesses: Nathaniel Parker and Wm. Parker.

2769. WEBSTER, JOHN (1780) #4617
EST. Hampstead esq. decd. testate. WILL: Drawn 4/14/1779. Legatees: Wife-Elisabeth; Sons-Joseph and Caleb; Dau-Sarah wife of Moses Kimball, Elisabeth wife of Edmund Worth, Mary wife of Robert Emerson and Anna wife of Moody Chase; Son-in-law Asa Page; Children of his dau. Sarah. Execs.-sons Joseph and Caleb. His sig. Witnesses: Ichabod Shaw, Joseph Pilsbury and John Calfe. CERT. WILL (D25:334): 4/27/1780. Presented by Execs. and witnesses Calfe, esq. and Pilsbury. INVY.: Appr. 6/12/1780. Comm.: Timothy Goodwin, John Harriman and Benjamin Pilsbury. Value not tallied. Esti. L5447.0.0+. Oaths 7/15/1780 Comm. and Execs. to John Calfe, JP.

2770. WEBSTER, JOHN (1784) #5048
EST. Chester esq. decd. testate. CAVEAT: 10/20/1784. The instrument proporting to be the last Will of John Webster, Chester esq. decd., was presented by Sarah Webster, the Exex. named. A Caveat having been laid before the judge, a hearing thereon was deferred to Nov. 18. Order: 11/18/1784. After appearance of all witnesses to the Will, who swore that in their best judgment he was of sound mind, and reading depositions and a multitude of witnesses relative to the deceased's sanity before and after signing his Will, the judge rules that John Webster was not of sound mind and sets aside and disallows the Will. On 11/27/1784 Sarah Webster, the named Exex., petitioned for an appeal against the Decree and gave bond. ADMIN.: 11/19/1784. Admr. John Webster, Chester gent. Bond L2000.0.0. Sureties: Josiah Flagg, esq. and Benjamin Page, physician, both of Chester. Witnesses: Ebenezer Flagg and W. Parker. RULING ON APPEAR: 4th Tues. of April 1785. The Superior Court of Judicature committed the Appeal of Sarah Webster to a jury, who returned the verdict that the proported Will is legal and valid and is to be approved and allowed. Cert. of Nathl. Adams, clerk. WILL: Drawn 5/25/1784. Legatees: Wife-Sarah; Sons-John, Samuel, Toppan and Edmund; Daus.-Sarah Wingate, Anna Flag, Mary Webster and Elizabeth Webster. Exec.-wife Sarah. His sig. Witnesses: John Moulton, Jabez Hoit and Isaac Blasdell. ADMIN.: 5/18/1785. Exec. Sarah Webster, Chester widow. Bond L1000.0.0. Sureties: John Wingate, North Hampton gent. and Christopher Toppan, Hampton esq. Witnesses: Elizabeth Parker and Nathl. Parker. ADMIN. D.B.N.: 5/10/1797. Admr. d.b.n. Thomas Sargent, Chester physician. Bond $3,000.00. Sureties: Edmund Webster and Enos Towne, Chester traders. Witnesses: Shearborn Dearborn and Jerahmiel Bowers. LETTER ADMIN. D.B.N. To Thomas Sargent.

2771. WEBSTER, NATHAN (1789) #5486
EST. Salem yoeman decd. intestate. ADMIN.: 9/16/1789. Admx. Hannah Webster of Salem. Bond L500.0.0. Sureties: Robert Campbell, yoeman and Nathaniel Gorrell, esq., both of Salem. INVY.: Appr. 1/13/1790. Comm.: Robert Campbell, Joseph Morrill and Nathl. Gorrell. Value L445. 7.7. Oaths 1/13/1790 Comm. and Admx. To Timothy Ladd, JP. DOWER: 4/16/1793. Comm.: Joseph Merril, John Smith, Jeremiah Dow, Samuel Kelly and Jesse Webster. Of Widow Hannah Webster. Oaths 4/17/1793 Dow, Kelly and Webster to James Gilmore, JP. Allowed. ACCOUNT: 9/17/1793. Of Admx. Allowed 12/18/1792 heirs having been notified. Account includes main. 2 children. APPR. WARR.: 1/4/1794. Comm.: Jeremiah Dow and Nathaniel Gorrell, esquires and Jesse Webster, gent., all of Salem. To view 2/3 of real est. to see if it can be div. Div. or appr. at present value. APPR.: 1/10/1794. Value L240.0.0. Oaths 1/13/1794 Gorrell and Webster to James Gilmore, JP. DECREE SETTLM.: 1/16/1794. Oldest son having refused, Nathan Webster, 2d son, having appeared and consenting, real est. settled on him, Nathan to pay L23.14.0 within 8 months, with interest, to each of his co-heirs-Isaiah Webster, Betty Hall, Bailey Webster, Jonathan Webster, Martha Webster, Abigail Webster, Hannah Webster, Benaiah Webster and Sarah Webster. BOND: 1/16/1794. Of Nathan Webster, Salem yoeman. Bond L500.0.0. To pay his co-heirs per Decree Settlm. Sureties: Elijah Hall, yoeman and Jesse Webster, gent., both of Salem. Witnesses: W. Parker and Saml. Parker.

2772. WEBSTER, NATHAN (1794) #5992
EST. Chester yoeman decd. testate. WILL: Drawn 1/21/1786. Legatees; Sons-Nathan Jr. and Moses. Daus.-Martha Richardson, Lois Morss and Lydia Webster. Exec.-son Nathan Jr. His sig. Witnesses: Jethro Colby, Samuel Wilson and Edmund Sleeper. CERT. WILL (D31:260): 4/17/1794. Presented by Exec. and witnesses Colby and Wilson. ADMIN.: 4/17/1794. Exec. Nathan Webster, Chester yoeman. Bond L1000.0.0. Sureties: Jethro Colby and Samuel Wilson, Chester yoemen. Witnesses: Josiah Bradly and Nathl. Parker. The file jacket for this est. mistakenly also lists Appr., Decree Settlm. and Bond, all of which belong to #5486, Nathan Webster (1789), this Nathan's father, and are with that est.

2773. WEBSTER, PETER (1771) #4351
GDP. Of the son of Peter Webster, Salem yoeman decd. PETITION: 3/20/1777. Of Anna Webster, Peter's mother. She declines Gdp. and requests appointment of Dr. Moody Morse. Witnesses: Joseph Kelly and Evan Jones. GDP.: 4/30/1777. Of Peter, a minor under 14. Gdn. Moody Morse, Salem physician. Bond L250.0.0. Sureties: Robert Young and Richard Dow Jr., Salem gentlemen. Witnesses: Nathl. Parker and W. Parker.

2774. WEBSTER, SAMUEL (1790) #5599
EST. Allenstown yoeman decd. ADMIN.: 11/17/1790. Admr. David Webster, Allenstown yoeman. Bond L1000.0.0. Sureties; Benja. Noyes, Bow gent. and David Quimby, Hawke esq. Witnesses: Samuel Parker and W. Parker. INVY.: Appr. 11/20/1790. Comm.: Richard Bartlett, John Cochran and Benja. Noyes. Value L95.17.8. Oaths 11/20/1790 Cochran and Noyes to Richd. Bartlett, JP. Oath 1/23/1791 Admr. to W. Parker, JP. PETITION: 5/16/1791. Of Admr. For Comm. Insolvency. Gives list claims of L120.19.10. and notes a problem about land sold by deed for which no title can be found. Also signed by Dorithy Webster and Samuel Webster. CLAIMS WARR.: 5/18/1791. Comm.: Benjamin Noyes of Bow, James Cochran, Pembroke, gent. and Theodore Shackford, Allenstown yoeman. On 11/16/1791 Comm. given 3 months longer. PETITION: 11/15/1791. Of Admr. The claims are not yet proved to satisfaction of Comm. Requests more time. PETITION: 3/21/1792. Of Admr. For div. of land in Allenstown held in common by decd. and Samuel Webster, Allenstown yoeman, so Dower may be set off. NOTIFICATION: 3/21/1792. To Samuel Webster, Allenstown yoeman. Of David Webster's Petition for Div. and hearing on it. CONSENT: 4/17/1792. Of Samuel Webster, Allenstown yoeman. For hearing on Petition at which he has right to make any objections he may have. CONSENT: 4/17/1792. Of Samuel Webster, Allenstown yoeman. To Petition. With Dorithy Webster and David Webster he appoints a Comm. for Dower and Div. of: Richard Bartlett, esq. and Capt. James Cochran, both of Pembroke; Capt. Robert Bunten, Theodore Shackford and Amos Carlton of Allenstown. CLAIMS: 2/8/1792. Total L43.4.8. Oaths 3/3/1792 Comm. to Richard Bartlett, JP. DIV.: 7/4/1792. Comm. as requested. Divisees: Heirs of Samuel Webster decd. and his son Samuel Webster. Oaths 7/4/1792 Bunten, Shackford and Cochran to Richard Bartlett, JP. Allowed. DOWER: 7/4/1792. Same Comm. Of Widow Dorothy Webster. Comm. also appr. income of 2/3 of real est. at $8.00. Oaths 7/4/1792 Shackford, Bunten and Cochran to Richard Bartlett, JP. Allowed. LICENSE (D30:277): 8/15/1797. To Admr. To sell real est. to amount of L66.0.0. Note: File #5704 Ephraim Moore (1791) contains a Petition on the bottom of which is a judge's memo that a License was granted to David Webster to sell real est. of est. Samuel Webster of Allenstown decd.

2775. WEBSTER, SARAH (1795) #6094
EST. Chester widow decd. testate. WILL: Drawn 2/17/1794. Legatees: Sons-Toppan and Edmund; Daus.-Sarah Robie wife of Edward Robie and Elizabeth Kitridge wife of Dr. Benjamin Kitridge; Grandson-John Smith Robie; Granddau.-Mary Robie; Grandchildren-William Hick, Sarah Sargent and Edmund Sargent; Sons-in-law- John Webster and Samuel

Webster; Dau.-in-law-Anna Flagg wife of Josiah Flagg, esq. Exec.-son Edmund. Her sig. Witnesses: Ebenr. Townsend, Simon Towle and John Dearborn. CERT. WILL (D31:517): 4/15/1795. Presented by Exec. and witnesses Townsend and Towle. Note: The men called "sons-in-law" and pos. the "dau.-in-law" are surely her step-children as she bequeaths to one grandson a desk which was her 1st husband's and to one of the in-law men a desk which was his father's. See #5048 John Webster (1784) for her husband's Will. ADMIN.: 4/15/1795. Exec.-Edmund Webster, Chester yoeman. Bond L1000.0.0. Sureties: Simon Towle, esq. and Thomas Sargeant, physician, both of Chester. Witnesses: John Morrison and W. Parker.

2776. WEBSTER, THOMAS (1772) #3945
EST. Kingston yoeman decd. testate. WILL: Drawn 12/19/1771. Legatees: Wife-Elisabeth. Daus.: Elisabeth Carter wife of John Carter, Sarah Bootman wife of Amos Bootman, Mary Carter wife of Thomas Carter, Martha Siever wife of Thomas Siever, Alice Opsilleway widow of Jacob Opsilleway and Mirriam Davis wife of Philip Davis; Grandson-Webster Davis son of Philip and Mirriam Davis. Exex.-wife Elisabeth. His sig. Witnesses: Ichabod Rowell, Jacob Hobbs and Thos. Clarke. CERT. WILL: 6/24/1772. Presented by Exex. and witnesses Rowell and Clarke. INVY. WARR.: 6/25/1772. Comm.: Thomas Clarke, Amesbury, Essex Co., MA gent. and Joseph Peaslee, Newton yoeman. INVY.: Appr. 6/29/1772. Value L155.17.8. Oaths 6/29/1772 Comm. and on 7/1/1772 Exex. to Ichabod Shaw, JP.

2777. WEED, DAVID(1787)#5314
EST. Poplin husbm. decd. testate. WILL: Drawn 12/15/1786. Legatees: Wife-Anna; Son-David; Daus.-Anna Jones, Judeth Cram, Sarah Jones and Susannah Weed; Heirs of dau. Betty Norris. Exex.-wife Anna. His mark. Witnesses: Joseph Mudget, Samuel Flanders. Benjamin Mudget and Saml. Shepard. CERT. WILL (D29:159):12/19/1787. Presented by Exex. and witnesses Flanders and Shephard. INVY.: Appr. 12/25/1787. Comm.: Biley Lyford and Ezekiel Godfrey. Value L351.11.3. Oath 12/27/1787 Exex. and on 3/10/1788 Comm. to John Scribner, JP.

2778. WEED, SARAH (1774) #4106
EST. Poplin widow decd. intestate. ADMIN.: 6/7/1774. Admr. Orlando Weed, Gilmanton, Strafford Co. gent. Bond L300.0.0. Sureties: Jonathan Gilman, Exeter esq. and Josiah Robinson, Poplin yoeman. Witnesses: Nathl. Parker and Wm. Parker Jr. INVY.: Appr. 6/7/1774. Comm.: Abraham Clark and Josiah Robinson. Value L70.14.8. Oaths 6/8/1774 Comm. to David Lawrence, JP. Oath 6/8/1774 Admr. to Wm. Parker, Jr.,

JP. LICENSE: 10/20/1774. To Admr. To sell sufficient real est. to pay debts. PETITION: 10/20/1774. Of Admr. For Comm. Insolvency. Allowed 10/20/1774 and judge appoints Comm. of John Dudley, esq. and Samuel Fellows. ACCOUNT: 10/1784. Of Admr. Allowed 10/20/1784.

2779. WEEKS, COMFORT (1786) #5233
EST. Greenland widow decd. testate. WILL: Drawn 5/14/1781. Legatees: Daus.-Thankful Rendall, Sarah Haines, Eleanor Mason, Comfort Mariner and Martha Doe. Execs.-son Dr. Ichabod and dau. Thankful Rendall. Her sig. Witnesses: Joshua Weeks, George Weeks and Clemt. Weeks. CERT. WILL (D29:88): 12/20/1786. Presented by Execs. and all witnesses. INVY.: Appr. 12/30/1786. Comm.: Wm. Weeks, Nathan Johnson, esquires and George Libbey. Value L88.9.6 1/2. Oaths 3/19/1787 Comm. and Execs. to Joshua Weeks, JP.

2780. WEEKS, JOSHUA (1776) #4212
EST. Given as Londonderry on file card with (?) by clerk. All papers say Loudon yoeman decd. intestate. RENUN.: 2/26/1776. Of Eloner Weeks, his mother, of Admin. Requests appointment of her son Nathaniel Weeks, Greenland (sic.) husbm. ADMIN.: 3/16/1776. Admr. Nathaniel Weeks, Stratham (sic.) yoeman. Bond L1000.0.0. Sureties: Daniel Pickering and John Foss, both of Stratham. Witnesses: Nathl. Parker and Wm. Parker. INVY. WARR.: 3/16/1776. Comm.: Orlando Weed and Benjamin Weeks, both of Gilmanton, Strafford Co. and Nathaniel Bachellor, Loudon, yoemen. Oaths 3/23/1776 Comm. to Nathan Bachelder, JP. INVY: Appr. 3/23/1776. Value not tallied. Esti. L76.0.0+. Oath 3/27/1776 Admr. to judge.

2781. WEEKS, WALTER (1772) #3914
GDP. Of the son of Walter Weeks Jr., Greenland yoeman decd. GDP: 3/23/1772. Of Walter, a minor over 14. Gdn. Nathan Hoag of Stratham. Bond L500.0.0. Sureties: Andrew Wiggin 3d and Jacob Jewett, both of Stratham. Witnesses: Samuel Parker and Stephen March.

2782. WEEKS, WALTER (1774) #4115
EST. Greenland husbm. decd. testate: WILL: Drawn 12/7/1773. Legatees: Wife-Comfort; Sons-Samuel, Ichabod and William; Daus.-Sarah Haines, Eleanor Mason, Comfort Weeks, Martha Doe and Thankful Randall; Grandson-Walter Weeks. Execs.-wife Comfort and son William. His sig. Witnesses: Samuel Sherburne, Thomas Lang and John Pickering Jr. CERT. WILL (D23:14): 7/11/1774. Presented by William Weeks, an Exec., the other Exec. renouncing, and all witnesses. RENUN.: 7/11/1774. Of Widow Comfort Weeks. Of Admin. in favor of her co-Exec. named in

Will, son William Jr. She also releases to Jehabod Weeks of Greenland all her right of dower in the land sold to him by her husb. and relinquishes right of dower in land sold to John Wedgewood by her husb. Witnesses: John Pickering Jr. and Saml. Hale Jr. INVY. WARR.: 7/11/1774. Comm.: William Weeks and Nathan Johnson, Greenland esquires. INVY.: Appr. 9/28/1774. Value L580.18.0. Judge notes "all sworn 9/28/1774."

2783. WEEKS, WARD COTTON (1789) #5439
EST. Exeter clothier decd. ADMIN.: 4/16/1789. Admx. Mary Weeks, Exeter widow. Bond L500.0.0. Sureties: Jabez Dodge, Exeter potter and Gilman Leavitt, Brentwood yoeman. Witnesses: Mary Sewall Parker and W. Parker. INVY.: Appr. 5/12/1789. Comm.: Paul Jewett and Jabez Dodge. Value L21.17.7. Oaths 8/10/1789 Jewett, on 8/11/1789 Dodge and on 8/18/1789 Admx. to W. Parker, Reg. PETITION: 8/18/1789. Of Admx. For Comm. Insolvency. Gives list claims of L27.9.6. CLAIMS: Dated by clerk 7/1790. Comm.: Eliphalet Hale and Wm. Parker Jr. Total L26.6.4. ACCOUNT: 7/29/1790. Of Admx. Allowed 7/29/1790. PROP. & SETTLM.: Claims L26.6.4. Amount to be proportioned L6.1.5. Allowed 7/29/1790 with order to Admx. to pay.

2784. WEEKS, COL. WILLIAM (1798) #6510
EST. Greenland esq. decd. testate. WILL: Drawn 9/25/1789. Legatees: Wife-Eleanor; Sons-Joshua, Clement, William, John, George and Jacob; Daus.-Eleanor Weeks, Martha wife of Daniel Rollings, esq., Mary Weeks, Anna Weeks and Hannah Weeks. Bequeaths negroes Casar and Dinah to wife. Execs.-sons Joshua, Clement and George. His sig. Witnesses: Ebenr. Smith, Ezra Smith and Benning Frost. Codicil: 12/18/1793. Makes changes in bequests to wife and son George, gives furniture to daus. after wife's death, gives wife horse to go with chaise formerly bequeathed and substitutes bequest to son Jacob from land to money. His sig. Witnesses: Jona. M. Sewall, Nathan Johnson and Mark Meloon. CERT. WILL (D32:542): 11/13/1798. Presented by Execs. and witness Ebenr. Smith, esq. to Will, Ezra Smith being out of state and Frost decd. Johnson and Meloon to Codicil. Also in file are what appear to be pages 1 and 2 of his orig. Will but may be a copy. INVY. (D33:40): 2/11/1799. Comm.: Ichabod Weeks, Joseph Clark and Josha. Brackett. Value $18,325.21. Oaths 2/18/1799 Weeks, Clark and Exec., to W. Parker, JP, except for some things omitted that were said to have been given away during lifetime of decd.

2785. WELLS, JOHN (1776) #4229
EST. Hampton Falls yoeman decd. testate. WILL: Drawn 3/19/1776. Legatees: Sons-Aaron and Joseph; Daus.-Eunice Wallace of Ipswich,

Essex Co., MA and Lucy Goodhue of Winchendon, Worcester Co., MA; Grandchildren-John Wells, Moses Wells and Mary Wells of Newburyport, Essex Co., MA children of his son Moses decd. Exec.-son Aaron. His sig. Witnesses: Samuel Perley, James Prescutt and Mary Prescutt. CERT. WILL: 4/24/1776. Presented by Exec. and witnesses Perley and James Prescutt. ADMIN.: 4/24/1776. Exec. Aaron Wells, Hampton Falls husbm. Bond L500.0.0. Sureties: Samuel Perley, clerk and James Prescutt, husbm., both of Hampton Falls. Witnesses: W. Parker and Moses Baker.

2786. WELLS, JOHN (1798) #6414
EST. Pelham yoeman decd. testate. PETITION: 1/13/1798. Of Hannah Wells, widow of John. She is satisfied with Will and requests it be accepted. WILL: Drawn 3/3/1797. Legatees: Wife-Hannah; Ebenezer Burbank and his wife. Exec.-Ebenezer Burbank. His mark. Witnesses: Nathan Butler, John Goodhue and Thomas Hovey. CERT. WILL (D32:419): 1/15/1798. Presented by Exec. and witnesses Butler and Hovey. ADMIN.: 1/15/1798. Exec. Ebenezer Burbank, Pelham yoeman. Bond $3,000.00. Sureties; Nathan Butler, Pelham gent. and Thomas Hovey, Dracut, Middlesex Co., MA gent. Witnesses Oliver Peabody and Wm. Parker.

2787. WELLS, JOSEPH (1773) #4008
EST. Portsmouth mariner decd. intestate. ADMIN.: 7/13/1773. Admr. Samuel Hale Jr., Portsmouth gent. Bond L500.0.0. Sureties: George Meserve, esq. and Joshua Brackett, physician, both of Portsmouth. Witnesses: Henry Rust and Samuel Parker. INVY.: Appr. 7/26/1773. Comm.: Joshua Brackett and Samuel Parker. Value L243.6.9. Oaths 7/26/1773 Admr. and Brackett and on 7/29/1773 Parker to judge. CLAIMS WARR.: 8/16/1773. Comm.: Joshua Brackett, physician and Joseph Peirce, gent., both of Portsmouth. CLAIMS: 2/9/1774. Total L149.0.8 3/4. Oaths 2/23/1774 Comm. to judge. ADMIN. D.B.N: 11/2/1780. Admr. d.b.n James Gooch, Portsmouth merchant. Bond L10000.0.0. Sureties: Eliphalet Ladd, merchant and Isaac Williams, both of Exeter. Witnesses: Wm. Fogg and Nathl. Parker. LICENSE(D26:202): 9/26/1781. To Admr. d.b.n. To sell sufficient real est. to pay debts. ACCOUNT: Of Admr. d.b.n. Allowed 10/31/1781. PROP. & SETTLM.: Claims L149.0.8 3/4. Amount to be proportioned L121.10.6. Allowed 10/31/1781 with order to Admr. d.b.n. to pay.

2788. WELLS, JOSEPH (1791) #5732
EST. Hampton Falls gent. decd. testate. WILL: Drawn 5/6/1791. Legatees: Wife-Eunice; Son-Moses; Daus.-Eunice Wells, Sally Wells and Nabby Wells; Thankful Hamilton, single woman. Execs.-wife Eunice and son

Moses. His sig. Witnesses: Abner Sanborn, Caleb Haskell and Saml. Weare. CERT. WILL (D30:170): 12/27/1791. Presented by Execs. and witnesses Sanborn and Haskell. ADMIN.: 12/27/1791. Execs.: Eunice Wells, widow and Moses Wells, yoeman, both of Hampton Falls. Bond L5000.0.0. Sureties: Abner Sanborn, husbm. and Caleb Haskell, physician, both of Hampton Falls. Witnesses: Nat Parker and W. Parker. INVY.: Comm.: Abner Sanborn, Benja. Pike and George Fifield. Value L2115.17.7. Oaths 3/14/1792 Comm. and on 3/19/1792 Eunice Wells, an Exec., to Caleb Tilton, JP. PETITION: 9/28/1829. Of Thankful Hamilton, Hampton Falls single woman. States that Moses Wells, an Exec., and both sureties died many years ago. Eunice Wells, the other Exec., has moved to Newburyport, Essex Co., MA and due to great age and infirmities of mind is unfit to Admr. By his Will, Joseph left Thankful a comfortable support as long as she remained unmarr. Though there is still a large est., Eunice neglects and refuses her the support due and she, Thankful, due to advanced age and sickness, is unable to support herself. Requests revokation of former admin. and appointment of a new Admr. Order: 10/14/1829. Eunice to be cited to appear for hearing. Cert.: 10/24/1829. Of Gilman White, Dep. Sheff., Essex Co., MA. That he handed Eunice copies of Citation and Petition. Decree: 11/11/1829. After a hearing, decreed that, due to her infirmity, the Letter of Admin. of Eunice Wells is revoked and Joseph Tilton Jr., Exeter esq., is appointed Admr. d.b.n. ADMIN. D.B.N.: 11/11/1829. Admr. d.b.n. Joseph Tilton Jr., Exeter esq. Bond $5,000.00. Sureties: Benjamin Dow, yoeman and Samuel George, esq., both of Seabrook. Witness Dudley Dodge. PETITION: 1/9/1830. Of Eunice Wells, Newburyport, Essex Co., MA widow by her atty. Sam. D. Bell. Requests appeal from Decree revoking her Letter of Admin. on the following grounds: 1. She is not unfit in mind and body to discharge duties; (2) The revokation was illegal; 3. The Will having been proved more than 38 years ago, the est. fully administered and divided among the heirs entitled to it, it is unnecessary and illegal for an Admr. d.b.n. 4. The legacy to Thankful being charged on the real and personal est., it is unnecessary for appointment of an Admr. to enable Thankful to obtain payment of the same legacy. 5. The appointment of the Admr. d.b.n. was illegal. Appeal granted 1/9/1830. BOND: 1/9/1830. Of Eunice Wells, Newburyport, Essex Co., MA widow. Bond $500.00. To appeal Decree revoking her Letter of Admin. Sureties: Benjamin Hale, Newburyport, Essex Co., MA gent. and James Burley, Exeter esq. Witnesses: J. Colman, S. Hale and S. D. Bell.

2789. WELLS, MOSES (1776) #4229
EST. Hampton Falls yoeman decd. testate. WILL: Drawn 3/19/1776. Legatees: Sons-Aaron and Joseph; Daus.-Eunice Wallace of Ipswich,

Essex Co., Mass. Bay and Lucy Goodhue of Winchendon, Worcester Co., Mass. Bay; Granddau.-Mary Wells of Newburyport, Essex Co., MA; Grandsons-John Wells and Moses Wells of Newburyport, Essex Co., MA sons of his son Moses decd. Exec.-son Aaron. His sig. Witnesses: Samuel Perley, James Prescutt and Mary Prescutt. CERT. WILL: 4/24/1776. Presented by Exec. and witnesses Perley and James Prescott. ADMIN.: 4/24/1776. Exec. Aaron Wells, Hampton Falls husbm. Bond L500.0.0. Sureties: Samuel Perley, clerk and James Prescutt, husbm., both of Hampton Falls. Witnesses: W. Parker and Moses Baker.

2790. WELLS, THOMAS (1774) #4125
EST. Chester yoeman decd. intestate. ADMIN.: 9/28/1774. Admx. Ruth Wells of Chester. Bond L1000.0.0. Sureties: Samuel Emerson, esq. and Jabez Hoit., gent., both of Chester. Witnesses: Robert MacMurphy and William White. INVY. WARR.: 9/28/1774. Comm.: Samuel Robie, esq. and Benjamin Hill, yoeman, both of Chester. Judge notes that he allows Saml. Emerson, esq. to take oath of assessors. INVY.: Appr. 12/22/1774. Value L138.0.6. Oaths 12/26/1774 Comm. to Saml. Emerson, JP. CLAIMS WARR.: 1/5/1775. Comm.: Samuel Emerson, esq. And Jabez Hoit, gent., both of Chester. CLAIMS: 7/5/1775. Total L24.19.1.1. Oaths 9/8/1775 Comm. to Wm. Parker Jr., JP. ACCOUNT: 8/21/1777. Of Admx. Allowed 8/21/1777.

2791. WENDELL, JOHN JR. (1799) #6603
EST. Portsmouth merchant decd. ADMIN.: 8/28/1799. Admr. John Wendell, Portsmouth esq. Bond $4,000.00. Sureties: Samuel Sherburne, esq. and George W. Wendell, merchant, both of Portsmouth. Witnesses: William Berry and Daniel Wendell. INVY.: 12/23/1799. Comm.: Jeremiah Libbey, George Wenworth and Samuel Penhallow Jr. Value $4,434.35. Affirm. and oaths 12/23/1799 Comm. to George Gains, JP. PETITION: 12/28/1800. Of Admr. For Comm. Insolvency. Gives claims already in of $9,136.00. Also for a License to sell all the real est., noting he is the sole heir. LICENSE: 12/31/1800. To Admr. To sell real est. to $3,000.00. CLAIMS WARR.: 12/3/1800. Comm.: Isaac Rindge, Jermiah Libbey and Rich'd. Cutts Shannon, Portsmouth esquires. On 7/22/1801. Comm. allowed 6 more months. Claims: 2/16/1802. Total $5,085.62. Affirms. Comm. to George Gains, JP., with notation that other claims were not allowed for lack of evidence, except the claim of Col. Samuel Sherburne, annexed. On examination of a statement of the claim made by decd. and several settlements made by themselves since, Comm. rules the transaction was settled. PETITION: 5/27/1801. Of Admr. For more time for Comm. Insolvency as many out-of-state claims not in. CLAIMS EXTENSION: 3/13/1802. The Comm. is allowed 3 months longer. Addl. Claims:

6/14/1802. Total $5,337.29. This last includes the Sargent claim. Affirms. 6/14/1802 Comm. to George Gains, JP. CLAIMS: Total $5,337.29. Has notation that the claims were returned 6/16/1802 and on the same day the Admr. objected to the claim of Daniel Sargent, esq. and on 7/2/1802 Sargent filed his Declaration against the Admr., which is now pending in the Superior Court. OBJECTIONS: 6/16/1802. Of Admr. To claim of Daniel Sargent, Boston, Suffolk Co., MA esq. Admr. claims that the promise of decd. to pay Sargent for goods delivered to a Saml. Haley has been paid and that on 5/1/1798 Sargent discharged Haley in full. Gives complicated list of details of several transactions between Wendell, Haley and Sargent. He refuses to pay the claim and advises Sargent to take recourse to the law. DECLARATION: 7/2/1802. Of Jere. Macon, atty for Daniel Sargent. A long narration of the history of his claim against est. Requests a copy of the Declaration be served on Admr. and he be notified to appear before the Superior Court of Judicature. Received and filed at the Probate office 7/2/1802. BILL: From Daniel Sargent. To John Wendell. Total $221.00. For goods delivered to Samuel Haley. CITATION: 7/2/1802. To Admr. To appear before the Superior Court of Judicature to answer Sargent's Declaration. CERT.: 7/2/1802. Of W. Parker, Reg. That a true copy of Declaration has been filed and notice given to Admr. to appear at Superior Court. ACCOUNT: 11/20/1804. Of Admr. By Citation at request of some of creditors. Allowed 11/21/1804 there being no objections. PROP. & SETTLM.: Claims $5,337.29. Amount to be proportioned $3,031.00. Allowed 12/3/1804 with order to Admr. to pay. Note: This file also includes a letter of 6/12/1803 from William Morse of Boston, Essex Co., MA to the judge regarding his inability to appear as cited as agent for the widow and children of Capt. Jose. It belongs with #6633 Capt. Michael Dennis Jose (1799)and is recorded there.

2792. WENTWORTH: DRISCO & MARK (1772) #3922
GDP. Of the children of Ezekiel Wentworth, Somersworth yoeman decd. GDP: 4/11/1772. Of Drisco and Mark, minors over 14. Gdn. Ephraim Kimball of Dover. Bond L1000.0.0. Sureties: Joshua Varney and John Kimball of Dover. Witnesses: Samuel Parker and Sarah Wentworth.

2793. WENTWORTH, ELIZABETH (1794) #6050
EST. Of Portsmouth, widow of Mark Hunking Wentworth esq., decd. testate. WILL: Drawn 11/11/1793. Legatees: Son-John, esq., late Gov. of Province of NH; Dau.-Ann Fisher wife of John Fisher; Grandsons-Charles Mary Wentworth son of her son John, John Fisher Jr. and John Wentworth; Granddaus.-Anne Sheafe, Elizabeth Wentworth alias Mimion dau. Of her son Thomas, Elizabeth Sheafe, Anna Bella Wentworth, Sarah Fisher and Frances Ann Fisher; Heirs of her grandson Charles Mary

Wentworth; Other heirs of her son John; Heirs of her grandson John Fisher Jr.; Widow Mary Fields now in her family; William Sheafe husb. of her granddau. Ann Sheafe. Execs.-Kinsman John Peirce and grandson John Fisher Jr. Her sig. Witnesses: Jonathan Warner, A. R. Cutter and George Gains. Codicil: Drawn 10/20/1794. Adds legacies to granddaus. Sarah Fisher and Frances Ann Fisher and a legacy to Widow Sarah Fellows. Witnesses: A. E. Cutter, Elizabeth Seawards and George Gains. CERT. WILL (D31:407): 12/2/1794. Presented by John Pierce, an Exec., the other being out of state, and witnesses Cutter and Gains. ADMIN.: 12/2/1794. Exec. John Pierce, Portsmouth merchant. Bond L2000.0.0. Sureties: Daniel Rindge and Ammi R. Cutter, Portsmouth esquires. Witnesses: Elijah Hardy and Nathl. Kennard. INVY. (D32:23): Appr. 7/16/1795. Comm.: A. R. Cutter, James Sheafe and D. R. Rogers. Value L16151.10.10. Comm. appraises lands outside of Portsmouth from best information available, not having seen them. Oaths 7/17/1795 Comm. and John Pierce, an Exec., to George Gains, JP. Note: The orig. Invy. is in file, but it is very fragile and in pieces and can be read only in the Docket book. LETTER: 8/25/1795. From John Fisher Jr. To William Parker, esq. Having been appointed an Exec. in Will, he wishes to qualify himself for the office. ADMIN.: 8/25/1795. Exec. John Fisher Jr, Portsmouth esq. Bond $6,000.00. Sureties: Daniel Rindge and Ammi Ruhamah Cutter, Portsmouth esquires. Witness Daniel Rindge Jr. LETTER ADMIN.: 8/25/1795. Of John Fisher. It states that at the time John Pierce was allowed to be Exec., power was reserved to make the same grant to John Fisher when he applied and is hereby granted. ADDL. INVY.: 10/13/1795. Value L290.18.3. Oaths 10/15/1795 Comm. to George Gains, JP. PETITION: Of William Sheafe, Portsmouth merchant and Ann his wife, a dau. of Thomas Wentworth, Portsmouth esq. decd. and an heir of Mrs. Elizabeth Wentworth decd. For div. of est. per Will. Requests Comm. of A. R. Cutter, James Sheafe, Daniel Rindge and Daniel Rogers, esquires and Peter Coffin, merchant, all of Portsmouth. Granted. DIV. WARR.: 6/1/1797. Comm. as requested. DIV.: Divisees: Ann Fisher, John Wentworth, Elizabeth Wentworth now Elizabeth Minchin, Ann Wentworth now Ann Sheafe and Annabella Wentworth now Annabella Gore. Oaths 7/12/1797 Rindge, Sheafe and Rogers to George Gains, JP. Allowed 7/14/1797 there being no objections. The following petition found in #5168 Hunking Wentworth (17860 belongs here. PETITION: 6/5/1802. Of John Wentworth, Portsmouth esq. States that he is a legatee of the Will of Mrs. Elizabeth Wentworth, widow of Mark Hunking Wentworth, esq. Elizabeth died about Oct. 1794. John Peirce and John Fisher Jr. were appointed Execs. and an Invy. taken July 1785. Since that time, he and his agent have repeatedly applied to Execs. to render an Account and satisfy the Petioner's thought that a large part of the residuary est. was not comprehended in the Invy., which must have been known to the Execs. through the same sources he has. He feels the unevaluated portion to be 50, if not 90, percent of his property, being a great loss to him as he is willing to prove in any way the judge wishes. Requests Execs. be cited to Account or allow Petitioner to sue Bond. of Admin. ORDER: 6/5/1802. Execs. to be cited to appear and exhibit Account. ACCOUNT: 12/3/1802. Of John Peirce. Of his services to ests. of both Mark Hunking Wentworth and Elizabeth Wentworth. ACCOUNT: Of John Peirce. Of Admin. est. Elizabeth Wentworth. Allowed 3/14/1803. Objections of residuary legatee John Wentworth esq. considered, and having been consented to by 7/8 of the legatees.

2794. WENTWORTH, GEORGE (1787) #5315
EST. Portsmouth mariner decd. testate. PETITION: 12/19/1787. Of George Wentworth. States that all of the est. that has come to his hands is real est. He has been at great expense to recover it and his demands against the est. are over L1000.0.0. Requests license so he can pay his and other claims. Granted. LICENSE (D29:159): 12/19/1787. To Admr. To sell sufficient real est. to pay debts. Note: This file contains a Petition and Cert. which, from the divisees, appears to belong with #5049 Hunking Wentworth (1784) and has been put there.

2795. WENTWORTH, HUNKING (1784) #5049
EST. Portsmouth esq. decd. testate. WILL: Drawn 9/6/1783. Legatees: Wife-Margaret; Dau-Elizabeth Warner widow of Saml. Warner, Portsmouth mariner decd.; Children of late dau. Sarah Penhallow decd. wife of John Penhallow, esq.; Children of dau. Elizabeth Warner. Exec.-John Penhallow. His sig. Witnesses: Saml. Penhallow, Joshua Brackett, Peter Man and Mark Nelson. CERT WILL: 10/20/1784. Presented by Jonathan Warner and witnesses Penhallow, Brackett, esq. and Man. RENUN.: 10/19/1784. Of John Penhallow. Of Executorship after he has presented the Will for proving. PETITION: 10/19/1784. Of Margaret Wentworth, widow of Hunking. As John Penhallow refuses to be Exec., she requests appointment of Jonathan Warner, esq. ADMIN. (D27:528): 10/20/1784. Admr. Jonathan Warner, esq. Sureties: Samuel Penhallow, esq. and Jonathan Sherburne, physician, all of Portsmouth. INVY.: Appr. 3/14/1785. Comm.: Wm. Knight, Jno. Parker and Isaac Rindge. Value L2092.10.7. Oaths 3/14/1785 Comm. to George Gains, JP. Oath 3/15/1785 Admr. to W. Parker, JP. PETITION: Dated by clerk 7/19/1786. Of Admr. States that income from est. not enough to support widow and dau. as in Will or to pay him for the expenses he has been advancing for them. Requests License. LICENSE: 7/19/1786. To Admr. To sell sufficient real est. to pay the legacies. ACCOUNT: 5/26/1788. Of Admr. LETTER:

8/18/1789. From Jonathan Warner and John Penhallow, esquires. To judge. Warner reports that he delivered judge's letter to Penhallow and as time is short, they have agreed that the Account lay until 3d Wed. in Sept., if agreeable to judge. ACCOUNT: 10/21/1789. Of Admr. Allowed 10/21/1789. PETITION: 5/1/1800. Of: Hunking Penhallow and Benjamin Penhallow, Portsmouth merchants. For div. of the real est. they hold in partnership with others, as provided in Will. DUPL. OF PETITION. APPR. WARR.: 7/14/1800. Comm.: Samuel Cutts, Isaac Rindge and James Sheafe, all of Portsmouth. To appr. the rent of the late dwelling house and land of decd. for the 5 1/2 years after 2/25/1788. Appr.: 7/16/1800. Value of rent is $24.00 = $132.00 for the 5 1/2 years. Oaths 7/16/1800 Cutts and Sheafe, esquires to Isaac Rindge, JP. OPINION: 7/28/1800. Of J. Mason. Of \terms of Will of Hunking Wentworth. He outlines that the Will provided for decd's dau. Elizabeth Warner widow of late Samuel Warner, Portsmouth, mariner decd.; The children of decd's late dau. Sarah Penhallow decd. wife of Jno. Penhallow, esq. and The children of decd's dau. Elizabeth. At the time of the Will, there were 8 children of Samuel Penhallow and 3 of Elizabeth Warner. Two Penhallow children died during Hunking's lifetime, one of which left children. At the death of the widow Margaret, there were still living 6 Penhallow children and 3 Warner children. The question asked of him, Mason, is what proportion are the children entitled to of what remained at the death of the decd's wife Margaret? He interprets the Will to mean that the children inherit in their own right and not as heirs of their mothers. Therefore, they are each entitled to 1/9 of the whole real and personal est. OPINION: 7/31/1800. Of Edw. St. Loe Livermore. Upon considering the Will, he is of opinion that the children of Sarah Penhallow living at the time of Hunking's death and the children of Elizabeth Warner share alike 1/9 to each. 2D ACCOUNT: 8/13/1800. Of Admr. Oath 8/13/1800 Admr. and consented to by Benj. Penhallow atty. to part of the heirs. Decree: Admr. to pay bal. of L473.7.2 to the children of John Penhallow, esq. and the children of Capt. Saml. Warner decd. who were living at the time of Hunking's death. DIV. WARR.: 8/15/1800. Comm.: Samuel Cutts, Isaac Rindge, James Sheafe, Supply Clap and Samuel Adams, Portsmouth esquires. To div. the dwelling house and its land, giving 2/3 to the children of John Penhallow and 1/3 to the children of Samuel Warner, who now hold the property in common. DIV.: 8/20/1800. Divisees per Warr. Oaths 8/20/1800 Cutts, Sheafe, Clap and Adams to Isaac Rindge, JP. Allowed 8/26/1800 no objection being made. PETITION: 9/26/1800. Of Admr. Requests appeal against some disallowances made by judge in his Account of 8/13. Granted 10/3/1800. BOND: 10/3/1800. Of Admr. Bond $150.00. To appeal the Decree disallowing part of his Account. Sureties: George Gains, esq. and Mark Nelson, merchant. Witnesses: Nathl. Banfill and Isaac Rindge. PETITION: 9/27/1800. Of Admr. He is dissatisfied with Div. Requests appeal. Granted 10/3/1800. BOND: 10/3/1800. Of Admr. Bond $150.00. To appeal the Decree allowing Div. Sureties: Geo. Gains, esq. and Mark Nelson, merchant. Witnesses: Nathl. Banfill and Isaac Rindge. PETITION: 3/16/1802. Of Benjamin Penhallow, Portsmouth merchant, a legatee. Claims the Admr. has received money for which he has not, and refuses to, account and refuses to allow the legatees to see his account books of admin. Requests Admr. be cited to Account. Order: 3/17/1802. Admr. to be cited to appear and exhibit Account. PETITION: 3/16/1802. Of Benjamin Penhallow, Portsmouth merchant for himself and his brethren. States that the Admr. had a hearing in Feb. 1801 before the Superior Court on his appeal against the judge's ruling on the Account of 8/13/1800, at which the judge's Decree was upheld, yet the Admr. still refuses to pay the legatees the bal. in the Account per the judge's order. Requests permission to sue Bond of Admin. Order: 3/17/1802. Admr. to be cited to appear and show cause why his bond should not be put in suit. Decree: 6/16/1802. Admr. shows no cause why Petition should not be granted. Petition granted. CITATION: 3/19/1802. To Exec. To appear and answer the Petition to sue his Bond of Admin. Marked as a copy. ADDL. ACCOUNT: 6/16/1802. Of Admr. Allowed persons interested having attended and been fully heard. Order: To Exec. To pay bal. in same manner as decreed for the 2d Account. BOND: 7/22/1802. Of Benjamin Penhallow, Portsmouth merchant. Bond: $200.00. To sue Bond of Admin. Surety: David Austin, Portsmouth merchant. Note: The following Petition and Cert. found in #5315 George Wentworth (1787), from the divisees, appears to belong here. PETITION: 4/18/1803. Of: George Wentworth, Joshua Wentworth, Jonathan Warner, John Penhallow Sr., Samuel Panhallow Jr., John Penhallow Jr., Hunking Penhallow, Benjamin Penhallow, Thomas Penhallow, Sarah Penhallow, Daniel Austin and Mary his wife, Daniel Warner and Elizabeth Sherburne, all of Portsmouth; Robert Cutts and Margery his wife, Andrew P. Wentworth, William Mugridge and Sally his wife, John Fernald, William W. Fernald, Samuel Fernald, Benjamin Fernald, Margery P. Wentworth, Mary Fernald, and Hannah Fernald, all of Kittery, York Co., MA/ME. They are seized in fee simple of 7/11 parts of an undiv. house and land in Portsmouth. George and Joshua Wentworth own 3/11; Warner 2/11; John Sr., Saml. Jr., John Jr., Hunking, Benja., Thomas, Sarah and Mary Penhallow, the Austins and Elizabeth Sherburne 1/11; The Cutts, Andrew P. Wentworth, Mudgridges and Fernalds 1/11. Owners of the other 4/11s unknown to Petitioners. Request div. Order: 4/21/1803. For hearing, Petitioners to publish Petition and Order. CERT.: 6/1803. Of Margaret Purcell, Portsmouth sempstress. As one of the owners of the real est. described in the Petition of George Wentworth and others, now pending before the Probate Court, she comes into court and says that Wentworth and the others are not seized of the premises as set forth in the Petition and prays that it may be dismissed.

2796. WENTWORTH, HON. JOHN (1773) #3977
EST. Portsmouth esq. decd. testate. WILL.: Drawn 10/20/1773. Legatees: Wife-Sarah; Son-Hugh Hall Wentworth; Daus.-Mary Clapham wife of John Clapham, Rebekah Butler wife of Gillam Butler and Sarah Purcell. Bequeaths negro woman Esther to dau. Mary and after Mary's death to her dau. Ann Appleton. Execs.- son Hugh Hall Wentworth and sons-in-law Gregory Purcell and Gillam Butler. Witnesses: Leverett Hubbard, Saml. Sherburne, Jr., Joseph Peirce, Samuel Hale Jr. and Samuel Parker. CERT. WILL: 11/30/1773. Presented by witnesses Sherburne, Peirce, Hubbard, esq. and Hale. INVY. WARR.: 3/20/1774. Comm.: John Wendell and Saml Hale Jr. INVY.: Appr. 6/3/1774. Value L507.13.5. Oath 6/3/1774 Gregory Purcell, an Exec., and Comm. to judge. Judge asked Comm. what happened to the negro woman Esther given to widow and Mary Appleton in Will? Comm. replied Mary was the property of Mary Appleton in her widowhood and so not appr. DEPOSITION: 5/30/1774. Of: Sarah Wentworth, Mary Wentworth, G. Purcell, Sarah Purcell and Rebecca Butler. They all cert. that John gave his negro girl Esther to his daughter Mary. PETITION: 3/19/1778. Of Rebecca Butler, atty. for Gillam Butler, gent, sole surviving Exec., who is now in Philadelphia. For License. She notes a Claims Comm. allowed claims of L427.9.10. LICENSE: 3/25/1778. To Gillam Butler, Exec.. To sell all the land in Rumney, Grafton Co. PETITION: 1/19/1779. Of Rebecca Butler. States that her husb. Gillam is now deceased and as his Exex. she now becomes Exex. also of est. of her father, John Wentworth. Requests License as his est. is insolvent. LICENSE: 1/21/1779. To Sarah Purcell, Exex. To sell sufficient real est. to pay debts. ACCOUNT OF DEBTS: Undated and not tallied. Esti. L385.0.0+

2797. WENTWORTH, GOV. JOHN (1780) #4600
TRUSTEESHIP Of the former Portsmouth Royal Gov., an absentee. RECEIPT: 3/30/1779. From: Nichl. Gilman, Treasurer. For L656.4.6 received from Joseph Badger and Caleb Hodgdon, esquires and John Burnham Hanson, a Comm. appointed by the NH General Court to dispose of property belonging to the absentees, being money raised by part of the effects of John Wentworth, esq. RECEIPT: 4/2/1779. From Jno. Taylor Gilman on behalf of Nicholas Gilman, esq., Treasurer. To same Comm. For L1404.3.0, money received on account of the sales of the Governor's library. ADMIN.: 2/24/1780. Trustee Saml. Gilman, Newmarket esq. Bond L200000.0.0. Gilman is appointed Trustee of the est. of John Wentworth, esq., late Governor of the Province of NH, an absentee from

the state whose est. is by law declared forfeit to the use of the state. Sureties: James Hill of Newmarket and Enoch Coffin of Epping, esquires. Witnesses: W. Parker and Nathl. Parker. INVY.: Appr. 3/14/1780. A list only with no appr. sums. List is too complicated to try to esti. Oath 3/14/1780. Of Trustee that the Invy. is all that has yet come into his hands. LICENSE: 3/15/1780. To Trustee. To sell all the real and personal est. he has already inventoried. ACCOUNT: 1/30/1782. Of Trustee. Of the confiscated est. Allowed 1/30/1782. ACCOUNT: 3/7/1782. Of: Col. Joseph Badger, Caleb Hodgdon and John B. Hanson, Comm. Of disposal of est. of John Wentworth, an absentee. Allowed 3/7/1782. Includes a note that they are waiting on Mr. Wentworth about the negroes. ACCOUNT: Of Trustee. Allowed 4/21/1783. ADDL. ACCOUNT: Of Trustee. Allowed 6/5/1783. LETTER: From Mark H. Wentworth, father of former Gov. John Wentworth. To judge. States that he feels that the demands against the est. and the mismanagement before it came into the hands of the judge, will render it insolvent. He has determined to withdraw his own demands so that the creditors may have their just demands paid. He reserves the right to reinstate his demands once the other creditors have been paid, if there is a surplus. He can vouch for all his demands, has paid off several creditors himself to a considerable amount since the Gov. left and has greatly augmented the value of the est. in Wolfeboro., to the profit of the creditors.

2798. WENTWORTH, MARK HUNKING (1786) #5168
EST. Portsmouth esq. decd. testate. WILL: Drawn 12/14/1785. Legatees: Wife-Elizabeth; Son-John; Dau.-Ann Fisher wife of John Fisher; Children of his son Thomas-Mark, John, Elizabeth and Anna Bella. Ref. to bro. Hunking Wentworth. Exex.-wife Elizabeth, or if wife decd., survivor of friend John Pierce and grandson John Fisher. His sig. Witnesses: Jonnathan Warner, George Gains and William Hart. CERT. WILL (D28:387): 1/18/1786. Presented by Exex. and all witnesses. ADMIN.: 1/18/1786. Exex. Elizabeth Wentworth, widow. Bond L20000.0.0. Sureties: Daniel Rindge, esq. and John Peirce, merchant. Witnesses: Jonathan Warner and Dan. R. Rodger. Note on back: Gov. Bartlett would be glad to hear the road called Richmond Hill if Miss Parker pleases. ADMIN.: 12/2/1794. Exec. John Peirce, Portsmouth merchant. Bond L2000.0.0. Sureties: Daniel Rindge and Ammi R. Cutter, Portsmouth esquires. Witnesses: James Rundlett and Daniel Rogers Jr. Note: this file contains a Petition which belongs with #6050 Widow Elizabeth Wentworth (1794). In her est. also is an Account for both ests.

2799. WENTWORTH, MARY (1790) #5519
EST. Portsmouth widow decd. testate. WILL: Drawn 1/9/1790. Legatees: Sister-Sarah Wentworth; Niece-Mary Clapham. Exec.-Nathaniel Adams; Her sig. Witnesses: A. R. Cutter, Margaret Purcell and Ann Purcell. CERT. WILL (D29:341): 2/17/1790. Presented by Exec. and all witnesses. ADMIN.: 2/15/1790. Exec. Nathaniel Adams, Portsmouth esq. Bond L200.0.0. Sureties: Ammi Cutter and Samuel Hill, both of Portsmouth. Witnesses: Jno. Parker and R. Champney.

2800. WENTWORTH, COL. MICHAEL (1795) #6152
EST. Portsmouth esq. and gent., decd. ADMIN.: 10/21/1795. Admx. Martha Wentworth, Portsmouth widow. Bond $3,000.00. Sureties: Joshua Brackett and Hall Jackson, Portsmouth esquires. Witnesses: Mary Wentworth and Joseph Willard. INVY.: Appr. 2/17/1796. Comm.: Joshua Brackett, Hall Jackson and George Wentworth. Value $1,360.48. Oaths 2/17/1796 Admx. and Comm. to Geo. Gains, JP. PETITION: 6/15/1794. Of Hall Jackson on behalf of Admx. For Comm. Insolvency. Gives claims already known as over $23,000.00. Granted. DUPL. PETITION but includes claims of $23,636.49. LIST OF CLAIMS: 10/8/1796. Signed by Jeremiah Libbey, who states they have not yet been examined and passed as just but are filed for that purpose. Total $19,469.72 2/3. A notation on back of real est. but no explanation. CLAIMS WARR.: 6/15/1796. Comm.: Supply Clap, Isaac Rindge and Jeremiah Libbey, Portsmouth esquires. Claims: 2/13/1797. Total $18,602.16. Affirms. 2/13/1797 Comm. to George Gains, JP. ACCOUNT: 3/9/1797. Of Admx. Oath 3/17/1797 Admx. to George Gains, JP. Allowed 3/20/1797. PROP. & SETTLM.: Claims $18,602.16. Amount to be proportioned $958.00. Allowed 3/20/1797 with order to Admx. to pay.

2801. WEST, NATHANIEL (1777) #4337 & (1775) #4177
EST. Concord gent. decd. intestate. RENUN. (#4177): 8/22/1775. Of Sarah West, Concord widow. Of Admin. Requests appointment of Timothy Walker Jr. Allowed 8/25/1775. ADMIN. (#4177): 8/26/1775. Admr. Timothy Walker Jr., Concord gent. Bond L1000.0.0. Sureties: Abiel Foster, Canterbury clerk and Daniel Sanborn, Sanbornton, Strafford Co. esq. Witnesses: Saml. Brooks and W. Parker Jr. INVY. (#4337): Appr. 4/22/1775. Comm.: John Fowle and Thos. Stickney. Value L164.7.3. Oaths 9/29/1776 Comm. to Timo. Walker, JP. DOWER WARR. (#4177): 3/25/1776. Comm.: John Fowle, Thomas Stickney, Benjamin Emery, Robert Davis and Richard Harbut, all of Concord. Of Widow Sarah West. DOWER (#4337):9/29/1777. Oaths 9/29/1777 Fowle, Stickney and Emery to Timo. Walker Jr., JP. Allowed 12/31/1777. LICENSE (#4337): 2/26/1775. To Admr. To sell sufficient real est. to pay debts. CLAIMS

WARR. (#4337): 11/27/1777. Comm.: Thomas Stickney, esq. and James Walker, gent., both of Concord. On 10/28/1778 Comm. allowed 4 months longer. CLAIMS (#4337): 8/31/1779. Total L266.15.7 1/2. ACCOUNT (#4177): Of Admr. Allowed 6/2/1780. ADDL. ACCOUNT (#4337): Of Admr. Allowed 6/14/1781. PROP. & SETTLM. (#4337): Claims L266.15.7 1/2. Amount to be proportioned L58.17.4. Allowed 6/29/1781 with order to Admr. to pay.

2802. WHEELER, JOHN SULLIVAN (1791) #5622
GDP. Of the son of Jona. Wheeler, late of Salem decd. GDP.: 2/27/1791. Of John Sullivan Wheeler, a minor over 14. Gdn.: Richard Kimball, Salem gent. Bond: L1000.0.0. Sureties: Deacon Jona. Massey and William Duty, esq., both of Salem. Witnesses: Nathaniel Perkins and Judith Perkins.

2803. WHEELER, JONATHAN (1777) #4411
EST. Salem gent. decd. testate. WILL: Drawn 11/14/1777. Legatees: Wife-Easter; Sons-Jonathan, Richard and John Sullivan Wheeler; Daus.-Chloe Wheeler, Tryphena Wheeler (2 oldest), Dille Wheeler, Anna Wheeler and Apphia Wheeler (3 youngest); Apprentice Boy-David Bussel. Exex.-Wife Easter. His sig. Witnesses: Walker Smith, Thomas Smith and Timothy Ladd. CERT. WILL (D24:161): 12/31/1777. Presented by Exex. and witnesses Walker Smith and Thomas Smith. INVY.: Appr. 2/4/1778. Comm.: Stephen Webster, James Webster and Jesse Smith. Value L1662.15.6. Oaths 2/5/1778 Comm. to Timothy Ladd, JP.

2804. WHEELER, NEHEMIAH (1796) #6285
EST. Epping esq. decd. testate. WILL: Drawn 6/29/1796. Legatees: Daus.-Anne Wheeler, Judith Wheeler and Elizabeth Lane; Daus.-in-law-Widow Sarah Chadbourne and Jane Brown wife of Benjamin Brown; Hunkin Wheeler son of Mary Meserve decd. Execs.-son-in-law Isaiah Lane and dau. Anne Wheeler. His sig. Witnesses: Enoch Coffin, Andrew Hanson and John Lunt. CERT. WILL (D32:223): 12/12/1796. Presented by Execs. and witnesses Hanson and Lunt. ADMIN.: 12/12/1796. Execs.-Isaiah Lane, joiner and Anne Wheeler, spinster, both of Epping. Bond $2,000.00. Sureties: Andrew Hanson and John Lunt, Epping yoemen. Witness W. Parker. INVY.: Appr. 12/23/1796. Comm.: Andrew Hanson, Thomas Norris and Ezekl. Godfrey. Value $558.17. Affirms. 12/23/1796 Norris and Hanson and oaths Execs. to Ezekl. Godfrey, JP.

2805. WHEELWRIGHT, DAMARIS (1780) #4662
EST. Portsmouth widow decd. ADMIN.: 10/25/1780. Admr. John Wheelwright, Portsmouth mariner. Bond L10000.0.0. Sureties: John Wendell of Portsmouth and Thomas Odiorne of Exeter, esquires. Witness

Nathl. Parker. INVY.: Comm.: John Wendell, Jno. Parker and Jacob Sheafe, Jr. Value L60.0.0 in land plus 200 Spanish milled dollars. Oaths 10/28/1780 Comm. and Admr. to Saml. Penhallow, JP. APPR. WARR.: 2/7/1781. Comm.: Pearse Long and John Parker, esquires; John Marshall, boatbuilder; Jacob Sheafe Jr. and Jeremiah Libbey, merchants, all of Portsmouth. To view the real est. to see if it can be div. among heirs. Div. Or appr. Appr.: Value L70.0.0. Oaths 7/31/1781 Marshall, Long, Sheafe and Libbey to Saml. Penhallow, JP. DECREE SETTLM.: 10/22/1782. John Wheelwright, only surviving son, appearing and consenting, real est. settled on him, John to pay his co-heirs: Heirs of his bro. Ebenezer Jose decd. L24.17.0, their double share and to his sisters Hannah and Mary L12..8.6 each, all within two months, with interest. BOND: 10/22/1782. Of John Wheelwright, Portsmouth mariner. Bond L1000.0.0. To pay his co-heirs per Decree Settlm. Sureties: Thomas Sheafe and James Sheafe, merchants. Witnesses: Mark Seavey and John Sheafe. ACCOUNT: 10/30/1782. Of Admr. Allowed 10/30/1782.

2806. WHEELWRIGHT, CAPT. JOHN (1784) #5039
EST. Portsmouth mariner decd. intestate. ADMIN.: 9/15/1784. Admr. Thomas Odiorne, Exeter esq. Bond L500.0.0. Sureties: John Ward Gilman, gent. and Thomas Gilman, yoeman, both of Exeter. INVY. WARR: 9/15/1784. Comm.: Jacob Treadwell and Jeremish Libbey, esquires and Jacob Walden, trader, all of Portsmouth. INVY.: Appr. 9/17/1784. Value L326.17.4. Oaths 9/17/1784 Comm. to George Gains, JP. PETITION: 1/19/1785. Of Admr. For License and Comm. Insolvency. Gives list claims of L340.12.1 1/4. LICENSE (D28:520): 1/19/1785. To Admr. To sell sufficient real est. to pay debts. CLAIMS WARR.: 1/19/1785. Comm.: John Parker, Jacob Treadwell and Jeremiah Libbey, Portsmouth esquires. Claims: Total L487.12.0 1/4. Oaths 11/5/1785 Comm. to Olivr. Whipple, JP. DOWER WARR.: 11/28/1785. Comm.: Richard Champney and Thomas Chadburn, esquires.; Peter Coues, mariner; John Fernald, brazier and Abner Blasdell, yoeman, all of Portsmouth. Of Widow Martha Wheelwright. ACCOUNT: 12/21/1785. Of Admr. Allowed 12/21/1785. PROP. & SETTLM.: Claims L487.12.0 1/4. Amount to be proportioned L150.6.4. Allowed 1/18/1786 with order to Admr. to pay. DOWER: 12/16/1785. Oaths 12/16/1785 Comm. to George Gains, JP. Allowed 3/15/1786.

2807. WHEELWRIGHT, JOHN (1784) #5040
GDP. Of the son of Capt. John Wheelwright, Portsmouth mariner decd. GDP.: 9/15/1784. Of John, a minor over 14. Gdn. Thomas Odiorne, Exeter esq. Bond L1000.0.0. Sureties: John Ward Gilman, gent. and Thos. Gilman, yoeman, both of Exeter. Witness W. Parker.

WHICHER. See also Whitcher, Whittier

2808. WHICHER, WILLIAM (1772) #3912
See #3912 William Whitcher (1772)

2809. WHIDDEN, JOSEPH (1794) #5976
EST. Portsmouth blacksmith decd. intestate. ADMIN.: 2/19/1794. Admx.: Mary Whidden, Portsmouth widow. Bond L1000.0.0. Sureties: Joseph Akerman and Nathaniel Banfill, Portsmouth yoemen. Witness John Ayers. INVY.: Appr. 4/14/1794. Comm.: Francis Marden, Thomas Beck and John Ayers. Value L258.3.0. Oaths 4/17/1794 Admx. and Comm. to George Gains, JP. PETITION: 1/8/1832. Of Daniel Whidden, son of Joseph, for Admin. D.B.N as Mary has died, the admin. of est. not completed and other heirs have for 3(?) years neglected and refused to admin. ADMIN. D.B.N: 1/8/1833. Admr. d.b.n Daniel Whidden of Portsmouth. Bond $500.00. Sureties: Joshua Johnson and Samuel Moulton, both of Portsmouth. Witness John Kelly.

2810. WHIDDEN, MARK (1799) #6527
EST. Loudon yoeman decd. ADMIN. (D33:27): 1/17/1799. Admr. Joseph Moore, Canterbury gent. Bond $2,000.00. Sureties: Parsons Whidden and Josiah Whidden, Canterbury yoemen. Witnesses: Jno. Parker and Wm. Parker. INVY. (D33:168): Appr. 1/21/1799. Comm.: Asa Foster, Saml. Piper and John Sutton. Value $715.34. Oaths 1/21/1799 Piper and Sutton and on 11/20/1799 Admr. to Asa Foster, JP. Note: The origs. of both the Admin. and Invy. are missing. In the file are old, poor photocopies, the bottom portion of the Invy. being unreadable. This file also contains a Gdp. which belongs with #6529 Eliphalet Gilman (1799) and is recorded there.

2811. WHIDDEN, MICHAEL (1773) #3995
EST. Portsmouth joiner decd. intestate. ADMIN.: 2/12/1773. Admr. Michael Whidden, Portsmouth joiner. Bond L500.0.0. Sureties: James Haslett, leather breeches maker and Richard Jackson, joiner, both of Portsmouth. Witnesses: John Taylor and Samuel Parker. INVY. WARR.: 2/12/1776. Comm.: George Hart, gent. and Richard Jackson, joiner, both of Portsmouth. INVY.: Appr. 2/13/1773 Value L194.0.6.1. Oaths 2/13/1773 Admr., Hart and Jackson to judge. ADDL. INVY.: Appr. 2/15/1773. Value L14.15.6. Oaths 3/13/1773 Comm. and Admr. to judge. LICENSE: 3/16/1773. To Admr. To sell sufficient real est. to pay debts.

2812. WHIDDEN, SAMUEL (1797) #6454
GDP. Of the son of James Whidden, Greenland gent. GDP.: 6/21/1797. Of Samuel, a minor under 14. Gdn. James Whidden, Greenland gent., his father. Bond $2,000.00. Sureties: Edward Gove, gent. and Josiah Akarman, baker, both of Portsmouth. Witnesses: Richd. Pickering and W. Parker.

2813. WHIPPLE, WILLIAM (1786) #5176.
EST. Portsmouth esq. decd. PETITION: 2/14/1786. Of: Kathn. Whipple, widow and Jos. Whipple, bro., of William. Request they be granted Admin. ADMIN.: 2/15/1786. Admrs.: Kathor. Whipple, widow and Joseph Whipple, esq., both of Portsmouth. Bond L2000.0.0. Sureties: Joshua Brackett, esq. and Richard Hart, merchant, both of Portsmouth. Witnesses: John Bartlett and Mary Tufton Moffatt. INVY.: Comm.: John Evans and William Gardner. Appr. 11/15/1788. Value L928.9.6. Oaths 11/15/1788 Comm. to Saml. Penhallow, JP. Oaths 11/18/1788 Admrs. to Geo. Gains, JP. DECLARATION: Of Katherine Whipple by her atty. T. Elwyn. She confesses that there has been left in her possession and she had the use and benefit of the items listed. Value L239.3.5. CITATION: 12/14/1811. To Admrs. To appear and exhibit Account in order for settlm. and distribution. Cert.: Of T. Elwyn. The Citation was read by Mrs. Whipple in his presence on 12/16/1811 and a copy left with "him", which he said would be sufficient. PETITION: 12/14/1811. Of Catharine Whipple by her atty Thomas Elwyn. Says Joseph had the whole management of the settlm. and asks that he be cited to Account for settlm. and distribution. ACCOUNT: 2/21/1812. Of Joseph Whipple, an Admr. Allowed 2/21/1812. Account includes a list of items Katharine had the use of. PETITION: 2/21/1812. Of Catherine Whipple by her atty. Thomas Elwyn. Requests appeal from Decree allowing Account as she had objections. Granted. BOND: 4/21/1812. Of Catharine Whipple. Bond $100.00. Surety Thomas Elwyn, Portsmouth esq. Witness John J. Parker.

WHITCHER. See also Whicher, Whittier

2814. WHITCHER, WILLIAM (1772) #3912 & #3947 (1772)
EST. Kingston blacksmith decd. testate. Note: This est. recorded 2 ways, as #3912 William Whicher (1772) and #3947 William Whittier (1772). As William's sig. on his Will is Whitcher, that is what is used here. WILL (#3912): Drawn 6/29/1769. Legatees: Wife-Sarah; Sons-Isaac and Nathaniel; Daus.-Abigail wife of David Morril and Phebe Whicher. Execs.-sons Isaac and Nathaniel. His sig. Witnesses: Jeremy Webster, Jacob Gale and Henry Blasdel. CERT. WILL (#3912): 3/5/1772 Presented by Execs. and witnesses Webster and Gale. INVY. WARR. (#3947):

3/3/1772. Comm.: Jeremy Webster, esq. and Nathaniel Bachellor, gent., both of Kingston. INVY. (#3947): Appr. 3/5/1773. Value not tallied. Esti. L490.0.0+. Oaths 6/17/1772 Comm. to Josiah Bartlett, JP. Oaths 6/27/1772 Execs. to W. Parker, JP.

2815. WHITE, DAVID (1776) #4242
EST. Chester yoeman decd. intestate. RENUN.: 5/31/1776. Of Mary White, widow of David. Of Admin. Requests appointment of her bro.-in-law Major William White. Witnesses: Stephen Derben, Samuel Dinsmor and Samuel White. INVY. WARR.: 5/5(prob. error)/1776. Comm.: Stephen Derben, David Weatherspoon and Samuel Robie, Chester gentlemen. ADMIN.: 6/5/1776. Admr. William White, Chester husbm. Bond L1000.0.0. Sureties: Robert Wilson of Chester and John Dudley of Raymond, esquires. Witnesses: Nathl. Parker and W. Parker. INVY.: Appr. 7/11/1776. Value L181.19.0. Oaths 12/4/1776 Robie and Derben to Saml. Emerson, JP. Oath 12/5/1776 Admr., esq. to judge. ACCOUNT: 1/31/1781. Of Admr. Allowed 1/31/1781. Account includes main. 3 children. LICENSE: 1/31/1781. To Admr. To sell sufficient real est. to pay debts. ADDL. ACCOUNT: 3/28/1781. Of Admr. Allowed 3/28/1781. ADDL. ACCOUNT: 3/28/1781 (sic.). Of Admr. Allowed 12/21/1791. DIV.: 12/11/1781. Comm.: Robt. Wilson, John Underhill, Stephen Derben, John Grimes and Ebenezer Basford. To div. real est. between 7 children, with double share to oldest son, and to the Widow Mary White her Dower. Divisees: Widow Mary White; Sons-David, Thomas, Abner and Samuel (oldest); Daus.-Mary White Jr., Lydia White and Jean White. Oaths 12/11/1781 Comm. to Saml. Emerson, JP. Allowed 12/18/1799.

2816. WHITE, JOHN (1777) #4340
EST. Londonderry yoeman decd. ADMIN.: 3/28/1777. Admx. Elizabeth White, Londonderry widow. Bond L500.0.0. Sureties: Georg Corning, yoeman and John Giles, carpenter, both of Londonderry. Witnesses: James Nesmith Jr. and Samuel White. INVY.: Comm.: Georg Corning, John Giles and James Nesmith Jr. Value L38.14.5. Oaths 5/28/1777 Admx. and Comm. to John Bell, JP.

2817. WHITE, JOHN (1797) #6340
EST. Pembroke yoeman decd. testate. WILL: Drawn 4/10/1778. Legatees; Wife-unnamed; Sister-Mary White; Nephew-Isaac Morrison. Exec.-nephew Isaac Morrison. His sig. Witnesses: Daniel Noyes, John Knox and Samuel Noyes. CERT. WILL (D32:304): 5/17/1797. Presented by Exec. And witnesses Daniel Noyes and Knox. ADMIN.: 5/17/1797. Exec. Isaac Morrison of Pembroke. Bond $2,000.00. Sureties: John Knox and Joseph Baker, both of Pembroke. Witnesses: Richard Bartlett and Nathl. Parker.

2818. WHITE, JOHN (1798) #6511
EST. Portsmouth cordwainer decd. CERT.: 11/2/1798. Of William Ham. That he was present, at the desire of John Marsh, and heard Mrs. Sarry White consent and agree to John Marsh as Admr. of the est. of her son John White of Portsmouth decd. Witnesses: Parry Hixon and Jerry Hixson. ADMIN. (D33:543): 11/14/1798. Admr. John Marsh, Barrington, Strafford Co. yoeman. Sureties: Samuel Bowles and Joseph Mann. INVY.: (D32:547): Comm.: George Gains, John Noble and James Hill. Value $149.77. Oaths 11/22/1798 Comm. and Admr. to Isc. Rindge, JP. ACCOUNT: 6/18/ 1800. Of Admr. Allowed 6/18/1800. Account includes boarding of the child.

2819. WHITE, MARY (1794) #5960
EST. Plaistow widow decd. testate, widow of Nicholas White, Plaistow esq. decd. WILL: Drawn 3/4/1790. Legatees: Sons-Joseph, John, Samuel and Heirs of William; Daus.-Mary Kent wife of Jacob Kent, Lydia Hale widow of Benjamin Hale, Elisabeth Ayers wife of Timothy Ayers, Martha White single woman and Abigail Davis wife of James Davis. Exec.-Son-in-law-James Davis. Her sig. Witnesses: Judith Clarke, Hannah Davis and Thomas Clarke. CERT. WILL (D31:163): 1/20/1794. Presented by Exec. and witnesses Davis and Thomas Clarke. ADMIN.: 1/20/1794. Exec. James Davis, Haverhill, Essex Co., MA yoeman. Bond L1000.0.0. Sureties: John White, Plaistow esq. and Robert Stuart, Newton gent. Witnesses: Thos. Clarke and W. Parker. INVY.: Comm.: Daniel Ayer, Joshua Dow and Jno. Ayer. Value L33.0.9. Oaths 1/30/1794 Comm. to John White, JP. Oath 12/24/1794 Exec. to judge. ACCOUNT: 11/16/1793. Of Admr. Allowed 11/16/1795 with order to Admr. to pay bal. to heirs.

2820. WHITE, NICHOLAS (1783) #4885
EST. Plaistow esq. decd. testate. WILL: Drawn 4/14/1776. Legatees: Wife-Mary; Sons-Noah, Ebenezer, Joseph, John, Samuel and Heirs of William; Daus.-Hannah, Mary, Lidea, Elizabetta, Abigail and Martha; Grandchildren-unnamed. He leaves 4 chares to John, John to care for Nicholas' affairs in his old age; Execs.-wife Mary and son John. His sig. Witnesses: William Ayer, James Huse and Daniel Ayer. Codicil: 12/23/1778. He spells out what his wife's Dower should be and provides house room for his two youngest daus. if either or both remain unmarr. Same witnesses. His sig. Proved 3/20/1783 on oaths of witnesses Daniel Ayer and William Ayer. INVY. WARR.: 3/20/1783. Comm.: John Ayer and David Bryent, both of Plaistow and James Davis of Haverhill, Essex Co., MA. Oaths 6/20/1783 Comm. to Joseph Welch, JP. INVY.: Value L1568.12.0. Oaths 6/25/1783 Execs. to W. Parker. CAVEAT: 3/24/1783. Of Saml. Blodget of Goffstown, Hillsborough Co. States that he and

several heirs, including Noah White, esq., have objections to the Will. Requests information from judge as to what steps they should take to assure the heirs will be present when the Will is presented. PETITION: 8/4/1783. Of Saml. Blodget, esq. on behalf of himself and others, children and heirs of decd. Requests an appeal against Decree allowing Will. Allowed 8/5/1785. REPORT: 10/18/1784. From: John Calfe, Joseph Johnson, Moses Greenough, Peter Clement and Henry White, a Comm. to div. 2/3 of real est. They decide it cannot be div. without much expense. Suggest that Mr. White have the liberty of purchasing lands at appr. value, White paying his co-heirs. If they must div., should they disregard the account book? Note: In his Will, decd. provided that there be deducted from each child's share any accounts owed to him according to his account book and if any child's account more than his or her share, the bal. to remain due est. APPR. WARR.: 10/20/1784. Comm.: John Calfe, esq.; Jesse Johnson, gent., both of Hampstead; Peter Clement, esq. and Moses Greenough, both of Atkinson and Henry Little of Salem. To appr. the real est. in order for it to be settled on son John White according to Will. DOWER: 4/8/1784. Comm.: Robert Stuart, David Bryent, gentlemen and John Ayer, cooper, of Plaistow; Samuel Ayer Jr. and James Davis of Haverhill, Essex. Co., MA. Of Widow Mary White. Oaths 1/6/1785 Comm. to John Calfe, JP. Allowed. APPR.: 1/6/1785. Exclusive of Dower, Comm. appraises homestead and bldgs. at L716.8.6; the land conveyed to son William decd. by Deed of Gift, entered in decd.'s book without a price, at L50.0.0 including bldg. Oaths 1/6/1785 Johnson, Clement, Little and Greenough to John Calfe, JP. Oath 1/6/1785 Calfe to Peter Clement, JP. Cert.: 3/15/1785. Of: Clement and Calfe. That within the appraisal part of the East Meadows belonging to the 2/3 of est they appraised and called homestead. ACCOUNT: 5/18/1785. Of Execs. Allowed 5/18/1785. PETITION: 5/31/1794. Of John White. For div. of Dower among children per Will, the Widow now decd. Order: For hearing, Petitioner to notify divisees. NOTIFICATION: 5/31/1794. To Heirs and divisees of decd. Of hearing on Petition. Cert.: 6 & 9/1794. Of (Consable?). He notified Joshua Hale, Timothy Ayer, Saml. White and Asa Tenney by reading notice to them. Gave copies to Jacob Kent, Ebenezer White and Nathl. White and left copy at dwelling in Haverhill, Essex Co. MA for Saml. Blodget. APPR. WARR. 9/15/1794. Comm.: John Calfe, esq. and John True, yoeman, both of Hampstead; Moses Greenough, Atkinson gent.; Robert Stuart, gent. and Eliphalet Bartlett, yoeman, both of Newton. To appr. Dower so it may be settled on son John White, esq. per Will. If John White is dissatisfied with appr. and refuses to take premises, they are to div. it among the children or reps. of those decd. in proportion as directed in Will, giving John four shares, each of the other sons two shares and one share to each dau. Appr.: 10/20/1794. Value

$17.00 per acre, there being 63 1/4 acres 30 rods, plus privileges and appertances. Oaths 10/20/1794 True, Greenough, Stuart and Bartlett to John Calfe, JP. ACCOUNT: Of John White, an Exec. Allowed 6/18/1798.

2821. WHITE, ROBERT (1773) #4060
EST. Pembroke yoeman decd. intestate. RENUN.: Of Aanes White, widow of Robert. Of Admin. Requests appointment of her son John White. ADMIN.: 11/30/1773. Admr. John White, Pembroke yoeman. Bond L1000.0.0. Sureties: Joseph Baker, gent. and Jonathan Dix, esq., both of Pembroke. Witnesses: Saml. Sherburne and Saml. Hale Jr. INVY. WARR.: 11/30/1773. Comm.: Joseph Baker and Saml. McConnell, gentlemen and David Abbot, yoeman, all of Pembroke. INVY.: Appr. 12/27/1773. Value L456.10.2. Oath 12/29/1773 Admr. to judge. ACCOUNT: 4/5/1774. Of Admr. Allowed 4/6/1774 with bal. of L25.10.3 to be apportioned among heirs. DOWER: 4/4/1774. Comm.: Joseph Baker, David Abbot, John Knox, Ephraim Blunt and Samull. McConnell. Of Widow Agness White. Oaths 4/4/1774 Comm. to Richard Bartlett, JP. ADDL. ACCOUNT: 12/29/1774. Of Admr. Allowed 12/29/1774 bal. of L207.12.2 to be distributed. ADDL. ACCOUNT: 11/1776. Of Admr. Allowed 11/27/1776. APPR. WARR.: 11/27/1776. Comm.: Joseph Baker, Samuel McConnel and Benja, Norris, gentlemen; David Abbot and Isaac White, yoemen, all of Pembroke. To appr. 2/3 of real est. to see if it can be div. into 4 equal parts. Div. or appr. APPR.: 12/2/1776. Value L127.13.0. Oaths 12/12/1776 Baker, Abbot, White and Norris to Richard Bartlett, JP. ADDL. ACCOUNT: 12/25/1776. Allowed 12/25/1776. BOND: 1/1/1777. Of John White, Pembroke husbandm. Bond L300.0.0. To pay his co-heirs per Decree Settlm. Sureties: Joseph Baker and Benjamin Norris, Pembroke gentlemen. Receipt: Of Mary White. She has received from Admr. L31.18.3 as her share in full of her father's real est. DECREE & SETTLM.: 3/27/1777. John White, only son, appearing and consenting, 2/3 of the real est. settled on him, John to pay each of his co-heirs L31.18.3-to dau. Mary White in one year, to the legal reps. of dau. Martha Morrison decd. when all the males reach 21 and the females 18, with interest. John receives double share.

2822. WHITE, ROBERT (1791) #5629
EST. New Castle mariner decd. ADMIN.: 3/16/1781. Admx. Mehitabel White, New Castle widow. Bond L1000.0.0. Sureties: John Simpson, gent. and Joseph Frost, merchant, both of New Castle. Witnesses: Samuel Frost and Betsy White. INVY.: (D30:191) Comm.: Josh. Frost, John Tarlton and Henry Sheafe Branscomb. Value L127.15.0. Oaths 9/19/1791 Comm. to Geo. Frost, esq. Oath 2/15/1792 Admx.

2823. WHITE, SAMUEL (1797) #6401
EST. Londonderry husbm. decd. testate. WILL: Drawn 9/18/1797. Legatees: Bros.-Ephraim and Thomas, if alive, or his children if decd.; Sister-Anis White; Cousin-Samuel Cox of Beverly, (MA?). Exec.-bro. Ephraim. His sig. Witnesses: John Bell, Robert Nesmith and David Smith. CERT. WILL (D32:411): 12/20/1797. Presented by Exec. and witnesses Bell, esq. and Smith. ADMIN.: 12/20/1798. Exec. Ephraim White, Londonderry husbm. Bond $3,000.00. Sureties: John Bell, esq. and David Smith, husbm., both of Londonderry. Witnesses: John Morrison and Nicholas Emery. INVY.: Appr. 3/15/1798. Comm.: Robt. Morrison, Robert Nesmith and Benjamin Corning. Value $2,025.64. Oaths 3/20/1798 Nesmith and Corning and on 4/14/1798 Exec. to John Bell, JP. INVY.: 4/14/1798. Of items sold before Invy. appr. Value $81.75. Signed by Exec. ACCOUNT: 12/16/1801. Of Exec. Allowed 12/16/1800, Eunice White, only other person interested, having no objections.

2824. WHITE, WILLIAM (1775) #4163
EST. Plaistow gent. decd. testate. WILL: Drawn 1/7/1775. Legatees: Wife-Mary; Sons-Abner Bayley White and Nicholas; Dau.-Mary; Selectmen of Newbury, Gloucester Co., NY. who are to dispose of his lands there when his son Abner is 21. Exex.-wife Mary. His sig. Witnesses: William Ayer, Daniel Ayer and James Huse. CERT. WILL: (D23:149) 3/29/1775. Presented by Exex. and witnesses Daniel Ayer and Huse. ADMIN.: 3/29/1775. Exex. Mary White, Plaistow widow. Bond L1000.0.0. Sureties: Daniel Ayer, Plaistow husbm. and Abner Bayley, Salem clerk. Witnesses: Wentworth Cheswill and Saml. Hale Jr.

2825. WHITE, WILLIAM (1777) #4360
GDP. Of the son of David White of Chester decd. GDP.: 5/28/1777. Of William, a minor over 14. Gdn. Stephen Dearborn, Chester gent. Bond L500.0.0. Sureties: Henry Moore of Chester and Walter Robie of Candia, esquires. Witnesses: Peter Sanborn and Wm. Parker.

2826. WHITE, WILLIAM JR. (1782) #4803
EST. Chester yoeman decd. ADMIN.: 4/24/1782. Admr. William White, Chester esq. Bond L500.0.0. Sureties: Robert McKinley of Chester and James Towle of Hawke, yoemen. Witnesses: Nathl. Parker and W. Parker. INVY.: 7/22/1782. Comm.: Stephen Chase, John Underhill and Wells Chase. Value L76.10.0. Oaths 12/12/1782 Underhill and Wells Chase to Saml. Emerson, JP. Oath 12/21/1782 Admr. to judge. ACCOUNT: 12/21/1791. Of Admr. Allowed 12/21/1791.

2827. WHITE, WILLIAM-CAPT. (1786) #5211
EST. Portsmouth mariner decd. ADMIN.: 8/28/1786. Admx.: Elizabeth White, Portsmouth widow. Bond L2000.0.0. Sureties: Joseph Green, mariner and Jonathan Shillaber, potter, both of Portsmouth. Witnesses: Sally Wamouth and George Shurburn. INVY.: Appr. 11/2/1786. Comm.: John Evans, Danl. Peirce and Jacob Walden. Value L204.17.1. Oaths 11/4/1786 Admx. and Comm. to Saml. Penhallow, JP. PETITION: Dated by clerk 5/1788. Of Admr. For License and Comm. Insolvency. Gives list claims of L199.6.9. Requests Comm. of Jery. Libbey esq., Daniel Peirce and John Evans. Granted. CLAIMS WARR.: 5/21/1788. Comm.: Jeremiah Libbey, esq., John Evans and Daniel Peirce, traders, all of Portsmouth. LICENSE (D29:193): 5/21/1788. To Admx., incorrectly called Mary. To sell sufficient real est. to pay debts. CLAIMS: 12/17/1788. Total L118.6.9. Oaths 12/17/1788 Evans and Peirce to Saml. Penhallow, JP. ACCOUNT: 3/18/1789. Of Admx. Includes board, support and funeral of Mr. Richd. White per agreement between Richard and William decd. Oath 3/18/1789 Admx. to judge. PROP. & SETTLM.: 4/15/1789. Claims L118.6.9. Amount to be proportioned L37.6.0. Allowed 4/15/1789 with order to Admx. to pay. PROP. & SETTLM.: Same as above but on back signatures of all those who received a proportion.

2828. WHITTEMORE, JOHN (1774) #4102
EST. Pembroke yoeman decd. intestate. ADMIN.: 5/10/1774. Admx. Ruth Whitomoe, Pembroke widow. Bond L1000.0.0. Sureties: James Head and Samuel Kimball, Pembroke yoemen. Witnesses: Joseph Baker and John White. INVY. WARR.: 5/10/1774. Comm.: Capt. Joseph Baker, gent. and David Abbot, yoeman, both of Pembroke. The judge notes that it will be acceptable to him, by his discretion, if Esq. Bartlet would swear the appraisers . Signed by Saml. Hale Jr., Reg. INVY.: Appr. 7/25/1774. Value L507.13.5. Oaths 8/25/1774 Comm. to Richard Bartlet, JP. Oath 8/31/1774 Admx. to judge. DOWER WARR.: 8/31/1774. Comm.: Joseph Baker and Saml. McConnel, gentlemen; Ephraim Blunt, David Abbot and Nathl. Head, yoemen, all of Pembroke. Of Widow Ruth Whittemore. DOWER: 12/23/1774. Oaths 12/23/1774 Baker, Blunt, Abbot and Head to Richard Bartlet, JP. PETITION; 12/28/1774. Of Admx. For License. LICENSE: 1/12/1775. To Admx. To sell sufficient real est. to pay debts. ACCOUNT: Of Thomas Baker and Ruth Baker, Admx. Allowed 6/25/1777. Account includes main. 2 children. ADDL. ACCOUNT: 6/30/1779. Of Thomas Baker and Ruth his wife, Admx. Allowed 6/30/1779. Account includes continuing main. 2 children. ADDL. ACCOUNT: 3/12/1794. Of Thomas Baker and Ruth his wife, Admx. Allowed 3/12/1794 with consent of Stephen Bartlett, Gdn. of one of sons, the other being out of state. Account includes continuing main. 1 child.

Also notes that rent of 2/3 real est. recd. since death of father of decd. to whom it was leased during father's lifetime and lifetime of wife, the rest being accounted for by Gdn. one of children. PETITION: 3/12/1794. Of Admrs. To sell all real est. Order: For hearing, Petitioners to serve notice to all persons interested. Stephen Bartlett, Gdn. of one of the two children, agrees granting of Petition would be beneficial to wards. BOND: 3/12/1794. Of Thomas Baker, Pembroke yoeman. Bond L300.0.0. With his wife, Admx., to account for proceeds of sale of real est. by License. Sureties: Stephen Bartlett, gent. and Richard Bartlet, esq., both of Pembroke. Witnesses _____? Wardell and Joseph Baker. LICENSE: 3/31/1794. To Admrs. To sell all of the real est. ADDL. ACCOUNT: 5/21/1794. Of Admrs. Allowed 5/21/1794 with consent of Gdn. of one of heirs, the other being out of state.

2829. WHITTEMORE, PETER (1769) A#3491
GDP. Of the son of Rev. Aaron Whittemore of Pembroke decd. ACCOUNT (D25:270): 2/21/1772. Of Peter Coffin of Boscawen, Hillsborough Co., Gdn. Allowed 9/29/1779. Orig. Archives file includes Gdp.

2830. WHITTEMORE, THOMAS (1791) #5661
GDP. Of the son of John Whitmore, Pembroke yoeman decd. GDP.: 5/18/1791. Of Thomas, a minor over 14. Gdn. Stephen Bartlett, Pembroke gent. Bond L500.0.0. Sureties: Richard Bartlet, esq. and Thomas Baker, yoemen, both of Loudon. Witnesses: Michl. McClary and Nathl. Parker.

2831. WHITTIER, COL. JOHN (1787) #5257
EST. Pembroke esq. decd. CAVEAT: 1/17/1787. Of David Bradley. He suspects that an instrument proporting to be the last Will of John Whittier, Pembroke esq. decd. will be presented for probate. Requests an opportunity to show that Whittier was not capable of making a will, and if he was, this instrument has been materially altered since it was written. WILL: Drawn 12/27/1786. Legatees: Widow Abigail Edes; John Whittier Ela. Exec.-John Whittier Ela. His sig. Witnesses: Richard Bartlet, Thomas Robinson and Daniel Lucas. Will presented 1/17/1787, but a caveat against proving laid against it, consideration postponed, at which time testimony for and against was heard. The witness to the Will testified that he had altered the Will by erasing and underling it without the knowledge of tesator. Will disallowed and Admin. ordered granted according to law. A PARTIAL COPY OF WILL. DEPOSITION: Of William Cochran. Testifies that on 1/6/1787 he was at the funeral of Col. Whittier where John W. Ely gave him the Will and asked him to read it. The Will appeared to be erased or scratched and written again, whether with the

same words or other words he did not know. He read the Will and returned it to Ely. Oath 2/12/1787. Of Deacon Cochran to Saml. Danniell, JP, being taken at request of David Bradley to be used in a cause depending before the Judge of Probate. John W. Ely was notified but not present. DEPOSITION: Of Elizabeth Lucas. Testifies that about 4 days before Col. Whittier died, John Whittier Ely, who was at the house, mentioned that the Col. had given Mrs. Edes 6 bushels of corn, 4 bushels of rye and 2 of wheat, 60 weight of pork and 40 weight of beef, which, Edes said, was too much by half and Ely would have it altered. Oath 2/12/1787 Lucas to Saml. Danniel, JP, Mr. Ely being present. Deposition to be used in Court of Probate. DEPOSITION: Of Abigail Edes. Testifies that after the Col. made his Will, John W. Ely was uneasy and said the Col. had given her too much in the Will and spoke to the Col. about it. The Col. answered that he had not given her enough, but if they could agree to have it altered, they might. But the Col. told her to take care of herself as she was not going to have as much as she should. She told Ely rather than have the swine, it should be altered because she wanted no contention about it. Ely then went to Esq. Bartlet and told him he had underlined the alterations so Bartlet's son could write a new Will. A while later, the Col. said to her he wanted no alteration and she was to take care of herself. Mr. Bradley, who was present, asked if Col. Whittier had sent Mr. Ely to Esq. Bartlet. She answered yes, but after Ely was gone, the Col. said Bartlet could do nothing without a line from him. When questioned, she replied that the Col. was very weak, but she did not know that he was wandering or out of his right mind. Oath 2/12/1787 Edes to Saml. Danniell, JP., John W. Ely being present and deposition taken at request of David Bradley to be used at Court of Probate. DEPOSITION: Of Daniel Lucas, a witness to the signing of Will. Testifies that when he was asked to sign the Will, he asked to read it in order to know what he was signing. He was told it was not customary. When he signed, the Will was folded so he saw only a part of it, but what he did see had no erasures or underlining and appeared to be clear and fair writing. Oath 2/12/1787 Lucas to Saml. Danniell, JP. Taken at request of David Bradley to be used at Probate Court and with Mr. Ely present. ADMIN.: 2/22/1787. Admr. David Bradley, Haverhill, Essex Co., MA gent. Bond L1000.0.0. Sureties: David Dexter, Hampstead yoeman and Simeon Ladd, Exeter gent. Witnesses: Nathl. Parker and W. Parker. INVY.: Comm.: Saml. Danniell and Joseph Emery. Value not tallied. Esti. 232.0.0+. Oaths 5/14/1787 Comm. to Richard Bartlet, JP. Judge notes that the securities represent principle only, with no interest, and omitted were a pew in Mr. Shaw's meeting house in Haverhill (MA?) and 1/4 right of land in Bakerstown, Cumberland Co., MA. PETITION: 12/17/1787. Of Admr. For Comm. Insolvency. Gives list claims of L162.4.9. CLAIMS WARR.: 1/16/1788. Comm.: Joseph Welch and John White, esquires and John

Ayer, yoeman, all of Plaistow. 6/18/1788 Comm. allowed 6 months longer. 1/21/1789 Comm. allowed 3 months longer. PETITION: Dated by clerk 7/1788. Of Admr. For License. Gives list claims of L292.15.8. LICENSE (D29:197): 7/16/1788. To Admr. To sell sufficient real est. to pay debts. CLAIMS: 7/9/1789. Total L187.13.8. Oaths 7/9/1789 White and Ayer to Joseph Welch, JP. NOTIFICATION: 8/18/1789. To: Nehemiah Emerson, gent.; Obadiah Ayer and Israel Carlton, yoemen, all of Haverhill, Essex Co., MA. The Admr. has submitted his Account and they may appear at hearing. Cert.: 8/26/1787. David Dexter, Emerson Jr., Carlton and Ayer that they have been legally notified. Clerk calls these men "heirs." ACCOUNT: 8/18/1789. Of Admr. Allowed 9/16/1789. PROP. & SETTLM.: Claims L187.13.8. Amount to be proportioned L115.12.9. Allowed 10/21/1789 with order to Admr. to pay.

2832. WHITTIER, JOSEPH (1798) #6417
EST. Nottingham yoeman decd. testate. WILL: Drawn 5/1/1794. Legatees: Wife- Betsy; Sons-Charles, John, Reuben, Chase and Joseph; Daus.-Dorotha French wife of Gould French, Sarah Elkins wife of Richard Elkins, Martha Moody wife of Abner Moody and Mary Chandler wife of John Chandler. Execs.-wife Betsy and Bradbury Cilley, Nottingham yoeman. His sig. Witnesses: Cutting Cilley, Simeon Ladd and Benjamin Cilley. CERT. WILL (D32:433): Presented by Betsy Whittier, an Exec., the other removed from state, and all witnesses. ADMIN.: 2/6/1798. Exex. Betsy Whittier, Nottingham widow. Bond $3,000.00. Sureties: Simeon Ladd and Moses Burnham, Nottingham yoemen. Witnesses: Josiah Dow and W. Parker. INVY.: Appr. 3/8/1798. Comm.: John Harvey, Simeon Ladd and Greenleaf Cilley. Value $384.05. Oaths 3/26/1798 Ladd and Cilley to Benja. Butler, JP. Oath 3/27/1798 Exex. to W. Parker. PETITION: 7/9/1798. Of Moses Burnham for Admx. For Comm. Insolvency. Gives claims already exhibited as $580.26. Granted. CLAIMS: 1/21/1799. Comm.: Thos. Bartlett, Greenleaf Cilley and Samuel Gile. Total $257.22. Oaths 1/21/1799 Comm. to Jos. Cilley, JP. PETITION: 2/4/1799. Of Exex. For License. Granted. LICENSE (D33:38). 2/4/1799. To Exex. To sell real est. to amount of $300.00.

2833. WHITTIER, JOSIAH (1776) #4230
EST. Candia yoeman decd. intestate. ADMIN.: 4/24/1776. Admr. Anna Whittier, Candia widow. Bond L500.0.0. Sureties: Moses Baker, gent. and Jacob Bagley, yoeman, both of Candia. Witnesses: William Baker and W. Parker. INVY.: Appr. 5/23/1776. Comm.: Moses Baker, John Moore and William Baker. Value L55.13.3 plus the real est. not tallied. Oaths 7/18/1776 Comm. and Admr. to Samuel Mooers, JP.

2834. WHITTIER, MARTHA (1782) #4775
EST. Wife of Joseph Whittier of Nottingham, decd. testate. WILL: Drawn 10/15/1780. Legatees: Husband-Joseph; Sons-John, Reuben, Chase and Joseph; Daus.-Dorathy French, Sarah Elkins, Martha Witcher and Molly Wicher; Grandsons-Philip McCrilles and Andrew McCrilles. Ref. to her father John Evans of Nottingham decd. Exec.-son Joseph, Nottingham gent. Her mark. Witnesses: John Banfill, Joseph Hodgdon, William Hook and Simeon Ladd. Consent (D26:272): 1/30/1782. Of Joseph Whittier to his wife's Will. Witnesses: Joseph Hodgdon and Simeon Ladd. CERT. WILL (D26:272): 1/30/1782. Presented by Exec. and witnesses Hodgdon and Ladd. INVY. WARR.: 1/30/1782. Comm.: Joseph Hodgdon and Simeon Ladd, both of Nottingham. INVY.: Appr. 4/22/1782. Value L84.0.0. Oaths 4/22/1782 Comm. to Thos. Bartlet, JP.

2835. WHITTIER, REUBEN (1790) #5534
EST. Raymond yoeman decd. testate. WILL: Drawn 1/31/1789. Legatees: Wife-Betty; Sons-Moses, Richard, Reuben, Joseph, Daniel, Aaron, Phinehas and Clark; Daus.-Mary wife of Charles Moore, Sarah wife of Joseph Glidon, Miriam wife of Zaccheus Clough and Deborah Whittier; Grandson-Richard Whittier. Exec.-son Aaron. His sig. Witnesses: Jona. Swain, Joseph True and Joseph True Jr. CERT. WILL (D29:360): 4/21/1790. Presented by Exec. and witnesses Swain and Joseph True. ADMIN.: 4/21/1790. Exec. Aaron Whittier, Raymond yoeman. Bond L500.0.0. Sureties: Jonathan Swain, Raymond esq. and Joseph True, Chester gent. Witnesses: Peter Clement and N. Parker. INVY.: Appr. 5/6/1791. Comm.: Joseph True and Thomas Gordon. Value L238.13.8. Oaths 5/8/1790 Comm. and Exec. to Jona. Swain, JP. DOWER: 4/26/1791. Comm.: Joseph True, Benjamin True, Jonathan Swain, Thomas Gordon and William Moore. Of Widow Betty Whittier. Oaths 4/28/1791 Joseph True, Benj. True and Moor to Jona. Swain, JP. Allowed 4/28/1791. ACCOUNT: 1/16/1792. Of Exec. Allowed 1/16/1792. Account includes a payment of L4.3.0. to widow, she "refusing to stand to the Will."

2836. WHITTIER, SARAH (1772) #3967
EST. East Kingston widow decd. testate. WILL: Drawn 6/26/1772. Legatees: Sons-Isaac and Nathl.; Daus.-in-law(sic.)-Phebe Currier wife of John Currier and Abigail Morrill wife of David Morrill. Exec.-son-in-law David Morrill. Her mark. Witnesses: Nathl. Bachellor, Henry Blazdel and David Gale. CERT. WILL: 11/10/1772. Presented by Exec. and witnesses Bachellor and Gale.

2837. WHITTIER, TIMOTHY (1789) #5408
EST. Newton yoeman decd. intestate. ADMIN.: 1/21/1789. Admr. Benjamin Whittier, Newton yoeman. Bond L1000.0.0. Sureties: Eliphalet Bartlet and Elijah Bagly, Newton yoemen. Witnesses: W. Parker and Nathl. Parker. INVY.: Appr. 4/9/1789. Comm.: Eliphalet Bartlet, Francis Chase Jr. and Jacob Peaslee. Value L447.18.11. Oaths 4/13/1789 Comm. to Matthias Bartlet, JP. Oath 4/15/1789 Admr. to W. Parker, JP. DOWER: 5/22/1789. Comm.: Robert Stuart, Nehemiah Sleeper and Samuel Hoit. Of Widow Sarah Whittier. Oaths 5/25/1789 Comm. to Matthias Bartlet, JP. Includes map. PETITION: 6/15/1789. Of Admr. Requests Dower be set aside and another Comm. appointed as the present Div. appears to give widow too large a proportion of the most fertile land, particularly grass land, to the prejudice of the other heirs. After a hearing, Div. was allowed, although marked by clerk "not allowed." PETITION: 6/17/1789. Of Widow Sarah Whittier; Benjamin Whittier, Admr.; Andrew Whittier; Mary Whittier; Allice Whittier and Martha Whittier. They complain that the Dower as set off by a recent Comm. is not satisfactory. They are mutually agreed there should be a new comm. Request appointment of Francis Chase and Capt. Moses Carleton, both of Newton; William Sleeper and Capt. Jacob Webster, both of Kingston; and Moses Flanders of South Hampton. PETITION: 7/14/1789. Of Widow Sarah Whittier. States she has received no information from the Admr. or Dower Comm. regarding her Dower and requests that the acceptance of it be put off until next probate day so she may obtain a copy of the return and satisfy herself about it. Witnesses: Timothy Whittier and Jacob Whittier. PETITION: 7/14/1789. Of: Andrew Whittier and Philip Whittier, children of decd., and Timothy Whittier and Benjamin Whittier, "children-in-law." They have been informed that the judge has been requested to appoint a Gdn. for their mother Sarah Whittier. They do not feel it is necessary as they all live with her and are ready and able to assist her if necessary. Also, they find it strange that two of their bros. support the Gdp., one of whom, an own son with whom Sarah lives, has "the whole case of her improvements" and has it in his power to see that justice is done for her. The income of her interest is more than sufficient for her support in sickness or health. DOWER: 7/3/1789. Comm. as requested in Petition. Oaths 7/3/1789 Comm. to Matthias Bartlett, JP. Judge recaps the dissatisfaction with former Dower, the request for new Comm. and request for delay of acceptance. The new return having been heard and objections considered allowed 8/18/1789. ORDER: 8/18/1789. To Admr. To deliver to Widow such articles as she chooses from the personal est. to the amount of L15.0.0. as appr. by Invy., including what she has already received. A License is granted to sell the rest of the personal est., for which Admr. to account. PETITION: 8/18/1789. Of Timothy Whittier. He objects to new Dower. Feels it is

inconvenient for his mother because: 1. She has not received an equal part of the wood on the homestead; 2. It will be inconvenient to fence, perhaps taking all of her part of woodlot; 3. Since the return of former Comm., she has been to considerable expense in making a garden, the principle part of which has been taken from her. Request a new dower not be accepted. PETITION: 8/18/1789. Of Admr. For Comm. Insolvency. Gives list claims of L374.10.2, including his own claim for 26 years of service in his father's employ. CLAIMS: 2/10/1790. Comm.: Nathl. Bachellor and Simmons Seccombe. Total L206.7.4. Oaths 2/10/1790 Comm. to Josiah Bartlett, JP. Includes dau. Mary's claim for 14 years service in father's employ after reaching 21. NOTIFICATION: 2/22/1790. To: Timothy, Andrew, Jacob and Philip Whittier, sons; Joseph Kimball, Nathaniel Cheeney and Daniel Hoyt who marr. daus. of decd.; Mary, Alice, Meriam and Martha Whittier, daus. They are notified the Admr. has filed his Account of Admin., on which a hearing will be held. They may be present to make objections to Account if they have any, to give bonds to pay their ratable shares of debts and to hear a Petition of Admr. to sell part or all of real est. The following signed that they had been notified: Joseph Kimball, Andrew, Allice, Mary, Miream, Martha, Elijah Bagley, Nathaniel Cheny and Philip Whittier. Cert.: 3/11/1790. Of Danl. Peaslee, Newton Constable. That he notified Timothy and Jacob Whittier. APPR.: 3/13/1790. Comm.: Matthias Bartlet and Benja. Hoit. They appr. income of 2/3 of the real est. for the last year at L6.12.0. ACCOUNT: Of Admr. Allowed 3/17/1790. LICENSE: 5/17/1790. To Admr. To sell real est. to the amount of L180.0.0. NOTIFICATION: 11/17/1790. To: Nathaniel Cheney of Plaistow; Timothy Whittier, Jacob Whittier, Molly Whittier, Alice Whittier, Andrew Whittier and Miriam Whittier, all of Newton. They are notified that Admr. to exhibit Addl. Account. Cert.: 11/22/1790. Of Daniel Morse. He notified Timothy Whittier. Of Elijah Bagley that he notified Jacob Whittier on 11/19. Of Benjamin Whittier that he notified Nathaniel Chaney, Andrew, Molly, Ellice and Mariam Whittier. ADDL. ACCOUNT: Of Admr. Allowed 12/6/1790. LICENSE (D29:448): 12/6/1790. To Admr. To sell real est. to amount of L16.0.0. CLAIMS WARR.: 2/1/1791. Comm.: Jeremiah Fogg and Ebenezer Clifford, esquires and Jeremiah Dearborn, joiner, all of Kensington. ADDL. ACCOUNT: 4/16/1792. Of Admr. Witness to Admr.'s mark Eliphalet Bartlet. Allowed 4/16/1792. PETITION: 6/16/1817. Of Timothy Whittier. States the Admr. is dead without fully finishing admin. The widow is also decd. and her Dower needs admin. As oldest son, requests Admin. D.B.N. and Invy. Comm. of John Chase of Plaistow and Matthias Bartlet, esq. and Thomas Peaslee, yoeman, both of Newton. INVY. WARR.: 5/21/1819. Comm.: As requested. ADMIN. D.B.N. (D45:526): 5/25/1819. Admr. d.b.n. Timothy Whittier, Newton husbm. Sureties: Jacob Whittier, Newton gent. and Jacob Gale of East Kingston. INVY.: Appr. 8/18/1819. Value $723.00. Oaths 8/18/1819 Chase and Peaslee to Matthias Bartlet, JP. PETITION: 11/10/1819. Of Jacob Whittier. For div. of mother's Dower in Newton and Kingston, of which he owns 3/11. PETITION: 11/10/1819. Of Philip Whittier. For div. of Dower, of which he owns 3/11. PETITION: 11/10/1819. Of Timothy Whittier. For div. of Dower, of which he owns 2/11 plus $23.00 more in value. PETITION: 11/10/1819. Of Elis Whittier, single woman. For div. of Dower, of which she owns 1/11. DIV. WARR.: 11/17/1819. Comm.: Matthias Bartlet, esq.; Caleb Peaslee, Benjamin Rowell and Eli Hoyt, all of Newton and Isaac Webster of Kingston. To div. Dower, giving Timothy 2/11 plus as much more of the shares of Andrew, Molly and Elis as the Comm. decides belongs to Timothy; Jacob 3/11; Philip 3/11; and to Andrew, Molly and Elis 1/11, deducting as much as Comm. decides to have been conveyed by deeds or otherwise to Timothy. DIV.: 4/28/1820. Divisees: Timothy, Jacob, Philip, Heirs of Molly, Elis and Andrew. Oaths 4/28/1820 Webster, Hoyt, Rowell and Peaslee to Matthias Bartlet, JP. Allowed 6/15/1820. ACCOUNT: 8/7/1820. Of Admr. d.b.n. Oath 8/9/1820 Admr. d.b.n. to Matthias Bartlet, JP. Allowed 8/10.1820.

2838. WHITTIER, WILLIAM (1772) #3947
EST. Kingston yoeman decd. testate (sic.). INVY. WARR.: 3/3/1772. Comm.: Jeremy Webster, esq. and Nathaniel Bachellor, gent., both of Kingston. To be shown by Execs. of will Isaac Whittier and Nathl. Whittier. INVY.: Appr. 3/5/1772. Value not tallied. Esti. L490.0.0. Oaths 6/17/1772 Comm. to Josiah Bartlett, JP. Oaths 6/27/1772 Execs. to W. Parker, JP. Note: There is no will in the jacket and none found in Docket.

2839. WIBIRD, ELIZABETH (1774) #4085
EST. Portsmouth widow decd. intestate. ADMIN.: 2/14/1774. Admr. John Penhallow, Portsmouth merchant. Bond L1000.0.0. Sureties: William Knight, merchant and Saml. Penhallow, esq., both of Portsmouth. Witnesses: John Parker Jr. and Saml. Hale Jr.

2840. WIBIRD, ELIZABETH (1785) #5070
EST. Portsmouth widow decd. TESTAMENT: 12/29/1784. Of: Ann Penhallow, Margaret Phillips and Sarah Phillips. They testify that they heard Widow Wibird, the day before she died, express in words her will that Mary Barns, now living with her, be supported from what is now due Mary from Elizabeth and also from Elizabeth's est., in a comfortable, decent manner during Mary's life. Oaths 1/24/1785 Ann Penhallow, Margaret Phillips and Sarah Phillips to Saml. Penhallow, JP. PETITION: 12/30/1784. Of: Oliver Wendell, only bro. of decd.; Ann Penhallow and

Margaret Phillips, sisters of decd. and John Penhallow, brother-in-law of decd. For themselves and on behalf of the other heirs, request that Samuel Penhallow, Portsmouth esq., be appointed Admr., it being impracticable for any of the heirs to attend to settlement of est. ADMIN.: 6/19/1785. Admr. Samuel Penhallow, Portsmouth esq. Bond L1000.0.0. Sureties: Samuel Brooks and Samuel Hobart, Exeter esquires. Witnesses: Theophilus Smith and W. Parker. INVY.: Appr. 3/2/1785. Comm.: Sam. Cutts and Francis Borland. Value L225.5.6. Oaths 8/16/1785 Comm. to George Gains, JP. Oath 8/17/1785 Admr. to W. Parker, Reg. ACCOUNT: 9/17/1788. Of Admr. Allowed 9/17/1788. Note: Evidently the Invy. is only for personal est. as the Account lists a house and land in Boston, rent of another house, income from Notes, etc., with a final bal. of L900.11.11 3/4.

2841. WIGGIN: AARON, CALEB AND POLLY (1774) #4100
GDP of the children of Andrew Wiggin, Stratham esq. decd. GDP: 4/27/1774. Of: Caleb, Aaron and Polly, minors under 14. Gdn. Dorothy Wiggin, Stratham widow, their mother. Bond L1000.0.0. Sureties: William Pottle and Stephen Piper, Stratham yeomen. Witnesses: Moses Clark and Josiah Robinson.

2842. WIGGIN, ANDREW (1774) #4099
EST. Stratham esq. decd. testate. WILL: Drawn 12/31/1773. Legatees: Wife-Dorothy; Sons-Andrew, Levi, Caleb and Aron; Daus.-Dolly Wiggin and Polly Wiggin. Exex.-wife Dorothy. His sig. Witnesses: William Pottle, Joseph Mason Jr. and Richd. Rust. CERT. WILL (D22:477): 4/27/1774. Presented by Exex. and witnesses Pottle and Mason. INVY.: Appr. 7/26/1774. Comm.: Stephen Bordman and Samuel Lane. Value L3175.8.3. Oath 9/26/1774 Bordman and on 9/30/1774 Lane and Exex. to judge. ACCOUNT: Of Exex. Allowed 10/20/1784. Account includes main. one child. PETITION: 6/25/1791. Of Exex. For Dower. Order: Sons to be cited to appear for hearing. Hearing postponed. DOWER WARR.: 8/15/1791. Comm.: Joseph Norris, Enos Hoag, Thomas Boardman, Samuel Lane Jr. and Jonathan Wiggin, all of Stratham. Of Widow Dorothy Wiggin. DOWER: 4/21/1795. Oaths 4/21/1795 Boardman, Lane and Norris to Andrew Wiggin, JP. Allowed 10/27/1795.

2843. WIGGIN, ANDREW 3D (1778) #4492
EST. Stratham yoeman decd. testate. WILL: Drawn 6/18/1773. Legatees: Wife-Mary; Sons-Nathan and Andrew; Daus.- Anna, Phebe and Lydia. Execs.: Deacon Stephen Boardman of Stratham and wife Mary. His sig. Witnesses: Samuel Lane, Andrew Jewett and Thomas Hatch. CERT. WILL: 10/28/1778. Presented by Execs. and witnesses Lane, esq. and

Jewett. INVY. WARR.: 10/28/1778. Comm.: Samuel Lane and Theo. Smith, esquires and Jona. Wiggin, gent., all of Stratham. Invy.: Appr. 11/20/1778. Value not tallied. Esti. L5840.19.0. Oaths 12/31/1778 Comm. and Exec. to judge.

2844. WIGGIN: HENRY & WEALTHAN & ANNA SHUTE (1787) #5245
GDP. Of the sons of Henry Wiggin, Newmarket housewright and dau. of Michael Shute decd. GDP.: 1/17/1787. Of Anna Shute, Henry Wiggin and Wealthan Wiggin, minors over 14. Gdn. Henry Wiggin, Newmarket housewright, father of Henry and Wealthan. Bond L500.0.0. Surety John Shute, Newmarket innholder. Witnesses: Nathl. Parker and W. Parker. Note: The Gdp. of Anna Shute has been recorded with #5641 Shute: Anna, Hiram, Lydia, Michael and William (1791), her siblings.

2845. WIGGIN, JEWETT (1789) #5496
GDP. Of the son of Andrew Wiggin, Stratham yoeman decd. GDP.: 11/18/1789. Of Jewett, a minor over 14. Gdn. Walter Weeks, Stratham yoeman. Bond L500.0.0. Sureties: Nathan Wiggin and Andrew Wiggin, Stratham yoemen.

2846. WIGGIN, JOSEPH (1788) #5373
EST. Stratham yoeman decd. RENUN.: 9/20/1788. Of Patience Wiggin, widow of Joseph. Of Admin. Requests appointment of her son Benjamin. Witness Thomas Wiggin. Renun.: 9/20/1788. Of Joseph Wiggin, oldest son and David Wiggin, 2d son. Of Admin. Request appointment of Benjamin. ADMIN.: 9/20/1788. Admr. Benjamin Wiggin, Hopkinton, Hillsborough Co. innholder. Bond L500.0.0. Sureties: Joseph Wiggin of Stratham and Bickford Kenison of Greenland, husbandmen. Witnesses: H. L. Langdon and W. Parker. INVY.: Appr. 1/8/1789. Comnm.: Joshua Avery and Bickford Kenison. Value L35.5.6. Oaths 1/8/1789 Comm. to Mark Wiggin, JP. Oath 1/21/1789 Admr. to judge. PETITION: 1/21/1789. Of Admr. For Comm. Insolvency. Gives partial claims of L39.4.0. CLAIMS WARR.: 1/21/1789. Comm.: Mark Wiggin, esq.; Jonathan Wiggin and Nathan Barker, gentlemen, all of Stratham. CLAIMS: Total L34.6.4. Oaths 8/18/1789 Comm. to Simon Wiggin, JP. ACCOUNT: 3/17/1790. Of Admr. Allowed 3/17/1790. PROP. & SETTLM.: Claims L34.6.4. Amount to be proportioned L25.1.2. Allowed 3/17/1790 with order to Admr. to pay.

2847. WIGGIN, JOSEPH (1796) #6171

EST. Exeter blacksmith decd. intestate. ADMIN.: 1/4/1796. Admr. Joseph Wiggin, Exeter blacksmith. Bond $3,000.00. Sureties: Benjamin Lamson, innholder and Robert Kimball, gent., both of Exeter. Witnesses: Simeon Ladd and Wm. Parker. INVY.: Appr. 2/22/1796. Comm.: Jere. Bachelder, Jere. Leavitt and Nathl. Gordon. Value L604.16.0. Oaths 2/22/1796 Comm. and Admr. to W. Parker, JP. APPR.: 6/25/1798. No Comm. Marked "Appr. For Div." One section called "To be settled on Joseph and Gideon L314.0.0., another section represents Dower at L157.0.0, the whole L471.0.0. APPR.: 3/12/1799. Comm.: Jere. Bachelder, Wm. Hale and Jeremiah Leavitt. They appr. 2/3 real est. at L314.0.0. Oaths 8/28/1799 Bachelder and Leavitt to judge. DOWER: 3/12/1799. Comm.: Jere. Backelder, Wm. Hale and Jeremiah Leavitt. Of Widow Lydia Wiggin. Oaths 8/11/1799 Bachelder and Leavitt to judge. Allowed. ACCOUNT: 6/21/1807. Of Admr. Allowed 2/1/1814 receipts from heirs having been submitted. Admr. notes real est. having been settled on him and he had paid co-heirs in full. No Decree Settlm. found.

2848. WIGGIN, NOAH (1789) #5413

GDP.: Loudon yoeman adjudge n.c.m. PETITION: 1/21/1789. Of William Wiggin, Stratham yoeman. States that his bro. Noah, Loudon yoeman, is n.c.m. and not capable of taking care of himself or est. Requests appointment of a Gdn. Order: 1/21/1789. To Loudon Selectmen. To make inquisition into condition of Noah. Report: 1/1789. Of Selectmen. They are of opinion that Noah needs a Gdn. and recommend his bro. William. Petition: 1/24/1789. Of Timo. Gleeson and Samuel Hill, Loudon Selectmen. They consent to William Wiggin as Gdn. together with Samuel Hill, Loudon yoeman. GDP.: 2/3/1789. Of Noah, Loudon yoeman, an adult adjudged n.c.m. Gdn. William Wiggin, Stratham yoeman. Bond L1000.0.0. Sureties: Jonathan Wiggin of Stratham and Nathaniel Goss of Greenland, yoemen. Witnesses: Elias Merrill and W. Parker. INVY. WARR.: 2/3/1789. Comm.: Capt. William Boynton and Lt. Samuel Piper, Loudon gentlemen. Includes oaths 2/6/1789 Comm. to Nathan Bachelder, JP. INVY.: 2/9/1789. Value not tallied. Esti. L99.0.0. CERT.: 5/19/1797. Of: John Dow and John Clough, Loudon Selectmen. They certify that Noah is now compos mentis and capable of caring for his property. RELEASE: 9/5/1797. Of Noah Wiggin. To William Wiggin, Gdn. They have settled all accounts and demands of the Gdp. Witness Nathl. Wiggin. Oaths 9/18/1797 Noah Wiggin and William Wiggin to Saml. Piper, JP.

2849. WIGGIN, SAMUEL (1790) #5586
EST. Stratham joiner decd. RENUN.: 10/19/1790. Of Penelope Wiggin, widow of Samuel. Of Admin. Requests appointment of her son Andrew Wiggin 3d. Witnesses: Mark Wiggin and Hitty Wiggin. ADMIN.: 10/20/1790. Admr. Andrew Wiggin 3d, Stratham yoeman. Bond L1000.0.0. Sureties: Elijah French and Stephen Wiggin, Stratham yoemen. Witnesses: Jonathan Warner and Saml. Drowne. INVY.: Appr. 1/13/1791. Comm.: Samuel Piper and Nathan Barker. Value L109.1.6. Oaths 1/19/1791 Comm. and Admr. to W. Parker, JP & Reg. DOWER: 11/25/1791. Comm.: Samuel Piper, Nathan Barker, Samuel Lane Jr., Tuftin Wiggin and Stephen Wiggin. Of Widow Penelope Wiggin. Oaths 11/29/1791 Comm. to Simon Wiggin, JP. Allowed 2/13/1792. PETITION: 3/21/1792. Of Admr. For License. Granted. LICENSE (D30:205): 3/21/1792. To Admr. To sell real est. to amount of L80.0.0. ACCOUNT: 4/16/1792. Of Admr. Allowed 4/16/1792. ADDL. ACCOUNT: 3/1793. Of Admr. Allowed 3/20/1793.

2850. WIGGIN, SAMUEL (1797) #6407
EST. Stratham yoeman decd. testate. WILL: Drawn 5/30/1797. Legatees: Wife-Anna; Sons-Daniel, Samuel and Thomas; Dau.-Anna Wiggin. Exec.-son Daniel. His sig. Witnesses: Phinehas Merrill, Nathaniel Wiggin 3d, Nathan Norton, Stephen Wiggin Jr. and Moses Wiggin. CERT. WILL (D32:404): 12/6/1797. Presented by Exec. and witnesses Merrill and Nathaniel Wiggin 3d. ADMIN.: 12/6/1797. Exec. Daniel Wiggin, Stratham yoeman. Bond $2,000.00. Sureties: Walter Weeks, gent. and Nathaniel Wiggin 3d, yoeman, both of Stratham. Witnesses: Phinehas Merrill and Wm. Parker. INVY. WARR.: 12/6/1797. Comm.: Phinehas Merrill and Richard Wiggin, yoemen and Walter Weeks, gent., all of Stratham. Invy.: Appr. 3/5/1798. Value $3,200.18. Oaths 3/10/1798 Weeks, Merrill and Exec. to W. Parker.

2851. WIGGIN, THOMAS (1782) #4812
EST. Epping husbm. decd. testate. WILL: Drawn 4/3/1782. Legatees; Wife-Dolley; Sons-Joshua, Thomas, Hubbert, John, Andrew, William and Elijah; Dau.-Sarah Wiggin. Exec.-son William. His sig. Witnesses: Henery Wiggin, Nathaniel Wiggin and James Brackett Jr. CERT. WILL (D26:401): 6/18/1782. Presented by Exec. And witnesses Henery Wiggin and Nathl. Wiggin. INVY. WARR.: 6/18/1782. Comm.: Josiah Burleigh and Asa Folsom of Newmarket and Chase Crockett of Epping. INVY.: Appr. 8/26/1782. Value L246.7.7. Oaths 8/26/1782 Comm. to Walter Bryent, JP. Oath 9/3/__ Exec. to W. Parker, Reg.

2852. WIGGIN, CORNET THOMAS (1785) #5164
EST. Stratham gent. decd. CITATION: 11/26/1785. To Mark Wiggin, Stratham esq. To appear and take admin. of his father's est. or it will be granted to another heir or person. ADMIN.: 12/21/1785. Admr. John Folsom, Stratham gent. Bond L500.0.0. Sureties: Joseph Wiggin Jr. and Nathan Barker, Stratham husbandmen. Witness: Jona. Poor. Note: the text names Enoch Barker as a surety, but the sig. is Nathan. INVY. WARR.: 12/21/1785. Comm.: Jonathan Robinson, Jonathan Piper, gentlemen and Chase Wiggin, yoemen, all of Stratham. INVY.: 3/9/1786. Value L302.17.0. Oaths 3/14/1786 Robinson and Wiggin to Mark Wiggin, JP. Oath 3/15/1786 Admr. to W. Parker, Reg. ADMIN. D.B.N: 5/6/1786. Admr. d.b.n. Nathan Barker, Stratham yoeman. Bond L500.0.0. Sureties: Jonathan Wiggin and Chase Wiggin, Stratham gentlemen. Witnesses: John Parker and W. Parker. INVY.: Comm.: Jonathan Wiggin, John Piper and Bickford Kennison. Value not tallied. Esti. L188.0.0+. Oaths 8/12/1788 Comm. to Simon Wiggin, JP. Oath 8/20/1788 Admr. d/b/n to W. Parker, Reg. PETITION: 8/1788. Of Admr. d.b.n. For Comm. Insolvency. Gives List claims of L326.4.0. LICENSE (D29:209): 8/20/1788. To Admr. d.b.n. To sell sufficient real est. to pay debts. CLAIMS WARR.: 8/20/1788. Comm.: Jonathan Wiggin and Andrew Wiggin, gentlemen and Samuel Lane Jr., tanner, all of Stratham. On 2/20/1789 Comm. allowed 2 months more. Claims: 5/20/1789. Total L318.9.5. Oaths 5/20/1789 Comm. to judge. ACCOUNT: 5/20/1789. Of Admr. d.b.n. Allowed 5/20/1789. PROP. & SETTLEM: Claims L318.9.5. Amount to be proportioned L88.7.9. Allowed 6/17/1789 with order to Admr. d.b.n. to pay.

2853. WIGGIN, TUFTON (1779) #4531
EST. Stratham yoeman decd. testate. WILL: Drawn 2/28/1776. Legatees: Son-Benjamin; Daus.-Judith Wiggin, Mehitable Wiggin and Sarah Wiggin. Notes that he has given the other children their shares. Exex.-wife Sarah, who is not a legatee in Will. His mark. Witnesses: Benjamin Wiggin, Bickford Kennison and John Foss. CERT. WILL: 3/31/1779. Presented by Exex. and Kennison, one of the witnesses, Foss, a witness, decd. and Benj. Wiggin absent. INVY.: Appr. 6/22/1779. Comm.: Daniel Pickering, John Piper and Thomas Brackett. Value L587.8.0. Oaths 6/22/1779 Comm. to Mark Wiggin, JP. Oath 6/30/1779 Exex. To judge.

2854. WIGGIN, CAPT. ZEBULON (1783) #4959
EST. Portsmouth mariner decd. ADMIN.: 12/17/1783. Admx. Ann Wiggin, Portsmouth widow. Bond L2000.0.0. Sureties: Jonathan Wiggin, gent. and Stephen Thurston, yoemen, both of Stratham. Witnesses: Josiah (Lunt?-unreadable) and Nathl. Parker. INVY.: Appr. 12/29/1783. Comm. Sam. Sherburne and Joseph White. Value L35.10.0. Oaths 1/15/1784

Comm. to Saml. Penhallow, JP. Oath 2/18/1784 Admx. to W. Parker, Reg. PETITION: No sig. For Comm. Insolvency. Gives list claims of L39.16.0. CLAIMS WARR.: 2/18/1784. Comm.: Samuel Sherburne and Joseph Ayers, yoemen and Joseph White, gent., all of Portsmouth. CLAIMS: Total L44.6.11. Oaths 8/17/1784 Comm. to Saml. Penhallow, JP. ACCOUNT: 8/18/1784. Of George Freese and Ann his wife, Admx. Allowed 8/18/1784. Account includes main. 2 children.

WILLEE. See also Willie

2855. WILLEE, SAMUEL (1753) A#1846
EST. Of Durham intestate. ACCOUNT (D21:423): Of Elijah Denbow and Sarah his wife, formerly Sarah Willee. Allowed 7/9/1772. Account includes main. 3 children. Orig. Archives file includes Admin. and Invy.

2856. WILLIAMS, ISAAC JR. (1793) #5906
EST. Exeter trader decd. ADMIN.: 7/1/1793. Admr. Isaac Williams, Exeter barber. Bond L500.0.0. Sureties: John Dean, hatter and Thomas Dean, trader, both of Exeter. INVY.: Appr. 3/21/1794. Comm.: Simeon Ladd, Wm. Parker Jr. and Bradbury Cilley. Value L44.0.1. Oaths Admr. and Comm. 3/12/11794 to W. Parker, JP. PETITION: Dated by clerk 3/21/1794. Of Admr. For Comm. Insolvency. Requests Simeon Ladd, Wm. Parker Jr. and Bradbury Cilley, esquires for Commissioners. Allowed. CLAIMS WARR.: 3/21/1794. Comm.: As requested. CLAIMS: 10/1/1794. Total L273.15.0. Includes Bill 7/2/1792 from Jeremiah Leavitt for L1.9.3. Signed by Ladd and Parker, Comm., as having been allowed by judge. Bill 2/10/1795. Of Thomas Dean for L2.17.4 signed by Ladd and Parker, Comm., as having been allowed by Judge. ACCOUNT: 9/4/1794. Of Admr. Order: 9/4/1795. To Admr. Bal. to be distributed to creditors. PROP. CLAIMS: 9/9/1795. Claims L213.15.0. Amount to be proportioned L32.0.0. Allowed 9/9/1795 with order to Admr. to pay.

2857. WILLIAMS, REV. SIMON (1793) #5943
EST. Londonderry minister decd. testate. Note: The Will gives res. as Windham. WILL: Drawn 6/22/1793. Legatees: Wife-Mary; Sons-George, Gilbert, Simon and John; Daus.-Katharine, Ann, Mary and Elizabeth; Grandson-Adam Williams; Friends-George Wood, Rev. Joseph McKeen of Beverly, MA and Dr. George Wood of Nottingham West, Hillsborough Co., to be editors of his manuscript works. Exec.-Son-in-law Deacon Elijah Sargent. His sig. Witnesses: Samuel Senter, Thomas Hardy and John Davidson Jr. CERT. WILL (D31:129): 12/18/1793. Presented by Exec. and witnesses Hardy and Davidson. ADMIN.: 12/18/1793. Exec.

Elijah Sargeant, Methuen, Essex Co., MA esq. Bond L1000.0.0. Sureties: Thomas Hardy, esq. and John Davidson Jr., yoeman, both of Windham. Witnesses: Joseph McKeen and N. Parker. INVY.: Comm.: John Davidson Jr., John Anderson and Eliphalet Ladd. Value L254.7.7. Oath 4/15/1794 Exec., Davidson and Ladd to James Betton, JP. PETITION: 3/19/1798. Of Mary Williams, widow of Simon. For Dower. Witnesses: Gilbert Williams and Martha Williams.

2858. WILLIAMS, THOMAS (1789) #5453
EST. Hampstead yoeman decd. testate. Will: Drawn 5/18/1787. Legatees: Wife-Susanna; Sons-Thomas, John and Moses; Dau.-Molley wife of Reuben Wells; Three grandchildren-children of his dau. Ruth and children of his dau. Sarah decd. Exec.-son Moses. His sig. Witnesses: Henry Johnson, Molley Calfe and John Calfe. CERT. WILL (D29:270): 5/20/1789. Presented by Exec. and witnesses John Calfe and Johnson. CERT.: 5/20/1789. Of Susanna Williams widow of Thomas. She accepts the things given her in Will and relinquishes all right of Dower. Witnesses: John Calfe and Henry Johnson. ADMIN.: 5/20/1789. Exec. Moses Williams, Hampstead yoeman. Bond L1000.0.0. Sureties: John Calfe, esq. and Henry Johnson, yoeman, both of Hampstead. Witness W. Parker. INVY.: Comm.: Wm. Marshall, Edmund Mooers and Timothy Goodwin. Value L341.2.7. Oaths 6/22/1789 Comm. to Edmund Mooers, JP. Oath 8/28/1789 Exec. To W. Parker, JP. Also oath 8/28/1789 Exec. to John Calfe, JP.

2859. WILLIAMS, WALTER (1777) #4378
EST. Hampton Falls mariner decd. ADMIN.: 7/29/1777. Admx. Mary Williams, Hampton Falls widow. Bond L500.0.0. Sureties: Meshech Weare, esq. and Hilyard Shaw, joiner, both of Hampton Falls. Witnesses Nathl. Parker and W. Parker. INVY. WARR.: 4/2/1777. Comm.: Dea. Abner Sanborn Jr., Hilyard Shaw and Dr. Joshua Chase. INVY.: Value not tallied. Esti. L25.0.0+. Oaths 9/30/1777 Comm. to Samll. Weare, JP. Oath 11/26/1777 Admx. to W. Parker, JP.

WILLIE. See also Willee

2860. WILLIE: HANNAH, LOIS, PENELOPE & SAMUEL (1772) #3949
GDP. Of the children of Samuel Willie, Durham yoeman decd. GDP.: 7/9/1772. Of Samuel, Hannah and Penelope, minors over 14. Gdn. James Willie, Lee yoeman. Bond L500.0.0. Sureties: Elijah Denbo, yoeman and Joseph Sias, esq., both of Lee. Witnesses: Daniel Lunt and Samuel Parker. GDP.: 7/9/1772. Of Lois, a minor under 14. Gdns.: Elijah Denbo and Sarah his wife, both of Lee. Bond L500.0.0. Sureties: Joseph Sias, esq. and James Willie, both of Lee. Witnesses: Daniel Lunt and Samuel Parker.

2861. WILLIE, WILLIAM (1772) #3930
EST. Durham yoeman decd. intestate. ADMIN.: 5/7/1772. Admr. John Willey, Barrington yoeman. Bond L500.0.0. Sureties: Joseph Young of Barrington and David Drew of Madbury, yoemen. Witnesses: Oliver Whipple and Saml. Hale Jr. INVY. WARR.: 5/7/1772. Comm.: David Drew of Madbury and Joseph Young of Barrington, yoemen. "To be shown by Bethia Willey, his widow, or John Willey, his son, one of whom is to be Admr." INVY.: Appr. 5/9/1772. Value L102.4.0. Oaths 5/27/1772 John Willy, Admr. and Comm. to judge. LICENSE: 5/26/1773. To sell sufficient land to pay debts. (Says, "est. in hands of William Willie, Admr.", evidently a clerk's error.)

2862. WILSON: AGGNIS, JAMES & JEAN (1791) #5651
GDP: Of the children of Samuel Wilson, Londonderry yoeman decd. GDP.: 4/21/1791. Of James, a minor over 14. Gdn. John Nesmith Jr., Londonderry gent. Bond L1000.0.0. Sureties: James Betton, esq. and William Simson, yoeman, both of Windham. Witnesses: Samuel Johnson and Nathl. Parker. GDP.: 4/21/1791. Of: Jean, a minor over 14 and of Aggnis, a minor under 14. Gdn. James Betton, Windham esq. Bond L1000.0.0. Sureties: William Simson, Windham yoeman and John Nesmith Jr., Londonderry gent. Witnesses: John Prentice and N. Parker.

2863. WILSON, BENJAMIN (1773) #4001
EST. Londonderry esq. decd. intestate. ADMIN.: 3/30/1773. Admrs.: James McGregor, gent. and James Evins, yoeman, both of Londonderry. Bond L1000.0.0. Sureties: Henry Moor, Chester esq. and John Langdon, Portsmouth merchant. Witnesses: Nathl. Rogers and Samuel Parker. REVOCATION OF ADMIN.: (D22:125) 4/6/1773. On 3/30/1883 Evins and McGregore represented to the judge there was no legal next of kin of Benjamin of sufficient capacity to be Admr. So the court was induced to appoint Evins and MacGregore. It now appears that Benjamin has a bro. qualified. Admin. granted to Evins and MacGregore is revoked and Admin. granted instead to the bro. John Wilson, Londonderry yoeman with Wilson requesting that Samuel Allison, Londonderry gent. join him as co-Admr. This was ordered. ADMIN.: 4/6/1773. Admrs.: John Wilson, yoeman and Samuel Allison, gent., both of Londonderry. Bond L500.0.0. Sureties: Matthew Thornton and Stephen Holland, Londonderry esquires. Witnesses: Jean Holland and Elizabeth Holland. INVY. WARR.: 4/6/1773. Comm.: James Betton, Windham esq. and Hugh Montgomery, Londonderry yeoman. INVY.: Appr. 4/16/1773. Total L335.3.6. Oaths 4/16/1773 Comm. to Stephen Holland, JP. Oath 4/21/1773 John Wilson, an Admr., to judge. LICENSE: 4/22/1773. To Admrs. To sell sufficient real est. to pay debts. ACCOUNT: 3/1774. Of Admrs. Allowed 3/30/1774.

ADDL. ACCOUNT: 11/28/1776. Of Samuel Allison, an Admr. Allowed 11/28/1776. ADDL. ACCOUNT (D24:45): 6/1777. Of Saml. Allison, an Admr. Allowed 6/25/1777. Note: This file also contains a single page of an Invy. which belongs with #4548 Rev. John Wilson (1779) and is recorded there.

2864. WILSON: BENJAMIN, EDWARD ELDER & JANE (1773) #4015
GDP. Of the children of Benjamin Wilson of Londonderry decd. GDP.: 3/31/1773. Of Benjamin, Edward Elder Wilson and Jane, minors under 14. Gdns.: Peter Patterson and Saml. Wilson, Londonderry husbandmen. Bond L1000.0.0. Sureties: James Betton, esq. and Samuel Campbell, husb., both of Windham. Witnesses: William Hogg, Thomas Patterson and James Campbell. GDP.: 5/6/1773. Of Benjamin, a minor over 14. Gdn. James McGregore, Londonderry gent. Bond L500.0.0. Surety Robert McNeill, Londonderry yoeman. Witnesses: Richard York and Samuel Parker. GDP.: 3/30/1774. Of Benjamin. dn. Hugh Montgomery, Londonderry yeomen. Bond L1000.0.0. Sureties: Samuel Allison, Londonderry gent. and James Betton, Windham esq. Witnesses: Samuel Hale Jr. and Nathl. Adams.

2865. WILSON, COLL TURNER (1797) #6396
GDP. Of the son of an Exeter cordwainer. GDP.: 11/21/1797. Of Coll Turner Wilson, a minor over 14. Gdn. Eliphalet Hale, Exeter gent. Bond $1,000.00. Sureties: Nathaniel Gilman and Nathaniel Parker, Exeter esquires. Witness W. Parker.

2866. WILSON, DAVID (1776) #4297
GDP of the son of Benjamin Wilson of Londonderry decd. GDP: 12/4/1776. Of David, a minor over 14. Gdn. John Holms, Londonderry gent. Bond L500.0.0. Sureties: Jonathan Reed, tanner and Samuel Gregg, yoeman, both of Londonderry. Witnesses: Robert Murrey and Jonathan Holmes. GDP. (D23:493): 3/-/1777. Of David, a minor over 14, son of Benjamin Wilson of Londonderry decd. Gdn. John Holms who gave bond.

2867. WILSON, GEORGE (1783) #4950
GDP. Windham yoeman adjudged n.c.m. GDP.: 11/19/1784. Of George Wilson an adult adjudged n.c.m. Gdn. Alexander Wilson, Windham gent. Bond L5000.0.0. Sureties: James Betton, esq. and Job Pingry, yoeman, both of Windham. Witnesses: James Wilson and Abner Foster. INVY.: Appr. 11/27/1783. Comm.: Capt. James Gilmore and Samuel Morison. Value L406.10.0. Oaths 11/27/1783 Comm. to James Betton, JP. Oath 5/17/1786 Gdn. To W. Parker, Reg. CERT.: 4/13/1787. Of: Benjamin Thom and James Davidson, Windham Selectmen. They certify that George has now become capable of taking care of his family and the Gdn. may be

called upon to settle his Account and be discharged from his Gdp. ACCOUNT: Of Gdn. Allowed 5/16/1787 after hearing objections of Robert Young, esq. on behalf of George. ADDL. ACCOUNT: 9/7/1788. Of Gdn. Allowed 9/17/1788.

2868. WILSON, INCREASE (1773) #4006
EST. Exeter yoeman decd. intestate. ADMIN.: 12/18/1773. Admx. Susanna Wilson, Exeter widow. Bond L500.0.0. Sureties: John Folsom and Benjamin Boardman, Exeter yoemen. Witnesses: David Gilman and Wm. Parker Jr. INVY. WARR.: 1/5/1774. Comm.: Charles Rundlet, esq. and Samuel Brooks, gent., both of Exeter. INVY.: Appr. 3/5/1774. Value L256.14.6. Oaths 2/9/1776 Comm. and on 2/15/1776 Admx. to W. Parker Jr., JP. PETITION: 2/28/1776. Of Saml. Harris, atty to Admx. For License. LICENSE: 2/28/1776. To Admx. To sell sufficient real est. to pay debts. PETITION: 4/23/1776. Of Priscilla Wilson, Exeter widow. States it is necessary that an Admr. D.B.N. be appointed. She declines and requests appointment of Saml. Harris of Exeter who is acquainted with est. proceedings. Creditors Winthrop Odlin, J. Emery and Peter Coffin Jr. join in Petition. ADMIN. D.B.N.: 4/24/1776. Admr. d.b.n. Samuel Harris, Exeter taylor. Bond L500.0.0. Sureties: Winthrop Odlin, gent. and James Rundlet, yoeman, both of Exeter. Witness Nathl. Parker. LICENSE: 5/28/1776. To Admr. d.b.n. To sell sufficient real est. to pay debts. ACCOUNT: 7/16/1788. Of Admr. d.b.n. Allowed 11/19/1788. Account includes main. one child. ACCOUNT: 7/16/1788. Of Susanna Wilson, decd. of her Admin. exhibited by Admr. d.b.n. Allowed 11/19/1788.

2869. WILSON, JAMES (1772) #3956
EST. Londonderry yoeman decd. testate. WILL: Drawn 4/20/1772. Legatees: wife-Jennet; Sons-Alexander, James, John, George and Samuel; Daus.-Jennet Willson and Ellenor Dickey; Grandsons-James Willson son of his son Alexander, James Willson son of his son James; Sons-in-law: Samll. Fisher, Thomas Nesmith and Daniel McDuffee. Exec.-son Samuel. His sig. Witnesses: John Durham, John Durham Jr. and James Mcgregore. CERT. WILL (D21:434): 7/30/1772 Presented by Exec. and witnesses Mcgregore and John Durham. ADMIN.: 7/30/1772. Exec. Samuel Wilson, Londonderry yoeman. Bond L500.0.0. Sureties: John Durham, yoeman and James Mcgregore, gent., both of Londonderry. Witnesses: Richd. Bartlet and Samuel Parker.

2870. WILSON, JAMES (1777) #4361
EST. Londonderry yeoman decd. testate. WILL: Drawn 4/24/1777. Legatees: Wife-Jennet; Children-Thomas, James, Robert, Alexander, David, Elizabeth Graham, Mary Smith, Martha Ferguson and Jean

Forsythe. Execs.: Capt. William Duncan and James Nesmith Jr. His mark. Witnesses: Francis Mitchell, James Thompson and Jane Dickey. CERT. WILL (D24:14): 5/28/1777. Presented by Execs. and witnesses Mitchel and Thompson. INVY.: Comm. Georg Corning, Archibald McMurphy and James Thompson. Value L418.12.10.2. Oaths 8/27/1777 Comm. and Execs. to John Bell, JP.

2871. WILSON, JAMES (1791) #5728
EST. Chester yoeman decd. testate. WILL: Drawn 7/2/1789. Legatees: Wife-Mary; Sons-David, James Jr. and Edward; Daus.-Martha, Elizebeth, Maryann (or Mary and Ann?), Rebecah and Jane. Exec.-wife Mary. His sig. Witnesses: Jethro Colby, Saml. Wilson and Robt. Wilson. CERT. WILL (D30:167): 12/21/1791. Presented by James Wilson, Exex. named refusing trust, and witnesses Colby and Samuel Wilson. RENUN.: 1/12/1792. Of Mary Wilson, widow of James. Of Admin. Requests appointment of her son James. Witnesses: Jethro Colby and Josiah Bradly. ADMIN.: 1/18/1792. Exec. James Wilson, Chester yoeman. Bond L1000.0.0. Sureties: Samuel Wilson and Benjamin Sleeper, Chester yoemen. Witnesses: Eliza. Parker and W. Parker. INVY.: Appr. 2/9/1792. Comm.: William White, Jethro Colby and Pearson Richardson. Value not tallied. Esti. L61.0.0+. Oaths 2/9/1792 Colby, Richardson and Exec. to Willm. White, JP.

2872. WILSON, REV. JOHN (1779) #4548
EST. Chester clerk decd. testate. WILL: Drawn 4/22/1760. Legates: Dau.-Ann Wilson; Sisters-Elisabeth Elleson of Pentecoora and Martha Taylor of Corride, Parish of Bally Kally; Bros.-James Wilson, Colrain innholder; Thomas Wilson of Harlow, Parish of Bally Kally, all Ireland; Cousin-Ann Miller Alles(?) Flemming. Execs.-Capt. James Sherala and Lt. Silvanus Smith, gent., both of Chester. His sig. Witnesses: Saml. Emerson, Benja. Wilson and Dorithy Emerson. Oaths 6/10/1779 Saml. Emerson, esq. and Dorithy Emerson, to W. Parker, Reg. & JP. CERT. WILL: 6/13/1779. Presented by Ann Wilson, one of Execs., the other named in Will being dead and the other refusing to accept trust. Note: The Will is very difficult to read and even checking with the Docket enry, the correct name of his cousin Ann is uncertain. The Will itself does not name his dau. Ann as an Exec. INVY. WARR.: 6/10/1779. Comm.: Robert Wilson and William White, esquires and John Sanborn Dearborn, gent., all of Chester. INVY.: Appr. 8/23/1779. Value not tallied. Esti. L9795.0.0. Oaths 8/23/1779 Wilson, White and Admr. to Saml. Emerson, JP. Note: In #4001 Benjamin Wilson (1773) there is an addl. page of the Invy. It, too, is in poor condition and unreadable except for the names of Wilson and White and a date for oaths of 8/23/177? at Chester.

2873. WILSON, JOSEPH (1781) #4747
EST. Londonderry yoeman decd. ADMIN.: 11/20/1781. Admr. Joseph Willson of Co has, Grafton Co. Bond L50000.0.0. Sureties: John Clark, Londonderry yoeman and James Betton, Windham esq. Witnesses: Robert Wilson and John Thomson. INVY. WARR.: 11/16(sic.)/1781. Comm.: John Clark, John Thomson and Saml. Thomson. Invy.: Appr. 3/29/1782. Value L20.0.0. Oaths 4/2/1782 John Clark and John Thomson to James Betton, JP.

2874. WILSON, PETER (1785) #5118
GDP. Of the son of Peter Wilson, Portsmouth mariner decd. GDP.: 6/22/1785. Of Peter, a minor over 14. Gdn. Noah Parker, gent. Bond L1000.0.0. Sureties: Nathaniel Melcher, whitesmith and William Sowersby, chaise trimmer. Witness W. Parker.

2875. WILSON, ROBERT, ET. ALS. (1784) #4976
See #4756 Benjamin Bachelder (1781)

2876. WILSON, ROBERT (1791) #5706
EST. Chester esq. decd. testate. WILL: Drawn 8/8/1791. Legatees: Wife-Jane; Sons-John, Jonathan and William; Daus.-Mary Moore, Susanna Towle, Margaret Gibbin, Anna Wilson, Sarah Wilson and Elizabeth Wilson. Execs.-sons John and William. His sig. Witnesses: Benja. Currier, Gideon Currier and Josiah Flagg. Proved 11/5/1791. CERT. WILL (D30:146): 11/16/1791. Presented by Execs. and witnesses Benjamin Currier and Flagg, esq. ADMIN.: 11/5/1791 Execs.: John Wilson and William Wilson, Chester yoemen. Bond L1000.0.0. Sureties: Josiah Flagg, esq. and Benjamin Currier, gent., both of Chester. Witness W. Parker. INVY.: Appr. 12/29/1791. Comm.: Benjamin Currier and James Wason. Value not tallied. Esti. L161.0.0 plus short list of Notes and Certificates. Oaths 12/29/1791 Comm. and Execs. to Josiah Flagg, JP.

2877. WILSON, SAMUEL JR. (1778) #4504 & #5507 (1790)
EST. Londonderry yoeman decd. testate. WILL (#4504): Drawn 10/22/1778. Legatees: Mother; Wife-Grizzel; His three children, only the son James named; Indentured servant Benjamin McCarty. Execs.-Thomas Nesmith and wife Grizzel. His sig. Witnesses: William Dickey, James Humphrey and James Betton. CERT. WILL (D24:435): 12/31/1778. Presented by Execs. and Witnesses Dickey and Humphrey. INVY. (#5507): Appr. 4/2/1779. Comm.: John Prentice, Robert Moor and John Nesmith. Value L10394.10.0. Oaths 4/2/1779 Comm. to Moses Barnett, JP. Oath 4/20/1790 Grizzel Simpson, an Exec., to James Betton, JP.

2878. WINGATE, AARON (1797) #6392
EST. Portsmouth mariner decd. RENUN.: 11/2/1797. Of Ruth Wingate, widow of Aaron. Of Admin. Requests appointment of her bro. John Wingate. ADMIN.: 11/3/1797. Admr. John Wingate, Madbury, Strafford Co. esq. Bond $3,000.00. Sureties: Jonathan Steele of Durham, Strafford Co. and George Sullivan of Exeter, esquires. Witnesses: Nabob Tucker and Nicholas Emery. INVY. WARR.: 11/3/1797. Comm.: Jeremiah Libbey, George Gains and George Wentworth, Portsmouth esquires. Invy.: Appr. 11/7/1797. Value $696.28 plus an insurance policy for $1,500.00. 11/7/1797 affirm. of Libbey and oaths Capt. Wentworth and Admr. to R. Cutts Shannon, JP. ACCOUNT: 6/18/1800. Of Admr. Allowed 6/18/1800 being consented to by Gdn. of heirs. Order: Admr. to pay widow $96.05 as full bal. of her Dower and remaining $400.00 to Gdn. of heirs. Account includes main. Aaron, Elizabeth, Jonathan, Ebenezer and James.

2879. WINGATE: AARON & JAMES (1798) #6495
GDP. Of the sons of Aaron Wingate, Portsmouth mariner decd. GDP.: 1/13/1798. Of: James and Aaron, minors under 14. Gdn. John Wingate, Madbury, Strafford Co. esq. Bond $3,000.00. Sureties: Samuel Kielle, esq. and Maul Hanson, husbm., both of Madbury, Strafford Co. Witnesses: Ezekiel Twombly and Elisha Hanson. PETITION: 4/16/1798. Of Ruth Wingate, widow of Aaron decd. and mother and natural Gdn. of her children Aaron and James. Requests appeal against Decree appointing John Wingate Gdn. And appointment of herself. Encloses a bond. Granted. BOND: 4/16/1798. Of Ruth Wingate, Portsmouth widow. Bond $100.00. To appeal Decree GDP. Sureties: Ebenezer Chadwick and Clement Jackson, Portsmouth merchants. Witnesses: Thomas Safford and Samuel Rundlet. GDP (D32:537): 9/20/1798. Of: James and Aaron, minors under 14. Gdn. Ruth Wingate, Portsmouth widow. Sureties: Ebenezer Chadwick and Clement Jackson, both of Portsmouth.

2880. WINGATE, JOHN (1792) #5822 & (1793) #5898
DIV. North Hampton gent. The following Petition is recorded as #5813 Daniel Gookin (1792) but belongs here. PETITION: 10/22/1792. Of Daniel Gookin, North Hampton esq. For div. of land in North Hampton which he holds in common with John Wingate, North Hampton gent. and on which he and Wingate now live. NOTIFICATION (#5822): 12/22/1792. To John Wingate, North Hampton gent. Of a hearing on petition of Daniel Gookin. Cert.: 11/6/1792. Of Simon Ward, Constable. He left a copy of Notification with Wingate. DIV. (#5898): Comm.: John Dearborn, esq.; Thomas Marston, gent.; and David Knowles, Morris Hobbs and Thomas Loveren, yoeman, all of North Hampton. Divisees:

Daniel Goodkin, esq. And John Wingate, gent. Oaths 4/2/1793 Dearborn, Marston and Knowles to Moses Leavitt, JP. Allowed.

WINSLE. See also Winslow

2881. WINSLE, SAMUEL (1787) #5264 1/2
EST. Kingston yoeman decd. testate. WILL: Drawn 9/29/1785. Legatees: Present wife; Sons-Ephraim, John, Jacob and Samuel; Daus.-Hannah Severance and Elisabeth Buswell. Exec.-son-in-law William Buswell. His sig. Witnesses: Jonathan Sleeper, Abigail Sleeper and Hannah Sleeper. CERT. WILL (D29:111): 3/21/1787. Presented by Exec. and witnesses Jonathan Sleeper and Abigail Sleeper. INVY.: Appr. 8/23/1787. Comm.: Israel Dimond, Jacob Webster and Simmons Seccombe. Value L480.11.10. Oaths 8/23/1787 Comm. to Solomon Wheeler, JP. Oath 9/20/1787 Exec. to W. Parker, JP.

WINSLOW. See Winsle
2882. WISE, KATHARINE (1774) #4091
EST. Portsmouth widow decd. testate. WILL: Drawn 3/11/1771. Legatees: Son-John Dennett; Grandson-Jeremiah Dennett son of her son Ephraim Dennett decd. She notes that all her other children have received their proportions. Exec.- son John Dennett. Her mark. Witnesses: Abraham Elliot, John Ayers 3d and Richard Cutts Shannon. CERT. WILL (D22:433): 3/12/1774. Presented by Capt. John Dennett, Exec. and witnesses Elliot and Ayers.

WITHERSPOON. See Weatherspoon

2883. WOOD, NATHANIEL (1773) #3993
EST. Chester husbandman decd. testate. WILL: Drawn 2/10/1772. Legatees: Wife-Elizabeth; Sons-Obediah and Nathaniel; Daus.-Luce Wells, Abigail Eaton and Ruth Porter. Exec.-son Nathaniel. His mark. Witnesses: Samuel Emerson, Stephen Derbon and Wells Chase. CERT. WILL (D22:28): 2/3/1773. Presented by Exec. and witnesses Emerson and Derbon. INVY. WARR.: 2/3/1773. Comm.: Stephen Derbon, gent. and Wells Chase, yeoman, both of Chester. INVY: Appr. 4/8/1773. Value L88.3.1. Oaths 10/2/1773 Comm. to Samuel Emerson, JP. Oath 10/11/1773 Exec. To judge.

2884. WOODBURN, JOHN (1791) #5652
EST. Londonderry yoeman decd. testate. WILL: Drawn 1/9/1779. Legatees: Wife-Mary; Sons-David and John; Daus. and Sons-in-law-Jane Woodburn, Edward Aiken and Margred his wife, John Wallace and Sarah

his wife, George Reid and Mary his wife, John Thomson and Martha his wife, James Thomson and Ann his wife, William Aiken and Elisabeth his wife, Robert Dickey and Hannah his wife; Grandson-John Anderson son of James Anderson; The other living children of James Anderson by his dau. Agness Anderson; Exec.-Thomas Patterson. His mark. Witnesses: John Clark, Ephraim Gregg and James Betton. CERT. WILL: 4/22/1791. Presented by James Thomson, the Exec. named declining, and witnesses Clark and Betton. RENUN.: 5/17/1790. Of Thomas Patterson. Of Admin. ADMIN.: 4/22/1790. Admr. James Thomson, Londonderry yoeman. Bond L1000.0.0. Sureties: John Dwinell, Londonderry yoeman and James Betton, Windham esq. Witnesses: John Prentice and Nathl. Parker. ACCOUNT: Of Admr. Oath 4/17/1793 Admr. to James Betton, JP. Allowed 4/17/1793. ACCOUNT: Of Admr. No allowance. May be part of previous.

2885. WOODBURY, EBENEZER (1774) #4107
EST. Salem yoeman decd. testate. WILL: Drawn 2/18/1774. Legatees: wife-Elizabeth; sons-Hasediah and Henry; daus.-Anna Corning, Hannah Pingree, Mary Smith, Elizabeth Ellinwood and Abigail Duty; Grandchildren-James, Ebenezer and John, children of his son Ebenezer; Granddau.-Lidea Field. Exec.-son Henry. His sig. Witnesses: David Nevins, John Giles and Timothy Emerson. There is no Cert. of Will nor any signed proving by the judge, only a notation which says Nevins and Emerson sworn 6/8/1774.

2886. WOODBURY, JONATHAN (1776) #4267
EST. Salem yoeman decd. ADMIN.: 9/25/1776. Admr. Benjamin Woodbury, Salem yoeman. Bond L500.0.0. Sureties: Jesse Merrill, gent. and Jonathan Massey, yoeman, both of Salem. Witness Nathl. Parker. INVY.: Appr, 10/23/1776. Comm. Jesse Merrill, Zachariah Woodbury and Jeremiah Dow. Value L160.13.8. Oaths 10/23/1776 Comm. to Timothy Ladd, JP. Oath 10/30/1776 Admr. to W. Parker, JP.

2887. WOODMAN, BENJAMIN (1784) #5001
EST. Canterbury yoeman decd. intestate. RENUN.: 4/14/1784. Of Samuel Morrison of Sanbornton, Strafford Co. States that Benjamin Woodman died leaving a widow, now wife of Morrison, and 4 minor children. The Admin. accrues to him, but requests appointment of Isaac Medar, who is the bro. of his wife. ADMIN.: 4/21/1784. Admr. Isaac Medar, Durham, Strafford Co. gent. Bond L500.0.0. Sureties: Edmund Pendergast of Durham, Strafford Co. and John Leavitt, Exeter husbm. Witnesses: Nathl. Parker and Saml. Hobart. INVY. WARR.: 4/21/1784. Comm.: Jacob Garland, John Durgan and Edmund Chapman. INVY.: Appr. 6/1/1784.

Value L3.5.0. Oaths 6/1784 Garland and Durgan to Thomas Gilman, JP. Oath 7/15/__ Admr. to W. Parker, Reg. CLAIMS WARR.: 7/15/1784. Comm.: Jeremiah Bryent, esq.; Wentworth Cheswill, gent. and Benja. Meed, trader, all of Newmarket. CLAIMS: Total L9.12.4 1/2. Oaths 4/19/1785 Comm. to Saml. Gilman, JP. ACCOUNT: 7/21/1785. Of Admr. Allowed 7/21/1785 having been sworn to by Admr. before.

2888. WOODMAN, HANNAH (1778) #4442
EST. South Hampton widow decd. ADMIN.: 3/27/1778. Admr. Jonathan Woodman, Deerfield yoeman. Bond L500.0.0. Sureties: Richard Jenness 3d and Job Jenness Jr., Rye yoemen. Witnesses: Nathl. Parker and W. Parker. INVY.: Appr. 6/5/1778. Comm.: Moses Flanders, Abel Brown and Isaiah Dole. Value L99.12.0. Oaths 6/5/1778 Comm. to judge. ACCOUNT: 9/30/1778. Of Admr. Allowed 9/30/1778.

2889. WOODMAN, HILTON (1768) A#3486,
EST. South Hampton yoeman decd. ADMIN. D/B/N (D25:263):3/27/1778. Admr. d/b/n Jonathan Woodman of Deerfield. Sureties: Richard Jenness 3d and Jobe Jenness, gent., both of Rye. Orig. Archives file includes Admin., Invy., Account, Warr. & Appr., Dower, Decree Settlm., Bond and Gdp. of Thomas.

2890. WOODMAN, JOSHUA (1791) #5642
EST. Kingston blacksmith decd. testate. WILL: Drawn 1/27/1789. Legatees: Wife-Eunice; Sons-Joshua, John, Moses, Jonathan, David, Joseph, Benjamin and Samuel; Daus.-Eunice wife of Daniel Watson, Hannah wife of William Bagley, Sarah wife of John Emmons and Mary Wife of Eliphalet Haskel. Exec.-son Samuel. His sig. Witnesses: Josiah Bartlett, Josiah Bartlett Jr. and Ezra Bartlett. CERT. WILL (D30:38): Presented by Exec. And witnesses Josiah Bartlett esq. and Ezra Bartlett.

2891. WOODMAN, LEVI (1777) #4323
GDP. Of the son of Hilton Woodman, South Hampton yeoman decd. GDP.: 3/5/1777. Of Levi, a minor over 14. Gdn. Josiah Rogers, South Hampton yoeman. Bond L500.0.0. Sureties: Isaac Brown, cordwainer and William Cooper, gent., both of South Hampton. Witnesses: William Graves and Isaac Brown Jr.

2892. WORTH, JOSEPH (1777) #4321
EST. Of Hampton Falls decd. testate. WILL: Drawn 10/20/1765. Legatees: sons-John, Obadiah and Joseph. Exec.-son Obadiah. His sig. Witnesses: Isaac Brown, Jona. Stuward, Josiah White and David Stuward. CERT. WILL: 2/26/1777. Presented by Exec. and witnesses Brown and Jonathan

Stuward. INVY.: Comm.: Abner Sanborn Jr., Joshua Chase and Isaac Brown. Value L370.13.0. Oaths 3/25/1777 Comm. to Winthrop Gove, JP. Oath 4/30/1777 Exec. to judge.

2893. WORTHEN, ABIGAIL (1774) #4113
GDP. Of the dau. of Jonahan Worthen of Concord decd. PETITION: 6/27/1774. Of Abigail. She states that there belongs to her part of her father's est. that needs taking care of. On the advice of friends and relatives, she requests the appointment of Capt. Ezekiel Worthen as her Gdn. Witnesses: Ezekiel Worthen Jr. and John Ward. Allowed 7/6/1774. GDP.: 7/7/1774. Of Abigail, a minor under 21 but now more than 14. Gdn. Ezekiel Worthen, Kensinton esq. Bond L1000.0.0. Sureties: Eliphalet Merril of South Hampton and Josiah Bartlett of Kingston, esquires. Witnesses: Saml. Hale Jr. and William Hale.

2894. WORTHEN, EPHRAIM (1763) A#3028
EST. Rumford yoeman decd. ACCOUNT (D22:78): Of John Chandler Jr., Admr. d.b.n. Allowed 2/17/1773. Account includes main. of Ezekiel and Jacob. Note: The following Petition and Div. found in #5499 Ebenezer Virgin (1789) belongs here. PETITION: 11/6/1790. Of John Hoit, Gdn. of Rebecca Worthen, a minor, dau. of Saml. Worthen late of Concord decd., and Ebenr. Virgin. To div. the real est. of Ephraim Worthen, late of Concord decd. Request Comm. of Timothy Walker, esq.; John Chandler and John Bradley, gentlemen; David Foster and Philbrook Bradley, yoemen. DIV.: 4/6/1791. Comm. as requested. To div. land in Concord, the est. of Ephraim Worthen, decd., in equal shares between Rebecca Worthen and Ebenezer Virgin of Concord. Because Virgin's part was included in Dower, he being given use of some of Rebecca's portion during the natural life of Widow Joanna Austin, the same to revert to Rebecca on Widow's death. Oaths 4/16/1791 Forster, John Bradley, Chandler and Philbrook Bradley to Timothy Walker, JP. Allowed 3/7/1794. Orig. Archives file includes Admin., Invy., License 1765, License 1767 and Admin d.b.n., Account, Pet. Div., Notice of Pet., Dower, Div. Warr. and Div. 1777.

2895. WORTHEN, CAPT. EZEKIEL (1783) #4951
EST. Kensington yoeman decd. testate. WILL: Drawn 9/23/1782. Legatees: Sons-Jacob, Exekiel, Samuel and Enoch; Daus.-Mary Worthen, Abigail Brown and Hannah James. Exec.-son Enoch. His sig. Witnesses: Jona. Brown, John True and Abel Brown. CERT. WILL (D27:336): Presented by Exec. and witnesses Jonathan Brown and Abel Brown. INVY. WARR.: 11/19/1783. Comm.: Jonathan Brown, yoeman; Joseph Brown, gent., both of Kensington and Moses French, South Hampton

joiner. INVY.: Appr. 11/21/1783. Value L591.3.0. Oaths 12/8/1783 Jonathan Brown and Joseph Brown to Ebenr. Potter, JP. Oath 2/18/1784 Exec. to W. Parker, Reg.

2896. WORTHEN, JONATHAN (1764) No A# & (1776) #4268.
EST. Of Rumford decd. INVY. (4268): Comm.: Timothy Bradley and John Chandler Jr. Value L2973.11.3. Oaths 2/26/1765 Comm. to Ezra Carter, JP. Oath 9/25/1776 Elizabeth Worthen, Admx. to judge. ACCOUNT: (#4268) 9/25/1776. Of Admx. Allowed. Account includes main. Mehitabel and Dorothy. Orig. Archives file includes only the Admin. with Elizabeth Worthen Admx. in which Jonathan' res. is given as Bow.

2897. WORTHEN, REBECKAH (1790) #5546
GDP. Of the dau. of Samuel Worthen, Concord gent. decd. PETITION: 5/17/1790. Of Mary Abbot. She chooses John Hoit to be Gdn. of her dau. Rebeckah Worthen, age 12. Oath 5/17/1790 Mary Abot of Loudon to Saml. Chamberlin, JP. Chamberlain supposes Hoit to be a suitable man for Gdn. GDP.: 5/19/1790. Of Rebeckah, a minor under 14. Gdn. John Hoit of Concord. Bond L500.0.0. Sureties: Chandler Lovejoy of Concord and Samuel Gerrish of Canterbury. Witnesses: James H. McClary and N. Parker.

2898. WORTHEN, SAMUEL (1778) #4506
EST. Chester yoeman decd. ADMIN.: 12/26/1778. Admx. Abigail Worthan, Chester widow. Bond L1000.0.0. Sureties: Stephen Lafken, yoeman and Nathan Fitts, gent., both of Chester and Isaac Blasdel, gent. Witnesses: Edmund Eliot and Jacob Elliot. INVY.: Appr. 3/1/1779. Comm.: Stephen Laufkin, Nathan Fitts and Isaac Blasdel. Value L541.11.1. Oaths 4/10/1779 Comm. to Robert Wilson, JP. Oath 10/26/1779 Admx. to Robert Wilson, JP. LICENSE: 4/25/1781. To Admx. To sell sufficient real est. to pay debts. ACCOUNT: Of Abigail Heath, late Abigail Worthen, Admx. Allowed 6/20/1787. Account includes maintenance of Aphia, David, Susanna and Sarah (who seems to have been born posthumously).

2899. WORTHEN, SAMUEL (1796) #6207
EST. Candia yoeman decd. ADMIN.: 4/27/1796. Admx. Betty Worthen, Candia widow. Bond $3,000.00. Sureties: Zechariah Clifford, gent. and Nathan Brown, yoeman, both of Candia. Witnesses; John Lane and Nath. Emerson. INVY.: Appr. 5/12/1796. Comm.: John Clay Jr., John Lane and Nathl. Emerson. Value $398.34. Oaths 5/12/1796 Clay and Lane to Nathl. Emerson, JP. PETITION: Of Zechariah Clifford on behalf of Admx. For

License and Comm. Insolvency. Gives list claims of $440.00. Granted 4/28/1796 with Comm. Insolvency of: Nathl. Emerson, Walter Robie and Ephraim Eaton. LICENSE (D32:155): 6/28/1796. To Admx. To sell real est. to the amount of $300.00. PETITION: 12/29/1796. Of Walter Robie on behalf of Admx. For License, noting that former one was insufficient. Gives claims still outstanding as $267.67. Granted. LICENSE (D32:234): 12/29/1796. To Admx. To sell real est. to amount of $290.00. DOWER: 7/14/1796. Comm.: Nathl. Emerson, Benja. Batchelder, Isaiah Rowe, John Lane and Walter Robie, esq. Of Widow Betty Worthen. Oaths 7/14/1796 Emerson, Batchelder, Rowe and Lane to Walter Robie, JP. Allowed. CLAIMS: 12/30/1796. Total $302.27. Oaths 2/20/1797 Emerson and Eaton to Walter Robie, JP. ACCOUNT: 3/15/1797. Of Admx. Allowed 3/15/1797. Account includes main. 3 children. PROP. & SETTLM.: Claims $302.27. Amount to be proportioned $267.00. Allowed 6/14/1797 with order to Admx. to pay.

2900. WORTHEN, THOMAS (1773) #4037
EST. Chester yeoman decd. testate. WILL: Drawn 3/2/1769. Legatees: Wife-Dorothy; Sons- Ezekiel and Samuel ; Daus.-Rhoda Fitts, Mary Clifford and Lydia Worthen; Grandsons- Michel Worthen and Thomas Worthen sons of his son David; Granddaus.-Sarah Worthen and Dolley Worthen daus. of his son David, Abigail Worthen, Mehetible Worthen and Dottey Worthen daus. of his son Jonathan. Exec.-son Samuel. His sig. Witnesses: Edmond Eliot, Simon Bayley and Saml Emerson. CERT. WILL (D22:274): 9/1/1773 Presented by Exec. and witnesses Bayley and Eliot. INVY. WARR.: 9/1/1773. Comm.: Nathan Fitts and Isaac Blasdell, Chester gent. INVY.: Appr. 9/23/1773. Value L238.12.6. Oaths 9/23/1773 Comm. to Saml. Emerson, JP. Oath 10/11/1773 Exec. to judge. DOWER: 5/28/1781. Comm.: John Underhill, Stephen Lufken, David Healy and Daniel Hodgkins. Of Widow Dorothy Worthen. Oaths 5/28/1781 Comm. to Saml. Emerson, JP.

2901. WRIGHT, MAJOR JOSEPH (1779) #4574
EST. Salem gent. decd. testate. WILL: Drawn 9/2/1779. Legatee: Wife-Mary. Exex.-wife Mary. His sig. Witnesses: Samuel Cole, Benjamin Woodbury and Olley Ladd. CERT. WILL: 9/29/1779. Presented by Exex. and witnesses Cole and Woodbury. ADMIN.: 9/29/1779. Exex. Mary Wright, Salem widow. Bond L2000.0.0. Sureties: Samuel Cole and Benjamin Woodbury, Salem yoemen. Witnesses: Nathl. Parker and W. Parker.

2902. WRIGHT, JOSEPH (1782) #4820

EST. Pelham husbm. decd. PETITION: 3/22/1782. Of Sarah Wright, widow of Joseph. States that her husb., who died about 6 years ago, was during his lifetime possessed of 1/2 of a house, barn and land in equal shares with the assignees of Jonathan Wright of Pelham decd. There are some debts due the est., mostly hers for bringing up 2 children until 7, and repairs needed, which she cannot do because she does not know what part belongs to est. Joseph's est. is small, the income just pays taxes, and she fears it may be insolvent. Requests div. and appointment of Jonathan Lyon as Admr. Witnesses: Jonathan Griffin and Edward Coburn. ADMIN.: 7/4/1782. Admr. Jonathan Lyon, Pelham yoeman. Bond L1000.0.0. Sureties: James Foster and Amos Johnson, both of Pelham. Witnesses: Thomas Hardy and J. Butler Jr. INVY. WARR.: 7/4/1792. Comm.: Thomas Hardy, gent.; John Ferguson and Abial Barker, all of Pelham. INVY.: Value not tallied. Esti. L77.0.0+. Oaths 10/23/1782 Hardy, Ferguson and Admr. to James Betton, JP. PETITION: 11/4/1782. Of Widow Sarah Wright and Admr. For div. of real est. held in common by heirs of decd. and Jonathan Lyon. Suggest Comm. of: Lt. Thomas Hardy, John Ferguson and Deacon Barnabus Gibson. DIV. WARR.: 11/16/1782. Comm.: Thomas Hardy, John Ferguson, Barnabus Gibson, Amos Gage and Josiah Gage. All of Pelham. To div. real est. as Petitioned. To div. land in Pelham in 2 equal parts. DIV.: 3/3/1783. Divisees: Heirs of Joseph Wright and Jonathan Lyon. Oaths 3/20/1783 Hardy, Josiah Gage and Gibson to James Betton, JP. Allowed 3/26/1783. ACCOUNT: Of Admr. Allowed 3/26/1783. Account includes main. 2 children. LICENSE (D27:189): 3/26/1786. To Admr. To sell sufficient real est. to pay debts. DOWER: 4/28/1783. Comm.: Same as Div. Of Widow Sarah Wright. Oaths 4/28/1783 Comm. to James Betton, JP. Allowed 4/16/1794.

2903. WRIGHT, MARY (1799) #6590

EST. Salem widow decd. testate, relict of Major Joseph Wright. WILL: Drawn 10/27/1779. Legatees: Children of Rev. John Page of Hawke-Joseph and Mary Page; Mary Page mother of Joseph and wife of Rev. John Page; Joseph Wright Rogers son of her who was Hannah Holt before marriage. Exec.-Rev. John Page. Her mark. Witnesses: Abner Bayley, Samuel Cole and David Messer. CERT. WILL (D33:108): 7/2/1799. Presented by Joseph Wright Page, the Exec. named being dead and witness Cole, the others being dead. ADMIN.: 7/2/1799. Exec. Joseph Wright Page, Salem yoeman. Bond $3,000.00. Sureties: John Page, Hawke hatter and Samuel Cole, Wilton, Hillsborough Co. yoeman. Witnesses: William S. Adams and W. Parker. INVY. (D33:161): Comm.: Samuel Webster, Farnum Hall and Richard Messer. Value $396.94. Oaths 9/9/1799 Comm. to Joseph Wardwell, JP. Oath 11/5/1799 Exec. to W. Parker, JP.

2904. WYMAN, AARON (1790) #5600
EST. Pelham gent. decd. intestate. PETITION: 11/23/1790. Of Asther Wyman, widow of Aaron. Of admin. Requests appointment of her sons Jesse Wyman and Josiah Wyman. Witnesses: James Gibson and Abigail Duty. PETITION: 11/24/1790. Of: Theodore Wyman and Benjamin Wyman, minors over 14, sons of Aaron. Theodore chooses Lt. John Ferguson to be his Gdn. and Benjamin chooses Nehemiah Butler to be his Gdn. ADMIN.: 11/26/1790. Admrs. Jesse Wyman of Cornish, Cheshire Co. and Josiah Wyman of Pelham, yoemen. Bond L1000.0.0. Sureties: James Gibson, esq. and James Hall, yoeman, both of Pelham. Witnesses: Mary Mansfield and William Parker. INVY.: Comm.: Barnabas Gibson, Eliphalet Hardy and Jesse Smith. Value L677.9.11. Oaths 3/10/1791 Comm. and on 4/20/1791 Josiah Wyman, an Exec., to James Gibson, JP. DIV.: 4/12/1794. Comm.: Barnabas Gibson, Eliphalet Hardy, Jesse Smith, James Gibson and James Hall. To div. the real est. Divisees: Granddau.-Zeviah Wyman, John Wyman, Jesse Wyman, Sally Wyman, Theodore Wyman, Benjamin Wyman, Phebe Wyman, Aaron Wyman, Mehetable wife of Israel Brient and Josiah Wyman. Oaths 4/12/1791 Barnabas Gibson, Hardy, Smith and Hall to James Gibson, JP. Allowed 4/18/1791. See #5623 for Gdp. of Benjamin and #5601 for Gdps. of Theodore and Sally.

2905. WYMAN, BENJAMIN (1791) #5623
GDP. Of the son of Aaron Wyman, Pelham gent. decd. GDP.: 3/10/1791. Of Benjamin, a minor over 14. Gdn.: Nehemiah Butler, Pelham yoeman. Bond: L1000.0.0. Sureties: James Gibson, esq. and James Hall, yoeman, both of Pelham. Witnesses: Josiah Wyman and Daniel Wyman. See #5600 Aaron Wyman (1790) for Benjamin's Petition for Gdp.

2906. WYMAN, DANIEL (1779) No#
GDP. Of the son of Thomas Wyman, Pelham yoeman decd. GDP. (D25:202): 6/29/1779. Of Daniel, a minor over 14. Gdn. Peirce Gage, Pelham yeoman. Sureties: Josiah Gage, esq. and Amos Gage, gent., both of Pelham.

2907. WYMAN, DAVID (1784) #4994
GDP. Of the son of Joseph Wyman of Pelham decd. GDP.: 4/16/1784. Of David, a minor over 14. Gdn. Asa Richardson, Pelham gent. Bond L1000.0.0. Sureties: Josiah Gage and James Gibson, Pelham esquires. Witnesses: Jesse Smith and Eliphelet Hardy. Note: This file includes the Admin. of the est. of Jacob Gale which belongs in File #4992 and is recorded there.

2908. WYMAN, JOSEPH JR. (1778) #4436
EST. Pelham husbm. decd. intestate. RENUN.: 3/16/1778. Of Mary Wyman, widow of Joseph. Of admin. Requests appointment of John Wyman, Joseph's bro., Pelham "copper," who she also appoints her atty. Witnesses: J. Butler Jr. and Jacob Kemp. ADMIN. (D24:242): 3/24/1778. Admr. John Wyman, Pelham yoeman. Sureties: Josiah Gage, esq. and Jacob Kemp, yoeman, both of Pelham. INVY. WARR.: 3/25/1778. Comm.: Jacob Kemp, Jacob Butler Jr. and Daniel Butler, all of Pelham. INVY.: Appr. 3/31/1778. Value L473.13.8. Oaths 5/18/1778 Comm. to Josiah Gage, JP. Oath 5/27/1778 Admr. to judge. DOWER: 6/4/1778. Comm.: James Ford, James Gibson, Jacob Kemp, Jacob Butler Jr. and David Butler. Of Widow Mary Wyman. Oaths 6/5/1778 Comm. to Josiah Gage, JP. Allowed. PETITION: 8/15/.1778. Of Admr. For Comm. Insolvency. Recommends Comm. of Josiah Gage, esq. and Jacob Butler Jr., both of Pelham. CLAIMS WARR.: 10/29/1778. Comm. as requested. LICENSE: 6/30/1779. To Admr. To sell sufficient real est. to pay debts. CLAIMS: Total L34.2.10.3. Oaths 6/21/1779 Comm. to Timothy Ladd, JP. ACCOUNT: 6/28/1781. Of Admr. Allowed 6/28/1781. PROP. & SETTLM.: Claims L34.2.10. Amount to be proportioned L8.17.0. Allowed 6/29/1781 with order to Admr. to pay. ADDL. ACCOUNT: 7/1786. Of Admr. Allowed 7/19/1786. ADDL. PROP. & SETTLM.: Claims L34.2.10. Amount to be proportioned L21.18.0. Allowed 8/16/1785 with order to Admr. to pay.

2909. WYMAN: SALLY & THEODORE (1790) #5601
GDP. Of the children of Aaron Wyman, Pelham gent. decd. GDP.: 11/26/1790. Of Theodore, a minor over 14. Gdn. John Ferguson, Pelham gent. Bond L1000.0.0. Sureties: James Gibson, esq. and James Hall, yoeman, both of Pelham. Witnesses: Josiah Wyman and Daniel Wyman. GDP.: 11/26/1790. Of Sally, a minor under 14. Gdn. Esther Wyman, Pelham widow. Bond L1000.0.0. Sureties: James Gibson, esq. and James Hall, yoeman, both of Pelham. Witnesses: Josiah Wyman and Daniel Wyman. See #5600 Aaron Wyman (1790) for Petition for Gdp. of Theodore.

2910. WYMAN, WILLIAM (1785) #5126
EST. Pelham yoeman decd. ADMIN.: 7/20/1785. Admrs.: Phebe Wyman, widow and William Wyman, yoeman, both of Pelham. Bond L500.0.0. Sureties: Daniel Richardson, gent. and Ebenezer Palmer, yoeman, both of Pelham. Witnesses: Nathaniel Abbot and Joshua Wyman. INVY.: Appr. 9/16/1785. Comm.: Asa Richardson, Ebenezer Palmer and Jacob Butler Jr. Value L761.10.0. Oaths 9/16/1785 Comm. and on 10/17/1785 Admrs. to Josiah Gage, JP.

2911. YEATON, JOHN DREW (1785) #5117
EST. Portsmouth yoeman decd. testate. WILL: Drawn 3/31/1785. Legatees: Wife-Mary; Niece Polly Yeaton and nephew John Yeaton children of Hopley Yeaton; Frederick Bell the boy who formerly lived with him. Execs.-wife Mary and Dr. John Jackson. His sig. Witnesses: Benja. Miller, Enoch Meloon and Luther Reed. His sig. CERT. WILL (D28:212): 6/15/1785. Presented by Execs. and witnesses Meloon and Reed. INVY. WARR. & INVY.: 6/15/1785. Comm.: Jeremiah Libbey, esq.; John Fernald and Joseph Akerman, all of Portsmouth. Appr. 6/24/1785. Value L150.14.2. Oaths 10/13/1785 Admrs. and Comm. to George Gains, JP. PETITION: 3/15/1786. Of Jno. Jackson, an Exec. For Comm. Insolvency. Gives list claims of L190.9.1. DOWER WARR.: 3/15/1786. Comm.: Richard Hart, merchant; Noah Parker, gent.; Isaac Rindge and Jeremiah Libbey, esquires and John Furnald, brazier, all of Portsmouth. Of Widow Mary Yeaton. Dower: 3/24/1786. Oaths 4/3/1786 Hart, Rindge and Libbey to George Gains, JP. Allowed.

2912. YOUNG, JEREMIAH (1793) #5862
EST. Newmarket trader and gent. decd. intestate. ADMIN.: 3/14/1793. Admr. James Cram, Newmarket blacksmith. Bond L1000.0.0. Sureties: Joseph Young, gent. and David Chapman, yoeman, both of Newmarket. Witnesses: Natl. Kidder and John Bryent. INVY.: Comm.: Nathl. Kidder, Eliphalet Smith and Paul Chapman. Value L311.9.2. Oaths 4/5/1793 Comm. to James Smith, JP. Oath 4/5/1793 Admr. to W. Parker, JP. PETITION: 5/8/1793. Of John Bryent for Admr. For Comm. Insolvency. Gives list claims of L625.13.11. Granted with Comm. of Josiah Adams and Nathl. Kidder. EXTENSION: 10/4/1793. Comm. Insolvency allowed 3 months longer. LIST OF NOTES: 11/27/1793. Of John Bryent for Admr. Notes left by decd. except for three or four given up on settlm. of Account where est. was in debt. Impossible to total or esti. because some are produce or lumber. DOWER WARR.: 12/2/1793. Comm.: Josiah Adams, esq.; Nathaniel Kidder, physician; Winthrop Smith, gent.; Daniel Smith and Paul Chapman, yoemen, all of Newmarket. Of Widow Sally Young. DOWER: 3/7/1794. Oaths 3/7/1794 Adams, Kidder, Smith and Chapman to James Smith, JP. Allowed. CLAIMS: 3/7/1794. Total L1051.10.11. Oaths 3/7/1794 Comm. to James Smith, JP. PETITION: 3/11/1794. Of Admr. For License. Granted. LICENSE (D31:205): 3/11/1795. To Admr. To sell real est. to amount of L850.0.0. ACCOUNT: Of Admr. Allowed 7/14/1794 with order to Admr. to pay bal. to creditors. PROP. & SETTLM.: Claims L1051.10.11. Amount to be proportioned L478.15.6. Allowed 8/23/1794 with order to Admr. To pay. ADDL. ACCOUNT: Of Admr. Allowed 10/28/1800. Note: A portion of the following Letter found in #5615 Josiah Brown (1791) belongs here.

LETTER: 4/19/1797. From Benja. Thompson, esq. To Wm. Parker, esq. Requests a copy of List of Claims against est. of Jeremiah Young late of Newmarket.

2913. YOUNG, JOHN (1788) #5324
GDP. Of the son of Daniel Young, Exeter yoeman decd. GDP.: 1/16/1788. Of John, a minor over 14. Gdn. Benjamin Boardman, Exeter esq. Bond L200.0.0. Surety Theophilus Folsom, Kensington yoeman. Witnesses: Thomas Folsom and James Thurston Jr.

2914. YOUNG, THOMAS (1772). #3962
EST. Rochester yeoman decd. testate. WILL: Drawn 5/4/1772. Legatees: Wife-Anna; Sons-Jonathan (oldest),Thomas, James and Moses; Daus.-Abigail, Anna, Mary and Susannah (all under age). Exec.-Son Jonathan. His sig. Witnesses: Moses Brown, James Bickford and Avery Hall. CERT. WILL : 9/30/1772. Presented by Anna Young, widow and relict, Jonathan being dead, and witnesses Bickford and Brown. ADMIN.: 9/30/1772. Admx. Anna Young, Rochester widow. Bond L500.0.0. Sureties: John Plummer, esq. and Jona. Dam, yoeman, both of Rochester. Witnesses: Theophilus Smith and Samuel Parker.

Note: Probate Minutes were a record of the actions coming before the court on the day indicated, together with the fees collected. Several Minutes were found in individual's files and have been recorded with those files.

2915. PROBATE MINUTES at Londonderry 1796.

2916. PROBATE MINUTES at Epsom 9/19/1798.

2917. PROBATE MINUTES for 2/1799, 4/17/1799 and 9/14/1799, no towns given.

INDEX

(EDITOR'S NOTE: Numbers are to the entry number not the page number)